FOURTH EDITION

INTERNET, PHONE, MAIL, AND MIXED-MODE SURVEYS

FOURTH EDITION

INTERNET, PHONE, MAIL, AND MIXED-MODE SURVEYS

The Tailored Design Method

Don A. Dillman
Jolene D. Smyth
Leah Melani Christian

WILEY

To
John Tarnai (1947–2012)
For his leadership of the Social and Economic Sciences Research Center
at Washington State University, the laboratory for our collaborative
efforts to develop and test the methods described in this book.

Janet Harkness (1948–2012)
For encouraging the further development of these methods
as Director of the Survey Research and Methodology (SRAM) Program
at the University of Nebraska–Lincoln.

Contents

Additional Resources

We are excited to share new developments in survey methods with our readers in this fourth edition of *Internet, Phone, Mail, and Mixed-Mode Surveys*. There were issues we could not address in the pages of the book because of space limitations and the constraints of the print format. Our solution, in part at the urging of our great editorial team at John Wiley & Sons, was to create a Book Companion Website for this new edition of the book: www.wiley.com/go/dillman.

On the web page, we have provided a set of materials that we hope readers will find informative and useful. We chose materials we thought would help readers see how the ideas we discussed in the book can be brought together in practical ways. The website contains:

- **Checklist and summary of principles**: 184 guidelines for designing drawn from the book that can be used as a brief refresher or even as a checklist when one is designing one's own questionnaire. The guidelines are organized under topical headings for quicker searching.
- **Visual design video presentation**, "Understanding Visual Design for Questions and Questionnaires" (47 minutes) that is suitable for classroom presentation. In this video we demonstrate key visual design concepts and their application to questionnaire design. The video format allows us to integrate a number of helpful examples and illustrations that would not work in the static pages of a book. We anticipate that this will be a highly valuable resource for those trying to better understand the visual design of surveys and those trying to figure out how to format their questions into a questionnaire.
- **Sets of real-world example survey materials**: Each set includes a brief overview of the goals and design of the study, a copy of the question-naire(s), copies of all implementation materials, and in some cases, copies of envelopes. These example materials illustrate how procedures have been brought together to create comprehensive designs that are consistent with our social exchange framework, are tailored to the specific study and population, and incorporate the visual design concepts presented in the book. The examples include both single- and mixed-mode surveys. These sample materials will be useful to those looking for examples of how we have applied ideas from the book to our surveys, as well as those looking for ideas about how to put together their own surveys.
- **An example of a 7″ × 8.5″ questionnaire** for those looking for an example of how this smaller booklet size can work.
- **Before-and-after images from a redesign of the USDA-sponsored Agricultural Resource Management survey** that demonstrates the application of many of the visual design ideas discussed in the book. This example shows how multiple visual design concepts and design strategies can be brought together to simplify an incredibly complex survey.

- An **example of a cognitive interview report** that demonstrates how this method can be used to inform questionnaire design. This report describes the motivation behind the interviews, procedures followed, and results and discussion. Readers can use it to better understand how this method works, see a real example of its application, and inform their own study design and procedures, or as an example of how a cognitive interview report can be put together.
- **Color versions of select figures** where we think the color will help convey the central idea better than can be done in the black-and-white format used in the print edition of the book.

We hope that you find these materials helpful. We wish to acknowledge the invaluable help of Morgan Millar in pulling these materials together, especially the example survey materials. Morgan compiled most of these example surveys and wrote most of the survey descriptions. As with the rest of the book, this website has benefited greatly from her assistance.

In addition to these materials, the editors at Wiley have arranged to provide on the Book Companion Website short PowerPoint presentations of the key concepts in each chapter as well as test questions for each chapter for use by instructors.

Preface

Writing the fourth edition of this book nearly four decades after preparing the first edition has brought into perspective how survey science has evolved. It has also led us to reflect on how each edition needed to be refocused in order to fit with dramatically changing times.

The first edition was written on a typewriter, when personal computers, fax machines, the Internet, and cell phones were mostly unimagined by those wanting to do surveys. The title of this 1978 book, *Mail and Telephone Surveys: The Total Design Method*, suggested what was then a revolutionary idea—sample surveys of the general public, which prior to that time were viewed as synonymous with in-person interviews, could be done in other ways. It proposed standardized step-by-step methods for conducting such surveys by either mail or by telephone. Those procedures contained the seeds of a bold idea, "For very little investment of money, almost any academic institution or agency can establish the capability for conducting credible mail and telephone surveys" (Dillman, 1978, p. 275).

Nearly 20 years elapsed before work began on the second edition. During those years dozens of experiments and field tests involving different survey populations were undertaken to refine the 1978 mail data collection procedures and test new ones. The main outcome was to realize the necessity of tailoring specific data collection strategies to different populations, survey situations, and topics rather than using the one-size-fits-all approach described in that first book. The title of the 2000 edition, *Mail and Internet Surveys: The Tailored Design Method*, concisely summarized the fundamental changes introduced there. More than half of the new book was devoted to tailored designs such as alternative ways to deliver questionnaires, how to achieve greater speed and efficiency, challenges specific to government surveys, and how to survey businesses. The last chapter to be drafted, and the first to go out of date, was about Internet and interactive voice response surveys, which seemed ready to revolutionize surveying. In addition, the idea of mixed-mode survey designs, using the strengths of one mode to assist another, was introduced. To make room for these changes, telephone data collection methods were removed. This book was about a 95% revision of the first edition.

Only 6 years elapsed before work began in earnest on the third edition with two new coauthors, Jolene Smyth and Leah Christian. The three of us had begun working together as a team in 2002 to systematically research the effects of visual layout and design on the ways people answered survey questions and how responses differed across aural and visual modes of response. In this edition, we were first able to articulate what we had learned as guidelines for designing questionnaires. It was also apparent that there were multiple barriers to the conduct of mixed-mode surveys, ranging from how surveyors tended to structure questions for use in particular modes to inherent differences between aural and visual communication that might not be amenable to solutions for some types of questions. This edition began and ended with a discussion about the turbulence being felt among surveyors with declining response rates, coverage problems with telephone surveys, and a concern that the Internet was not yet ready to replace telephone as a stand-alone data collection mode, especially for household surveys. When bringing closure on this substantial rewrite in early 2008, we were also examining soon-to-be published results from a new kind of experiment we had done, which was a significant departure from the measurement and question wording issues that constituted much of our focus in this revision. These preliminary results seemed to show that we could use address-based sampling (our best source of coverage for household surveys in the United States) with mail contact and effectively encourage many people to respond over the Internet. These results (Smyth, Dillman, Christian, & O'Neill 2010) were included in this 2009 edition as having potential for surveying the general public by Internet using a mixed-mode design.

Work began on the fourth edition of this book, only 4 years after publication of the previous edition, and it was quickly apparent to us that the revisions would need to be nearly as substantial as the changes between the second and third editions. The telephone as an independent survey mode was continuing to face difficulties, and seemed on the verge of being rejected for certain national as well as state and smaller area surveys. It was also clear that the Internet had still not yet achieved the use and comfort levels that would allow it to be a sole data collection mode for many, and perhaps most, surveys. In addition, new challenges to designing and getting people to respond to Internet surveys had arisen because of the quick adoption of smartphones and tablets as devices for accessing the Internet. And mail, which was once our least expensive mode but had the poorest coverage, had become the mode with the best coverage of households but had also become a higher-cost mode. These were the new issues we were grappling with in the constantly changing survey landscape.

The most significant change in this edition is bringing the telephone back into the book after leaving it out of the 2000 and 2009 editions. This decision may seem curious at a time when most surveyors are moving away from the telephone mode. But it is apparent to us that the telephone is still necessary for certain types of surveys and, perhaps more importantly, that there are many ways it can be used in mixed-mode designs to overcome the weaknesses of single contact and/or response mode surveys. Including the telephone in this edition reflects our commitment to integrating some of the main themes of the previous edition—tailored design and mixed-mode surveys—throughout the book, rather than assigning them to individual chapters. In this edition we have also expanded the theoretical underpinnings of our approach to asking people to cooperate with survey requests and updated the social exchange framework used in all previous editions, placing more emphasis on trust and its response consequences in today's rapid-fire communication environment. Rethinking this framework was critical to laying a base for showing how different modes of contact, different response modes, and their coordinated use each provides potential for improving survey response rates and response quality.

Much more is understood now about the different processes of communicating aurally and visually than when previous editions were written, and our comfort with blending aural and visual modes together has increased. Thus, an entire chapter is now devoted to these issues. It brings together the past 15 years of published research and will be invaluable to those designing both single- and mixed-mode surveys. Stand-alone telephone, web, and mail data collection methods are presented in individual chapters, because they are still relevant for certain survey situations; those chapters are also a prelude to their integration in mixed-mode designs.

This book ends on a note of uncertainty about exactly what lies ahead but also conveys our belief that the fundamental ideas of social exchange and tailored design that have evolved through all editions of this book will continue to be relevant and helpful for figuring out how to conduct surveys in the face of significant cultural and technological changes. Survey methods will undoubtedly continue to change and successful change will depend upon reconciling the needs and desires of surveyors with those of the people being surveyed. The ideas of social exchange and tailored design will be useful in figuring out how to do that. This edition draws heavily upon our own research experiences and experiments. Some of this research was conducted when we were working together at Washington State University with assistance from the Social and Economic Sciences Research Center (SESRC), but this edition also draws heavily on our separate experiences and research foci since that time. This includes Don's continued work at the SESRC, Jolene's experiences at the Survey Research and Methodology Program, the Department of Sociology, and the Bureau of Sociological Research at the University of Nebraska–Lincoln and Leah's experiences at the Pew Research Center and Nielsen.

For the first time we have developed a companion website for this book that contains additional materials. On the website you will find example survey materials (i.e., questionnaires, contact materials, descriptions of implementation, etc.) for web, mail, telephone, and mixed-mode surveys; resources developed to demonstrate good survey visual design; color versions of many of the figures from throughout the book; and a cognitive interview example report. Readers can access these materials at www.wiley.com/go/dillman.

This book is dedicated to two consummate professionals—John Tarnai and Janet Harkness—both of whom were taken from us too early. Each has influenced our work in ways neither may have realized.

As the Assistant Director and Director of the SESRC from 1981 to 2012, John, more than any individual, nurtured the development of the web, mail, and telephone data collection capabilities of the SESRC, which provided the survey infrastructure that made it possible for us to conduct dozens of experiments that are reported in this book. Without his entrepreneurial leadership, our joint research could not have been done. His quiet demeanor and insights inspired us to do our best work and to share our survey experiences openly with others. He also collaborated on one of the first efforts to articulate the need for mixed-mode survey designs (Dillman & Tarnai, 1988), which set the tone for 25 years of follow-up experiments on the strengths and limitations of such designs that made this book possible.

Janet Harkness, served as a faculty member and later the Director of the Survey Research and Methodology Program at the University of Nebraska–Lincoln from 2005 to 2012, and in that role was a strong supporter of much of the research reported in this edition of the book. In her research Janet was grappling with many incredibly complex issues involved in cross-national and cross-cultural survey research; her contributions in these areas will continue to influence our field for decades to come as more and more surveys are conducted across cultural and national borders.

Survey methodology and our abilities as a profession to tackle new ideas has benefited from the work of these colleagues. We thank them for inspiring us both personally and professionally.

For more than a decade the National Center for Science and Engineering Statistics (NCSES) has funded much of our work to invent and apply new mixed-mode methodologies and test their applicability to government surveys. For this we are especially grateful to the NCSES Division Director, Lynda Carlson, who initiated this work, and her successor, John Gawalt, who continued it and the many NCSES staff who worked with us. This funding provided support for many graduate students whose much appreciated contributions to this research appear in the book references—Michael Stern, Arina Gertseva, Taj Mahon-Haft, Nicholas Parsons, Bryan Rookey, Allison O'Neill, Benjamin Messer, Morgan Millar, and Michelle Edwards. We also wish to acknowledge the contributions of graduate students in the Sociology Department Survey Practicum at Washington State University, and in Data Collection Methods and Questionnaire Design courses at the University of Nebraska–Lincoln.

Don would also like to thank the many staff of the SESRC who regularly, and often with great patience, solved the innumerable design challenges associated with the experimentation necessary for testing many of the ideas presented here. Special thanks goes to Tom Allen, study director for most experiments, for his ability to solve the visual design and communication issues associated with working across survey modes, and Rita Koontz, SESRC Administrative Manager, for her commitment to making the SESRC an effective and much appreciated work environment. He would also like to thank Edith deLeeuw for conversations that influenced rewriting the theoretical approach used in this book.

Jolene would like to thank Kristen Olson for being a wonderful colleague and friend who shares her time generously and is always willing to talk through ideas and undertake new research projects. She would also like to thank Amanda Richardson and the staff of the Bureau of Sociological Research for the many insightful survey discussions that have influenced her thinking in recent years, and Dan Hoyt and Julia McQuillan for their ongoing support and leadership. Finally, Jolene has had the privilege of working directly with many wonderful graduate students in recent years who have made valuable contributions to her research and thinking. She appreciates each and every one and would like to especially thank Nuttirudee Charoenruk, Alian Kasabian, Amanda Libman, Rebecca Powell, Kay Ricci, Ashley Richards, Mathew Stange, Lauren Walton, Heather Wood, and Quan Zhou.

Leah would like to thank Scott Keeter, her mentor and collaborator at the Pew Research Center, as well as Jim Bell and the many other colleagues who eagerly tackled the methodological challenges the center faced. Special thanks go to Leah's new colleagues at Nielsen, who provided encouragement and guidance as she spent time on the final manuscript.

The intensive writing process benefitted greatly from the help of several individuals. We appreciate Kristen Olsen critically reviewing the sampling and coverage chapter and Amanda Richardson providing a thorough review of the telephone chapter. In addition, Mathew Stange provided assistance with some of the figures. We especially want to thank Morgan Millar, who brought her expertise with survey methods and excellent editorial skills to bear on all aspects of reviewing, preparing, and submitting the final manuscript. Her attention to detail, organization, and encouragement ensured we were able to deliver a final manuscript.

Finally, we want to thank our families. Joye Jolly Dillman has memorably experienced with Don the writing of all four editions of this book as spouse, parent, and

Washington State University faculty colleague. His appreciation for her support is both deep and long lasting.

Kristi and Tyson Chambers were both invaluable sources of support and inspiration during the writing of this book. They did more than their share of the chores when Jolene was tied to the computer, stayed patient with the process, and always seemed to have the right answer, usually a laugh or a hug, at the right time. She hopes they know how much she loves and appreciates them.

Eugene MacIntyre has helped Leah throughout her work on this book; she deeply appreciates his unwavering support. She also thanks Leilani, who lights every day and reminds Leah of all the really important things in life, and who gave up very important playtime with Mommy so she could work on the book.

Don A. Dillman
Washington State University
Pullman, Washington

Jolene D. Smyth
University of Nebraska–Lincoln
Lincoln, Nebraska

Leah Melani Christian
Nielsen
Atlanta, Georgia

Sample Surveys in Our Electronic World

Hundreds of times every day someone decides to create a survey. The variety of organizations and individuals who make this decision is enormous, ranging from individual college students to the largest corporations. Community service organizations, nonprofit foundations, educators, voluntary associations, special interest groups, research scientists, and government agencies also all collect needed information by conducting surveys. The topics of these surveys vary greatly, from questions about health, education, employment, and political preferences to inquiries about television viewing, the use of electronic equipment, and interest in buying a new car, among many other things.

The reasons for deciding to conduct a survey are as diverse as the range of survey sponsors and topics. Sometimes, the justification is that the sponsors do not know the opinions or beliefs of those they want to survey. More typically, the sponsor has interests that go much deeper, wanting to know not just how many individuals in a group have a particular attitude, but how that attitude varies with other respondent characteristics that will be asked in the survey, such as across men and women or across different age or socioeconomic groups.

While the need to know something that is unknown drives the decision to conduct most surveys, the uses of survey results are as diverse as those who sponsor them. For example, one of us recently completed a community survey that was used to decide what facilities to include in a new neighborhood park that was about to be developed. University leaders use results from surveys of students to revise their undergraduate and graduate education programs. Public opinion pollsters use results from surveys of likely voters to predict who will win national and local elections. The Federal Reserve uses estimates of the unemployment rate produced monthly in the Current Population Survey to help set economic policy. Data from this same survey are used by individuals and businesses throughout the United States to make investment, hiring, and policy decisions. Market researchers use surveys to provide insights into consumer attitudes and behaviors. Nonprofit groups use surveys to measure attitudes about issues that are important to them and support for possible programs the group might pursue.

Surveys are both large and small. For example, over the course of a year the U.S. Census Bureau asks a few million households to respond to the American Community Survey. Others ask only a few hundred or even fewer individuals to respond. The survey response mode also varies, with some surveys being conducted by a single mode—in-person, web, telephone, or paper—while others provide multiple modes for answering questions. Sometimes respondents are asked to respond only once, while in other surveys a single individual may be asked to answer questions repeatedly over months or years, and surveys may be conducted in just a few weeks or over several months or years. In some cases people are asked to provide information about themselves or their households, and in other cases they are asked to provide information about a particular business or other organization with which they are affiliated.

Despite this diversity, all surveys still have a lot in common. Each is motivated by the desire to collect information to answer a particular question or solve a particular problem. In some cases the desired information is not available from any other source. In other cases, the information may be available, but it cannot be connected to other important information—such as other characteristics or related attitudes and behaviors—that need to be known in order to solve the problem or answer the question.

In most surveys only some of those in the population of interest are asked to respond. That is, the survey is based on a *sample* rather than being a *census* of every member of the target population. In addition, those who respond are asked questions they are expected to answer by choosing from among predetermined response categories or, occasionally by providing open-ended answers in their own words. These commonalities and the enormous amount of money and effort now spent on surveys point to their importance as a tool for learning about people's characteristics, opinions, and behaviors, and using those results to inform and direct public policy, business decisions, and for many other purposes.

Other nonsurvey means, both quantitative and qualitative, are available to social scientists, marketing professionals, government officials, special interest groups, and others for collecting useful information that will produce insight into the attitudes and behaviors of people and the groups they are a part of. These include unstructured interviews, focus groups, participant observation, content analyses, simulations, small group experiments, and analyses of administrative records or organic data such as birth and death records, sales transactions, records of online searches, social media, and other online behavior. Each of these methods can yield different types of information, and for some questions they are more appropriate than surveys or may be used in combination with surveys to answer the research question or community problem.

The feature of the probability sample survey that distinguishes it from these other methods of investigation is that it can provide a close estimate of the distribution of a characteristic in a population by surveying only some members of that population. If done correctly, it allows one to generalize results with great precision, from a few to the many, making it a very efficient method for learning about people and populations.

The efficiency and importance of the probability sample survey might best be illustrated by considering an alternative way to learn about a population—a census. Every 10 years the U.S. Census Bureau attempts to contact and survey every household in the United States, as required by our Constitution. The resulting information is used to reapportion the U.S. House of Representatives so that each member represents about the same number of U.S. residents. This massive survey, known as the Decennial Census, costs billions of dollars to conduct. A smaller organization that wants to know the opinions of all U.S. residents on a particular issue could hardly afford such an undertaking. But with a probability sample survey, it can learn those opinions for considerably lower costs by selecting only some members of the population to complete the survey.

Even on a smaller scale, few would be able to afford to survey every undergraduate student at a large university in order to assess students' satisfaction in the education they are receiving. If this were necessary, studies of student satisfaction would seldom, if ever, be done. But probability sample surveys allow us to be much more efficient with our resources by surveying only a sample of students in a way that enables us to generalize to the entire student population.

Whatever the target population or research question, limiting our data collection to a carefully selected sample of the population of interest allows us to concentrate limited resources (e.g., time and money for follow-up communications, data cleaning, and analysis) on fewer individuals, yet obtain results that are only slightly less precise than they would be if every member of the population were surveyed.

Our purpose in this book is to explain how to conduct effective probability sample surveys. We discuss the fundamental requirements that must be met if one wants to generalize results with statistical confidence from the few who are surveyed to the many they are selected to represent. We also describe specific procedures for designing surveys in which one can have high confidence in the results. Regardless of whether your interest in surveys is to understand one of the many national surveys that are conducted for policy purposes or to gain knowledge of how to design your own survey of organization members, college students, customers, or any other population, it is important to understand what it takes to do a good survey and the multiple sources of error that can reduce the accuracy of the survey results—or completely invalidate them.

FOUR CORNERSTONES OF QUALITY SURVEYS

In general, survey error can be thought of as the difference between an estimate that is produced using survey data and the true value of the variables in the population that one hopes to describe. There are four main types of error that surveyors need to try to minimize in order to improve the survey estimates.

1. *Coverage Error* occurs when the list from which sample members are drawn does not accurately represent the population on the characteristic(s) one wants to estimate with the survey data (whether a voter preference, a demographic characteristic, or something else). A high-quality sample survey requires that every member of the population has a known, nonzero probability of being sampled, meaning they have to be accurately represented on the list from which the sample will be drawn. Coverage error is the difference between the estimate produced when the list is inaccurate and what would have been produced with an accurate list.

2. *Sampling Error* is the difference between the estimate produced when only a sample of units on the frame is surveyed and the estimate produced when every unit on the list is surveyed. Sampling error exists anytime we decide to survey only some, rather than all, members of the sample frame.

3. *Nonresponse Error* is the difference between the estimate produced when only some of the sampled units respond compared to when all of them respond. It occurs when those who do not respond are different from those who do respond in a way that influences the estimate.

4. *Measurement Error* is the difference between the estimate produced and the true value because respondents gave inaccurate answers to survey questions. It occurs when respondents are unable or unwilling to provide accurate answers, which can be due to poor question design, survey mode effects, interviewer and respondent behavior, or data collection mistakes.

We consider reducing the potential for these errors as the four cornerstones of conducting successful sample surveys. Surveyors should attempt to limit each to acceptable levels. None of them can be ignored. As such, each receives detailed attention in the chapters that follow. Because these sources of error are so essential for defining survey quality, we describe each of them here in more detail.

Coverage Error

As we previously mentioned, the strength of a probability sample survey is that it allows us to collect data from only a sample of the population but generalize results to the whole, thus saving considerable time, money, and effort that would be incurred if we had to survey everyone in the population. However, in order to draw a sample, one has to have a sample frame, or a list of members of the target population, and any errors in that list have the potential to introduce coverage error into the final estimates that are produced. If some units from the target population are not included on the sample frame (i.e., undercoverage) *and* they differ from those that are in ways that are important to the survey, the final estimates will contain error.

For example, all other error sources aside, a landline random digit dial telephone survey would likely overestimate the prevalence of higher socioeconomic status because the well-off are more likely than the poor to have landline telephone service (i.e., the well-off are more likely to be on the landline random digit dial sample frame) (Blumberg & Luke, 2013). In fact, one of the challenges now being faced in conducting household telephone surveys is that only about 58% of households still have landlines (Blumberg & Luke, 2013), the traditional source of random digit dialing samples, and those who have them are quite different from those who do not on a number of important characteristics. Using the landline telephone frame alone (without supplementing it with a cell phone frame) for a national household survey would leave out significant portions of the population who are likely to differ in important ways from those included on the frame.

Similarly, conducting a national household survey by Internet would leave out significant portions of the population because, as of May 2013, only 73% of American adults have Internet access in the home (Pew Internet & American Life Project, 2013b). In comparison, an Internet survey of undergraduate students at a university, where all students are required to use the Internet, would likely have little coverage error, provided a list of all students could be obtained. In Chapter 3 we discuss in detail the threat of coverage error, its likely sources, and how to limit it.

Sampling Error

The extent to which the precision of the survey estimates is limited because only some people from the sample frame are selected to do the survey (i.e., sampled) and others are not is known as sampling error. If we have a sample frame with complete coverage (i.e., the list matches the population perfectly), we can say that sampling error is the difference between the estimates produced and the true value because we survey only a sample of the population and not everyone. The power of probability sampling, which is also discussed in detail in Chapter 3, is that estimates with acceptable levels of precision can usually be made for the population by surveying only a small portion of the people in the population. For example, a researcher can sample only about 100 members of the U.S. general public and, if all 100 respond, achieve estimates with a margin of error of +/−10%. Successfully surveying a sample of 2,000 individuals reduces the margin of error to about +/−2%. Surveying 100 or even 2,000 people rather than the approximately 315 million people in the United States represents an enormous and desirable cost savings, but doing so means that one has to be willing to live with some sampling error in the estimates.

Sampling error is an unavoidable result of obtaining data from only some rather than all members on the sample frame and exists as a part of all sample surveys. For this reason, we describe the importance of reducing survey error to acceptable levels, rather than being able to eliminate it entirely. By contrast, censuses—in which all members on the sampling frame are selected to be surveyed—are not subject to sampling error.

Many novice surveyors find sampling error to be somewhat nonintuitive. They find it difficult to imagine only needing to survey a few hundred or thousand to learn about millions of households or individuals. Yet, during each presidential election in the United States, surveys of between 1,000 and 2,000 likely voters are conducted that correctly estimate (within the limits of sampling error) the votes for each candidate. For example, across polls conducted in the final week of the 2012 campaign, the average error for each candidate was about 2 percentage points. Just as nonintuitive for some beginning surveyors to grasp is that in order to predict the outcome of a local election for a particular state or medium sized U.S. city with perhaps 50,000 voters, nearly as many people need to be surveyed as are needed for predicting a national election.

The exact sampling error is easily calculated mathematically, as described in Chapter 3. However, the ease of making those calculations and the mathematical preciseness of the result leads to overreliance on it as a singular measure of the amount of error in a survey statistic. This tendency should be avoided. Sampling error calculations reflect the completed sample size, that is, only received responses are considered. The larger the number of responses, the greater the reported precision and statistical confidence. But they ignore the possibility for coverage error as well as the fact that many and sometimes most of the invited participants did not respond, which raises the potential for a third source of error, nonresponse error.

Nonresponse Error

Many sponsors think of a survey's response rate (the proportion of sampled individuals that respond to the survey) as the major indicator of survey quality. A major focus of this book is how to obtain high response rates to surveys. However, taken by itself, the response rate is only an indirect indicator of survey quality. The more important response quality indicator is nonresponse error, which occurs when the characteristics of respondents differ from those who chose not to respond in a way that is relevant to the study results. For example, if a survey on environmental attitudes obtained responses mostly from those individuals who have positive attitudes toward the environment and those who have negative attitudes are underrepresented, then that survey's results would be biased because of nonresponse error.

The common mistake sometimes made by novice surveyors is to consider response rate as an adequate indicator of whether nonresponse error exists. Comparisons across many surveys have shown that nonresponse error may occur in surveys with higher as well as lower response rates (Groves & Peytcheva, 2008). For example, in 1989 a study was conducted in Dallas County, Texas, to learn about people's thoughts and behaviors related to acquired immunodeficiency syndrome (AIDS). Sampled individuals were asked to complete a self-administered survey and have a blood sample drawn by a phlebotomist. This study achieved a remarkable 84% response rate: A rate that some might think is a clear indication of high quality. But to ascertain whether there was nonresponse bias, the researchers went back to a random sample of the nonrespondents and were able to get some to participate (some were not asked to give the blood sample at this stage). This effort revealed that the prevalence of human immunodeficiency virus (HIV) risk behaviors like intravenous (IV) drug use and male-to-male sex were underestimated in the original data collection effort. Only 3% of those who initially participated reported engaging in IV drug use compared to 7% of those who participated in the follow-up. Similarly, only about 5% of the initial participants reported engaging in male-to-male sex compared to about 17% of those in the follow-up (Centers for Disease Control and Prevention, 1991). Despite an impressive 84% response rate, the initial estimates were biased because those who responded differed from those who did not respond on characteristics of interest in this study.

While the study just described demonstrates that higher response rates do not guarantee minimal nonresponse error, it is important to recognize that higher response rates do reduce the likelihood of nonresponse error and thus provide greater credibility to surveys' results than do lower response rates. In addition, higher response rates result in larger completed samples, thereby increasing the precision of the estimates in that way. Thus, designing surveys in ways that produce higher response rates can be a helpful tool in reducing nonresponse error.

Response is a function of contact and cooperation. That is, in order to obtain a response, we first have to make contact with sample members and then we have to convince them to cooperate with our request to complete the survey. Using multiple contact attempts and varying the timing, delivery method, and mode of those attempts are a few ways we discuss in this book of increasing the likelihood of making contact with sample members. Respondent-friendly questionnaires, shorter (rather than longer) survey instruments, the use of incentives, follow-up requests that target likely nonrespondents, and switching survey modes are a few of the many features of survey design discussed in this book that are intended to increase the likelihood of sample members cooperating with our request. All of these strategies have the parallel objectives of increasing response while simultaneously reducing nonresponse error. Chapter 2 introduces the discussion of implementation procedures and a theory for guiding those decisions. The majority of this book, from Chapter 4 forward, focuses on many aspects of survey design that can reduce nonresponse as well as measurement error.

Measurement Error

Survey objectives are realized by asking questions to which respondents provide accurate answers. However, in designing a survey that will achieve valid and reliable measurement, one faces a gauntlet of measurement challenges. One of the challenges to asking a good survey question is making sure that it adequately measures the idea or concept of interest. An example occurred in a survey in which the sponsor wanted to obtain a measurement of household wealth. He had tentatively decided to use household income for the previous year as a measure of wealth until a colleague pointed out that annual income is likely to decrease sharply when a person retires, but wealth typically does not. Similarly, a community survey sponsor proposed using length of time individuals had lived in their current residence as a measure of length of time in the community, but soon discarded the idea because of the likelihood that many people may have moved from one residence to another in the same community. When a question does not measure what it was intended to, as in these cases, it is typically referred to as having specification error (also known as low construct validity). Considerable time and effort can be spent deciding what format of question to use, what type of scale to provide, how to label answer categories, whether to offer a "don't know" option, and any number of other details, but all of that effort is useless if the question does not measure the concept called for by the study objectives.

Once one has selected an acceptable way to measure a specific concept, there are many different ways that accuracy of the estimate may be compromised, resulting in measurement error.

- The substance of the question may encourage a response that, because of perceived societal norms, puts the respondent in a more favorable light to the interviewer and/or survey sponsor. Questions about sex and illegal behaviors are examples.
- The question may be unclear to the respondent because it uses words that are not understood or phrases that are confusing.
- The question structure may encourage certain answers that another structure would not. For example, items that ask respondents to mark all that apply tend to result in fewer selections among later categories than those that ask for an explicit positive or negative answer for each item (i.e., a forced-choice or yes/no format).
- The order in which questions are asked may produce different answers to specific questions than would another order.
- The visual layout of a question may increase the likelihood that certain answers are chosen and others are not, or that some items are overlooked altogether.
- Some types of respondents may be less likely to give accurate answers than others.
- Perception of the expectations of interviewers or the sponsor may also influence answers.
- Interviewer characteristics, such as gender or race, may influence the answers people provide.
- The choice of survey mode may also influence answers to surveys. For example, research has consistently shown that scalar questions are likely to be answered differently in visual versus aural surveys.

These problems can result in two types of measurement error. The first is response bias, in which estimates are systematically shifted one way or the other. Two common examples are underestimating socially undesirable behaviors, like drug use and criminal activity, and overestimating socially desirable behaviors, like volunteering and voting. The second type of measurement error is response variance, which is akin to the idea of low reliability. That is, if the measurement were taken over and over multiple times, it would produce a different result each time.

A great deal of terminology is often used to indicate why some questions and not others exhibit measurement error, including social desirability, primacy/recency, acquiescence, clarity of figure/ground relationships, the Law of Pragnanz, the norm of evenhandedness, and much more. We mention these many sources of potential measurement differences because writing effective questions requires simultaneously working on many fronts in an effort to reduce measurement problems in surveys to obtain accurate answers to all questions. We discuss this further in Chapters 4, 5, 6, and 7.

Total Survey Error

The need to focus on many design considerations at once sometimes results in ignoring one source of error, a mistake that can have devastating repercussions for a survey. For example, a faculty member concerned with reports of classroom cheating decided to take advantage of the web survey software available in her university and design a survey of students to get their perceptions about whether classroom cheating was happening and to learn what they thought would be appropriate punishment. It was her hope that conducting a probability sample survey of students would produce data she could report to the appropriate university officials to inform new policies for dealing with cheating cases. To avoid the challenge of sending sample members e-mails with individual passwords that would allow only those sampled to respond, she sent generic e-mails and set up the survey website so that anyone who knew about the survey could complete it. She soon learned that the e-mails sent to the carefully selected sample of students had been forwarded to other students and that some students with particularly strong viewpoints had filled out the survey multiple times (i.e., stuffed the ballot box!), which breaks from the requirement for a probability sample that only the people selected for the survey can provide a response and that each person can respond only once. In trying to simplify the administration of this survey, the faculty member ended up making a decision that undermined the probability nature of the sample and discredited the survey's results.

We have also observed situations in which survey designers became excessively concerned over resolving issues with small consequences. Upon learning that a sample of household addresses for a community survey would only reach about 95% of the households in the community, one surveyor became obsessed with how to manually add the missing addresses. To do so would have required tremendous costs and effort, including cross-checking records and potential personal visits to areas in the community to check to see if there were addresses there. In this case, the error from missing 5% of households was likely to be small, and the resources that would be required to fix it were excessive in relation to the likely benefit. It would have been more beneficial to focus on reducing other potential errors.

In another situation this may not be the case. Surveyors designing a national survey that will produce data used to allocate government funds may decide that even though small, the extra precision obtained by enumerating the missing 5% of addresses is worth the extra effort because it will help ensure that federal funds are fairly distributed.

One mistake some survey designers make is to worry most about what error source they know best. The research-based knowledge for dealing with specific sources of error comes from different academic disciplines. Sampling theory and concepts for defining and understanding coverage effects come principally from statistics. Measurement issues are more likely to be dealt with by the disciplines of psychology and sociology. Nonresponse research draws concepts from all of the disciplines. While understanding of the behavioral reasons for nonresponse as relied heavily on sociological and psychological thinking, potential solutions for such response issues, such as imputing missing responses for individual items or calculating weighting adjustments to mitigate unit nonresponse have been developed primarily by statisticians. Economists, political scientists, and market research professionals have also contributed significantly to the literatures in these areas. Survey error is fundamentally a multidisciplinary problem and nowhere is that more evident than in efforts to reduce multiple sources of survey error. Good survey design requires giving balanced concern to error sources, regardless of one's inclination to focus mostly on what he or she knows best.

This state of affairs has encouraged the development and use of the Total Survey Error (TSE) framework. This term refers to attempting to design surveys in a way that maximizes data accuracy within constraints that cannot be ignored, such as costs and the time available for completing the survey (Biemer & Lyberg, 2003). Reducing total survey error involves careful survey planning, sample selection, questionnaire design, implementation, and data analysis. It is about simultaneously controlling all four sources of error to the extent practical and possible, within the time, cost, and other constraints of the survey. Survey error cannot be completely eliminated, but with diligence to all four types it can be kept to reasonable levels. Our emphasis throughout this book is on how reducing total survey error can be accomplished in large and small surveys alike, including those with generous as well as quite limited budgets.

Often reduction of total survey error focuses on discrete actions that can be taken separately to reduce each type of error, but in other cases a much broader systematic change to the survey design may be undertaken. For many years, the National Household Education Survey conducted by the National Center for Educational Statistics was conducted in a two-step process. Random digit dial telephone surveys (landline numbers only) were used to identify households with children. Then the identified households were surveyed again, also by telephone, to collect detailed information. It became evident early in 2007 that not only were response rates falling dramatically (Montaquila, Brick, Williams, Kim, & Han, 2013), but increasing portions of the nation's children were being raised in homes without landline connections. The proportion of children growing up in cell-only households has continued to increase, and is now over 45% (Blumberg & Luke, 2013). The survey sponsors were concerned about both coverage and nonresponse error and were worried about the costs associated with beginning to call cell phones to reduce the coverage error. A proposal to consider a possible change to address-based sampling using mail methods was met with considerable skepticism. In addition to not being sure it would improve response, changing to mail also meant that questions would need to be asked in different ways, changes that might impact trend lines from data accumulated over many years. But, after extensive testing, it was decided to make the switch based on considerations across multiple types of error.

Making these changes to the National Household Education Survey instead of continuing to try to fix the problems associated with the telephone survey was a major decision that took a lot of guts and hard work. It required extensive institutional change to switch from dealing with telephone to mail, as well as substantial changes to the survey itself to make it work in a visual rather than aural survey mode. Because this undertaking was so enormous, initial reluctance was only overcome after several years of testing. Ultimately, this testing showed that the new methods were more suitable for the changing survey landscape we now face, and that they were beneficial from a total survey error perspective.

WHAT IS DIFFERENT ABOUT SURVEYING IN THE 2010s?

When the first edition of this book appeared in 1978, personal computers, the Internet, cell phones, and fax machines existed only as ideas that might someday be a part of people's lives. Surveys were limited to landline telephone, mail, and in-person interviews. When the second edition appeared in 2000, the Internet and another intriguing development, telephone Touchtone Data Entry, which eventually evolved into Interactive Voice Response, were added in a single chapter. At this time surveyors were just beginning to consider their possible uses.

Rapid technological development in the past 15 years has changed this situation substantially so that there are now many means for contacting people and asking them to complete surveys. Web and cellular telephone communication have undergone rapid maturation as means of responding to surveys. In addition, voice recognition, prerecorded phone surveys that ask for numerical and/or voice recorded responses, fillable PDFs, smartphones, tablets, and other devices have increasingly been used for data collection. Yet, for many reasons traditional phone, mail, and in-person contacts have not disappeared, and are often being used in combination to maximize the potential of reaching people. In addition, offering multiple ways of responding (e.g., web and mail in the same survey) is common. It is no longer practical to talk about a dominant mode of surveying, as in-person interviews were described in the middle of the 20th century and telephone was referred to from about 1980 to the late 1990s.

The situation faced by surveyors in this decade is in some ways ironic. We can now connect with a huge portion of a survey population in multiple ways; about 98% of U.S. households have either a landline or cellular telephone (Blumberg & Luke, 2013), around 96% have U.S. Postal Service mail delivery (Iannacchione, 2011), and 85% of adults in the United States use the Internet and 73% have Internet access in their homes (Pew Internet & American Life Project, 2013b, 2013c). Individual household access for in-person surveys is harder to estimate because of locked apartment buildings and gated communities that prevent interviewers from gaining access. However, while surveyors now have multiple ways to contact people, their efforts are often thwarted by buffers designed to keep unsolicited messages at bay. Receptionists or guards prevent access to buildings. Answering machines, voice mail, and caller ID technology filter telephone calls. E-mail filters and the ability to preview e-mails without opening them make e-mail survey requests less likely to be seen and answered. Thus, the technology that makes unprecedented and speedy access possible also provides the means of avoiding or ignoring it. In addition, cultural norms have evolved so that control over whether a survey request is received and responded to rests increasingly with the individual to whom the request is being made, and not with the individual making it.

Many years from now when the history of electronic communication is written, it is likely that one of the major themes will be its role in the elimination of intermediaries. Tasks that once required help—making a bank withdrawal, reserving a room in a hotel or a seat on an airplane, leaving a phone message, and purchasing groceries—can now be done quite well without the assistance of another person. In this environment, why should surveyors expect that positioning an interviewer as a necessary intermediary between the surveyor and respondent remain the most prevalent way of conducting a survey? It should not be surprising that many telephone-only surveys now obtain response rates in the single digits (Keeter, Christian, Dimock, & Gewurz, 2012).

However, the rapid decline of telephone interviewing as a dominant stand-alone way of conducting household and other surveys is occurring for other reasons as well. The shift away from landlines as the predominant method of telephone communication means that the traditional sample frame for random digit dialing that was depended upon to cover the U.S. population no longer covers a considerable portion of households. Combining landline and cell phones poses difficult sampling challenges, some of which occur because many people have both landlines and cell phones, and because landlines tend to be household-based and cell phones tend to belong to individuals. In addition, the portability of cell phone numbers across geographic areas adds to the challenge when one wants to conduct a survey of a specific geographic area like a city or region. Those who keep a cell phone number from another area when they move into the area being surveyed will not appear on the sample frame, and those who kept their local number when they moved out of the area will be erroneously included in the frame. Also, the need to ask all respondents additional questions to establish eligibility is made difficult by the conflicting need to make questionnaires shorter, due to today's culture of people being less willing to reveal information about themselves to a stranger over the telephone.

Many surveyors were optimistic in the late 1990s that as telephone response rates fell, a smooth transition could be made to conducting most surveys over the Internet. This transition has not been as effective as it was envisioned. Not all households have Internet access, and the fact that individuals who do not use the Internet differ sharply (older, less education, and lower incomes) from those who do, makes it difficult to achieve adequate representation for many surveys. Perhaps even more importantly, there are no sample frames for household surveys that allow direct e-mail contact, like traditional random digit dialing for the telephone or address-based lists for mail. Even when e-mail addresses are available (e.g., lists of clients, students, and organization members), contact only by e-mail often produces response rates that are similarly low to those achieved in telephone surveys.

As a result, optimism about the potential for web surveys has more recently given way to puzzlement. Even casual observation in airports, shopping malls, and meetings make it evident that people are increasingly receiving and sending messages on smartphones and a myriad of other electronic devices. Full screen laptops or desktop computers with keyboards are no longer the predominant way that many people connect to the Internet.

While purse and pocket devices provide convenient ways to connect to the Internet, their small screens and input devices make reading and responding to survey requests quite difficult. Obtaining responses to a questionnaire in today's environment often requires getting an electronic survey request successfully through a prescreening on a smartphone (i.e., read but not deleted), and then returned to on a laptop, desktop, or tablet where respondents can more easily view and respond to the survey request. Complicating matters further, as many young people continue to replace e-mail communication with texts or social networking status updates, it has become harder to reach this group. For these reasons, successfully shifting to electronic communication for all survey requests continues to be very challenging.

Mail surveys have also undergone a significant transformation. Although modern mail survey methods were being developed at the same time that random digit dialing enabled the telephone to become a prominent mode, mail has long been considered a less desirable and lower response rate alternative. This survey mode is also not well suited for the intensive branching that now characterizes many survey questionnaires. But substantial advancements in printing capabilities mean that the personalization and customization of paper surveys and mailing materials have advanced well beyond where they were just a decade ago.

The situation for mail also improved considerably when the U.S. Postal Service began routinely releasing a list of residential addresses of all households receiving delivery of postal mail. Improvements in the proportion of households with city addresses, as opposed to simplified addresses that were somewhat imprecise, now mean that about 95% to 97% of U.S. households are accessible to surveyors by mail (Iannacchione, 2011). At the same time, research has shown that responses to postal surveys have not declined as significantly as responses to telephone surveys (Messer & Dillman, 2011; Rookey, Le, Littlejohn, & Dillman, 2012; Smyth, Dillman, Christian, & O'Neill, 2010).

Ironically, mail has moved from being the lowest response rate mode for many survey designs to now having response rates that are significantly higher than telephone and being competitive with well-financed in-person surveys. It has also shifted from having the poorest coverage for household surveys to having the most comprehensive household sample frame. Mail surveys were also once considered the lowest cost method for conducting surveys but are now a somewhat higher cost method, especially when compared to an e-mail-only contact web survey. That said, mail continues to have its challenges, such as ensuring that the mail is actually delivered to the household and opened by someone in the household and that the person receiving it can read and comprehend it in the language(s) provided.

In sum, single mode surveys, regardless of mode, tend not to be as effective as in years past for many, if not most, survey situations. And increasingly, more than one mode may need to be used to contact and survey different individuals to ensure that various members of the population are represented.

WHY EMPHASIZE MIXED-MODE DATA COLLECTION?

Our emphasis in this book on mixed-mode survey designs stems from our desire to create designs that are most likely to keep the four major sources of error to acceptably low levels while also reducing survey costs. Mixing modes allows us to take advantage of the strengths of certain modes to overcome the weaknesses of others in order to minimize total survey error as much as possible within resource and time constraints. How exactly we mix modes depends heavily on our motivation for mixing them; that is, it depends on what sources of error we are trying to minimize or if we are trying to reduce costs or collect the data quickly.

One goal a surveyor might have is to reduce the costs of their survey. In fact, a recent study of national statistical agency surveys conducted in Europe and the

United States by Luiten (2013) found that reducing costs was the primary reason for the increasing use of mixed-mode designs. A common way to mix modes to reduce costs is to collect as many responses as possible in a cheaper mode before switching to a more expensive mode to try to obtain additional responses. This strategy was used by the U.S. Census Bureau for the 2010 Decennial Census. Paper questionnaires were first mailed to nearly every address in the United States and about 74% of them responded (U.S. Census Bureau, n.d.). Only then were more expensive interviewers sent out to try to obtain responses from households that did not respond by mail. The Census Bureau was able to save considerable money by getting most households to respond by mail and minimizing the number that would need to be visited by in-person interviewers.

However, there are many other reasons that multiple modes of survey response are used. Sometimes the goal is to improve coverage. While it is theoretically possible to contact sampled individuals in many different ways—cell phone, office phone, home phone, home postal delivery, office postal delivery, or through multiple e-mail addresses—it is quite uncommon for our available sampling frames or lists to include all types of contact information for each unit. The lack of available contact information for multiple modes can be due to the inability to match contact information from different frames or because people are unwilling to voluntarily provide multiple types of contact information to organizations requesting it (e.g., some people might provide a phone number, others an e-mail address, and still others a postal mailing address). In this context, developing a sample frame for a single-mode survey often means excluding members of the target population for whom the desired mode of contact is not available, potentially increasing coverage error. Mixing modes is a way to ensure most members of the target population can be included on the sample frame and thus have an opportunity to be sampled.

Sometimes a second or third mode is offered to individuals in hopes they will find an alternative mode particularly appealing or they will be able to respond to it when they are unable to respond by a different mode. An example is that individuals who cannot respond on a computer because of not having developed those skills may be quite comfortable responding by paper or by telephone. Some individuals may not pick up their mail or answer a landline phone but will check their e-mail and answer their cell phone. In cases such as these, using multiple modes can improve response rates and reduce nonresponse error by appealing to different kinds of respondents. In still other instances, one response mode is offered initially, such as web or telephone, and then followed by another (e.g., mail) to improve the speed of response and facilitate quicker processing of results.

Mixing survey modes does not necessarily mean offering people more than one way of completing a survey questionnaire. Different modes can also be used to contact sample members with the survey request even when only one mode is used for collecting responses. Traditionally, people were contacted by the same mode that was also used to complete the survey. However, research has long shown that contacting individuals by mail ahead of a telephone or in-person interview can improve response rates (de Leeuw, Callegaro, Hox, Korendijk, & Lensvelt-Mulders, 2007); similarly, follow-up telephone calls to remind people to respond can sometimes improve response rates for postal surveys.

In fact, in today's survey environment, using multiple survey modes as a means of communication to encourage response in a single mode may be a more powerful way of mixing modes to improve survey response and the quality of those responses than simply providing an alternative mode for responding to a survey. Several decades of experimentation has consistently shown that sending a token cash incentive of a few dollars with a mail survey request improves response dramatically for that mode (Church, 1993). Recent research has now demonstrated that sending a postal letter with such an incentive and a request to respond over the web improves response over the web more so than with a request to respond to a paper questionnaire (Messer & Dillman, 2011). In these instances, mixing contact modes allows surveyors to incorporate other response-inducing strategies into their surveys.

Perhaps even more important is the potential for creating synergy between contacts via different modes to encourage survey responses. For example, while a postal request containing an incentive can be quite effective at getting people to complete a web survey (Smyth et al., 2010), recent research has shown that following a postal request with an e-mail containing an electronic link to the web survey can improve response rates even more (Millar & Dillman, 2011). Thus, one important area of potential for mixed-mode survey designs is using multiple types of contact information to produce contacts in different modes that work together in synergistic ways to convince sample members to respond.

In the third edition of this book we presented a model proposing four types of mixed-mode surveys:

> Type 1: Use one survey mode to encourage response by another mode. For example, use a postal letter to encourage cooperation when an interviewer calls to administer a telephone survey.
>
> Type 2: Use two modes to collect responses from the same respondent. For example, to provide privacy for answering a subset of sensitive questions such as those about sexual behavior or drug use, allow respondents to an in-person interview to answer these questions using a self-administered paper or computer questionnaire.
>
> Type 3: Use two different modes to collect responses from different people in the same survey population. For example, use a telephone survey to obtain responses from individuals who have not responded to a previously sent mail questionnaire.
>
> Type 4: Use two different modes to obtain responses from the same person at different times. A common example is to switch from in-person interviews at time 1 to web follow-ups at time 2, as is sometimes done in longitudinal surveys.

This typology was presented in order to convey how different combinations of contact and response modes may affect costs, coverage, nonresponse, and measurement errors. Whereas Types 1, 3, and 4 are primarily focused on improving coverage and response while controlling costs, Type 2 is primarily focused on improving measurement by reducing social desirability. In addition, Types 3 and 4 have significant implications for measurement error, especially if both aural and visual modes of surveying are used. These risks are likely to be even more serious when attempting to precisely measure change over time as in Type 4.

It is now evident that the mixing of survey modes is likely to be far more complex than suggested by this simple model. Increasingly, modes are being mixed at both the contact and data collection stages. For example, we are aware of a number of surveys that use multiple modes of contact to encourage and facilitate response in one or more modes of data collection (i.e., Type 1 used in combination with Type 3) in an attempt to maximize response and minimize nonresponse error, improve coverage, or control costs. Examples of mixing modes of contact with and without mixing response modes will be discussed repeatedly in this book.

Although we focus on mixed-mode survey designs, it is important not to ignore single-mode data collection. Often mixed-mode designs are impractical or will not necessarily improve data quality. It is possible, and sometimes most effective, to limit survey contacts and data collection to only one mode. For example, telephone-only preelection surveys will likely continue in the future because of the timeliness with which they can be conducted. In addition, many organizations (i.e., businesses, professional organizations, universities, etc.) that have accurate and complete lists of members' e-mail addresses will likely continue to conduct successful web-only surveys with e-mail contacts. Likewise, contacting households by mail and asking them to complete a paper questionnaire, which will be discussed in this book, has produced response rates and nonresponse error attributes that are as good, or better, than those that can be achieved by mixed-mode designs, and thus will likely continue to be used in the years to come.

In sum, mixed-mode design, from the most simple to the most complex, is about reducing multiple sources of error, with each way of mixing modes having different implications for each source of error. Mixed-mode designs are also justified by the desire for lower costs, achieving greater timeliness of response, and making the response task easier for the recipient of the survey request. These concerns, plus the wide variety and complexity of ways of mixing modes for contact and response, underscore the need to establish criteria for developing specific survey designs.

WHAT IS TAILORED DESIGN AND WHY IS IT NEEDED?

A key premise of this book is that in order to minimize total survey error, surveyors have to customize or tailor their survey designs to their particular situations. This can be illustrated by an experience one of us recently had in a survey design workshop. The workshop participants had just finished a lengthy discussion of topics already discussed in this chapter. One participant responded somewhat impatiently, "You have explained the problems, but you haven't told us how to solve them. The reason I am here is to find out what specific procedures and techniques I should use for my survey in order for it to be a success, whether mixed mode or not."

By asking him to describe his survey problem and then inviting others to share examples of the challenges they were facing, as well by providing additional examples that have come up in other workshops, a list of examples was produced that illustrated the diversity of challenges surveyors face. These included the following:

- An extension service entomologist wanted to survey beekeepers in his state to find out the extent to which they were experiencing winter die-off, and what they were doing to prevent it.
- A university researcher had funding to survey the general public in different parts of the United States in order to understand household water conservation practices. He explained, "I had planned to do a telephone survey

with a 20-minute questionnaire until someone told me I would get a poor response rate."

- A graduate student working on her doctoral dissertation wanted to survey rural and urban people to understand differences in the visual landscapes people preferred for the area in which they lived. "I have to use pictures," she said.
- A federal agency employee wanted to survey a nationally representative sample of home owners in order to better understand effects of the recent recession on their financial well-being.
- Another federal agency employee was concerned with how to find and survey households with children, pointing out that nearly half of the children in the United States are being raised in households without landline telephones.
- An employee of a large corporation wanted to survey consumers about a potential new product and the features they might like or dislike.
- An employee of a large cultural history museum had been asked to develop a way of surveying samples of visitors to measure their satisfaction and collect suggestions for improvement.

Our response to those seeking answers to specific situations such as these is that there is not a simple set of design procedures that if applied to every situation will be most effective in reducing survey error. The populations to be sampled and surveyed, the kinds of questions that need to be asked, the resources available for doing the survey, and other constraints imposed by survey sponsorship differ greatly across individuals and organizations who wish to do surveys. It should be apparent, even from this small list of situations, that the same procedures will not work for all surveys. But how does one go about deciding which procedures to use and not use, and by what criterion does one choose certain methods for collecting data over others? Also, under what conditions should one choose a single survey mode, and under what conditions is it better to use multiple modes?

Tailored design refers to customizing survey procedures for each survey situation based upon knowledge about the topic and sponsor of the survey, the types of people who will be asked to complete the survey, the resources available, and the time frame for reporting results. Tailored design is a strategy that can be applied in the development of all aspects of a survey to reduce total survey error to acceptable levels and motivate all types of sample members to respond within resource and time constraints.

Underlying this general approach are three fundamental considerations. First, tailored design is a scientific approach to conducting sample surveys with a focus on reducing the four sources of survey error—coverage, sampling, nonresponse, and measurement—that may undermine the quality of the information collected. Second, the tailored design method involves developing a set of survey procedures (including the recruitment contacts and the questionnaire) that interact and work together to encourage all sample members to respond to the survey. Thus, it entails giving attention to all aspects of contacting and communicating with people—few, if any, aspects of this process can be ignored when using a tailored design strategy. Finally, tailoring is about developing survey procedures that build positive social exchange and encourage response by taking into consideration elements such as survey sponsorship, the nature of the survey population and variations within it, and the content of the survey questions, among other things.

At first glance, this challenge of tailored design may hardly seem different from that faced for decades by survey researchers. However, the dizzying array of mode possibilities now available, individually and in combination with one another, and each with quite different cost and time implications, adds to the complexity of the situation. In addition, the dramatic changes occurring in the presence or absence of human interaction, trust in the legitimacy of surveys, and changes in people's control over whether and how they can be contacted make what once may have been a more simple survey design situation much more difficult. We utilize tailored design as a means of helping identify which survey procedures are effective and which ones are ineffective within each specific survey context.

We develop our tailored design approach by using an understanding of what causes people to behave in certain ways and not others. Specifically, we use a *social exchange* perspective on human behavior, which suggests that respondent behavior is motivated by the return that behavior is expected to bring, and in fact, usually does bring, from others. It assumes that the likelihood of responding to a questionnaire, and doing so accurately, is greater when the person trusts that the expected rewards for responding to a survey will outweigh the anticipated costs of responding.

Our social exchange approach underlies certain decisions made regarding coverage and sampling (e.g., obtaining sample frame and contact information), heavily influences the way we write questions and construct questionnaires, and determines how we design contacts that will produce the intended representative sample. We explain this social exchange approach in Chapter 2 and discuss how it might be applied to a wide variety of practical survey design situations.

CONCLUSION

The compelling concern that has guided revising this book is that mixed-mode surveys have shifted from being an occasional survey design issue to becoming an enduring concern for many, if not most, survey designers. Even when one decides that a single-mode survey is adequate for her survey needs, consideration of mixed-mode, mixed-device, and/or mixed-communication possibilities often precedes that decision.

Because of this substantial change in the survey landscape, in this edition we have introduced mixed mode front and center in this first chapter, and we treat it as part of the fundamental framework for this book rather than waiting to introduce it until the middle of the book, as was done in the previous edition. It has been presented here as a solution to the inadequacy of individual modes used to recruit sample members to respond and to collect responses.

The mixed-mode framework we have presented focuses the search for high-quality sample survey procedures on finding alternatives for telephone-only, web- and e-mail-only, in-person-only, and mail-only data collection designs. The nature of that approach considers traditional modes as communication mediums in addition to being potential response modes. Tailored design refers to fitting the communication and response modes to the survey topic, population characteristics, and the implementation situation one faces. Using multiple modes in a tailored design framework does not imply a one-size-fits-all approach to surveying. It means getting inside the heads of respondents, to understand what appeals to them and why, and adjusting survey procedures accordingly.

We begin that process with Chapter 2, where we answer the question of why people do and do not respond to sample surveys and provide suggestions for how to increase response rates. In Chapter 3 we focus on issues related to sampling and coverage, or finding and choosing who to survey, for each of the survey modes and for mixed-mode designs. Chapters 4, 5, and 6 are devoted to the topic of designing survey questions and questionnaires. Specifically, in Chapter 4 we cover issues common to all questionnaires; in Chapter 5 we provide guidance for designing specific types of questions; and in Chapter 6 we discuss the differences between aural and visual questionnaires and provide specific guidance for how to design for visual surveys. Chapter 7 is focused on how to order questions in the questionnaire and how to pretest them. These first seven chapters contain information that applies broadly to multiple survey modes.

We then turn to strategies for designing and implementing surveys for specific survey modes: Chapter 8 discusses telephone surveys, Chapter 9 web surveys, and Chapter 10 mail surveys. These chapters will be very useful to readers who are trying to design and carry out single mode surveys but also to those who are using these modes in mixed-mode designs. Chapter 11 then discusses designing questionnaires, contacts, and implementation strategies for mixed-mode surveys, building upon each of the individual mode chapters. Finally, in Chapter 12 we look ahead to how surveyors might respond to technological and societal changes in pursuit of conducting better sample surveys.

Reducing People's Reluctance to Respond to Surveys

Survey sponsors and the people they ask to respond to their surveys often have contrasting views of the situation. Designing quality surveys requires understanding those differences and how to reconcile them.

For many recipients of survey requests, the invitations come as annoying intrusions into their lives, such as unwanted phone calls, postal letters, or junk e-mails. "Why me?" and "How do I make this go away?" are common quick and decisive reactions from sample members, resulting in a hang-up, a toss into the wastebasket, or a deletion.

If the recipient should begin to study the invitation, these feelings may be amplified by thoughts such as disinterest in the topic, uncertainty about who is making the request, or concern about opening an electronic link from an unknown source that could infect his computer. If a survey request survives these initial perils, other considerations are likely to arise, with individuals wondering, how long is this survey going to take to complete, will the results be useful, do the questions—especially the first ones—make sense, is this request legitimate, and will my name be placed on a mailing list that produces even more annoyances?

The survey sponsor, on the other hand, often sees herself as facing a huge task of contacting hundreds or thousands of individuals and getting them to answer burdensome questions. She also wants to do it quickly, efficiently, and at minimal cost. The surveyor's thinking is often focused on what kind of communications can be written that cover all possible information that someone in the sample might like to know and how all the contacts can be produced in the least costly way. This thinking often leads to practices such as sending only two or three requests by e-mail, only using bulk rate postal mail, or repeating word-for-word in follow-ups the same information that was provided earlier. The content of these communications often focuses on the survey problem as the survey sponsor sees it, even to the point of becoming defensively prepared messages such as "My agency is required to find out what the health improvement needs of people are, and therefore I must ask you to tell us your concerns."

The questionnaire may include dozens of questions, with the list continuing to grow as new possibilities are created. The most critical questions for the planned analyses may be asked first, especially in web surveys, in case people decide to quit after answering only a few questions. This kind of reasoning sometimes results in starting with open-ended questions, such as "How much was your total household income last year?" The sponsor asks for the exact amount, to the last dollar, instead of offering broad categories, because it is deemed essential to the survey's purpose that measurement be as precise as possible. When only a few people respond to these requests, surveyors are often disappointed, concluding, "People just aren't interested in helping with important surveys." At times, the sponsor's perspective on surveys appears to be, "It's all about me."

It is sometimes hard to know who is most annoyed with follow-up phone calls that are made one after another, over a period of days and weeks: the recipient of the call, who has learned to avoid them, or the surveyor, who cannot understand why those calls are not getting answered. Figure 2.1 provides a few examples of what surveyors sometimes do, and common respondent reactions to what is read

FIGURE 2.1   Why respondents may not complete surveys.

What surveyors sometimes do ...	... and what the respondent may think or do
Send a brief e-mail from an unknown organization; it gets to the point quickly by asking recipients to click on a link to complete a survey about crime in their community.	**How do I know this is legitimate? There is no address or telephone number, and I wonder if this link will connect me to some malware that will infect my computer.**
Send a letter emblazoned with "Survey enclosed. Respond immediately."	**This is advertising. I'm not interested.**
"This is Jane calling for the Smithfield Polling Company. I am not selling anything and I only need to ask you a few questions."	**Uh, oh. She hasn't said *why* she is calling, and I think I need to be really careful here. The easiest thing for me to do is hang up ... click!**
Include a lengthy consent form at the beginning of a web survey that requires an *x* to indicate that the respondent has agreed to complete the survey.	**I have not yet seen the questions. I don't know if I am willing to complete all of the questions. What is so worrisome about this survey that this kind of consent is needed?**
Write in the invitation to respond: "I have included $5 to pay for your time in completing this brief survey."	**My time is worth more than this. This is a paltry amount to be paid.**
Start the survey request with "My agency is required to report types of individuals we serve, so please answer the demographic questions so we can fulfill that requirement."	**Just because an agency is required to do something does not mean that I am required.**
Include "To unsubscribe click here" at the end of an e-mail request.	**Oh, this is spam and I can just unsubscribe so I do not get the same e-mail tomorrow and the next day.**
Program the web survey to require an answer to every question.	**None of these answer categories fit me; I don't know what to do. Should I quit or just make something up?**

or heard. These negative reactions are often in response to quite specific aspects of the survey invitation materials or questionnaire.

These behaviors on the part of the surveyor may individually or collectively produce incomplete answers or no response at all. In addition, if responses come only from those especially interested in talking about a particular topic—for example, views about abortion, a particular election outcome, or climate change—the survey cannot accomplish its intended purpose. When we examine surveys in this way, it is easy to understand why survey response rates are frequently quite low—sometimes in the single digits—with considerable nonresponse error regardless of survey mode.

How to obtain acceptable response rates and response quality from a sample that will allow the precise estimation of characteristics in the population of interest is the focus of this chapter. We describe specific steps that can and should be taken by survey designers to develop respondent-friendly questionnaires and implementation procedures that accommodate the concerns and interests of potential respondents to help them find reasons for responding. To do this we develop a perspective that considers what happens when an organization or individual asks a randomly sampled stranger to complete a survey and how multiple communication attempts can be utilized to encourage a positive response when the first request falls short.

We are guided in our design efforts by a sociological perspective on what causes humans to behave as they do in normal daily life, known as social exchange theory. The basic idea is that surveyors need to consider potential benefits and costs that accrue as a result of responding (or not responding), and work to create trust that these benefits will be realized by the respondent during the response process and afterward. Although this perspective has been utilized in previous editions of this book, the specific recommendations for survey design presented here go well beyond those introduced earlier, taking into consideration the massive changes in technology and how people communicate with others that are occurring all around us.

In light of these changes, mixed-mode surveys are increasingly needed and are emphasized here. The use of multiple modes to make contact provides surveyors with additional opportunities to present the survey request and reasons for responding to it. Offering alternative modes for providing the response also becomes possible. Together these possibilities increase the opportunities for multiple efforts at communication that are comfortably within societal norms for interaction, and that allow a surveyor to improve the balance of rewards and costs as well as enhance feelings of trust. To begin introducing this framework, we consider results from a recently completed mixed-mode survey.

EXAMPLE OF A SURVEY WITH A HIGH RESPONSE RATE

A recent survey was conducted to obtain responses from nearly 600 doctoral students at Washington State University (WSU) about their dissertation work and graduate training. The study was targeted toward students who had successfully completed their required preliminary examinations and had only to finish the dissertation in order to meet their degree requirements. Data collection needed to be completed within about a month. After learning that we could obtain both e-mail and postal contact information for the sampled individuals, we proposed the following implementation design:

- *Day 1:* Send a postal letter asking students to respond over the web. Enclose a $2 incentive with this request.
- *Day 4:* Send an e-mail that builds upon the information contained in the invitation letter, while emphasizing that the sender is following up by e-mail to provide an electronic link to the survey with the hope that this will make responding easier.
- *Day 10:* Send a second e-mail request.
- *Day 18:* Send a postal letter offering the option of responding via mail. Include a paper questionnaire and an addressed and stamped return envelope.
- *Day 22:* Send a final e-mail follow-up.

Our initial proposal elicited some hesitation. A faculty member reminded us, "These are graduate students. They are all highly skilled with computers, have e-mail and check it all or most days. Why would you even consider starting with a postal contact and offering a paper questionnaire as a follow-up?" He suggested that it would be just as effective to use only e-mails. Also, $2 sounded like a waste of money; it would barely buy a cup of coffee. Why not save money by giving $5 only to those who responded? He also argued that if we insisted on using web as well as mail, that we should give people a choice of response modes in the first contact to improve the initial response. After considering these objections, we decided to proceed as planned.

Figure 2.2 shows the cumulative response rate over the course of the study. The figure highlights the increase in response achieved after each of the

FIGURE 2.2 Cumulative response rate by day and mode for the 2013 WSU Doctoral Student Experience Survey, showing contribution of each contact to final response rate.

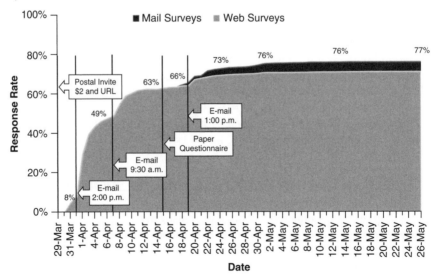

Source: Adapted from *Determining Whether Research Is Interdisciplinary: An Analysis of New Indicators* (Technical Report 13-049), by M. M. Millar, 2013, Pullman: Washington State University, Social and Economic Sciences Research Center.

five contacts. Importantly, each contact produced an additional increment of response. Most striking perhaps is the effect of the quick e-mail follow-up sent a few days after mailing the initial postal contact. The response rate from the initial postal mail-out had reached 8% by 2 p.m. on Day 4 when the first e-mail contact was sent. From then until midnight, a period of only 10 hours, the response rate jumped to nearly 30% and continued to climb over the next few days so that at the time of the next contact on Day 10 it had already reached 49%. The e-mail sent on Day 10 produced a smaller increase, with total response reaching 63% the day the paper questionnaire was mailed.

The combined effect of the second postal contact and the final e-mail follow-up pushed the overall response up to 77%. About half of the additional responses came in the form of paper questionnaires, and the rest were additional Internet returns stimulated primarily by the quick follow-up by e-mail. To put this final rise of 14 percentage points in context, nearly a third of the approximately 200 students who were sent the follow-up contacts containing the paper questionnaire responded by paper or the web.

We expected this approach to be effective as earlier research suggested that combining these implementation elements would produce a good response (Millar & Dillman, 2011). This previous research showed that offering people an initial choice of survey modes (which we had been encouraged to do but did not) tends to decrease final response rates, perhaps because it makes the response decision more complex, and leads to individuals delaying response.

We return to this example at the end of this chapter with a full discussion of why and how social exchange concepts, as described in the next section, were systematically applied to all aspects of the survey design to achieve such high response, which was well beyond the 20% to 30% range that student surveys conducted at this university typically achieve.

USING SOCIAL EXCHANGE CONCEPTS TO MOTIVATE POTENTIAL RESPONDENTS

There is no shortage of theory and research suggesting how respondents might be motivated to respond to surveys. Among those efforts are these:

Cognitive Dissonance Theory: Approach people in a way that encourages cognitive consonance with a previous behavior, expecting that people who responded to other surveys will feel the need to respond to your survey (Festinger, 1957).

Reasoned Action Theory: Appeal to people's positive attitudes toward surveys and the existence of subjective norms that favor responding, both of which produce behavioral intentions that are likely to encourage a positive response (Ajzen & Fishbein, 1980).

Adult-to-Adult Communication Style: Use an adult-to-adult style of communication rather than an adult-to-child interaction style that potential respondents will find demeaning, for example, "You must respond to this request today!" (Comley, 2006).

Influence Theory: Communicate scarcity of opportunity to respond, emphasize consistency with previous behavior, facilitate reciprocation for a favor already performed, focus on enjoyment of task and social proof, and describe what other people have done or are perceived as doing in the face of similar opportunities (Cialdini, 1984).

Leverage-Saliency Theory: Be attentive to the fact that survey features can have a positive effect on the response decision for some sample members and a negative effect for others (leverage). Make positive features more salient and negative features less salient in follow-ups to increase the likelihood of obtaining a response (Groves, Singer, & Corning, 2000).

Cost–Benefit Theory: Focus explicitly on respondent costs and benefits. Reducing costs of responding is desirable but insufficient; people choose to act when, in their subjective calculus, the benefits of doing so outweigh the costs (Singer, 2011).

Gamification Theory: Make responding to surveys fun by making them appear like games with awards like badges or points that can be earned by engaging in certain behaviors (Lai, Bristol & Link, 2012), graphics that make questions more visual, and other elements that appeal to people's emotions and desire to have an enjoyable experience (Puleston, 2012a, 2012b).

Each of these theories provides us with different concepts and tools to use in thinking about survey response. One thing they have in common is that they all place an emphasis on what appears to be going on in the potential respondent's head as she weighs whether or not to respond. That is, they are psychological in nature. There is less emphasis on how well the survey materials fit with the general culture in a way that affects response behavior, something that cannot easily be articulated by the recipient of the survey request. Because of this, these theories do not provide guidance about how multiple features of each survey such as the mode(s) of contact and response, content of communications, questions asked, question order and presentation, and the timing of contacts should be designed to create a holistic data collection protocol that will improve response rates and data quality. That is, these theories do not tell us much about how to connect response-encouraging elements together into a comprehensive design. In particular, they have not addressed how surveyors might use multiple modes of contact and response modes to increase the likelihood that recipients of survey requests will attend to those requests and respond.

The first edition of this book (Dillman, 1978) introduced social exchange as a means of connecting multiple design issues, some of which are dealt with in isolation by the aforementioned theories, in order to obtain high survey response rates, but did so primarily in a single-mode context. In this edition, we apply social exchange theory to the mixed-mode context that characterizes much of survey research today.

The concept of social exchange is quite simple. It is that people are more likely to comply with a request from someone else if they believe and trust that the rewards for complying with that request will eventually exceed the costs of complying. Social exchange was developed by Blau (1964), Homans (1961), and Thibaut and Kelley (1959) as a general model for understanding how people behave in their interactions with one another, and to understand how social norms develop to guide those interactions. This framework was used to explain how people realize their self-interests as well as achieve effective interaction with others in social groups, from communities to the society in which they live. Social exchange concepts provide a means of reconciling philosophical views of the human desire to find meaning through interactions with others and the human desire to achieve self-interests (e.g., Roloff, 1981) from which they also draw satisfaction.

Social exchange is not the same as economic exchange. Social exchanges are different from economic ones because there is only a general expectation of a positive return. The exact nature of benefits and why they will be provided are often not specified in advance; instead, they are left open, based upon trust that they will be delivered. As noted by Stafford (2008), social exchanges involve trust in a likely outcome, rather than relying on explicit bargaining, and are more flexible. In addition, social exchanges involve various types of as-yet undelivered benefits (e.g., social, psychological, etc., in addition to economic benefits) as well as any immediate ones. In contrast, economic transactions rely only on assigning a monetary value to the service or product to be transferred in the exchange.

Social exchange is also not a rational behavior model. It does not assume that individuals are balancing only benefits and costs to determine what action to take to maximize their personal advantage (Friedman, 1953). Reciprocity, trust, and altruism are not usually a part of rational behavior models, but all three are central to social exchange theory and how social behavior occurs.

Applying social exchange to survey response encourages us to think about multiple aspects of how a request from a stranger is viewed, and what features of that request, which may be communicated in different ways over time, influence whether a questionnaire is completed and returned. We assume that for most people the decision to participate in a survey (and to continue their participation) involves multiple considerations that take into account perceived benefits, perceived costs, and trust that in the long run the benefits will outweigh the costs.

However, it is a mistake to think that all of the decisions people make about social interactions or whether to respond to a questionnaire are always, or even mostly, the result of a lengthy, careful consideration of dozens of features. Social interaction decisions are sometimes made quickly while considering only a few of many potential issues. So are survey decisions; for example, an individual may simply think "The interviewer seems sincere" or "This questionnaire looks like it could be interesting." Quick decisions to respond or not might also get made because one is trying to be helpful to someone else, supporting a good cause, wanting to experience something interesting, wary of the size of the request, or for a number of other reasons that can be triggered by something embedded in the request or related to the person's background and interests.

The decision to respond to a self-administered web or mail survey is typically made in the first day or two with many sample members deciding almost immediately whether to respond. The decision to respond to a telephone survey is also immediate, in the first seconds or minute of the interaction. These decisions are often spur-of-the-moment and based on quick impressions. It is certainly not the norm to prepare a detailed list of reasons to respond or not respond to a survey in order to balance all of the pros and cons. But at the same time, people generally do not look at a questionnaire printed on pretty green paper or a dynamically constructed web page and decide to respond regardless of other considerations such as what questions are asked or who is asking. Rather, the spur-of-the-moment decision is generally based on quick impressions of multiple aspects of the survey request. Thus, the chances of eventually convincing sample members to respond are higher when many aspects of the survey request work together to encourage response. Our use of social exchange recognizes that cultural influences, respect for the requestor, spending one's time in interesting ways, and many other issues intertwine to influence the behavior of people asked to become respondents.

Does Social Exchange Still Apply in Today's Asynchronous and Rapid-Fire Communication Environment?

When the social exchange perspective on human behavior was developed in the mid-20th century, the way that people behaved and interacted was considerably different than it is today. People's lives were more likely to be focused on communities and organizations that contributed to the maintenance of societal-wide norms. They were also more likely to communicate by phone or through postal mail and make many decisions in a slower manner. As just one example, having dinner out with friends was usually the result of a very deliberate decision-making process and then making the arrangements to do so took considerable planning.

Nowadays we have more technology at our disposal that allows short and quick communications to happen instantly. The in-depth communications of the past have been largely supplanted by brief e-mails, text or voice messages, tweets, or posts that get read and responded to very quickly, often while the recipient is engaged in other activities like walking down the street, waiting in line, or during pauses in work and play activities. Our social interaction has also become more spontaneous, with meetings and activities being based upon spur-of-the-moment decisions. For many, deciding to go out to dinner with friends is now done spontaneously, arrangements are made within minutes, and behavior may be modified immediately (e.g., I was on my way home when I decided to head across town to meet Kris for dinner).

We can now socially interact with people hundreds or thousands of miles away as easily, and in some cases even more easily, than with someone sitting next to us on a city bus or living in our same neighborhood. In addition the messages we receive in any given day include requests from close friends as well as from complete strangers. We often decide whether to ignore, delete, postpone, or respond to these requests based on quick assessments of only a few written words. And we do so with the understanding that answering or forwarding some unsolicited messages can have unanticipated disastrous consequences. For example, one might accidentally share a private message, picture, or privileged digital address with strangers, making previously private information public. Or one might inadvertently click on one of the many links in a message disguised as legitimate that is really intended to steal their identity, such as in this message that one of us recently received in an e-mail from a sender claiming to be our bank: "Your credit card has been used by someone else. Click here to confirm your receipt of this message and help us protect your credit rating."

It is in this environment of rapid-fire communications with messages from multiple sources (some less scrupulous than others) that surveys are now undertaken to assess public opinion, identify employment practices and rates, and gather knowledge on a host of public policy issues, ranging from education access to overt discrimination. The critical question this raises for surveyors is how to create effective communication that will reach sampled individuals, be processed by them, create an understanding of why they are being asked to respond to a particular survey, and motivate them to comply with the request and offer thoughtful honest answers to survey questions.

In sum, our methods of social interaction are now much more quick and asynchronous and much of the content of that interaction has changed significantly. These changes have altered our behavior in many important ways. Given these substantial changes, it is reasonable to ask whether social exchange still applies to predicting and understanding the reasons for human behavior, including survey response decisions. Some may wonder if it is an outdated way of looking at things.

Individuals are as likely to make decisions based on considerations of cost, benefits, and trust in today's environment as in times past. In fact, with more decisions to make, less time to make them, and, in many cases, serious consequences at stake, social exchange concepts may be even more important in today's decision-making processes than in earlier times. For example, the potential costs of decisions are a frequent concern in a world where the information one shares has the potential to exist and be easily accessible in digital space seemingly forever. Likewise, with so many requests that require decisions to be made, the immediate benefits of taking a particular action may be particularly important in deciding which requests to process and respond to. As these examples demonstrate, the costs and benefits of doing some things and not others are as much a part of our daily environment as they ever were.

Perhaps more importantly though, trust, which has received little to no direct attention in the theories discussed earlier, has likely become even more salient than it was in the past. In earlier times, when lives were more constrained to the immediate geography, people learned who they might trust and not trust through personal interaction and accumulated experiences. Institutions developed reputations that, once created, were slow to change. A misspoken word in a conversation or letter was typically slow to reach others. Technology, especially the Internet, did not provide the immediate access to one's past that is now available. Sharing of one's words could not be done so quickly and effortlessly, making the types of misinterpretation that results from the information becoming increasingly removed from the source as people tell and retell it less common. In addition, in the past people were not typically asked to make decisions in a quick response environment with individuals or organizations whose characteristics and intent were being communicated through digital media.

It is against this background that we must think about perceptions of cost, benefits, and trust associated with responding to a survey request. Costs, benefits, and trust affect both whether people attend to the survey request at all and, once they do, whether they are persuaded to respond.

Increasing the Benefits of Survey Participation

The benefits of responding to a survey have been, and are likely to remain, limited. Responding is usually voluntary and can easily be disregarded. But, this does not mean that benefits are completely absent and will not be provided. Many of the things that humans do in life, and from which they feel satisfaction, involve helping others. These actions are particularly satisfying if the beneficiaries are individuals or groups (school, community, country) to which someone belongs, or from which they receive long-term benefits. People also seek to have personal, and perhaps selfish, interests realized.

In their development of social exchange principles, Blau (1964) and Homans (1961) indicated that many people feel a sense of reward from knowing they have helped others. Showing positive regard for others can also be rewarding.

Thibaut and Kelley (1959) proposed that time-consuming assistance is often appropriately repaid simply by verbal appreciation or returning a small favor later. Being able to provide requested consultation is also something that many people consider rewarding, and people enjoy doing tasks that they find interesting. Individuals also have a tendency to reciprocate when people make a special effort to provide benefits, even if they are of a token nature. There are many specific ways that a survey design can take advantage of these characteristics to increase the modest benefits some people may feel from responding to survey requests. These include the following.

Specify How the Survey Results Will Be Useful

Is it possible or likely that survey results will influence a community or organization decision? Is public policy a likely beneficiary? Many people feel a significant benefit when contributing to something that benefits others, even if they do not believe they will personally benefit directly. Many, but not all, surveys are undertaken specifically in hopes of affecting practical decisions. Other surveys may stop short of that, focusing on why something does or does not happen, but have implications for individual or group decisions that can be emphasized in communications to sampled members. Describing those potential benefits may encourage individuals to respond and carefully answer the survey questions.

Ask for Help or Advice

As noted by both Homans (1961) and Blau (1964), people often feel good when others ask them for advice or assistance that only they can provide. Moreover, because the increased specialization of occupational skills and tasks in today's organizations necessitates collaboration to get work done, asking for and providing assistance or advice is an essential feature of our modern society. In addition, group actions and decisions are a fundamental part of today's school and work culture. When people are asked for assistance or advice, it conveys the value of their contribution to the group activities as much or more today than it ever did.

This cultural and psychological phenomenon can be applied to the survey context. Most surveys are done because the information being requested is not available from other sources. Thus, it is natural to ask people for help or advice that they are situated to provide. Generally speaking, people will take interest from being asked, and it will not be inconsistent with other social experiences they commonly have.

Ask Interesting Questions

Enjoying a particular activity can be a powerful determinant of human behavior, as suggested by Cialdini (1984). When questions are interesting, and it can be explained in communications that the questionnaire will be interesting, people are more likely to feel they benefit from answering them. However, what is interesting to one person may be of little interest to another. Thus, an essential part of questionnaire design, as discussed later, is contemplating what questions have broad appeal, and which may be of limited interest. This may mean reordering questions so that those with broad appeal and interest appear earlier in the questionnaire, as discussed in Chapter 7, or even adding interest-getting questions relevant to one's topic to a survey to better engage people early in the questionnaire.

Puleston (2012a, 2012b) suggested following gaming theory by changing the style of asking questions. For example, surveyors could substitute graphical representations for words, and tell respondents from the outset of a survey that they would like them to play a survey game, as opposed to completing a survey. Gamification seems to be a novel way of connecting with some respondents, particularly younger people who enjoy and have extensive exposure to computer games. However, Puleston (2012b) also notes that although response rates are likely to increase, "the impact on the data is not inconsiderable. Often the results can be measurably different." Further, initial results from using gamification techniques, such as badges, to encourage people to respond to an online or mobile TV diary have shown little benefit, and even then only among very young adults, and may actually be confusing to older respondents (Lai et al., 2012).

The gaming approach raises important questions about measurement validity and reliability, but serves as an important reminder of why surveys often do not get answered. There is little doubt that answering interesting questions is seen by respondents as a benefit to answering a survey. Because of our concern with obtaining valid and reliable measurement, rather than using gamification to motivate response, in this book we approach this issue by focusing on the addition of topically relevant questions that may be of particular interest to respondents and strategic ordering of survey questions.

Utilize Sponsorship by a Legitimate Organization

The sponsor of a survey can affect the decision to respond in two ways: by making it more rewarding to do so and by lending legitimacy to the survey and inducing trust (discussed in more detail later in this chapter). To the extent that people want to help an organization, having sponsorship from that organization will increase the likelihood that sample members will respond. In many instances, sponsorship by religious, professional, philanthropic, political, or a number of other types of organizations that have a positive relationship with the population being surveyed can produce a sense of reward in that responding to the survey can be seen as doing something helpful for that group. In these cases, the sponsorship should be emphasized.

One of the challenges associated with today's society is that virtually all organizations can muster the capability to survey nationwide, and even internationally, via e-mail and the web. However, this means that people may increasingly be asked to respond to surveys that come from an organization that is unknown to them. The better known an organization is to potential respondents, the greater the likelihood they will respond, provided the recipients of the request see it as a legitimate organization and do not view it in a negative way.

Stress That Opportunities to Respond Are Limited

Individuals perceive doing something as more valuable when the opportunities to do so are only available to some people (Cialdini, 1984). This is great for sample surveys because they, by nature, ask some people to respond but not others. Telling sample members that only a small number of people have an opportunity to participate can be motivational. This may particularly help those who simply think someone else, with more time or knowledge of the topic, should respond instead. In addition, explaining—in a friendly and non-patronizing way—that there are relatively few opportunities to respond and that they need to respond soon can also encourage people to participate.

Convey That Others Have Responded

Much of human behavior is normatively oriented, and recognizing that one is behaving in a manner consistent with others in groups they are part of can be seen as rewarding (Cialdini, 1984). Thus, knowing that others have completed a survey can encourage people to participate. The use of social networking sites, such as Facebook or Twitter, to share status updates about what they have done and express their thoughts on the behavior suggests that this normative aspect of influencing others to try something—or avoid it—remains relevant in the information age. Many social networking sites reveal the identities of people engaged in various behaviors to entice others to try them (e.g., Christina reached level 50 on Candy Crush Saga). Revealing the identity of survey respondents in this way is almost always unethical, but statements can be added to contacts to more generally communicate that others have responded (e.g., a number of people have responded to this survey and provided valuable information …).

Use Cash and Material Incentives to Encourage (but Not Require) Reciprocity

One of the reasons that token cash incentives sent with a survey request have been shown consistently to be one of the most effective ways of improving survey response is that the surveyor has given something to the recipient, and he in turn sees it as appropriate to return the favor by completing the questionnaire, even though it is not required or mandatory.

The social reward value of modest incentives with the request, in comparison to post-survey rewards, was recently shown experimentally in a mail survey conducted in Russia (Avdeyeva & Matland, 2013). A control group received no incentive, a second group received 50 rubles (~$1.65) with the survey request, and a third group was promised 6 times that amount (300 rubles) would be paid if the questionnaire was returned. The response rate for the group receiving 50 rubles was 37% compared to only 24% for the group that received 300 rubles, while the no incentive response rate was only 10%. In addition, a combined social and economic exchange group that received both a prepaid token incentive and the postpaid contingent incentive produced a 48% response rate. This study is noteworthy in that the experimental comparison between the large postpayment and the much smaller token cash incentive sent with the survey request revealed that the smaller advance incentive was considerably more effective. However, the combined effect of both incentives was the largest, leveraging social and economic exchange. These findings are consistent with the social exchange framework, which seeks to combine social and self-interests to explain human behavior.

In a comprehensive meta-analysis, Church (1993) showed that token cash incentives provided in advance produce a substantial positive effect on survey response. Gifts or material incentives (e.g., ball point pens) have a smaller positive effect, and cash payments afterward produce an even smaller effect. In a recent review of the extensive literature on incentive use in surveys, Singer and Ye

(2013) updated the work by Church (1993) by conducting an extensive literature review of incentive studies for all modes. Consistent with Church's findings, they concluded that incentives increased response rates to surveys in all modes, with monetary incentives sent in advance having larger effects than either gifts sent with the request or promised incentives and lotteries that are contingent upon completion of the survey. However, it is important to note that prepaid incentives are difficult to offer in web and telephone surveys.

Singer and Ye (2013) also present evidence that providing incentives can impact the demographic composition of the completed sample by inducing certain demographic groups to participate. In some cases, members of groups that are typically underrepresented in surveys participated at higher rates when incentives were provided, thus reducing the potential for nonresponse error. Further, they found that relatively few studies have examined data quality (i.e., item nonresponse and length of open-ended responses), but the available ones indicate that providing an incentive does not seem to have a substantial effect on data quality. There can be little doubt that token cash incentives are one of the most important ways of providing benefits to individuals asked to complete surveys.

Recognize That Benefits Both Have Additive Effects and Can Reinforce One Another

The strategies discussed here for increasing response rates can have additive effects, meaning that using several of them will increase response rates more than using just one. For example, the Avdeyeva and Matland (2013) study discussed earlier showed that providing the incentive and using stationery and envelopes that conveyed sponsorship by a legitimate organization (a university) each individually contributed to increasing the response rate. That is, the stationery featuring the sponsor increased the response rate in addition to the gains realized from using the incentive. Response also appeared to improve further by the use of multiple contacts.

In addition, certain aspects of survey design can act as gateways for allowing other aspects to have a positive effect. Positive institutional recognition on the outside of envelopes can get envelopes opened. Token cash incentives inside envelopes can get letters that would otherwise be discarded read. Interesting questions pave the way for getting other questions answered. As such, inattention to certain beneficial aspects of completing surveys may reduce other benefits that the surveyor attempts to include.

In mixed-mode studies, one of the ways that cash incentives may be particularly impactful is to get people's attention so they will read cover letters and/or listen to an interviewer's appeal. The small cash incentive used in the Doctoral Student Experience Survey introduced earlier in this chapter undoubtedly had a major impact on response rate, with the effect coming when the e-mail follow-up arrived to reinforce the earlier contact and ease the task of responding by providing an electronic link to the web survey (Millar, 2013). This mixed-mode approach can be used when both postal and e-mail addresses are available to overcome the limitation of sending prepaid cash incentives electronically.

Do Not Deny the Existence of Benefits

On multiple occasions, we have observed surveyors explicitly telling respondents, often at the urging of an Institutional Review Board, "There are no benefits to you for responding to this survey." Such statements are provided in e-mails, cover letters, or even consent statements that respondents are required to sign. It is unwise to make such statements to survey recipients. To do so denies the possibility, and indeed the likelihood, that some respondents enjoy completing surveys, providing answers to questions they find interesting, and/or contributing to research that may be helpful to others.

Decreasing the Costs of Participation

In contrast to the benefits of survey participation being relatively small and diffuse, the costs of participation are likely to be sharply evident and may be substantial for respondents. Chief among these costs is the burden of responding to surveys that are long and detailed with questions the respondent either does not understand or cannot answer. In addition, surveys often ask for information that the respondent considers inappropriate to provide. Added to this are objections to being surveyed by particular modes, such as telephone—which for many is no longer a normative way to provide information to strangers—and the web, which some still lack access to or the ability to use well. Other costs include frustration with how often the surveyor attempts to contact individuals with a request for participation and the sense that surveyors are not considerate of people's time. In addition, whereas the benefits of someone participating in a survey accrue largely to the survey sponsor, the costs of responding are experienced mostly by the respondent. As with benefits, there are a number of specific ways that the costs of responding can be reduced for respondents.

Reduce the Burden of Length

Survey designers often want enormous detail from respondents, because they consider it essential for their analyses. Instead of asking one or two questions about people's satisfaction with their health care, a surveyor may want to ask a dozen or more items that are part of a previously tested scale that deals with a variety of aspects of health care. We have also observed cases of surveyors asking respondents to complete less than 100 questions, but upon examining the subquestions under them, each of which would require an answer, the survey turned out to ask for 300–400 responses, with the exact number depending upon the specific branching pattern that applied to each respondent.

Length, independent of all other considerations, is a huge cost of being a respondent. The insistence on designing long questionnaires, driven by investigator interests, is often the largest cost experienced by respondents who complete surveys. In addition to questionnaires not being returned, this feature often leads to mid-survey terminations or increased item nonresponse as people skip items. A division of labor sometimes exists in conducting surveys, wherein the survey designers are uninvolved in the actual data collection, so they often are separated from the angst that lengthy questionnaires cause for most respondents.

On occasion we have observed mail surveyors attempt to reduce the impression of length by squeezing questions together on fewer pages. However, this is little more than an attempt to disguise length and it offers no response advantage. For example, research has shown that Decennial Census questionnaires that spread questions out over more pages obtained similar response rates to questionnaires that placed more questions on fewer pages (Dillman, 2000; Leslie, 1997).

Reducing length takes on increased importance as a way of reducing cost in today's society. With outlets such as text messaging and Twitter, which require packing ideas into very few words, it becomes normative to substitute frequency of messages for length. There may also be a tendency for attention spans to be more limited as people become used to rapid changes in what appears on computer and smartphone screens.

Reduce Complexity

Length is only part of the concern about burden. Complexity is also an enormous source of burden for respondents. In the American Community Survey, instead of asking for the previous year's income in a single question, people are asked for precise income from each of seven sources, with categories ranging from the combined total of "interest, dividends, net rental income, royalty income, or income from estates and trusts" to "veteran's payments, unemployment compensation, child support, or alimony." These questions are asked separately for each member of the household, which in contemporary society is likely to include unrelated adults.

For one person to provide all of that information for each household member is very difficult. In addition to the combination of categories, the request for exact amounts and the need for families to report for each person individually make the question impossible for some to answer. It should not be surprising when a well-intentioned respondent gives up and does not respond to these items or abandons the survey entirely.

The U.S. Census Bureau has the authority of the U.S. government under Title 13 to require people to respond to the American Community Survey, which helps their ability to persuade people to respond. But we once met with a prospective surveyor who wanted to ask these same income questions in a university survey. Requesting this detail would have had a significant negative effect on response rates in this setting where responses cannot be required, something the investigator had difficulty understanding.

As another example, the U.S. Consumer Expenditure Survey asks respondents to recall details of all expenditures for all members of the household during the previous three months. For large expenditures like cars and washing machines it is usually possible to obtain reasonably accurate answers. However, people cannot usually recall the needed level of detail for expenditures on clothing items, household supplies, and other smaller items. Faced with the request from an interviewer for detail they cannot possibly supply, people mentally withdraw from the in-person interview, a fact that should not be surprising (National Research Council, 2013).

Clearly, the time required to answer questions is a significant cost to the respondent, and many do not take the time required to respond. However, the realization by the respondent that he cannot provide accurate answers to questions increases the sense of burden further. The desire of surveyors to obtain answers to increasingly detailed questions needed for complex modeling of attitudes and behaviors appears often to be in conflict with the limitations and patience of respondents for providing answers. It is important to realize that this is happening at a time in which everyday communications seem to be becoming much shorter and quicker and in an environment in which terminating the response requires little more than a simple push of a button or click of a mouse. Finding a balance between what respondents are asked to provide and what respondents are able to provide is an increasingly necessary way to reduce burden.

We often see surveyors trying to include as many questions as possible, often with each asking for extensive detail, into their surveys. Sometimes the additional questions and detail are included just in case, with no clear plan to use them. This is typically done because the surveyor does not know when or if he will get another opportunity to conduct a survey and wants to get as much information out of the current one as possible. Each of us has had this tendency ourselves and continues to resist it in our own research. The problem with this approach is that the researcher's anxiety is directly translated into increased respondent burden, and thus, probably into decreased response and lower data quality. In addition, in our own experience and from watching others do this as well, more times than not the extra questions go unanalyzed and the detailed responses are aggregated into more general measures because once data collection is finished, there is insufficient time or resources to analyze everything that was collected.

Rather than using this researcher-centric strategy of trying to collect everything at once at the expense of respondents, surveyors should collect only the level of detail that is needed and ask only the questions that are necessary to be able to do the analyses required to answer the research questions that motivated the survey in the first place (with the exception of interest getting questions as discussed in Guideline 7.2). Even then, they may have to compromise to ensure that the questions they ask are ones respondents are actually able to answer. The payoff will be higher response and more thoughtful and accurate answers from respondents.

Use Visual Design Principles to Make Questionnaires Easier to Complete

Internet and mail questionnaires are often much more difficult to complete than they need be because they do not clearly guide respondents in how questions should be answered and in what order. Research has shown that following principles of visual design and layout make it easier for respondents to process and complete questionnaires (e.g., Dillman & Christian, 2005; Jenkins & Dillman, 1997). Extensive experimentation conducted on response rates to U.S. Census questionnaires in the early 1990s showed that visual layout in a respondent-friendly design was 1 of only 5 factors (of 16 total tested) that significantly improved response rates (Dillman, 2000). Thus, designing questionnaires to enhance usability and minimize respondent burden can decrease the costs of responding to the survey. In Chapter 6 we discuss these principles in considerable detail.

Avoid Subordinating Language

People prefer not to feel that they are dependent upon others, and Blau (1964) argued they will expend great effort to avoid feeling subordinated. Yet many surveyors include subordinating language in their communications with sample members. Consider these contrasting statements that might be included in a letter or e-mail to potential respondents:

- "For us to help solve the school problems in your community, it is necessary for you to complete this questionnaire."

- "Will you please be a part of helping to solve the school problems in your community? Your responses can assist this community in fully understanding the issues facing schools here."

The first statement subordinates the respondent to the surveyor using what Comley (2006) might consider an adult-to-child style, whereas the second statement makes the respondent feel that the surveyor is dependent on him or her. Asking a person for help or assistance (discussed here as a benefit) reverses the relationship—subordinating the sponsor to the potential respondent, rather than vice versa—and is a way to decrease the costs (and increase the rewards) to the respondent for her participation.

This concern remains as salient today as at any time in the past. Today's increasingly service-oriented culture places a great emphasis on being respectful of other people. This is often enforced through the increasing use of video and audio recordings of transactions in stores and elsewhere that can be examined to ensure that customers and clients were treated appropriately. In addition, stories and even videos of disrespectful encounters can spread quickly through social media sites, leading to mass public scorn for those who acted inappropriately.

In the past, survey recipients likely felt more compelled to respond regardless of the attitude conveyed in the request. But now that it is culturally acceptable to decline such requests and people are more comfortable doing so, disrespecting and subordinating sample members is even more important to avoid. Sensitivity to this issue may be especially important when surveying hard-to-reach populations and those who are disadvantaged or experience discrimination.

Make It Convenient to Respond

One of the most effective ways of decreasing costs is making it as easy as possible for people to respond to a survey. In mail surveys, this involves sending a business reply or stamped return envelope, the absence of which would certainly lower response (as demonstrated by Armstrong & Lusk, 1987). In today's world this may also entail offering a desired mode of responding that fits the population or, for web surveys, e-mailing people a link that will open their browser and conveniently take them to the survey when clicked, as was done in the WSU Doctoral Student Experience Survey discussed earlier in this chapter.

Avoid Requiring Respondents to Provide Answers in a Survey Mode That Is Uncomfortable for Them

Most people are now capable of responding to mail, web, and/or telephone surveys. However, it is also clear that some people are more comfortable responding to some modes than others (Olson, Smyth, & Wood, 2012). People's comfort with responding over the telephone has certainly decreased over time, as evidenced by low response rates to this mode (Curtin, Presser, & Singer, 2005) and the increasing use of text messages in place of voice calls, especially among certain demographic groups (Lenhart, Ling, Campbell, & Purcell, 2010), yet when asked, some people indicate that they prefer that mode. It is also the case that some individuals have a strong preference for responding over the web, while others have a strong aversion, or even an inability to respond by web. However, those who are averse to the web mode will often respond by telephone (Olson et al., 2012).

In the case of mail, there are increasing numbers of people who indicate that taking a return envelope to a mail box down the street is decidedly inconvenient. Understanding people's mode preferences, the strength of those preferences, and especially barriers associated with each mode of responding is important for understanding the costs some people experience when asked to respond by a particular survey mode. We discuss mode preferences further in Guideline 11.14.

Recognize That Offering a Choice of Response Modes May Lower Response Rates

Concern with eliminating costs of being asked to respond by a particular survey mode could lead one to the conclusion that offering a choice of modes would improve survey response rates. However, a strong body of evidence has emerged that demonstrates that offering people that choice simply does not improve response, and in some instances can even lower response rates (e.g., Gentry & Good, 2008; Millar & Dillman, 2011; Smyth, Dillman, Christian, & O'Neill, 2010). Indeed, a meta-analysis of these and other studies showed in 17 out of 19 previous experimental tests that offering a choice of responding by web or mail resulted in a decline in response rates compared to only offering mail (Medway & Fulton, 2012). Schwartz (2004) provided a possible explanation for these results, suggesting that offering a choice complicates the decision-making process, making it likely that some people will take no action at all. This could also explain why offering a choice of telephone, as is sometimes done, seldom results in more than a handful of recipients calling to request a phone interview. Going from a letter or e-mail to the telephone to make a call to an unknown person also involves significant cost.

The effects of offering choice, when juxtaposed with evidence that people have mode preferences, as described earlier, make it clear that certain ways of reducing respondents' costs to participate might in practice impose other costs. This connection underscores the fact that reducing the costs of responding to a survey is significantly more complicated than simply individually applying each of the considerations we have listed here. We discuss the negative effects of offering a choice of modes further in Guideline 11.15, and suggest specific ways of overcoming them.

Minimize Requests to Obtain Personal or Sensitive Information

Surveys often ask for information that some people do not want to reveal such as their income and other financial information, their health and medical history, and their past sexual behavior or drug use. Asking for sensitive information like this should be avoided whenever possible because it increases costs for respondents, but when obtaining sensitive information is absolutely necessary, there are several things that can be done to reduce the costs to respondents of providing it. These include asking the questions in a self-administered mode that provides more privacy for responding (Tourangeau & Smith, 1996), asking them later in the survey to allow time for trust and rapport to develop, providing simple explanations for why responses to these questions are important and how the information will be protected, and softening the requests for personal information with other modifications to the question wording. We return to this topic in Chapters 7 and 11.

Show Similarity to Other Requests to Which a Person Has Responded

People have a desire to be consistent in their attitudes, beliefs, and actions. There is a psychological cost associated with feeling inconsistent (Festinger, 1957). Therefore, people who have committed themselves to a position may be more likely to comply with requests to do something consistent with that position and less likely to comply with requests to do something inconsistent with that position (Groves, Cialdini, & Couper, 1992). This inclination to behave consistently means that in some cases surveyors can offer arguments that point out how responding to a particular survey is consistent with something one has already done. For example, a survey of members of a particular organization may include the following statement: "We really appreciate your support through the recent payment of dues, and we want to be responsive to your expectations. Completing this web survey will give us guidance on how best to serve you and your fellow members."

The need to be consistent may also explain why, in panel surveys, once people respond to the initial request, it is much easier to get them to respond to subsequent requests (Lynn, 2009; Otto, Call, & Spenner, 1976). Consistency may also explain why the foot-in-the-door technique, where people are more likely to perform a large task if they are first asked to perform a smaller task, is effective (Mowen & Cialdini, 1980). A survey of national park visitors successfully used this technique by first asking people to respond to three short questions upon entering the park, and then asking them to complete a questionnaire at the end of their visit (Dillman, Dolsen, & Machlis, 1995).

Establishing Trust

Perhaps the single most important issue affecting response to questionnaires in today's world, as surveyors attempt to move from telephone and mail to the Internet, is trust. A wrong click can infect one's computer with a virus or other malware, and the consequences may be disastrous, rather than just inconvenient. As people increasingly depend upon computers and smartphones for their social and business transactions, it seems natural for them to receive e-mails from their bank, cable company, credit card provider, parcel delivery service or other businesses or even government agencies that are part of their lives and to provide information to these organizations online. The increasingly conventional use of e-mail and the web for these types of interactions has provided an easy opportunity for imposters to attempt to ascertain sensitive private information by imitating these businesses or organizations.

Most of us have heard the stories of those who made the mistake of clicking on a fraudulent link and providing the requested information only to have their accounts cleaned out, their credit card bill run up, or new credit accounts opened using their identity. In this environment, the safe response, as we are regularly told in public service messages, is not to respond to any request from an unknown source. That is, we live in a technological environment in which it often pays to be skeptical and suspicious. At the same time, most of the survey requests that one receives are from organizations unknown to them. That means that the safe response to such requests is not to respond at all.

The issue of trust carries over to all survey modes. While much of the public's attention has been focused on online scams, it is not uncommon to hear news of people being scammed over the telephone by criminals impersonating an official organization or a family member or of people learning when debt collectors start calling that someone has taken personal information from their postal mail and used it to steal their identity for financial gain. In addition, increasingly, people may ask whether surveys they have been told are useful really are, and breeches in confidentiality or other improprieties in the use of survey data can easily be publicized, and made known to all who have the patience to do an Internet or media search.

Sample members need to have confidence that their data will be kept safe and the benefits promised by a survey will be realized. For example, if a surveyor says, "Results of this survey are confidential," steps need to be taken to ensure that they are. When one suggests in a letter that "This survey will help our company do a better job of providing service to its customers," or "This survey will help state legislatures make decisions about how to allocate funding for higher education," there is usually no way to guarantee that the results of the survey will actually deliver the return as expected. Respondents are more likely to complete the survey when they trust that the sponsor will provide the benefits as promised. Trust is critical to believing that in the long run the benefits of completing the survey will outweigh the costs of doing so, as in other social interactions.

Among the actions that can be taken to instill trust that responding to a survey is beneficial and worth the costs of responding, are these:

Provide Ways for Sample Members to Assess the Authenticity of a Survey Request and Ask Questions About It

The Internet is one source of fake surveys that, if answered, can have negative consequences, but fake surveys are not new as a result of the Internet. Marketers have often telephoned people with a request to complete a brief survey as a means of introducing a product they wished to sell. Special interest groups have used survey questions to elicit interest in their purpose before asking for donations or to promote their position during election seasons. One thing many of these fake surveys have in common is that they do not provide contact information or other means for finding out whether the request is real. As such, an e-mail that contains little more than an electronic link and an instruction: "Please help me out by completing this survey. You will enjoy answering these questions" should not be answered, and would not be answered by most people.

Legitimate surveys have sponsors who are willing to identify themselves and answer questions about their survey. Doing this provides a signal to sample members that the survey request can be trusted. There are many ways that a surveyor can provide information that legitimates their survey. One is by providing a physical address where the sponsor is located. Another is by listing a toll-free number that sample members can call to talk to a real person in order to obtain information about the survey. Here it is important that those calling in not be sent down an answering tree to a recorded message. Another option is to include a web address where sample members can find additional information about the sponsor, background on the survey, and even results from previous surveys. Also, a specific e-mail address for asking questions should be made available. Ideally, several of these methods should be used.

Certainly, it is possible to provide a false telephone number or other contact information. However, providing multiple ways for sample members to contact someone to obtain information about the sponsor and the survey gives them multiple ways to assess the legitimacy of the survey and protects both legitimate surveys and respondents from surveys with nefarious purposes. The more ways that potential respondents have of obtaining information about the survey, its purpose, who is conducting it and the reasons why, the greater the likelihood that trust will be achieved.

Emphasize Sponsorship by a Legitimate Authority

People are more likely to comply with a request if it comes from an authoritative source that has been legitimized by larger society to make such requests and to expect compliance (Cialdini, 1984; Groves et al., 1992). Therefore, it is not surprising that for some time, government-sponsored surveys have achieved higher response rates than those sponsored by marketing research firms (Heberlein & Baumgartner, 1978), and that this trend continues today. In general, it is considered legitimate for government agencies to ask questions that are needed to help the government operate effectively. In contrast, private organizations lack that broad legitimacy. Government organizations also have the resources to make sure that sample members have a way to make sure the request is authentic and to ensure that their data is protected. The fact that employees of government agencies face significant fines and penalties for disclosing survey data may also contribute to the perception that they can be trusted more so than private organizations. In addition, the unique authority that some government agencies have to inform people that their response to a survey is mandatory helps improve response for government surveys of both businesses (Tulp, How, Kusch, & Cole, 1991) and individuals (Dillman, Singer, Clark, & Treat, 1996).

Universities are also authoritative sources that are legitimized by the larger society and as such university sponsorship also tends to increase response rates compared to marketing and private organization sponsorship (Dillman, 1978; Fox, Crask, & Kim, 1988; Groves et al., 2012). However, there is some evidence that the effect of university sponsorship may be more localized than that of government sponsorship. For example, Jones (1979) found that university sponsorship increased response rates in areas near the university, but decreased response rates in areas near a competing university. Similarly, Edwards, Dillman, and Smyth (2013c) found that sponsorship of a survey from an in-state university increased response rates compared with sponsorship by an out-of-state university.

The fact that government and university sponsorship is generally associated with higher response rates does not mean that those who are not associated with the government or a university cannot take advantage of survey sponsorship to help increase response inducing trust. Rather many organizations that can sponsor surveys are seen as legitimate and trustworthy by various populations. If the survey sponsor is generally viewed in a good light, seen as legitimate, and trusted by the target population, that sponsorship should be emphasized. If information is also given to allow sample members to verify the legitimacy of the survey so they can be sure it is legitimate, the sponsorship should have a positive effect on the decision to respond.

Build Upon Previously Established Relationships and Friendships

Most surveys are *not* conducted by government agencies like the U.S. Census Bureau with visibility and legitimacy and are not surveys of the general public. Companies survey their customers, universities survey their students, and associations often survey their members. In these instances and many others, there is an implicit understanding of who the survey sponsor is, and often this relationship can be leveraged to provide a reason for responding. For example, surveys by professional associations of their members for the purpose of improving the association's service to members have a legitimacy that helps them to be successful because they can build upon their preexisting relationship. Likewise, student surveys with the aim of improving the student experience at the university have a claim for legitimacy that surveys from other sponsors do not have. The Doctoral Student Experience Survey introduced earlier in this chapter had the advantage of being conducted by the university where students were enrolled. The survey protocol was designed to capitalize on the established relationship between the surveyor and students, all of whom were part of the university, to encourage response.

Some organizations have built visibility and legitimacy with the general public. An example is the Gallup Organization, which has for many decades conducted polls of the American public. It has visibility that provides legitimacy with a broad segment of the population. This visibility and legitimacy can be used to encourage response to survey requests.

Provide a Token of Appreciation in Advance

A few dollars included with a survey request increases rewards, as discussed earlier in this chapter, but it also creates value in the social exchange process by helping to establish trust. By providing the incentive with the request, before the survey is completed, the researcher demonstrates trust in potential respondents—who could pocket the money without completing the survey. In addition, emphasizing that the incentive is a "small token of appreciation" is consistent with conveying trust and respect for the respondent. The sending of such an incentive with the request to respond represents a behavioral commitment on the part of the surveyor. As noted by Molm, Takahashi, and Peterson (2000), a behavioral commitment provides a means of reducing the uncertainty of benefits based upon reciprocity.

A factor that makes these token incentives work is that they are neither too small nor too large. To engender trust, incentives need to be commensurate with the request. Research has consistently shown that general populations are far more likely to respond to an incentive of a dollar than no dollars, and may be somewhat more likely to respond to slightly higher incentives, but this effect diminishes quickly (e.g., James & Bolstein, 1990; Trussell & Lavrakas, 2004). An advance incentive that is too good to be true (say, $15 for a two-page questionnaire) is more likely to create suspicion than trust and may become a deterrent to response.

Assure Confidentiality and Protection of Data

Of considerable concern for some survey respondents is how the information they provide will be used, and who will have access to it, particularly if they are disclosing information that is personal or sensitive. The rise of the Internet has also brought increased attention to the security of electronic information, especially with respect to whether surveyors can guarantee that people's responses will remain confidential. The public's increasing concern about information security has been demonstrated recently by the incredible amount of attention and critique levied at the National Security Administration for secretly collecting people's telephone records and at a large national retailer for a breach of security in which millions of shoppers' electronic financial information was stolen. In light of this increased concern among the public, one way surveyors can establish trust is by explaining the efforts that will be taken to ensure the confidentiality and security of people's survey responses.

At the same time, one needs to be careful not to overdo it. Work by Singer, Hippler, and Schwarz (1992) showed that going to great lengths and detail to explain how confidentiality will be assured when the survey is not terribly sensitive is more likely to raise concerns about the data being collected than to resolve such concerns. In this case, confidentiality assurances can deter response. In later work, Singer, von Thurn, and Miller (1995) showed that strong confidentiality assurances can be beneficial, increasing response, when the survey topic is sensitive. Much like the use of incentives, when assuring confidentiality and data protection, there is a need to achieve optimal levels, but not make respondents suspicious by offering excessive amounts of money or overexplanations of confidentiality and protection.

Design Communications With Professionalism in Mind

Many surveys try to appeal to people on the basis that something important will ultimately happen as a result of the survey. Making each contact appear important can help establish trust in the survey sponsor and trust that the results will have the impact the surveyor says they will. Printing personalized cover letters on letter-head stationery, including a carefully chosen, relevant color picture on the front of the questionnaires, and providing information about the survey project can make the survey appear credible and help establish trust in the survey sponsor. In contrast, form letters produced on copy machines and questionnaires that are poorly designed or contain questions that are difficult to understand suggest that a survey and the sponsor are relatively unimportant. However, balance is needed here too. Information that is too slick, giving a brochure-like look and feel, may have the opposite effect. Communications need to find an appropriate balance between being professional and well done, but not overdone.

It's More Than Just Getting People to Respond

We have provided here considerable guidance on ways to increase the benefits and decrease the costs of responding as well as increase trust in order to encourage people to respond to a survey, but we also want to offer a note of caution that one should always be thinking about both response rates and nonresponse error. It does little good to increase response rates if doing so only brings in a certain type of respondents, thereby biasing estimates. A recent experiment on the effects of sponsorship by Groves et al. (2012), for example, shows that sponsorship by the March of Dimes and the University of Michigan both resulted in an overrepresentation of people who are supportive of the March of Dimes in the completed samples, but that the degree of overrepresentation was more severe when the survey sponsor was the March of Dimes. As a result, estimates of volunteering and fundraising activities were strongly biased upward in this treatment. In this case, the March of Dimes sponsorship appealed more strongly to people who support the March of Dimes and similar organizations than to those who did not, thus increasing their participation and therefore the amount of nonresponse bias in the estimates related to support for the organization.

As this example illustrates, it is important to ensure that any steps taken to increase benefits, decrease costs, or build trust do not have differential appeal (or lack of appeal) across different types of sample members in ways that are related to outcomes of interest in the survey. For example, while it might make perfect sense to emphasize March of Dimes sponsorship of a survey focused on how the March of Dimes can better interact with supporters, it would be advisable to deemphasize March of Dimes sponsorship of a survey focused on estimating volunteerism or barriers to volunteerism because in the latter case responses are needed from both those who volunteer and those who do not.

Figure 2.3 provides a summary of the ways we have described here of increasing benefits, decreasing costs, and building trust. As this image suggests, we view trust as the base upon which the decision to respond depends. Obtaining a response will be most likely if sample members can trust that the promised benefits will come to fruition and if the perceived costs have been minimized such that the benefits outweigh the costs.

PUTTING THE PARTS TOGETHER: SOME GUIDELINES FOR APPLYING SOCIAL EXCHANGE

It is one thing to provide a list of actions one might take to offer rewards, reduce costs, and engender trust that responding to a survey request will contribute to a positive outcome, as we have done in the last section. It is quite another to decide which of these to use for a particular survey, and when to use them. A number of considerations need to guide the process of going from these various disparate parts into a meaningful and effective whole survey design.

FIGURE 2.3   Summary of ways to increase benefits, reduce costs, and establish trust.

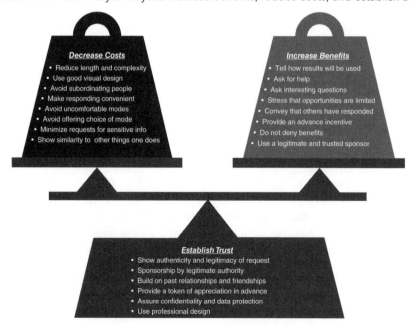

Much of this book is devoted to presenting guidelines for writing questions, preparing questionnaires, and deciding on specific implementation procedures. In the remainder of this chapter we present the first of these guidelines, all of which are aimed at applying the social exchange framework in tailored designs in order to improve response rates and data quality.

Guideline 2.1: Use a Holistic Approach to Design

Discussions with hundreds of individuals—from students and community leaders to agency statisticians and corporation executives—suggest to us that one of the major barriers to improving response is a tendency to focus on only a few aspects of costs, benefits, and/or trust, and ignore others. This concern surfaced with one of the authors many years ago when an individual sought a meeting to discuss improving his survey results, and only asked one question, "Will I improve response by putting commemorative stamps on the envelopes I use for the study?" The response was, "Perhaps a little bit," but what was disappointing about this discussion is that it was so singularly focused on one small issue while ignoring other design features.

In today's technological environment it is more common for surveyors to focus on questions such as, "What subject line will get people to read the e-mails I am going to send?" or "Since long e-mails don't get read, what's the shortest message I can send?" Rather than focusing on singular issues such as these, one should consider all features of the survey effort that the sample member is likely to experience and how these features connect with one another and are likely to affect the sample member's combined assessment of costs, benefits, and trust.

The research literature reporting experimental tests of factors that might influence response is often unhelpful in thinking about holistic design of the implementation process. Articles tend to report tests of specific issues, showing whether, for example, an altruistic approach to e-mails is better than an ego-centered approach (Fazekas, Wall, & Krouwel, 2013), whether each dollar of additional incentive produces greater response rates (Trussell & Lavrakas, 2004), or whether shorter electronic messages are better than long ones (Kaplowitz, Lupi, Couper, & Thorp, 2012). This research has been successful in identifying specific design features that tend to have larger versus smaller effects, but generally leaves unanswered how all elements of a design fit together or how the specific design feature being tested works with other aspects of the survey design.

In building a holistic approach it is important to recognize that communication occurs in multiple places within the letters, e-mails, and/or interviewer script, the questionnaire and the individual questions, and any other information provided during the survey process. Envelopes and subject lines affect whether messages are opened, and the first words from an interviewer may be enough to produce a hang-up. In the case of mail surveys, not only the letter requesting a response, but any enclosure that provides background information on the study, the cover page of the questionnaire, the look and feel of the entire questionnaire (color vs. black and white, staples vs. saddle stitch, and apparent length), whether the first questions are understandable and perhaps interesting, and a return envelope with real stamps to return the questionnaire all communicate to respondents. Web survey requests sent by e-mail also include multiple ways that information is communicated to respondents, from the subject line, to the wording of the request, the presentation of a clickable URL, where to enter passwords, the appearance of additional instructions and/or study information, and the first questions in the survey. Failure to connect the many aspects of a survey's design results in a disjuncture that affects how people perceive the benefits, cost, and trust.

Multiple contacts, which are a critical part of a well-designed survey, provide additional opportunities to communicate the features of a study and reasons for responding so that the same information does not need to be presented in each contact. One does not have to communicate every possible reason for responding, information about how to respond, and details of how confidentiality is protected, in every communication. The more information that one tries to present, the less likely it is to be processed and remembered. Just as different features of each contact provide an opportunity to put the right information in the right place, multiple contacts allow surveyors to divide out information across contacts in a way that does not overwhelm sample members or increase the difficulty of understanding the survey request.

Using a holistic approach also means avoiding the common practice of repeating the same stimulus over and over in the same way. Several years ago we encountered an organization's purchasing officer responsible for placing requests for printed materials who informed the survey designer that the most efficient way to send a follow-up reminder would be to double print the initial request so it could be sent a second time to nonrespondents with "second notice" printed on the outside of the envelopes. This means nonrespondents would have received identical content twice. We have also had organizations tell us that operationally they cannot remove respondents from the list for subsequent requests so all follow-up contacts were mailed to both nonrespondents and those who had already responded. Conversations between individuals do not normally progress well when one of the parties keeps repeating the same argument over and over, and neither do survey requests. Thus, while it is important for respondents to be able to recognize that each new contact is connected to the previous contact (which requires duplication of some information) it is also important to vary the contacts in order to maximize the chances of convincing people to respond. We discuss specific contact designs for single-mode telephone, web, and mail surveys in Chapters 8–10 and for mixed-mode surveys in Chapter 11.

Guideline 2.2: Social Exchange Concepts Should Be Applied Differently Depending on the Survey Population, Topic, Sponsorship, and Survey Mode(s) Available

A holistic approach to applying social exchange concepts does not mean that the same elements will be used in every, or even most, situations. Some surveys require using a particular mode to accomplish their objectives. For example, the U.S. Current Population Survey, which measures the nation's unemployment rate each month, first recruits people at sampled addresses using in-person interviews in order to maximize coverage and response rates. Thereafter, whenever possible, monthly follow-up interviews are conducted by telephone using phone numbers collected during the initial interview to obtain responses more quickly and at a lower cost than in-person interviews. Data collection by mail would be too slow and Internet would likely result in too much coverage and nonresponse error. Moreover, switching from in-person (i.e., an aural mode) to mail or Internet (i.e., visual modes) would likely introduce measurement differences. By comparison, a longitudinal survey we are familiar with measures attitudes using telephone calls at every data collection wave in order to keep measurement as consistent as possible over time so that changes in attitudes can be examined. As a third example, the Decennial Census and American Community Survey start with a postal contact and employ multiple modes of data collection, the choice and sequencing of which are driven primarily by cost considerations.

Each of these designs provides different opportunities for communicating with sampled members and trying to affect costs, benefits, and trust. When postal contacts and e-mails are used, there tend to be many contact opportunities that can be utilized to appeal in different ways to people. When only telephone contacts can be used, the opportunities to deliver different kinds of appeals may be severely limited, sometimes to only a single contact that ends in a quick hang-up. When written materials are sent, it is possible to deliver certain kinds of information and encouragement that cannot usually be delivered to an uncooperative telephone respondent.

Likewise, for some surveys it is inappropriate or impractical to use cash incentives while for others it is unlikely that reasonable response rates and data quality can be obtained without them. In the early 1990s when the U.S. Census Bureau was searching for ways to turn around response rates for the Decennial Census, one of us was asked to serve on a committee to discuss whether response might be improved by including token cash incentives. The idea was quickly dismissed for multiple reasons including size and security, as well as cultural and political sensitivities, but it contributed to a successful focus on how other techniques might be used to improve response rates.

In another situation, the possibility of sending a token cash incentive to employees of large organizations in the aerospace industry was rejected because of rules within the companies that would have required reporting of those gifts. However, in a survey of another occupational group, farmers, it was concluded that sending a $20 cash card redeemable at an ATM with the survey request was warranted because of survey length (nearly two hours) and because the costs of the incentives would be offset by savings realized as more responses came in by mail and fewer needed to be collected by in-person follow-up (Dillman, Gertseva, & Mahon-Haft, 2005).

Consistent with the tailored design concept introduced in Chapter 1, survey designs need to take into account sponsorship, the population to be surveyed, and other aspects of the survey situation. Bringing together the benefit, cost, and trust elements will need to be done differently for these varying situations. In the remainder of this book, we provide examples from both large and small surveys involving a wide variety of survey populations and sponsors.

Guideline 2.3: Identify and Evaluate Whether to Change or Eliminate Design Constraints That Are Especially Likely to Have a Negative Impact on Response and Data Quality

While our efforts to improve response rates and response quality are focused on multiple aspects of the survey design and implementation processes, it is also the case that certain design features may have singular importance in preventing a survey from obtaining a satisfactory response rate, and ultimately for data quality. Some of these are those that sponsors insist be included in the final design of surveys, but others may also be due to system or operational constraints or simply by inadvertent errors.

Recently one of us was asked to complete a faculty survey being conducted by students at our university. The first question asked was, "Are you 18 years or older?" It's easy to understand why that question was included—the university does not allow students under 18, of which there are some, to be asked to complete surveys without parental permission, and the surveyors thought that would also be required in a faculty survey. But, the question seemed particularly strange to faculty members who saw it, none of whom were under 18, and provided an early signal that the survey may not be worth answering. We have also observed some large-scale surveys, including some national ones, obtain excessively large web cut-offs when the first question asked respondents to read a consent form and agree to complete that survey as well as follow-ups at a later date.

In another example, a friend expressed his frustration with a survey that arrived in the mail, with this item as the first question:

Our records show that you got care at the clinic named below

32005004922

Is that right?

□ Yes
□ No → If No, go to #44

Even if he had received medical care only at one clinic, the presumption that the number provided was sufficiently clear for the respondent to answer this question or others in the questionnaire was strange. That alone resulted in the questionnaire being discarded.

In still other cases, we have observed web surveys that fail because answers were required to every single question, and mail surveys that fail because people were asked to fax their response or provide their own return envelope and postage. We have also observed surveyors who send letters or e-mails to individuals requesting phone numbers, in hopes that most of them will respond, something that is unlikely to happen.

However, the most common feature of surveys that make obtaining satisfactory response difficult is the extremely heavy burden associated with length and complexity. We have been shown surveys that use dozens (and in one case over 300) of attitudinal or belief items. These items are almost always used because they have previously been used and validated in classroom settings; however, it is quite unlikely that one can get people outside of a classroom environment to complete these lengthy surveys.

Many surveys go through a very long creation-to-implementation process involving dozens or even hundreds of people in different work groups, from those who create the questions to those who do computer programming to make the surveys work. In between are editors, mode specialists, administrative staff, and others, many of whom have little experience with the process of asking and responding to questions. Parts of a survey or questionnaire are sometimes examined in detail and changes made independently from others. It is not surprising to us that many surveys include features that disproportionately affect the cost–benefit–trust evaluations they make. Efforts to find and eliminate, or at lease reduce, these features are a major concern that we return to in later chapters of this book.

MIXED-MODE DESIGNS PROVIDE NEW OPPORTUNITIES FOR APPLYING SOCIAL EXCHANGE

The need to consider mixed-mode survey designs has largely developed out of concern over coverage and low response, but the concept has not been enthusiastically accepted by many because the complexities of designing and implementing such surveys are considerable. Our view of mixed mode designs is that they provide an important and perhaps unprecedented opportunity to more effectively balance surveyor needs and respondent concerns because of the various ways social exchange principles can be applied in mixed-mode designs.

One of the most important things to understand about mixed-mode designs is that modes can be combined in different ways with varying implications for the benefits, costs, and trust calculus as well as for minimizing different sources of error. This will be discussed in considerably more depth in Chapter 11. Here we focus on the two main ways for mixing modes and the rationale for using them.

Guideline 2.4: Use Multiple Modes of *Communication* to Gain More Opportunities to Increase Benefits, Decrease Costs, and Build Trust

The first general way to mix modes to improve response is to use multiple modes of contact in the recruitment phase of the survey. In the late 1980s when the idea of mixing modes to improve survey response was being introduced for mail and telephone surveys (e.g., Dillman & Tarnai, 1988), the mode of response was thought of as synonymous with the mode of contact for most surveyors; mail surveys required postal mail recruitment and telephone surveys required telephone recruitment. This was reinforced by the tendency for mail and interview work to be assigned to different divisions or teams and the related difficulty of passing information back and forth in this era when electronic communication was still in its infancy. Even today, significant cultural and system barriers remain that inhibit the ability of different operational groups and computer systems to work together effectively.

When the web was developing as a survey mode in the late 1990s, it was natural to continue this tradition and think of using e-mails as the means for convincing people to respond over the web. However, the lack of e-mail sample frames for many surveys limited the web surveying possibilities. In addition, the difficulty of getting people to go from e-mails to the web proved to be considerable, so that response rates to web surveys relying only on e-mail contact were low, corresponding in many ways to the low response rates for random digit dial (RDD) telephone surveys.

A distinct limitation of these single-mode designs is that it is difficult to develop trust or convey the benefits of responding and how costs are being minimized when messages sent by e-mail are likely to be ignored or quickly deleted or when telephone calls are abruptly terminated and later calls are not answered. Using multiple modes provides additional opportunities to inform respondents of the benefits of responding, communicate how costs are being minimized, and build trust. In other words, it allows one to build a more holistic implementation protocol, as discussed in Guideline 2.1, in which synergy is developed between modes of contact (e.g., a postal letter on letterhead with an enclosed incentive might be used to provide a reward and encourage trust while a follow-up e-mail is used to deliver an electronic link to a web survey thereby removing a barrier to response).

Guideline 2.5: Use Multiple Modes of *Response* to Increase Benefits, Decrease Costs, and Build Trust

Providing an alternative response mode is the second way that mixed-mode designs can improve survey response. Some sample members may be unable to respond by one mode but able to respond by another. For example, someone who does not have Internet access cannot complete a web survey and someone who is vision impaired will likely have considerable difficulty completing a mail survey. Others prefer some modes to others and are less likely to answer in modes they do not prefer (Olson et al., 2012), as discussed further in Guideline 11.14. Still others may be able and generally willing to respond by a mode, but object to honestly answering sensitive questions in that mode. Providing an additional mode of response can help overcome these reasons for not responding or for giving inaccurate responses to these questions. In addition, a new mode can provide a different stimulus. For example, some sample members may be reluctant to answer a telephone survey because they do not know what will be asked of them, but after being able to preview the questions in a mail or web version of the questionnaire may decide to respond. We have learned in many instances of people who decide to respond to a web questionnaire only after receiving a paper questionnaire that they can use to preview the questions and as a rough draft. This is especially likely to happen in business surveys where it is necessary for the respondent to gather information from records (Snijkers, Haraldsen, Jones, & Willimack, 2013). In these cases, the paper survey is much easier to use than a web survey that unfolds one question at a time.

Using multiple modes of communication and multiple modes of response are the two most general ways survey modes can be mixed to improve response. In Chapter 11 we return to this theme and present specific strategies for mixing modes of communication and response. For example, in some surveys multiple modes of communication are used with a single response mode, and in others multiple modes of communication are used with multiple response modes. In addition, multiple response modes can be offered simultaneously or in sequence. In Chapter 11 we also include a more thorough discussion of how different mixed-mode designs can be expected to impact different sources of survey error. While these details are incredibly important, our main point here is that using multiple modes of communication and/or response provides surveyors with more ways to apply the social exchange concepts and improve survey response than using a single mode alone.

Guideline 2.6: Utilize Knowledge From Past Research and Feedback From Early Contacts to Adapt Implementation Procedures in Order to Reduce Nonresponse Error

In addition to improving response rates, mixed-mode survey designs may be especially helpful in reducing nonresponse error for a couple of reasons. First, communications that arrive via a different mode from previous communications are less likely to be dismissed than one via the original mode. This provides an opportunity to focus later communications on the types of individuals that did not respond to the earliest communications to improve the representativeness of the responding sample. Second, different modes of response may appeal to different types of sample members. For example, a series of recent studies have shown for household surveys that when both web and mail modes of response are used, quite different individuals respond to each mode, with mail respondents being older and having less education and income than web respondents (Messer & Dillman, 2011; Rookey, Hanway, & Dillman, 2008; Smyth et al., 2010). These studies suggest that using multiple modes can spread the appeal of the survey to different kinds of respondents, potentially reducing nonresponse error compared to what would be obtained in a single-mode survey. Multiple modes can be used at both the recruitment and response phases to appeal to different types of sample members, thereby reducing the potential for nonresponse error.

Strategies such as these have been discussed to some degree as *adaptive design* or *responsive design*. Adaptive design is a relatively new concept that is gaining a following in many survey design situations (Groves & Heeringa, 2006; Schouten, Calinescu, & Luiten, 2013; Wagner, 2008). It refers to adjusting procedures during the data collection process based upon observations made about the types of individuals who are responding and not responding and the estimates that are being produced. For example, if it is learned that younger people in the population are responding in disproportionately small numbers, procedures can be introduced that are specifically targeted at improving response among that age group.

An example of doing this from an earlier time occurred in the 1990s with a periodic mail survey that involved surveying individuals who had turned in an out-of-state driver's license in order to obtain one in Washington State (Salant & Dillman, 1994). Those records also provided the age and sex of each sampled person. In the first round of surveying, when no incentives were used, the response rate for people under 35 was 40%, compared to between 40% and 50% for 36- to 60-year-olds and 72% for those who were 61+ (Miller, 1996). When the next set of names was provided 3 months later, the surveyor decided that a $2 token cash incentive would be included in hopes of reducing nonresponse error on these characteristics since they were critical to the planned analysis. This incentive resulted in increasing the less than 35 response rate to 60%, while all other groups, including the 61+ respondents, had a response rate of 71%. As a result, the final response rate was increased significantly and the completed sample was more representative of the survey population.

Today's adaptive design goes far beyond simply changing strategies between cohorts. Information about how the characteristics of early respondents compare to those of nonrespondents and to the entire sample is used to identify what kinds of respondents might be specifically targeted later in the field period in order to obtain more representative results. In some instances the information needed for these comparisons comes from auxiliary data on the sample file, such as information from administrative records, for example, of students, customers, or members of an organization. In other instances, such as for public opinion surveys, one might use data collected from other surveys like the American Community Survey to make such comparisons.

One of the reasons that such adjustments can be made is that the technology now used to conduct surveys in all survey modes makes it possible to know quickly who is responding and not responding, and to use that information for targeting follow-up efforts with different communications, different offers of a response mode, and perhaps differential incentives. In addition, the collection of paradata for the answering process may identify troublesome spots in questionnaires that can be changed, such as questions that are being skipped, answered incorrectly, or taking inordinate amounts of time to answer (Couper, 1998; Kreuter, 2013). Of course, there are some operational constraints to adaptive design. One has to have the time and capability to identify what type of sample members are responding and what type are not as well as if any nonresponse is manifest as error on measures of interest. In addition, one has to have the ability to do this very quickly and to make changes to the implementation protocol that may impact multiple systems (i.e., mail tracking, computer-assisted telephone interviewing (CATI) system, etc.). It is also usually difficult to accommodate major changes in implementation protocols within budget limits, which are typically determined at the start of the project and are often inflexible.

RETURNING TO THE WSU DOCTORAL STUDENT EXPERIENCE SURVEY: WHY IT OBTAINED SUCH A HIGH RESPONSE RATE

The WSU Doctoral Student Experience Survey discussed earlier in this chapter provides an example of connecting the parts of a survey design effectively within the social exchange framework, as well as tailoring the design to the survey situation.

The survey was sponsored by a research center at Washington State University, providing a certain amount of legitimacy (increase benefits and trust), especially since the population of interest was students completing a doctorate degree at that university. The invitation letter asking recipients to respond over the Internet was printed on official university stationery and also provided names and contact information for the study director and office from which the study was being implemented, providing further legitimacy (increase trust). An additional aim was to create trust that something useful to future graduate students would result from the study (a potential benefit because of the identity some students were developing with their department). The inclusion of the $2 bill with the request and referring to it as a "token of appreciation" was aimed at communicating the importance of each response (a benefit) and providing a direct and unconditional benefit to the recipient (increase trust), although this was less of a concern in this survey situation than it might have been in others because the survey originated from within the university.

The immediate e-mail follow-up, that can be thought of as e-mail augmentation of the paper contact in order to provide an electronic link was designed to reduce the effort needed for sample members to transfer the URL and password from the paper letter to the computer (reduce costs). The wording in this e-mail emphasized this attempt to reduce the cost of time and effort by providing an electronic survey link and explaining that it was included to make it easier to respond, as illustrated in Figure 2.4. The additional follow-ups each conveyed new information and discussed the usefulness of the study with different words to spread the appeal (cf. Millar, 2013).

The fourth contact (the second via mail) included a paper questionnaire, the first page of which is presented in Figure 2.5. Its purpose was to appeal to different types of sample members (new benefits) and to cut the costs of responding for those who might find mail more convenient or confidential (decrease costs) than the web mode. This version of the questionnaire was designed to be attractive,

FIGURE 2.4   Initial communications sent to students asked to complete the WSU Doctoral Student Experience Survey (inside addresses have been altered).

First contact: Postal letter

WASHINGTON STATE UNIVERSITY

Social and Economic Sciences Research Center

March 29, 2013

Jane Doe
123 Cougar Road
Pullman, WA 99163

Dear Jane,

I am writing to ask for your help with an important survey we are conducting of WSU doctoral students. I understand that you have successfully completed your preliminary examinations and are now at the stage of needing to complete a dissertation.

My colleague, Morgan Millar, and I have been working with the National Science Foundation to better understand how the needs of doctoral training in the U.S. are changing. We are hoping you could spend a few minutes sharing some of your experiences in your doctoral program. In particular, we are interested in factors that may affect bringing the dissertation writing process to a successful conclusion.

To this end, we would greatly appreciate if you would answer a few questions for us. To do so, simply go to this website: www.opinion.wsu.edu/phdexperience

In order to begin the survey, you will need to enter this access code: «RESPID».

We think it should only take about ten minutes to complete the questionnaire.

The survey is confidential. Your individual answers will not be linked with your name or department in any reports of the data. Your participation is voluntary and if you come to any question you prefer not to answer, you are welcomed to skip it and go on to the next. Should you have any questions or comments, please contact me (dillman@wsu.edu) or Thom Allen, the study director (509) 335-1722 or ted@wsu.edu.

We very much appreciate your help with this study, and a small token of appreciation is enclosed with this letter as way of saying thank you.

Many Thanks,

Don A. Dillman
Regents Professor and Deputy Director
Social and Economic Sciences Research Center
Washington State University

Research and Administrative Offices, 133 Wilson-Short Hall
PO Box 644014, Pullman, WA 99164-4014 • 509-335-1511 • Fax: 509-335-0116

Public Opinion Laboratory, 1425 NE Terre View, Suite F
PO Box 641801, Pullman, WA 99164-1801 • 509-335-1721 • Fax: 509-335-4688

included communication on the front to link it to the web version (increase benefits), and was sent with a stamped return envelope (decrease costs). The e-mail follow-up to this paper mailing conveyed that a response over the web was also fine.

However, it is not just the judicious mixing of postal and e-mail contacts with a pre-incentive that contributed to the success of the study. The primary purpose of this study was to assess the extent to which students' doctoral dissertations were interdisciplinary in nature. However, we were concerned that focusing only on this topic in the letters and the questionnaire would result in students with interdisciplinary interests being more likely to respond, resulting in nonresponse error. As a result, we included interest-getting questions about satisfaction with the dissertation process and the student's doctoral program in general, how their

FIGURE 2.4 (*continued*).

Second contact: E-mail

> **From**: Don Dillman [don.dillman@wsu.edu]
> **Sent**: Monday, April 1, 2013 2:00 PM
> **To**: Jane Doe [jane.doe23@wsu.edu]
> **Subject**: WSU Doctoral Student Survey
>
> Dear Jane,
>
> Earlier this week we sent you a letter asking for your help with an important survey. We are conducting this study of WSU doctoral students to learn more about the processes they go through to complete their dissertations and finish their degrees.
>
> I am following up with this e-mail to provide you with an electronic link to the survey website. I hope this link makes it easier for you to respond. It should only take a few minutes to complete the questionnaire.
>
> Simply click on this link and you will automatically be logged into the survey:
>
> http://www.opinion.wsu.edu/phdexperience
>
> And enter your personal Access Code in the space provided: <<RESPID>>
>
> The results of this study will help us better understand the needs and experiences of students as they work on their dissertation research. Your participation is very important, and we appreciate you considering our request.
>
> Sincerely,
>
> Don A. Dillman
> Regents' Professor and Deputy Director
> Social and Economic Sciences Research Center

work was supported financially, and the amount of encouragement for their work provided by faculty, all of which are relevant to all doctoral students regardless of interdisciplinary status (increase benefits), and would be of added value to the researchers as well. Some of these questions were placed prominently in the early portion of the questionnaire because they seemed likely to be of great interest to most dissertating students.

We were also concerned that a long questionnaire would produce mid-questionnaire cutoffs, so the questionnaire was kept reasonably short (reduce costs) and limited to 44 questions (about a 10-page paper questionnaire or 47 web screens). The initial page of the paper questionnaire (as shown in Figure 2.5) contained an appealing but vague title, "Understanding the Doctoral Experience at WSU," which gave the questionnaire a localized identity (increase benefits). This same title was also used in the web version of the questionnaire to convey connectivity, should a sample member look at the questionnaire in both modes.

Thus, many aspects of the study design and implementation system were shaped in relation to one another in ways that we hoped would produce positive responses from those asked to participate. These are summarized in Figure 2.6. We were *not* relying on shaping only one or two features as a means of encouraging response while ignoring everything else; rather, we were creating a holistic design.

FIGURE 2.5   First page of the paper version of the WSU Doctoral Student Experience Survey, designed to attract interest.

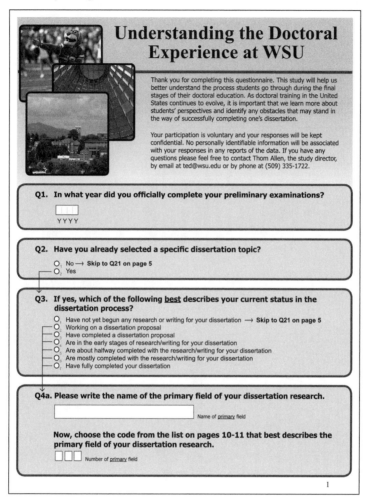

We were also tailoring our design to the particular situation where the sponsor and the respondents were at the same university and where both e-mail and postal addresses were available.

This survey obtained a 77% response rate—a 63% response was achieved from the initial two contacts, with a 30 percentage point increase happening in a 10-hour period following the e-mail sent after the initial postal letter. The final 14 percentage point increase in the overall response came from the third and fourth contacts. The success of this study in receiving such a high response illustrates how a mixed-mode design can produce results that were unlikely to be achieved by using only postal contacts requesting response to a paper survey or only e-mail contacts requesting a web response. It also produced results quickly, a much desired goal of the study. Doing that was achieved by making many separate decisions and connecting them together in ways suggested by the social exchange framework.

FIGURE 2.6 Summary of elements used to build trust, maximize benefits, and minimize cost in the WSU Doctoral Student Experience Survey.

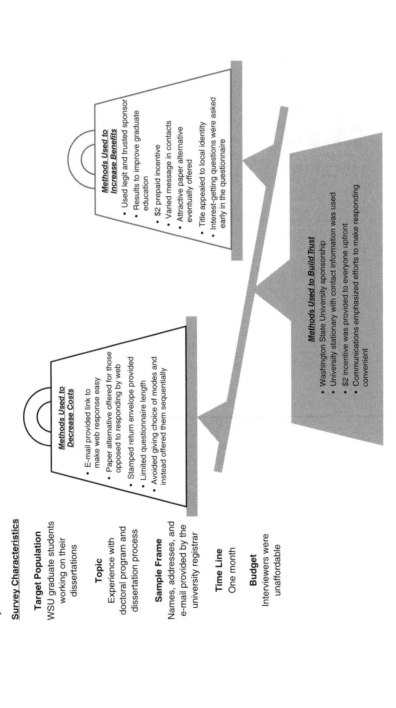

CONCLUSION

The interests of sample members and of surveyors need not be as oppositional as they often become and were portrayed at the beginning of this chapter. The core idea we have considered here is that social exchange—with its emphasis on increasing benefits, reducing costs, and increasing trust that the benefits will outweigh the costs of responding—remains a useful framework for identifying aspects of surveys that can be shaped to improve response and reduce nonresponse error, even in this new communication era.

An important change in how this framework is applied in this era is the need for placing a greater emphasis on the creation of trust that the research is legitimate and that benefits valued by the respondent will likely come to fruition. Trust is an essential component, now especially threatened by the electronic environment in which most communication occurs, that connects the providing of benefits and reducing costs with increased response.

Although single-mode surveys are often conducted and will continue, we contend that mixed-mode survey designs have the potential to provide new, and much needed, ways for improving the effective application of these social exchange concepts in ways that will improve survey response and data quality. Offering an alternative mode for answering survey questions may encourage certain types of individuals to respond who could not or would not respond by another survey mode. In addition, the use of additional contacts by a second or third mode improves the opportunity to provide sponsor explanations for why each person's response is needed, and to target those appeals more precisely to different types of individuals. Mixed-mode surveys provide new means of attempting to close the gap between the way survey sponsors think about imposing their survey on others and how respondents react when they encounter the survey request and questionnaire.

LIST OF GUIDELINES

Guidelines for Applying Social Exchange

Guideline 2.1: Use a holistic approach to design

Guideline 2.2: Social exchange concepts should be applied differently depending on the survey population, topic, sponsorship, and survey mode(s) available

Guideline 2.3: Identify and evaluate whether to change or eliminate design constraints that are especially likely to have a negative impact on response and data quality

Guidelines for Applying Social Exchange in Mixed-Mode Surveys

Guideline 2.4: Use multiple modes of *communication* to gain more opportunities to increase benefits, decrease costs, and build trust

Guideline 2.5: Use multiple modes of *response* to increase benefits, decrease costs, and build trust

Guideline 2.6: Utilize knowledge from past research and feedback from early contacts to adapt implementation procedures in order to reduce nonresponse error

Covering the Population and Selecting Who to Survey

The 2010 Census enumerated 308.7 million people in 116.7 million households across the United States. It cost about $13 billion to conduct, $97 per household (Government Accountability Office, 2012). The cost of conducting the Census has roughly doubled each of the past few decades even as the length of the questionnaire has decreased. In 2010, the Census questionnaire asked only four questions about the household and six more for each person living in it. The cost increases are largely driven by population growth and people becoming increasingly difficult to reach. The U.S. Census is a massive undertaking in time and resources, with people spread all over the country to carry out the effort. Although it only takes 5 months to conduct the actual enumeration, the preparation, planning, and analysis for each cycle takes about 10 years to complete.

Most surveyors do not have $13 billion to spend, 5 months to collect data, or 10 years to plan for the survey and analyze the data. But thankfully most researchers also do not have to conduct a census, which entails selecting everyone in the target population. Instead, most people can conduct a sample survey, which involves selecting a sample or subset of the population rather than asking everyone to participate. Surveys allow for the characteristics of thousands or millions of people to be estimated with considerable precision by collecting information from only a few hundred or thousand rather than everyone in the population. This allows surveyors to focus their resources on maximizing response among those who are selected and ensuring the responses collected are as accurate as possible.

There are certain principles one needs to follow to be confident that those who are selected for the survey are *representative* of the population one is interested in describing. These basic principles apply regardless of whether the population is households in the United States, residents of a local community, students at a high school or university, members of an organization, or people who attended a conference or training program. These principles are the focus of this chapter, which will cover the specific procedures used to select people for a survey as well as strategies for minimizing coverage and sampling error. In addition, this chapter discusses how the final data may need to be adjusted or weighted to correct for variations in how people are selected and/or if the final sample of people who respond differs from the population of interest on certain characteristics.

ESSENTIAL DEFINITIONS AND THEIR USE

To introduce the basic sampling concepts, we will describe the design of a survey of households in the state of Washington conducted in 2009 (the Washington Economic Survey) using address-based sampling in which sample members were initially asked to complete the questionnaire on the web and later offered a mail alternative (Messer & Dillman, 2011). The survey's *target population*—the group that the survey aimed to describe and generalize results to—was the approximately 2.5 million households in the state of Washington (American Community Survey [ACS], 2008). The *sampling frame*—or list that the sample was drawn from—was the U.S. Postal Service computerized delivery sequence file (CDSF) that contained mailing addresses for households in the state of Washington. This frame includes about 96% of Washington households; this is an estimate of the *coverage* of the sampling frame. But even with the vast majority of households covered on the list, *coverage error* may still occur if households in the state of Washington that were excluded from the sampling frame (e.g., newly constructed homes may not be on the CDSF yet) differ from those that were included on some of the variables of interest (for this study, financial status and technology were two such variables). Coverage error is a property of the survey's sample frame.

Before the sample was selected from the frame, the surveyor requested that addresses designated as business, seasonal, or vacant be removed because the population of interest was households containing people who are full-time residents of the state of Washington. The 2,100 residential addresses selected from the CDSF for inclusion in the study constitute the *sample* for the survey. For this survey, the sample was stratified. *Stratification* refers to grouping the units on the sample frame into subgroups, called strata, based on certain characteristics, so that sampling can be performed independently for each stratum; if desired, units can then be selected using different procedures and/or at different rates from each stratum.

In this case, the addresses on the frame were stratified based on whether they were located in an urban or a rural area because a goal of this survey was to assess the impact of the recession in urban and rural areas and to compare experiences across these areas. Addresses in rural areas were oversampled, or sampled at a higher rate than they exist in the target population, to ensure that there were enough households from rural areas for the final analysis. As a result, the sample drawn for this survey consisted of 50% of the addresses coming from urban areas and 50% coming from rural areas (even though about 67% of the state's population lives in urban areas and 33% lives in rural areas, according to the 2008 ACS). *Sampling error* results from selecting only a subset of, rather than all, households from the sampling frame. It is the difference in the estimate produced when sampling some of the households, compared with the estimate if all households on the frame were surveyed.

Since the CDSF is a list of addresses (or households) that may contain more than one resident and the surveyor for this study did not need responses from everyone in the household, a procedure was needed to select one adult to complete the survey from each sampled household. If a household only had one adult, that adult was asked to complete the survey. For households with more than one adult, the adult with the most knowledge of the household's economic situation was asked to complete the survey.

Questionnaires were returned by respondents from 969 households, or about half of the contactable sample (1,932 of the 2,100 sampled addresses were in service, not returned to sender). This response rate is based on the American Association for Public Opinion Research's (AAPOR) RR3 calculation—for more on calculating response rates, see AAPOR's standard definitions (AAPOR, 2011).

The 969 households who completed the survey questionnaire constituted the *completed sample* or the respondents to the survey. Survey data is often adjusted or weighted to account for the fact that units in the population may have been sampled at different rates or that some types of people are more likely to respond than others, resulting in the completed sample not matching the target population on key characteristics. The *survey weights* for this survey adjusted the final sample based on parameters from the 2008–2009 American Community Survey to account for the fact that addresses had different probabilities or chances of being included in the sample based on whether they were in urban versus rural counties. Those in urban counties received a larger weight than those in rural counties.

For many surveys, additional weighting to demographic characteristics is performed to help correct for differences in nonresponse across different types of people (e.g., older individuals are typically more likely to respond than younger people). This type of poststratification weighting ensures that the final weighted survey sample is representative of the population of interest. The weighting process can introduce additional variation in the final weighted estimates (i.e., *weighting error*), which can be estimated and taken into account when reporting the sampling error. This loss of precision increases the sampling error.

For a completed sample of this size, one could have 95% confidence that the true value (if everyone in the population was surveyed) is within plus or minus 3.9 percentage points of the survey's estimate. This margin of error accounts for the loss of precision introduced by the weighting that was used to correct for the disproportionate sampling (the design effect was 1.56, which increased the margin of error from 3.2 to 3.9 percentage points). It is important to remember that even though surveys often report a margin of error for the survey as a whole (using a common formula or by taking a mean across a selected set of key questions in the survey), coverage and sampling error vary for each statistic estimated from the survey.

For a summary of the common coverage and sampling terms, as well as a definition and example from the preceding study for each, see Figure 3.1.

CURRENT COVERAGE AND ACCESS CONSIDERATIONS

Coverage of each survey mode is influenced by both who has access to the mode and what lists or frames are available that can be used to sample members of the target population. The first surveys were mostly conducted through in-person conversations with people, often in their homes but sometimes in other places, and nearly everyone was able to participate. The rise of a variety of new technologies has changed the way people communicate. As a result, survey conversations are now often mediated through various devices, including landline telephones, mobile phones and smartphones, tablet computers, laptops, and desktops. But often not everyone in the survey population has access to each device, so the

FIGURE 3.1 Coverage and sampling terms: Definitions and examples.

Term	Definition	Example from a Sample Survey
Target population	All of the units (e.g., individuals, households, organizations) to which one desires to generalize the survey results	Households in the state of Washington
Sample frame	The list of units in the population that the sample will be drawn from	List of addresses from the U.S. Postal Service CDSF
Coverage rate	The proportion (often estimated) of the target population that is included in the sample frame	96% of households in the state of Washington
Coverage error	The difference on a variable of interest between those covered in the sample frame and those not covered multiplied by the coverage rate	Highly mobile people or those who live in newly constructed homes not covered by the address frame may have experienced the recession differently than those who were covered
Sample	All units of the population that are drawn for inclusion in the survey	2,100 residential addresses selected from the sample frame
Sample selection	How units are chosen from the sampling frame; every unit in the population must have a known chance of being included in the sample, but the rate at which different units are sampled can vary	The frame was stratified by urbanicity, with the sample allocated equally to urban and rural areas (rather than proportionate to their size in the population)
Completed sample	All of the units sampled that complete the survey questionnaire	969 households that completed the survey questionnaire
Sampling error	The difference on a variable of interest between those who were sampled and those who were not; sampling error results from collecting data from only a subset, rather than all, of the units in the sampling frame	Plus or minus 3.9 percentage points

FIGURE 3.1 (continued).

Term	Definition	Example from a Sample Survey
Survey weights	Adjustments that correct for differences in selection probabilities and response rates among different groups in the sample	To correct for probability of selection of the household because of the disproportionate sampling
Weighting error	Loss of precision due to postsurvey adjustments; it can be estimated and taken into account when reporting the margin of sampling error	The survey's design effect was 1.56, which increased the sampling error from 3.2 to 3.9 percentage points

choices surveyors make about which communication devices to use to contact and survey potential respondents impacts who will be covered by and respond to the survey.

As of December 2013 nearly 98% of all households in the United States had access to a landline or mobile phone. This means only about 2% did not have access to a phone of any kind (Blumberg & Luke, 2013). In fact, telephone surveys have covered 90% or more of the population for the past few decades, which has contributed to their widespread use in survey research. But the past decade has seen a significant shift in the types of phones people use (see Figure 3.2 for a summary of these trends). For example, in 2003, 95% of households had a landline telephone and 46% had a cell phone (Blumberg & Luke, 2006). Only 3% of households had only a cell phone while 42% had both a landline and cell phone (dual households). In 2013, far fewer households, 58%, had a landline phone, and the proportion having a cell phone nearly doubled to 89%. Further, 39% of households have only a cell phone now while 50% have both a cell phone and landline phone. Among the 50% who have both a cell phone and landline phone, 32% rely on their cell phone for all or almost all of their calls. These "wireless mostly" households comprise 16% of all households in the United States (Blumberg & Luke, 2013).

This steep growth in the number of people with only a cell phone and no landline telephone is important because people who are cell-only lead different lifestyles than their landline counterparts, meaning bias can result if they are excluded from the survey's sample. For example, they are more likely to be young, racial and ethnic minorities, renting their homes, living in poverty, living in the South, and can have very different attitudes and behaviors than those accessible by landline telephone (Blumberg & Luke, 2013; Christian, Keeter, Purcell, & Smith, 2010). For telephone surveyors, this has meant that to obtain adequate coverage, cell phone numbers must be included in the sample, especially to reach certain demographic groups.

Telephone surveys must also deal with the fact that people are generally less amenable to answering survey questions over the telephone than they used to be. The increase in unsolicited telephone calls, and the adoption of technologies designed to limit those types of calls, have created important challenges for telephone surveyors and have led to decreased contact and cooperation rates.

FIGURE 3.2   Trends in household landline and cell phone coverage.

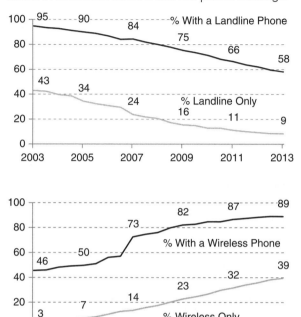

Source: *Wireless Substitution: Early Release of Estimates from the National Health Interview Survey, January–June 2013*, by S. J. Blumberg and J. V. Luke, 2013, National Center for Health Statistics. Retrieved from http://www.cdc.gov/nchs/data/nhis/earlyrelease/wireless201312.pdf. Based on households in the United States.

Internet surveys also face coverage problems in that Internet access remains lower than that for telephones. According to the Pew Research Center in 2013, 85% of adults in the United States use the Internet at least occasionally (Pew Internet & American Life Project, 2013c), and 73% do so at home (Pew Internet & American Life Project, 2013b). One encouraging trend for those conducting web surveys is that 70% of adults now have a high-speed or broadband connection at home, which may vastly improve the experience for those responding to today's web surveys. Broadband penetration has doubled in the past 5 years (Pew Internet & American Life Project, 2013b). However, taken together this still means that 15% of adults are completely left out of Internet surveys since they don't use the Internet at all, 30% do not have high-speed Internet service at home, making them less likely to complete a survey online, and even more may not use the Internet enough to be willing to respond to a web survey.

Even more importantly, there are differences between those who have access to the Internet and those who do not. Seniors age 65 and older, non-Whites, people with lower education levels, and those with lower incomes are less likely to use the Internet than their counterparts (Pew Internet & American Life Project, 2013d). Therefore, these groups are less likely to be covered by Internet surveys. These same groups, as well as those living in rural areas, are also underrepresented among those with high-speed Internet service at home (Zickuhr & Smith, 2013).

The increasing use of mobile phones to access the Internet, especially among non-Whites and those with lower education and income levels, has helped to reduce these gaps, but they still persist. In addition, for some, mobile phones have become their primary Internet source, which raises new challenges for conducting web surveys. When surveys are not designed effectively for mobile devices, it can impact both response rates and measurement error. Some question types may not display correctly, there may not be enough space to input a response by touch, or many people may open the survey but then quickly abandon or leave the survey when they discover it is not viewable on their mobile device (Callegaro & Macer, 2011). We discuss designing questions for mobile devices more in Chapters 4, 5, 6, and 9.

Access to technology is less of a problem for in-person surveys, where the survey conversation is face-to-face, although high-rise residences with security entrances and gated communities still pose challenges for face-to-face surveys. Likewise, access to technology is not terribly problematic for mail surveys since nearly everyone is familiar with receiving and opening mail and dealing with paper.

Language and literacy issues also limit some people's ability to be included in a survey. Nearly everyone can carry on a conversation in their native language, but in-person surveys will only include people who speak the language(s) the survey is being offered in. For example, if a survey is only offered in English, anyone who cannot speak English has virtually no chance of actually being able to respond to the survey.

According to the Census Bureau in 2007, 20% of people in the United States age 5 and older speak a language other than English at home, and 5% do not speak English at home and say they speak English "not too" or "not at all" well (Shin & Kominski, 2010). However, offering Spanish in addition to English can cover nearly two thirds of this group, thereby significantly reducing the potential for nonresponse bias since many people are provided the survey in a language they can understand.

Paper and web surveys not only have to deal with language issues, but also with literacy. As of 2003, the National Center for Education Statistics estimated that 5% of adults (11 million) in the United States cannot read and write in English and another 10% score below the basic level of ability to read prose (Baer, Kutner, & Sabatini, 2009). According to Kutner et al. (2007) 12% of the U.S. adult population also score at a below basic level in ability to locate basic information and follow simple instructions in forms and documents. As such, literacy can be a significant barrier to people being able to participate in paper and web surveys. However, literacy should be considered when designing survey questions for all modes as an even greater share of adults may have trouble interpreting complex questions (see Chapters 4 and 5 on crafting survey questions).

COMMON SAMPLING FRAMES AND ASSESSING HOW WELL THEY COVER THE POPULATION

To select people to survey, surveyors need a list or frame that contains units or members of the population. Since the sample for the survey is selected from the frame, it is important to understand how well the frame covers the population and whether certain types of units are systematically missing or excluded from it.

Currently there are a number of sample frames available to surveyors, each with its own strengths and weaknesses.

Area Probability Sampling

Area probability samples are most often used for in-person data collection, where field interviewers are sent onsite to complete the interview with the sampled unit. The process of creating an area probability sample is quite expensive and time-consuming; however, it can usually provide near complete coverage of the population of interest. These types of sampling designs are frequently used in countries where no address or population list is available that can be used as a sampling frame.

Figure 3.3 shows an example of the steps of an area probability sample using a hypothetical state. First, the state is split into clusters—in this case counties—and a probability sample of the clusters is selected. Second, each of the

FIGURE 3.3   Design of a multistage area probability sample.

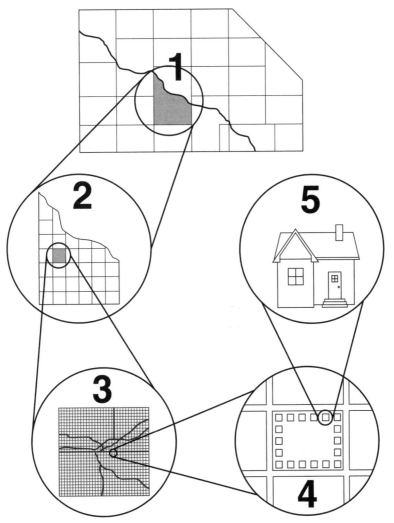

selected counties is split into smaller geographic areas. In the United States, this is typically done using Census geography, such as Census tracts. A probability sample of these smaller geographic areas within each selected county is then selected. Third, each of the selected areas is split into even smaller geographic areas such as Census blocks, and a sample of the blocks is selected, again using probability means. Finally, houses that are located on the selected block are listed. This is often accomplished by sending a person to walk the block and list every household that is on it or by sending someone with an existing list of addresses from that block and having him update the list by adding or removing any addresses as needed. A probability sample of these households is then selected to be surveyed. One of the benefits of area probability samples is that while the entire geographic area one is sampling from is covered by the frame, only the houses in the selected blocks have to be listed. This saves considerable time and resources, compared to those that would be expended if every house in the entire geographic area—in this case the state—had to be listed. Area probability samples are most often employed for sampling housing units but can also be used to sample establishments, such as businesses or schools.

Not only can constructing area probability samples be costly and take a lot of time, but it also can involve significant challenges as well, especially when relying on a diverse field staff to accurately implement the sampling procedures. First, the boundaries of the clusters or areas are sometimes hard to define. Once the areas are defined, it can be difficult to accurately identify what is an eligible unit. For example, it is not always clear whether a building is a housing unit or a business or commercial unit, and sometimes housing units are not visible from the street (e.g., a basement apartment or back cottage). Similarly, it may be unclear how many units are in a multiunit structure. Clear procedures need to be implemented for how to handle group living quarters, such as dorms, assisted living facilities, group homes, and prisons. It also may be difficult to clearly identify living arrangements within a structure. For example, one rule we have seen used for cross-national surveys is that each cooking area constitutes a separate unit or household. Lastly, area probability samples that select an individual from the housing unit face the same difficulties of determining who is a member of the household and executing household selection procedures as surveys by other modes (for more see Identifying Household Members and Within-Household Respondent Selection later in this chapter).

Increasingly, address-based lists, particularly the U.S. Postal Service's computerized delivery sequence file, are replacing area probability sample frames. In addition, some organizations are using address lists as a foundation for their samples and then enhancing the lists using area probability methods (Eckman & Kreuter, 2011). Addresses listed on the address-based sample frame are verified and any missing addresses are added to provide more complete coverage. Address-based lists do have weaknesses, especially in covering rural areas, Native American reservations, military bases, and new development zones. In these places, in-person enumeration may be necessary to ensure adequate coverage.

Address-Based Sampling

The use of residential address lists for survey samples has increased dramatically over the past decade. This change was accelerated when the U.S. Postal Service made its CDSF available in the 1990s for surveyors to use to update and correct existing mailing lists. Another driver of the increased use of residential address lists has been advances in computer technologies, which have helped facilitate the creation and maintenance of large-scale address lists. In the past 10 years, address-based sampling (ABS) has replaced RDD telephone sampling for many surveys. Some of the larger national surveys that are now conducted using ABS are GfK Knowledge Network's KnowledgePanel, Nielsen's TV diary survey, and the National Household Education Survey. In addition, ABS is now being used for surveys such as the General Social Survey and the American National Election Study, where the CDSF frame is supplemented using in person enumeration.

The CDSF is an electronic file containing all delivery point addresses serviced by the U.S. Postal Service (USPS). In other words, it contains the address of every delivery stop on every postal carrier's route, with the exception of general delivery (i.e., having mail held for pickup at the post office). As of 2013, the USPS CDSF included a total of 140,028,225 residential delivery points (USPS, 2013).

The CDSF can only be used to update and correct an existing mailing list that can be demonstrated to already contain 90% of the current mailing addresses in a designated area. Thus, organizations without an existing mailing list are not allowed to receive the CDSF (Iannacchione, 2011). Lists that have been updated using the CDSF are made available to the public through a few commercial vendors who have met strict licensing guidelines with the USPS and pay a subscription fee to have their lists regularly updated.

Some advantages of sample frames based on the CDSF are that they contain a variable to differentiate between business and residential addresses (a task that can be difficult or time-consuming in other commonly used sampling frames). There are also indicators for other types of addresses, such as P.O. boxes, vacant addresses, and seasonal or vacation home addresses. When ordering an ABS, you can specify what types of addresses you want to include and exclude.

In addition, because addresses allow geocoding to near-exact GPS coordinates, ABS is especially useful for geographic stratification and targeting specific populations at even the lowest geographic levels (e.g., surveying the homes in one neighborhood), as well as for targeting people with certain characteristics who tend to concentrate in particular geographic areas (e.g., areas with high incidence of Spanish speakers). Having an address for each unit in the sample file also makes it easier to append other types of data, such as voter registration records and consumer or other types of transaction data, for people living at that address.

The CDSF also has some limitations as a sampling frame. For one, it does not include names associated with the addresses. Although names can be appended, they cannot be matched to every address, and those that are matched are often subject to some of the same biases associated with listed telephone directories (which is discussed in more detail later). Second, the CDSF is available only through private commercial list vendors, each of whom has different protocols for managing and updating the lists, resulting in differences in the lists across vendors (Link et al., 2005). However, vendors that specialize in survey sampling have been working to enhance and improve the CDSF for use as a sampling frame.

Coverage of the CDSF overall is quite high—between 95 and 99% of all U.S. households (Iannacchione, 2011; Iannacchione, Staab, & Redden, 2003; Marketing Systems Group, 2013). But, as mentioned earlier, coverage can be lower in rural areas, areas in transition or where there is a lot of new development, and on Native American reservations and military bases (Iannacchione, 2011; Link et al., 2005; O'Muircheartaigh, English, & Eckman, 2007; Steve, Dally, Lavrakas, Yancey, & Kulp, 2007). However, coverage in rural areas is increasing because of E-911 programs that encourage local governments to replace unlocatable addresses (e.g., "Occupant, Charlo, MT 59824," "Occupant, Route 1 Box 211b, Charlo, MT 59824") with city-style addresses (e.g., "123 Happy Street, Charlo, MT 59824") that make it easier for emergency responders to find a household (Iannacchione, 2011).

Additionally, addresses for multiperson dwellings such as apartment complexes are sometimes listed as only one drop point and thus can result in large groups of people being left off the list. Similarly, people with more than one address (e.g., a regular home address and a vacation home address, or a street address and a PO Box) can be overrepresented, giving them a higher probability of being selected. However, the negative effects of such duplication can be reduced by sampling only certain address types.

Address-based sampling has been shown to be effective for single- and mixed-mode cross-sectional surveys (Link, Battaglia, Frankel, Osborn, & Mokdad, 2008; Smyth, Dillman, Christian, & O'Neill, 2010), including surveys that are screening for a particular population (Brick, Williams, & Montaquila, 2011; Montaquila et al., 2013) and for recruiting people to become part of longitudinal research panels (DiSorga, Dennis, & Fahimi, 2010). Most often initial contacts to households are made by mail, but also sometimes in person. Also, landline telephone numbers can be matched to the addresses in order to add telephone contacts as well. However, in general, only about 45% to 55% of addresses can be matched to a telephone number (Amaya, Skalland, & Wooten, 2010). Match rates can also vary substantially by location (e.g., match rates will be lower in areas with a higher proportion of cell-only households because the matches are typically only to landline numbers).

Address-based sampling can be used to conduct surveys by each of the four major survey modes. Interviewers can go to an address for an in-person survey or the address can be sent a paper survey by mail or information about how to complete a survey online or by calling a toll-free number. In addition, at the first contact, telephone numbers or e-mail addresses can be collected to facilitate follow-up contacts by alternative modes. Indeed, part of the appeal of address-based sampling is the flexibility it provides for conducting surveys by a variety of modes and for conducting mixed-mode surveys.

RDD Sampling

The widespread adoption of telephone surveys in the 1980s and 1990s was facilitated not only by high coverage rates, but also by the development of RDD procedures that allowed telephone numbers to be easily sampled (Waksberg, 1978). In RDD sampling, area codes and prefixes (also known as exchanges) are selected based on the geographic area to be surveyed, and then a number of four-digit combinations are randomly generated and appended to the area code/exchange combinations to produce a random sample of all possible 10-digit numbers within each selected area code/exchange combination (e.g., 404-202-xxxx). See Figure 3.4 for an overview of the components of telephone numbers. While these procedures produce random samples of telephone numbers, calling these numbers can be quite inefficient due to the increasingly large proportion of ineligible units

FIGURE 3.4   What is in a telephone number?

404-202-1500	
Area code	404
Prefix/exchange	202
1000-block	404-202-1000 to 404-202-1999
100-block	404-202-1500 to 404-202-1599

(e.g., businesses) and nonworking numbers. In a typical RDD sample, drawn using equal probability methods, only about 25% to 30% of numbers will be working residential numbers.

To increase efficiency, list-assisted RDD methods are often used, in which landline telephone numbers are first grouped or clustered into banks that each contain 100 contiguous phone numbers (i.e., the first eight digits are the same such as 404-202-1020, 404-202-1021, etc.). Then, only those banks with a certain threshold of listed numbers are included in the sample frame. The most commonly used approach is to only include banks in which one or more of the 100 possible numbers are listed telephone numbers (although some surveys we have seen only include banks with three or more listed numbers). These methods can improve efficiency by about 50% to 60%. However, these efficiencies come at a cost, which is reduced coverage of the RDD landline frame since some numbers in the excluded banks do actually belong to households (e.g., unlisted numbers that have been assigned to a household). Recent research suggests that only calling numbers from banks with at least one listed number can result in excluding between 5% and 20% of households (Boyle, Bucuvalas, Piekarski, & Weiss, 2009; Fahimi, Kulp, & Brink, 2009).

Although RDD techniques were first developed for landline telephone numbers, they have now been adapted for cell phone numbers. RDD methods are used to select cell phone numbers from dedicated wireless and shared service banks (with no listed landline numbers). Similar to landline phone numbers, cell phone numbers are often grouped into banks of 100 contiguous phone numbers to facilitate sampling.

Telephone surveys, especially national ones, are increasingly employing a dual-frame sampling approach—sampling from both an RDD landline and RDD cell phone frame. Dual-frame sampling has increased the complexity of employing RDD sampling methods. One important consideration in dual-frame RDD sampling is how to handle the overlap between the two frames, since people who have both a landline and cell phone are included in both frames. One approach is to screen out those who have a landline but are reached using the cell sample as part of the data collection process. An alternative approach is to screen out those who have a cell phone from the landline frame. This approach has been used less often due to the higher cost of conducting interviews via cell phone, as discussed further later in this chapter, but we expect interest in these types of designs to continue to increase, especially since more people in the United States now have cell phones than landline phones. In these types of screening designs, the goal is to remove any overlap between the frames by only interviewing people with both a landline and cell phone in one of the frames (and terminating the interview with people with both types of phones in the other frame). The more common approach to dual-frame RDD surveys is to conduct interviews with everyone reached in both frames. This approach is often chosen because some of the demographic groups that are hardest to reach by landline telephone are more easily accessible by cell phone (e.g., young people, non-Whites, and less educated adults). If this approach is used, the postsurvey weighting needs to include an adjustment to correct for the fact that some respondents could be covered in both frames (to deal with the frame overlap). Further, accepted rules are still being developed about how much of the sample should come from, or be allocated to, each frame.

Although dual-frame (i.e., landline and cell phone) RDD telephone surveys can adequately cover the population, calling and interviewing people on cell phones raises new challenges. Contact rates can be lower because many people do not want to answer unidentified calls on their cell phones. Furthermore, people tend to be less cooperative with surveyors when reached on cell phones (Brick et al., 2007). In addition, the cost of conducting cell phone interviews is often higher because of legal rules in the U.S. that require mobile numbers to be hand dialed (rather than auto dialed) and because compensation is often offered to reimburse respondents for any costs they might incur for using their cell phone minutes while on the call. Additionally, many minors (under age 18) have cell phones, and they must be screened out of surveys targeting adults (AAPOR, 2010). Also, calling protocols, including calling schedules and how many attempts should be made, need to be revisited when conducting cell phone surveys (see Chapter 8 for further discussion of implementation procedures for telephone surveys, including for dual-frame landline and cell phone surveys). Lastly, survey length is an additional consideration, as people may be less likely to complete longer interviews on their cell phone.

Cell phones also introduce challenges when sampling smaller geographic areas, such as states, metro areas, or counties. The area codes and exchanges in a cellular telephone number may not align well with these smaller geographic areas. Unlike most landline phone numbers, people often keep their cell phone numbers after they move to a new location, or they may purchase their cell phone in a different location from where they actually live. A study by one of the authors in 2009 found that 10% of people live in a different state from what their cell phone number would indicate, and nearly 40% live in a different county (Christian, Dimock, & Keeter, 2009).

Furthermore, the accuracy of cell phone area codes and exchanges for identifying where people live can vary substantially by location. For example, this problem is much greater in Washington, DC, and New York City than in other areas (Skalland & Khare, 2013). A surveyor whose target population is residents of the Washington, DC, metro area would need to account for the fact that this area crosses multiple states and includes a number of area codes. In addition, the more mobile nature of the target population means that many have telephone numbers with area codes outside those assigned to the DC metro area. This likely would introduce substantial undercoverage, as many people living in the area would not be included on the sample frame. The same issues that affect geographic sampling can introduce significant biases for any stratification based on geography. For example, for a sample stratified by Hispanic density, someone whose area code suggests he lives in an area with a high proportion of Hispanics may actually live in a different area with fewer Hispanics and should be assigned to a different stratum.

Taken together, the geographic challenges with sampling cell phone numbers have meant that people who are interested in surveying a particular city or county should consider alternatives to RDD sampling that would provide more precise ability to geographically target the survey sample and better coverage of the target population. For example, an address-based sample would allow clear boundaries to be defined because the geographic information provided with the sampling frame is very precise, and would not suffer the coverage issues associated with sampling cell phone numbers described here.

Telephone Directories

Telephone directories, which also often include complete mailing addresses, provide another alternative for sampling households via telephone (or by mailing paper questionnaires or requests to complete a survey online). Although the majority of landline telephone numbers are listed, about 40% are not (Lavrakas, 2008), and in many large urban areas, 50% or more of numbers may not be listed. People who are older, live in the suburbs, and have medium household incomes are more likely to have listed phone numbers. In addition, cell-phone-only households are generally not listed in such directories at all, and, as was already discussed, these households can differ substantially from those with landlines. As a result of these issues, telephone directories provide inadequate coverage for most general population surveys.

Lack of General Population Internet Frame

The Internet can be a useful mode for conducting surveys targeted at very specific populations, such as college students and certain groups of professionals, for which comprehensive lists that include e-mail addresses are available for sampling. But using the Internet to survey the general public can be much more challenging. In addition to the fact that segments of the population lack Internet access, there is no list of all (or even most) known members of the population (i.e., a sampling frame). Moreover, there is no simple procedure available for drawing samples in which individuals or households have a known, nonzero chance of being included, like RDD methods provided for telephone surveys. This inability is partly the result of widely different e-mail address structures. Examples of the many ways one person's address might vary range from complete full name or nickname to a descriptor that has nothing to do with one's name. For example: Elizabeth.Fern.Thompson@domain .com, EFT@domain.com, thompsonef@domain.com, ethompson@domain.com, thompson005@domain.com, liz@domain.com, FloppyEars@domain.com, and busymom@domain.com. In addition, some people share e-mail addresses with a partner or spouse (e.g., lizandhank@domain.com), and many individuals have multiple addresses, sometimes from different providers (e.g., xxxxx@gmail.com, xxxxx@university.edu, and xxxxx@yahoo.com).

Even if such addresses could be sampled, there are legal and cultural barriers to contacting randomly generated e-mail addresses. Because Internet service providers are private rather than public entities, surveyors do not have the assumed right to contact people as is the case with landline telephones, nor do professional associations of surveyors support sending e-mails to populations with which the surveyor has no preexisting relationship. The Council of American Survey

Research Organizations (CASRO), for example, states in its code of standards that "Research Organizations are required to verify that individuals contacted for research by e-mail have a reasonable expectation that they will receive e-mail contact for research" (CASRO, 2011, p. 8). A preexisting relationship is necessary for respondents to have such a "reasonable expectation." For panel surveys, sometimes surveyors even ask for permission to contact the panelist by e-mail.

In response to these challenges, web surveyors have increasingly come to rely on self-selected panels of respondents or intercepting people while they are online and asking them to complete surveys. People willing to join panels and fill out surveys provide their contact information voluntarily and are thereafter asked to respond periodically to surveys on a variety of topics until they leave the panel. Some web panels contain tens and even hundreds of thousands of active panel members at a time, which has helped circumscribe the challenges discussed earlier of finding and contacting web survey respondents. Similarly, surveys can be administered to people as they go about using the Internet.

However, nearly all of these online methodologies rely on some form of non-probability sampling, and thus it is more difficult to estimate how representative they are of the general population, as is discussed further later in this chapter. Moreover, the easy access that the web provides to large numbers of willing potential respondents, and the very low marginal costs for collecting data from each additional respondent, have led to sampling a large number of potential respondents. In these instances, even if only a small proportion of the sampled people complete the survey, the completed sample size is still quite large. This all too often leads to the unfortunate situation where reporting that surveys have been completed by tens of thousands of people gives the impression that estimates are quite precise. However, what gets overlooked in many of these cases is that it is not possible to calculate sampling error because of the nonprobability nature of the sample to begin with, and in almost all cases there is substantial risk of high nonresponse error (Baker et al., 2013).

Other Alternatives

Other alternatives to telephone directories and the CDSF also may exist for more local general population surveys (i.e., at the regional, state, or county level). In some states, sampling can be accomplished by obtaining driver's license or voter registration lists. Because these lists do not contain all members of the population (they only cover drivers or voters in that state), they may not be suitable for surveys wishing to generalize to the full adult population. These lists can also often become outdated since the people on them only update their information when they are renewing a driver's license or voting in an election.

Consumer lists can also be used as sampling frames or to supplement other sampling techniques. Increasingly, general public lists are being compiled by combining information from a large variety of sources: credit card holders, telephone directories, city directories, magazine subscribers, bank depositors, organization membership lists, catalog and online customers, and so on. Although these lists are not representative of the general population and, therefore, should not be used as sampling frames, the information they contain can sometimes be linked with samples drawn from more representative lists, such as the CDSF. For example, by matching addresses from a CDSF-based sample with addresses on these lists, it may be possible to learn the names of people who live at selected addresses or to obtain phone numbers or e-mail addresses associated with selected addresses that can be used for follow-up contacts with nonrespondents. However, these lists are subject to a variety of biases that must be understood if they are to be used as part of any sampling design. Ethnic name lists also are available, where first and last names thought to be of specific ethnic backgrounds are flagged and separated into lists that can be used for sampling. These lists also do not usually provide full coverage of an ethnic group but may be used in combination with other frames (such as CDSF or RDD) in surveys of various hard-to-reach populations or to help identify which households may need to be contacted in a language other than English.

Researchers may also encounter situations where they want to survey a population for which a good sampling frame does not exist. One of the most prominent populations of this type is voters in an election. To sample voters, exit polls have been conducted for decades now that survey people as they are leaving their polling location (Edison Research has conducted the national exit polls in the United States since 2003). However, sampling voters has gotten more complicated now as many vote by mail or in person before Election Day. To overcome these challenges, a telephone survey is conducted in the weeks leading up to the election to survey people and ask whether they have voted.

Other populations for which no adequate list already exists are visitors to national parks and museums, users of airports, and attendees at open houses. For such populations, coverage is not a problem if people can be sampled as they experience the place, event, or activity of interest. For example, national park or museum visitors can be surveyed while entering or exiting (Dillman, Dolsen, & Machlis, 1995; Rookey, Le, Littlejohn, & Dillman, 2012). Similarly, area probability samples are an example of how to develop a frame that provides adequate coverage of the population when a list does not already exist.

Reducing Coverage Error

Although the issue of finding a good general public population sampling frame is of concern to the larger field of survey methodology and to those who field large-scale national surveys, many people who conduct surveys are interested in specialized groups such as store customers, employees of organizations, members of special interest organizations, and service subscribers. Computer technologies have made it possible to compile and maintain enormous up-to-date lists for these types of populations, but there are some serious challenges associated with using these lists as sample frames. The following section focuses on the questions that must be considered before deciding whether a list provides an adequate sample frame for the target population and how it can be used to effectively survey members of that population.

Most of these types of lists are developed by organizations for their own administrative uses such as sending out advertisements, requesting donations, or asking people to renew their memberships. The primary use of the list will dictate what information is included on it and how often that information is updated. In addition, legal and ethical concerns sometimes cause certain information to be added to or subtracted from a list (or for different versions of lists to be maintained). Some listings may have telephone numbers and e-mail addresses, whereas others do not. Sometimes the list is divided into sublists for an organization's needs, with the result that individual names may appear on several of the sublists.

Moreover, lists are often formatted for particular mailing equipment in a way that makes their use for other purposes difficult. For example, some lists are formatted entirely in capital letters, which needs to be changed for writing cover letters. Knowing the details of how a specific list is compiled, maintained, and managed is essential for understanding whether it will provide an adequate sample frame, and what information it can provide for contacting and surveying potential respondents.

The following five questions can be used in assessing how well a sampling frame covers the survey's target population.

1. Does the Sample Frame Contain Everyone in the Survey Population?

An essential first step in evaluating a sample frame is to determine whether all members of the survey population are included. Members of the population might be excluded for a variety of reasons. For example, one of us was provided a list that was said to contain all members of a health maintenance organization; however, any members who selected not to have their names shared with outside organizations were excluded. Another example is when one of us was asked to evaluate a membership list and members for whom an address was not available were excluded, even if other contact information was available. Similarly, one of us was provided a list of employees but it only included those who received benefits and thus would likely not include part-time employees, who are generally not eligible to receive benefits, and employees who elect not to receive benefits. These examples demonstrate why it is important to understand how well the sampling frame covers the population.

Sometimes when a sampling frame does not adequately cover the population, it may be feasible to try to complete the list and include the remaining people. For example, a cable company's billing list may only include current subscribers. But if the survey is focused on customer satisfaction, the surveyor might want to also include people who are no longer subscribers as part of the sample frame (i.e., people who have discontinued service recently). If it is not possible to include everyone in the population on the sample frame, it is important to evaluate how those not covered differ from those who are covered. Surveyors should ensure that the survey findings appropriately define the population that was actually surveyed, and discuss any ways in which it might differ from the target population.

2. Does the Sample Frame Include Names of People Who Are Not in the Study Population?

Not only do sample frames often exclude people who should be included, but they may also include people who are not part of the target population and thus should be excluded. For example, a university alumni list provided to one of us included some people who had not attended the university (many had donated money to the university) as well as people who may have only attended for a semester or two. Similarly, a list of employees may include consultants or independent contractors who might be ineligible, and thus need to be screened out of the entire survey or screened out of questions that do not apply to them (such as those asking about the physical workspace or specific policies and procedures they may not encounter). When coverage issues like this are identified up front, the appropriate screening questions can often be included in the questionnaire to ensure that only those who are eligible complete the entire survey. However, this involves identifying all of the possible reasons why someone could be ineligible so that appropriate questions can be developed.

3. Are the Same Sample Units Included on the Frame More Than Once?

Not only is it important to ensure that each member of the target population is included, and that those who are ineligible are excluded, but oftentimes members may be listed more than once on the sampling frame. When doing customer surveys, we have sometimes been given lists that have the same address, or nearly the same address, for several names or the same name associated with several addresses. Investigation of this phenomenon for one such list revealed that the list was compiled from customer orders made over the course of several years and there were often slight variations in the names and addresses. This may also be a problem in address-based samples if people have more than one address (e.g., a P.O. box and a residential address or two residential addresses) or in telephone surveys where people have more than one phone number (e.g., a landline and cell phone or two cell phones).

A district-wide survey of the parents of school children presented the problem of duplication in a different way. The keeper of the list created a separate listing for each parent. If a child had two parents with different last names or two parents living in separate residences, each parent had a separate entry on the address list. However, if the parents had the same last name and lived together, they were listed as one entry. The sample was designed on the basis of individual children being the sample unit, so that all children were to have an equal chance of their parent (or parents) being drawn in the sample. Sampling from this address list would have given each child with parents with different last names or with parents living at different addresses twice the probability of being included in the sample as children whose parents had the same last name and lived together. The solution required matching parent names to each child and then deciding randomly which parent should be asked to respond to the survey. These types of situations highlight why it is important to remove duplicates from the frame before selecting the sample for the survey.

4. How Is the Frame Maintained and Updated?

Frames are maintained in many different ways. For example, the CDSF is updated every week or two, and rates of mail being returned as undeliverable tend to be the lowest just after it is updated (Iannacchione, 2011). However, other frames may only be updated every 6 months, annually, or less often than that. Sometimes address lists are actively updated by regularly resending undeliverable correspondence with address correction requests. In other instances, updating contact information is left up to individual members or subscribers, thus eliminating the costs to the organization of having to employ people to update the information. For example, membership lists are often only updated annually or when the member initiates an update. Finally, some lists sit unused for years, with only new names and contact information being added and with little to no attempt made to update information for people already on the list (so that names added in earlier years are less likely to have up-to-date contact information).

One issue we encountered when surveying university students is that they are often responsible for reporting any address and phone number changes to the university. Unfortunately, many never do, resulting in poor quality lists. For example, for many students, their listed mailing address was that of their parents' home rather than their local campus address. It is especially important for surveyors wishing to ask questions about a particular event or transaction (such as a recent concert or hotel stay) to know how often the attendee or customer list is updated and to clearly define the target population.

Knowing these characteristics of a sample frame allows one to evaluate the likelihood of unintended coverage error creeping into one's survey results (e.g., fewer valid addresses for older members on a survey about retirement saving or new members likely being underrepresented in a survey about what direction the organization should move in). In difficult cases of this nature, we have sometimes sent letters to a sample of members, or even everyone on the list, with "Address Correction Requested" on the envelope in order to learn from the U.S. Postal Service how many addresses were invalid.

5. Does the Frame Contain Other Information That Can Be Used to Improve the Survey?

Many frames contain other information that can be used to improve the survey. For example, a sample frame of addresses used to contact people for a mail survey may also contain telephone numbers that can be used in follow-up contacts to reach people who are less likely to open their mail. Similarly, if a sample frame of telephone numbers used to call people to complete a telephone survey also includes e-mail addresses, these might be used to contact nonrespondents who do not pick up or talk on the phone very much. Multiple modes are increasingly being used in these ways to contact and/or survey sampled members (for more on this, see Chapter 11). It is only by assessing what types of contact information are available (telephone numbers, e-mail addresses, postal addresses, etc.) that an appropriate contact strategy can be developed.

In addition to contact information, some lists contain information, such as gender, age, or race that might be used to stratify the sample to ensure that particular groups are represented in the survey. Other information, such as number of orders submitted during the past year, length of employment, or membership level, may be available for stratifying the sample in other ways. In addition, this type of sample information can also be useful for evaluating whether the survey sample is representative of the target population and identifying potential nonresponse bias in the completed sample.

Coverage Outcomes

The coverage considerations we have discussed here highlight the importance of ensuring that every member of the population is included in the sampling frame, that every member is included only once, and that only members of the population are included (i.e., every effort is made to screen out ineligibles). It is important to assess the coverage of the sample frame before selecting the sample and designing how the survey will be implemented.

Frequently, a coverage analysis of potential sample frames may produce a conclusion that no one frame or list is completely adequate for one's purpose.

One alternative that has become increasingly popular is the use of multiframe surveys (Lohr, 2009), where multiple sampling frames are used to reduce the coverage limitations of any one frame (e.g., combining landline and cell phone RDD frames, combining different types of organization lists, etc.).

Similarly, even if only one frame is used for sampling, multiple modes are often used to contact and/or survey respondents. For example, one might conduct a survey primarily via the Internet but also send a paper questionnaire through the mail or call people on the phone to provide an alternative way for people who do not have Internet access to respond to the survey, thereby reducing the threat of coverage error. Additionally, mixed-mode surveying provides one solution to the challenge of respondents exercising more and more choice about what contact information they make available and of different people providing different types of information.

In some cases, not even a combination of sampling frames may be available, or the budget may not be large enough to accommodate the additional complexity of a mixed-mode survey. Then, the surveyor is faced with a decision about whether plans for the survey should be abandoned or whether a certain amount of coverage error is acceptable. Such decisions usually involve a consideration of whether any alternatives exist (frequently they do not), the cost of those alternatives, and whether any methods exist for evaluating the extent of any resultant error.

PROBABILITY SAMPLING

The remarkable power of the sample survey is its ability to closely estimate the distribution of a characteristic in a population by obtaining information from relatively few elements of that population. It is *probability sampling*, where every member of the sampling frame is given a known, nonzero chance of being included in the sample that allows a survey's results to be generalizable to the full target population, even though only some members of the population are selected. *Sampling error* occurs because only a sample of the population is asked to complete the survey, rather than everyone in the population, and because every possible sample one could draw from a sample frame can produce slightly different estimates. In most cases, the estimates will be close to the true value, although the amount of sampling error is highly dependent on sample size and how the sample is designed.

The effects of sampling error can usually be estimated with considerable precision. As a result, it is commonly used as an indicator of the survey's quality and is often reported when survey results are presented.

Drawing a sample can be fairly simple or remarkably complex, depending on the sampling design employed. *Simple random sampling* is when each member of the population is given an equal chance of being included, members are selected randomly, and their selection is independent of one another. Since all members have an equal chance of being selected, simple random sampling is fairly easy to execute, especially with basic computer programs that now make it very easy to randomly select units from the sampling frame.

Sampling statisticians have also developed various modifications or deviations from simple random sampling. These approaches are usually used to help increase fielding efficiencies and reduce costs, but can also increase sampling error.

- Clustering—Sample units are grouped (or clustered) and then the groups are randomly sampled, rather than each unit sampled independently.

For example, addresses are grouped into counties and then counties are selected for sampling. Clustering typically increases sampling error.

- Stratification—Sampled units are divided into groups (strata) prior to selection. For example, a list of addresses can be grouped into five strata ranging from highest to lowest population density. Stratification typically decreases sampling error.
- Proportionate sampling—Groups or strata are sampled at rates equal to their size in the population. For example, in the survey discussed at the beginning of this chapter, 33% of the state's population lived in rural areas so if proportionate sampling was used, 33% of the sample would be drawn from rural areas.
- Disproportionate sampling—Groups or strata are sampled at rates unequal to their size in the population (i.e., some groups are oversampled and others are undersampled). Looking again to the survey discussed at the beginning of this chapter, disproportionate sampling was used where 50% of the addresses selected were in rural areas, rather than 33% (the portion of the state's population living in rural areas).

Clustering is most often used for surveys that are conducted in person (or where in-person interviewing is employed as part of a mixed-mode survey). It is typically used because grouping sampled units into particular geographic areas can substantially reduce interviewing costs and increase productivity by decreasing the distance interviewers have to travel between sampled households. It is important to note, though, that clusters often represent preexisting relationships or connections—such as housing units on a block or schools in a district. For mail, web, and telephone surveys, the geographical distance between respondents usually has little to no effect on costs, so clustering is not usually necessary.

Stratification with either proportionate or disproportionate sampling is common in all types of survey modes, since it helps surveyors control the representation of key groups of interest in the sample. Proportionate sampling helps ensure that important groups are represented in the sample at the same rate as in the population. That is, it eliminates the possibility that exists in simple random sampling of happening to draw a sample in which groups are not accurately represented. Disproportionate sampling is typically done when researchers want to be able to draw conclusions about low incidence populations. Oversampling helps ensure that enough members of these subpopulations will be surveyed so that estimates can be reported for these groups with a reasonable amount of precision, and differences between subgroups can be compared.

Clustering and stratification are often combined in what is called multistage sampling. For example, imagine one wants to survey high school seniors. Enumerating a list of all the high school seniors in the state would be quite an undertaking. Instead, one might decide to sample districts and then within the selected districts sample schools. This would mean the surveyor only has to enumerate and sample the high school seniors in the selected schools, rather than in the entire state, a much more attainable goal. In this case, the high school seniors are clustered within the schools, and the schools are clustered in the selected districts. If the researcher expects seniors from urban schools to differ from seniors from rural schools, before sampling the districts she might want to create two strata—urban districts and rural districts—to make sure that districts (and thereby schools and seniors) of each of these types are represented in the final sample.

Cluster sampling usually increases sampling variance relative to simple random sampling. This happens because units within a cluster tend to have a lot in common (since they are often naturally occurring groupings), which means that each additional unit from a cluster drawn in to the sample does not bring in as much unique information as would a unit drawn from outside the cluster. Because of this, more units will be needed in a cluster sample to get the same amount of information as a simple random sample with fewer units. The example of surveying high school seniors can help explain this. Within a high school, students typically share a lot of experiences such as attending the same classes, playing on the same sports teams, or singing in the same choir. They may even have a shared school identity ("Go Jaguars!"). Students within a school are also likely to share other characteristics related to their neighborhoods, such as being of the same race or similar social class. We can each think back to our own high school experience and see many ways that the students who attended our school were similar to each other and different from the students attending a neighboring school. Because of this commonality, drawing an additional student from the same school, as is done in a cluster sample, will yield less information than drawing an additional student from a different school, as might be done in a simple random sample.

We now focus on the general relationship between sample size and the reduction of sampling error in the context of simple random sampling. In what follows, we do not discuss the statistical theory and proofs that underlie the development of these types of designs because they are beyond the scope of this book. Many excellent texts focus exclusively on the various types of sampling designs used in survey research and provide far more detail than can be covered here (these include Levy & Lemeshow, 2008; Lohr, 1999; Maxim, 1999). In addition, the classic sampling texts by Kish (1965) and Cochran (1977) are helpful in describing the foundation of these sampling methodologies. Our goal is to give the reader a sense of the basics underlying sample designs, sample size, and the resulting sampling error.

How Large Should a Sample Be?

One of the first key decisions in sampling is deciding how large of a sample needs to be drawn. What is an appropriate sample size will be determined by

- The desired level of confidence one wishes to have in the estimates
- How much sampling error can be tolerated
- How much variation there is in the population on the characteristic of interest
- The size of the population from which the sample is to be drawn

If, for example, one wishes to estimate the percentage of people who have a college education in a small county of 25,000 adults within 3 percentage points of the actual percentage 95% of the time, a completed sample of about 1,100 respondents is needed. If one wants to estimate this characteristic for a small state of 2 million adults with the same confidence, then about 1,100 respondents also are needed. If this information is sought for the entire United States, then the same number—about 1,100—is needed.

These examples demonstrate one of the primary characteristics of probability sampling: It is the size of the sample that affects precision, not the size of the population. The formula below can be used to determine what size completed sample is needed, when a simple random sample is employed. The formula takes into account how much confidence is needed for the estimates, the expected distribution for the characteristic of interest being measured in the survey, the amount of sampling error that is desired, and the size of the population.

$$n = \frac{(z^2 * p * q)}{MoE^2}$$

where
    n = completed sample size needed for desired level of precision
    p = the proportion being tested
    q = $1 - p$
MoE = the desired margin of sampling error
    z = the z-score or critical value for the desired level of confidence

To explain further, n is the sample size needed for the size of the survey population. p is the proportion being tested, and q is derived from p (i.e., $1 - p$); they are measures of the variation in answers to the question of interest. Often, margins of error are reported for the survey overall, where p is set at the most conservative value possible, 50% (i.e., the expectation that 50% of the people in the population answer "yes" to a question and 50% answer "no"). However, it is important to remember that sampling error varies for each statistic or question that the survey produces.

MoE is the level of sampling error that is acceptable for the study. z is the z-score or critical value associated with the amount of statistical confidence one desires to have in the estimates. The most widely used level of confidence is 95%, where 95 out of 100 times that a random sample is drawn from the population, the estimate obtained from the completed sample will fall within the margin of sampling error. For 95% confidence, the z-score is 1.96 (1.645 for 90% confidence and 2.58 for 99% confidence).

Thus, for a question with a 50/50 split, a completed sample size of 544 cases is needed to be sure that the estimate of interest will be within ±3 percentage points 95% of the time:

$$n = \frac{(1.96 * .5 * .5)}{.03^2}$$
$$n = 544$$

To put it another way, one can conclude for a yes/no question in which one expects respondents to be split 50/50 (the most conservative assumption that can be made about variance) that 95 out of 100 times that a random sample of 544 people is selected from the total population of 1,000, the sample estimate will be within 3 percentage points of the true population value.

Although many surveys are conducted with larger samples and the preceding formula works fine, when populations are small, one may want to consider adjusting this formula by including the finite population correction (*fpc*), which accounts for the size of the target population in the calculation. The *fpc* adjusts for the fact that in smaller populations, a given sample size provides proportionately more information than a sample of the same size in larger populations (represents a greater share of the total population). In practice though, most surveyors ignore the *fpc* when estimating sample sizes. Following is the formula that includes the finite population correction (where N is the size of the target population):

$$n = \frac{(N * p * q)}{\left\{ (N - 1) * \left(\frac{MoE}{z} \right)^2 + (p * q) \right\}}$$

When this formula with the finite population correction is used, and the population of interest is small (in this case $N = 1,000$), the estimated sample size needed is somewhat smaller, 516 cases (for a proportion with a 50/50 split where one wants to be confident that the true value will fall within plus or minus 3 percentage points of the estimate 95% of the time).

$$n = \frac{(1000 * .5 * .5)}{\left\{ 999 * \left(\frac{.03}{1.96} \right)^2 + (.5 * .5) \right\}}$$

$$n = 516$$

Our example used a yes/no question, but not all questions are yes/no items. Moreover, the amount of variation that exists in a population characteristic differs from one population to another. For example, the variation in age of first-year students at a major university may be quite small, mostly 17- to 19-year-olds, whereas the variation in age in the general public is much larger. If a surveyor is trying to determine the mean age of first-year students, adding more and more students to the sample is not going to change the estimate much because they are all a similar age. A low sample size will likely come close to the desired estimate. However, if one is trying to determine the mean age of the general population, she will need a larger sample to estimate the mean age with the same amount of precision. In general, the greater the variation, the larger the sample size needed for making population estimates. For this reason, the examples presented here assume maximum heterogeneity (a 50/50 split) on a proportion in the population from which the sample is to be drawn.

If we experiment with different parameters in the preceding equation, we discover several somewhat nonintuitive premises about sample size that need to be understood in order to make wise sampling decisions. These premises are reflected in Figure 3.5, which was derived from the preceding sample size equation for simple random sample surveys that includes the finite population correction. The figure is presented here less because of its practical use for surveyors than for the general perspective it provides about sample sizes needed for conducting surveys. If no finite population correction is used, the estimated sample sizes needed will be similar to those for populations of 1,000,000 or more, because as the population size increases, the finite population correction has little effect.

Relatively Few Completed Questionnaires Can Provide Surprising Precision at a High Level of Confidence

This is the reason that survey sampling is such a powerful tool. Figure 3.5 shows that if one could be satisfied with being 95% confident that an estimate from a sample survey is within ±10 percentage points of the true population value,

FIGURE 3.5 Completed sample sizes needed for various population sizes and characteristics at three confidence interval widths (margins of error).

Population Size	Sample Size for the 95% Confidence Interval					
	±10%		±5%		±3%	
	50/50 Split	80/20 Split	50/50 Split	80/20 Split	50/50 Split	80/20 Split
100	49	38	80	71	92	87
200	65	47	132	111	169	155
400	78	53	196	153	291	253
600	83	56	234	175	384	320
800	86	57	260	188	458	369
1,000	88	58	278	198	517	406
2,000	92	60	322	219	696	509
4,000	94	61	351	232	843	584
6,000	95	61	361	236	906	613
8,000	95	61	367	239	942	629
10,000	95	61	370	240	965	640
20,000	96	61	377	243	1,013	661
40,000	96	61	381	244	1,040	672
100,000	96	61	383	245	1,056	679
1,000,000	96	61	384	246	1,066	683
1,000,000,000	96	61	384	246	1,067	683

Note. These are estimated sample sizes for simple random samples that include the finite population correction.

that estimate could be calculated by obtaining completed surveys from a random sample of only about 100 individuals. What this means is that in a properly conducted national survey with a completed simple random sample of 100 individuals, in which 50% of the respondents say they own the home in which they are living, one could state with 95% confidence that between 40% and 60% of the entire population owns the home in which they live, assuming there is no error from nonresponse, measurement, or coverage.

Among Large Populations There Is Virtually No Difference in the Completed Sample Size Needed for a Given Level of Precision

This premise is also reflected in the sample size numbers presented in Figure 3.5, and is shown visually in Figure 3.6, which graphs the completed sample sizes that are needed to make estimates within ±3, ±5, and ±10 percentage points by population size. For each of these lines, when the population size gets large (i.e., 6,000+), the lines level off considerably, meaning that the differences in the needed completed sample size are quite small among large populations. It is only when the population size decreases to a few thousand or less that the number of completed surveys needed for a given margin of error begins to change significantly. It is for this reason that one can estimate within ±3 percentage points the percentage of people who have a high school education in a small county of 25,000 adults with 1,023 completes and can measure the same thing among the entire U.S. population of more than 300 million by obtaining only 44 more completes.

FIGURE 3.6 Completed simple random sample sizes needed by population size and desired margin of error (95% confidence level with 50/50 split).

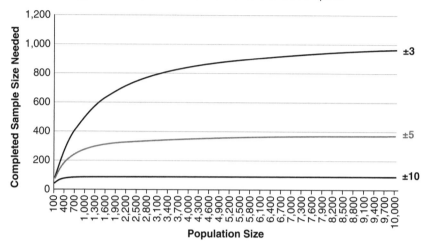

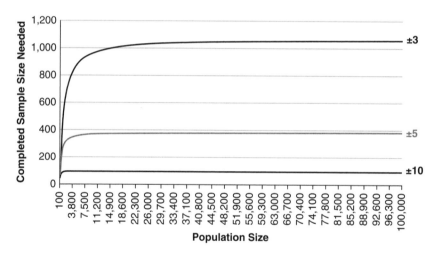

Within Small Populations, Greater Proportions of the Population Need to Be Surveyed (i.e., Completed) to Achieve Estimates Within a Given Margin of Error

Frequently survey sponsors ask why, if about 1,200 people will provide an estimate within 3 percentage points in a national poll, they cannot get by with only a small fraction of that number when their entire survey population is only one county or small city. This question returns us to our original point that it is not the size of the population, but the size of the sample, that matters. The proportion that must be sampled changes across population sizes and is much higher among small populations.

This raises the question of whether one should sample at all in smaller populations, or instead attempt to survey everyone (i.e., take a census of the population). This question is especially critical for self-administered surveys, in which the marginal costs of contacting additional people are usually less than for interview surveys. In these cases, survey sponsors frequently make quick decisions to survey everyone in their small populations, but as a consequence they usually have to spread their resources thinner, so that other sources of error do not get minimized to the extent possible.

There is nothing to be gained by surveying all 1,000 members of a population in a way that produces only 350 responses (a 35% response rate) versus selecting a random sample of only 500 and surveying them in a way that produces the same number of responses (a 70% response rate), because the potential of nonrespondents being different from respondents on important survey items (i.e., nonresponse error) may be greater when the response rate is lower. In cases like this, considering only the relationship between *completed sample size* and statistical precision, and overlooking the potential for nonresponse error, leads to unwise decisions in which survey sponsors simply trade small amounts of sampling error for potentially large amounts of nonresponse error. That said, surveying everyone in the population may be useful when the budget is large enough to also minimize coverage, nonresponse, and measurement error, or when the population is so small that the additional costs of surveying everyone are fairly negligible.

At Higher Sample Sizes, Increases Yield Smaller and Smaller Reductions in the Margin of Error

Figure 3.7, shows the margin of error that can be expected as the completed sample size increases from 2 to 1,002 in a population of 1,002 (50/50 split in the proportion being estimated at the 95% confidence level for a simple random sample and including the finite population correction). This graph shows that the margin of error is drastically reduced from ±69.3 points to ±13.6 points as the completed sample size increases from 2 to 52. As the completed sample size is increased from 52 to 102, the margin of error continues to decrease, but much less drastically,

FIGURE 3.7 Rate of decrease in margin of error resulting from increases in completed sample size in a population of 1,002 (95% confidence level with 50/50 split).

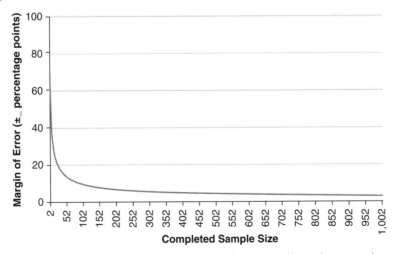

Note. The margins of error shown here are based on a simple random sample, are calculated for estimates of proportions (they may differ for estimates of means), and apply only to analyses including the full sample (i.e., not subgroup analyses).

to ±9.7 points. In this example, the sampling error drops below 5 percentage points at a completed sample size of 385. Surveying the entire population would require one to survey hundreds more, thus substantially increasing costs, but could only reduce the margin of error 5 percentage points under the best conditions. As pointed out earlier, the additional resources might better be allocated to improving response rates among a smaller sample.

Completed Sample Sizes Must Be Much Larger If One Wants to Make Precise Estimates for Subgroups of Populations

The discussion up to this point has assumed that the surveyor is interested in making estimates only for the survey population as a whole. If, in a statewide survey of adults, one desires to make estimates for women only with a precision of ±3 percentage points using the 95% level of confidence, then one needs slightly more than 1,000 women respondents in the survey. If one wants this much precision at the same level of confidence for women who are between 18 and 34 years old, the same reasoning applies (i.e., one needs more than 1,000 women who are within that specific age group). The desire for substantial precision in making estimates for subgroups of populations is typically a powerful factor in pushing sample sizes as high as can be afforded, while balancing the trade-offs with other design considerations.

Identifying Household Members and Within-Household Respondent Selection

Thus far we have discussed the importance of ensuring that every member of the target population is covered by the sample frame (i.e., minimizing coverage error) and of selecting sample members from the frame using probability methods. We have discussed these two topics somewhat independently, but in surveys where the target population is adults but the sample frame contains household listings (i.e., addresses or landline telephones), they become entangled. In this case, once households are selected with probability means, additional steps need to be taken to ensure that every eligible member of each sampled household has a chance to be selected as the respondent (i.e., is covered) and that selection of a respondent from each household is done using probability or quasiprobability methods.

Some of the common methods require an explicit listing of eligible household members while others require people to think about all eligible household members, but not necessarily to list them. Whether it is done explicitly or implicitly, all within-household selection methods start by determining who qualifies as a member of the household. One of the simplest rules for determining whether someone is a household member is if he lives at the residence the majority of the time. Another commonly used criterion is whether a person considers the home to be his permanent residence. But within these broad definitions, special situations arise and it is important that the sampling procedures clearly specify how to handle these types of cases. Following are some of the frequently encountered situations that should be considered when developing the sample design:

- Students who live away (at boarding school, college, etc.)
- People who live away at other institutions (e.g., nursing home, psychiatric facility, prison, etc.)

- People who travel frequently
- People who have multiple residences (especially children with multiple residences, such as those in joint custody arrangements)
- Members of the Armed Forces
- People who live in the household in exchange for a fee/services (e.g., renter, nanny, housekeeper)

Once qualifying members of the household have been identified, surveyors typically sample one member from each household. In interviewer-administered surveys, the interviewer can guide household informants to ensure that they understand the selection procedures and execute them correctly. In addition, they can provide encouragement and accountability if the person needs to get someone else in the household to complete the survey. When the questionnaire is administered over a computer, such as in computer-assisted personal interviewing (CAPI) or computer-assisted telephone interviewing (CATI), the computer can be programmed to guide the interviewer through the selection process and, with some input, to select the correct respondent, thereby reducing interviewer burden. However, in self-administered surveys, recipients must be able to clearly understand and execute the selection procedures on their own, without help from an interviewer. In web surveys the computer can be programmed to help them through some of the steps, but the household informant still has to understand the procedure well enough to enter needed information into the computer so it can make the proper selection.

Three of the most common approaches to selecting individuals from within a household are the Kish, Rizzo, and birthday methods. The Kish method (1949) involves listing all members of a household, by gender and age (or sometimes name and age), and then selecting one member from the list using previously developed random selection tables. This method is considered the most comprehensive method, and is usually considered a true probability-based procedure (although it does not allow equal chance of selection in households with more than six adults). The Kish method was originally developed for in-person surveys. It is used for telephone surveys, but only limitedly because it requires the collection of information that may be considered sensitive before allowing respondents to become engaged in and committed to the survey, and it takes a lot of time. The Kish method is rarely used in self-administered paper and Internet surveys because it is complex, and in these modes there is no interviewer present to guide the household informant through the selection process.

An alternative to the full Kish method is the Rizzo method. Rizzo, Brick, and Park (2004) recognized that most households in the United States (about 85%) have only one or two adults. In these households simple random selection can be used and the laborious and sometimes sensitive task of enumerating all household members and using complicated tables to select one of them can be avoided. The Rizzo method starts by asking a household informant how many adults live in the household. For households with only one adult, that person is selected to complete the survey. If there is more than one adult in the household, the informant is selected with probability $1/N$, where N is the total number of adults in the household. If the informant is selected, the within-household selection procedure is finished and the survey can commence. If the informant is not selected, then in two-adult households, the other adult is automatically selected. For households with three or more adults, when the informant is not selected, additional selection procedures such as the Kish method or a birthday method (described below) are used. In this case, the household informant is excluded because she has already had a chance to be selected in the previous step. Since less than 15% of households in the United States have three or more adults, a much smaller number of households are asked to complete the full Kish enumeration, or alternatively, to implement one of the birthday methods.

The birthday methods involve selecting the adult in the household who has had the most recent birthday (when using the last birthday method) or who will have the next upcoming birthday (when using the next birthday method) to be the respondent. Although this method theoretically allows all members of the household to have an equal chance of selection, it is more of a quasiprobability method because it relies on the assumption that birthdays are randomly distributed throughout the year and across respondent characteristics. When this assumption is not met, such as when one is measuring characteristics that have a cycle, season, or periodicity to them, these methods can introduce bias. For example, estimates produced by a survey of college students about their drinking and drug behaviors right after spring break or by a survey of voters where age eligibility is determined by the date of the election would likely be affected by the use of the birthday methods.

Nevertheless, this approach is one of the most prevalent within-household selection methods used, especially for self-administered surveys, because it is easy for people to complete on their own when there is not an interviewer present to help guide them. A sentence can easily be inserted in the cover letter and even on the questionnaire that says, "In order for the results of this survey to accurately represent all adults in the state, it is important that the questionnaire be completed by the adult (18 years or older) who currently lives in this household who has had the most recent birthday."

This technique, when used over the telephone, has produced an overrepresentation of women (Groves & Lyberg, 1988), which may occur because women are somewhat more likely than men to answer home telephones. Similar findings have been reported for mail surveys (Battaglia, Link, Frankel, Osborn, & Mokdad, 2005; Olson, Stange, & Smyth, forthcoming). Moreover, in both telephone and self-administered modes, there is some risk that the request for the person with the most recent birthday will be ignored or misunderstood, resulting in the wrong person being selected (Battaglia et al., 2005; Gaziano, 2005; Lavrakas, Stasny, & Harpuder, 2000). According to a study conducted by one of the authors, the birthday household selection methods were executed correctly by only about 66 to 71% of households, but this includes one-person households, which are guaranteed to make accurate selections. Only between 53 and 63% of households with two or more adults (i.e., those households that could possibly make an error) selected the correct person to respond (Olson, Stange, & Smyth, forthcoming; Stange, Olson, & Smyth, 2013). Nevertheless, in the absence of better alternatives that can be easily understood and executed by respondents, the birthday method seems to be among the best within-household selection methods for self-administered surveys.

Lastly, some surveyors use a nonprobability method, such as quota sampling, where individual household members are selected to meet certain predetermined characteristics, such as needing 51% of the completed sample to be women or 14% to be Hispanic. Other survey designs use an at-home method where a household member is selected from among those who are at home at that time, and sometimes may also involve asking for a person who fits a combination of gender and age characteristics and who is now at home. An example is the youngest male/youngest female method used by the Pew Research Center, where interviewers randomly ask half the sample first for the youngest male who is now at home and then if there is no male available, for the youngest female. The other half of the sample starts with the youngest female and if she is not home, then asks for the youngest male. This approach helps overcome the common problem of surveys underrepresenting young adults. It is used more in telephone surveys than in other modes where it may be difficult to call back the household and reach the selected individual (which would be necessary for the other selection methods). Nonprobability approaches like these are subject to biases. For example, the at-home method underrepresents those who are away from the home more, such as those who are employed outside the home or who engage in many activities outside the home.

Some household surveys are not aimed at obtaining a representative sample of the adult population. Instead, the topic of interest may be a household behavior, in which case the person with the greatest responsibility for that area of activity should complete the questionnaire. For example, a survey on telephone service appropriately requested the following: "The adult most responsible for making decisions about the telephone services provided to your household should complete the enclosed questionnaire." This line of reasoning can be extended to many areas of activity, from shopping for groceries to purchasing automobiles to making investment decisions. It also applies to businesses where the desired respondent may be the one most responsible for recommending or making decisions about, for example, the purchase of computers. In these types of surveys, where an individual is selected based on his knowledge or position, the potential for coverage error is limited to the household or business level.

Sometimes letters are addressed to an individual within the household or organization who is not necessarily the person who should complete the questionnaire. This often happens when the sample frame contains addresses, each with only one corresponding name (i.e., households are initially sampled), but the target population is all adults (i.e., an adult within the household needs to be randomly selected).

Letters intended for households that are addressed to an individual provide a special problem in this regard because that person may immediately take ownership of the questionnaire (it also often results in a higher number of undeliverables since the USPS is matching on name and address). When the first edition of this book was published, general public samples drawn from telephone directories typically produced a higher proportion of male respondents than female respondents, even though letters requested that an adult female complete the questionnaire in half the households. The overrepresentation of male respondents stemmed from the fact that men's names were more likely to be listed than their spouses' names in telephone directories, so the envelopes were often addressed to them (Dillman, Christenson, Carpenter, & Brooks, 1974). In contrast, women were somewhat more likely to participate in telephone surveys because they were more likely to answer the telephone, and it was sometimes difficult to get access to another household adult. To avoid these biases, we recommend not addressing the materials to a named household member if a different person in the household might be selected as the respondent. Other types of personalization may still be used, such as "Dear (CITY) Resident" or even "Dear (NEIGHBORHOOD) Resident."

As these various procedures outline, sampling procedures are employed not only for selecting units (households or businesses), but also for selecting individuals within those units. Due to variations in household size and selection procedures, individuals vary in their chance of being selected. For example, people in larger households have a smaller chance of being selected than those in smaller households (e.g., an adult in a household with two adults has a 50% chance of being selected whereas an adult in a household with five adults has a 20% chance of being selected). When within-household selection procedures are used, it is important to collect information about how many adults are in each household so that the probability of each sample member being selected can be known. This information will be used in the weighting process.

Here are a few key tips for guiding households through within-household selection procedures:

- Clearly define who should be considered a household member
- Ask for the number of household members (can often can just ask for number of adults)
- Decide on which selection procedure to use
- Describe how to execute the procedure clearly and concisely in simple terms
- Provide motivation to help the person understand why doing this is important

Household selection procedures are often a key step in the sampling process. It is important to not only use probability-based sampling methods to select units from the sample, but these methodologies also need to be applied when selecting individuals from within the sampled units.

In many ways, planning a sample is a guessing game in which one tries to determine the type and size of sample that will yield acceptably precise estimates while staying within budget but without knowing what type(s) of sample members or how many will respond. While one can and should make informed and smart sampling decisions from the outset, the quality of the final sample in terms of how well it represents the population of interest and how precise the estimates are cannot be determined until after the data are collected. Depending on what happens during data collection, the final margin of error may differ from what was initially planned. We turn next to methods for postsurvey adjustments (i.e., weighting) and calculating the actual sampling error.

POSTSURVEY ADJUSTMENTS AND CALCULATING SAMPLING ERROR

Weighting

Many surveys involve weighting to help ensure that the final sample represents the target population as closely as possible. First, one of the most important steps in weighting survey data is creating the *base weight*. This weight corrects for any differences in sampled members' chances of being selected into the sample. In the simplest form, the base weight is the inverse of the probability of selection for each sample member. The base weight should include adjustments for probability of selection, at each stage of sampling, including any clustering, stratification, and within-household selection.

For example, in a survey that uses simple random sampling to select 1,000 addresses from the frame of 10,000 addresses, the probability of selection for all addresses would be 1/10. This number would then need to be multiplied by the probability of selection of each individual within her household to account for the within-household selection. Individual residents within the addresses selected would have different probabilities of selection, depending on the household size. A person in a household with two adults would have a within-household probability of selection of 1/2, which, when multiplied by 1/10 yields an overall probability of selection of 1/20. This person's base weight would be 20, which is the inverse of the overall probability of selection (i.e., the inverse of $1/20 = 20$). By comparison, a person in a household with five adults would have a within-household probability of selection of 1/5, which when multiplied by 1/10 yields an overall probability of selection of 1/50. Thus, this person's base weight would be 50 (see Figure 3.8 for a summary on calculating base weights).

The weights reflect how many people in the target population are represented by each completed interview. For example, when a person has a weight of 20, his responses represent those of 20 people from the target population, whereas the data from someone with a weight of 50 represent 50 people from the target population.

Some surveys also adjust for differential nonresponse among subgroups as part of the weighting. Sample-based *nonresponse adjustments* can help to reduce the potential bias from the fact that not everyone sampled responded to the survey. One way to calculate a nonresponse weight is to take the inverse of the response rate for each group. Alternatively, propensity models can also be used to generate nonresponse weights (Levy & Lemeshow, 2008).

Lastly, *poststratification* weighting or raking can be employed to improve the representativeness of the survey sample by adjusting for the fact that some groups were less likely to respond than others. These methods weight the final sample to match the population on characteristics such as gender, age, race/ethnicity, education, and region. For example, if only 46% of the sample was male but in the population 51% are male, the weight would be higher for males (and lower for females) to compensate for this underrepresentation. For this step, the characteristics of the target population must be known from another source. The most commonly used sources for population parameters in the United States are high-quality surveys, such as the American Community Survey, Current Population Survey, and the National Health Interview Survey, as well as the Decennial Census.

Weighting generally requires one to have data sources other than responses from the survey itself. For sample-based nonresponse weighting, the characteristics used in weighting need to be known for both respondents and nonrespondents

FIGURE 3.8 Calculating base weights.

	Probability of Selection of the...			Base Weight
	Household	Adult in the Household	Combined	(Inverse of Probability of Selection)
One adult in household	1/10	1/1	= 1/10	10
Two adults	1/10	1/2	= 1/20	20
Three adults	1/10	1/3	= 1/30	30
Four adults	1/10	1/4	= 1/40	40
Five or more adults	1/10	1/5	= 1/50	50

so the response rate for each group can be calculated. This means that this type of nonresponse weighting can only be done for characteristics that are included or appended to every record on the frame. For poststratification weighting, one needs a high-quality data set to produce the population parameters. In this case, one can only weight for characteristics that are measured in that data set and also asked about in the survey. Most surveys are weighted only to demographic characteristics because these are the most widely available measures available on sample files and in the data sets people weight to.

This brings us to an important limit of weighting. Weighting on any characteristic will ensure that the sample is representative with respect to that characteristic and to characteristics that are correlated with it, but it will not ensure that the sample is representative with respect to characteristics that are not correlated with the characteristic used for weighting. This means that within the same survey, weighting can improve some estimates, have no effect on others, and potentially even bias others.

For example, imagine a survey in which the researcher is trying to estimate average yearly income and the proportion of people who use the Internet. Assume also, that, as is commonly the case, women responded to the survey at higher rates than men. If the researcher uses the collected data without any adjustments, she is likely to underestimate average yearly income because there are too many women in the sample and women make less money on average than men. To produce a less biased estimate of average yearly income, she will want to weight the data on gender. This will help ensure that men's and women's incomes are represented in the estimates in the right proportion, reducing the bias in the estimate. But what effect will weighting on gender have on the estimate of the proportion of people who use the Internet? The answer is that it will not have any effect. This is because the same proportion of men and women use the Internet (about 85%). If the researcher wants to reduce the bias in the estimate of the proportion using the Internet, it will make more sense to weight on age because young people (who are likely to be underrepresented in the final survey because they are less likely to respond to surveys in general) are more likely to use the Internet than older people (i.e., age is associated with Internet use whereas gender is not). Incidentally, weighting on age will also probably reduce the bias in the estimate of average yearly income because income is correlated with age as well.

Thus, weighting is not guaranteed to improve all estimates, and data that are weighted are not necessarily more representative than data that are not weighted. The effectiveness of the weighting depends very strongly on what characteristics are used for weighting and how those characteristics are related to the variables of interest. In addition, it is important to also understand that nonresponse adjustments and poststratification weighting may decrease biases, but they do so at the cost of increasing the variability of the estimates, which results in loss of precision.

Calculating Sampling Error

The margin of sampling error provides an estimate of the range that we expect the true value to fall within, and can be used to test whether one value is significantly larger than another. The margin of error is frequently discussed in preelection polling to determine whether a candidate has a statistically significant lead. For example, in a survey in October 2012, 52.4% of likely voters supported the Democratic candidate while 45.2% backed the Republican candidate. The margin of sampling error for this survey was plus or minus 3.5 percentage points. In other words, the research firm that conducted this poll could be 95% confident that between 48.9% and 55.9% of likely voters supported the Democratic candidate while between 41.7% and 48.7% supported the Republican candidate. In this case, this meant that the Democratic candidate's 7.2-point lead over the Republican candidate was statistically significant (just barely passed at the 95% confidence).

Calculating sampling error is relatively simple. It requires knowing:

- The amount of confidence desired in the estimates
- The point estimate being tested (proportion or mean)
- The size of the sample selected

$$MoE = z * \sqrt{\frac{(p * q)}{n}}$$

where
MoE = the margin of sampling error
z = the z-score or critical value for the desired level of confidence
p = the proportion being tested
$q = 1 - p$
n = the sample size

Thus, for a question with a 50/50 split in a sample of 1,000, one can be 95% confident that the estimate will be within plus or minus 3.1 percentage points of the true value.

$$MoE = 1.96 * \sqrt{\frac{(.5 * .5)}{1000}}$$

$$MoE = 3.1$$

The finite population correction can be applied for surveys of small populations. An example would be if we were estimating votes in a mayoral race in a city of 1,000 people with a completed sample size of 200. Using the preceding formula would show that the margin of error without the finite population correction is plus or minus 6.9 percentage points at the 95% confidence level. The finite population correction can be calculated, as shown in the following formula and then multiplied by this margin of error to yield the new adjusted margin of error, which in this case is 6.1 percentage points.

$$fpc = \sqrt{\frac{(N - n)}{(N - 1)}}$$

where
N = the size of the target population
n = completed sample size needed for desired level of precision

$$fpc = \sqrt{\frac{(1000 - 200)}{(1000 - 1)}}$$
$$fpc = .89$$
$$MoE = 6.9 * .89$$
$$MoE = 6.1$$

The preceding equations assume a simple random sample. As we have mentioned previously, both the sample design and weighting procedures employed can have a substantial impact on the precision of the estimates produced by the survey. Clustering during sampling as well as nonresponse and poststratification weighting can all significantly decrease the precision of the estimates. Similarly, employing stratification with disproportionate sampling can result in a loss of precision if the large weights that may need to be employed to correct for the disproportionate sampling rates are not correlated with the important survey variables. The preceding formula for the *MoE* does not account for the additional losses in precision associated with these more complex sampling designs.

A *design effect* is a measure of the loss of precision in a sample design compared to a simple random sample of the same size. Thus, any time one is analyzing data from a survey that used a sampling method other than a simple random sample, she should account for the design effect. Otherwise, statistical tests may be wrong. There are various formulas for calculating the design effect, depending on the sampling design employed, and most statistical packages offer commands or modules that can account for the design effect in analyses of such complex survey data. It is also important to remember that this design effect will vary for each estimate or statistic produced by the survey. Or thinking about it another way, the impact of the sampling design differs for each estimate.

When sampling error is reported, it should also incorporate the design effect. The preceding sampling error formula can be modified to incorporate the design effect as follows:

$$MoE = \sqrt{deff} * z * \sqrt{\frac{(p * q)}{n}}$$

where
MoE = the margin of sampling error
$deff$ = design effect
z = the z-score or critical value for the desired level of confidence
p = the proportion being tested
$q = 1 - p$
n = the sample size

For example, in a question with a 50/50 split in a sample of 1,000 with a design effect of 2.0, one can be 95% confident that the estimate will be within plus or minus 4.4 percentage points of the true value.

$$MoE = \sqrt{2.0} * 1.96 * \sqrt{\frac{(.5 * .5)}{1000}}$$
$$MoE = 4.4$$

In this example, including the appropriate design effect in the calculation increased the margin of error from 3.1 to 4.4 percentage points. Heeringa, West, and Berglund (2010) and Valliant, Dever, and Kreuter (2013) provide very comprehensive reviews of how to account for the design effect (including the appropriate formulas to use) when analyzing survey data from complex survey designs.

NONPROBABILITY SAMPLING

Some surveyors, especially those conducting web surveys, are increasingly turning to nonprobability sampling methods rather than relying on probability sampling for conducting surveys. Since there is no available sample frame of Internet users, a variety of methods have been used to intercept people while they are online and ask them to complete a survey or join a panel. These methods can be much less expensive than probability sampling methods, especially for certain populations, and often can yield results very quickly (in a matter of hours or days).

There are a variety of different nonprobability sampling methodologies, including intercept surveys, snowball sampling, respondent driven sampling, network sampling, and sample matching. The assumptions and procedures for creating nonprobability samples and adjusting the data vary considerably for these different methods. Thus, unlike probability sampling there is no single unifying framework that could cover all types of nonprobability sampling (Baker et al., 2013). Nonprobability methods range from simple to sophisticated and differ greatly in their quality.

But all nonprobability methods share a common set of obstacles because they usually exclude large numbers of people from the selection process and they rely mostly on people who volunteer to participate (and whose selection probabilities are unknown). They also suffer from very low participation rates, often lower than for surveys that use probability sampling methodologies. As a result, modeling and statistical adjustments are often needed to compensate for these selection biases, but the effectiveness of these adjustments depends on being able to identify variables that are correlated with each of the variables of interest and include them in the adjustments to see if they improve the estimates (Baker et al., 2013). Some of the most promising work in this area focuses on leveraging data from probability based surveys for selecting or adjusting the nonprobability sample.

For researchers interested in producing population estimates and being able to generalize results to a larger target population, a probability sampling method is needed. However, nonprobability sampling methods are increasingly being used for testing and experimentation as well as for surveys that need a quick turnaround. Thus, it is important to establish the goals for the survey before deciding whether the sample will be drawn using probability or nonprobability methods.

CONCLUSION

The power of a sample survey is in the ability to select a small number of people to be able to accurately describe the target population with a great deal of precision. This stands in contrast to conducting a census and surveying the entire population of interest, which is usually quite expensive and time-consuming. However, selecting a sample introduces sampling error and requires attention to the details of how the sample frame is created, how the sample is drawn, how the final data are weighted for analysis, and ensuring that analyses properly account for the sampling design and weighting. Understanding coverage and sampling error is central to one's ability to conduct a quality survey. This chapter provided a foundation for understanding both of these types of error and how they affect survey quality.

Because sampling error can be calculated by applying mathematical formulas (when probability samples are used), some people tend to use it as the primary standard for drawing conclusions about survey quality. Others tend to focus solely on survey response rates (i.e., the ratio of completed sample to total sample) as the quality indicator, reasoning that low response rates equate to high nonresponse error and therefore poor survey quality.

Both of these practices are problematic. Relying on sampling error alone ignores the fact that estimates may also be affected by the presence of coverage, nonresponse, and measurement error. Similarly, focusing solely on response rates as measures of survey quality ignores potential error attributable to sampling, measurement, and coverage. Further, nonresponse error is not a direct function of low response rates (Groves, 2006) but results from those who do not complete the survey *differing in attitudes, beliefs, behaviors, and characteristics* from those who do *on the item or items of interest*. It is possible, therefore, for a survey with a very low response rate to adequately represent the survey population, or for a survey with very high response rates to fail to represent the intended population. Likewise, it is possible, and quite likely, that the amount of nonresponse error within a single survey will differ across questions and question topics (Groves, 2006; Keeter, Christian, Dimock, & Gewurz, 2012).

Although technically a larger sample is always better from the standpoint of sampling error, it is important to balance the expenditure of resources for minimizing sampling error against potential expenditures for reducing the other three sources of error. It makes little sense to push sampling error to an extremely low level if it comes at the cost of not trying to lower levels of other types of error (or, worse yet, increasing other types of error).

Conducting quality self-administered surveys means simultaneously attempting to hold error levels of all four types to low levels, which requires an optimal allocation of resources, as discussed in detail by Groves (1989). As of yet, there is no accepted way of providing a meaningful combined measure of the effect of the four sources of error on overall accuracy. Minimizing all four types of survey error is perhaps the most difficult challenge of surveying. We now turn our attention in the remaining chapters to focus on strategies for minimizing measurement and nonresponse error, first through designing survey questions and questionnaires, and then through implementation procedures.

The Fundamentals of Writing Questions

Asking questions of a sample of individuals and deriving estimates from them sounds simple in theory. However, in reality, to generate a good estimate, we have to write a question that every potential respondent will be willing to answer, will be able to respond to accurately, and will interpret in the way the surveyor intends. We then have to organize those questions into a questionnaire that can be administered to respondents by an interviewer or that respondents can process on their own. We also have to find and convince sample members to complete and return the questionnaire. Doing these things requires us to make many design decisions. Making the right decisions will minimize measurement and nonresponse error, while making the wrong decisions might increase them.

The decisions one will have to make require considerable knowledge about question writing, questionnaire design, and implementation. In this and the remaining chapters, we provide many best practices and specific guidelines that will help make these decisions. Underlying every one of these guidelines is the idea that in order to develop a successful questionnaire and implementation procedure, one needs to *get into a respondent state of mind*. By this we mean to consider what the questions, questionnaire, and invitation contacts will look like from a respondent perspective. What will the respondent see or hear first? What next? Will he think responding is important? How will he know where to start and what the navigational path is through the questionnaire? Will he be able to understand the questions? Will he be able and willing to answer them? How will he interpret a question if it is presented in isolation versus as a group with other questions? Where will he need extra help to avoid making errors or to find and correct those already made?

Getting into a respondent state of mind means we should consider whether each possible design feature will help people in some way. If the answer is "yes," the feature should be used; if the answer is "no," it should not be used. After all, a questionnaire that is absolutely perfect from the researcher's perspective will be useless if it does not communicate well with respondents.

Writing questions requires attending to a lot of details at once. In this chapter, we first focus on issues that should be considered prior to writing each survey question, and then discuss the major format alternatives and the parts of a survey question. The rest of this chapter presents fundamental guidelines for writing survey questions that apply to all such items. In the chapters that follow, we turn our attention to how to write specific types of questions (e.g., nominal, ordinal, etc.), how aural versus visual presentation should be considered during question writing, and how to bring all of these considerations together to craft questionnaires for paper, web, telephone, and mixed-mode surveys.

ISSUES TO CONSIDER WHEN STARTING TO CRAFT SURVEY QUESTIONS

What Concepts Do I Need to Measure?

Almost everyone who has conducted a survey or utilized survey data has wished that at least one more question had been asked. It is tempting in the beginning to jump right in and start writing questions. However, pausing to first think hard about what one needs to measure, although it involves a considerable investment in time and energy, will help ensure that the survey covers the needed concepts.

The first step is to write clear research questions or statements that identify what will be studied. The concepts that need to be measured will flow from these questions. As a simple example, suppose our research question is, "How does education affect well-being?" (as shown in Figure 4.1). The two key concepts in this research question are education and well-being.

Both of these are big concepts that cannot be measured well with single questions; thus, we need to elaborate both of them more fully. This involves defining what we mean and do not mean by each concept and identifying important domains and subdomains of each (Hox, 1997). For example, education can be formal or informal. Formal education might consist of the number of years one went to school, whether she attended private or public school, the size of the school, and the classes that she took. Informal education might include on-the-job training, apprenticeships, workshops, mentoring, and so on.

We need to continue to break down the concepts of interest until we get to domains or subdomains that can be measured with a single question. For example, number of years of schooling can be measured with a single question, but the concept of size of school will need further elaboration.

The same process can be undertaken with well-being. For example, three domains of well-being might be physical health, mental health, and financial health. Each of these can be further broken down to get to a specific aspect that can be measured, as shown in Figure 4.1. Many of the concepts on the right side of Figure 4.1 can be even further broken down.

Clearly defining the goals of the survey (i.e., the research question to be answered) and identifying the concepts of interest and their domains and subdomains will help in a number of ways. First, it will help us think about what we really want to measure (i.e., do we only need to know about formal education or is informal education important as well?). Second, it will help reduce the likelihood that we forget to ask about an important concept. And third, it will help ensure that we ask questions that measure what we intend to measure (i.e., minimize specification error). After all, spending all the time and effort in the world developing a perfect question will not matter at all if the question is not measuring what we intend it to be measuring. The process of identifying the research question and important concepts will help ensure that ultimately the research questions can be answered with the data that are collected.

When specifying the concepts you want to measure, it is also often helpful to explore whether there are measures for the essential concepts that have been

FIGURE 4.1 Example of deriving measurable concepts from a research question.

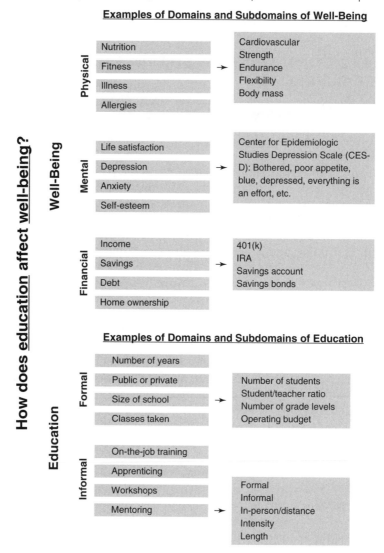

asked in other surveys. For example, a commonly used measure of depression is the Center for Epidemiological Studies Depression Scale (CES-D) (Radloff, 1977), which is referred to in Figure 4.1. It is possible that preexisting measures such as this will meet the needs of the survey sufficiently, saving the considerable time and resources required developing a new measure. However, having been used on a previous survey or even validated within a specific context does not guarantee that a question is effective, or will work for a new purpose or in a new context. So while it is useful to explore preexisting measures, they should only be adopted if they are well written and suit the particular need of the survey. Established measures can be found in existing surveys as well as in archives and question banks such as the Inter-University Consortium for Political and Social Research (ICPSR) and the Roper Center for Public Opinion Research's iPOLL Databank.

What Type of Information Is the Question Asking For?

It is easier to get accurate answers for some types of survey questions than others. For example, almost everyone knows how old they are, as people are frequently asked to give that information to others. Because people already have an answer in their heads when asked about their age—assuming they are willing to disclose it—they can easily provide it and can do so in a number of different ways, as shown in Figure 4.2. Because the information is readily available to the respondent, most surveyors can accurately collect such data as age and other *factual or demographic information* regardless of how they ask for it; however, as we discuss later in this chapter, people can still be encouraged, through question design, to report the answer in a particular format.

Surveys also frequently ask for information that people may have thought little about and will need more time to answer, such as questions about *attitudes and opinions*. The second example in Figure 4.2 seeks to understand how effective respondents think citizens' groups are in helping to solve environmental problems.

FIGURE 4.2 What type of information is the question asking for?

A question that people can easily answer regardless of how it is asked

What year were you born?

[ ] Year born

How old are you?

[ ] Age

What is your date of birth?

[ ] [ ] [ ]
Month Day Year

A question where people are often more likely to be influenced by context

In your opinion, how effective do you think citizens' groups are in helping to solve environmental problems?

○ Very effective
○ Somewhat effective
○ A little effective
○ Not at all effective

In your opinion, how effective or ineffective do you think citizens' groups are in helping to solve environmental problems? (Please mark an X on the line).

Very effective   Very ineffective

In your opinion, how effective are citizens' groups in helping to solve environmental problems?

○ A great deal
○ A fair amount
○ Not very much
○ Almost none at all

Most respondents will not have a ready answer available for this type of question, and may have to do considerable work to formulate one. Some may consider generally whether they think people can effect change, whereas others will think about examples of environmental citizens' groups or various types of environmental problems that people have tried to help solve.

For these types of questions, more so than for factual or demographic questions, respondents can be substantially influenced by the context (a topic we return to in Guideline 7.6) as they work their way through the response process of comprehending the question, recalling relevant information, forming a judgment, and reporting their answer (Tourangeau, 1992). Different elements of the question that can influence the answering process include what questions came before it, what type of response is being asked for (e.g., choose one category, mark an X on the scale), the wording of the question and response options (e.g., "a great deal" or "somewhat effective"), and the visual layout, each of which we will consider in detail in this and the following chapters.

Other questions that are prone to such context effects are those asking about *behaviors and events*. Surveyors ask about many aspects of people's behavior, such as what they have done, how often (number of times or relative frequency), and when. Frequently survey designers want respondents to provide far more detail about past behaviors than can be recalled, and as a result, they write questions respondents find difficult, if not impossible, to answer. Doing this causes respondents to draw even more on features of the questions' context rather than their real experiences in formulating their answers, as is the case in Figure 4.2.

To avoid this tendency, surveyors should consider three recall problems. First, memory tends to fade over time. Second, individual episodes or occurrences of regular and mundane events are generally not precisely remembered (Rockwood, Sangster, & Dillman, 1997; Tourangeau, Rips, & Rasinski, 2000). And third, people usually do not categorize information by precise month or year.

Given these limitations, respondents are unlikely to be able to accurately report how many days they drove more than 1 mile during the past 6 months. But they can probably very accurately report how many days they drove their car during the past week or drove more than 200 miles at a time in the past 3 months.

Asking questions about behaviors that people can easily recall because they are recent or more memorable can help improve the accuracy of the information people report. In addition, using definitions and examples can also help improve recall (Martin, 2002; Schaeffer & Presser, 2003). However, definitions must be easy for respondents to understand, and examples should be selected carefully so as not to influence respondents' answers in unintended ways. For example, previous research has shown that when asked about the consumption of different types of foods, examples of frequently consumed foods (e.g., beef, pork, and poultry as examples of meat) elicit higher reports of the number of servings consumed than examples of less frequently consumed foods (e.g., lamb, veal, and goat as examples of meat) (Redline, 2011).

What Survey Mode(s) Will Be Used to Ask the Questions?

How one writes a survey question should depend strongly on how that question is going to be delivered to respondents. Each mode has features that enable some designs and constrain others. The key features to keep in mind are whether the mode has an interviewer present or not, relies on aural or visual communication, and is computerized or not.

Presence Versus Absence of an Interviewer

Interviewer-administered surveys are inherently more social than self-administered surveys. This has several implications for measurement. First, the interviewer can provide extra motivation and assistance to respondents when needed. For example, they can clarify the meaning of questions or probe for more complete answers.

However, by virtue of an interviewer being involved, the respondent has less control over the delivery of the survey questions. The interviewer, not the respondent, sets the pace of the survey and controls the order in which the questions are administered. While having the interviewer control question order can eliminate many of the difficulties involved with getting respondents to navigate skip patterns correctly, that control can also significantly impact how question order may affect responses and how much time respondents spend answering each question. Interviewer-administered surveys typically progress quicker than self-administered surveys, giving respondents less time to work through the response process thoroughly.

The social nature of interviewer-administered surveys also means there is more risk for social norms to be evoked in ways that impact measurement. Two such normative phenomena are social desirability and acquiescence.

Social desirability is the tendency to provide answers that put one in a good light with the person who asks the question; it is often motivated by wanting to make a good impression in a social interaction (or avoid a negative one). It can occur when respondents falsely deny engaging in socially undesirable behaviors such as drug use or cheating on one's spouse, or when they falsely claim to have engaged in desirable behaviors like voting or volunteering.

One study, for example, asked the question "How often do you drive a car after drinking alcoholic beverages? Frequently, Occasionally, Seldom, Never, or Don't Know." Respondents were more likely to deny driving a car after drinking in an interviewer-administered telephone survey (63% said "never") than in a self-administered paper survey (52% responded "never") (Dillman & Tarnai, 1991). Similarly, respondents have been found to be more willing to admit to having shoplifted something from a store when asked in self-administered than in interviewer-administered surveys (Aquilino, 1994; de Leeuw, 1992; de Leeuw & van der Zouwen, 1988; DeMaio, 1984; Dillman, Sangster, Tarnai, & Rockwood, 1996).

Social desirability effects are an even greater concern when the interviewer is closely linked to the topic of the questions. This often occurs in customer satisfaction surveys when organizations use their own staff as interviewers because of cost constraints. For example, many years ago the administrator of a large regional hospital in Florida asked for advice on two customer satisfaction surveys of similar samples of former patients. Results had been obtained by a paper survey sent by mail and by telephone interviews, but the paper questionnaires showed much lower satisfaction ratings. The hospital had tentatively decided to discontinue the paper survey because of the belief that only unhappy patients seemed to be responding, but the sponsor wondered why that was the case. When asked for more information about the procedures, the hospital administrator indicated that in order to keep costs low, the telephone sample had been interviewed by nursing staff on the evening shift, many of whom had cared for the former patients they were asked to call. In light of this information, these results were not surprising. It seemed likely that patients would offer more positive, socially desirable answers by telephone when interviewed by the nursing staff. In that way, respondents' answers reflected what they thought the person who had provided the service hoped to hear.

Social desirability sometimes operates at a threshold far below what one thinks of as sensitive behavior. Even very ordinary questions that seem on the surface to have little social desirability consistently exhibit this effect. For example, consider the following: "How would you describe your current health? Excellent, Good, Fair, or Poor." Compared to interviewer-administered surveys, self-administered surveys consistently produce lower proportions of respondents who choose "excellent" (Biemer, 1997; Hochstim, 1967). This is consistent with general U.S. norms. When one person meets another on the street and offers the conventional American greeting "How are you?" the person typically responds "Fine," regardless of how she is truly feeling. A more negative answer requires additional and oftentimes an awkward explanation, and so is usually not given.

When designing questions, one should routinely expect social desirability to occur on sensitive questions and even on some less sensitive questions. These effects will likely be stronger in interviewer-administered modes than in self-administered modes.

The second normative phenomenon that is more likely to occur in interviewer-administered modes is *acquiescence*, or the tendency to agree with someone rather than disagree. Acquiescence is culturally based. In most cultures, it is easier to agree than to disagree, especially when interacting with another person (Javeline, 1999). For example, a classic interview experiment by Schuman and Presser (1981) showed that 60% of one national sample of respondents agreed with the following statement: "Individuals are more to blame than social conditions for crime and lawlessness in this country." However, 57% of a control group agreed with the exact reverse of this statement: "Social conditions are more to blame than individuals for crime and lawlessness in this country." That these numbers add up to well over 100% indicates that acquiescence was likely at play. Five months later respondents were resurveyed and given the opposite statement of the one they had in the initial survey. A quarter of respondents agreed to both of these opposing statements across these two data collection periods, further indicating a tendency toward agreement. Moreover, changing the question structure to a forced choice between the two items produced lower levels on endorsement for each.

In another example, an experiment by Dillman and Tarnai (1991) found telephone respondents were significantly more likely than a comparable sample of respondents contacted by mail to agree that seven different proposals for increasing seatbelt use would work. Differences ranged from 5 to 23 percentage points. A similar pattern was observed by Jordan, Marcus, and Reeder (1980). However, a meta-analysis by de Leeuw (1992) failed to detect any differences across modes, revealing that the literature is not entirely consistent on this issue. Nonetheless, surveyors should be aware of the potential for differences across modes on agree/disagree types of questions.

These examples of social desirability and acquiescence focus on how the presence of interviewers can affect responses on individual questions, but interviewers can also evoke social norms that affect answers across multiple questions. For example, normative question order effects occur when respondents adjust their answers to later questions to take into account their answer to early questions in an attempt to put themselves in a positive light with the interviewer (see Guideline 7.6 for examples of normative question order effects).

All of these are examples of *bias*, which is a systematic shift in estimates away from the *true value* (e.g., a change in a mean or proportion). When the shift in estimates can be attributed to the presence of interviewers, we call it *interviewer bias*.

For example, in one recent study, researchers used school records to verify respondent answers and found that 20% of web survey respondents denied having ever received a D or F in college when in fact they had received one of these grades (i.e., a false negative) (Kreuter, Presser, & Tourangeau, 2008). This shift away from the true value, which in this case should be everyone reporting accurately (no false negatives), is bias. In the same study, 33% of telephone survey respondents falsely denied having ever received a D or F in college (see Figure 4.3). The 13 percentage point increase in the telephone version compared to the web version is likely a result of interviewer bias, due to more respondents denying this socially undesirable outcome to improve their presentation of self in the presence of an interviewer. The percent falsely reporting earning a grade point average less than 2.5 and receiving a warning or probation was also higher in the telephone survey than the web survey.

Interviewer bias also arises when fixed interviewer characteristics affect how respondents answer questions. Common examples are interviewer gender and interviewer race. For example, Groves and Fultz (1985) found that respondents in a telephone survey gave more optimistic reports about the future of the economy to male interviewers than to female interviewers. Similarly, Catania, Binson, Canchola, Pollack, and Hauck (1996) found that both men and women were more likely to report engaging in extramarital sex when interviewed by a same sex interviewer than when interviewed by an opposite sex interviewer. Men were also more likely to report more sexual violence when the interviewer was male.

Research on race of interviewer effects has shown that African Americans tend to be more humble about their achievements, less likely to voice political complaints, and more warm, trusting, and friendly when talking to White interviewers compared with Black interviewers (Hyman, Cobb, Feldman, Hart, & Stember, 1954; Schuman & Converse, 1971). Similar effects are found for Whites in that they are more likely to give pro-Black attitudes (i.e., supportive of interracial marriage, school integration, and African Americans moving into their neighborhood) when interviewed by a Black interviewer than when interviewed by a White interviewer (Hatchett & Schuman, 1975).

In more recent research, Krysan and Couper (2003) found that race of interviewer effects are more likely to occur on questions about current hot button issues, particularly those regarding racial policies and perceptions of discrimination. In general, gender and race of interviewer effects are more likely to occur when the questions are sensitive and are directly related to the characteristic of interest (i.e., race or gender). For the vast majority of survey questions, they will likely not be an issue.

Interviewer experience can also impact the answers respondents provide. However, the literature is often mixed as to whether more experienced interviewers have a positive or negative effect, and it can depend on what measure of success one is using. Experienced interviewers are often better at encouraging participation and getting respondents to complete or finish the survey. The effect

FIGURE 4.3 Social desirability bias in telephone surveys.

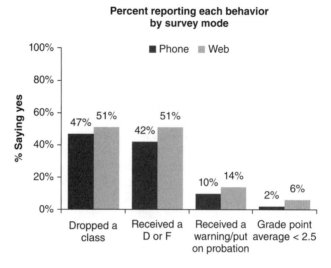

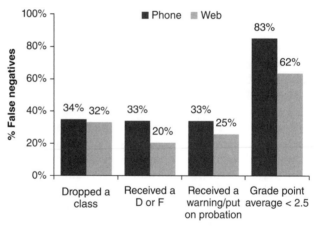

Source: Adapted from "Social Desirability Bias in CATI, IVR and Web Surveys," by F. Kreuter, S. Presser, and R. Tourangeau, 2008, *Public Opinion Quarterly, 72*, pp. 847–865.

of interviewer experience on data quality is less clear, but the evidence generally suggests that interviewer experience can have a negative effect on the quality of the answers respondents provide.

A recent study found that more experienced interviewers conducted the interviews faster (Olson & Peytchev, 2007). However, this study was unable to assess what effect the interview length had on the quality of the responses. For example, the interview could be shorter because interviewers deviated less from the script and stayed on task, or because they did not execute probing or other techniques to help ensure quality answers.

Other studies have demonstrated that respondents interviewed by more experienced interviewers have higher item nonresponse rates (Bilgen & Belli, 2011) and a greater tendency to acquiesce or agree than respondents interviewed by less experienced interviewers (Olson & Bilgen, 2011). Also, Bradburn, Sudman, and Blair (1979) found that experienced interviewers were less likely to read questions exactly as worded and deviated more from protocols.

The mechanisms behind these differences are still unclear. It could be that experienced interviewers are less careful about reading questions exactly as instructed and may deviate more from standard protocols or that they communicate that approximate (rather than exact) answers are acceptable. And this may be especially pronounced in telephone surveys, especially among interviewers who are skilled at encouraging cooperation, because interviewers want to keep respondents moving through the survey rather than allowing them to pause and consider discontinuing their participation. Lastly, often the incentive or reward structure for interviewers is based on getting respondents to cooperate, the time to complete the interview, and other productivity measures, rather than on quality factors, such as getting accurate or complete responses, that may be harder or more costly to measure.

Interviewer bias occurs when all interviewers have a similar effect on respondents, leading to systematic shifts in estimates. It is also possible for different interviewers to have different effects on respondents; that is, for different interviewers to influence the estimates in different ways. As a simple example, imagine we ask the question "How many pets do you have?" One interviewer might instruct respondents to consider only indoor dogs and cats. Another might instruct them to consider both indoor and outdoor dogs and cats. Yet another may instruct them to also include rabbits, gerbils, guinea pigs, mice, and rats. Still another might add reptiles to the list of creatures to be considered pets. And maybe another encourages respondents to count farm animals like horses and chickens as pets. In this case, each interviewer is influencing responses in a unique way. The result will be increased variance in the mean number of pets people have. Because this increased variance is attributable to interviewers, it is called *interviewer variance*.

As this example illustrates, interviewer variance is typically the result of lack of standardization in the administration of a question across interviewers. That is, interviewers administer the question in different ways. This can often be a result of poor questionnaire design (e.g., questions that are too difficult to administer in their original form), poor interviewer training (e.g., interviewers do not understand that they need to read questions exactly as written), or lack of motivation to abide by interviewing rules. Interviewer variance is likely to be higher on questions that are vague, and as a result require a great deal of clarification, or on questions that require probing to obtain an acceptable response. Ways to reduce the potential for interviewer variance through question and questionnaire design will be discussed in Chapters 6, 7, and 8. Interrviewer training and monitoring will be discussed in Chapter 8. For more information on interviewer variance, including how to measure it, see Biemer and Lyberg (2003).

Because of variation across interviewers in how they administer the questions and provide feedback to respondents, two interviews conducted by the same interviewer are often more similar than two interviews conducted by different interviewers. Thus, similar to the effects of clustering on sample variance, interviewer effects reduce the amount of information each new completed interview from the same interviewer provides. Also, just like in clustering, the intraclass correlation (rho) can be used to estimate the tendency for responses from the same interviewer to be correlated with one another, compared with responses from other interviewers, and thus the effect that interviewer variance has on each of the survey estimates (Groves, 1989; Kish, 1962). Interviewer workload is also important in estimating the effect of interviewer variance on the final estimates; interviewers who complete more interviews are likely to have a greater impact on the estimates than those who complete fewer interviews.

That said, it is often difficult to disentangle the effects interviewers may have on how people respond from actual differences between respondents of different interviewers. A recent study demonstrates how differences in estimates across various interviewers may stem less from interviewer-related measurement and more from interviewer-related nonresponse error (i.e., different interviewers get different types of people to respond, which influences the estimates) (West & Olson, 2010). The good news is that to reduce interviewer variance, researchers can standardize the questionnaire and scripts used by interviewers in telephone (and face-to-face) surveys, ensure that the questions are designed well and the response task is clear, train interviewers on how to administer the survey and respond to different situations that may arise, and monitor interviewer performance and quality throughout the interviewing process, topics we return to in Chapter 8.

Aural Versus Visual Communication

Whether respondents receive survey questions aurally or visually can have a tremendous influence on how they process questions, and as such, on how the questions need to be designed. For example, in telephone interviews, respondents give and receive information through spoken words and the hearing system. As a result, words, inflection, tone, and other paralinguistic features of the interviewer's voice take on extra importance. Memory also becomes a significant factor to be considered because respondents have to hold all of the information in their working memory and cannot refer to a written questionnaire to help remind them. By comparison, on the web and in paper questionnaires, information is transmitted through the visual system, making visual design elements much more important. The visual presentation of words and other elements impacts responses to written questions, just as voice characteristics influence answers to aurally administered questions.

We discuss the differences between aural and visual communication in more detail in Chapter 6. Here we limit our focus on how these differences might affect measurement in a particular way—through primacy or recency effects. *Primacy* refers to the tendency to more frequently choose from among the first categories offered regardless of their content, while *recency* refers to the tendency to more frequently choose from among the last categories offered regardless of their content. Whether primacy or recency is more likely to occur depends in part on how the categories are received by respondents (i.e., aurally versus visually).

According to the cognitive elaboration model of response order effects, each response option is a short persuasive communication that brings to mind either confirming or disconfirming cognitive elaborations. The more time respondents have to think about each item, which is a direct function of the survey mode and the position of the item in the list, the more confirming or disconfirming information will come to mind (Schwarz, Hippler, & Noelle-Neumann, 1992; Sudman, Bradburn, & Schwarz, 1996). In self-administered (i.e., visual) survey modes, respondents can deeply process items appearing early in the list, but as they move through the list their minds become more cluttered and their ability

FIGURE 4.4 Cognitive elaboration model of response order effects.

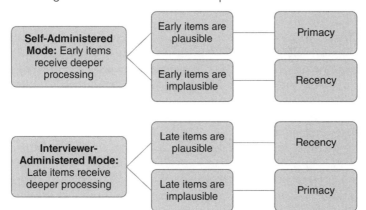

Source: Adapted from "A Cognitive Model of Response Order Effects in Survey Measurement," by N. Schwarz, H. J. Hippler, and E. Noelle-Neumann,1992, in N. Schwarz and S. Sudman (Eds.), *Context Effects in Social and Psychological Research* (pp. 187–201), New York, NY: Springer-Verlag.

to process becomes increasingly limited (Krosnick & Alwin, 1987). Thus, if early response options are plausible and bring to mind confirmatory thoughts, they are more likely to be endorsed, resulting in primacy effects (see Figure 4.4). However, if early items are implausible and bring to mind disconfirming thoughts, later items are more likely to be selected, resulting in recency effects.

The expectations are a bit different for interviewer-administered surveys without show cards (i.e., aural interviews). In these modes there is typically not enough time for respondents to process all of the response categories as they are being read by the interviewer. Consequently, when the time comes to respond, the last categories that are heard are more likely to be remembered and are processed more deeply than the earlier ones (Krosnick & Alwin, 1987). Thus, if the last categories are plausible, a recency effect is expected, but if they are implausible, a primacy effect is expected. Under typical survey conditions, in which researchers try to avoid providing implausible response options, one would expect primacy effects in self-administered surveys and recency effects in interviewer-administered surveys.

Evidence for the existence of pure primacy/recency effects is decidedly mixed. Although recency effects have been observed in telephone surveys by several researchers (Moore, 1997; Schuman & Presser, 1981), these same authors have also noted exceptions. Relatively few mixed-mode comparisons have been done (for one exception, see Schwarz et al., 1992). However, an analysis of 82 experiments (in 12 separate surveys conducted in seven states) found that primacy and recency effects occurred in both paper and telephone surveys and the most likely outcome was not to occur at all in either mode (Dillman, Brown, et al., 1995).

We conclude that despite the extensive discussion of these effects in the literature, much remains to be learned about the conditions under which primacy and recency occur in surveys, some aspects of which may be entangled with other effects of visual versus aural communication of survey questions. The occurrence of primacy effects in self-administered surveys and recency effects in telephone surveys is far from predictable, and further experimentation is needed until this issue is settled.

Computerization

The final feature that sets modes apart in ways that affect how we write questions is whether the questionnaire is administered through a computer or not. Web surveys and most telephone (and many in-person) surveys are computerized, but paper surveys are not. Also, we know of several instances where people are administering a telephone survey using a printed paper questionnaire. Computerization is important because it allows us to automate some of the more challenging aspects of questionnaires, and it also opens up the opportunity to use some advanced questionnaire design features.

One of the most complex features of paper surveys is skip patterns, in which respondents are only supposed to answer certain questions if they meet some specific criteria as established through prior questions. Even on simple skip patterns, respondents regularly make skip errors, answering questions they are not supposed to (i.e., errors of commission) or failing to answer those they are supposed to (i.e., errors of omission). More complex patterns where the follow-up question is contingent on answers to multiple prior questions are incredibly difficult to include in paper surveys, and result in even higher error rates.

Computerization eliminates this problem because rather than leaving it up to interviewers or respondents, who inevitably make errors, the computer itself can be programmed to present the correct question based on previous answers. Moreover, provided the programming can be done correctly, very complex combinations of previous answers can be used to determine what question comes next. The computerization of questionnaires requires additional steps in the testing phase to ensure that all programming is functioning correctly (for more detail, see Chapters 8, 9, and 11).

Similarly, computerization allows for other features to be used that are difficult, if not impossible, to use when there is no computerization. Fills are one example. A fill is when an answer from a previous question, or even from a previous data collection, is inserted into a later question to customize it. Similarly, with computerization, sets of response options can be customized based on previous answers. A simple example would be asking respondents to report which of a list of hotels they have stayed at, and then in a follow-up question asking them to rate their satisfaction with each of the hotels they previously selected. Validating answers using previous questions is also possible with computerization. For example, if a respondent enters 1984 as her year of birth and then subsequently reported in 2014 she is 20 years old, the computer can be programmed to recognize that there is a discrepancy and to ask for a correction. These are but a few of the automated features that can be used in computerized modes. In paper surveys, some of these features can only be used if the information is known ahead of time (e.g., fills and validations) and others must be minimized and simplified (e.g., skip patterns) because respondents have considerable difficulty carrying them out.

Is This Question Being Repeated From Another Survey, and/or Will Answers Be Compared to Previously Collected Data?

The answer to this question will influence how much, if any, the question can be changed. If a particular question has been used in another survey and the main objective is to replicate the previous survey or make the new results comparable in some other way, usually no changes or only minimal changes can be made.

Examples are government surveys, adolescent and youth surveys, and public opinion and election polls that have asked the same questions repeatedly, sometimes for decades, to produce time-series data. For self-administered surveys, this means trying to replicate not only the question wording but also the other aspects of the visual design and layout of the questions. For interviewer-administered surveys, it may mean fully understanding how interviewers administered a question and any instructions or probes that were provided.

Less obvious, but equally important, is that any questions that will be used for weighting should also be asked similarly to how they were asked in the data that one is weighting to. For example, if the final data will be weighted by age, sex, and education to Census estimates from the ACS, the questions measuring age, sex, and education should be asked similarly in the survey to how they were asked in the ACS.

Will Respondents Be Willing and Motivated to Answer Accurately?

Ensuring that respondents are motivated to respond to each question is a major concern, especially when there is no interviewer present to encourage respondents to carefully select and report complete answers. Without proper motivation, respondents may ignore instructions, read questions carelessly, or provide incomplete answers. Worse yet, they may skip questions altogether or fail to complete and return the questionnaire.

In some instances, motivational problems stem from poor question design, such as when questions are difficult to read and understand, instructions are hard to find, or the response task is too vague. In other instances, the question topic itself may be the source of motivational problems. This is often the case with questions pertaining to personal financial information. For example, people are more likely to report their income when provided with broad categories from which to choose rather than asked to provide an exact value; however, sometimes a survey, such as the American Community Survey, requires an exact number, and anything else is unacceptable.

Respondents are also often reluctant to answer questions about behaviors that they may find embarrassing or threatening, such as sexual or criminal activity. When asking for sensitive information about people's past or current behavior, changing the wording of the question can encourage reluctant respondents to answer. For example, instead of asking "Have you ever shoplifted anything from a store?" one might ask "Have you ever taken anything from a store without paying for it?" Another strategy is to include the question with others—such as "How often do you go shopping?" and "What types of stores do you shop at?"—so that it may appear in context and seem less objectionable. Although steps can be taken to improve the design of sensitive questions, it may still be difficult to collect accurate information from all respondents.

What concepts need measured, what type of information the question is asking for, what survey mode will be used, whether changes can be made to questions, and whether respondents will be willing and motivated to answer are all pieces of background information that will help a surveyor make informed decisions about how to craft each question.

In addition, we find it helpful when writing questions to think about the process respondents will go through when trying to answer them. Doing so helps us

FIGURE 4.5 A common model of the survey response process.

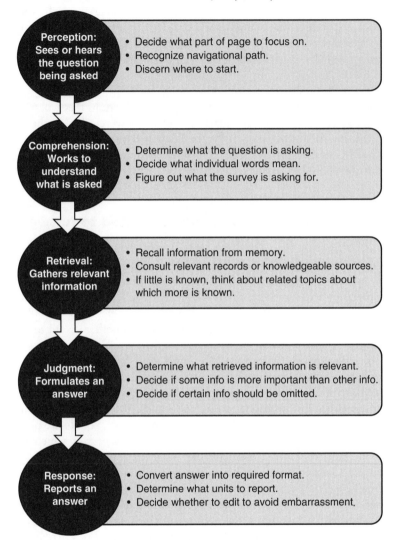

Perception:
Sees or hears
the question
being asked
- Decide what part of page to focus on.
- Recognize navigational path.
- Discern where to start.

Comprehension:
Works to
understand
what is asked
- Determine what the question is asking.
- Decide what individual words mean.
- Figure out what the survey is asking for.

Retrieval:
Gathers relevant
information
- Recall information from memory.
- Consult relevant records or knowledgeable sources.
- If little is known, think about related topics about which more is known.

Judgment:
Formulates an
answer
- Determine what retrieved information is relevant.
- Decide if some info is more important than other info.
- Decide if certain info should be omitted.

Response:
Reports an
answer
- Convert answer into required format.
- Determine what units to report.
- Decide whether to edit to avoid embarrassment.

Source: Adapted from "Towards a Theory of Self-Administered Questionnaire Design," by C. R. Jenkins and D. A. Dillman, 1997, in L. E. Lyberg, P. Biemer, M. Collins, E. D. de Leeuw, C. Dippo, N. Schwarz, and D. Trewin (Eds.), *Survey Measurement and Process Quality* (pp. 165–196), New York, NY: Wiley-Interscience; *The Psychology of Survey Response*, by R. Tourangeau, L. J. Rips, and K. Rasinski, 2000, New York, NY: Cambridge University Press.

identify where things can go wrong and what types of changes might solve a problem once we have diagnosed it. The five steps of a common model of the response process that we use are shown in Figure 4.5.

The first step, perception, is particularly important in self-administered questionnaires because it is where respondents start to try to understand the questionnaire itself (Jenkins & Dillman, 1997). We will return to this topic in much more detail in Chapter 6. Once respondents have perceived the questionnaire and the overall layout and navigational flow, they can focus on individual questions and proceed through the remaining steps of the response process. In the comprehension stage, respondents try to make sense of what is being asked of them. Most people writing survey questions focus a lot on comprehension, which is good, but it is also important to consider the remaining steps in the response process. Respondents also have to retrieve relevant information, use that information to formulate a judgment, and report their answer, each of which requires them to make several important decisions, as elaborated in Figure 4.5 (Tourangeau, 1992; Tourangeau et al., 2000). Respondents can work through these steps in order, or they can move back and forth through them (e.g., moving from comprehension to retrieval and then back to comprehension before moving on). Ultimately we want respondents to thoroughly undertake each of these steps. When they do so, we say they are *optimizing*, meaning they are doing all of the necessary mental work to provide a high-quality and truthful answer. However, if we design a poor questionnaire or fail to motivate our respondents appropriately, they may *satisfice* (i.e., shortcut the response process) to reduce their cognitive burden (Krosnick, 1991). *Weak satisficing* consists of taking small shortcuts such as not working hard to understand what a question is asking, failing to retrieve all of the relevant information needed to formulate an answer, estimating rather than providing precise answers, or providing answers in the wrong format. In other cases, respondents may skip entire steps of the response process, leave questions blank, or provide made-up answers. These are all cases of *strong satisficing* (Krosnick, 1991), and they are all behaviors we want to try to avoid by writing reasonable questions in the first place.

THE ANATOMY OF A SURVEY QUESTION AND TYPES OF QUESTION FORMATS

Survey questions come in different formats and are made up of multiple parts that must work together in concert to produce high-quality data about the topic of interest. If one part of the question fails or provides a conflicting message with another part, it can undermine the accuracy of people's responses. Crafting good survey questions requires understanding each of the different question formats and how each component of the question conveys meaning independently to respondents, as well as how all of the parts work together to convey meaning.

The most important part of any survey question is the *question stem*, or the words that form the actual query itself. The question stem for the second question shown in Figure 4.6 is "How many years have you lived in Nebraska?" The question stem provides the most explicit and direct information about what the question is asking (e.g., how long you have lived in Nebraska) and how respondents should provide their answer (e.g., in years). It may also include *additional instructions*, definitions, or examples that will help respondents comprehend the meaning of the question or of key concepts. Additional instructions might include verbal instructions (e.g., "Select only one" or "Please round to the nearest whole year"), or they may consist of numbers, graphics, or symbols that further inform respondents how to answer (e.g., $, #, YYYY). Each question has *answer spaces or choices* that provide additional information to respondents about what responses are possible and how to record their answer. Answer choices limit the available possibilities from which respondents can choose (e.g., very satisfied, somewhat satisfied, etc.) and often provide cues about the type and number of answers to provide (e.g., size of answer space, reminder of units requested). Throughout this book, we use the specific terms italicized in this paragraph for each of the particular parts, and we use the term *question* to mean the entire anatomy of the survey question, including all of the parts.

There are two broad types of question formats: open-ended and closed-ended. *Open-ended* question formats allow respondents to formulate their answer how they want. In self-administered surveys, this involves providing a blank space or box where respondents type or write in their response using their own words (or numbers). In interviewer-administered surveys, respondents speak their answer to the interviewer, who subsequently records it in detail. In contrast, *closed-ended* question formats provide respondents with a list of answer choices from which they must choose one or more responses.

The strength of the *open-ended question format* is that it allows respondents to freely answer the question as they want without limiting their response, such as "What is the most important problem facing Nebraska today?" (see first question in Figure 4.6). Thus, this format is preferable when the surveyor does not want to influence respondent answers by providing a set of answer choices. For example, an open-ended question format should be used when the goal is to collect rich, detailed information from respondents, or when the surveyor is questioning about topics for which little information is known ahead of time. Additionally, an open-ended format in which respondents provide a numerical response can sometimes be easier for respondents and yield more precise information because they report an exact number rather than choose from categories with vague labels or ranges of values (such as the second question in Figure 4.6).

However, there are also several limitations to open-ended question formats. In self-administered surveys, more respondents skip open-ended question formats than closed-ended formats because they require more work to answer. Issues of item nonresponse bias arise because some types of respondents may be more likely to skip these questions than others. This may be an even bigger problem for people taking surveys on mobile devices, where typing can often be difficult. Initial research suggests there is often high item nonresponse to open-ended questions on mobile devices (Buskirk, Gaynor, Andrus, & Gorrell, 2011; Peytchev & Hill, 2010).

If respondents do answer the question, they may provide only a short response or a response that does not actually answer the question. In interviewer-administered surveys, open-ended questions are less burdensome to respondents, but more burdensome to interviewers as they are the ones who must type in the response. Countless times we have observed interviewers struggle to type in responses as quickly as respondents are speaking them. Those who cannot keep up must find ways to paraphrase the answers and may have to ask respondents to repeat portions of their response, both processes that likely result in increased interviewer variance.

Once collected, responses to open-ended questions must be coded before they can be analyzed; responses to paper surveys must also be typed or entered before coding. The data entry and coding process is often complicated by poor spelling, the use of abbreviations, and, in paper surveys, messy handwriting. In addition to the time to code responses to open-ended questions, there is often a lot more variation in respondents' answers, so it may be more difficult to analyze and interpret the data; depending on the range of variation, it may not even be possible to create a variable based on the responses. In contrast, responses to closed-ended questions can be analyzed immediately (or with only minor transformations to the data or recoding of responses), and results can be produced quickly.

FIGURE 4.6 Examples of question formats and the components of a question.

<u>*Open-ended questions*</u>

Question stem **What is the most important problem facing Nebraska today?**

Answer space

Question stem with verbal and numeric instructions **How many years have you lived in Nebraska?**
Please report only whole numbers. For example, if you have lived in Nebraska 20 months, please round to 2 years.

Answer space with verbal and symbolic instruction
☐ Years lived in Nebraska

<u>*Closed-ended ordinal question*</u>

Question stem **Overall, how satisfied are you with living in Nebraska?**

Answer choices
○ Completely satisfied
○ Very satisfied
○ Somewhat satisfied
○ Not too satisfied
○ Not at all satisfied

<u>*Closed-ended nominal question*</u>

Question stem **What is your current marital status?**

Answer choices
○ Married
○ Living with a partner
○ Divorced
○ Separated
○ Widowed
○ Never married

<u>*Partially closed-ended question*</u>

Question stem **What are your favorite women's sports at the University of Nebraska?**

Answer choices
☐ Basketball
☐ Cross Country
☐ Gymnastics
☐ Soccer
☐ Softball
☐ Swimming and Diving
☐ Tennis
☐ Volleyball
☐ Other: Please specify

A *closed-ended question format* should be used when surveyors want respondents to provide an answer after considering or evaluating a specified set of answer choices. Because researchers provide answer categories in closed-ended questions, the response options they choose have significant impact on how respondents interpret the questions. Closed-ended question formats can utilize nominal or ordinal categories.

In *nominal* questions, respondents are asked to compare a set of categories with no natural order underlying the categories, such as "What is your current marital status?" in Figure 4.6, where the response options are married, living with a partner, divorced, separated, widowed, and never married. Because the categories lack an inherent ordered relationship, the difficulty of processing nominal items increases as the number of categories that need to be compared at one time increases. This difficulty can be exacerbated in telephone surveys, where respondents need to hold the categories in their memory while deciding on a response While some nominal items require respondents to choose only one answer, others may allow the selection of multiple answers (e.g., check-all-that-apply and ranking questions). Examples of nominal questions that may allow multiple responses include which grocery stores one has visited, websites one frequently visits, and brands of personal care products purchased.

Surveyors may order these variables alphabetically or group them by type, but any such ordering or grouping is completely subjective and based on sets of criteria that are external to the categories themselves. Such ordering is usually done to help make answering the question easier for respondents. For example, when asking what state one resides in, it is often helpful to list the states in alphabetical order. This works well because respondents usually know what state they live in. They only need to find their own state; they do not need to read and process all of the other options. An alphabetical ordering may be less helpful for questions in which respondents have to read and consider all of the response options before settling on one of them. We have also seen instances in which surveyors subgroup the response options by type or theme in self-administered surveys to help respondents narrow in on an appropriate response more easily. However, one difficulty discussed in the conclusion of Chapter 6 is that such subgrouping introduces additional visual cues that can sometimes cause confusion about how an item should be answered.

In contrast, *ordinal questions*, sometimes called scales, provide an ordered set of answer categories, and respondents must decide where they fit along the continuum. A common ordinal scale asks about levels of satisfaction (e.g., see Figure 4.6 about satisfaction with living in Nebraska), where each category represents a higher degree or level of satisfaction but the exact interval between categories is unknown. Someone who is "completely satisfied" is more satisfied than someone who is "very satisfied," but it is not known how much more satisfied. Another common type of ordered scale asks about frequency of behaviors or events (e.g., all of the time, most of the time, some of the time, none of the time), where each category represents a greater or lesser frequency, but again the interval between the categories is unknown. As a result, one must be careful during analyses and reporting to avoid assuming that there is an equal interval between each scale point (e.g., by reporting a mean for these types of questions, which assumes equal distance between categories). Moreover, because there is an inherent order to the categories, respondents are particularly influenced by how the categories are distributed and by the overall layout of the response scale, both points we return to in Chapters 5 and 6.

A *partially closed-ended question format* is a hybrid of the open- and closed-ended formats that includes a set of response categories and an "other" response, thus allowing respondents who do not fit into the provided response categories to specify a different category that they do fit. This format is often used when it would be too burdensome to ask respondents about the entire set of items. For example, in the question in Figure 4.6 asking "What are your favorite women's sports at the University of Nebraska?", if one of the respondent's favorite sports was basketball, he would select that sport and move to the next question. However, if one of his favorite sports was rowing, which is not one of the options provided, he would select "other" and write or type "rowing" in the adjacent answer space. The value of this question format is that it reduces the number of items respondents have to consider at once and still collects data for the key items of interest. However, respondents are more likely to select the options provided than to write or type their own other responses. Therefore, categories should be included for all of the key items of interest, and care should be used when comparing "other" categories provided in the open-ended field with those that are explicitly provided. That is, it is not accurate to draw conclusions that compare listed to unlisted options, such as "Respondents were 10 times as likely to say basketball is one of their favorite women's sports as rowing." We will now turn to guidelines that will help surveyors write questions that can be understood and answered without introducing undue burden for respondents.

GUIDELINES FOR CHOOSING WORDS AND FORMING QUESTIONS

Guideline 4.1: Choose the Appropriate Question Format

One of the fundamental writing tools that exist for creating survey questions is to shift questions from one format to another. There are several reasons we might want to shift question formats. First, the question format we choose will affect how the respondent must answer the question. As a result, it will affect what type of data we receive and the types of variables we can create for our analyses. In order to ensure we collect the data needed, it is very important to think about and plan our key analyses before finalizing our question design, including what variables will be needed for the analysis and what types of questions will best collect the data needed to create these variables. This might involve thinking from the outset about how one wants to display the results, and perhaps even creating shells of the tables or graphics (i.e., titles, column headings, row labels, chart type, what will be shown on each axis, etc., but with mock data). One can then work backward from the desired tables or graphics to determine what question format is needed for each item that will be used in the analysis. Further, it is useful to think about the types of variables that will be best for any multivariate analyses one wishes to conduct.

Second, often questions that do not work in one question format can be converted to another format to more effectively measure the concept. For example, one of us was once asked to help a university committee that was preparing a questionnaire to evaluate a dean's performance. All of the questions proposed by the committee intermingled nominal and ordinal categories, and many of them included multiple concepts. As illustration, the first item from this questionnaire is shown in Figure 4.7. Because of the way the questions were structured, people just could not answer them, and the final results would have been very difficult to interpret. The proposed solution to the university committee was to break the question apart and to ask two ordinal closed-ended questions that focused on how often or to what extent the dean had demonstrated leadership and innovation. Then ask people a nominal closed-ended question where the dean's abilities to lead and innovate were directly compared. Separating leadership and innovation into separate questions and asking the direct comparison question allowed the committee to test its stated objectives of finding out how the faculty evaluated the dean separately on leadership and innovation, and on which attribute she performed better.

Another option for revising the question would have been to replace it with two open-ended questions that asked separately about the dean's ability to lead and innovate and perhaps still follow up with the direct comparison of leadership and innovation in the nominal closed-ended question. Which strategy should be used depends on the ultimate purpose for asking the question and how the data will be used. The open-ended questions would have produced more descriptive data on how faculty evaluated the dean's abilities independently; however, the ordered closed-ended questions would have allowed the committee to measure the dean's abilities using a common scale so that results could be easily summarized and compared.

In addition to highlighting how different question formats can be used to improve measurement and ensure that the data that are collected will answer the research question, this example also provides nice context for the warning to not get stuck using just one question format. Oftentimes people fall into a pattern of formulating questions in the one format they are most familiar and comfortable with. It is okay, and even advisable, to vary the question format within the survey in order to improve measurement and ensure the usefulness of the final data. Doing so may also add variety and interest for respondents.

Each survey mode has features that enable or constrain the use of different question formats. This means that in some cases, the decision of which question format to use for a question will be influenced by the survey mode being used. For example, in all modes we can formulate basic open-ended, ordinal, and nominal questions such as those shown in Figures 4.6 and 4.7, but because of the computerization underlying web and most telephone surveys, we have additional ways to present question formats in these modes, such as with visual analog scales, drop-down menus, drag-and-drop, and automatic calculation tools. We discuss these in Guidelines 5.2, 5.8, and 5.9.

Other times, the necessity of using a particular question format may limit one's options for which survey modes can be used. For example, while it is possible to administer complex formats such as check-all-that-apply and ranking questions in the paper and web modes, these formats do not work well in the telephone mode because there is no visual communication to support them. These formats are discussed at length in Guidelines 5.9 and 5.12.

Guideline 4.2: Make Sure the Question Applies to the Respondent

Imagine you are responding to a survey that asks, "Do you use your cell phone at least daily for voice calls, to access the Internet, or to send text messages?" (see Figure 4.8), but you do not have a cell phone. How do you respond? What if

FIGURE 4.7 Choosing the appropriate question format.

Nominal closed-ended

Which of these five statements best describes the dean?

○ Innovative but lacking leadership qualities
○ About the same on innovation and leadership qualities
○ Stronger on leadership than innovation
○ A born leader
○ A real innovator

Ordinal closed-ended for each concept

To what extent has the dean demonstrated strong leadership qualities?

○ All of the time
○ Most of the time
○ Some of the time
○ None of the time

To what extent has the dean demonstrated an ability to innovate?

○ All of the time
○ Most of the time
○ Some of the time
○ None of the time

Nominal closed-ended—revised to achieve direct comparison of concepts

Which one of the following do you feel best describes the dean?

○ A strong leader
○ A strong innovator
○ Both a strong leader and innovator
○ Neither a strong leader nor innovator

Open-ended for each concept

How would you describe the dean's leadership abilities?

How would you describe the dean's ability to innovate?

you did not make dinner at home last night but are asked, "If you prepared dinner last night, about how many minutes did it take" These kinds of questions are less common in modes where surveyors can take advantage of computerization to automate skip patterns (i.e., telephone and web). But they commonly occur in paper surveys because of the desire of the question writer to reduce the overall number of questions (i.e., save space) and avoid the need for skip instructions.

These two questions have another common problem in question design—they do not require answers of every respondent—but the source of the problem is slightly different for each. The first question contains an embedded assumption of having a cell phone that may not be true for all respondents. The second avoids

FIGURE 4.8 Example of asking questions that do not apply to everyone and asking more than one question at a time.

A question that some respondents cannot answer

Do you use your cell phone at least daily for voice calls, to access the Internet, or to send text messages?

☐ Yes
☐ No

A revision that uses a filter question and asks about one item at a time

Do you have a cell phone?

○ Yes
○ No

(If yes) Do you use your cell phone at least daily for each of the following?

	Yes	No
For voice calls	○	○
To access the Internet	○	○
To send text messages	○	○

making assumptions by including an "if" statement, but does not apply to those who do not fit the "if" criteria. Even if a "does not apply" box were provided, respondent confusion will likely still occur because the use of the word *if* implies that no response is needed from those who did not prepare dinner the previous night.

Aside from potentially confusing respondents, the methodological problem with these questions is that it is impossible to distinguish between those who did not respond because they were unmotivated (i.e., nonrespondents) and more motivated people who, nonetheless, did not respond because the question did not apply to them. These types of questions may even lower respondent motivation to complete future questions. Questions such as these are also particularly damaging in web surveys that require a response to every item. In this case, respondents have to either quit the survey altogether or enter false information.

A good rule to apply is that in order for an inquiry to constitute a survey question, it must require an answer from each person of whom it is asked. The two previous questions should only be asked of respondents who answer "yes" to filter questions such as "Do you have a cell phone?" or "Did you prepare dinner last night?"

Guideline 4.3: Ask One Question at a Time

On first take, the advice to ask one question at a time seems like a no-brainer, yet it is striking how often what appears to be one question actually contains two or more components. For example, the cell phone use question just discussed and shown in Figure 4.8 asks about three very different activities-voice calls, accessing the Internet, and sending text messages-in one question. Questions that contain multiple concepts like this are called double- or triple-barreled questions. As this question is written, it poses problems for respondents who use their cell phones for voice calls but not for text messages or to access the Internet. Do they answer "yes" or "no"? The question also poses a problem for anyone using the resulting data, as they will not know which activity or activities the respondents were referring to when they marked "yes" or "no."

One possible solution to this problem, as demonstrated in the revision shown in Figure 4.8, is to ask about each activity separately. This can be done using the forced-choice format shown in the revision, or by splitting these activities into three entirely separate questions (e.g., Do you use your cell phone at least daily for voice calls? … to access the Internet? … to send text messages?).

Guideline 4.4: Make Sure the Question Is Technically Accurate

Asking a question that is not technically accurate can confuse respondents and make answering difficult. For example, if a survey of horse owners asks, "How many feet tall is your horse?" respondents likely will be confused about how to answer because horses are often measured in a different unit—hands (one hand equals 4 inches). A more appropriate way to ask this question would be "How many hands tall is your horse?" Also, using specialized terms, accepted among the survey population, will likely produce more accurate measurement. For example, in a survey of physicians, asking "Have you ever conducted a coronary artery bypass?" is often preferred to "Have you ever conducted a bypass surgery?"

Ensuring that questions are technically accurate becomes more challenging when one is asking questions about topics that apply to very specialized populations such as equestrians or physicians. For these types of surveys, we recommend consulting experts and even members of the target population. Failing to do so can compromise the quality of responses (thereby increasing measurement error) as well as diminish the perceived credibility and legitimacy of the surveyor, possibly resulting in reduced motivation or even break-offs on the part of respondents.

Guideline 4.5: Use Simple and Familiar Words

One way to establish legitimacy and credibility with respondents is to present them with a formalized and professional questionnaire. Generally this is good practice. One way it can backfire, however, is if efforts to formalize the questionnaire lead to the use of complex words or phrases and technical terminology that not all respondents will understand. Many complex words and phrases can be easily replaced by more generally understood terms, as seen in Figure 4.9. When drafting questions, it may be advisable to consult sources that specialize in grammar and writing, as they commonly provide more extensive lists of replacement terms for complex words and wordy phrases. A good rule of thumb is that when a word exceeds six or seven letters, a shorter and more easily understood word can probably be substituted. However, it should not automatically be assumed that all shorter words are acceptable. For example, it would not be advisable to substitute *deter* for *discourage*.

Another common tendency, especially in government surveys, is to inadvertently use abbreviations or specialized phrases that are commonplace for the survey sponsor but require some translation for respondents. An example is shown in Figure 4.10. Although the survey sponsors may know that Form SS-4 is needed to request an employer identification number, many general public respondents

FIGURE 4.9   Words and phrases that can often be simplified.

Replacing complex with simple words	
Exhausted	Tired
Candid	Honest
Top priority	Most important
Leisure	Free time
Employment	Work
Courageous	Brave
Rectify	Correct
Replacing complex with simple phrases	
Occupants of this household	People who live here
Your responses	Your answers
Postschool extracurricular activities	What you do after school
Subnational region	Area of the country

FIGURE 4.10   Use of simple and familiar versus complex or specialized words.

Unnecessary use of specialized words and abbreviations

Have you filed Form SS-4 with the IRS?

   ○ Yes
   ○ No

A simplified revision

Have you filed an application for an employer identification number (Form SS-4) with the Internal Revenue Service?

   ○ Yes
   ○ No

may not. Others may not immediately know, or recall, what *IRS* stands for, further confusing them and making it even harder to figure out what Form SS-4 is. A clearer statement of the question is provided in the revision, in which the form is referred to by its full name and *IRS* is replaced with *Internal Revenue Service*.

In most instances it is desirable to replace complex and specialized words, but there are instances when this is not necessary. Virtually all occupational groups share a particular vocabulary that is not understood by outsiders but facilitates efficient communication within the group. Replacing this specialized vocabulary with simpler words would only confuse matters for these groups. In a survey of city planners, for example, it seems quite reasonable to talk about "annexation" instead of "an addition." Similarly, in a survey of physicians, it seems reasonable to talk about "pharmaceutical companies" instead of "companies that sell medicines." To do otherwise may even suggest a lack of knowledge and understanding of the topic of the survey.

However, the fact remains that people who write questionnaires are far more likely to overestimate than underestimate the knowledge and vocabulary of respondents. Thus, when in doubt, it is prudent to use the simpler of the available alternatives. Ultimately, though, the best way to determine if the vocabulary is appropriate is to pretest questions with members of the population of interest to identify potential difficulties, a topic we return to in Chapter 7.

Guideline 4.6: Use Specific and Concrete Words to Specify the Concepts Clearly

Suppose you are interested in different elements of family cohesiveness and you pose the first question in Figure 4.11 to a sample of parents with school-age children. One strength of this question is that it clearly specifies a reasonable time referent and the units in which one should report an answer. The problem, however, is that it contains several vague concepts. What does "eat" mean? Should we count snacks? What if we all gathered for a smoothie a couple hours before dinner; does that count, even though some may consider it a beverage more than a meal? And what does "together as a family" mean? Does the lunch we got from the drive-thru and ate in the car on the way to Grandma's house count? What about the pizza we ate in the living room while watching a movie on Saturday night? Do we count the end-of-season potluck for the baseball team at which we were all present but interspersed with other families?

One respondent might take a very liberal interpretation of this question and include all gatherings where her whole family was present and food or drinks were consumed, whereas another may take a very conservative view and count only full meals for which the family was gathered at home around the kitchen table. The problem is that the two interpretations would most likely result in quite divergent answers that are due to different interpretations of the question, not differences in family cohesiveness. This question could be improved by specifying that you are interested in meals consumed at home, as in the first revision. It could be made even more specific by specifying that you are interested in sit-down meals shared as a family, as in the second revision.

This example illustrates a common problem for many writers of survey questions. Once the units are specified, many concepts such as age, height, and weight are very straightforward. Others, however, are not as straightforward as they seem. It seems like everyone would know what it means to eat together as a family, but as the example shows, once one begins to factor in the complexity of family life in this day and age, the concept of eating together as a family is opened up to much

FIGURE 4.11　Use specific and concrete words to specify the concepts clearly.

Question with vague concepts

How many times did you eat together as a family last week?

　☐　Number of meals

A revised question with more specific and concrete concepts

How many meals did you eat together as a family at home last week?

　☐　Number of meals

A more specific revision

How many meals did you sit down to eat at home as a family last week?

　☐　Number of meals

interpretation. Thus, it is important to make sure the concepts in survey questions are clearly defined and communicated in order to minimize the amount of interpreting and defining that respondents need to do.

Guideline 4.7: Use as Few Words as Possible to Pose the Question

Part of writing simple questions is keeping them short and to the point. The longer the question, the more information respondents have to take in and process, and the higher the likelihood that they will not fully process or understand the question. This is especially important in thinking about how we ask questions in different modes. Telephone surveys have encouraged the use of shorter questions, a tendency that has often continued with web surveys and especially now mobile surveys, where long questions may result in the entire question stem not being visible on the screen.

When presented with the question in Figure 4.12, for example, one respondent in a cognitive interview answered, "I don't have any idea how many people live in the United States." As a result of this and other interviews, the well-intentioned second sentence that explained the reason for the directions about those to include and exclude was removed (Dillman & Allen, 1995).

The goal of keeping questions short sometimes contradicts the previously stated goals of using familiar and simple words and using specific and concrete words to specify concepts clearly. Substituting several simpler words for a more complex word or carefully specifying concepts can lengthen questions. In these instances, we recommend first ensuring that the questions use simple and familiar words as well as specific and concrete words. Once questions are written with words chosen that are understood by virtually all respondents and the concepts

FIGURE 4.12 Use as few words as possible to pose the question.

Long question with potentially confusing information
How many people were living or staying at this residence on Saturday, March 3rd, 2000? To make sure each person in the United States is counted only once, it is very important to:
Include everyone who lives here whether related to you or not, and anyone staying temporarily who has no permanent place to live; **But not include** anyone away at college, away in the Armed Forces, in a nursing home, hospice, mental hospital, correctional facility, or other institution.
A shorter revision with potentially confusing information removed
How many people were living or staying at this residence on Saturday, March 3rd, 2000? Please:
Include everyone who lives here whether related to you or not, and anyone staying temporarily who has no permanent place to live; **But do not include** anyone away at college, away in the Armed Forces, in a nursing home, hospice, mental hospital, correctional facility, or other institution.

FIGURE 4.13 Eliminating wordy and redundant expressions.

Due to the fact that	Because
At this point in time	Now
A small number of	A few
A considerable number of	Many
Small in size	Small
Has the ability	Can
Ascertain the location of	Locate
Concerning the matter of	About
If conditions are such that	If
In the majority of instances	Usually
Make a decision	Decide
Take into consideration	Consider

are clearly specified, then a final review is helpful to see if any unnecessary words can be removed.

There are several ways to do this. One way is to replace wordy and redundant expressions such as those shown in Figure 4.13 with simpler wording. More comprehensive lists of commonly used wordy expressions and their replacements can be found by searching sources that specialize in grammar and writing.

Guideline 4.8: Use Complete Sentences That Take a Question Form, and Use Simple Sentence Structures

It is tempting to save space by using incomplete sentences for paper surveys. It is true that few people will misunderstand "Your name" or even "Age." However, the series of questions in Figure 4.14 once caused many respondents to provide erroneous answers to the second and third questions. Nearly 20% of the respondents listed the number of years they had lived in the city or town and the county. In addition, several other respondents listed "United States" for *county*, a word that is only one letter different from *country*. Writing each question as a complete sentence would have helped solve both problems. In addition, in the revision "county" is changed to "Idaho county" in order to minimize the possibility of listing the United States as the respondent's county of residence.

Using complete sentences is even more important in telephone surveys and in web and mobile surveys with page-by-page construction. When there is only one question presented at a time, respondents can easily lose track of the context in which an inquiry is made. Here, incomplete sentences become isolated in ways that can make their meaning even less clear. Moreover, the inflection at the end of a question gives a clear indication to a listener that they are expected to speak a response. Thus, using actual questions (e.g., "What month and year were you born?") rather than imperative sentences (e.g., "Please enter the month and year you were born.") and using complete sentences are key strategies for avoiding interruptions or awkward pauses and ensuring that the turn taking in telephone surveys proceeds smoothly. Using questions with complete sentence structures should be the norm throughout a questionnaire; incomplete sentences should be avoided and imperative sentences should only be used in exceptional situations.

When asking for very specific information, it is tempting to add extra clauses onto the sentence to help specify the focus of the question; however,

FIGURE 4.14 Use complete sentences.

Common use of incomplete sentences

Number of years lived in Idaho

[ ] Years

Your city or town

[ ] City or Town

Your county

[ ] County

A revision using complete sentences

How many years have you lived in Idaho

[ ] Years

In what city or town do you live?

[ ] Name of City or Town

In what Idaho county do you live?

[ ] Name of Idaho County

these may confuse respondents or result in their misunderstanding the question. The problem with doing this is that reading sentences with multiple clauses or a complex sentence structure requires more skill than reading sentences with simple structures. Just as with wording, it is advisable to avoid complex sentence structures and replace them instead with simple structures.

Guideline 4.9: Make Sure "Yes" Means Yes and "No" Means No

It seems obvious that questions should not include double negatives, or, in other words, require a respondent to say "yes" to mean no as in the following question: "Should the city manager not be directly responsible to the mayor?" Yet such questions are commonly asked in surveys. One of the reasons they are so prevalent is because voters are often asked in elections to vote for measures where a yes vote would result in something not being done, as illustrated by the tax approval question in Figure 4.15. Surveyors are often reluctant to pose the question differently than it will be expressed on the ballot. However, because people tend to read questions quickly, it is likely that some people will miss the word *not*. In addition, the mental connection of favoring a "not" is difficult for most people.

Two different solutions for this problem might be considered. The first revision simply asks whether people favor or oppose requiring 60% approval by voters

FIGURE 4.15   Make sure "yes" means yes and "no" means no.

A question containing a double negative

Do you favor or oppose not allowing the state to raise taxes without approval of 60% of the voters?

○ Favor
○ Oppose

A revision with no double negative

Do you favor or oppose requiring 60% approval by voters in order to raise state taxes?

○ Favor
○ Oppose

A revision that preserves important wording

In the September election you will be asked to vote on this referendum: "No state tax can be raised without approval by 60% of those voting in a statewide election." If the election were held today, would you vote for or against approval?

○ For
○ Against

---

in order to raise state taxes. To help clarify, the answer categories specify what *favor* and *oppose* mean for the purposes of this question. This wording would seem appropriate during discussion of an issue before it has reached the ballot measure stage. A second revision, indicating that a vote will be taken, specifies the measure exactly as it will appear on the ballot and asks whether respondents are for or against approval of the measure. The change in the categories from favor/oppose to for/against is also an attempt to bring the language of the question more in line with that of the voting situation.

Guideline 4.10: Organize Questions in a Way to Make It Easier for Respondents to Comprehend the Response Task

The goal underlying this guideline is efficiency for whoever is reading the question (i.e., the interviewer or the respondents). Dillman, Gertseva, and Mahon-Haft (2005) applied the design principles described by Norman (1988) for everyday things to the survey context. One of these principles is to simplify the structure of tasks. With respect to questionnaires, this means presenting the information in the question in a logical way such that each new piece of information can be made sense of within the context of the overall question.

Figure 4.16 shows an example of a question re-created from the 1993 U.S. Census of Agriculture in which this is not done well. In this item, respondents were given great detail about what land to consider in their answer before even knowing what the question was asking. The inevitable result is that it is necessary to reread this information after discovering what the question is asking.

FIGURE 4.16   Poor information organization with unclear navigational path.

Poor information organization and lack of navigational path:

CENSUS USE ONLY	035	036	037	038	039	040	041	042

SECTION 1	**ACREAGE IN 1992** – Report land owned, rented, or used by you, your spouse, or by the partnership, corporation, or organization for which you are reporting. Include ALL LAND, REGARDLESS OF LOCATION OR USE – cropland, pastureland, rangeland, woodland, idle land, house lots, etc.
S1	

If the acres you operated in 1992 changed during the year, refer to the INFORMATION SHEET, section 1.   None | Number of acres 043

1. All land owned ....

Better information organization and creation of clear navigational path:

1. **How many acres of land did you own in 1990? You should report all land (crop land, pasture land, rangeland, woodland, idle land, house lots, etc.), regardless of location, owned by you, by your spouse, or by the partnership, corporation, or organization for which you are reporting.** *(If the acres you operated in 1990 changed during the year, refer to the information sheet, Section I.)*

_____Number of acres owned

In a self-administered survey, the drawback to such inefficiency is that respondents may become frustrated and unwilling to retrace those steps and therefore may give a wrong answer or no answer at all. In an interviewer-administered survey, such disorganization forces the respondent to hold considerable detail in working memory before they even understand why they need to know this information, and while they are also hearing the question itself. Few will be able to do this well.

A more effective organization of the information is shown in the revision in the bottom panel of Figure 4.16. The revision allows respondents to know at the beginning that they are being asked to report the number of acres they own; they are then given instructions on what to include and exclude.

Another tendency some have is to present response options prior to the survey question itself by embedding them in the middle of the question stem, as in the example shown in Figure 4.17: "Are you very likely, somewhat likely, somewhat unlikely, or very unlikely to visit Yellowstone National Park again?" In this example, the response options interrupt the question stem and can make it harder for the respondent to understand what the question is asking. In addition, the response options may not make sense without understanding the full context of what the question is asking. Presenting the response options first is particularly problematic in telephone surveys, in which respondents do not have the ability to review the response options after hearing the actual question unless they ask the interviewer to repeat them. Including the full question stem first, as is done in the first revision in Figure 4.17, allows the respondent to understand what the question is asking before having to process and differentiate among the response options.

For these reasons, we recommend placing the response options at the end of the question stem in interview-administered modes (or even simply removing them from the question stem and instructing the interviewers to read the options that are visually displayed on the screen below the question stem). In self-administered modes, they do not need to be included as part of the question stem since they will be visually displayed below the question stem where the respondent provides a response as shown in the second revision in Figure 4.17. Constructing questions in this way also helps provide a common stimulus across modes, since the full question stem will be presented before the response options in all modes.

FIGURE 4.17   Include response options after the question stem.

Embedding response options in the question stem

Are you very likely, somewhat likely, somewhat unlikely, or very unlikely to visit Yellowstone National Park again?

- ○ Very likely
- ○ Somewhat likely
- ○ Somewhat unlikely
- ○ Very unlikely

A revision for a telephone survey

How likely or unlikely are you to visit Yellowstone National Park again —very likely, somewhat likely, somewhat unlikely, or very unlikely?

- ○ Very likely
- ○ Somewhat likely
- ○ Somewhat unlikely
- ○ Very unlikely

A revision for a paper or web survey

How likely or unlikely are you to visit Yellowstone National Park again?

- ○ Very likely
- ○ Somewhat likely
- ○ Somewhat unlikely
- ○ Very unlikely

CONCLUSION

Writing good survey questions requires attending to many details at once. You need considerable knowledge about the different question formats, the strengths and weaknesses of each, and how the parts of the survey question work together. But crafting effective survey questions that measure concepts well is also something that takes a great deal of practice and experience, and requires considerable up-front work. If one just sits down and begins writing questions without carefully thinking through such issues as what concepts need to be measured, what type of data will ultimately be needed, and what mode will be used, the results will surely be disappointing. And the process does not end when one has drafted the initial questions, as it is important to test the survey questions to evaluate how well they perform (see Chapter 7 for more on testing questionnaires).

This chapter has provided some fundamental tools and strategies needed to get started writing good survey questions, as well as some guidelines and best practices for wording and forming questions that apply broadly across modes and across different question types. But once a question format has been chosen and the basic wording of the question developed, there are many more decisions that need to be made. These decisions are specific to whether the question will be asked as an open- or closed-ended question, and whether the question will be perceived aurally or visually by the respondent. In the next chapter, we discuss guidelines that are specific to open- and closed-ended question formats. In Chapter 6, we then turn to discuss how questions are impacted by whether the respondent perceives the information aurally or visually, and guidelines for designing questions for visual surveys.

LIST OF GUIDELINES

Guidelines for Choosing Words and Forming Questions

Guideline 4.1: Choose the appropriate question format
Guideline 4.2: Make sure the question applies to the respondent
Guideline 4.3: Ask one question at a time
Guideline 4.4: Make sure the question is technically accurate
Guideline 4.5: Use simple and familiar words
Guideline 4.6: Use specific and concrete words to specify the concepts clearly
Guideline 4.7: Use as few words as possible to pose the question
Guideline 4.8: Use complete sentences that take a question form, and use simple sentence structures
Guideline 4.9: Make sure "yes" means yes and "no" means no
Guideline 4.10: Organize questions in a way to make it easier for respondents to comprehend the response task

How to Write Open- and Closed-Ended Questions

In this chapter we turn our focus from the challenges faced in writing every question, to the more specific tasks faced in writing specific types of survey questions. Many important decisions have to be made in order to write good survey questions. These decisions differ depending on the intent and format of the question that is being written. In addition, what might seem like an insignificant decision can strongly impact respondents' answers. To illustrate this point, we present findings from student surveys we have conducted where we obtained very different results depending on how we asked the question. For example,

1. Only about 28% of students are very satisfied with their university as a place to go to school … or is it 55%? It depends on what scale we provide.
2. This same campus offers a library instruction resource to students. Either 20% or 52% of students have used this resource, depending on how the response options are ordered.
3. Seventy-one percent of students study over 2.5 hours per day if you ask the question one way. But if you ask it another way, only 30% study over 2.5 hours per day. Ask it yet a third way, and 58% report studying this long.
4. Either 54% or 63% of students think their university is a "farm/agriculture school" and 26% or 37% think it is "outdoors oriented," depending on how we present the response options.
5. When given a list of 12 possible descriptions of their university, students, on average, thought that just over a third of them applied. But when we formatted the question a different way, they thought over half of the exact same descriptions applied.

These examples illustrate the strong impact that the decisions we make while crafting questions can have on the survey's final results. And the impacts may not be inconsequential. Should we invest in the library instruction program, or cut it and its staff if only 20% of students are using it? What if 52% are using it? When the estimates we provide may have considerable impact on both students and staff, we need them to be as good as possible. We return to each of these examples throughout this chapter to discuss what features of the questions resulted in such large differences, and how to decide which is the best way to ask them (Example 1 is in Guideline 5.18, 2 is in Guideline 5.7, 3 is in Guideline 5.21, and 4 and 5 are in Guideline 5.12). We start with guidelines for writing open-ended questions, followed by guidelines for writing closed-ended nominal and closed-ended ordinal questions.

GUIDELINES FOR WRITING OPEN-ENDED QUESTIONS

When many people think of open-ended questions, only one type comes to mind: the *descriptive open-ended question*, in which respondents are asked to provide in-depth information on the topic of the question. Examples might include a question asking how a local restaurant can improve the dining experience it provides or what is the most important problem facing the country today.

However, there are two other ways in which surveyors ask respondents a question and allow them to formulate their response in an open-ended way. Perhaps the most common of these circumstances, and one that many overlook when they think about open-ended questions, is when the surveyor asks respondents to report a *numerical response* such as a date, frequency, monetary value, count, amount, or scalar value. Another way in which open-ended answer boxes are provided is when surveyors ask respondents to provide a *list of items* such as grocery stores they frequent, organizations they volunteer for, classes they have taken, or businesses they would like to see move into their area.

The measurement goal of each of these types of open-ended questions is different. Only a number is desired in one, in another only a list of items is desired and any extra elaboration or description is unnecessary, and in the third the surveyor wants as much elaboration and description as possible. However, they have in common that their answer spaces provide the respondent with an immense amount of flexibility in the answer that can be supplied, and thus it is important to guide respondents about how they should report their answers throughout the entire question in all open-ended questions.

Guideline 5.1: Specify the Type of Response Desired in the Question Stem

The first place for communicating the type of information respondents should provide is in the wording of the question stem. The way this will be done differs across the types of open-ended questions. Imagine, for example, that we ask, "In an average week, how often do you cook dinner at home?" Some respondents to this question might answer using a number, as was intended by the researcher (e.g., "5"). Others may provide more vague responses, such as "most of the time" or "rarely." Still others may get very specific: "I cook dinner at home on Monday, Tuesday, and Thursday. My partner cooks dinner on Wednesday, Friday, and Sunday. We eat out every Saturday night." The problem here is that each respondent has a different idea about the type and specificity of information he should report. An effective way to reduce such differences in numeric open-ended items is to specify a response unit in the question stem. Along these lines, we might rewrite this question as, "In an average week, how many days do you personally cook dinner at home?"

Specifying the type of response desired in the question stem is particularly important for telephone surveys. Because respondents to telephone surveys cannot see the answer spaces (which might provide clues about how to respond), the only cues they receive about what is expected from them are from the wording

FIGURE 5.1   How specificity of question wording affects reports about when students began their studies.

Question Wording (Telephone)	% Reporting Month and Year	% Reporting Season/Semester
When did you begin your studies at Washington State University?	13.4	57.3
What date did you begin your studies at Washington State University?	49.5	32.3
What month and year did you begin your studies at Washington State University?	83.7	11.0

Source: "Helping Respondents Get It Right the First Time: The Influence of Words, Symbols, and Graphics in Web Surveys," by L. M. Christian, D. A. Dillman, and J. D. Smyth, 2007b, *Public Opinion Quarterly, 71*(1), pp. 113–125.

of the question. In one study, we wanted to know the month and year students began their studies at Washington State University. When we asked, "*When did you begin your studies at Washington State University?*" only 13% of students told us the month and year, and 57% reported a season or semester such as "Fall 2006" (Figure 5.1). This is not surprising, given that academic years are strongly organized around semesters (or quarters) that tend to correspond with seasons. When the question stem specified, "*What date did you begin your studies … ?*" about half reported a month and year and 32% reported a semester or a season. Finally, when we got very specific in the question stem and asked, "*What month and year did you begin your studies … ?*" nearly 84% reported the desired month and year and only 11% reported a semester or season (Christian, Dillman, & Smyth, 2007b). Specifying the type of response desired in the question stem helped ensure that we collected the type of information we needed, but it also serves another important role in telephone surveys—it helps the telephone interview proceed smoothly by reducing the need for clarifications and corrections, which can take interviewers off-script and result in increased interviewer variance.

Although the measurement intent is different, the question stem can also be used to communicate response expectations for list-style open-ended items. For example, in one study, we were interested in knowing what businesses students would like to see come to their local area, which was made up of two nearby cities, Pullman, Washington, and Moscow, Idaho. In one version we asked, "What businesses would you most like to see in the Pullman and Moscow area?" In the other we asked, "What three businesses would you most like to see in the Pullman and Moscow area?" Reaching this level of specificity in the question stem is particularly important for those conducting telephone surveys or mixed-mode surveys with a telephone component. In fact, in this experiment, the percentage of respondents reporting three or more businesses over the telephone increased by 32 percentage points when we provided the more specific question stem (Smyth, Dillman, & Christian, 2007b).

Guideline 5.2: Avoid Making Respondents (or Interviewers) Calculate Sums; When Possible, Have the Computer Do It

A surveyor might want to ask a series of numerical open-ended questions in which the answers add up to a specific value. An example is shown in Figure 5.2.

FIGURE 5.2 Example of a question requiring a sum.

Example of question requiring respondent to calculate a sum

4. Between the hours of 8:00 a.m. and 8:00 p.m., how many hours do you spend on each of the following activities in an average day? *Answers should add up to 12 hours.*

	Hours
Work for pay	8
Housework	1
Child care	2
Leisure	1
Other	0

Example of question with automatic calculation of a sum

4. Between the hours of 8:00 a.m. and 8:00 p.m., how many hours do you spend on each of the following activities in an average day? *Answers should add up to 12 hours.*

	Hours
Work for pay	8
Housework	1
Child care	2
Leisure	1
Other	0
Total	12

In this case, respondents are being asked to allocate a known amount of time, 12 hours, across a number of tasks. A common variant of this type of question involves asking respondents to report percentages that must sum to 100. In other cases, responses must sum to an answer from a previous question, such as when someone is asked how many hours she worked last week and then asked to allocate that time to different work days or tasks. These types of questions can be very burdensome to respondents, especially those who struggle with math.

As a general rule, one should avoid asking questions that require respondents to do math, but in cases where they cannot be avoided, providing an automatic calculation tool, as shown in the revision in Figure 5.2, will make responding easier and reduce errors. The automatic calculation tool keeps a running total or tally to help respondents know how much total time they have allocated so far across the different categories.

The limited research on automatic calculation tools suggests that they are helpful to respondents. For example, in one study, only about 85% of respondents provided answers that summed to the target value when no accuracy feedback was given, but about 97% did so when an automatic calculation tool displayed a running total that updated each time a respondent entered new information (Conrad, Couper, Tourangeau, & Galesic, 2005). Moreover, respondents were more likely to have their answer sum correctly on the first try and were able to achieve this more quickly when they were provided with a running total. Another study found that respondents who were shown a tally were less likely to leave items blank, enter zeros, or provide rounded answers than those not shown a tally

(Conrad, Tourangeau, Couper, & Zhang, 2010). Of course, automatic calculation tools can only be used in computerized modes such as web and telephone; they cannot be used in paper questionnaires.

Guideline 5.3: Provide Extra Motivation to Respond

One of the fundamental problems with descriptive open-ended questions is that they require respondents to exert a great deal of effort to report their response (i.e., increased costs). Closed-ended questions only require respondents to choose a response from an existing list, whereas descriptive open-ended questions require that they formulate an answer in their own words. Further, in self-administered surveys, there is no interviewer present to motivate respondents to answer the question, and respondents must write or type their response themselves. Providing thorough answers to these questions takes a lot of time as well as both mental and physical energy, so supplying a short and very basic answer is much easier. As a result, respondents may need extra motivation to answer descriptive open-ended questions well.

One way to keep motivation for these questions high is to use them sparingly, and only for important topics about which descriptive information is necessary. Another way is to provide clarifying and motivating material with the question. In one research example, we asked university students the following: "In your own words, how would you describe your adviser(s)?" A randomly selected subset of the respondents to the web survey received the following introduction prior to the question: "This question is very important to understanding the Washington State University student experience. Please take your time answering it." In two different comparisons, we found that including the additional explanation increased response length between 5 and 15 words, and increased the percentage of respondents who elaborated in their response between 12 and 20 percentage points. Respondents who received the motivational explanation also took more time to provide their answers (between 20 and 34 seconds) (Smyth, Dillman, Christian, & McBride, 2009).

Oudejans and Christian (2011) tested the effectiveness of a motivational statement on four questions in a web survey of Dutch panel members. Overall, they found similar effects, in that the version with the motivational statement produced higher quality answers. Importantly, they also found that the statement was most effective on the early questions and lost effectiveness for the later questions. Thus, including such a statement on one or two items can be very effective, but may lose its effectiveness if used on several questions in the survey.

If space is an issue, further research into the use of introductions has shown that using a shorter introduction (e.g., "This question is very important to understanding the Washington State University student experience") has nearly the same benefits as using the longer version (i.e., the preceding introduction with "Please take your time answering it" added). Informing respondents that their answers are important, and clarifying why they are important, gives them a reason to expend the time and energy needed to produce good open-ended responses. These types of motivational statements can be particularly helpful in self-administered surveys where there is not an interviewer present to motivate them to respond.

Guideline 5.4: Use Nondirective Probes to Obtain More Information on Open-Ended Items

The value of open-ended items is that they capture respondents' thoughts without influencing or constraining them with closed-ended response options. However, it is sometimes challenging to get respondents to completely articulate their thoughts, resulting in incomplete answers. In these instances, following up with a probe can encourage them to say more.

As an example, we once asked students in a telephone survey, "What businesses would you most like to see in the Pullman and Moscow area that are currently not available?" A random half of students received a follow-up probe asking, "Are there any others?" after their initial response. Those who did not receive the probe listed an average of 1.8 businesses, while those who received the probe listed an average of 2.4 businesses (Smyth et al., 2007b).

Our research has also shown that probes are effective in descriptive open-ended questions. When we asked students, "Why did you choose to attend Washington State University?" those who did not receive a probe gave us an average of 1.6 reasons in their answer, but those whose initial response was probed with "Is there anything else?" gave an average of two themes. Using the probes got us more information (Smyth, Dillman, Christian, & McBride, 2006).

There are two important points one must keep in mind about probing. First, any probes used must be nondirective or neutral. This means they should seek more information without biasing responses. When we ask students what businesses they would like to see in the area, it is very appropriate for interviewers to follow up with "Are there any others?" but it would be wildly inappropriate for them to follow up with "Wouldn't you like to have a Taco Bell?" as this would strongly bias responses. Fowler and Mangione (1990) suggest that interviewers be taught to use one of the following three nondirective probes for descriptive open-ended questions: "How do you mean that?" "Tell me more about that." and "Anything else?" (p. 42).

This brings us to the second important point to keep in mind, which is that the type of probe used will strongly impact the amount and type of information received. For example, we asked students, "In your own words, how would you describe your adviser or advisers?" After their initial response, half of the students were given the probe "Is there anything else?" and the other half were given the probe "Can you tell me more about that?" Only about 18% of students who received the "anything else" probe responded to it. Most simply said, "No," leaving the interviewer to go on to the next question. In comparison, 82% of students who received the "tell me more" probe responded with additional information, including new ideas or themes as well as elaboration on previously reported themes (Smyth et al., 2006).

Based on this research, the "tell me more" probe seems far superior, but imagine we were asking the list-style question about what businesses students wanted to see in the area. In this case, asking, "Can you tell me more about that?" would probably lead to unwanted elaboration about the previously listed businesses rather than mentions of additional businesses. With the measurement intent behind this question being to obtain a thorough list of businesses students want, the probes "Are there any others?" or "Is there anything else?" will almost certainly be more productive.

In the past, probing has been an activity reserved for interviewer-administered surveys, but research has begun to explore what happens when surveyors include probes in web surveys. In a study one of us conducted, undergraduate students at the University of Georgia were asked two open-ended questions to gauge their interest in topics related to a new major—Latin American and Caribbean Studies. For each question, once they submitted their answer, a probe appeared asking for more information. An example of one of the questions can be seen in Figure 5.3.

FIGURE 5.3 Example of probing in a web survey.

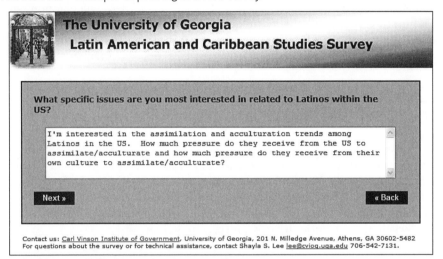

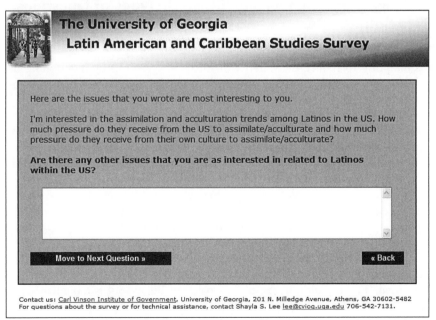

Source: The Influence of Interactive Probing on Response to Open-Ended Questions in a Web Survey, by J. Holland and L. M. Christian, October 2007, Raleigh, NC. Paper presented at the Southern Association for Public Opinion Research Annual Conference.

Results of the study indicated that, compared to a version without the probe, the version with the probe produced significantly longer answers with significantly more themes, but no increases in elaboration (Holland & Christian, 2007). That the percentage of respondents elaborating was not increased significantly is probably due to the fact that the probe was worded in a way that elicited more themes but not necessarily more elaboration, as discussed earlier.

Oudejans and Christian (2011) also found probing on the web yielded slightly longer answers with more themes. Thus, it appears that using a probe can improve response quality to open-ended questions on the web as well. However, inasmuch as such probes may increase the burden of an already burdensome question type, it is advisable to reserve this technique for only the most important questions. Indeed, Oudejans and Christian (2011) found that probing was most effective on the first few questions in which it was used and less effective thereafter.

GENERAL GUIDELINES FOR WRITING ALL TYPES OF CLOSED-ENDED QUESTIONS

We now turn our attention to closed-ended questions, where respondents are provided a list of categories to choose from, and are asked to choose one or more responses that apply. We first discuss general guidelines that apply to all closed-ended questions. We then present separate guidelines for nominal closed-ended questions, where the categories are unordered, and for ordinal closed-ended questions, where the categories have an inherent underlying order.

Guideline 5.5: When Asking Either/Or Types of Questions, State Both the Positive and Negative Side in the Question Stem

It is tempting to reduce the number of words in questions by mentioning only one side of an issue. For example, the question in the top panel of Figure 5.4 asks only if one favors congressional term limits, without any mention that one might oppose them. Mentioning only the positive option implicitly suggests that favoring term limits is the "right" answer, which will magnify any preexisting tendencies to acquiesce, as discussed in Chapter 4. Stating both sides of the question, as is done in the improved design shown in Figure 5.4, rebalances the question so that neither favor nor oppose is given priority.

In addition, this revision creates a better match between the question stem and the response options. The original question stem implied incorrectly that the response options should be "yes" or "no," but the revised question stem implies correctly that the response options should be "favor" or "oppose."

The same guideline applies to ordinal questions, although in practice it is implemented in slightly different ways, depending on the type of ordinal scale being used. The question in the middle panel of Figure 5.4 is a bipolar scale in which the categories allow respondents to express satisfaction or dissatisfaction. The question stem asks the extent to which people are satisfied with service, but leaves out any mention of dissatisfaction. Substituting "satisfied or dissatisfied" into the question stem, as in the improved design, helps convey to the respondent that the response options will include categories that allow them to express satisfaction or dissatisfaction. The bottom panel of Figure 5.4 shows an example

FIGURE 5.4   State both positive and negative sides in the question stem.

Poor Designs	*Improved Designs*
Do you favor congressional term limits of four years?	**Do you favor or oppose congressional term limits of four years?**
○ Favor ○ Oppose	○ Favor ○ Oppose
How satisfied are you with the overall service you have received from your financial consultant?	**How satisfied or dissatisfied are you with the overall service you have received from your financial consultant?**
○ Very satisfied ○ Somewhat satisfied ○ Somewhat dissatisfied ○ Very dissatisfied	○ Very satisfied ○ Somewhat satisfied ○ Somewhat dissatisfied ○ Very dissatisfied
How concerned are you that you will get a computer virus while using the Internet?	**How concerned, if at all, are you that you will get a computer virus while using the Internet?**
○ Very concerned ○ Somewhat concerned ○ Slightly concerned ○ Not at all concerned	○ Very concerned ○ Somewhat concerned ○ Slightly concerned ○ Not at all concerned

of a unipolar scale, asking how concerned one is about getting a computer virus, where the categories express different gradations of concern (see Guideline 5.13 for discussion of unipolar versus bipolar scales). In this case, we added "if at all" to the question stem to communicate to the respondent that the scale ends with "not at all concerned," and to indicate that this response is acceptable.

Guideline 5.6: Develop Lists of Answer Categories That Include All Reasonable Possible Answers

The question in Figure 5.5, which asks respondents to choose one answer that describes how they heard about a tornado, suffers from several very common problems. One of the most notable is that it is missing some important news sources: the Internet and newspapers. Inasmuch as both the Internet and newspapers are common sources of news, they too need to be offered as options in this question, as is done in the revision. Otherwise, people who heard about the tornado from these sources would have great difficulty answering this question. To avoid encouraging respondents to skip questions, every question should include all reasonable possible answers so that every respondent can find an applicable answer.

This brings us to the topic of response options like "don't know," "no opinion," and "undecided." Some argue that such options provide those who cannot put themselves into one of the offered categories a way to register an honest response (Converse & Presser, 1986). Without a nonsubstantive option, these

FIGURE 5.5 Exhaustive and mutually exclusive questions.

A question that is not exhaustive or mutually exclusive

From which one of these sources did you first learn about the tornado in Derby?

- ○ Radio
- ○ Television
- ○ Someone at work
- ○ While at home
- ○ While traveling to work

A revision that is exhaustive and mutually exclusive

From which one of these sources did you first hear about the tornado in Derby?

- ○ Radio
- ○ Television
- ○ Internet
- ○ Newspaper
- ○ Another person

Where were you when you first heard about it?

- ○ At work
- ○ At home
- ○ Traveling to work
- ○ Somewhere else

---

respondents would have to select an untrue answer or skip the question, neither of which is a desirable outcome. Others argue that providing these response options makes it easier for respondents to satisfice; that is, that respondents will select the nonsubstantive option rather than doing the mental work necessary to report their true response (Krosnick, 2002).

Considerable research has been conducted on this topic, especially for attitude and opinion questions, and has found support for both of these notions. Some people select the nonsubstantive options because they are the most accurate, and others select them because they are an easy out. As such, there is no simple answer to the question of whether one should provide nonsubstantive response options.

Rather than automatically providing or not providing such options, we advise that survey designers consider whether these options should be provided for each question. If it is plausible that many respondents will not know the answer to a question, as might be expected with many knowledge or factual questions, providing a "don't know" or "not sure" option may be advisable. For questions about topics that we expect virtually everyone to know about or have an opinion about, it may be better to withhold these types of options.

Guideline 5.7: Develop Lists of Answer Categories That Are Mutually Exclusive

The image that often comes to mind when discussing the lack of mutually exclusive categories is when ranges overlap, as in age categories such as the following: 35 or younger, 35 to 50, 50 to 65, and 65 and older. Although the overlap is minor, it can be very annoying to people who happen to fall on the line, and it can very easily be fixed by offering categories like 35 or younger, 36 to 50, 51 to 65, and 66 and older. Alternatively, one may prefer to ask age as a numerical open-ended question where respondents specify their age in years.

Questions measuring income can be even more challenging to write because the numbers can get very large, and large numbers can be difficult to read aloud, as would be required in a telephone survey. The top panel in Figure 5.6 shows a telephone survey income question in which the response options are not mutually exclusive. If one were to solve this problem in the same way as suggested for the age item just discussed, the result would be the question in the middle panel of this figure, in which the response options are now adjusted to be mutually exclusive. The problem with this revision becomes immediately clear once one tries to read the categories aloud (e.g., less than nine thousand nine hundred ninety-nine dollars, ten thousand to nineteen thousand nine hundred ninety-nine dollars, twenty thousand to twenty-nine thousand nine hundred ninety-nine dollars, etc.). This item will not work well in a telephone survey. The final revision in Figure 5.6 shows a slightly different way of designing the response options that makes them both mutually exclusive and easier to administer in a telephone survey.

FIGURE 5.6   How to make response options in income questions mutually exclusive and also conducive to telephone surveys.

Income question lacking mutual exclusivity in the response options

| Last year, that is, in 2013, what was your total family income from all sources, before taxes? Just stop me when I get to the right category. [READ] | 1 ⊙ Less than $10,000
2 ⊙ 10,000 to $20,000
3 ⊙ 20,000 to $30,000
4 ⊙ 30,000 to $40,000
5 ⊙ 40,000 to $50,000
6 ⊙ 50,000 to $75,000
7 ⊙ 75,000 to $100,000
8 ⊙ 100,000 to $150,000 [OR]
9 ⊙ 150,000 or more
10 ⊙ [VOL. DO NOT READ] Don't know/Refused |

Income question with mutually exclusive response options that make administration difficult

| Last year, that is, in 2013, what was your total family income from all sources, before taxes? Just stop me when I get to the right category. [READ] | 1 ⊙ Less than $9,999
2 ⊙ 10,000 to $19,999
3 ⊙ 20,000 to $29,999
4 ⊙ 30,000 to $39,999
5 ⊙ 40,000 to $49,999
6 ⊙ 50,000 to $74,999
7 ⊙ 75,000 to $99,999
8 ⊙ 100,000 to $149,999 [OR]
9 ⊙ 150,000 or more
10 ⊙ [VOL. DO NOT READ] Don't know/Refused |

Income question with mutually exclusive response options that simplify administration

| Last year, that is, in 2013, what was your total family income from all sources, before taxes? Just stop me when I get to the right category. [READ] | 1 ⊙ Less than $10,000
2 ⊙ 10 to under $20,000
3 ⊙ 20 to under $30,000
4 ⊙ 30 to under $40,000
5 ⊙ 40 to under $50,000
6 ⊙ 50 to under $75,000
7 ⊙ 75 to under $100,000
8 ⊙ 100 to under $150,000 [OR]
9 ⊙ $150,000 or more
10 ⊙ [VOL. DO NOT READ] Don't know/Refused |

Our main concern with mutual exclusivity is when it is used for response categories of survey questions where there is considerable likelihood that its presence will go unnoticed. To illustrate this point, we return to Figure 5.5. Another problem with the question in its original form is that the choices include both sources of the news and location. Respondents are supposed to select only one answer, but it is very possible that some heard about the tornado on the radio while traveling to work or on the television while at home. Therefore, in addition to adding missing response options, the revision breaks the one question into two: one about source and the other about location (for more about asking one question at a time see Guideline 4.3).

It may seem from these examples that mutual exclusivity is only an issue in single-answer questions. But drawing the conclusion that mutual exclusivity does not matter in multiple-answer questions would be a mistake. On the contrary, lack of mutual exclusivity in multiple-answer questions can cause significant bias in responses.

The second example from the introduction to this chapter comes from an experiment we conducted in the spring of 2003, in which we administered a student experience survey that contained the following question: "Which of the following resources have you used at Washington State University? Please check all that apply." This was followed by 10 university resources, the group of which was taken from the university's web page (see Figure 5.7). When the response options were

FIGURE 5.7 Subtraction effects in multiple-answer questions.

Which of the following resources have you used at WSU? Please check all that apply.			
	%		%
Original Order	**Endorsing**	**Reverse Order**	**Endorsing**
Libraries	95	Counseling Services	
Computer Labs		Library Instruction	52
Student Health Center		Campus-Sponsored Tutoring	
Academic Advising		Career Services	
Student Recreation Center		Internet/E-Mail Access	
Internet/E-Mail Access		Student Recreation Center	
Career Services		Academic Advising	
Campus-Sponsored Tutoring		Student Health Center	
Library Instruction	20	Computer Labs	
Counseling Services		Libraries	93

Which of the following forages are used during the winter months to feed your cattle? (Check all that apply.)			
	%		%
Original Order	**Endorsing**	**Reorder**	**Endorsing**
Native range	70	Silage	2
Deferred grazing (save pasture for fall and winter)	37	Deferred grazing (save pasture for fall and winter)	48
Hay	84	Winter pasture	36
Silage	1	Native range	30
Winter pasture	29	Hay	79
Other	14	Other	15

Source: Top panel adapted from "The Use of Client Side Paradata in Analyzing the Effects of Visual Layout on Changing Responses in Web Surveys," by M. J. Stern, 2008, *Field Methods, 20*(4), pp. 377–398. Bottom panel adapted from "Can Response Order Bias Evaluations?" by G. D. Israel and C. L. Taylor, 1990, *Evaluation and Program Planning, 13*, pp. 1–7.

presented in their original order, the first option was "libraries" and the ninth option was "library instruction." In this order, 20% of respondents checked that they had used library instruction. When we reversed the order of the options so that "library instruction" appeared in the second position and "libraries" in the 10th, substantially more respondents selected it—about 52%. A similar pattern of results was also found in a forced-choice version of this same question.

When "library instruction" appeared after the broader category of "libraries," many respondents interpreted it narrowly, as a part of the broader set of services offered in the library. Because they had already selected "libraries," they did not need to select "library instruction" unless they had, in fact, used this very specific service. But when "library instruction" appeared first, respondents seemed to interpret it more broadly (i.e., as libraries) and therefore selected it, not realizing that the category "libraries" was going to be an option later in the list.

Additional analyses of computer paradata suggested that some respondents caught their mistake. Respondents who initially checked the first library option they came to were 7 times more likely to go back and uncheck it when they got to the second library option when "library instruction" appeared first than when "libraries" appeared first (Stern, 2008). In this case, having response options that lacked mutual exclusivity drastically altered the results and meant that they more strongly reflected the poor design of the response options than actual use of resources at the university.

A similar type of result was obtained from Florida beef producers in a question about what forages were fed to cattle in winter months (see the bottom panel of Figure 5.7) (Israel & Taylor, 1990). Switching the "native range" option from first to fourth on the list decreased the percentage checking that answer from 70% to only 30%, a 40-percentage-point drop. The options "winter pasture" and "deferred grazing," which were moved to the third and second positions, respectively, were both subject to increased endorsement. The likely reason for this change is that "native range" is such a broad category that, when listed in the first position, respondents who would otherwise have selected "winter pasture" or "deferred grazing" picked it and then mentally subtracted that from the answers they would have otherwise given. By comparison, "silage," which is a distinctively different type of livestock feed from any of the other pasture choices, received the same proportion of endorsements regardless of whether it was in the fourth or first position.

The same fundamental problem underlies both of these examples. University officials knew the difference between libraries and library instruction. Likewise, Florida extension agents knew the difference between native range, deferred grazing, and winter pasture. But in both cases, respondents did not fully understand these distinctions. To the respondents, the response options were not mutually exclusive. Thus, in addition to providing a cautionary tale about mutual exclusivity, these examples illustrate the importance of designing questions to fit the understanding of respondents as well as the understanding of the experts.

Guideline 5.8: Consider What Types of Answer Spaces Are Most Appropriate for the Measurement Intent

One of the important features of closed-ended questions is whether they allow only one answer or multiple answers to be given. In all modes, question wording and possibly extra instructions can be used to try to encourage respondents to give the proper number of responses. This is particularly important in mail surveys, where this is the only cue respondents will get about how to answer.

In contrast, in telephone surveys using the CATI software system, closed-ended questions can be programmed to allow only one or to allow multiple answers. Although interviewers can communicate this information to respondents if they are aware of it, we recommend using the question stem to convey whether one or multiple responses are requested, even in interviewer-administered surveys, to help guide respondents and reduce variation among interviewers. On the web it is also possible to rely on computerization and software to ensure the correct type of responses are given. For example, when only one response is allowed, HTML radio buttons can be provided. With radio buttons, once an option has been selected, selection of another option will replace the first so that only one response can be registered. In contrast, when multiple responses are allowed, HTML check boxes can be used. With this input form, additional selections do not change prior selections so multiple responses can be given.

Web surveys also offer several question formats that are a bit more dynamic or interactive than a series of radio buttons or check boxes. One such format is the visual analog scale, also known as a slider scale (for an example see Figure 5.8). In *visual analog scales* respondents can interactively slide a marker to the position on the scale that best describes their answer. These scales can be designed to emulate an ordinal closed-ended question format, in which respondents can choose from a limited number of points on the scale, or they can be designed to collect interval-level data (e.g., a scale ranging from 0 to 100). The parallel in a paper survey would be placing a mark such as an *X* on a continuum.

In two early studies of visual analog scales on the web, Couper, Tourangeau, Conrad, and Singer (2006) found no differences in the response distributions between visual analog scales and ordinal scales presented horizontally with radio buttons, and Thomas and Couper (2007) found similar validity and self-reported accuracy ratings between visual analog scales and scales presented vertically with radio buttons. Both studies demonstrated that the visual analog scales took longer to complete than the scales with radio buttons. In a more recent study, Funke, Reips, and Thomas (2011) showed that compared to radio button items, slider scale items took longer to complete and produced higher break-off rates.

FIGURE 5.8 Examples of visual analog scale and drop-down menu formats.

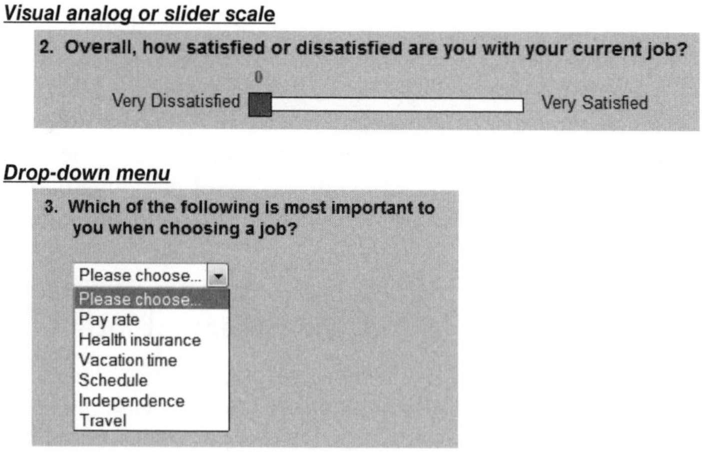

The break-off rates were particularly high for the slider scale version among those with less than a college degree. These types of slider scales can often be quite difficult for those completing a web survey on a mobile device, as the touch input for most smartphones and tablets means respondents can struggle with trying to accurately provide a response.

Another format possible in a web survey (and also in CATI surveys) is a *drop-down menu*. A drop-down menu provides respondents with a list of options from which they select one or sometimes multiple responses. However, respondents cannot view the options until they click on the menu, and then they generally have to scroll to find the answer they want to select, often from long lists of options.

Several studies have experimentally examined the effects of formatting items in the drop-down menu format versus in radio buttons (Couper, Tourangeau, Conrad, & Crawford, 2004; Healey, 2007; Heerwegh & Loosveldt, 2002b). Across these studies, there are mixed results pertaining to which format takes the longest to complete, but none suggest that either format is considerably better in this regard.

However, two additional studies do reveal problems with the drop-down menu format. First, Couper et al. (2004) found that respondents who were provided with a drop-down box with half of the response options immediately visible were more likely to select the visible response options than respondents who had to activate the menu to see any of the options. This finding indicates that it is important to avoid presenting drop-down menus with only some response options visible from the outset. This is especially important for items in which respondents need to see all of the response options in order to formulate a response, as is the case with many attitude and opinion questions. It is less important when respondents know their answer immediately after reading the question stem and without looking at the response options. An example is one's state of residence.

The second important finding is that drop-down menus can be particularly problematic for respondents using a scrolling mouse (Healey, 2007) as they are particularly prone to inadvertently change their answers. This has been confirmed by Gendall and Healey (2008), who found that web survey respondents who were asked to report their age using a drop-down menu were much more likely to err toward older reports (consistent with downward scrolling) while those reporting using an open-ended answer box were more likely to err toward younger reports. This pattern likely emerged because once an item has been selected in a drop-down menu, respondents have to click outside of the drop-down menu to deactivate it before scrolling. Any scrolling while the menu is still activated will change the selection rather than move the screen.

An additional consideration is that drop-down menus can accommodate multiple answers, but respondents have to hold down the Ctrl button (or Apple key) on their keyboard while clicking items with their mouse to register more than one answer. This task is difficult, even for some experienced computer users. On mobile devices, long drop-down menus can be difficult because they require scrolling across multiple screens to find the desired response. Selecting multiple answers is also quite difficult on mobile devices because of the touch input.

Because of these challenges, we recommend avoiding drop-down menus when possible, and especially for multiple-answer questions. We only recommend using drop-down menus in instances where there are too many options to display with radio buttons in one screen, respondents will know their answer before they see the response options, and/or when typing the answer would be slower and more difficult than searching through a long list of items.

Those who decide to use the drop-down format should label the boxes with what type of information is being requested and only make specific items visible once the box is clicked, such as in the example in Figure 5.8. In addition, for items in which respondents will need to consider every response option to formulate their answer, surveyors must ensure that all of the options are visible on the screen at one time (i.e., to avoid making respondents scroll to see some of them), so that all options can be processed equally. As mentioned earlier, this often means only a few options are visible for respondents completing a survey on a mobile device.

Each of these formats has its strengths and weaknesses. What is important is that surveyors understand what formats are available to them and what response behavior is allowed or disallowed by each format. As a general rule, we use the conventional response formats for most questions and only use the more dynamic and interactive features when we are sure they will provide better data without increasing respondent burden too much. This is especially critical for mixed-mode surveys, where response formats such as visual analog scales and drop-down menus may not be available in all modes, and thus their use in one mode, but not another, may introduce measurement error.

GUIDELINES FOR NOMINAL CLOSED-ENDED QUESTIONS

Closed-ended questions with nominal response options can range from fairly easy to quite challenging for respondents to answer, as shown in Figure 5.9. The first question in this figure, for example, is quite simple, as it contains only two options from which to choose. The most common question of this type is the yes/no question (e.g., "Do you own a car, or not?") or the favor/oppose question (e.g., "Do you favor or oppose allowing gays and lesbians to marry legally?"). Choosing from among many categories, however, can be quite complex, as suggested by the second and third questions in Figure 5.9. Responding to either of these questions entails a great deal of effort. Answering the question about the highway bypass requires absorbing considerable detail, identifying differences between the choices, and then selecting the most preferred route. The final question asks respondents to compare eight groups, then seven, then six, and so forth to complete the ranking. In both cases, providing answers necessitates substantially more effort than is usually the case for closed-ended questions with ordered categories. Yet these are precisely the types of questions that can sometimes provide the most useful information to survey sponsors.

Guideline 5.9: Ask Respondents to Rank Only a Few Items at Once Rather Than a Long List

In ranking questions, such as the community problems question in Figure 5.9, each answer choice adds another concept that must be compared with other choices. Ranking questions such as these can be incredibly difficult for respondents to understand and complete correctly. This is especially true in telephone surveys during which they have to remember all the items to be ranked while they compare them and keep track of their ranking. When the community problems question in Figure 5.9 was administered to a random sample of community residents as part

FIGURE 5.9 Examples of closed-ended questions with unordered response options.

Most simple form: Two categories

While growing up did you live mostly on a farm or mostly elsewhere?

❏ Farm
❏ Elsewhere

A more difficult form: Multiple complex categories

If the highway bypass is to be built on one of these routes, which would you most prefer?

❏ A north route that starts west of the city at Exit 21 (Johnson Road) off Highway 30, crosses Division at North 59th Street, and reconnects to Highway 30 three miles east of the city at River Road.
❏ A modified north route that starts further west of the city at Exit 19, crosses Division at 70th Street, and reconnects to Highway 30 three miles east of the city at River Road.
❏ A south route that begins west of the city at Exit 19, crosses Division at South 24th Street, and reconnects to Highway 30 east of the city at River Road.

Another difficult form: The ranking question (Stern, 2006)

Which of these do you believe are the largest and smallest problems facing residents of the Lewiston and Clarkston area? Use "1" for the largest problem, "2" for second largest problem, and so forth until you have completed all eight.

___ Lack of community involvement
___ Taxes are too high
___ Lack of affordable health care
___ Lack of money for local schools
___ Lack of affordable housing
___ Lack of good jobs
___ Too much crime overall
___ Too much drug use

of an experiment in a mail survey, nearly a quarter of them failed to complete it correctly (Stern, 2006). The same question would not have worked at all in a telephone survey.

On paper or on the screen, a question that lists 15 items to be ranked from top to bottom may not look much more difficult than one that has only 6 items to be ranked, but the respondent demand is obviously far greater. If all 15 options need to be presented, then the question might be simplified by asking for a ranking of only the top three. Another alternative is to present respondents with a paired comparison in which they are asked to compare only two options (and thus two concepts) at a time until they have compared each option against each other option. The surveyor can then use the results to form the ranking for each respondent.

As an abbreviated example, let us assume a respondent is given the following comparisons and asked to indicate which item in each pair is the more important problem residents of his community face. The underlined options are those that our hypothetical respondent feels are most important.

Lack of community involvement	<u>Taxes are too high</u>
Taxes are too high	<u>Lack of affordable health care</u>
<u>Lack of affordable health care</u>	Lack of community involvement

We can now use these results to form a list that ranks the importance of these items for this respondent from most to least important:

1. Lack of affordable health care
2. Taxes are too high
3. Lack of community involvement

Sometimes it is also possible to make ranking questions less burdensome through creative use of technology. For example, the items to be ranked in a paper survey might be printed on peel-and-stick labels that the respondent can peel up and place into a ranked order, a method used by Rokeach (1973) to assess 18 competing values. Such a method allows respondents to actually locate each item relative to the others, and as such provides a clearer visual reminder of their ordering as they work through the items. Physically rearranging the items in the desired order makes it much less mentally burdensome for respondents to keep track of their ordering than trying to keep track of a numbering system applied to items that are physically out of order.

Two similar techniques for ranking questions are now being used on the web (see Figure 5.10). One is a drag-and-drop method where respondents use their mouse to move items into a rank order. The second is an arrow method in which respondents click either an up or down arrow next to each individual item in the list to shift its location. A recent web study compared both of these methods to the more traditional method of placing numbers next to static items and found that the arrow and drag-and-drop methods resulted in higher percentages of respondents answering the ranking question completely, but also took longer to complete than the numbering method (Blasius, 2012). The same study also found, however, that respondents were less likely to move items from the very top to the very bottom of the list or vice versa in the arrow method than in the number or drag-and-drop methods, presumably because doing so requires a fairly high number of clicks. The arrow method also took longer to complete than the drag-and-drop method, leading the author to recommend the drag-and-drop method for ranking items in web surveys. However, drag-and-drop methods are particularly difficult for respondents on mobile devices, where the touch input easily allows one to drag the item but makes it much more difficult to drop it in place in the list.

Considerations of whether to employ these technologies should carefully weigh the impact they will have on download times, the likelihood that respondents' computers will be enabled to operate them, and respondents' computer and Internet skill levels.

Ranking questions are often avoided in telephone surveys. However, sometimes one can ask multiple questions and use the responses to create a ranking, at least of the top two or three most important items. This can be done by providing a short list of options (e.g., five to six items) and asking which is the

FIGURE 5.10 Examples of ways to create ranking items in web surveys.

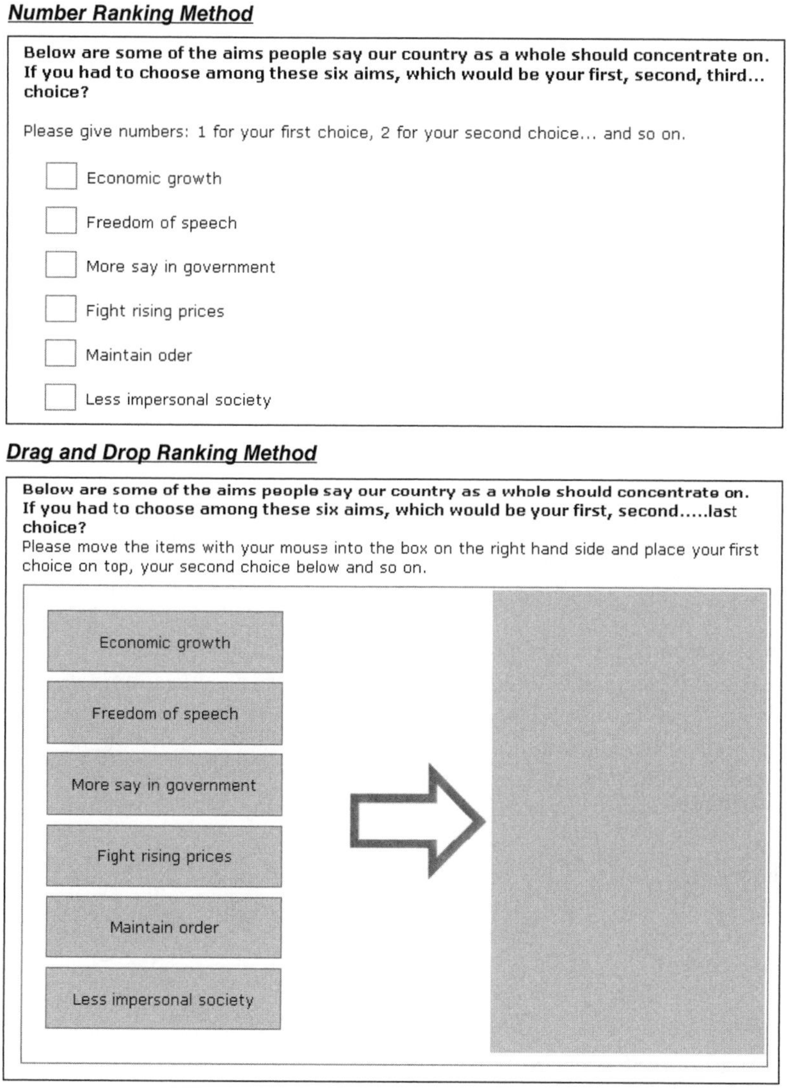

<u>*Number Ranking Method*</u>

Below are some of the aims people say our country as a whole should concentrate on. If you had to choose among these six aims, which would be your first, second, third... choice?

Please give numbers: 1 for your first choice, 2 for your second choice... and so on.

- [ ] Economic growth
- [ ] Freedom of speech
- [ ] More say in government
- [ ] Fight rising prices
- [ ] Maintain oder
- [ ] Less impersonal society

<u>*Drag and Drop Ranking Method*</u>

Below are some of the aims people say our country as a whole should concentrate on. If you had to choose among these six aims, which would be your first, second.....last choice?
Please move the items with your mouse into the box on the right hand side and place your first choice on top, your second choice below and so on.

Economic growth
Freedom of speech
More say in government
Fight rising prices
Maintain order
Less impersonal society

Source: "Comparing Ranking Techniques in Web Surveys," by J. Blasius, 2012, *Field Methods, 24*(4), pp. 382–398. http://fmx.sagepub.com. Copyright © 2012 by The Author. Reprinted by permission of SAGE Publications.

"most important," and then which is the "next most important." For example, a question we asked during the 2012 presidential election was "Which one of the following issues matters most to you in deciding your vote for president this year? Jobs, the budget deficit, health care, Social Security, immigration, or same-sex marriage?" We then followed up with, "And what would be the next most important issue?" after which the options were read again, excluding the response to the first question. This allowed us to create rankings of the top two issues that mattered to each respondent.

FIGURE 5.10 *(Continued)*

Arrow Ranking Method

Below are some of the aims people say our country as a whole should concentrate on. If you had to choose among these six aims, which would be your first, second, third... choice?

Please move the items with the mouse (klick on the arrow signs) and place the first item on top of the list, the second below that, the third below that and so on.

1. Economic growth   [↓]

2. Freedom of speech   [↓] [↑]

3. More say in government   [↓] [↑]

4. Fight rising prices   [↓] [↑]

5. Maintain order   [↓] [↑]

6. Less impersonal society   [↑]

Guideline 5.10: Avoid Bias From Unequal Comparisons

Closed-ended questions with unordered categories can become unbalanced, thus biasing responses. Consider the wording of the question in Figure 5.11, which was designed to find out what respondents think is most responsible for outbreaks of gun violence in schools. The term *irresponsible* places a value connotation on the first category, while *lenient* does so for the last category. Such connotations are not present in the other choices. Although it is unclear whether unbalancing questions in this way leads to more or less frequent selection of such categories (Schuman & Presser, 1981), the credibility of responses to these questions is inevitably open to critique.

The difficulty of revising such questions is that true balance may be extremely difficult to achieve. The first revision uses less emotionally charged words (i.e., "the way children are raised by parents"), but results in a category with many more words than the school and television choices. It also removes "lenient" from the "gun laws" item. The other two categories could be made more specific by mentioning school discipline policies and violent television programs, but it is unclear without extensive pretesting whether that would improve or detract from the balance. The challenge of achieving balance on such closed-ended questions often leads to reducing choices to simple nouns (*parents, schools, television, gun laws*), a solution that also increases the vagueness of the categories. One might, for example, wonder what aspect of television is being referenced: its use in schools, how much television children watch, or the content of the programming. Still another revision that might be considered is to completely restructure the question, converting to a closed-ended ordinal question structure with a detailed concept presented in the stem of the question, so response for each can be directly compared, as shown in the final revision offered in Figure 5.11.

Guideline 5.11: Randomize Response Options If There Is Concern About Order Effects

Sometimes the order in which response options are placed can affect their likelihood of being selected. Two examples of subtraction order effects due to the

FIGURE 5.11 Avoid bias from unequal comparisons.

Unequal comparison

Which of the following do you feel is most responsible for recent outbreaks of gun violence in America's schools?

- ○ Irresponsible parents
- ○ School policies
- ○ Television programs
- ○ Lenient gun laws

A revision with more neutral response options

Which of the following do you feel is most responsible for recent outbreaks of gun violence in America's schools?

- ○ The way children are raised by parents
- ○ School policies
- ○ Television programs
- ○ Gun laws

A simplified revision

Which of the following do you feel is most responsible for recent outbreaks of gun violence in America's schools?

- ○ Parents
- ○ Schools
- ○ Television
- ○ Guns

Still another revision retaining more complex descriptions

To what extent do you feel that the way children are raised by parents is responsible for recent outbreaks of gun violence in America's schools?

- ○ Completely responsible
- ○ Mostly responsible
- ○ Somewhat responsible
- ○ Not at all responsible

And so forth for the remaining concepts

---

content of the options are demonstrated in Figure 5.7. Another potential cause of response category order effects can be memory and cognitive limitations. In self-administered surveys, early response options may be processed more deeply, and thus may be more likely to be selected (i.e., primacy), because respondents' minds become more cluttered as they continue through a list and have more information to keep track of. In interviewer administered surveys, early response options may be forgotten or subject to less deep processing as later response options are read, making them less likely to be selected (i.e., recency) (Schuman & Presser, 1981; Tourangeau, Rips, & Rasinski, 2000). Another potential cause of primacy or recency is lack of motivation. Respondents with low motivation levels or those who have to finish quickly because of some other obligation may choose the first defensible answer they come to rather than the best answer (i.e., they may satisfice) just to get the survey finished (Krosnick, 1991). We discussed primacy and recency effects and satisficing in greater detail in Chapter 4.

A final type of response option order effect is anchoring. This occurs when an early response option forms a standard of comparison for later response options. For example, in one study, respondents were asked, "Which food is more typically German?" with response options of "potatoes" and "rice." When the item potatoes was listed after rice, 48% said it was more German, but when it was listed before rice, only 30% said it was more German (Noelle-Neumann, 1970). Having rice, which is clearly not German, as a standard of comparison made potatoes seem more German.

The dynamism of web and computer-assisted telephone surveys, and now of advanced database and printing technologies for paper surveys, provides surveyors with the ability to randomize response options. For estimates like means and proportions, such randomization will average out the order effects. That is, any effect due to an item being located early in the list for some respondents will presumably be cancelled out by the effects of the same option appearing late in the list for other respondents. Thus, when the end goal is only to produce such estimates, randomization of response option order is one way to reduce bias. However, this type of randomization can affect the relationship between variables (i.e., correlations). Thus, the decision of whether to randomize response option order should be made only after considering how the data will be used.

Guideline 5.12: Use Forced-Choice Questions Instead of Check-All-That-Apply Questions

A multiple-answer question can generally be asked in one of two formats, and traditionally these two formats have been used interchangeably under the assumption that they elicit similar answers. In the check-all-that-apply format, respondents are provided with a list of items and asked to select each one that applies to them. An example is shown in the top panel of Figure 5.12. The check-all format has traditionally been used in paper and web surveys because it is space efficient and easily processed and completed.

The forced-choice format, by comparison, has traditionally been used in interviewer-administered surveys, especially telephone surveys. In this format the respondent is presented with one option and asked to make a judgment about it before moving to the next. An example is shown in the bottom panel of Figure 5.12. The advantage of the forced-choice format for telephone surveys is that it lets the respondent focus memory and cognitive processing efforts on one option at a time.

Although these two question formats have long been used interchangeably, a close look at them reveals that they require a fundamentally different response task. Whereas the check-all format provides respondents with a group of items and asks them to choose those that apply from the group, the forced-choice format requires respondents to make an explicit judgment about each item independently. To satisfy the requirements of a check-all question, a respondent simply has to mark a few of the options, but to satisfy the requirements of a forced-choice question, a respondent has to consider and come to a judgment about every item.

FIGURE 5.12 Replacing check-all-that-apply questions with a forced-choice format.

Check-all-that-apply formatted question

Which of the following items do you have? Please check all that apply.

❏ Desktop computer
❏ Laptop computer
❏ Cell phone
❏ E-reader
❏ Tablet computer
❏ iPod or MP3 player

A revision converting to the forced-choice format

Do you have each of the following items or not?

Yes	No	
○	○	Desktop computer
○	○	Laptop computer
○	○	Cell phone
○	○	E-reader
○	○	Tablet computer
○	○	iPod or MP3 player

Comparisons of these two response formats have provided evidence that they are not as interchangeable as was once assumed and that their differences may trace directly back to the different response tasks that underlie them. In one study, we compared 16 questions in both web and paper surveys and found that the forced-choice format consistently resulted in more options being endorsed (Smyth, Dillman, Christian, & Stern, 2006a).

For example, when university students were asked whether a number of descriptions described their university, respondents to the forced-choice format endorsed an average of 6.6 descriptions compared to only 4.4 among respondents to the check-all format, as shown in Figure 5.13. Further, across all 198 items in these 16 questions on a variety of topics, 61% of the items were marked affirmatively significantly more often when they appeared in the forced-choice format than when they appeared in the check-all format. Not a single item was marked affirmatively significantly more often in the check-all format (see Figure 5.13).

For example, 63% of respondents to the forced-choice format endorsed the description "farm/agriculture school" and 37% endorsed "outdoors oriented"; however, among respondents to the check-all format only 54% endorsed "farm/agriculture school" and 26% endorsed "outdoors oriented." The fourth and fifth examples used at the start of this chapter come from this experiment.

Additional analyses of these experiments revealed that the difference in endorsement across these two formats came from about 66% of respondents to the check-all format. These respondents seemed to be using a satisficing response strategy. They answered relatively quickly and were more likely to select the items appearing in the top half of the list than the bottom, regardless of what those items were (i.e., primacy). In contrast, respondents to the forced-choice format, even those who responded quite quickly, appeared to have processed all of the response options.

FIGURE 5.13 Endorsement outcomes for individual items within check-all and forced-choice experimental comparisons.

	Mean # of Items Selected	% Marked Significantly More Often in That Format
Check-all (paper and web)	4.4	0%
Forced-choice (paper and web)	6.6	61%
Check-all (web)	3.8	0%
Forced-choice (telephone)	4.4	35%
Forced-choice (web)	5.5	0%
Forced-choice (telephone)	5.5	0%

Source: Adapted from "Comparing Check-All and Forced-Choice Formats in Web Surveys," by J. D. Smyth, D. A. Dillman, L. M. Christian, and M. J. Stern, 2006, *Public Opinion Quarterly, 70,* pp. 66–77.

The results are similar with respect to the use of the forced-choice and check-all formats across telephone and web surveys, as shown in Figure 5.13. The mean number of options marked in the check-all format in a web survey was 3.8, compared with an average of 4.4 items in the forced-choice format in a telephone survey. In the telephone forced-choice format, 35% of 54 items were marked affirmatively significantly more often than in the web check-all format. No items were marked significantly more often in the telephone forced-choice format.

Subsequent experimentation has also shown that the forced-choice question format transfers very well across web and telephone modes (Smyth, Dillman, & Christian, 2008). In nine comparisons of the forced-choice format across web and telephone surveys, including 101 items, the mean number of options endorsed was the same (5.5 items for the forced-choice format in web and telephone). Further, only 4% of the items were selected significantly more often in the web mode, and only 6% were selected significantly more often in the telephone mode, figures that are close to what one might expect by chance, given the total number of items being compared (see Figure 5.13).

These results indicate that the forced-choice question format works very well in both telephone and web surveys, and, combined with the evidence that the check-all format is prone to satisficing response strategies, they form the basis for our recommendation to substitute the forced-choice format for the check-all format in most instances. However, in the rare circumstances when the information being asked is very factual and respondents are likely to know their answers without having to read the list of items, it may be advisable to retain the check-all format because it is less burdensome. For example, we would use the check-all format when asking respondents to report their race or the language one speaks at home, with the caveat, of course, that if the race question is to be used for weighting, it should be asked similarly to how it was asked in the comparison data.

GUIDELINES FOR ORDINAL CLOSED-ENDED QUESTIONS

Ordinal questions are one of the most commonly used types of survey questions because they can measure gradations of a variety of opinions, attitudes, behaviors, and attributes. There are two general types of closed-ended ordinal scales—those that offer vague quantifier response options (e.g., very satisfied, somewhat satisfied, etc., or always, often, occasionally, etc.) and those that offer response options using a natural metric (e.g., once, twice, three times, etc., or none, 1 to 5 hours, 6 to 10 hours, etc.).

The problem with vague quantifiers is that they are vague; that is, there is not a single and clear meaning for each of the labels in the same way there is with natural metrics. As a result, they are sometimes used inconsistently across question topics and across individual respondents (Bradburn & Miles, 1979). For example, having gone on three vacations in a year might constitute vacationing "often" while having gone grocery shopping 26 times in a year would not constitute "often." In this case, "often" means something very different depending on the topic of the question.

It is also possible that "often" could mean something very different depending on the frequency with which individual people engage in behaviors. For example, grocery shopping once every 2 weeks might constitute "often" for someone who has to make a special 2-hour-long trip to do it, but not for someone who drives past several grocery stores on her way home from work every day or for someone who works at a grocery store.

There is some amount of error that is inherent in questions using vague quantifiers. Yet despite this, they are still commonly used because they greatly reduce the burden on respondents. It is incredibly difficult for respondents to precisely quantify attitudes, opinions, subjective states, and behaviors as well as events that happen very frequently. Rating these types of items using scales with vague quantifiers is much easier for respondents, and may even result in less error than one would get from asking respondents to be more precise than they possibly can be. The reality is that it may be impossible to get precise measures of some constructs, and using vague quantifiers may be the best we can do.

That does not mean, however, that we cannot minimize the error as much as possible in these questions. Guidelines 5.13 through 5.21 discuss ways to design these questions in ways that minimize error. We then turn to guidelines for items that use a natural metric.

Guideline 5.13: Choose Between a Unipolar or a Bipolar Scale

Unipolar ordinal scales measure gradation along one dimension where the zero point falls at one end of the scale (e.g., *very successful* to *not at all successful*—see Figure 5.14). By comparison, *bipolar* ordinal scales measure gradation along two opposite dimensions, with the zero point falling in the middle of the scale, or where it tips from positive to negative (e.g., *very satisfied* to *very dissatisfied* or *very likely* to *very unlikely*—see Figure 5.14). In other words, bipolar scales measure both direction (i.e., positive or negative) and the level or magnitude (i.e., *how* positive or how negative) of opinions.

The decision of whether to use a bipolar or unipolar scale largely depends on the underlying construct that is being measured. Some constructs naturally start at zero and increase in value from there. For example, if we ask someone how often he goes grocery shopping, it makes conceptual sense to have the lowest frequency label be "never" and to increase from there. Negative frequencies are nonsensical in this instance. Thus, a unipolar scale would be necessary for this item. For other constructs, it may be more appropriate to include both the negative and positive side of the scale.

FIGURE 5.14 Examples of unipolar and bipolar scales.

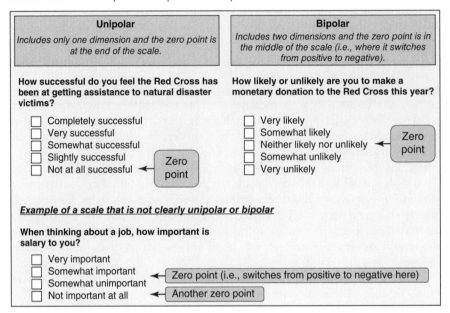

And often many types of questions are asked both ways. For example, we frequently see people measure satisfaction with a unipolar scale (e.g., completely satisfied, mostly satisfied, somewhat satisfied, not too satisfied, not at all satisfied), and we also see surveyors frequently use a bipolar scale (e.g., very satisfied, somewhat satisfied, somewhat dissatisfied, and very dissatisfied). We sometimes prefer a unipolar scale for measuring concepts like satisfaction to ensure that the categories are spread far enough apart and do not overlap. For example, it may be difficult to distinguish between "somewhat satisfied" and "somewhat dissatisfied" in the bipolar scale.

The response scale in the question in the bottom half of Figure 5.14 is not clearly unipolar or bipolar. As the figure shows, there are two zero points, one where the scale tips from "important" to "unimportant" (between the second and third categories) and another at the end of the scale (the "not at all important" option). Mixing unipolar and bipolar scales in this way is problematic because it interrupts the ordinality of the scale. In the unipolar scale in the top of Figure 5.14, each scale point is more successful than all of the points below it and less successful than all of the points above it. For example, "somewhat successful" is more successful than both "not at all" and "slightly," and less successful than "very" and "completely." The same cannot be said for the scale in the bottom of Figure 5.14. To avoid problems such as this, it is important to use a purely unipolar or purely bipolar scale and not to mix them as is done in this example.

Guideline 5.14: Choose an Appropriate Scale Length—In General, Limit Scales to Four or Five Categories

Ordinal scales can measure as few as 2 points and as many as 10 or even 100 points. The challenge in choosing an appropriate scale length is to provide enough categories that respondents will be able to place themselves on the scale but not so many that the categories begin to lose their meaning or become ambiguous. Offering too few scale points results in more respondents skipping the item or marking two adjacent answers because their true answer falls between them; offering too many scale points results in clustering of responses around certain points, such as around the 0 categories (i.e., 20, 50, 80, etc.) on a 100-point scale.

In addition, respondents can only hold a limited number of categories in their head at once, so offering fewer categories can help reduce the cognitive complexity involved in providing a response, especially over the telephone. In other words, one must provide a scale that is long enough to represent the entire continuum of possible answers, but without so many categories that they begin to burden respondents or that the difference between any two categories becomes so small as to be practically meaningless.

For bipolar scales, which measure both the direction (e.g., satisfied or dissatisfied) and the intensity (e.g., very, somewhat) of the construct, the optimal number of response categories seems to be from five to seven, which allows for two or three levels of differentiation on either side of the middle or neutral category. For unipolar scales, which measure different levels or gradations (e.g., very, somewhat, not too, not at all) but not direction, optimal scale length is four or sometimes five categories. Scales of these lengths have been shown to be more reliable and valid (more scale points yield only modest gains in reliability and validity) as well as to provide meaningful distinctions for analysis (i.e., differentiation of the construct) (Krosnick & Fabrigar, 1997). Figure 5.15 shows examples of 5- and 7-point bipolar scales and 4- and 5-point unipolar scales.

In some cases, it is advisable to reduce the number of scale points that are used in order to reduce respondents' cognitive burden. For example, telephone respondents may have difficulty remembering seven scale points, especially if they are labeled in complex ways. Interviewers also have difficulty reading all of the categories without stumbling over words and adding considerable length to the interview, especially when multiple questions with many scale points are asked.

FIGURE 5.15 Types of scalar questions and scale lengths.

A 5-point bipolar scale	*A 7-point bipolar scale*
How likely or unlikely are you to make a monetary donation to the Red Cross this year?	**How likely or unlikely are you to become a Red Cross volunteer this year?**
○ Very likely ○ Somewhat likely ○ Neither likely nor unlikely ○ Somewhat unlikely ○ Very unlikely	○ Very likely ○ Somewhat likely ○ Slightly likely ○ Neither likely nor unlikely ○ Slightly unlikely ○ Somewhat unlikely ○ Very unlikely
A 4-point unipolar scale	*A 5-point unipolar scale*
How important do you feel it is to volunteer your time with organizations like the Red Cross?	**How successful do you feel the Red Cross has been at getting assistance to natural disaster victims?**
○ Very important ○ Somewhat important ○ Slightly important ○ Not at all important	○ Completely successful ○ Very successful ○ Somewhat successful ○ Slightly successful ○ Not at all successful

In this case, it may be advisable to reduce the scale to five or even fewer points as we have suggested.

A common question for those using bipolar scales is whether they should include an explicit midpoint such as a "neutral" or "neither/nor" midpoint as is done in Figure 5.15. Note that this type of midpoint is different from an undecided or "don't know" response; nonsubstantive responses should not be used as a midpoint, but should be placed at the end of the scale (for example see Willits & Janota, 1996). Those in favor of offering midpoints argue that some respondents may really be neutral and thus need this point. Without it, they will have to either select an inaccurate response option or skip the question. However, others argue that the midpoint can be an easy out for those who do not want to do the mental work to provide a response or for those who have a true opinion, but want to appear neutral in their presentation of self (Krosnick & Fabrigar, 1997). In interviewer administered surveys, respondents are more likely to select a midpoint when it is explicitly offered than when they have to volunteer it (Schuman & Presser, 1981). However, while many people agonize over the decision of whether or not to offer a midpoint, the literature suggests whether one offers a midpoint has little effect on the resulting data quality and conclusions drawn from the data (Andrews, 1984; Krosnick & Fabrigar, 1997; Schuman & Presser, 1981).

We are also often asked whether to present the positive or negative end of the scale first. Tourangeau, Couper, and Conrad (2004) suggested that most respondents expect the most positive category to be presented first ("up means good" heuristic). However, recent research showed that there were no differences in responses in a web survey when all of the scales were presented with the most positive category or the most negative category first (Christian, Parsons, & Dillman, 2009), but respondents answered the question more quickly when the positive category was presented first. There are two possible reasons people answer more quickly when the positive answer is listed on top. The first is that this arrangement is consistent with the expectation that the positive category should be at the top of the list. The second is that ordinal questions are often written such that most respondents will have a positive answer (i.e., the responses to many ordinal scale questions tend to be positively skewed). As a result, most respondents will find their answer more quickly when the positive end of the scale is presented first.

Whether the positive or negative end of the scale is presented first seems like a fairly minor concern to us. What is more important is ensuring that the scales are presented in a consistent direction across questions throughout the entire survey. We have seen examples where the direction of the scale was switched in the middle of a survey (intentionally and unintentionally) after respondents had come to expect them to always start with the positive or negative end of the scale first. When this happens, many respondents fail to notice the change and therefore select the wrong response option. These types of errors occur because respondents do not expect survey designers to make such illogical changes in the design, not necessarily because they are being lazy respondents (Israel, 2013; Schwarz, 1996).

Guideline 5.15: Choose Direct or Construct-Specific Labels to Improve Cognition

Oftentimes surveyors pose a question in a way that does not match the response scale, so that respondents have to convert their responses from how they were asked in the question stem to fit the categories offered in the scale. The first

FIGURE 5.16   Use construct-specific scales whenever possible.

Questions with multiple constructs	*Construct-specific questions*
Construct of interest: accessibility of instructors	

To what extent do you agree or disagree that your instructors are accessible outside of class?

- ○ Strongly agree
- ○ Agree
- ○ Neutral
- ○ Disagree
- ○ Strongly disagree

How accessible or inaccessible are your instructors outside of class?

- ○ Very accessible
- ○ Somewhat accessible
- ○ Neutral
- ○ Somewhat inaccessible
- ○ Very inaccessible

Construct of interest: perceived durability of mountain bike

How satisfied are you with the durability of the mountain bike you purchased?

- ○ Very satisfied
- ○ Somewhat satisfied
- ○ Neither satisfied nor dissatisfied
- ○ Somewhat dissatisfied
- ○ Strongly dissatisfied

How would you rate the durability of the mountain bike you purchased?

- ○ Very high
- ○ Somewhat high
- ○ Average
- ○ Somewhat low
- ○ Very low

example in Figure 5.16 shows two ways of attempting to measure the accessibility of students' instructors outside of class. Putting this question in the agree/disagree framework requires respondents to process an extra concept because they first have to decide how accessible their instructors are and then convert that judgment into a different concept (i.e., how much they agree or disagree). In the revised construct-specific measurement, the question stem and response options both focus directly on the construct of interest, thus directly measuring levels of accessibility/inaccessibility and easing the response task. Another poor example of the use of an agree/disagree format is "To what extent do you agree or disagree that you enjoyed the movie?" It is much easier to answer this question when it is phrased more directly: "How much, if at all, did you enjoy the movie?"

Many surveyors default to the agree/disagree format as shown in Figure 5.16 for multiple items because it allows them to save space in a questionnaire by only introducing the scale once and/or arranging the items in a grid rather than providing them as individual, stand-alone items. Others use the agree/disagree format out of habit, because it is a widely used and familiar scale in the field (i.e., a strong tradition), or because they are borrowing an established battery of items that use this scale.

However, research has also shown that construct-specific scales reduce acquiescence response bias and cognitive burden relative to agree/disagree scales, making it easier for respondents to map their judgment to the response options in the reporting stage of the response process, and resulting in less measurement error (i.e., higher reliability and validity) (Saris, Revilla, Krosnick, & Schaeffer, 2010). In addition, the agree/disagree scale itself has been shown to increase acquiescence

(Schuman & Presser, 1981). As a result, we specifically recommend against using the agree/disagree scale, and we strongly advocate the use of construct-specific scales in place of any more generic scale like agree/disagree or satisfied/dissatisfied (when agreement or satisfaction are not the key construct of interest).

Writing a construct-specific question requires one to very clearly define the construct of interest and its dimensions. We offer one more example in Figure 5.16 to help surveyors think about using construct-specific scales. In the second example, the first version focuses on satisfaction/dissatisfaction with the durability of a mountain bike, whereas the construct-specific version goes directly to the concept of interest—the durability of the bike—and eliminates the satisfied/dissatisfied concepts.

Again, the difficulty with identifying construct-specific measurements is determining which construct one is actually trying to measure. In the mountain bike example, if the surveyor wants to know how durable a recently purchased bike is, the proper question to ask is the construct-specific one in Figure 5.16. Other research goals may dictate the use of other types of questions and response options. For example, one might elect to use the satisfied/dissatisfied question if the goal were to determine how much durability (as pre-rated at the bike shop) is required to satisfy customers.

Guideline 5.16: If There Is a Natural Metric (e.g., Frequencies, Amounts, Sizes, etc.), Use It Instead of Vague Quantifiers

In many cases, numbers are less open to interpretation and therefore more reliable than vague quantifiers. For example, imagine asking someone, "Do you attend religious services regularly, occasionally, rarely, or never?" Some respondents might interpret "regularly" to mean attendance at least weekly. Others might think that attending on major religious holidays year after year is regular, even if they do not generally attend outside of these holidays. Rather than vague quantifiers like these, a more concrete time metric should be used. For example, we could ask how often one attends religious services and provide categories such as "never," "a few times per year," "about once a month," "two to three times a month," "about once a week," and "more than once a week." Alternatively, we could be even more concrete and ask how many times they attended religious services in the past 30 days. For this question we could provide response options (e.g., 0, 1, 2, 3, ... 10 or more) or we could simply provide a number box to collect open-ended reports.

While using natural metrics in place of vague quantifiers is recommended when possible, one should also be aware of some of the challenges that can arise. For example, when respondents are asked to report numbers such as frequencies, dollar amounts, or number of days, we tend to see reference point effects in the data. This occurs because some numbers come to mind more easily than others, making them more likely to be reported. For example, on a scale of 1 to 100, numbers like 25, 50, 75, and 100 are likely to come to mind easily.

Another instance when we might expect to see reference point effects is when asking for the value of big ticket items like cars and houses. Round amounts like $15,000, $20,000, $25,000, and so on are what most people will associate with prices of cars and amounts like $200,000, $250,000, $300,000, and so forth are what most people associate with home prices. Of course the actual values that occur to respondents will depend strongly on the market in the area being surveyed, but the bigger point stands: Round numbers often serve as reference points in these instances, and therefore come to mind more easily and are more likely to be reported. A final type of reference point effect occurs when asking about time. In these instances, expect to see more reports that follow calendar prototypes like multiples of 7 or 30 days (a week and a month respectively).

Guideline 5.17: Provide Balanced Scales Where Categories Are Relatively Equal Distances Apart Conceptually

Another important element in choosing category labels is ensuring that all of the verbal labels are relatively equal distances apart conceptually. In addition, it is important to provide balanced bipolar scales. This means that there are an equal number of positive and negative categories and the positive half of the scale is labeled symmetrically to the negative half of the scale.

Consider, for example, the question about the quality of retail shops available in the upper left side in Figure 5.17. The scale provided with this question is unbalanced, such that three categories are positive ("excellent," "very good," and "good"), one is about average ("fair"), and only one is negative ("poor"). In addition, the conceptual distance between "excellent" and "very good" is much smaller than the distance between "fair" and "poor." The revision in the right side in Figure 5.17 provides two positive and two negative categories on each side of the average, or middle, category, making it a more balanced scale. It also has equal distances between all of the categories on the scale.

In fact, we found that respondents provided different answers to this question depending on the scale that was provided. The percent saying the quality of retail shops available was "good" or better was 37% for the unbalanced version

FIGURE 5.17 Provide balanced scales with categories that are evenly spaced conceptually.

Unbalanced scales with uneven distance between categories	*Balanced scales with more even distance between categories*
How would you rate the quality of retail shops available to you in the Pullman/Moscow area?	**How would you rate the quality of retail shops available to you in the Pullman/Moscow area?**
○ Excellent ○ Very good ○ Good ○ Fair ○ Poor	○ Very good ○ Good ○ Fair ○ Poor ○ Very poor
What do you think we should do about the country's defense budget?	**What do you think we should do about the country's defense budget?**
○ Increase it ○ Keep it the same ○ Decrease it a little ○ Decrease it some ○ Decrease it a lot	○ Increase it a lot ○ Increase it a little ○ Keep it the same ○ Decrease it a little ○ Decrease it a lot

(combining responses to "excellent," "very good," and "good"), compared with 23% for the balanced version (combining responses to "excellent" and "good") (Dillman & Christian, 2003). For another question using a similar scale, the pattern was similar, with more providing positive ratings to the unbalanced than balanced version (80 vs. 67% saying "good" or better). Thus, providing more positive than negative categories results in more overall positive ratings than when an equal number of positive and negative categories are provided.

In the second example in Figure 5.17, which asks about the defense budget, the scale on the left is unbalanced with one positive category and three negative categories. The revision on the right is balanced with two positive and two negative categories, and the conceptual distance between the categories is more equal in this revision. As an added consideration, providing relatively equally spaced categories is a prerequisite for treating scalar results as interval-level variables (i.e., assign a 1 to *strongly oppose*, 2 to *somewhat oppose*, a 3 to *neither*, etc.) in data analyses.

Guideline 5.18: Verbally Label All Categories

The ordinal scales we have discussed up to this point are all fully labeled and have verbal labels for each response category (see first question in Figure 5.18). However, telephone surveyors often shorten scales by having respondents report a number that corresponds to their answer and verbally labeling only the endpoints or positive and negative categories of the scale, particularly for longer scales

FIGURE 5.18   Fully labeled and polar-point labeled scales.

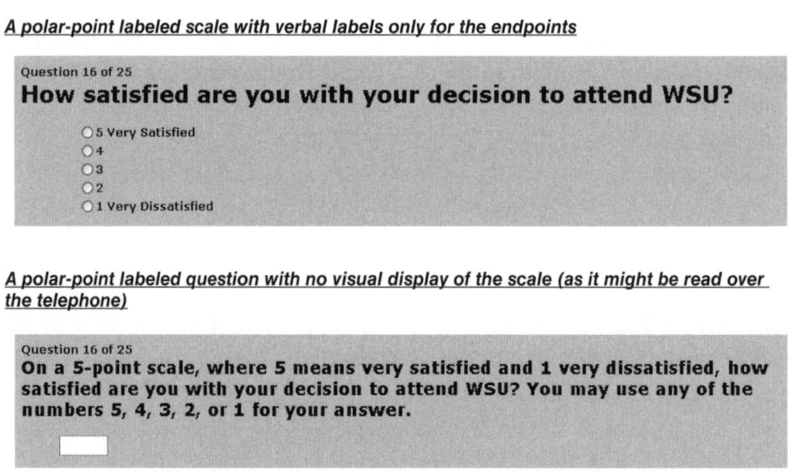

A fully labeled scale with verbal labels for all of the categories

Question 16 of 25
How satisfied are you with your decision to attend WSU?

○ Very Satisfied
○ Somewhat Satisfied
○ Neutral
○ Somewhat Dissatisfied
○ Very Dissatisfied

A polar-point labeled scale with verbal labels only for the endpoints

Question 16 of 25
How satisfied are you with your decision to attend WSU?

○ 5 Very Satisfied
○ 4
○ 3
○ 2
○ 1 Very Dissatisfied

A polar-point labeled question with no visual display of the scale (as it might be read over the telephone)

Question 16 of 25
On a 5-point scale, where 5 means very satisfied and 1 very dissatisfied, how satisfied are you with your decision to attend WSU? You may use any of the numbers 5, 4, 3, 2, or 1 for your answer.

Source: The Influence of Visual Layout on Scalar Questions in Web Surveys, by L. M. Christian, 2003. Unpublished master's thesis, Washington State University, Pullman, WA.

(as shown in the third revision in Figure 5.18). Polar-point scales are easier for interviewers to administer over the telephone, and some surveyors argue that a numeric range is easier for respondents to hold in their memory than a full set of verbal category labels.

However, one difficulty with polar-point labeled scales is that the meaning of the unlabeled categories is open to respondents' interpretation, and different respondents can interpret the middle categories differently, often increasing measurement error. In contrast, verbally labeling each category on the scale gives the surveyor more control over how the points are interpreted, and helps ensure that respondents interpret them similarly. In addition, when all the points are labeled, each category is given the same verbal and visual weight so no one category stands out more or less compared to the other categories. Lastly, because few people hold or express their opinions in numerical terms, numbers can be removed from fully labeled scales to eliminate the extra processing step of converting opinions to numeric terms. For these reasons, surveyors tend to prefer fully labeled scales, and these can be used effectively in all survey modes for most scales containing five or fewer categories (see Guideline 5.14 about scale length).

In addition, fully labeled scales rate higher on reliability, validity, and respondent preference, and they are less susceptible to context effects (Krosnick & Fabrigar, 1997). In fact, a recent eye-tracking study revealed that fully labeled scales have higher reliability than polar-point labeled scales, even though respondents to fully labeled scales do not read the labels for all of the scale points (Menold, Kaczmirek, Lenzner, & Neusar, 2013). The information that is provided in the verbal labels of scale points other than the end point seems to help respondents understand the scale, even if they do not read all of the labels. Polar-point scales provide less information to help respondents fully understand the scale.

Previous research has shown that fully labeled scales elicit more positive ratings than polar-point scales in mail, web, and telephone surveys (Christian, 2003; Christian & Dillman, 2004; Christian, Dillman, & Smyth, 2008; Dillman & Christian, 2005). This is illustrated by the first example at the start of this chapter, in which we found widely varying estimates in the percentage of students who are very satisfied with their university. When we ask the question in a fully labeled format, 55% report being "very satisfied" and 38% "somewhat satisfied"; when we ask it in a polar-point format, only 28% report being "very satisfied" but 57% report being "somewhat satisfied." Because fully labeled scales elicit more positive ratings, we suggest using caution when switching between the fully labeled and polar-point labeled scales, either within a questionnaire or between questionnaires where data will be combined or compared. It is important for surveyors to be consistent in how scales are formatted, particularly when comparing their responses to those from other surveys.

In self-administered surveys, visually displaying the response categories can help respondents more easily understand the overall layout of the scale. Removing the visual display, as in the third question in Figure 5.18, can make the question more difficult for respondents, as they first have to think whether they are satisfied or dissatisfied, and they then have to figure out what number best corresponds to how satisfied or dissatisfied they are. Moreover, research has shown that in response to scales with no visual display, respondents have trouble determining which end of the scale is positive and which end is negative, have difficulty matching a number to a category label, and take more time to respond (Christian

& Dillman, 2004; Christian, Parsons, et al., 2009; Dillman & Christian, 2005). However, this question stem most closely approximates the stimulus that telephone respondents receive when asked polar-point questions. For these reasons, we think it is easier for respondents when scales are fully labeled so each category can be read or presented to them.

Guideline 5.19: Remove Numeric Labels From Vague Quantifier Scales Whenever Possible

Another tendency that some people have when creating scales is to provide numeric labels, either in addition to the verbal labels or instead of some of the verbal labels, as discussed in the previous guideline. Numbers are often used to reinforce to respondents that the categories are intended to be equal distances apart.

Unless there is a specific and intentional purpose behind including the numbers, we recommend against this practice, as the numbers are simply one more piece of information respondents must attempt to make sense of, and doing so adds significantly to response time (Christian, Parsons, et al., 2009). Respondents who are following the norms of conversation will expect each contribution made by the researcher to be unique and relevant (Schwarz, 1996). Thus, they will try to make sense of the numeric labels provided with scales in addition to the verbal labels. If a survey designer is unaware of what the numbers mean, chances are respondents will also be confused by them or, worse yet, will attribute unintended meaning to them that will affect responses, thus negatively impacting how well the question performs.

If numeric labels are provided, the effects on respondents' answers need to be evaluated carefully, as numbers can be powerful sources of information respondents draw upon when responding to ordinal scale questions. One of the best examples of how including numbers can affect measurement comes from studies on the use of only positive versus positive and negative numbers to anchor a scale. In one study, respondents were asked to rate their success in life so far on a scale ranging from "extremely successful" to "not at all successful." Of respondents who were presented with a scale ranging from 0 to 10 on a show card, 34% rated themselves between 0 and 5 (Schwarz, Knäuper, Hippler, Noelle-Neumann, & Clark, 1991). When presented with the scale ranging from −5 to 5, only 13% rated themselves in the comparable categories of −5 to 0.

Further study revealed that respondents interpreted the label "not at all successful" to mean the absence of success when it was accompanied by a 0, but to mean the presence of explicit failure when it was accompanied by −5. The decidedly negative connotation of "explicit failure" seemed to push people higher up the scale. Thus, the numbers selected to anchor this scale entirely changed the way the scale labels, and thereby the entire scale range, were interpreted (and whether the scale was interpreted as a unipolar vs. bipolar scale). Tourangeau, Couper, and Conrad (2007) confirmed this effect in web surveys, but found that the effect of the numbers was reduced when all of the categories were verbally labeled.

In attitude scales, respondents also expect the highest numbers to be associated with the most positive ratings. Research has shown that contradicting this expectation by associating high numbers with negative ratings does not necessarily, in and of itself, have negative effects (Christian, Parsons, et al., 2009). Respondents usually figure out what happened and their answers are not affected, unless they are being asked to provide a numeric response by entering it into an open-ended space or number box (Christian & Dillman, 2004), or to an interviewer. However, any numbering needs to be done consistently across questions. Switching the way the numbers are assigned within a questionnaire will affect responses, as some respondents will miss the fact that a switch was made and continue to answer as if the direction had not changed.

Guideline 5.20: Consider Branching (or Decomposing) Bipolar Scales to Ease Respondent Burden and Improve Data Quality

Consider the question "Overall, how satisfied or dissatisfied are you with the car you purchased? Very satisfied, somewhat satisfied, slightly satisfied, neutral, slightly dissatisfied, somewhat dissatisfied, or very dissatisfied." To answer a question using a bipolar ordinal scale like this, respondents have to figure out two things: (1) the direction of their assessment (i.e., satisfied, dissatisfied, or neutral) and (2) the intensity of their assessment (i.e., slightly, somewhat, or very satisfied or dissatisfied). One way to ease the cognitive burden of answering this type of item is to decompose it into two questions, one that asks for the direction of the assessment (i.e., Overall, are you satisfied or dissatisfied with the car you purchased, or are you neutral?), and a second that asks for an intensity rating (i.e., Would you say you are slightly, somewhat, or very [satisfied/dissatisfied]?). In fact, research has shown that branching bipolar scalar questions in this manner increases reliability and validity and that respondents can answer the two decomposed questions more quickly than the single unbranched question (Krosnick & Berent, 1993; Malhotra, Krosnick & Thomas, 2009). The research also shows that it is not necessary to ask those initially selecting a neutral category which direction they are leaning; rather, those who initially select the middle category truly seem to belong there (Malhotra et al., 2009).

While this research would seem to suggest that branching is a desirable practice, there are several instances in which we would urge caution in employing it. The first is in paper surveys because asking the proper follow-up question requires the use of skip instructions, which are difficult for many respondents to follow (we return to this topic in Chapter 6). If there is no computerization to automate the process, branching should probably be avoided. We also advise caution in using the branching technique when final data will be combined or compared with other data collected where branching was not used. This might happen, for example, in mixed-mode surveys or when tracking trends. Because branching yields different distributions, combining data from branched and unbranched scales is problematic, as is comparing data collected via these two means of measurement (Christian, 2007).

Guideline 5.21: Provide Scales That Approximate the Actual Distribution of the Characteristic in the Population, or Ask the Question in an Open-Ended Format to Avoid Biasing Responses

Many respondents use the response scale as a guide to help them formulate their answer. As a result, the values included in the response scale can bias reports. Such was the case in the third example at the opening of this chapter, in which

FIGURE 5.19   Percentage of students reporting studying 2.5 hours or less and more than 2.5 hours, for three different question formats.

	Low Scale	High Scale	Answer Box
Up to 2½ hours	½ hour or less From ½ to 1 hour From 1 to 1½ hours From 1½ to 2 hours From 2 to 2½ hours	2½ hours or less	
Over 2½ hours	More than 2½ hours	From 2½ to 3 hours From 3 to 3½ hours From 3½ to 4 hours From 4 to 4½ hours More than 4½ hours	

Percent who report studying up to and over 2½ hours by each response format			
Up to 2½ hours	70%	29%	42%
Over 2½ hours	30%	71%	58%

Source: Adapted from "Context Effects in Web Surveys: New Issues and Evidence," by J. D. Smyth, D. A. Dillman, and L. M. Christian, 2007a, in A. Joinson, K. McKenna, T. Postmes, and U. Reips (Eds.), *The Oxford Handbook of Internet Psychology* (pp. 427–443), New York, NY: Oxford University Press.

we obtained conflicting estimates about what percentage of students study over 2.5 hours per day (Smyth, Dillman, & Christian, 2007a). We obtained these widely varying estimates because we provided three different sets of response options with the question: a low scale, a high scale, and an open-ended format, as shown in Figure 5.19. Technically, all three ways of asking the question could accommodate students studying anywhere from 0 to 24 hours, but the low and high scales emphasized different, slightly overlapping portions within that range, whereas the open-ended version did not emphasize any of the range. When we used the low scale, fewer students (30%) reported studying over 2.5 hours per day; when we used the high scale, more students (71%) did so. The open-ended version produced the more moderate estimate of 58% studying over 2.5 hours per day.

Why did the different scales have such a large effect? If respondents use only the words in the question stem and the category numbers to interpret the meaning of the question, the answers across these three versions of the question should be the same. Because the answers vary widely, it is apparent that respondents are drawing extra information from the response categories and using that information to help formulate their answers. In other words, respondents are using information well beyond the numbers that are provided to define the parameters of each response option.

For many students, exactly how many hours per day they study is not something they can recall in the same way that they can recall whether they live in a student dormitory or own a car. As a result, they have to estimate how many hours per day they study, and doing so probably requires them to average across days during the week and on weekends, and possibly even across times of year (i.e., a normal day vs. a day during the week of final exams). When respondents have to do this type of mental work to formulate their answers, they often look to the question and its accompanying response options for clues.

When asked how many hours per day they study, respondents might assume that the range emphasized by the scale represents how many hours most students study. As a result, someone who gets the low scale might conclude that *most* students study between 0.5 and 2.5 hours, whereas someone who gets the high scale might conclude that most students study between 2.5 and 4.5 hours. Another assumption that respondents may make is that the middle option(s) represents the amount that the *average* student studies; thus, those who receive the low scale might assume that the average student studies between 1 and 2 hours, but those who receive the high scale would assume that the average student studies from 3 to 4 hours. Rather than actually counting the hours they study, respondents can instead decide whether they study more, the same, or less than most typical students. In this type of estimating, different assumptions made based on the scale range and midpoint are bound to influence answers.

The scale range might also bias responses if it affects how respondents define a vague concept. For example, surveyors commonly ask frequency questions about things like experiencing anger or going shopping. Both of these are rather vague concepts. There are many degrees of anger ranging from minor to severe, and there are many types of behaviors that might be considered shopping (e.g., visiting the mall to purchase a new outfit, grocery shopping, online purchases, or just picking up a packet of peanuts in the convenience store while gassing up the car). For questions like these, respondents have to determine what counts; that is, what is the threshold for considering a negative emotion to be anger, and what types of purchases are considered shopping. A low scale range might suggest a high threshold (i.e., only severe anger counts; only department store or mall purchases count) while a high scale range might suggest a lower threshold (i.e., even minor anger instances count; every purchase counts). In this case, the scale range will affect how respondents comprehend the construct of interest, which then influences what instances they retrieve and count in the response process.

One thing all three of these examples have in common is that they refer to activities that people frequently engage in and that are often mundane (studying, shopping, and to a lesser degree experiencing anger). When we are asking about frequent and mundane activities, it is more difficult for respondents to recall and count individual occurrences, making them more likely to turn to estimation response strategies (Tourangeau et al., 2000). Thus, we expect more scale range effects for these types of items. In contrast, respondents will more easily be able to recall and count rare and memorable events (e.g., car accidents, childbirths, etc.), making scale range effects less of a problem on these items. Thus, especially when asking about frequent or mundane occurrences, it is important to provide category ranges that approximate the expected distribution of the characteristic of interest. When we do not know the distribution of a characteristic—often determining this information is the purpose of the survey in the first place—it is best to ask the question in an open-ended format to avoid the risk of providing a scale that biases responses.

The Challenges of Writing Ordinal Closed-Ended Questions

When writing ordinal questions, several decisions need to be brought together to design a question that best measures the attitude, opinion, or behavior of interest. What may seem like a simple opinion question (e.g., "How satisfied are you with the community in which you live?") actually involves thinking through a series of details about how this question should be asked. Research presented here overwhelmingly demonstrates that one must choose the response categories carefully and that respondents gain meaning from the overall distribution of the scale.

Therefore, designing good ordinal questions requires thinking about each component of the question, and about how the response options work together to form a scale. In Guidelines 5.13 to 5.21, we presented best practices for constructing ordinal closed-ended questions. Here, we summarize those guidelines in a checklist that may be helpful as you review your questionnaires to ensure that ordinal scales are constructed in the best way to measure the concept of interest:

- Will a unipolar or bipolar scale be used?
- Does the scale only include four or five categories? If more are used, is there a justification for it?
- Do the question stem and response categories match? Are construct-specific response categories used?
- Is there a natural metric underlying the scale that can be used for the response categories?
- Are the positive and negative ends of the scale equally balanced?
- Are all the categories verbally labeled? If not, is there a justification for using a polar-point or other type of scale construction?
- Are numeric labels included? If so, are they needed, or can they easily be removed?
- Is the question too complex? Should a branching or multiple-step format be used?
- Will the response options bias the responses? Should an open-ended question be used instead?

Nearly all surveys include several ordinal scale questions; thus, it is important to ensure that these questions are designed effectively to measure the concept of interest and that they are designed in a way that minimizes respondent burden.

CONCLUSION

Although crafting survey questions may seem simple, in this chapter we have demonstrated how this task requires attending to many details at once to help ensure that respondents process all of the component parts and comprehend the question as intended so that they can report an accurate answer. As the examples at the start of the chapter and throughout the guidelines illustrate, many of the decisions about how to design survey questions may seem inconsequential, but these decisions can have substantial impacts on how respondents answer survey questions, and therefore on the conclusions ultimately drawn from the survey results. The guidelines presented in this chapter are intended to help surveyors make decisions that will minimize measurement error.

The guidelines we have provided thus far have mostly focused on specific parts of questions, but we want to end this chapter by cautioning that one should not get consumed with a single part of a question at the expense of considering how all the parts fit together as an overall measurement stimulus. That is, one should take a *holistic approach* and make sure all parts of the question communicate a consistent message. The question stem has to clearly state the response task and the response format and/or options provided, in addition to any instructions, and must match the task as it is stated in the question stem. Figure 5.20 shows several examples of

FIGURE 5.20   Examples of questions with inconsistent designs.

1. **How many days in January did you miss work because of illness or injury?**
   - ☐ Always
   - ☐ Most of the time
   - ☐ Sometimes
   - ☐ Rarely
   - ☐ Never

2. **What are your job responsibilities?**
   - ☐ Delivery
   - ☐ Pick-up
   - ☐ Invoicing
   - ☐ Loading and unloading
   - ☐ Customer service
   - ☐ Maintenance

3. **Please check all of the descriptions you think describe your immediate supervisor.**

	Yes	No
Open-minded	☐	☐
Fair	☐	☐
Honest	☐	☐
Personable	☐	☐
Productive	☐	☐
Expert	☐	☐

4. **Are you satisfied with your current job?**
   - ☐ Very satisfied
   - ☐ Somewhat satisfied
   - ☐ Neither satisfied nor dissatisfied
   - ☐ Somewhat dissatisfied
   - ☐ Very dissatisfied

5. **Which of your university employees took research ethics training in 2013?**
   a. Executive and administrative employees (e.g., deans, provosts, chairs, directors, etc.)
      ☐ All   ☐ Most   ☐ Some   ☐ None
   b. Tenure track faculty
      ☐ All   ☐ Most   ☐ Some   ☐ None
   c. Nontenure track faculty
      ☐ All   ☐ Most   ☐ Some   ☐ None
   d. Professional staff
      ☐ All   ☐ Most   ☐ Some   ☐ None
   e. Secretarial/clerical staff
      ☐ All   ☐ Most   ☐ Some   ☐ None
   f. Student employees
      ☐ All   ☐ Most   ☐ Some   ☐ None

questions that are not holistically designed. Before reading further, see if you can find the problem with each one.

The problem with the first question is that the question stem specifies that respondents should provide the number of days in the month, but the response options ask for more vague assessments of how often work was missed. Respondents who formulate an answer before reading the response options will have trouble at the reporting stage of the response process because they will have to convert the answer they formulated into a new format. This is inefficient and burdensome.

Question 2 is written as an open-ended question, but clearly has closed-ended response options. Thus, the query the respondent hears is not what she is being asked to do. This is a very common mistake. In self-administered surveys, it is inefficient and increases response burden in much the same way as occurred in Question 1. In telephone surveys, it is problematic for the same reasons, but also for an additional, and perhaps more important, reason. After hearing the open-ended question stem, respondents will often start to answer in their own words. This takes the interviewer off script and puts them in the uncomfortable position of having to interrupt the respondent and explain that there are categories that need to be read before they can answer. This process is socially uncomfortable for both parties. Moreover, when this happens early in the interview, respondents tend to become hesitant to answer questions that are phrased in an open-ended way. When an open-ended response is actually needed on an item, interviewers often have to use additional prompts to get the respondent to answer. In essence, this question breaks down normal conversational cues, resulting in confusion and a more awkward conversation thereafter. As we discuss in Guideline 8.6, it is important to provide clear cues about when it is the respondent's turn to talk; this item does the opposite.

Question 3 also contains a mistake that we commonly encounter when reviewing questionnaires: The response options are clearly formatted in a forced-choice way, but the question stem is written for a check-all-that-apply question. Our own research has shown that this mistake can be costly in terms of data quality. Compared to a holistically designed forced-choice item, when a check-all question stem is paired with forced-choice response options, respondents endorse fewer items, are more likely to treat the question as a check-all question by ignoring the "no" column and only marking in the "yes" column, and are more likely to leave items blank (net of those marking only in the "yes" column). For example, we asked respondents what descriptions describe Washington State University with forced-choice formatted response options and the following experimental question stem wordings:

- Forced-choice wording: "Please indicate whether you think each of the following descriptions does or does not describe WSU."
- Check-all wording: "Please check all of the descriptions that you think describe WSU."

Those who received the check-all wording selected an average of 5.7 options, compared to 6.2 for those who received the forced-choice wording. Perhaps more troubling, 17.4% of those receiving the check-all wording treated the item like a check-all item compared to only 3.6% of those who received the forced-choice wording. This resulted in an average of about 1 item per respondent being left blank with the check-all wording compared to only 0.27 items per respondent being left blank with the forced-choice wording (Smyth, 2008). Forced-choice formatted items need forced-choice worded question stems. The question stem should include the phrase "each of the following," as this tells respondents they need to attend to every item in the list. To remain balanced, it should also mention both possible responses for each item (e.g., does or does not describe).

Question 4 in Figure 5.20 is a yes/no question with response options other than "yes" and "no." This question is going to create the same type of response inefficiencies and burden as the first question, in that respondents are likely to generate a "yes" or "no" response initially, only to find out later when they look at the response options that they are supposed to report the degree of their satisfaction or dissatisfaction. It will also create the same types of awkward and inefficient interviewer–respondent interactions in a telephone survey as Question 2, in that before the response options can be read, many respondents will interrupt with an answer of "yes" or "no." The interviewer will then be forced to do the repair work that should have been done at the question design stage.

Finally, Question 5 is written as an open-ended item, but has closed-ended response options. Perhaps more importantly, the question stem suggests that respondents will only have to report what types of employees took the training, but the response options add a whole new dimension to the information that is being requested—how many of each type of employee took the training. This type of mistake is commonly made in paper surveys because people are trying to save space. But like the other examples, it creates additional response burden and inefficiencies. In addition, the question stem does not guide the respondents in interpreting the purpose of the ordinal response options. Thus, some respondents might interpret these boxes as asking how many of each type of employee took the training and others might interpret it as how much of the training was taken by these types of employees. A clearer question stem might be, "How many of each of the following types of university employees took research ethics training in 2013?"

In each of the examples in Figure 5.20 there is some sort of mismatch between the questions respondents are asked and the answers they are expected to give. Not only does this open the door for respondents to interpret and answer the questions in different ways, but it can be frustrating to both the interviewer and the respondent. And, in self-administration it slows down the respondent, and there is no interviewer to help resolve any confusion.

A holistic design approach encourages surveyors to revisit each question, looking at all of its parts to make sure they are sending a clear and consistent message to respondents. Making sure all of the words in the question stem, instructions, and response options send a clear and consistent message is a necessary first step toward achieving holistic design. But it is not the only thing that needs to be done. In the next chapter, we discuss how people process aural and visual information and present guidelines for improving how people perceive information in surveys.

LIST OF GUIDELINES

Guidelines for Writing Open-Ended Questions

Guideline 5.1:   Specify the type of response desired in the question stem
Guideline 5.2:   Avoid making respondents (or interviewers) calculate sums; when possible, have the computer do it
Guideline 5.3:   Provide extra motivation to respond
Guideline 5.4:   Use nondirective probes to obtain more information on open-ended items

General Guidelines for Writing All Types of Closed-Ended Questions

Guideline 5.5:   When asking either/or types of questions, state both the positive and negative side in the question stem
Guideline 5.6:   Develop lists of answer categories that include all reasonable possible answers
Guideline 5.7:   Develop lists of answer categories that are mutually exclusive
Guideline 5.8:   Consider what types of answer spaces are most appropriate for the measurement intent

Guidelines for Nominal Closed-Ended Questions

Guideline 5.9:   Ask respondents to rank only a few items at once rather than a long list
Guideline 5.10:   Avoid bias from unequal comparisons
Guideline 5.11:   Randomize response options if there is concern about order effects
Guideline 5.12:   Use forced-choice questions instead of check-all-that-apply questions

Guidelines for Ordinal Closed-Ended Questions

Guideline 5.13:   Choose between a unipolar or a bipolar scale
Guideline 5.14:   Choose an appropriate scale length—in general, limit scales to four or five categories
Guideline 5.15:   Choose direct or construct-specific labels to improve cognition
Guideline 5.16:   If there is a natural metric (e.g., frequencies, amounts, sizes, etc.), use it instead of vague quantifiers
Guideline 5.17:   Provide balanced scales where categories are relatively equal distances apart conceptually
Guideline 5.18:   Verbally label all categories
Guideline 5.19:   Remove numeric labels from vague quantifier scales whenever possible
Guideline 5.20:   Consider branching (or decomposing) bipolar scales to ease respondent burden and improve data quality
Guideline 5.21:   Provide scales that approximate the actual distribution of the characteristic in the population, or ask the question in an open-ended format to avoid biasing responses

Aural Versus Visual Design of Questions and Questionnaires

To create a truly holistic design requires us to think not just about what the questions and response options communicate, but *how* they are communicated and how that might affect people's ability to answer our questions. In telephone surveys, the respondent and interviewer must rely entirely on aural communication for exchanging information; there are no visual cues whatsoever to help aid respondents (as can be used in face-to-face surveys through show cards or other means). Thus, the words that the interviewer reads to the respondents are of primary importance. In paper and web surveys, where respondents perceive the information visually, the visual design and layout of the questionnaire is also very important.

Whether the primary communication channel is aural versus visual has an important impact on how questions should be designed, because people perceive aural and visual information differently. Engaging in aural communication requires different abilities and skill sets than engaging in written communication. For example, at the perception stage of the response process, receiving aural information requires hearing and listening skills while receiving visual information requires one to have sight and reading abilities. General research on aural versus visual communication indicates that information that is read is more likely to be comprehended and remembered than information that is heard (Haug, 1952; Wilson, 1974). While differences are small for comprehension of simple information, they increase as the complexity of the information grows (Chaiken & Eagley, 1976). Thus, how information is received at the perception stage will impact respondents' ability to comprehend the questions, retrieve relevant information, formulate judgments, and report answers. That is, it will affect the entire response process (as shown in Figure 4.4) and thereby measurement.

In surveys where information is received through the aural channel (i.e., in a telephone survey), respondents experience increased cognitive burden and demand for memory capacity compared with information that is received through the visual channel (i.e., in a web or paper survey). This is because aural survey modes do not have the same type of information permanence and accessibility respondents have when they can look at the question as many times or for as long as they need to. Telephone respondents, for example, cannot revisit questions, instructions, answers, and response options as easily as paper or web respondents. To do so, they have to ask the interviewer to reread information.

In a sense, telephone respondents are double burdened; they have to remember the question, instructions, and response options while also trying to comprehend what is being asked of them, recall relevant information, form a judgment, and report their answer. They also have to remember the flow and direction of the survey conversation as they proceed from question to question. Further, distractions may affect this process. We often hear people cooking dinner or watching TV while completing a survey, and now with cell phones, people can be even more mobile than the cordless telephone allowed, and may be out in public places. Thus, for aural modes, designing in ways that reduce cognitive burden and demands on memory is imperative.

The skills and abilities needed to register responses also differ across these two communication types. Responding orally requires speaking skills, which most people have. The interviewer takes care of recording the spoken response. In contrast, responding in a written mode requires respondents to be able to write, type, touch, and/or use a mouse to record their own responses. These are more specialized skills than speaking. As such, respondents to telephone surveys may find perception and comprehension more difficult, while respondents to paper and web surveys may find reporting more difficult.

Further, in self-administered surveys, surveyors only have to focus on ensuring that one person, the respondent, can understand and answer the survey questions. However, in interviewer-administered surveys there are two people to consider—the interviewer and the respondent. While interviewers can have substantial positive impacts on respondent behavior by helping motivate and guide them as they complete the questionnaire, interviewer confusion or misunderstanding about what they are supposed to do can also have enormous negative impacts on respondents, and thereby contribute to measurement error.

As Japec (2008) pointed out, interviewers have to proceed through mental processes in order to administer questionnaires, much like respondents do in order to respond to them. Interviewers also experience burden, which increases substantially when they have to deal with respondent confusion. When that burden is too great, they look for ways to reduce it, such as by skipping over questions; rewording items; or failing to clarify, probe, or otherwise work to obtain the optimal answer from respondents (i.e., interviewer satisficing). All of these behaviors have great potential to result in increased measurement error (i.e., interviewer bias and/or variance), and as such, should be avoided as much as possible. For more on the interviewer's role in delivering the questionnaire and implementing telephone surveys, see Chapter 8.

While the primary meaning in both aural and visual surveys comes from the words that make up the questions and instructions, these types of surveys differ in sources that add additional meaning beyond the words. In aural surveys this meaning can be communicated through interviewer as well as through paralinguistic features of the interviewer's voice, such as emphasis or tone. Thus, in telephone surveys, significant consideration needs to be given to how to design questions that can easily be delivered aurally by interviewers, that communicate all the necessary information needed to answer, that are easily understandable to respondents, and that help keep the conversation between the interviewer and respondent on track. Most of this can be accomplished through careful wording that adheres to common rules of conversation and by minimizing the effects of interviewer behavior on respondents' answers.

In visual surveys, graphical features and layout communicate additional information to respondents. The visual design of survey questions has been shown to significantly impact how people respond. Visual design features of the questions—such as the size and labeling of answer spaces, the layout of response categories and the spacing between them, the location of special instructions, and the overall layout of the questionnaire page or screen—can impact the answers respondents provide to those questions. Visual design is especially important in helping respondents complete self-administered questionnaires because there is not an interviewer present to help guide them. Thus, while memory and cognitive burden are among the primary concerns in telephone surveys, visual design becomes a primary concern in web and paper surveys.

In this chapter, we discuss key visual design concepts and how they can be applied to questionnaire design. We then provide guidelines for the visual design of individual questions and of questionnaire screens or pages. These guidelines are based on applying visual design concepts to questionnaire construction, and are rooted in the research to date on how visual design features of questions impact respondent behavior. Together, they provide the tools for helping to ensure respondents process the survey information in a consistent manner and that the words and visual layout send a consistent message in paper and web surveys.

As we discussed, telephone surveys need to be designed to minimize burden on both the respondent and the interviewer and to make their interaction as easy and smooth as possible. The guidelines presented in Chapter 4 provide the foundation for designing effective questions for telephone surveys (e.g., ask one question at a time, use simple and familiar words, use specific and concrete words, use as few words as possible, use complete sentences, etc.). However, additional considerations are needed to ensure that all of the information respondents need in order to answer is provided to them aurally and in a way that helps reduce the memory and cognitive burden of responding to telephone surveys.

In addition, it is important that the design of telephone questionnaires ensures that interviewers have all the information they need to deliver the questionnaire effectively, and to help to ensure questions are delivered similarly across different interviewers. Given the importance of understanding the role of the interviewer in designing telephone questionnaires, we present guidelines that cover these additional considerations for designing effective questions for telephone surveys in Chapter 8, after we have more fully discussed the impact of interviewers in telephone surveys.

Although most of the guidelines for designing telephone surveys presented in Chapter 8 focus on ways to word questions to help respondents and interviewers, we also believe that the visual layout of the questions and questionnaire for telephone surveys is important because good visual design can make interviewers' jobs easier to do. Very little research has examined the visual design of CATI screens, but it stands to reason that many of the concepts and guidelines for paper and web surveys that we discuss in this chapter could be applied to the design of telephone surveys to make them easier for interviewers to administer.

Understanding how questions are presented in aural and visual modes is especially important for mixed-mode surveys. In this chapter, and in Chapter 8, we address some of the challenges and opportunities for modifying how questions are asked in both aural and visual modes in order to facilitate mixed-mode data collection. We present specific guidelines for designing mixed-mode surveys in Chapter 11.

THE IMPORTANCE OF VISUAL DESIGN IN SELF-ADMINISTERED SURVEYS

Prior to the 1990s, most of the survey methodology research focused on how the wording of questions influences how respondents answer them; with very few exceptions, the importance of visual design and layout of questions was overlooked. In the 1990s, survey methodologists increasingly began to realize that the visual design of questions and questionnaires can significantly impact whether and how people respond to surveys (DeMaio & Bates, 1992; Dillman, Sinclair, & Clark, 1993; T. W. Smith, 1993). As researchers began to discover ways in which visual design impacted nonresponse and measurement, they started to incorporate knowledge from other disciplines, such as psychology and the vision sciences, into survey methodology. This helped to identify important visual design concepts that were used to start building a theory of visual design for surveys (Jenkins & Dillman, 1997). The concepts and theory of visual design allowed survey methodologists to think more systematically about the visual design of questions and questionnaires, and to develop experiments to test the effectiveness of different visual designs (Christian & Dillman, 2004; Christian, Dillman, & Smyth, 2007a; Jenkins & Dillman, 1997; Redline & Dillman, 2002; Redline, Dillman, Dajani, & Scaggs, 2003; Tourangeau, Couper, & Conrad, 2004; Tourangeau, Couper, & Conrad, 2007). It is now widely accepted that, in addition to question wording, visual design can have substantial impacts on survey response and measurement.

What is the purpose of visual design in self-administered surveys? In self-administered surveys, respondents do not receive assistance from interviewers; rather they are on their own to determine how to navigate the questionnaire, including complex skip patterns, and figure out what the questions are asking for and how to answer them. This is where visual design comes in. Good visual design in self-administered surveys can work much like interviewers do and help respondents as they complete these tasks.

Visual design is important at both the page or screen level and at the level of individual questions. At the page or screen level, visual design is used to help respondents gain entry into and understand the pages, and to coax them into processing all of the relevant information in the prescribed order. This helps ensure that every respondent perceives the survey questions in the same way, which is considered essential for obtaining quality survey data.

At the individual question level, visual design can be used to assist respondents through the stages of the response process. For example, images might be used to help respondents understand exactly what the question is asking for and retrieve relevant information, or graphics and symbols might be used to help them figure out how to map their response and report it in the questionnaire. Likewise, questions and their subcomponent parts can be arranged in ways that encourage respondents to process all of the parts in the prescribed order.

Visual design done well can minimize measurement error and item nonresponse, but if it is done poorly it can increase both of these. While the primary purpose of visual design is to help respondents process the questionnaire, it can also be used to make the questionnaire more appealing, provided any stylistic elements do not interfere with the functionality of the questionnaire.

VISUAL DESIGN CONCEPTS AND THEIR APPLICATION TO SURVEYS

In this chapter, we discuss survey visual design at both the page level and at the level of individual questions. But to really understand how visual design works at these two levels in a survey, it is necessary know some basic concepts from the vision sciences and Gestalt psychology. Additional information about many of these concepts and ideas can be found in the works of Palmer (1999), Hoffman (2004), and Ware (2004).

Survey questionnaires include four types of visual design *elements* that communicate meaning to respondents (see Figure 6.1): words, numbers, symbols, and graphics. *Words* are the most powerful source of meaning that respondents draw upon when answering survey questions, but *numbers* used in the question stem, in instructions, and in labels for answer choices also communicate additional meaning. *Symbols* can also be used to add special meaning, often without occupying very much physical space in a questionnaire. For example, an arrow may communicate to respondents where to focus their attention next. Finally, *graphics* (e.g., text boxes, check boxes, radio buttons, shaded backgrounds, etc.) are another type of visual design element that can be used in designing survey questions. In addition, graphics can include more complex images and logos that layer various elements. The use of these types of graphics has increased, particularly in web surveys, because of the ease and affordability of including them, but also in paper surveys because the cost of printing them has decreased.

FIGURE 6.1 The basic building blocks of visual communication.

Visual design elements **that communicate information to respondents**

Words are the fundamental source of meaning that help respondents understand what is being asked of them.

Numbers are used to convey meaning and sequence or order to respondents.

Symbols are figures that add special meaning based on what they represent to respondents.

Graphics are shapes and visual images that can be simple or complex and convey meaning to respondents.

Visual design properties **that modify how elements are presented visually and the meaning respondents assign to them**

Size: Changes in the size of elements influence how they are perceived and whether they stand out visually.

Font: Changes in the shape and form of elements influence the legibility of words and how they are perceived.

Brightness/Contrast/Color: Changes in shading and color influence how elements are perceived and whether they stand out visually from the background.

Location: How near or far elements are from one another (the spacing and alignment) influences whether they are perceived as related or unrelated.

Each of the four visual design elements (words, numbers, symbols, and graphics) can be presented in different ways: They can be large or small, light or dark, close to one another or far apart, static or in motion, grayscale or in color. Thus, in addition to using the four types of visual design elements, surveyors can also manipulate the *properties* of each of these types of elements to increase or decrease the attention given to them and change the meaning respondents assign to them. Visual design properties include size, font, brightness or contrast, color, location or proximity, shape, orientation, and motion. For example, attention can be drawn to particular words, numbers, or symbols by changing their size, contrast, or color in relation to the surrounding text (e.g., **bolding** or *italicizing* an important word or phrase in the question stem). A dollar symbol ($) could remind respondents to report their income in dollars. Symbols can also be located in proximity to the answer spaces where respondents will need to use them at the time of response. In addition, differently shaped graphics for response scales, for example, a ladder versus a pyramid shape, can influence how respondents interpret and respond to the scales (Schwarz, Grayson, & Knäuper, 1998).

When a person is presented with visual information, whether in a newspaper, web site, or survey questionnaire, many separate actions take place very quickly as the eye takes in the information and the brain processes it to make sense of the page or screen. People do not assign meaning to information all at once. Instead, they process and give meaning to visual elements and their properties in multiple steps, although often quite quickly. Figure 6.2 provides definitions of the three basic steps of visual processing, as well as definitions for concepts related to the attention and visual processing that takes place in the steps.

In the first step, respondents gain an understanding of the ***basic page layout***. To do this, they use *preattentive processing*, which is subconscious, to quickly scan the page. Here they will notice certain visual properties (e.g., number, size, shape, contrast, enclosure, color hue and intensity, etc.) that stand out from the other information on the page, and this will give them a general understanding of the scene. This step is dominated by *bottom-up processing*, where only the visual scene itself influences how information is perceived (i.e., they are using the vision system alone and are not drawing on the context of the situation or applying any cultural knowledge at this step).

In the second step, entitled ***information organization*** in Figure 6.2, respondents gain an understanding of how the information is organized on the page. Here they divide or segment the page into basic regions based on shared visual properties. Once the page is divided into regions, any contours and boundaries help respondents distinguish figures or objects from the background. This process of *figure/ground orientation* helps respondents differentiate the individual visual elements that will be used in further processing. Then, respondents begin to perceive groups among visual elements. For example, respondents might begin to perceive elements of similar contrast that are located close in proximity, such as a set of response options, as a group. In this step, respondents move from preattentive to *attentive processing*, a more conscious processing where elements are more actively attended to and cognitively processed. During this step, respondents utilize both bottom-up and *top-down processing*, where the context of the situation and respondents' cultural knowledge, prior experiences, and expectations also influence the meaning assigned to visual information.

After respondents perceive and organize the basic visual elements of the questionnaire, they begin the third step, ***task completion***. It is during this step that respondents shift their attention from the entire page to a much smaller area for

FIGURE 6.2   Visual processing steps and important concepts.

Three steps of visual processing

Basic page layout: The first step where respondents quickly scan the page and preattentively process basic visual properties, such as color and size, to gain a general understanding of the basic layout of the page. This step is dominated by bottom-up processing.

Information organization: In the second step, respondents begin to organize the information by segmenting the page into basic regions, differentiating individual visual elements from the background, and perceiving groups or relationships among elements. This step involves both preattentive and attentive processing, and respondents move from bottom-up to top-down processing.

Task completion: In the final step, attention is on the task of answering individual questions. Respondents focus on a smaller area of the page and begin attentively processing the components of each individual question. Top-down processing occurs in this step; the survey context and respondents' prior knowledge influence interpretation.

Attention and visual processing concepts

Preattentive processing: Broad, rapid visual analysis of the entire field of available information that determines which visual elements are attended to in later stages, according to certain properties that are noticed subconsciously and stand out because they deviate from other information on the page.

Attentive processing: Conscious visual processing where the visual field narrows and the focus is on a few elements that enter visual working memory and are more easily recalled.

Foveal view: The sharpest and most detailed area of vision during attentive processing. Made up of about 2 degrees of visual angle or 8 to 10 characters in width.

Useful field of vision: The visual space attended to during attentive processing. Contains the foveal view, where vision is sharpest, plus up to about 13 more degrees of visual angle in which items can be detected, but vision is less sharp. Is smaller when we are stressed or the visual information is dense, and larger when the visual information is less dense.

Bottom-up processing: Visual information is quickly processed by the visual system alone, and only the visual stimulus itself influences perception.

Top-down processing: Visual information is processed based on the context of the situation and the viewer's cultural knowledge, prior experiences, and expectations.

Figure/ground orientation: The organization of the visual scene into what is object and what is background, determined by the contours of the visual elements, and determining order of attention during processing, with figures attended to first.

more focused processing, and that they first begin to read the text on the page in any detail. Here the visual processing is attentive and conscious. The visual field (i.e., *the useful field of vision*) narrows to less than 15 degrees of visual angle, with the most focused visual processing happening in the *foveal view*, which is made up of only about 2 degrees or 8 to 10 characters in width. This narrowing of the visual field means that attention is focused on only a few elements. During this attentive processing, respondents sequentially attend to the components of each individual question, and these components enter working memory and are more easily remembered. The task completion step is dominated by top-down processing, where the survey context and the respondents' prior cultural knowledge and experiences influence how they interpret the visual information. For example, respondents bring to bear cultural understanding of any symbols used in the questionnaire, such as dollar signs and arrows.

In Figure 6.3, we demonstrate how respondents process a questionnaire by showing images of what respondents might perceive in each of the three steps. We utilize a United States Department of Agriculture Survey of Farm Operators to illustrate the steps that respondents go through when processing a survey questionnaire (see Dillman, Gertseva, & Mahon-Haft, 2005, for more information about this questionnaire). During the first step, respondents notice the basic horizontal and vertical layout of information on the page; distinguish changes in contrast and color; and notice the dark, medium, and light gray and white areas on the questionnaire page (the Step 1 image in Figure 6.3). Respondents perceive multiple dark gray features of different shapes and sizes (a circle, rectangle, and five small squares), three medium gray rectangles of different sizes at the top of the page, and white spaces in the lower right and bottom areas of the page.

We show two images of Step 2 to differentiate early Step 2, where preattentive and bottom-up processing still dominate, from late Step 2, where more active attention begins and respondents use top-down processing. In early Step 2, respondents use the boundaries and contrast to segment the page into two regions. Once the page is segmented, respondents focus on the darker gray and white elements and let the light gray recede into the background (the Step 2a image). In this early step, respondents notice even more elements located in different areas of the page and their varying sizes, shapes, and contrast. In late Step 2 (the Step 2b image), respondents attend to these various elements, grouping them and using prior knowledge and experiences to assign meaning to them. Respondents distinguish the header region with the logos, contact information, title of the survey, and instructions from the question region, which contains the section heading and instructions, five questions, and the answer spaces (respondents may also briefly notice the "office use only" area in light gray at the bottom of the page).

In the final task completion stage, respondents focus their attention on perceiving the first question and completing the other steps in the response process. As this example illustrates, the three steps of visual processing correspond to the perception stage of the survey response process shown in Figure 4.5. How respondents perceive the information in the question influences the remaining four steps of the response process: comprehension, retrieval, judgment, and response. Then they move on to the next question.

Throughout these three steps, the properties of the visual design elements or how they are displayed can strongly influence the meaning respondents assign to them, and thus the ease with which they gain entry into the page, understand individual questions, and navigate between questions. As such, surveyors need to apply these properties so that they create meaningful connections and patterns

FIGURE 6.3   How respondents perceive a questionnaire page during each step of visual processing.

Step 1: Determining the Basic Page Layout

among elements in order to help respondents understand the basic screen or page layout as well as individual questions as intended.

The Gestalt psychology principles of pattern perception can help surveyors understand how properties can be strategically applied to elements to influence whether respondents perceive them as conceptually related or conceptually distinct, thereby creating meaningful visual grouping and connection among them.

Figure 6.4 gives a simple demonstration of how these Gestalt grouping principles can be applied in design. In the first row of Figure 6.4, there is no grouping among the circles. In the subsequent rows, grouping is established through the application of visual properties following Gestalt grouping principles.

FIGURE 6.3 *(continued)*.

Step 2a: Segmenting the Page into Regions and Distinguishing Figure/Ground

According to the principle of proximity, locating elements close to each other creates the perception that they are part of the same group, that they are physically and conceptually related, while locating them further apart encourages respondents to see them as distinct. We apply the principle of proximity in the second row of Figure 6.4 to create three distinct groups, each with two circles. Similarly, surveyors can use similarity of size, shape, or contrast to encourage respondents to perceive elements as a group, as is done in the third, fourth, and fifth rows. Conversely, surveyors can use dissimilarity in these properties or added distance between items to give the impression of distinctness.

FIGURE 6.3 *(continued).*

Step 2b: Grouping and Organizing the Information on the Page

NATIONAL
AGRICULTURAL
STATISTICS
SERVICE

**2003 AGRICULTURAL RESOURCE
MANAGEMENT SURVEY**

ERS ∷∷
ECONOMIC RESEARCH SERVICE

U.S. Department of Agriculture
Rm 5829, South Building
1400 Independence Avenue, S.W.
Washington, D.C. 20250-2000
1-800-727-9540
Fax: 202-690-2090
e-mail: nass-dc@nass.usda.gov

Form Approved O.M.B. Number 0535-0218
Approval expires 12/31/03
Project Code 904 VERSION 3 CORE

YOUR REPORT IS CONFIDENTIAL
and it will only be used for statistical purposes.
Your report **CANNOT** be used for purposes of
taxation, investigation, or regulation. The law also
provides that copies retained in your files are
immune from legal processes.

Please make corrections to label name, address, and zip code if needed.

Results from this important data collection will be mailed to all respondents in July 2004

SECTION A: LAND in FARM/RANCH

Please report farm/ranch land owned, rented, or used by you, your spouse, or by the partnership, corporation or organization for which you are reporting in 2003. *(Include all cropland, idle land, CRP, pastureland, woodland, wasteland, etc.)*

		NONE	NUMBER OF ACRES

1 How many acres of farm and ranch land are <u>owned</u>? ....

2 How many acres of farm and ranch land are <u>rented</u> or <u>leased</u> from others...*(Exclude land used on an AUM or fee per head basis under a grazing permit)*

   a) for a <u>fixed cash</u> payment? ....

   b) for a <u>flexible cash</u> payment?
    (Rent paid depends on prices and/or yields, or otherwise not a fixed amount) ...

   c) for a <u>share</u> of crop or livestock production?
    (Include hybrid rental arrangement where rent paid is based on a fixed cash payment plus some shared production) ....

   d) rented for <u>free</u>? ....

Add these five

         SUBTOTAL

3 SUBTOTAL *(Items 1+2a+2b+2c+2d)* ....

Subtract item 4 from item 3

4 How many acres of farm and ranch land are rented or leased <u>to others</u>? *(Include land rented for cash, for a share of crop or livestock production, or rent free)* ....

| NONE | NUMBER OF ACRES |

5 TOTAL ACRES in this operation in 2003 *(subtract item 4 from item 3)* ....

Office Use Only	Response Code	Reporting Unit	MM/DD/YY	Name/Address Change

Respondents also perceive elements that are enclosed in a common region, such as a box or an area with a common background color, as a group, as shown in the sixth row. Likewise, connecting visual elements by using another element, such as a line, as shown in the seventh row, encourages respondents to perceive the connected elements as a group.

Elements that continue smoothly (i.e., continuity) will also be perceived as a group. In the eighth row, the two horizontal arrows will be perceived as belonging together because the arrow on the right continues smoothly from the arrow on the left. In contrast, the downward pointing arrow departs at an angle. As a result,

FIGURE 6.3 (continued).

Step 3: Perceiving and Answering
Individual Questions

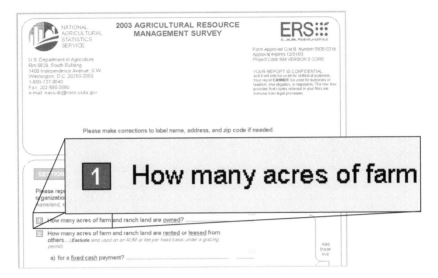

it does not continue as smoothly and will be perceived as separate from the other two arrows.

The principle of closure says that people will perceive a whole object even when it is incomplete. The image in the ninth row of Figure 6.4 is of a piece of graffiti one of us snapped a photo of while walking to the office one day that nicely demonstrates how the law of closure works. Enough of the panda bear's features are present to allow us to perceive exactly where its head should be, even though there is no line drawn to show us where the head is. We are mentally filling in the blanks to perceive the panda's head.

Finally, the principle of common fate is demonstrated in the tenth row of the figure. Here the first, second, fifth, and sixth circles are perceived as belonging together because the arrows indicate they will move the same direction. The third and fourth circles are perceived as a separate group because their arrows indicate they will move a different direction.

As these examples show, altering properties in line with the Gestalt grouping principles creates the perception of groups. An even stronger impression of grouping can be created by layering these properties as is done in the final row of Figure 6.4.

The following example illustrates how visual design elements and properties used in accordance with the Gestalt grouping principles can improve responses to a simple survey question. In an article based on a series of experiments, we found that visual design changes to the question "What month and year did you begin your studies at WSU?" increased the percentage of respondents reporting their answer in the desired format (i.e., two digits for the month and four digits for the year) from 55% to 96%, an increase of 41 percentage points (Christian, Dillman, & Smyth, 2007b). In a follow-up study, Christian (2007) reported the sequential impact of a series of visual and verbal manipulations to the same question. The results of this study can be seen in Figure 6.5. In the initial version at the top of

FIGURE 6.4   Applying Gestalt psychology principles to create grouping and connectedness among visual elements.

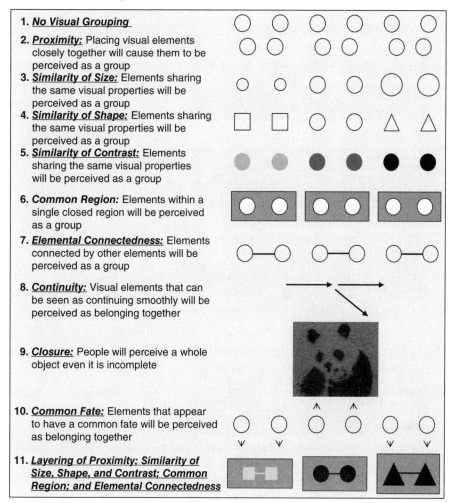

1. *No Visual Grouping*

2. *Proximity:* Placing visual elements closely together will cause them to be perceived as a group

3. *Similarity of Size:* Elements sharing the same visual properties will be perceived as a group

4. *Similarity of Shape:* Elements sharing the same visual properties will be perceived as a group

5. *Similarity of Contrast:* Elements sharing the same visual properties will be perceived as a group

6. *Common Region:* Elements within a single closed region will be perceived as a group

7. *Elemental Connectedness:* Elements connected by other elements will be perceived as a group

8. *Continuity:* Visual elements that can be seen as continuing smoothly will be perceived as belonging together

9. *Closure:* People will perceive a whole object even it is incomplete

10. *Common Fate:* Elements that appear to have a common fate will be perceived as belonging together

11. *Layering of Proximity; Similarity of Size, Shape, and Contrast; Common Region; and Elemental Connectedness*

Figure 6.5, respondents were provided with two equal size boxes for the month and year, and only 44% responded in the desired format. However, when the size of the month box was reduced by half (consistent with the expectation that the month be reported in half the number of digits as the year), more respondents reported the year using four digits, raising the percentage using the desired format to 57%. Thus, the size of the answer boxes communicated additional meaning to respondents, beyond the graphics alone, about how many digits they should use in providing their answer.

In the next manipulation, adding the verbal instruction to "Please provide your answer using two digits for the month and four digits for the year" resulted in a 21-percentage-point increase, bringing the percentage responding in the desired format to 78%, and demonstrating that respondents were processing the words in the instruction and applying them when providing their response. Placing the verbal instruction directly after the question stem helped to ensure that respondents would see and process it just prior to providing their answer.

FIGURE 6.5 Example of the influence of visual design on how respondents report date information.

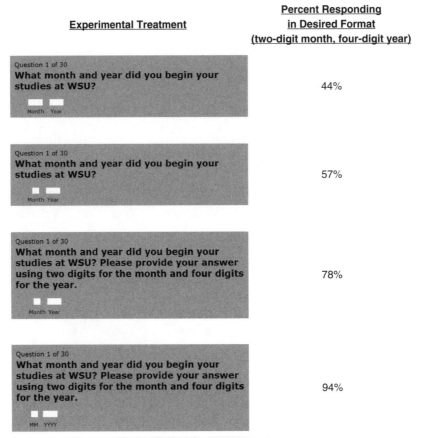

Source: Adapted from *How Mixed-Mode Surveys Are Transforming Social Research: The Influence of Survey Mode on Measurement in Web and Telephone Surveys*, by L. M. Christian, 2007. Unpublished doctoral dissertation, Washington State University, Pullman, WA.

Finally, replacing the word labels "Month" and "Year" with a symbolic instruction MM YYYY beneath their respective boxes increased the percentage responding in the desired format to 94%. The symbolic instruction was designed so that the letter M was used to represent month and Y to represent year, with the number of letters indicating the number of digits to use when reporting the month and year. In this version, respondents gained additional meaning from the symbolic instruction about the number of digits to use in their response. Locating the instruction near the answer spaces and within their foveal view also helped to ensure that respondents would notice and apply the instruction when reporting a response.

In the previous experiment reported by Christian et al. (2007b), providing the symbolic instruction with the answer spaces had the highest impact on use of the desired format (increased use by 35 and 42 percentage points in the two experiments), but there was no additional instruction presented with the question stem. That the instruction was so important in Christian's (2007) experiment (see Figure 6.5) without the MM YYYY symbol to indicate the desired number of digits suggests that verbal instructions are particularly effective in the absence of adequate visual information. Results of telephone experiments confirm this conclusion: The instruction to respond in the desired format on the telephone, where there is no visual information available, raised the percentage reporting in the desired format from less than 1% to 59% (Christian, 2007). Nevertheless, in self-administered surveys, it is now clear that the use of visual information is key to obtaining desired responses and can contribute to this effort above and beyond the wording of the question and instructions.

GENERAL GUIDELINES FOR THE VISUAL PRESENTATION OF SURVEY QUESTIONS

We now turn to describing general guidelines for the visual presentation of survey questions that apply to designing nearly all types of questions. We continue to use the visual design concepts we just discussed in presenting these guidelines. We will use the poorly designed question in the top panel of Figure 6.6 to demonstrate the application of the first four general guidelines. This question would undoubtedly turn many respondents off. Some might not even be able to understand that this is a survey question or what it is asking, making it difficult to provide an answer. The overall problem with this question is that it is unorganized and cluttered; there is no clear message sent by the visual design. But such a broad observation does not necessarily give us enough information to start revising the question. When we look closer, however, we can identify a number of more specific problems that we can begin to address:

- It is difficult to tell where the question stem ends and the response options begin.
- The response options run together.
- It is not immediately clear how one should mark an answer.
- Certain options stand out more than others, making them more likely to be selected.
- The purpose of the bolding, underlining, and reverse print (white text on a black background) are unclear.
- One would have to process the "other" option before processing all of the options provided by the surveyor.

The revision is clearly an improvement on the original design. To construct it we used the following four guidelines.

Guideline 6.1: Use Darker and/or Larger Print for the Question Stem and Lighter and/or Smaller Print for Answer Choices and Answer Spaces

The first change that needed to be made to the question in Figure 6.6 was to create subgrouping. Good subgrouping helps the respondent quickly recognize and process the parts of the question. In this example, we used the design property of *contrast* to create separation between the question stem and the response options. To create differences in contrast, we bolded the question stem but not the response options. This is the standard use of bolding that we have adopted for most of

FIGURE 6.6 Implementing general visual design principles to construct individual questions.

Poor design

Which one of the following best **describes** the reason for your most *recent visit* to the Southgate Mall? ♡ **Shopping** for fun/entertainment ▷ Shopping for a needed item [ ]MALL WALKING/Exercise □ Other _____ ○Dining at the mall ☆Hanging out with friends Meeting new people ♧ *Conducting Business*

Revision with improved design

Which <u>one</u> of the following best describes the reason for your most recent visit to the Southgate Mall?

□ Shopping for fun/entertainment
□ Shopping for a needed item
□ Mall walking/exercise
□ Dining at the mall
□ Hanging out with friends
□ Meeting new people
□ Conducting business
□ Other [_____]

Poor design

How much do you favor or oppose implementing a merit-based pay system for elementary school teachers? ① Strongly favor ② Somewhat favor ③ Neutral ④ Somewhat oppose ⑤ Strongly oppose

Revision with improved design

How much do you favor or oppose implementing a merit-based pay system for <u>elementary</u> school teachers?

□₁ Strongly favor
□₂ Somewhat favor
□₃ Neutral
□₄ Somewhat oppose
□₅ Strongly oppose

the examples throughout this book. If we wanted to reserve bolding for another purpose in our questionnaire, however, another property we could manipulate is text size (see the bottom example of Figure 6.6). Increasing the size of the text in the question stem but not the response options helps differentiate these two parts of the question.

Guideline 6.2: Use Spacing to Help Create Subgrouping Within a Question

The Gestalt psychology principle of *proximity* states that items located close to one another will be perceived as belonging to a group, and items located farther apart will be perceived as separate from one another. We applied this principle to help reinforce the subgrouping within the question. We started by moving the first response option onto its own line of text and adding some extra space between it and the question stem. We then moved each response option onto its own line and arranged them vertically underneath the question stem so that they would no longer blend together. To help create the impression that the response options were all part of one group, we placed them in close vertical proximity to one another and spaced them equally. We also indented them a few spaces to the right underneath the question stem to reinforce the subgrouping we were creating.

Guideline 6.3: Visually Standardize All Answer Spaces or Response Options

Another problem with the poorly designed question that we needed to address was that some response options stood out visually more than others, making them more likely to be seen and selected. "Shopping" stood out because it was bolded, "dining" because it was in reverse print, and "hanging out with friends" because it was underlined. Our solution to this problem was to standardize the design properties of all of the response options. First we made sure they were all the same text size with the same character spacing. We then changed them all to the same font.

We chose Calibri because of its readability and professionalism (i.e., compared to the ***Disney Script*** used for "conducting business"). Finally, we removed variations due to color, contrast (bolding), underlining, and reverse print. The resulting uniformity makes the response options easier to process and helps ensure that they will be processed equally. The similarity across response options also helps them appear as a subgroup within the larger question group (i.e., the Gestalt psychology principle of *similarity* says that items that appear regular and like each other will be perceived as belonging together). In addition to making these changes, we reordered the response options so that the "other" option was located at the end of the list. This allows respondents to process all of the substantive response options first, so that by the time they reach the "other" option they know if they need to use it.

Guideline 6.4: Use Visual Design Properties to Emphasize Elements That Are Important to the Respondent and to Deemphasize Those That Are Not

In the poor design of the first question in Figure 6.6, the words "describes" and "recent visit" in the question stem are emphasized with bolding and italics, respectively. However, these words seem no more important to respondents' understanding of the response task or the question than any others in the stem. As a result, the bolding and italics were removed in the revised design. Instead of emphasizing these words, we opted to use underlining to emphasize the word "one" in order to draw respondents' attention to the fact that they should select only one of the response options.

The choice of underlining for this purpose works quite well for paper surveys, but should be carefully considered for web surveys because underlining already has a predefined meaning on the Internet (i.e., a clickable link), especially when combined with the color blue. Nevertheless, we use underlining in the same way in the merit-based pay example in the bottom of the figure to draw respondents' attention to the fact that this question is about elementary school teachers only.

In this second example we also face another common problem: the need to include extra information for survey processing reasons. In this case, the extra information is numbers located inside the check boxes to assist with data entry of the paper surveys. Because they are unimportant to the respondent, these numbers should be deemphasized if they cannot be eliminated altogether. We do this by manipulating the properties of size, contrast, and location. The numbers are made smaller and lighter to make them less obvious, but still visible to the astute data enterer. They are then relocated from the center to outside the check box, where they are less likely to be noticed by respondents but can still easily be used for data entry.

A similar strategy is used for key codes in the questionnaire shown in Figure 6.3. In addition, in this questionnaire, the "Office Use Only" section is deemphasized through its placement at the bottom of the page, the use of gray text, and the lack of a colored background (Dillman et al., 2005).

Guideline 6.5: Choose Font, Font Size, and Line Length to Ensure the Legibility of the Text

Even a very well-worded question can be difficult for respondents to process if it is not designed in a legible way. Enhancing legibility means choosing an appropriate font, font size, and line length.

Examples of how font variations can impact reading efficiency are shown in Figure 6.7. As the figure suggests, one should avoid script fonts because they can

FIGURE 6.7 Examples of font variations that affect reading difficulty.

Name of Font	Appearance of Font	How Font Affects Reading Difficulty
Brush Script Edwardian Script Freestyle Script	*In what year were you born?* *In what year were you born?* *In what year were you born?*	Script fonts are very difficult to read
Courier New Lucida Console	In what year were you born? In what year were you born?	Monospace fonts make the shape of words harder to recognize
Calibri Times New Roman Arial	IN WHAT YEAR WERE YOU BORN? IN WHAT YEAR WERE YOU BORN? IN WHAT YEAR WERE YOU BORN?	Using all capital letters makes reading inefficient because the words lack shape
Calibri Times New Roman Arial	In what year were you born? In what year were you born? In what year were you born?	Proportionally spaced fonts and lowercase letters make the shape of words easier to recognize
Times New Roman Garamond Century	In what year were you born? In what year were you born? In what year were you born?	Added detail at the end of letters (i.e., serifs) in serif fonts can make them hard to read on some computer monitors
Calibri Arial Tahoma	In what year were you born? In what year were you born? In what year were you born?	Sans serif fonts are easier to read on computer monitors because they do not have serifs

be very difficult to read. Instead, serif or sans serif fonts should be used. Serif fonts have added detail, or *serifs*, at the end of the strokes that make up the structure of the letters. In contrast, sans serif fonts do not have the added details. Although both serif and sans serif fonts work well on paper, sans serif fonts are commonly preferred for web surveys because they are more readable than serif fonts, especially on low resolution monitors.

Generally, one should also choose proportionally spaced fonts rather than monospace fonts. The reason for this is that we recognize the most common words we read by their overall shape, not by sounding out each letter in them. The shape of the words is more apparent with proportionally shaped fonts, which will make reading more efficient. For the same reason, we recommend against using all capital letters (although all caps is sometimes used for interviewer instructions or other information on the CATI screen in telephone surveys).

One additional point to keep in mind about fonts for web surveys is that for the font to display, it has to be installed on the user's computer. If the user does not have the correct font installed, the browser will default to a font the user does have (usually in the same font family). For this reason, it is advisable to stick to common fonts that nearly all users will have, such as Calibri or Arial.

To some degree, the font size one chooses will depend on the survey population. A good rule of thumb is to use 10- to 12-point fonts for most populations, but larger fonts for older populations. An additional consideration for web surveyors is that font preferences are often set on the user's computer, giving the designer little control. Additionally, font sizes appear different on screen than on paper, and the same font size may appear larger or smaller depending on factors such as the user's screen resolution. Thus, web designers are advised to seek additional resources on how to ensure legibility of text.

With respect to line length, readers may have difficulty tracking along the lines, reading evenly, and finding their place at the beginning of the next line on the return sweep when text lines are too long. In comparison,

excessively short
lines of text require
almost constant eye
motion and frequent
return sweeps that
can become overly
burdensome.

Thus, a more moderate line length of 3 to 5 inches is recommended.

Guideline 6.6: Integrate Special Instructions Into the Question Where They Will Be Used, Rather Than Including Them as Free-Standing Entities

Frequently it is necessary to provide a special instruction to clarify a question. This leads to the undesirable practice of placing instructions outside of the question and emphasizing them with boxes or perhaps a different color. The problem with this practice is that once people have gotten into the routine of completing a questionnaire, the marking of an answer leads to the immediate search for the next question. As a result, free-standing instructions tend to be skipped entirely because they are outside of the established navigational path of the questionnaire. The example in Figure 6.8 shows that such instructions are most likely to be properly applied if

FIGURE 6.8 Integrate special instructions into the question stem.

Instruction placed outside of the navigational path

8. **Have one-on-one meetings with professors contributed significantly to your WSU education?**

   ❏ Yes
   ❏ No

   If you haven't had many one-on-one meetings, just skip to Question 9.

   40% marked "No"
   5% left it blank

   11% left Question 9 blank

A revision with the instruction placed within the navigational path

8. **Have one-on-one meetings with professors contributed significantly to your WSU education?**

   If you haven't had many one-on-one meetings, just skip to Question 9.

   ❏ Yes
   ❏ No

   19% marked "No"
   26% left it blank

   3% left Question 9 blank

Another revision with the instruction integrated with the question stem and visually distinguished using italics

8. **Have one-on-one meetings with professors contributed significantly to your WSU education?** *If you haven't had many one-on-one meetings, just skip to Question 9.*

   ❏ Yes
   ❏ No

Source: "The Influence of Graphical and Symbolic Language Manipulations on Responses to Self-Administered Questions," by L. M. Christian and D. A. Dillman, 2004, *Public Opinion Quarterly, 68*(1), pp. 58–81.

they are expressed as part of the query itself rather than placed as a separate entity (Christian & Dillman, 2004).

In the first layout, an instruction to skip this question and move on to the next if it does not apply is located below both the question stem and the response options. In this design, 40% marked "no" and only 5% left the question blank and moved on. In the second layout, the instruction is moved up to a more integrated location between the question stem and the response options. Placing the instruction here resulted in 19% marking "no" and 26% leaving the question blank and moving on.

When the instruction was located where it was needed to help respondents decide whether and how they should answer the question, more people were able to successfully apply it. In contrast, when the instruction was located as a freestanding entity outside the question stem and answer categories, many respondents had probably already marked an answer before they even noticed it. The fact that 11% of respondents to this version (compared to 3% when the instruction was integrated) left the next question (Question 9) blank suggests that when some respondents got to the instruction located below the response options, they applied it to the wrong question altogether. The third layout, which has shown some promise in cognitive interviews, is another possible way the instruction could be integrated with the question stem. These types of effects are likely to be exacerbated when instructions are included in free-standing booklets or sheets that accompany the questionnaire.

As this example demonstrates, it is not enough to simply move instructions from the front of the questionnaire or from a separate booklet into the appropriate question subgrouping. Rather, even within a single question, in order to be effective, instructions need to be strategically located where they will be used.

Guideline 6.7: Separate Optional or Occasionally Needed Instructions From the Question Stem by Font or Symbol Variation

When respondents begin to fill out a questionnaire, they are learning how the questionnaire works, including what must be read and what can be skipped. Requiring them to read through a great deal of material that does not apply or that can be skipped without negative consequences encourages the habit of skipping words and phrases. For these reasons a distinction should be made between words that are essential for every person to read and those that may be needed by only some respondents.

There are many different reasons that reading a particular instruction may be optional. Perhaps it is because the instruction "put an X in the appropriate box" is the same instruction used for a previous question, and many respondents will remember that. It may also be that only a few respondents need the information, such as in the case of the instruction used in Figure 6.8 ("If you haven't had many one-on-one meetings, just skip to Question 9"). To avoid presenting information that respondents already know, or that applies to relatively few of them, distinguish this information from the query by the use of either italics (as shown for the second revision in Figure 6.8) or a symbol variation (e.g., putting it in parentheses).

This same type of issue occurs in telephone surveys, but in a slightly different way. In this case, the challenge is finding visual ways to communicate to interviewers what content on the screen they must read aloud, what content is optional, and instructions that are for them but should never be read aloud. We discuss ways to use visual design to do this in Chapter 8.

Creating an Effective Question Layout

Creating an effective question layout involves applying multiple visual design elements and properties at one time and ensuring that they work well together. For example, applying these four visual design guidelines we just discussed to the questions in Figure 6.6 helped us organize all of the information to make them more easily perceived and processed and, most importantly, to make it easier to provide a response. In addition to easing the response task, these changes also made the questions appear more professional, thereby increasing the likelihood that they would be taken seriously by potential respondents (i.e., perhaps increasing rewards and trust).

Other examples of poor question layouts are shown in the top and middle rows of Figure 6.9 (color image shown in Mahon-Haft & Dillman, 2010). The question layout in the first row uses a purple background with different elements on the page shaded in different colors (red, yellow, and green). The shading helps to group information but is not used to necessarily group related information (e.g., the question stem is shaded in red, whereas the answer spaces are shaded in yellow). Further, the use of different colors means each competes for respondents' attention, and the use of multiple colors that do not work well together interrupts the visual rhythm. Further, some information is right justified, some is centered, and still other information is left justified; this makes it hard for respondents to know where to focus their attention first and how to navigate the question. For example, some respondents will focus first on the left side and see the answer spaces/response options before the question stem, while others may first focus on the question stem since it is centered and highlighted in red (and since the question stem and answer spaces are not aligned they are unlikely to be grouped together, especially because of the differences in shading mentioned earlier).

FIGURE 6.9   Examples of bad and good design.

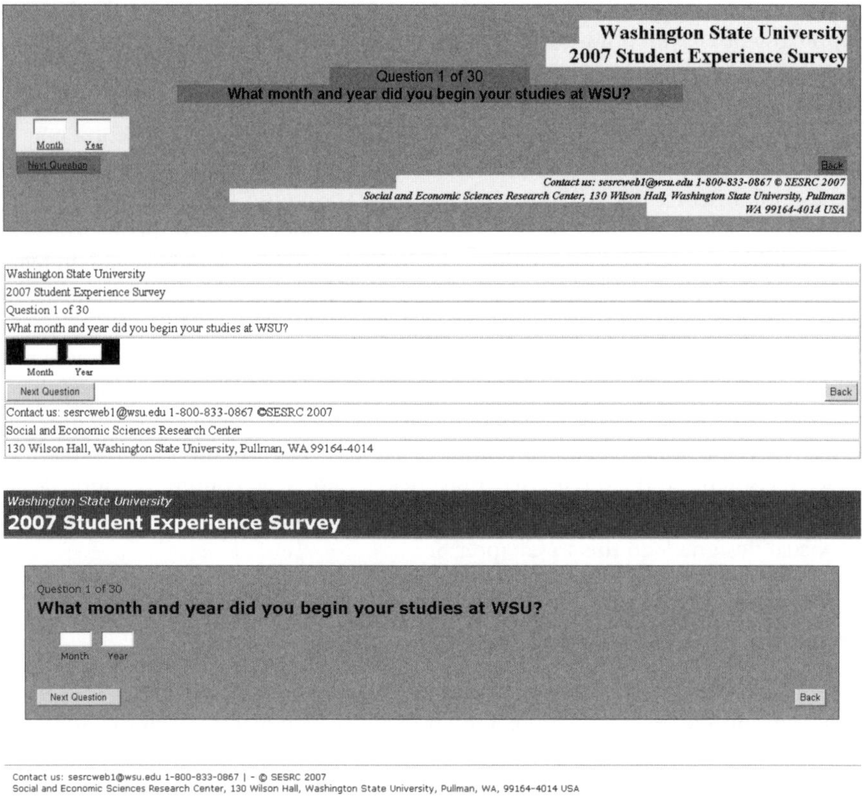

Source: "Does Visual Appeal Matter? Effects of Web Survey Screen Design on Survey Quality," by T. Mahon-Haft and D. A. Dillman, 2010, *Survey Research Methods, 4*(1), pp. 43–59.

FIGURE 6.9 (continued).

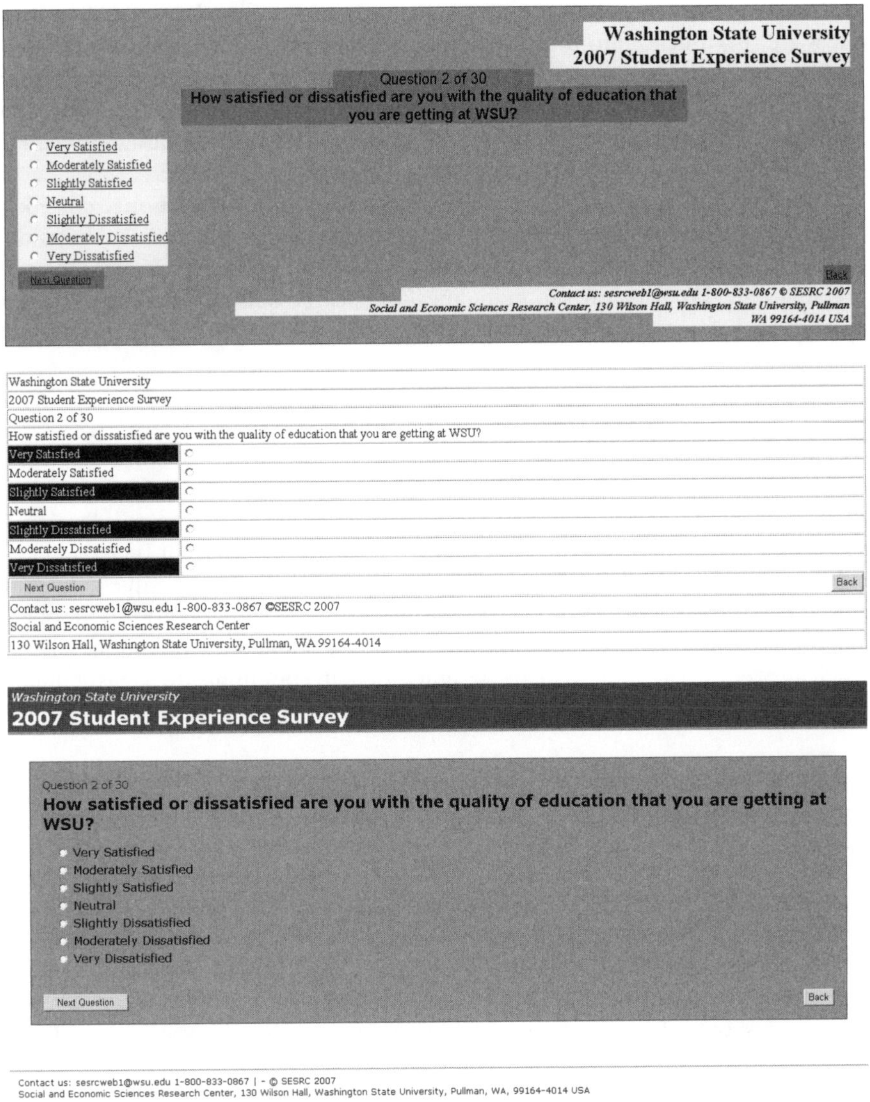

The example in the middle row in Figure 6.9 also is difficult for respondents to process but for different reasons. Here, there is very little variation among the different visual elements on the page, making it difficult for respondents to know which information to group together. For example, the question stem is in the same font and color as the sponsorship information, survey name, and question counter. Further, the black shading around the answer spaces and some of the response options will likely draw respondents' attention to these elements before they have read the question stem.

The final example in the third row in Figure 6.9 shows these screens redesigned applying the guidelines discussed thus far. This layout creates effective subgrouping between the sponsorship information, the question area, and the contact information. Further, the sage green background of the question area helps respondents focus their attention on the most critical elements they need to answer the question and navigate to the next question. The bolding of the question stem helps respondents focus their attention on it first, especially since the answer spaces are also indented to the right somewhat underneath the question stem—to encourage respondents to process them after the question stem. In fact, research by Mahon-Haft and Dillman (2010) showed that respondents spent more time per page on the poorly designed questions in Figure 6.9, and the design in the top row also resulted in higher item nonresponse rates.

Once a general question layout has been determined, additional considerations are still needed to effectively design different types of survey questions (e.g., open-ended vs. closed-ended questions) and to organize questions across screens/pages. We now turn to guidelines for specific question types and for the visual design of questionnaire pages and screens.

GUIDELINES FOR THE VISUAL PRESENTATION OF OPEN-ENDED QUESTIONS

In Guidelines 5.1 to 5.4, we discussed strategies for ensuring that respondents provide the right type and specificity of answers to the three different types of open-ended questions. These guidelines focused on the wording of the question stem and the answer box labels. However, the visual design of the answer boxes for open-ended questions is also important. The following guidelines highlight ways in which answer boxes can be visually designed to help communicate to respondents what type of response is needed, and how much information they should provide.

Guideline 6.8: Provide a Single Answer Box If Only One Answer Is Needed and Multiple Answer Boxes If Multiple Answers Are Needed

Since the three main types of open-ended questions ask for different types of responses (i.e., descriptive, numeric, or list style), their answer boxes should be designed accordingly. For example, a descriptive open-ended question should be accompanied by one large box in which respondents can provide a relatively long narrative response. In contrast, a very effective way to communicate that multiple answers are needed—and also how many are needed—for a list-style open-ended item is to provide multiple answer boxes arranged as one might arrange a to-do list or a grocery list.

The images in Figure 6.10 are from an experiment in which we tested the effectiveness of this strategy. When we provided multiple boxes instead of one large box, students listed more items. The number of students listing three or more businesses in response to the question increased by 15 percentage points when they were provided with three individual boxes rather than one large box (Smyth, Dillman, & Christian, 2007b). Moreover, responses to the multiple-box treatments contained less unnecessary extra detail and elaboration. Our findings also suggest that surveyors should provide as many boxes as they would like answers. Among respondents who were given three individual boxes, only 5% listed five or more businesses, but among those provided with five individual boxes, 18% listed five or more businesses. One caveat, however, is that providing too many boxes may make the response task appear too burdensome. Indeed, increasing from three to five boxes in the aforementioned experiment resulted in a nearly 5 percentage point increase in item nonresponse for this question.

FIGURE 6.10 The effect of answer space design on responses to list-style open-ended questions.

	Listed 3+ Items	Listed 5+ Items
A list-style question as commonly designed		
	32%	12%
List-style questions with multiple answer boxes		
	47%	5%
	44%	18%
A list-style question with labeled answer boxes		
	51%	2%

Source: Improving Response Quality in List-Style Open-Ended Questions in Web and Telephone Surveys, by J. D. Smyth, D. A. Dillman, and L. M. Christian, 2007, May. Paper presented at the annual conference of American Association for Public Opinion Research, Anaheim, CA.

In some instances, multiple boxes are also recommended for numeric open-ended items. For example, Couper, Kennedy, Conrad, and Tourangeau (2011) tested the effectiveness of providing separate boxes for the month and year inputs of a date item, compared to one single box, and found that respondents were much less likely to fail to report either the month or the year when they received two separate month and year boxes (<2%) than when they received a single box (~22%). The multiple boxes help respondents recognize what pieces of information are being requested, and whether or not they have provided all of the pieces.

Guideline 6.9: Provide Answer Spaces That Are Sized Appropriately for the Response Task

Another way to encourage respondents to answer in the way desired and to discourage them from providing invalid answers is to appropriately size the answer space for the type of information desired. For example, the best response to a descriptive open-ended question will contain considerable detail and elaboration. This means respondents are going to need space to write. A small box such as the one shown in the top example in Figure 6.11 communicates to respondents that the surveyor is looking for a short answer. In comparison, the larger box shown in the revision suggests that a longer answer is desired. Incidentally, the scroll bar shown in the revised item may provide an additional cue to computer-savvy respondents that they can enter more text than the size of the box suggests.

FIGURE 6.11 Answer spaces for descriptive open-ended items.

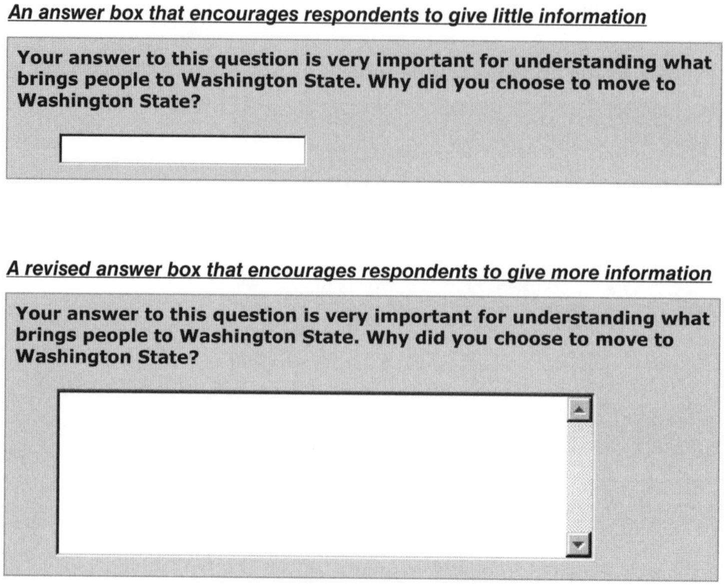

An answer box that encourages respondents to give little information

Your answer to this question is very important for understanding what brings people to Washington State. Why did you choose to move to Washington State?

A revised answer box that encourages respondents to give more information

Your answer to this question is very important for understanding what brings people to Washington State. Why did you choose to move to Washington State?

One of the earliest studies of the effects of answer box size of which we are aware was somewhat of an accident. In 1954, Gallup and the National Opinion Research Center (NORC) jointly fielded the same survey. Although they used a common questionnaire, in the printing process NORC provided 5 times more space for recording open-ended answers than did Gallup. When the data came back, the answers recorded by interviewers on the NORC questionnaires were 4 to 10 words longer than those recorded on the Gallup questionnaires (T. W. Smith, 1993).

In more recent experimentation, Christian and Dillman (2004) compared answers in a paper survey from three questions for which respondents were randomly assigned to receive either a small answer box or a large answer box. They found that responses in the large box, which was twice the size of the small box, were two to six words longer and contained more themes than responses in the small box. Another study using a paper survey compared responses to open-ended questions with seven different box heights ranging from 0.28 to 1.68 inches. This study also found that as box size increased so too did response length (Israel, 2010).

In additional research, we found that increasing answer box size in web surveys can encourage longer answers from late responders (i.e., those who put off responding until late in the fielding period and therefore probably already lack motivation to respond) (Smyth, Dillman, Christian, & McBride, 2006; Smyth, Dillman, Christian, & McBride, 2009). In comparisons of responses to small- and large-box versions of four questions, there was no difference in the number of words and themes provided, or in the percent elaborating on their response (i.e., extra explanation about a topic) entered by early responders. Among late responders, those who received the large box gave answers similar in length to those of early responders. However, those who received the small box gave responses that were three to seven words shorter and contained fewer themes. The percentage of late responders who elaborated on their responses was also 5 to 17 percentage points lower when they received the small box. It appears, from these findings, that larger box sizes can encourage more complete answers from the least motivated respondents.

In situations where answer boxes cannot be made large enough to accommodate the amount of information the surveyor hopes to collect, including a note indicating that one can write more than the answer box appears to hold may help. For example, we have experimented with including the explanation, "You are not limited in the length of your response by the size of the box" in questions of this sort. Two experimental tests of this explanation resulted in response length increases of 6 to 19 words, more themes, and increases in elaboration on the scale of 20 to 26 percentage points (Smyth, Dillman, Christian, & McBride, 2006; Smyth, Dillman, et al., 2009).

In contrast to descriptive open-ended items, in number-box items, extra description or elaboration increases data entry and cleaning costs and puts one in the situation of having to make somewhat subjective decisions about what to code as the final numeric response. As such, this type of information should be discouraged in these types of questions, and respondents should be encouraged to only report numbers. One way to do this is to limit the answer box for these items to the size needed to provide only the requested number, thereby encouraging respondents to format their responses correctly and minimize extra description and elaboration. For example, in the date study discussed earlier (see Figure 6.5), respondents were more likely to enter the requested number of digits for a date question (two digits for the month and four digits for the year) when the month box was half the size of the year box (Christian, 2007; Christian et al., 2007b). Another example of providing an appropriately sized answer box for number box items is shown in Figure 6.12.

Additional research has shown that the size of the answer box has little effect for items in which the response format is relatively clear and straightforward (i.e., there are few ways to format responses about how often one sees a doctor, sees a dentist, exercises, or drinks alcoholic beverages), but has greater effect for items in which the response format is more ambiguous (i.e., amount spent on prescription and nonprescription drugs)—(Couper, Kennedy, et al., 2011). As is the case with writing dates, there are many ways one can format dollar amounts (i.e., with or without decimal places, with or without dollar signs, etc.). Taken together, these studies suggest that when the format of the answer is fairly straightforward and clear, box size may not matter as much, but when the format is more ambiguous, such as when reporting dates or dollar amounts, respondents will look for extra cues about how to respond; in these cases, the size of the answer box will likely be one such cue.

FIGURE 6.12   How to improve numeric open-ended questions.

An uninformative answer space

In an average week, how many days do you cook dinner at home?

A revision with a more informative answer space

In an average week, how many days do you cook dinner at home?

Days per week (0–7)

Guideline 6.10: To Encourage the Use of Proper Units or a Desired Response Format, Provide Labels and Templates With Answer Spaces

Providing word instructions in the question stem will go a long way toward encouraging the proper type of responses, but some respondents may overlook these instructions. Others may get distracted thinking about the topic of the question and forget them. Locating labels near the answer spaces provides backup for these situations and makes the information immediately available during the reporting stage of the response process (when it is most needed).

An example of the provision of unit labels with answer spaces is given in Figure 6.12. To help ensure that the respondent sees the unit label, we locate it very close to the end of the answer space. Along with the unit labels, we also provide the range of values one is expected to enter to help clarify the intent of the question.

Labels can also be used with list-style open-ended questions, as shown in Figure 6.10. Providing the labels "Business #1," "Business #2," and "Business #3" alongside answer spaces for this question helped respondents focus their answers substantively resulting in more responses that included specific business names rather than general business types. In three experiments comparing unlabeled to labeled boxes, students reported significantly fewer general business types (e.g., a home improvement store) and, in two of the three experiments, significantly more specific business names (e.g., Home Depot) when the boxes were labeled (Smyth et al., 2007b). In hindsight, the students could probably have been helped even more by more specific labels such as "Business Name #1" or "Business Type #1" Depending on the type of the response desired.

Sometimes it is also necessary to clarify for respondents how their answer should be formatted. There are many acceptable ways of formatting certain types of information such as dates, telephone numbers, and dollar amounts. This is illustrated by the following seven ways of writing a single date.

- 3/18/2013
- 3.18.2013
- 3-18-2013
- 03/18/13
- March 18, 2013
- 18 March 2013
- 18-Mar-2013

When collecting these types of information, one should provide a visual template to communicate to respondents which of the conventional formats should be used. Helping respondents understand what format to use will reduce the likelihood that they will receive frustrating error messages in web surveys, and will reduce the amount of data cleaning and reformatting that is necessary in paper surveys.

Visual templates often consist of a combination of visual elements and properties arranged to communicate what format is desired. In some cases, they may also include text labels. Figure 6.13 shows examples of common date, telephone number, and dollar amount formats, each with a corresponding template. These templates layer together several of the guidelines we have mentioned previously

FIGURE 6.13   Examples of templates that can be used to solicit specific reporting formats.

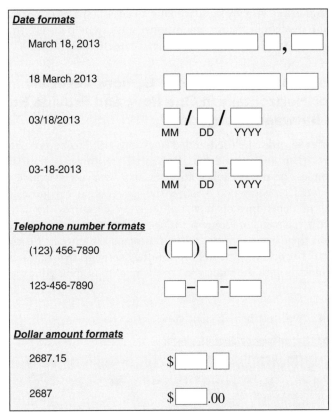

to formulate strong cues about how answers should be formatted. For example, the templates use multiple boxes when multiple pieces of information are needed, the boxes are sized appropriately for the information one should enter into them, and, in some templates, labels indicate what should go into the boxes.

The effectiveness of well-designed templates for date items was demonstrated by the experiment shown in Figure 6.5, in which the percentage of respondents using the correct format increased from 44% to 94%. Couper, Kennedy, et al. (2011) have shown that templates also work well for dollar amounts. In their experiment, they compared answers collected using a template like the last one displayed in Figure 6.13 to answers collected in a single text box with no dollar sign or ".00" label. About 96% of respondents who received the template used the intended format compared to only about 80% of those who received the single text box.

GUIDELINES FOR THE VISUAL PRESENTATION OF CLOSED-ENDED QUESTIONS

As was the case with open-ended questions, the visual aspects of closed-ended questions should be designed to support the message communicated through their wording and the measurement intent of the questions. A fundamental challenge in achieving this is to ensure that no response option stands out more or less than the others in ways that will influence the likelihood that it is selected. In Guideline 6.3, we recommended visually standardizing all answer spaces or response options. The following guidelines focus on additional ways to help ensure that the visual presentation of the items supports their measurement intent.

Guideline 6.11: Align Response Options Vertically in One Column or Horizontally in One Row, and Provide Equal Distance Between Categories

The categories in ordinal closed-ended questions need to be presented in a way that supports their inherent order. Presenting response options in multiple-column, double-, or triple-banked formats may result in respondents selecting different answers depending on whether they process the categories horizontally or vertically, or depending on how the designer organizes the categories. For example, in the top panel of Figure 6.14, respondents who are pretty satisfied with the education they are receiving and who process the options horizontally may choose "good" because it is the first option they come to that captures their view. Other respondents with the same view of the quality of their education who read

FIGURE 6.14 Align response options vertically in one column.

Triple-banked answer categories—Vertical

Q5. Overall, how would you rate the quality of education that you are getting at WSU?

- Excellent
- Very Good
- Good
- Fair
- Poor

Triple-banked answer categories—Horizontal

Q5. Overall, how would you rate the quality of education that you are getting at WSU?

- Excellent
- Fair
- Very Good
- Poor
- Good

A revision with vertically aligned answer categories

Q5. Overall, how would you rate the quality of education that you are getting at WSU?

- Excellent
- Very Good
- Good
- Fair
- Poor

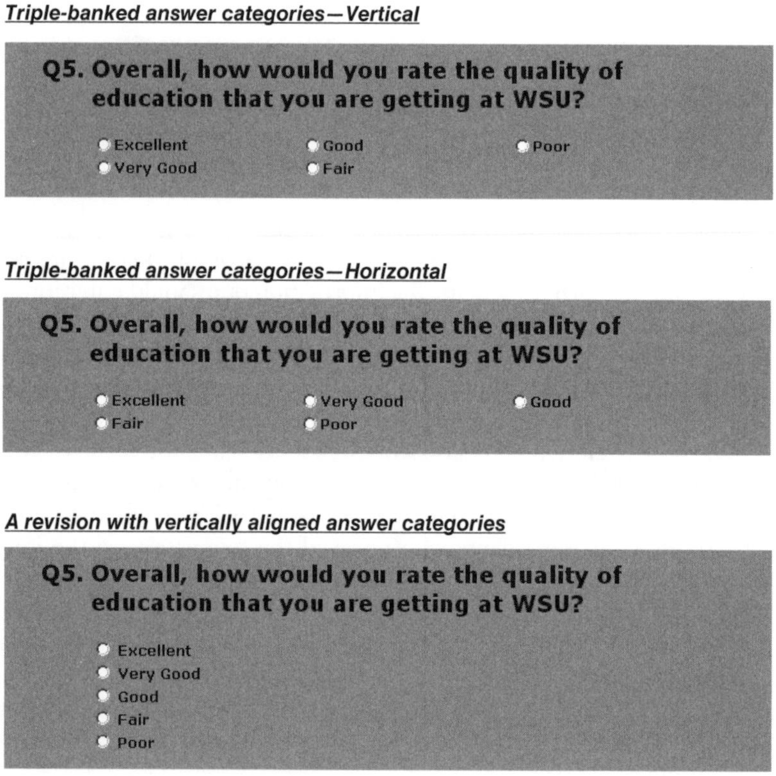

Source: "The Influence of Graphical and Symbolic Language Manipulations on Responses to Self-Administered Questions," by L. M. Christian and D. A. Dillman, 2004, *Public Opinion Quarterly, 68*(1), pp. 58–81.

vertically will probably mark "very good" for the same reason. Although their judgments are the same, the way they map them onto the response scale differs because they process the options in a different order.

Results from both paper and web experiments indicate that respondents process the categories differently when they are presented in multiple columns and that people are more likely to select the second category on the first row, regardless of its label (Christian, 2003; Christian & Dillman, 2004; Toepoel, Das, & van Soest, 2006, 2009).

The simple solution to these problems is to retain the inherent order of the categories in the visual layout of the scale by presenting them equally spaced in one vertical column, as is done in the final example in Figure 6.14, or in one horizontal row. Doing so encourages respondents to process categories in a consistent manner from top to bottom (or left to right). Even if some respondents choose to process the list from bottom to top, they will not be skipping categories, and they will be processing the list in a way that reflects their natural ordering from lowest to highest or highest to lowest.

Evenly spacing the response options in one vertical column is generally preferred for web surveys designed for smartphones or other mobile devices because it minimizes the horizontal scrolling required. Further, for mobile surveys it is important to leave enough space between response options so that when respondents touch the response, it is not easy to accidently touch an adjacent category.

In addition to helping respondents process response options in the right order, visual design can also impact the way respondents interpret and give meaning to response options. In particular, the spacing between answer categories conveys extra information about what a category means. Giving one category more space suggests that it is more important or that its portion of the scale is greater than that of the other categories, and thereby encourages more people to select it. This happens in both nominal and ordinal questions.

Consider the example in the top panel of Figure 6.15, in which the response options are spaced closer together on the left side of the scale and further apart on the right side. Experiments with spacing like this have resulted in more people choosing the options on the right side of the scale than occurs when options are evenly spaced, as in the revision (Tourangeau et al., 2004). In this case, the options on the right appear to account for a larger portion of the scale. In addition, the option to the immediate right of the midpoint appears closer to the spatial midpoint of the scale, thus making it seem less extreme and making it more likely to be endorsed. Several studies have shown that respondents draw heavily on the visual midpoint of scales in interpreting the meaning of scale points (Christian, Parsons, & Dillman, 2009; Tourangeau et al., 2004). As such, it is important to ensure that the conceptual midpoint of the scale (i.e., the "average" point in the item in Figure 6.15) is located at the visual midpoint.

Another example with nominal rather than ordinal response options is shown in the bottom portion of Figure 6.15. When the unevenly spaced version of this question was administered to university undergraduates, nearly 38% chose the option "To have a life partner with whom you have a satisfying relationship." In comparison, only 31% chose this option when the evenly spaced version was administered (Christian & Dillman, 2004). Thus, it appears the extra space associated with this option drew more people to it. Findings such as these reinforce the importance of providing equal spacing between answer categories for both ordinal and nominal questions.

FIGURE 6.15 Space response options evenly.

Uneven spacing of answer choices in an ordinal question

Compared to other veterinary services you have received, how would you rate the pricing at Pet Vet?

Very overpriced	Somewhat overpriced	Slightly overpriced	Average	Slightly underpriced	Somewhat underpriced	Very underpriced
O	O	O	O	O	O	O

Revised even spacing of answer choices

Compared to other veterinary services you have received, how would you rate the pricing at Pet Vet?

Very overpriced	Somewhat overpriced	Slightly overpriced	Average	Slightly underpriced	Somewhat underpriced	Very underpriced
O	O	O	O	O	O	O

Uneven spacing of answer choices in a nominal question

Thinking about your life after completing your education, which one of these do you consider most important?

- ☐ To have a life partner with whom you have a satisfying relationship
- ☐ Enjoy your work
- ☐ Earn a high income
- ☐ Raise a family

38% selected the first option

Revised even spacing of answer choices in a nominal question

Thinking about your life after completing your education, which one of these do you consider most important?

- ☐ To have a life partner with whom you have a satisfying relationship
- ☐ Enjoy your work
- ☐ Earn a high income
- ☐ Raise a family

31% selected the first option

Source: Bottom panel adapted from "The Influence of Graphical and Symbolic Language Manipulations on Responses to Self-Administered Questions," by L. M. Christian and D. A. Dillman, 2004, *Public Opinion Quarterly, 68*(1), pp. 58–81.

Guideline 6.12: Place Nonsubstantive Options After and Separate From Substantive Options

In Guideline 5.6 we discussed the use of nonsubstantive response options like "not sure," "don't know," and "no opinion." When offered, it makes a great deal of difference where these categories are placed. An experiment by Willits and Janota (1996) compared results from the placement of an "undecided" category in the middle and at the end of the following scale: strongly agree, somewhat agree, somewhat disagree, strongly disagree. When the "undecided" option was located in the middle of the scale, an average (across 13 questions) of 13% of respondents selected it, compared to only 5% when it was located at the end of the scale. Locating the "undecided" option at the end of the scale encouraged neutral respondents to choose a substantive option because they had to read through these options first, and presumably only those who were truly undecided selected that option. In addition, when they are located in the middle of scales, nonsubstantive items break up the ordinality of the scale, a practice that should be avoided.

It is also important to graphically separate nonsubstantive from substantive options. Experimental work by Tourangeau et al. (2004) has shown that respondents utilize a number of interpretive heuristics in processing survey questions. One of those heuristics, "middle means typical," reflects the assumption that the middle category represents the average or typical. However, as mentioned earlier, their experimentation has indicated that respondents are more heavily influenced by the *visual* midpoint of the scale than by the *conceptual* midpoint. In fact, respondents seem to assume that the visual and conceptual midpoints are aligned, as is the case in the first question in Figure 6.16. Thus, when a scale is changed visually but not conceptually, respondents continue to use the visual midpoint as their reference point, thus skewing results. This issue is particularly important for ordinal scales in which the categories represent an inherent order or gradation of response.

One way that the visual and conceptual midpoint of a scale can become misaligned is by adding response categories such as "don't know" and "no opinion" directly onto the end of the scale, as in the second example in Figure 6.16. In this example, the conceptual midpoint of the scale is still the "neither" option, but because the nonsubstantive options increase the visual length of the scale, the visual midpoint has shifted down to the "somewhat disapprove" option. Tourangeau et al. (2004) showed that when shifts like this occur, respondents are more likely to select the "somewhat disapprove" category (i.e., they are drawn to the visual rather than conceptual midpoint). In other words, shifting the visual midpoint down the scale causes respondents to give more negative responses.

In the final question in Figure 6.16, the separation of nonsubstantive options from the substantive options shifts the visual and conceptual midpoints back into alignment. In this case we used additional space to create the separation. Another way to do this is to insert a horizontal separator line between the substantive and nonsubstantive options. Additional research has shown that varying the distance between the middle category and the other categories on each side of the midpoint does not impact responses as long as the visual and conceptual midpoint remain aligned (Christian, Parsons, et al., 2009).

Guideline 6.13: Consider Using Differently Shaped Answer Spaces (Circles and Squares) to Help Respondents Distinguish Between Single- and Multiple-Answer Questions

Paper survey designers have traditionally used the same answer space for closed-ended questions throughout their entire questionnaire. This has most commonly been a square check box, or sometimes when optical scanning is used, a circle to be filled in. In contrast, web survey designers typically use HTML form fields for answer spaces. Two common form fields are round radio buttons and square check boxes. Radio buttons only allow respondents to select one response option. If they attempt to select another, their original answer is erased and replaced with the new one. Check boxes, in contrast, allow respondents to select multiple answers.

Because these two HTML form fields work differently, they have come to be used for different types of questions in web surveys—radio buttons for

FIGURE 6.16 Align the conceptual and visual midpoints of the scale.

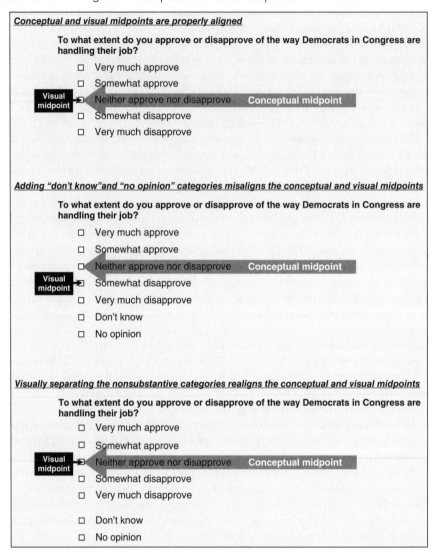

single-answer questions and check boxes for multiple-answer questions. While this is primarily a function of programming abilities and limits, we believe that the different shapes of radio buttons and check boxes provides a valuable visual cue to respondents about how many answers they can provide, and they can work in combination with clear question wording to help clarify the response task.

Consider, for example, the two questions presented in the top panel of Figure 6.17. In these designs, there is very little indication that the two questions differ in the number of options one can select. Unless respondents read very carefully, they are unlikely to catch the fact that the one on the left is a single-answer question and the one on the right is a multiple-answer question. In comparison, the differently shaped answer spaces in the revised version of these questions provide a visual cue that the response task has changed. In addition to altering the answer spaces, these questions could be further improved by rewording the single-answer version as follows: "Of the following considerations, which *one* is the most important to you when purchasing a new car?"

FIGURE 6.17   Use answer spaces to help distinguish between single- and multiple-answer questions in web surveys.

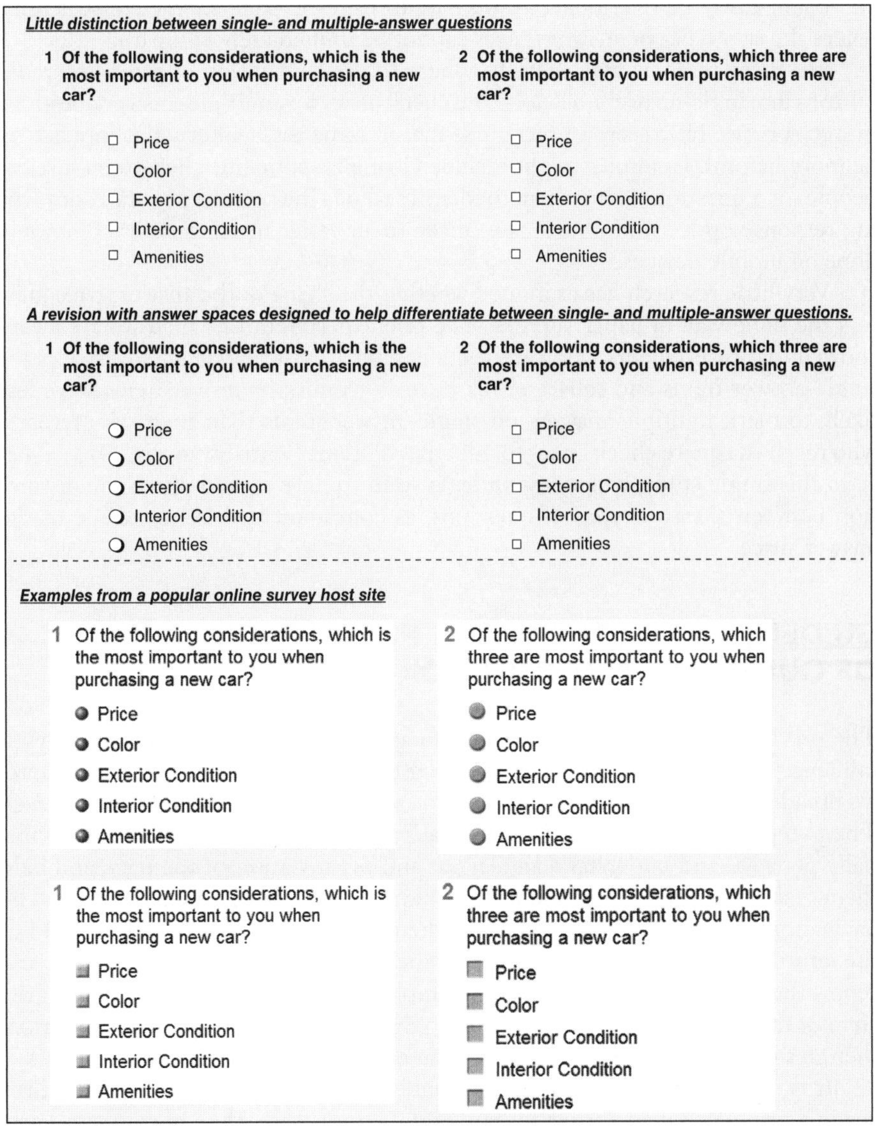

If web survey programmers were still largely limited to radio buttons and check boxes, including this guideline in this edition of the book would be unnecessary. But web programming has become much more sophisticated in recent years, allowing designers more latitude to alter the properties of answer spaces. A somewhat alarming trend that has arisen out of this new programming ability is the standardization of design properties across single- and multiple-answer spaces.

Examples from an online survey host service are provided in the bottom panel of Figure 6.17. Here, depending on the overall design theme chosen for a survey, surveyors get either round or square answer spaces, regardless of whether the question allows only one or multiple answers. To be fair, there are slight differences in the properties of the answer spaces. Properties such as coloring and shadowing are applied to the single-answer spaces to make them appear as if they protrude off the screen, whereas those applied to the multiple-answer questions make them appear more flat. But compared to differences in shape, these differences are very subtle and could easily be overlooked, especially in page-by-page survey constructions where the two types of answer spaces cannot be immediately compared.

For these reasons, we generally adhere to the convention of providing radio buttons for single-answer questions and check boxes for multiple-answer questions in web surveys. However, we recognize that in some cases, alternative inputs may be more helpful. Examples might include having respondents click on pictures of people for a question asking them to identify who is the secretary of state, or turning response options into buttons to make them easier to select, as is commonly done on mobile devices.

Very little research has examined whether the shape of the answer space matters the same way in paper surveys. The one experiment of which we are aware showed that respondents who received a combination of circle answer spaces for single-answer items and square check boxes for multiple-answer items were less likely to mark multiple answers on single-answer items than their counterparts who received square check boxes for all types of items (Witt-Swanson, 2013). That is, in this single study, paper respondents seem to have picked up on the distinction between the two types of questions, as communicated by the shape of the answer space.

GUIDELINES FOR THE VISUAL PRESENTATION OF QUESTIONNAIRE PAGES OR SCREENS

The previous guidelines in this chapter focused on how visual design and layout influence people when they are responding to individual survey questions. Here, we broaden our focus to how visual design can be used at the page or screen level. The two primary goals of visual design at this level are to help respondents initially perceive and understand the layout and organization of the page and help them recognize and be able to follow the navigational path through the page. The navigational path is the course we want them to follow so that they receive all of the information at the right time, answer the questions in the intended order, and report their responses correctly. A very simple navigational path might start at the stem of the first question, proceed first to the response options for this question, then to the answer spaces, next to the stem of Question 2, and so on.

It is important to note that as respondents proceed through the visual processing steps described earlier to gain entry into a page, they move from fairly automatic and effortless subconscious processing to conscious processing, which is intentional and takes effort. As survey designers, we want them to be able to figure out as much as they can about the basic page layout and navigational path of the survey during the easier subconscious processing stage, so that by the time they start consciously expending effort, they are ready to focus that effort on answering the questions. Stated another way, we would rather have them expending their conscious effort understanding and answering the questions than trying to figure out where we hid them on the page. The guidelines presented in this section are intended to help surveyors design pages or screens that make it easier for respondents to gain entry and navigate the page or screen. These guidelines apply generally to visual questionnaires. Guidelines specific to web questionnaires are provided in Chapter 9, and guidelines specific to paper questionnaires are given in Chapter 10.

Guideline 6.14: Establish Grouping and Subgrouping Within and Across Questions in the Questionnaire

We have seen many questionnaires in which it is not clear to respondents where they should begin and how questions are organized. In these questionnaires, respondents have to consciously expend effort searching the page to figure out how to navigate between questions. In addition to using grouping and subgrouping within each question, as is demonstrated in Guideline 6.2, it is important to create distinctions between questions. Establishing effective grouping and subgrouping of questions and their components can go a long way toward helping respondents move between individual questions. We suggest placing more space between questions than between their subcomponent parts to help make it clear where each question grouping ends and the next begins.

Additionally, we recommend indenting the answer spaces or response categories underneath the appropriate question stem (see example in Figure 6.18). This format helps respondents to easily establish a hierarchy (Lidwell, Holden, & Butler, 2003), where they first process the query, then the categories or answer spaces, before moving to the next question. The indentation will help make it very obvious where one question ends and the next begins. We cannot emphasize enough the effective use of blank space in the questionnaire for helping respondents organize the information on the page and group related information.

FIGURE 6.18   Example of the use of proximity, indentation, consistency, and vertical alignment to create effective grouping and subgrouping within and across questions in order to assist navigation.

```
10. What is your sex?

      ☐ Male
      ☐ Female


11. In what year were you born?

      ┌──────────┐
      │          │ Year born (YYYY)
      └──────────┘


12. Which income category describes your total
    family income in 2013?

      ☐ Under $20,000
      ☐ $20,000–$39,999
      ☐ $40,000–$59,999
      ☐ $60,000–$79,999
      ☐ $80,000–$99,999
      ☐ $100,000 or more


13. What is the highest degree or level of school you
    have completed?

      ☐ No diploma
      ☐ High school diploma/GED
      ☐ Some college, but no degree
      ☐ Technical/Associate/Junior college
      ☐ Bachelor's degree
      ☐ Graduate degree
```

Guideline 6.15: Establish Consistency in the Visual Presentation of Questions, and Use Alignment and Vertical Spacing to Help Respondents Organize Information on the Page

In addition to creating effective grouping, it is also important to display questions consistently within and across pages or screens of the questionnaire. The Gestalt principle of Pragnanz posits that visual information that is regular is easier to process and remember. We can take advantage of this by ordering the question components (i.e., question stem, answer spaces, response options, and instructions) consistently across questions. Doing so will reduce the amount of reorienting respondents need to do every time they turn a page or advance a screen, making navigation of the questionnaire more habitual and less effortful. This will allow them to get into a response rhythm, often observed in cognitive interviews of well-designed questionnaires, where respondents automatically and efficiently move from the answer space of one question to the beginning of the next question. Inconsistent arrangement of question parts often interrupts this response rhythm and leads to misunderstanding. Figure 6.19 displays an example of a web questionnaire in which questions are displayed consistently on the page and across screens to help respondents navigate each screen effectively.

In addition to displaying questions consistently, aligning them is a powerful tool in helping respondents to process and organize the questions on the page (Jenkins & Dillman, 1997; Lidwell et al., 2003). When presenting multiple questions on the page or screen, we suggest vertical alignment in which the question stems all begin along a common vertical line and the answer spaces or response options all begin along another common vertical line. This vertical alignment is consistent with the natural reading order in most languages, in which people begin

FIGURE 6.19   Example of consistent page layout for a web questionnaire.

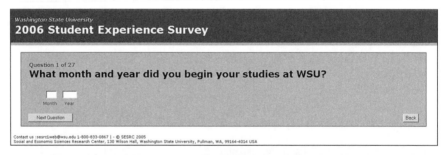

in the upper left-hand corner of the page, move horizontally across the page, and then continue this process vertically down the page, and will help make finding the start of the next question more automatic.

If only one question is shown per screen, as in many web surveys, it is helpful to begin each question in the same location (i.e., vertical and horizontal coordinates) on the screen. When this is done, respondents can effortlessly find the start of the question on each new screen. Indenting the answer spaces or response categories underneath the question stem is still advised even when there is only one question on the screen because it helps create the appropriate subgrouping within the question (see Figure 6.19).

Overall, displaying questions consistently throughout the questionnaire and aligning questions and their corresponding answer spaces or categories vertically helps respondents organize the information on the page and maintain a sense of order as they move across questions. Perhaps even more important, a vertical alignment helps encourage respondents to process the questions in the intended order and decreases the likelihood that items will be inadvertently missed.

Guideline 6.16: Use Color and Contrast to Help Respondents Recognize the Components of the Questions and the Navigational Path Through the Questionnaire

Color is a powerful tool for helping people organize information and understand the meaning of specific visual elements (Lidwell et al., 2003; Ware, 2004). Using color consistently throughout the questionnaire can help respondents clearly identify related information, and can ease the task of answering the questions. Color can also contribute to respondent motivation and the overall visual appeal of the questionnaire. When color cannot be used, contrast can be varied in grayscale to achieve many of the same goals.

A lightly shaded background, as is shown in Figures 6.3 and 6.19, can help respondents in several ways. First, it creates a region in which the respondent can focus attention (the use of regions to assist processing will be discussed in Guideline 6.17). Second, a shaded background allows for the use of white answer spaces, the benefit of which is discussed in the following. Finally, black font color for the text can easily be perceived and processed on a variety of lightly shaded backgrounds.

Lighter shades of blues and greens are often used as background colors in surveys because they are pleasing and calming. Oftentimes darker shades of the background color (or a shade of gray as in Step 2b of Figure 6.3) can then be used for keypunch codes or other information used by the surveyors but not needed by respondents. For example, 20% of a certain shade of blue might be used for the background, and then 80% of that same shade can be used for agency information in order to make it visible to someone looking for it (e.g., a coder or data entry person) but to reduce the likelihood that it will be seen and used by the respondent.

When smaller white answer spaces are enclosed within a lightly colored or shaded area, they tend to be perceived as figure, or the elements that people focus their attention on, and the larger colored area recedes into the background (Dillman et al., 2005; Hoffman, 2004; Jenkins & Dillman, 1997). Consistently displaying all answer spaces in white on a lightly colored background will, therefore, help respondents quickly and clearly identify where they should record their answers, and can also help them identify the overall navigational path through the survey in the early stages of visual processing (Jenkins & Dillman, 1997). Moreover, white answer spaces can help respondents more easily focus their finger, mouse, pencil, or pen on the space, and in paper surveys they can encourage respondents to constrain their marks within the answer spaces, thereby enhancing legibility and facilitating optical processing. Lastly, having all answer spaces appear in white helps respondents quickly scan their responses to see if they have completed all of the question(s) on the page.

Guideline 6.17: Visually Group Related Information in Regions Through the Use of Contrast and Enclosure

Grouping information into larger "chunks" helps respondents to easily process and organize the information on the screen or page (Lidwell et al., 2003). The Gestalt principle of Common Region tells us that enclosing elements together in a region will give the impression that they are related. As survey designers, we can strategically use contrast and enclosure to divide a page into meaningful regions that group related information, such as the title and introduction to the survey or groups of related questions. However, regions need to be chosen carefully so they aid in the completion process. It is important not to group questions or other information into arbitrary regions that have little or no meaning, because respondents might infer a meaning and alter their responses as a result.

The bilingual version of the 2010 Decennial Census is an example of a multiple-page questionnaire that used contrast and enclosure to create regions in order to help respondents navigate the questionnaire (U.S. Census Bureau, 2010a). This questionnaire used a blue background for the English versions of the questions, which appear in the left column of each page, and a green background for Spanish versions, which appear in the right column. The use of color and boundaries created regions to likely help English and Spanish speaking respondents focus their attention on their language of interest.

Another effective use of regions is from the 20-page U.S. Department of Agriculture Agricultural Resource Management Survey, a 2.5-hour-long paper survey that asks detailed questions about farm operations. Grouping related questions into regions and sections is especially important in this survey because some sections do not need to be filled out by specific types of farmers, and the sections are unlikely to be filled out in a specific order or at one time (e.g., some farmers may complete all of the sections they can without consulting records and then leave the remaining sections to be completed once they have compiled the relevant information) (Dillman et al., 2005).

The first page of this questionnaire, shown in Figure 6.3 (Step 2b), has three regions: the first region contains the title, sponsorship information, and general instructions; the second region groups several related questions (labeled "Section A"); and the third region groups several spaces for agency use only (see Guideline 6.4 for more information about visually deemphasizing this type of information).

The regions are defined using large rectangular enclosures with contoured edges to group the related information. The contoured edges help the regions lift off the page and become the objects of visual attention (Hoffman, 2004). In addition, lightly colored shading is used to demarcate the two regions on which respondents need to focus their attention, whereas no shading is used for the agency-only information because the surveyors wanted this area to recede from respondents' attention (Dillman et al., 2005).

Regions can also play a powerful role in helping respondents organize information in web surveys, even when only one question is shown per page. The web survey images in Figure 6.19 have three strategically designed regions. The top region includes the title and sponsor of the survey. This region tells the respondent that they are still in the survey as they move from question to question. Unless something goes wrong, it is likely to be ignored after the first screen or two, similar to the banners included on many web pages (i.e., banner blindness).

The middle region contains the question and its component parts as well as the navigation buttons. We refer to this as the "respondent region" because it contains everything the respondent needs to answer questions and move through the survey. Very quickly, respondents will learn that they can focus their attention in this region and ignore everything else on the screen unless they have a problem.

Finally, the bottom region includes information about how to contact the survey sponsor. It uses a white background to help decrease its visual importance; it is there for those who need it, but should not distract those who do not need it. Cognitive interviews have shown that respondents who completed a 25-item questionnaire using this screen layout do not recall having seen the information at the bottom of each page about how to contact the sponsor in case of a problem. Yet, if the screen froze and they needed help, it's likely that they would be able to find it.

Guideline 6.18: Consistently Identify the Beginning of Each Question and/or Section

In both paper and web surveys, it is important to clearly identify the beginning of each question and the beginning of each section (if sections are used to group questions). Norman (1988) argued that people will have less difficulty using a product if what is required of them is consistent with knowledge or skills they already have. In everyday life, we use numbers to keep track of all kinds of things, including order. Thus, numbering questions in surveys leverages knowledge and experiences that people already have in order to help them understand the organization and ordering of questionnaire components (Dillman et al., 2005).

Question numbers, and sometimes section headers, help surveyors communicate order, identify the start of each new question, and communicate where respondents should skip to when applying branching instructions. In Figure 6.3 (Step 2b), reverse print is used to display question numbers and section letters and titles. The consistent use of reverse print to identify the beginning of each section and each question will be picked up early in visual processing (i.e., preattentive processing) to help respondents recognize the navigational path, and will remain effective at communicating the navigational path during attentive processing so respondents can easily navigate through the questionnaire (Dillman et al., 2005; Jenkins & Dillman, 1997).

Although paper questionnaire designers almost always use numbers to identify each new question, web survey designers have often been reluctant to do this for two reasons. One is that when page-by-page construction is used, the navigation is automatic—with the next question appearing when the respondent clicks the button to advance the survey. The second concern is that respondents may notice when they are branched over questions that do not apply to them because question numbers are skipped (and may even go back and modify their responses to see if they are then asked the questions they were previously branched past). Thus, many web designers avoid numbering questions, even if their questionnaires do not involve complex skips.

However, there is considerable value to numbering items in many web surveys. In addition to serving the purposes just discussed, numbering helps respondents communicate with the survey sponsor about specific items or know where they previously left off when they return to a survey. In addition, question numbers can help surveyors communicate back to respondents.

A somewhat frustrating experience one of us recently had illustrates this well. It occurred while answering a web survey with multiple questions per page that did not have question numbers. Upon clicking the "next" button at the bottom of the page, an error message appeared insisting it was necessary to provide an answer to Question 23, but there was no way to know which question was number 23. Clearly the survey designers were using numbers as a tool to help themselves keep track of the content of the survey, but they did not provide this same tool to respondents. Doing so would have easily avoided much of the frustration caused by this error message.

Numbering questions in web surveys is also useful when a paper questionnaire is to be used by respondents to prepare answers ahead of time that will then be entered into a web survey. This is particularly common in establishment surveys, in which information may need to be compiled across multiple people or even divisions within an establishment (Snijkers, Haraldsen, Jones, & Willimack, 2013).

To overcome the concern about respondents noticing when they are branched over questions, one can use an outline style of numbering. For example, a series of follow-up questions after question number 5 could be numbered 5a, 5b, 5c, and so forth, and the next question that everyone would answer could be numbered 6. Respondents who are branched over the follow-up items would proceed from question number 5 to 6, a move that would seem completely normal to them. For those not branching past the follow-up items, progressing from question number 5 to 5a would also be unlikely to raise suspicions.

Outside of skip instructions, we suggest numbering questions simply and consecutively from beginning to end. Restarting numbering in each section should be avoided, especially when references need to be made to questions in other sections.

We have noted some surveys in which the designers place a large graphical question mark at the beginning of each question because they do not want to use numbers. The problem here is that symbols such as question marks have specific cultural meanings. Using them in ways that are inconsistent with their established meaning is confusing to people. Thus, question marks should not be used in place of numbers.

Guideline 6.19: Use Visual Elements and Properties Consistently Across Questions and Pages/Screens to Visually Emphasize or Deemphasize Certain Types of Information

While varying visual properties is a good way to emphasize certain information, doing so should be done carefully and consistently throughout the entire questionnaire, so as not to cause confusion and increase response burden. Because elements that appear similar in color, size, and shape are perceived as related (i.e., the Gestalt psychology principle of similarity), it is easier for respondents to navigate the questionnaire and complete the questions when similar types of information are presented consistently across pages. This consistency helps respondents connect related information and enhances the usability of the questionnaire (Lidwell et al., 2003), which can ease comprehension and speed up the answering process.

Conversely, inconsistency can undermine processing of the questionnaire. For example, it is distracting and frustrating to respondents when they are expected to provide their response to the same types of questions in different ways, such as checking answer boxes in one section, putting marks on answer lines in another section, and circling numbers in yet another section. Yet we have often seen such changes in formats on different pages of questionnaires for no apparent reason. These types of changes force respondents to actively search out answer spaces and may lead to some being overlooked, which can result in increased item nonresponse.

One way to ease the task for respondents is to have them report responses to similar types of questions in the same way throughout the questionnaire. In addition, if one is using white answer spaces on a shaded background, it is important to ensure that all answer spaces are actually white spaces. We have observed a tendency among many surveyors to use white answer spaces for most items, but to only provide a line on the shaded background for write-in type answers, as is shown in Figure 6.20. These answer spaces are considerably less visible and more likely to be overlooked.

It is even more common for questionnaire designers to use underlining or bolding to emphasize words or phrases in a question in one part of a questionnaire and then use capital letters or even italics for the same purpose later in the survey. Surveyors commonly use such properties for quite different purposes. Each time the property applied to the word or phrase changes, respondents have to take time to understand why the visual presentation is different, and what the change in presentation means. This inconsistent use of visual properties undermines the

FIGURE 6.20 Examples of inconsistent and consistent use of white answer spaces on a shaded background.

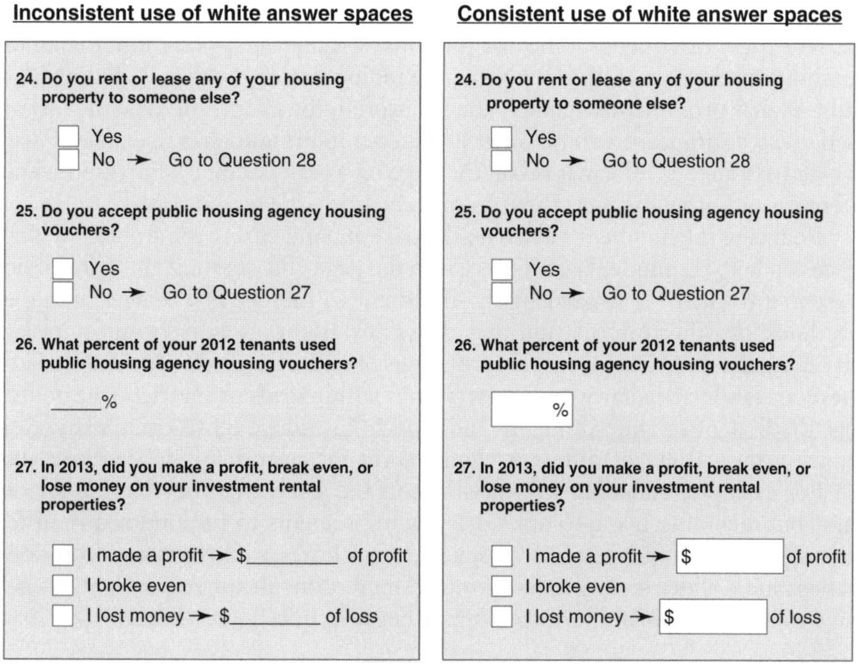

Inconsistent use of white answer spaces

24. Do you rent or lease any of your housing property to someone else?

☐ Yes
☐ No → Go to Question 28

25. Do you accept public housing agency housing vouchers?

☐ Yes
☐ No → Go to Question 27

26. What percent of your 2012 tenants used public housing agency housing vouchers?

_____%

27. In 2013, did you make a profit, break even, or lose money on your investment rental properties?

☐ I made a profit → $_____ of profit
☐ I broke even
☐ I lost money → $_____ of loss

Consistent use of white answer spaces

24. Do you rent or lease any of your housing property to someone else?

☐ Yes
☐ No → Go to Question 28

25. Do you accept public housing agency housing vouchers?

☐ Yes
☐ No → Go to Question 27

26. What percent of your 2012 tenants used public housing agency housing vouchers?

[%]

27. In 2013, did you make a profit, break even, or lose money on your investment rental properties?

☐ I made a profit → [$] of profit
☐ I broke even
☐ I lost money → [$] of loss

purpose of using them in the first place—to help simplify the response task—since respondents have to relearn the meaning of the properties at each use.

Instead, surveyors should use each design element or property for only one purpose. Even if the meaning of a design element or property is not immediately intuitive, the respondent has a better chance of learning its meaning and applying it throughout the questionnaire if it is used consistently, both within and across questions. An example could consist of the following: No matter what question or what part of the question it is used in, underlining is only used to draw attention to important words, white square boxes are only used as answer spaces, and bolding is only used to distinguish between the question stem and the answer options. One can choose to use these design properties to convey different meanings than those listed here, but the important thing is that they be used with consistency and regularity.

For each survey, we recommend setting rules for when to use various visual properties (underlining, capital letters, italics, bolding, reverse print, size of text, color, etc.) so that information is presented similarly throughout the questionnaire. Often a construction rule book describing which properties will be manipulated to display certain types of information can help ensure consistency in how visual information is presented, particularly for longer or more complicated questionnaires. For example, when redesigning the Agricultural Resource Management Survey mentioned earlier, surveyors created a rule book to guide the consistent and regular use of visual information, which then could be applied by all those working on the questionnaire (Dillman et al., 2005).

Many of the rules for visual presentation may be the same from one questionnaire to the next; however, some rules are created for specific issues in a survey and may not apply for other questionnaires, and thus construction or design rule books are likely to vary, at least somewhat, from questionnaire to questionnaire.

Guideline 6.20: Avoid Visual Clutter

We often see questionnaire pages designed with too much information jammed onto the pages or screens. Some designers may use only an 8-point font to fit more questions on the page. Others engage in branding, which involves including logos and text that prominently identify the sponsor(s), the client, the type of software used, the security features, and other extraneous information on the pages. Excessive and extraneous information on the page or screen competes for respondents' attention and often distracts them from completing the task at hand.

Reducing the number of items on the page and increasing the amount of blank space can help respondents gain entry into the page and organize the information presented to them. It is particularly important to remove any images, unnecessary lines, or other information that may draw attention away from the task of answering the questions. Complex groupings of questions, such as grid and matrix questions (and particularly unnecessary lines within grids or matrices), also interrupt the flow of the questionnaire and tend to introduce more complexity. Also, reducing the variety of different elements on the page helps to decrease clutter. For example, including five questions of the same type may be fine for one page, but including five questions that ask respondents to respond in five different ways—such as with text answer spaces, check boxes, radio buttons, drop-down menus, and a slider scale—makes it much more difficult for respondents to perceive where to begin and how to navigate between questions.

Another strategy for reducing clutter is to selectively emphasize only a limited amount of information, no more than 10% of the total visual scene (Lidwell et al., 2003). As a greater number and variety of elements and their properties are manipulated, it becomes more difficult for the viewer to distinguish those that deviate from the other elements on the page (Ware, 2004). For example, if red is used to draw attention to a particular word or phrase, it will become more difficult for the respondent to easily process the change in color as the number of other colors on the page increases. Overall, reducing visual clutter improves the visual appeal of the questionnaire, increasing people's motivation to respond and helping them to focus on the task of answering the questions.

Decreasing visual clutter is absolutely essential when designing surveys for smartphones. Oftentimes the visual scene should be reduced to just the question itself. Because the size of the screen that the survey designer has to work with is so small, the question itself generally takes up the full screen—and for many questions, multiple screens—requiring respondents to scroll to answer a single question.

Guideline 6.21: Avoid Placing Questions Side by Side on a Page so That Respondents Are Not Asked to Answer Two Questions at Once

In Guideline 4.3, we discussed the importance of not asking respondents to answer more than one question posed as a single question. Here we are concerned with the related, yet distinctly different, issue of arranging two or more questions on a page (i.e., page layout). Questionnaire designers are often tempted to ask respondents to simultaneously answer two or more different questions that are arranged side by side on a page. To some extent this practice is a holdover from the days when paper questionnaire designers did everything possible to reduce questionnaire page length by simultaneously introducing two questions that used some of the same information and then displaying them so that respondents were encouraged to process both at the same time. For example, Figure 6.21 shows a multiple-part question in which women in farm and ranch families were first asked how often they do each job and then were asked if they would prefer to do each job less, the same, or more.

Such questions exhibit two problems. One is that they require a respondent to make a choice between toggling back and forth between items or answering one question and then reprocessing each item over again to answer the other. Some respondents choose one path, whereas others take a different route, thus completing the question in different sequences. In addition, frequent testing of such questions has led us to the conclusion that they are difficult and more likely to produce item nonresponse. In this particular example, 11% of respondents left at least one item in Question 11 (frequency of doing the job) unanswered, and fewer than 1% skipped the question entirely. However, 35% of respondents left at least one item in Question 12 (preferred frequency) unanswered, and, even with the additional reminder to go back and answer this question, 5% skipped it altogether.

This is consistent with the findings of an experiment reported by Couper, Tourangeau, Conrad, and Zhang (2013), in which splitting two items, one measuring how often respondents eat 13 kinds of fruit and the other measuring how much they usually ate, across separate web screens versus presenting them side by side on the same screen resulted in lower item nonresponse rates. Importantly,

FIGURE 6.21 Example of double question grid format.

11. Please indicate whether you regularly, occasionally, or never do each type of work listed below. If a type of work is not done on your farm/ranch, please mark Does Not Apply and continue to the next type.

Type of Work	Does Not Apply	How often do you do each job?			Would you prefer doing each job…		
		Reg.	Occ.	Never	Less	Same	More
Plowing, disking, planting or harvesting	☐	☐	☐	☐	☐	☐	☐
Applying fertilizers, herbicides, or insecticides	☐	☐	☐	☐	☐	☐	☐
Driving large trucks	☐	☐	☐	☐	☐	☐	☐
Doing fieldwork without machinery	☐	☐	☐	☐	☐	☐	☐
Caring for horses	☐	☐	☐	☐	☐	☐	☐
Doing farm/ranch work with horses	☐	☐	☐	☐	☐	☐	☐
Checking cattle	☐	☐	☐	☐	☐	☐	☐
Calving/pulling calves	☐	☐	☐	☐	☐	☐	☐
Feeding cattle	☐	☐	☐	☐	☐	☐	☐
Vaccinating cattle	☐	☐	☐	☐	☐	☐	☐
Branding, dehorning, or castrating cattle	☐	☐	☐	☐	☐	☐	☐
Running farm/ranch errands	☐	☐	☐	☐	☐	☐	☐
Fixing or maintaining equipment	☐	☐	☐	☐	☐	☐	☐
Making major equipment purchases	☐	☐	☐	☐	☐	☐	☐
Marketing products	☐	☐	☐	☐	☐	☐	☐
Bookkeeping, records, finances, or taxes	☐	☐	☐	☐	☐	☐	☐
Supervising the farm/ranch work of others	☐	☐	☐	☐	☐	☐	☐
Caring for garden or animals for family use	☐	☐	☐	☐	☐	☐	☐
Caring for children or elderly family members	☐	☐	☐	☐	☐	☐	☐
Working on another family/in-home business	☐	☐	☐	☐	☐	☐	☐

12. Now, if you haven't already done so, please return to the list of jobs above and indicate in the right hand columns whether you prefer to do each job less, the same amount, or more than you currently do.

Couper et al. (2013) also found lower rates of motivated underreporting (i.e., not reporting something because one knows it will trigger follow-up questions) when the items were split across screens.

Although the number of pages is less of a concern with web surveys, the horizontal orientation of computer screens sometimes tempts designers to place questions side by side in this manner. Some web survey software programs even advertise the ability to do this as a benefit. As the Couper et al. (2013) findings suggest, this practice should be avoided and instead items should be presented separately, and a single vertical navigational path should be established through the questionnaire to encourage all respondents to process the questions in the intended order.

Guideline 6.22: Minimize the Use of Matrices and Grids, and When They Cannot Be Avoided, Minimize Their Complexity

When multiple questions that have a common set of response options and/or question stems need to be asked, many surveyors will format them in a grid or matrix in order to save space and avoid repeating the same information multiple times. Figure 6.22 shows an example of a grid in which the same set of response options is applied to nine different items.

While grid and matrix formats help save space, they are among the most difficult question formats for respondents to answer. These formats require people to match information in rows with information in columns, a task that is quite

FIGURE 6.22 Example of a grid format using the same response options for multiple items.

Top labeled grid

14. Please indicate how satisfied or dissatisfied you are with the availability of each of the following in your community.

	Very Dissatisfied	Dissatisfied	Neither Satisfied nor Dissatisfied	Satisfied	Very Satisfied
Parks	☐	☐	☐	☐	☐
Bicycle paths	☐	☐	☐	☐	☐
Outdoor areas to hunt, fish, or hike	☐	☐	☐	☐	☐
Sporting events	☐	☐	☐	☐	☐
Restaurants	☐	☐	☐	☐	☐
Fine arts (museums and theatres)	☐	☐	☐	☐	☐
Cell phone service	☐	☐	☐	☐	☐
Internet access	☐	☐	☐	☐	☐
Libraries	☐	☐	☐	☐	☐

Fully labeled grid

14. Please indicate how satisfied or dissatisfied you are with the availability of each of the following in your community.

	Very Dissatisfied	Dissatisfied	Neither Satisfied nor Dissatisfied	Satisfied	Very Satisfied
Parks	☐Very Diss.	☐Diss.	☐Neither	☐Sat.	☐Very Sat.
Bicycle paths	☐Very Diss.	☐Diss.	☐Neither	☐Sat.	☐Very Sat.
Outdoor areas to hunt, fish, or hike	☐Very Diss.	☐Diss.	☐Neither	☐Sat.	☐Very Sat.
Sporting events	☐Very Diss.	☐Diss.	☐Neither	☐Sat.	☐Very Sat.
Restaurants	☐Very Diss.	☐Diss.	☐Neither	☐Sat.	☐Very Sat.
Fine arts (museums and theatres)	☐Very Diss.	☐Diss.	☐Neither	☐Sat.	☐Very Sat.
Cell phone service	☐Very Diss.	☐Diss.	☐Neither	☐Sat.	☐Very Sat.
Internet access	☐Very Diss.	☐Diss.	☐Neither	☐Sat.	☐Very Sat.
Libraries	☐Very Diss.	☐Diss.	☐Neither	☐Sat.	☐Very Sat.

Source: "Exploring the Impact of Mode Preference on Measurement," by A. Kasabian, K. Olson, and J. D. Smyth, 2012, May. Paper presented at the annual conference of the American Association for Public Opinion Research, Orlando, FL.

complex since it requires them to work both vertically and horizontally at the same time (Dillman et al., 2005). Doing so becomes even more difficult when respondents are working toward the right side or bottom of the matrix or grid where the two pieces of information they are trying to connect are the furthest apart.

Two additional challenges of matrices are that the request to fill them out and the instructions for how to do so are often difficult to understand, and the structure of the matrix leaves it up to the respondent as to whether to navigate it and fill in answers primarily in columns, in rows, or some combination of both. So while they do save space, grids and matrices are subject to high rates of item nonresponse, and some people also satisfice by straight lining (i.e., giving the same answer to every item in the grid) due to their complexity (Couper et al., 2013; Tourangeau et al., 2004). By choosing to use these question formats, the survey designers trade data quality for space efficiency.

Even with these substantial difficulties in mind, we propose reducing rather than eliminating the use of grids and matrices because in some surveys the complexity of the information asked for can best be communicated in this format, and some survey populations are used to thinking about information presented this way (e.g., accountants responding to establishment surveys). However, we have seen matrix questions that required the respondent to remember as many as seven different specifications (through the use of subheadings in both columns and rows and additional definitions or instruction booklets) in order to fill in a single cell (Dillman, 2000). Most people can only remember four to five pieces of information at once, and the likelihood of errors being made when so much information must be connected is enormous.

When grids and matrices cannot be avoided, conscious efforts should be made to simplify them as much as possible. It is important to limit the number of items in the grid or matrix, and the number of pieces of information that must be processed in order to provide a single answer. One survey we saw recently had 19 items on a single screen, and each item was to be rated on a scale of 1 (*poor*) to 10 (*excellent*). That is 190 radio buttons on one screen! The length of this grid alone made it tedious and highly burdensome since items at the bottom of the grid were very distant from the column headings at the top.

In addition to reducing the amount of information contained in them, a number of steps can be taken to help minimize some of the difficulties respondents have in completing grids and matrices. In grids, for example, it is conventional to arrange the items in rows and the response options in columns, and to put the items on the left side of the grid and the response options on the right side. Breaking these conventions can increase response time and missing data (Galesic, Tourangeau, Couper, & Conrad, 2007).

In addition, large grids can be broken up into a series of smaller grids to minimize the distance between the answer spaces for an item and the column headings that give the space meaning. Alternatively, the column headings themselves can be repeated after every five to seven items. This is especially important on the web, where it is possible for respondents to scroll far enough that the column headings at the top of the grid are no longer visible on the screen.

Labeling every answer space in the grid as shown in the bottom panel of Figure 6.22 is another option for easing the response task, as doing so eliminates the need to work both vertically and horizontally to connect necessary pieces of information (Dillman, 1978). While this design appears more visually dense, initial evidence has shown that it decreases item nonresponse within the grid (Kasabian, Olson, & Smyth, 2012).

Visual cues can also be provided to help respondents move horizontally across the grid and keep them on the right row. A series of dots (i.e., leader dots) can connect the item on the left side of the grid with its corresponding answer spaces on the right side. Horizontally shading every other row in the grid or matrix can create the same horizontal connection. On the web, it is also possible to use a feature called *hover* that highlights the row and/or column that the respondent's mouse is on at any given time or to gray out rows as they are completed so that respondents can easily see what is left to do (see Couper et al., 2013, and Kaczmirek, 2011).

Allowing the gridlines (i.e., the borders of the rows and columns) to show through is a common mistake made with grids. The gridlines create separation between parts of the grid that should be connected, and they add considerable visual complexity to the grid (Dillman et al., 2005). As such, they should be suppressed. In addition, answer columns should all be the same width to avoid giving a false impression that some categories should be given more weight than others.

Many of these same types of design strategies can be used with matrices. For example, Dillman et al. (2005) showed and described a complete redesign of matrices used in the Agricultural Resource Management Survey, in which their goal was to create a simplified visual design that encouraged respondents to process the matrix both horizontally and vertically. The "before" and "after" versions of this matrix are shown in Figure 6.23. Because this particular matrix required respondents to remember and use many of pieces of information, the first task of the redesign was to eliminate unnecessary information such as extra column numbering and headings. The researchers then created more distinct answer spaces by

FIGURE 6.23 Redesigned matrix from the Agricultural Resource Management Survey.

Before

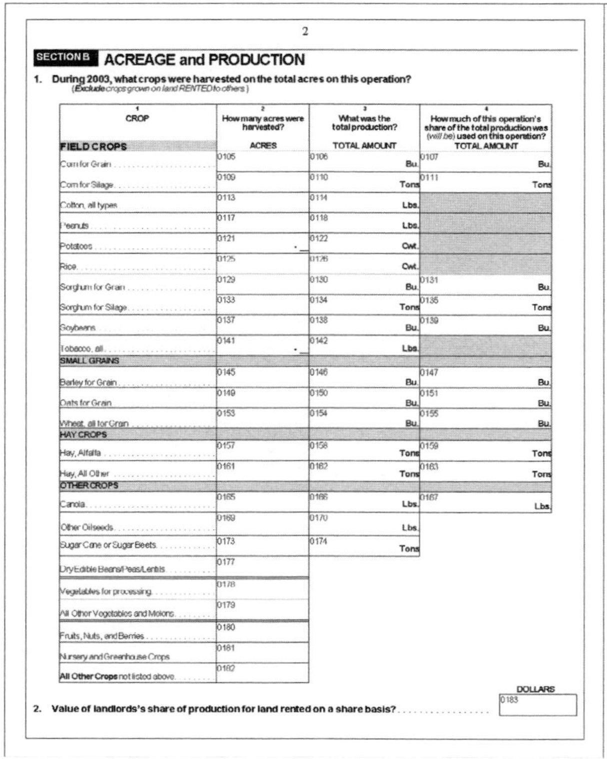

After

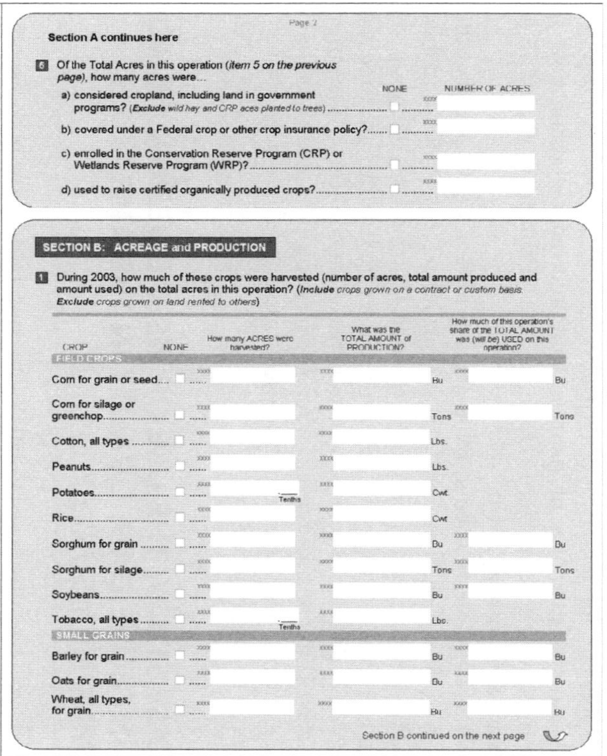

Source: "Achieving Usability in Establishment Surveys Through the Application of Visual Design Principles," by D. A. Dillman, A. Gertseva, and T. Mahon-Haft, 2005, *Journal of Official Statistics, 21*(2), 183–214.

designing them as white boxes on a green background. Doing this allowed them to eliminate the gridlines, which were impeding horizontal processing. Dark horizontal lines and leader dots were added to encourage horizontal movement across the grid. In addition, the answer spaces were placed farther apart horizontally than vertically to help establish the perception of columns of answer spaces that belong together. The result is a considerably simplified matrix that simultaneously drives the respondent horizontally and vertically.

Additional examples of matrices and information about how to design them are provided elsewhere (Dillman, 2008; Dillman et al., 2005; Morrison, Dillman, & Christian, 2010).

One final point to keep in mind about grids and matrices is that they do not work well on mobile devices. With the smaller screens of many mobile devices, typically respondents can either see the items in the first column or the answer categories across the top row; they can rarely see both at the same time. This makes it incredibly difficult to select an answer space that connects the appropriate item and answer category. As a result, when the survey will be completed by people on mobile devices, grids should not be used. Instead, the items should be presented as a series of single questions.

A CASE STUDY: THE USE OF VISUAL DESIGN PRINCIPLES TO IMPROVE DATA QUALITY IN THE AMERICAN COMMUNITY SURVEY

This chapter has introduced visual design concepts to show how respondents perceive survey questionnaires and how various visual design elements and properties can be applied effectively when designing individual questions and survey screens and pages. Many of the guidelines presented involve thinking about not only how a single visual design element may affect respondents, but also how different visual design features work together to impact how respondents navigate survey questionnaires and respond to individual questions.

Applying these guidelines to practical questionnaire design issues involves thinking about many of them simultaneously, and how they should be used together to design effective survey questionnaires. One of us was asked by Deborah Griffin at the U.S. Census Bureau if visual design theory might be able to account for why two different designs of the household roster in the American Community Survey produced different levels of item nonresponse in an experimental test she had conducted (D. Griffin, personal communication, March 14, 2006). The household roster asks for demographic information about every person who lives in the sampled household. Both versions of the household roster questionnaire pages are shown in Figure 6.24. For both versions, there were two facing pages of a booklet paper questionnaire, with each page measuring about 10.25 inches by 10.5 inches.

Missing data rates for each of the questions in the household roster are shown in Figure 6.25. These numbers reveal that across multiple items, one of the designs produced higher levels of item nonresponse than the other design (Griffin & Clark, 2009). Before reading further, look at the two designs in Figure 6.24 closely and see if you can figure out what caused the differences and which version produced lower item nonresponse rates. The visual design concepts and specific guidelines presented in this chapter have provided the tools to answer this question.

The answer is that Design A was best. Close inspection of the item nonresponse rates in Figure 6.25 will reveal that the biggest differences between the two

FIGURE 6.24 American Community Survey household roster designs.

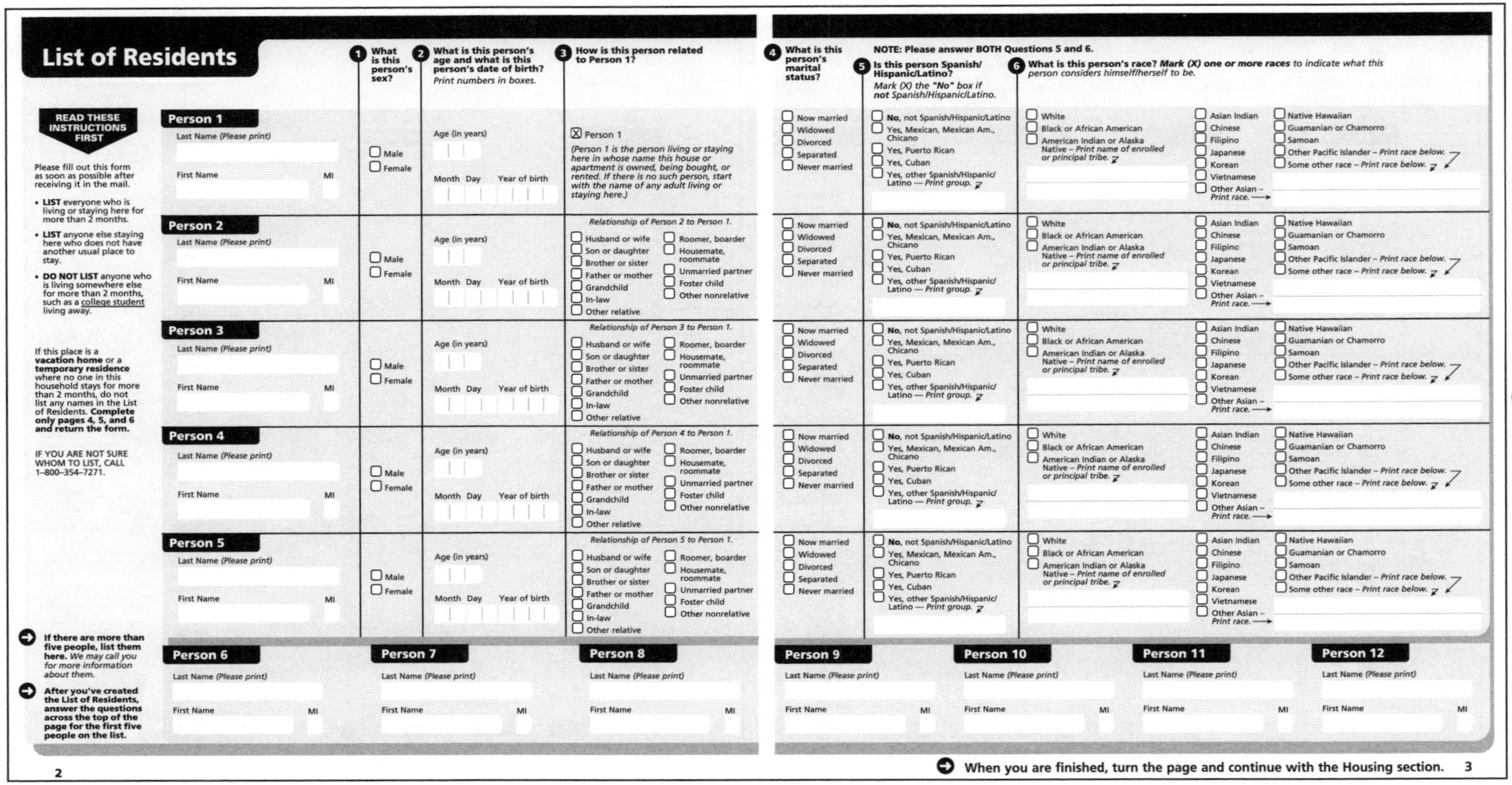

Source: "Respondent Effects Associated with Questionnaire Designed to Accommodate Survey Processing," by D. H. Griffin and S. L. Clark, 2009, May 15. Paper presented at the annual conference of the American Association for Public Opinion Research, Hollywood, FL.

FIGURE 6.24 (continued).

Design B

13191028

List of Residents

READ THESE INSTRUCTIONS FIRST

Please fill out this form as soon as possible after receiving it in the mail.

- **LIST** everyone who is living or staying here for more than 2 months.

- **LIST** anyone else who is living or staying here who does not have another usual place to stay.

- **DO NOT LIST** anyone who is living somewhere else for more than 2 months, such as a college student living away.

If this place is a **vacation home** or a **temporary residence** where no one in this household stays for more than 2 months, do not list any names in the List of Residents. **Complete only pages 4, 5, and 6 and return the form.**

IF YOU ARE NOT SURE WHOM TO LIST, CALL 1-800-354-7271.

If there are more than five people, list them here. We may call you for more information about them.

After you've created the List of Residents, answer the questions across the top of the page for the first five people on the list.

① What is this person's sex?
Male / Female

② What is this person's age and what is this person's date of birth? Print numbers in boxes.
Age (in years) / Month Day / Year of birth

③ How is this person related to Person 1?

Person 1
(Person 1 is the person living or staying here in whose name this house or apartment is owned, being bought, or rented. If there is no such person, start with the name of any adult living or staying here.)

Relationship of Person 2 to Person 1:
- Husband or wife
- Son or daughter
- Brother or sister
- Father or mother
- Grandchild
- In-law
- Other relative
- Roomer, boarder
- Housemate, roommate
- Unmarried partner
- Foster child
- Other nonrelative

Person 1 — Last Name (Please print) / First Name / MI
Person 2 — Last Name (Please print) / First Name / MI
Person 3 — Last Name (Please print) / First Name / MI
Person 4 — Last Name (Please print) / First Name / MI
Person 5 — Last Name (Please print) / First Name / MI
Person 6 — Last Name (Please print) / First Name / MI
Person 7 — Last Name (Please print) / First Name / MI
Person 8 — Last Name (Please print) / First Name / MI

2

13191036

④ What is this person's marital status?
- Now married
- Widowed
- Divorced
- Separated
- Never married

⑤ Is this person Spanish/Hispanic/Latino? Mark (X) the "No" box if not Spanish/Hispanic/Latino.

NOTE: Please answer BOTH Questions 5 and 6.

- No, not Spanish/Hispanic/Latino
- Yes, Mexican, Mexican Am., Chicano
- Yes, Puerto Rican
- Yes, Cuban
- Yes, other Spanish/Hispanic/Latino — Print group.

⑥ What is this person's race? Mark (X) one or more races to indicate what this person considers himself/herself to be.

- White
- Black or African American
- American Indian or Alaska Native — Print name of enrolled or principal tribe.
- Asian Indian
- Chinese
- Filipino
- Japanese
- Korean
- Vietnamese
- Other Asian — Print race.
- Native Hawaiian
- Guamanian or Chamorro
- Samoan
- Other Pacific Islander — Print race below.
- Some other race — Print race below.

Person 9 — Last Name (Please print) / First Name / MI
Person 10 — Last Name (Please print) / First Name / MI
Person 11 — Last Name (Please print) / First Name / MI
Person 12 — Last Name (Please print) / First Name / MI

→ When you are finished, turn the page and continue with the Housing section.

3

FIGURE 6.25   Item missing data rates from two versions of the American
Community Survey household roster items.

Item	Design With Higher Item Nonresponse	Design With Lower Item Nonresponse	Difference
Sex	6.2%	4.0%	2.2%
Age	3.4%	2.4%	1.0%
Relationship	3.0%	2.5%	0.5%
Marital Status	9.6%	5.1%	4.5%
Hispanic Origin	13.2%	7.6%	5.6%
Race	10.8%	6.3%	4.5%

Source: "Respondent Effects Associated with Questionnaire Designed to
Accommodate Survey Processing," by D. H. Griffin and S. L. Clark, 2009, May 15.
Paper presented at annual conference of the American Association for Public Opinion
Research, Hollywood, FL.

designs occurred on marital status, Hispanic origin, and race: the three questions
that are located on the second page. This suggests that on one version, respondents
were having difficulty making it horizontally past the fold between the two pages.
Design A does a better job of encouraging respondents to process horizontally,
even across the fold. This is achieved through the use of several visual grouping
principles.

In Design A, the dominant black line at the top and the green lines at the
bottom of the page create a sense of continuity across the two pages, giving the
impression that they belong together (i.e., the Principle of Continuity), and help
respondents treat them as a group rather than separately. The lines are absent
in Design B, and there are black lines that frame each page, creating the distinct
impression that the two pages are separate from each other (the Principle of Common Region), rather than related. These lines act as a visual barrier that limit
processing to one page at a time. Another important difference between the two
designs is that there is less white space between the two pages on Design A than
on Design B. This is important because of the Principle of Proximity, which says
that items that appear close together will be perceived as belonging to the same
group. The smaller white space on Design A helps define the pages as belonging
together, whereas the larger white space on Design B contributes to the perception that they are separate. Design A could be further improved by eliminating the
white space between the pages to further encourage the continuous flow horizontally across them.

While the dominant horizontal lines, lack of lines framing each page, and small
white space between the pages on Design A help direct the respondent horizontally
across the two pages, the more prominent vertical lines help create the needed vertical connection between the questions at the top of the page and the answer spaces
below. This design feature takes advantage of the Principle of Elemental Connectedness, which says that elements that are connected by other elements will be
perceived as belonging together. Taken together, these design features effectively
help respondents to Design A process the questionnaire pages horizontally, thus
increasing the likelihood that they see and answer the second page of questions.

Design B was designed as a replacement for Design A because it could be
processed optically instead of requiring manual key punching. The vertical and

FIGURE 6.26 Revised version of the American Community Survey household roster that uses a person-by-person design rather than a matrix.

13247028

Person 1

(Person 1 is the person living or staying here in whose name this house or apartment is owned, being bought, or rented. If there is no such person, start with the name of any adult living or staying here.)

1 **What is Person 1's name?**
Last Name *(Please print)* First Name MI

2 **How is this person related to Person 1?**
☒ Person 1

3 **What is Person 1's sex?** *Mark (X) ONE box.*
☐ Male ☐ Female

4 **What is Person 1's age and what is Person 1's date of birth?**
Please report babies as age 0 when the child is less than 1 year old. Print numbers in boxes.
Age (in years) Month Day Year of birth

NOTE: Please answer BOTH Question 5 about Hispanic origin and Question 6 about race. For this survey, Hispanic origins are not races.

5 **Is Person 1 of Hispanic, Latino, or Spanish origin?**
☐ **No,** not of Hispanic, Latino, or Spanish origin
☐ Yes, Mexican, Mexican Am., Chicano
☐ Yes, Puerto Rican
☐ Yes, Cuban
☐ Yes, another Hispanic, Latino, or Spanish origin – *Print origin, for example, Argentinean, Colombian, Dominican, Nicaraguan, Salvadoran, Spaniard, and so on.*

6 **What is Person 1's race?** *Mark (X) one or more boxes.*
☐ White
☐ Black, African Am., or Negro
☐ American Indian or Alaska Native — *Print name of enrolled or principal tribe.*
☐ Asian Indian ☐ Japanese ☐ Native Hawaiian
☐ Chinese ☐ Korean ☐ Guamanian or Chamorro
☐ Filipino ☐ Vietnamese ☐ Samoan
☐ Other Asian – *Print race, for example, Hmong, Laotian, Thai, Pakistani, Cambodian, and so on.*
☐ Other Pacific Islander – *Print race, for example, Fijian, Tongan, and so on.*
☐ Some other race – *Print race.*

Person 2

1 **What is Person 2's name?**
Last Name *(Please print)* First Name MI

2 **How is this person related to Person 1?** *Mark (X) ONE box.*
☐ Husband or wife ☐ Parent-in-law
☐ Biological son or daughter ☐ Son-in-law or daughter-in-law
☐ Adopted son or daughter ☐ Other relative
☐ Stepson or stepdaughter ☐ Roomer or boarder
☐ Brother or sister ☐ Housemate or roommate
☐ Father or mother ☐ Unmarried partner
☐ Grandchild ☐ Other nonrelative

3 **What is Person 2's sex?** *Mark (X) ONE box.*
☐ Male ☐ Female

4 **What is Person 2's age and what is Person 2's date of birth?**
Please report babies as age 0 when the child is less than 1 year old. Print numbers in boxes.
Age (in years) Month Day Year of birth

NOTE: Please answer BOTH Question 5 about Hispanic origin and Question 6 about race. For this survey, Hispanic origins are not races.

5 **Is Person 2 of Hispanic, Latino, or Spanish origin?**
☐ **No,** not of Hispanic, Latino, or Spanish origin
☐ Yes, Mexican, Mexican Am., Chicano
☐ Yes, Puerto Rican
☐ Yes, Cuban
☐ Yes, another Hispanic, Latino, or Spanish origin – *Print origin, for example, Argentinean, Colombian, Dominican, Nicaraguan, Salvadoran, Spaniard, and so on.*

6 **What is Person 2's race?** *Mark (X) one or more boxes.*
☐ White
☐ Black, African Am., or Negro
☐ American Indian or Alaska Native — *Print name of enrolled or principal tribe.*
☐ Asian Indian ☐ Japanese ☐ Native Hawaiian
☐ Chinese ☐ Korean ☐ Guamanian or Chamorro
☐ Filipino ☐ Vietnamese ☐ Samoan
☐ Other Asian – *Print race, for example, Hmong, Laotian, Thai, Pakistani, Cambodian, and so on.*
☐ Other Pacific Islander – *Print race, for example, Fijian, Tongan, and so on.*
☐ Some other race – *Print race.*

2

13247036

Person 3

1 **What is Person 3's name?**
Last Name *(Please print)* First Name MI

2 **How is this person related to Person 1?** *Mark (X) ONE box.*
☐ Husband or wife ☐ Parent-in-law
☐ Biological son or daughter ☐ Son-in-law or daughter-in-law
☐ Adopted son or daughter ☐ Other relative
☐ Stepson or stepdaughter ☐ Roomer or boarder
☐ Brother or sister ☐ Housemate or roommate
☐ Father or mother ☐ Unmarried partner
☐ Grandchild ☐ Other nonrelative

3 **What is Person 3's sex?** *Mark (X) ONE box.*
☐ Male ☐ Female

4 **What is Person 3's age and what is Person 3's date of birth?**
Please report babies as age 0 when the child is less than 1 year old. Print numbers in boxes.
Age (in years) Month Day Year of birth

NOTE: Please answer BOTH Question 5 about Hispanic origin and Question 6 about race. For this survey, Hispanic origins are not races.

5 **Is Person 3 of Hispanic, Latino, or Spanish origin?**
☐ **No,** not of Hispanic, Latino, or Spanish origin
☐ Yes, Mexican, Mexican Am., Chicano
☐ Yes, Puerto Rican
☐ Yes, Cuban
☐ Yes, another Hispanic, Latino, or Spanish origin – *Print origin, for example, Argentinean, Colombian, Dominican, Nicaraguan, Salvadoran, Spaniard, and so on.*

6 **What is Person 3's race?** *Mark (X) one or more boxes.*
☐ White
☐ Black, African Am., or Negro
☐ American Indian or Alaska Native — *Print name of enrolled or principal tribe.*
☐ Asian Indian ☐ Japanese ☐ Native Hawaiian
☐ Chinese ☐ Korean ☐ Guamanian or Chamorro
☐ Filipino ☐ Vietnamese ☐ Samoan
☐ Other Asian – *Print race, for example, Hmong, Laotian, Thai, Pakistani, Cambodian, and so on.*
☐ Other Pacific Islander – *Print race, for example, Fijian, Tongan, and so on.*
☐ Some other race – *Print race.*

Person 4

1 **What is Person 4's name?**
Last Name *(Please print)* First Name MI

2 **How is this person related to Person 1?** *Mark (X) ONE box.*
☐ Husband or wife ☐ Parent-in-law
☐ Biological son or daughter ☐ Son-in-law or daughter-in-law
☐ Adopted son or daughter ☐ Other relative
☐ Stepson or stepdaughter ☐ Roomer or boarder
☐ Brother or sister ☐ Housemate or roommate
☐ Father or mother ☐ Unmarried partner
☐ Grandchild ☐ Other nonrelative

3 **What is Person 4's sex?** *Mark (X) ONE box.*
☐ Male ☐ Female

4 **What is Person 4's age and what is Person 4's date of birth?**
Please report babies as age 0 when the child is less than 1 year old. Print numbers in boxes.
Age (in years) Month Day Year of birth

NOTE: Please answer BOTH Question 5 about Hispanic origin and Question 6 about race. For this survey, Hispanic origins are not races.

5 **Is Person 4 of Hispanic, Latino, or Spanish origin?**
☐ **No,** not of Hispanic, Latino, or Spanish origin
☐ Yes, Mexican, Mexican Am., Chicano
☐ Yes, Puerto Rican
☐ Yes, Cuban
☐ Yes, another Hispanic, Latino, or Spanish origin – *Print origin, for example, Argentinean, Colombian, Dominican, Nicaraguan, Salvadoran, Spaniard, and so on.*

6 **What is Person 4's race?** *Mark (X) one or more boxes.*
☐ White
☐ Black, African Am., or Negro
☐ American Indian or Alaska Native — *Print name of enrolled or principal tribe.*
☐ Asian Indian ☐ Japanese ☐ Native Hawaiian
☐ Chinese ☐ Korean ☐ Guamanian or Chamorro
☐ Filipino ☐ Vietnamese ☐ Samoan
☐ Other Asian – *Print race, for example, Hmong, Laotian, Thai, Pakistani, Cambodian, and so on.*
☐ Other Pacific Islander – *Print race, for example, Fijian, Tongan, and so on.*
☐ Some other race – *Print race.*

3

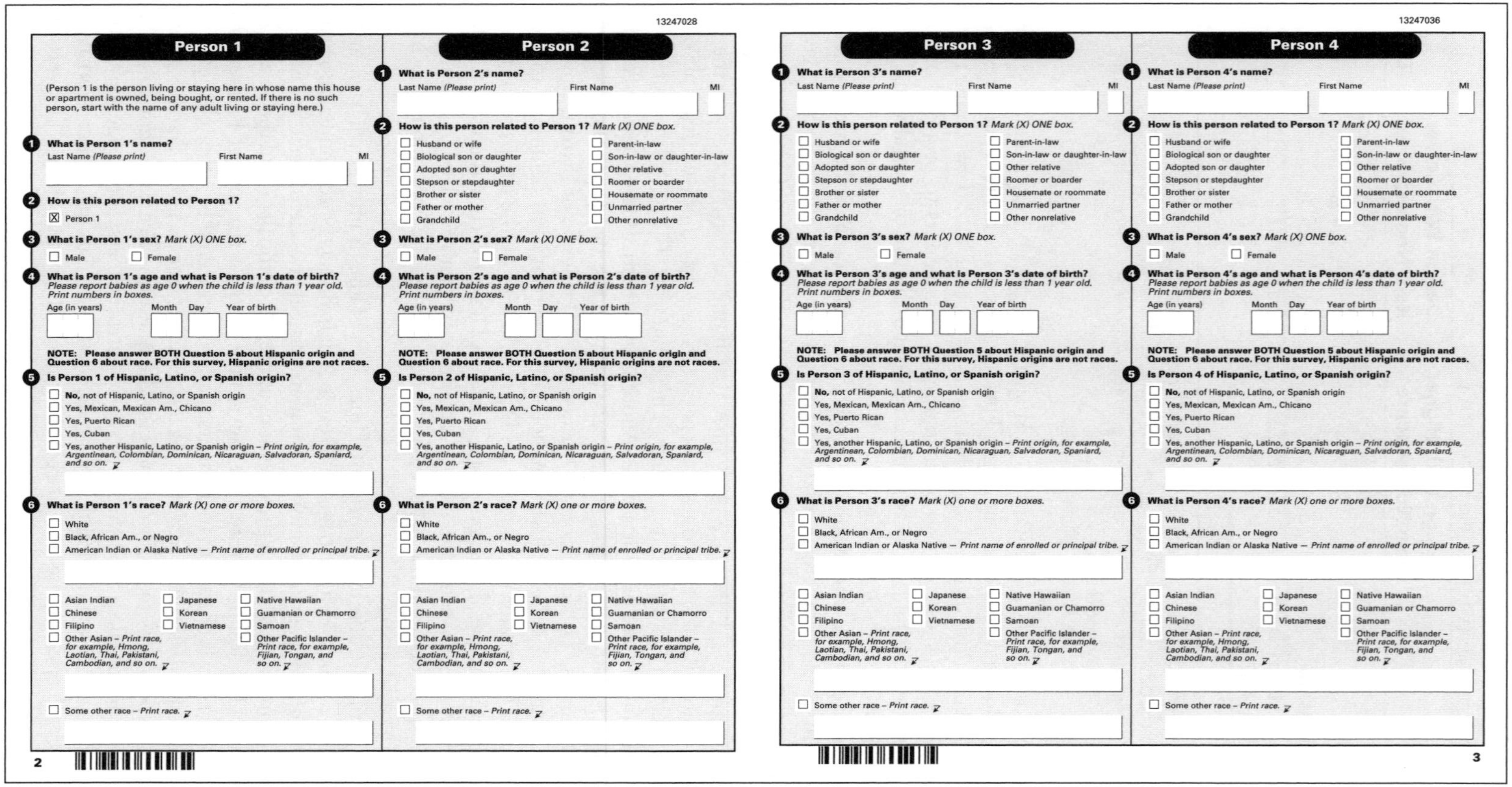

Source: American Community Survey Questionnaire, U.S. Census Bureau, 2011. Retrieved from http://www.census.gov/acs/www/Downloads/questionnaires/2011/Quest11.pdf

FIGURE 6.26 (*continued*).

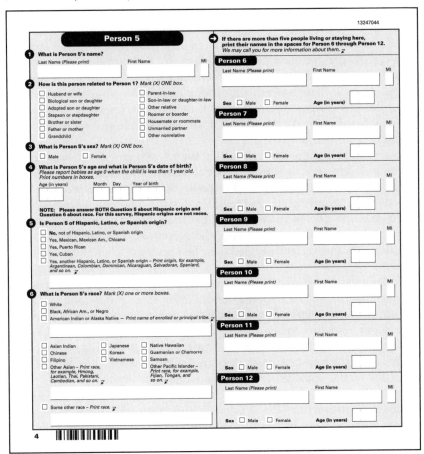

horizontal lines surrounding the fields were placed to provide precise locations that could be triangulated with specific data points in the response fields in order to specify the responses to be processed. The lesson from this experience was that designing optimally for optical scanning resulted in fewer respondents answering the questions (increasing item nonresponse). Another form was designed in an attempt to still allow the optical processing to work but overcome the item nonresponse issues.

Yet the most effective design thus far for these items is the one shown in Figure 6.26, in which the matrix format is eliminated altogether (consistent with our recommendation in Guideline 6.22) and instead respondents are asked the characteristics for one person at a time, as had been adopted previously for the 2000 Census short form. In this version, the questions for each member of the household are placed in their own vertical column, which clarifies the navigational path for answering rather than leaving it up to the respondent to decide whether to work vertically or horizontally. When compared to the matrix designs, this version yielded a slightly increased response rate and lower item nonresponse rates (Chesnut, 2008), and was therefore adopted for use by the U.S. Census Bureau.

CONCLUSION

In order to create a coherent organization for this book, we have dealt separately with the issues of how to word questions and their parts (in Chapters 4 and 5) and how to visually present them (here in Chapter 6). But in reality, these two tasks are usually done at the same time when designing a questionnaire. The words and the visual elements that make up an individual question or a questionnaire need to send consistent messages to respondents. If they do not, respondents are likely to become confused and make mistakes that will increase the amount of error in the final estimates produced with the data.

The example in Figure 6.27, which is from a web experiment we conducted based on a design used in a large national survey, illustrates this point. In the national survey, the designers sorted response options into two groups based on their content. Cognitive pretesting revealed that the subgrouping caused respondents to make mistakes in answering the question. Many respondents attempted to mark multiple answers, but because the survey was only designed to accept one answer, they inadvertently erased their first response when they entered their second.

We designed the treatments in Figure 6.27 to experimentally test the effects of such visual subgrouping on response options using a web survey (Smyth, Dillman, Christian, & Stern, 2006b). For this item, we wanted respondents to provide us with only one response. When the response options were subgrouped as in the top image, 70% of respondents marked answers within both groups, compared to only 41% when the response options were not subgrouped, as shown in the middle image. Clearly, the visual subgrouping had an enormous impact on respondent behavior.

Adding the instruction "Please select the best answer" to the subgrouped version in an attempt to get respondents to select only one option only reduced the number of respondents marking answers within both groups to 66%. However, when the instruction was added, more respondents limited themselves to selecting one option from each subgroup instead of multiple options from each subgroup. Thus, it appears that the visual design of this treatment influenced the way respondents interpreted the instruction wording. Rather than interpreting the instruction as "select the best answer," they seem to have interpreted it as "select the best answer *from each group.*"

This experiment provides an excellent example of how verbal and visual elements can contradict one another, leading to errors in responses. Perhaps more important, though, it demonstrates the importance of stepping back and looking at question construction holistically to ensure that both the words and the visual design of the question are sending a consistent message.

Achieving holistic design in visual modes is fairly complicated, but things get even more complex in mixed-mode surveys, where it is necessary to ensure that the visual and verbal stimulus given in a self-administered mode is similar to the aural stimulus given in an interviewer-administered mode. Because aural modes are more cognitively challenging for respondents, it is often necessary to give priority to the guidelines for designing aural surveys in both modes and then try to apply visual design to the self-administered mode in ways that will not make it substantially different from the aural mode. We return to this complex topic in

FIGURE 6.27   Example of how inconsistent verbal and visual design can encourage poor response behavior (or how consistent verbal and visual design can encourage good response behavior).

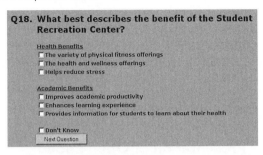

70% of respondents marked at least one answer in both the top and bottom halves of the response options when they were subgrouped

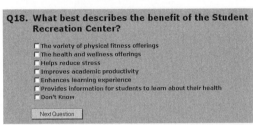

41% of respondents marked at least one answer in both the top and bottom halves of the response options when they were not subgrouped

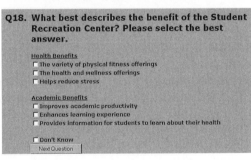

66% of respondents marked at least one answer in both the top and bottom halves of the response options when there was an instruction to select the best answer

Source: "Effects of Using Visual Design Principles to Group Response Options in Web Surveys," by J. D. Smyth, D. A. Dillman, L. M. Christian, and M. J. Stern, 2006, *International Journal of Internet Science, 1*(1), pp. 6–16.

Chapter 11, after first discussing how to order questions and some specific guidelines for designing and implementing telephone, web, and mail surveys.

LIST OF GUIDELINES

General Guidelines for the Visual Presentation of Survey Questions

Guideline 6.1:   Use darker and/or larger print for the question stem and lighter and/or smaller print for answer choices and answer spaces

Guideline 6.2:   Use spacing to help create subgrouping within a question

Guideline 6.3:   Visually standardize all answer spaces or response options
Guideline 6.4:   Use visual design properties to emphasize elements that are important to the respondent and to deemphasize those that are not
Guideline 6.5:   Choose font, font size, and line length to ensure the legibility of the text
Guideline 6.6:   Integrate special instructions into the question where they will be used, rather than including them as free-standing entities
Guideline 6.7:   Separate optional or occasionally needed instructions from the question stem by font or symbol variation

Guidelines for the Visual Presentation of Open-Ended Questions

Guideline 6.8:   Provide a single answer box if only one answer is needed and multiple answer boxes if multiple answers are needed
Guideline 6.9:   Provide answer spaces that are sized appropriately for the response task
Guideline 6.10:   To encourage the use of proper units or a desired response format, provide labels and templates with answer spaces

Guidelines for the Visual Presentation of Closed-Ended Questions

Guideline 6.11:   Align response options vertically in one column or horizontally in one row, and provide equal distance between categories
Guideline 6.12:   Place nonsubstantive options after and separate from substantive options
Guideline 6.13:   Consider using differently shaped answer spaces (circles and squares) to help respondents distinguish between single- and multiple-answer questions

Guidelines for the Visual Presentation of Questionnaire Pages or Screens

Guideline 6.14:   Establish grouping and subgrouping within and across questions in the questionnaire
Guideline 6.15:   Establish consistency in the visual presentation of questions, and use alignment and vertical spacing to help respondents organize the information on the page
Guideline 6.16:   Use color and contrast to help respondents recognize the components of the questions and the navigational path through the questionnaire
Guideline 6.17:   Visually group related information in regions through the use of contrast and enclosure
Guideline 6.18:   Consistently identify the beginning of each question and/or section

Guideline 6.19: Use visual elements and properties consistently across questions and pages/screens to visually emphasize or deemphasize certain types of information

Guideline 6.20: Avoid visual clutter

Guideline 6.21: Avoid placing questions side by side on a page so that respondents are not asked to answer two questions at once

Guideline 6.22: Minimize the use of matrices and grids, and when they cannot be avoided, minimize their complexity

Ordering Questions and Testing for Question Order Effects

Consider for a moment how potential respondents would react to and answer this series of questions (presented here in abbreviated form, without answer categories) in what a surveyor has described as an important questionnaire about their health.

1. What was your total family income from all sources in 2013?
2. Do you support or oppose making immigration into the United States more difficult?
3. What is your favorite sport to watch on television?
4. (If employed) Does your employer provide you with health insurance?
5. How satisfied are you with your current employment?
6. How satisfied are you with your life as a whole?
7. Have you ever taken prescription drugs that were not prescribed to you?
8. Are you a Republican, Democrat, Independent, or something else?
9. How much exercise do you get at work?
10. How would you rate your overall health compared to others your age?
11. How would you rate your health 10 years ago?
12. Should marijuana be legalized in the United States?
13. What year were you born?
14. Do you own or rent the place where you live?
15. All things considered, do you think your health could be better than it is now?

Imagine the reaction respondents would have when they see that the first question is about income—information that many people consider to be very personal and do not like to share. Oftentimes surveyors place the income question first so that if the respondent quits part way through the questionnaire they are sure to have collected this information, which is often deemed as critical. But asking for this sensitive information initially might prevent a number of sample members from ever starting the questionnaire in the first place. Furthermore, the two questions on immigration and one's favorite sport to watch on television could have been placed next because the surveyor thought they would be interesting and fun for the respondent to answer, but they may cause some to question the real purpose of the survey because they have nothing to do with the stated topic of health. These and other questions are likely to get some respondents focused as much on why they are being asked to answer questions unrelated to health as on coming up with accurate answers.

The first health question does not appear until number 4, but is still only tangentially related to health as it asks about the health insurance provided by one's employer. In addition, asking this just ahead of the question about employment satisfaction (number 5) is likely to bias that answer, which in turn may bias the following question about overall life satisfaction. That is, employer-provided health insurance will be more likely to be included in assessments of satisfaction with one's current employment than would be the case if this question did not immediately precede the employment satisfaction question. Likewise, satisfaction with current employment will be more likely to be included in assessments of overall life satisfaction than would otherwise be the case.

The next question about taking prescription drugs that were not prescribed asks the respondent to report a behavior that may not reflect positively on them as a law-abiding citizen. This question is followed by another question that some may find sensitive (political identification). After eight topic changes in the first eight questions, the topic then changes once again for the question about exercise at work. Respondents will then experience more health questions where question order effects will likely come into play, albeit in a slightly different way. Question 10, on how one's health compares to others their age, may lead respondents to erroneously include a comparison to people their own age in answering the next question, in which they are to rate their health 10 years ago.

The next question about legalizing marijuana is the second public policy opinion question and the only one related to health, and is followed immediately by age, a question that most respondents will be able to recognize as being related to health. But from respondents' perspective, the next question about owning or renting the place where they live jumps far afield. The questionnaire then moves to a vague inquiry about whether one's health could be better than it is now.

These questions are more like a list of potential questions that might be considered for a study than they are actual questions that will form a survey conversation that encourages respondents to methodically engage with each question and formulate reasonable answers. But many questionnaires cover a wide variety of topics, ask sensitive questions, and ask related questions as is done in this example; to make them successful requires considerable attention be given to how the questions are ordered in an effort to encourage thoughtful, valid, and accurate answers. Question order is the topic of this chapter. In addition, we discuss how to test draft questionnaires for question order effects and respondent reactions to individual questions.

QUESTION ORDER

While most surveyors intend for and assume that answers to individual questions are complete and able to stand alone, it is important to recognize early on that a questionnaire cannot be viewed as a compilation of completely independent questions that have no effects on one another. Rather, each question and the responses it receives must be evaluated not only on the basis of its individual content but also with regard to the larger context in which it is situated. Question order plays an enormous role in setting that larger context. A good question order will both motivate respondents to complete the question and questionnaire (i.e., reduce item and unit nonresponse) and minimize question order effects (i.e., measurement error that results from early questions unintentionally influencing answers to later questions).

Guideline 7.1: Group Related Questions That Cover Similar Topics Together

A questionnaire should be organized much like a conversation, which typically evolves in accordance with societal norms (Schwarz, 1996). Most conversations tend to follow a logical order in which people respond to what other people are saying with information that is relevant to the topic at hand. If someone jumps to a new topic immediately after every response you give, it appears as if this person is not listening to or caring about what you said, which can be a serious disincentive to continue the conversation and can make it incredibly difficult to keep up with and contribute to the conversation.

Within a questionnaire, grouping related questions is consistent with normal conversation and makes it easier for respondents to answer because they can use retrieved information to answer all of the questions on a topic before moving to a new topic that requires them to recall new information. Switching between topics means that people's answers are less likely to be well thought out, as new topics are more likely to evoke top-of-the-head responses. In addition, constantly changing topics back and forth within a questionnaire, such as in a list of questions at the beginning of this chapter, makes it appear that no effort was made to order the questions in a meaningful way (i.e., the questionnaire appears unprofessional and therefore unimportant).

Guideline 7.2: Begin With Questions Likely to Be Salient to Nearly All Respondents and Choose the First Question Carefully

Once related questions are grouped, it is often best to begin with questions that are most salient and interesting, and then move to those that are less salient. Psychologists have long known that once a person makes a decision to act in a certain way, they are likely to continue acting in that way even when the costs of doing so rise (Cialdini, 2009). Asking the more salient questions early in a questionnaire will help convince sample members to respond and will give them time to build commitment to the questionnaire, reducing the likelihood that they will quit when the questions become less interesting.

Choosing the right question to start the survey off is absolutely crucial, as the first question strongly influences whether sample members choose to participate. In web surveys that only have one question per screen, the first question is particularly important because people cannot easily browse through the subsequent questions the way they can in paper surveys. The initial set of questions, and especially the first question itself, should not be long, boring, difficult to understand, tedious to answer, or potentially embarrassing. Rather, they should apply to everyone to give the sense that the questionnaire is relevant. They should also be easy to read, comprehend, and answer to reduce the perceived burden of the questionnaire. Questions that are interesting to answer will increase the perceived rewards and decrease the perceived costs of completing the survey. Finally, first questions need to be connected to the purpose of the questionnaire to give the survey a feeling of consistency and help promote trust. The income question mentioned in the introduction to this chapter does not meet these criteria.

In some cases, one may even consider adding interest-getting questions to a survey for the sole purpose of developing commitment. For example, one of us was once asked to provide advice for a particularly difficult survey of licensed commercial salmon fishermen that focused mostly on the somewhat sensitive topics of the size of their boats and investment in their equipment. After much discussion with the survey sponsor, an introductory section was added to the survey that asked about the fishermen's views of the future of salmon fishing, whether they would advise young people to enter this occupation, and other issues that were described as the core issues facing the business. The first question asked whether respondents felt that the benefits of being a salmon fisherman were getting better, getting worse, or staying about the same. This was an easy, closed-ended question that nearly everyone in the sample would have an opinion about and would find interesting. This strategy worked; the response rate for this study of individuals, many of whom had not completed high school, was well over 50%.

Oftentimes surveyors want to start their questionnaires with questions that will determine if a sample member is, in fact, eligible to complete the survey (i.e., screener questions). However, leading with interest-getting questions will even be beneficial in some of these surveys. For example, members of web panels are often rewarded for the number of surveys they complete. They are also very familiar with screening procedures and understand that if they are screened out, they may not have an opportunity to complete the survey and receive the reward. Some respondents will attempt to fool the screening procedure and answer the questions even though they do not apply in order to collect the rewards. In this case, interest-getting questions might serve as a useful distraction from the screening task.

Relatedly, with mail surveys, it is important for those who are deemed ineligible to return the questionnaire. This allows the surveyor to distinguish those who are ineligible from those who are nonrespondents, which is helpful for calculating response rates and understanding nonresponse error in the final estimates. Respondents who have answered a small handful of interest-getting questions before being screened out are more likely to feel that returning the questionnaire is useful and helpful than those who have provided no information in the questionnaire because they are screened out at the first question.

Some are opposed to adding interest-getting questions because doing so increases monetary costs and does not always help answer the research questions. These questions add length to the questionnaire, which, depending on the survey mode, can require additional programming, space on the questionnaire, interviewer time, data entry, and/or data cleaning. But what is important to remember is that while they may not be useful from a measurement perspective, interest-getting questions are intended to reduce coverage and nonresponse error.

Guideline 7.3: Place Sensitive or Potentially Objectionable Questions Near the End of the Questionnaire

In addition to choosing the first question carefully, it is important to place sensitive or potentially objectionable questions near the end of the questionnaire. This way, respondents get to them after they have had an opportunity to become engaged with the questionnaire, have established rapport with the surveyor, and have answered the more salient and interesting questions. Respondents who have already spent 5 to 10 minutes answering the questionnaire are less likely to quit if at that point they are asked the potentially objectionable questions. Moreover, some questions may seem less objectionable in light of questions already answered, and placing sensitive questions near the end avoids interrupting the flow of the questionnaire as would happen if they were asked abruptly at the beginning or in the middle. Pretesting can help identify questions that people might object to answering, such as those about income, sexual behavior, criminal activity, medical history, and so on.

Guideline 7.4: When a Series of Filter and Follow-Up Questions Are to Be Used, Ask All of the Filter Questions Before Asking the Follow-Up Questions

Respondents are often asked a filter (or branching) question to determine if they are eligible to receive follow-up questions on the same topic. For example, Kreuter, McCulloch, Presser, and Tourangeau (2011) asked respondents a series of filter questions that determined if they had purchased a coat, shirt, pants, suit, or dress in the past 3 months. For each item, respondents who reported a purchase were asked as follow-up items to describe the item, for whom it was purchased, when it was purchased, and what it cost. A concern when one has multiple filter and follow-up question sequences like this in the questionnaire is that respondents will get savvy to the procedure and intentionally provide answers to the filter questions that will not trigger the follow-up questions (e.g., failing to report purchases to avoid having to give the details about them). This behavior is called *motivated underreporting*.

Research has consistently shown that this concern is justified. When the filter and follow-up questions are presented in an interleafed format, as shown in Figure 7.1, respondents are more likely to answer the filter question in a way that lets them avoid the follow-ups than when the filter questions are all asked together as a group before any follow-ups are asked (also shown in Figure 7.1) (Duan, Alegria, Canino, McGuire, & Takeuchi, 2007; Kessler et al., 1998; Kreuter et al., 2011). This effect is even stronger when the follow-up questions are more difficult (Kreuter et al., 2011).

Thus, when one is using a survey mode(s) in which a computer can keep track of previous responses and feed out the correct follow-up items, it is advisable to ask all filter questions together as a group prior to asking follow-up questions. It might also be helpful to split sets of filter and follow-up questions across different sections, because respondents do not seem to apply follow-up question avoidance strategies across sections. That is, within a section, respondents learn how to use filter questions to avoid follow-up questions, but when they start a new section, they seem to set this knowledge aside, unless it is reinforced by a new series of filter and follow-up items (Kreuter et al., 2011).

In mail surveys where there is no computer to assist with skip instructions, the strategy of asking all of the filter questions before any of the follow-up questions, as is done in Figure 7.1, should not be used because it would greatly complicate the skip instructions respondents would need to follow. In this mode, an interleafed design is necessary. This presents a major challenge when designing surveys that mix mail and web survey modes, which we describe in Chapter 11.

FIGURE 7.1   Examples of interleafed and grouped filter and follow-up questions.

Grouped version

In the past 3 months, have you purchased a coat?
In the past 3 months, have you purchased a shirt?
In the past 3 months, have you purchased pants?
In the past 3 months, have you purchased a suit?
In the past 3 months, have you purchased a dress?

> FOR EACH ITEM ABOVE ANSWERED "YES":
> Briefly describe your most recent [item] purchased.
> For whom was it purchased?
> In what month did you purchase it?
> How much did it cost?

Interleafed version

In the past 3 months, have you purchased a coat?
> Please briefly describe your most recent coat purchased.
> For whom was it purchased?
> In what month did you purchase it?
> How much did it cost?

In the past 3 months, have you purchased a shirt?
> Please briefly describe your most recent shirt purchased.
> For whom was it purchased?
> In what month did you purchase it?
> How much did it cost?

etc.

Source: Figure 1 (page 90) from "The Effects of Asking Filter Questions in Interleafed Versus Grouped Format," by F. Kreuter, S. McCulloch, S. Presser, and R. Tourangeau, 2011, *Sociological Methods & Research, 40*(1), 88–104. http://smr.sagepub.com. Copyright © 2011 F. Kreuter, S. McCulloch, S. Presser, and R. Tourangeau. Reprinted by permission of SAGE Publications.

Guideline 7.5: Ask Questions About Events in the Order the Events Occurred

An effort should also be made to order questions in a way that will be logical to the respondent. In particular, people find it easier to respond to questions about events in the order the events happened. For example, if asking a series of questions about previous and current employment positions, it can be helpful to walk through the different positions with respondents in chronological order (i.e., from the least to the most recent, or from the most to the least recent).

Asking about events in the order they occurred is helpful because autobiographical memories are often hierarchically linked in a network so that remembering one event can facilitate accurate recall of the next event in the sequence (Belli, 1998). In addition, more accurate and complete recall about each position can be facilitated by having respondents answer where they worked, in what position, the nature of the position, and how long they were in that position before responding to questions about what they liked most or why they left the position.

Guideline 7.6: Avoid Unintended Question Order Effects

Schwarz (1996) detailed how, in the normal give-and-take of regular conversations, people tend to give answers that take into account things they have already said. The same is true in surveys; respondents often draw on surrounding questions and consider their previous answers as they attempt to interpret and answer a given question. A simple example can illustrate this. Imagine a survey item that asks, "How many hours did you watch television yesterday?" Most of us can fairly easily come up with an answer to this question. But now imagine that the survey first asked, "When the television is on, how much of your time is spent actively watching it as opposed to just listening to it or letting it play in the background while you do other things?" and then asked, "How many hours did you watch television yesterday?" With the first question as context, our interpretation of the second question will change significantly, and our response will likely change as well. As this simple example, as well as the example at the beginning of this chapter, illustrates, the way the content unfolds throughout the questionnaire can strongly impact responses.

The effects of earlier questions on answers to later questions are referred to as *question order effects*. Although the cause of a question order effect can vary, the outcome is usually one of two types: a *contrast effect*, whereby the responses to questions become more different; or an *assimilation effect*, whereby the responses become more similar. Both of these types of effects become increasingly likely to occur when the questions are closer to one another, both in terms of topic and physical proximity on the page or screen.

Figure 7.2 summarizes various causes of assimilation and contrast effects. As the figure illustrates, question order effects can occur when early questions influence the cognitive processing of later questions (i.e., a *cognitive-based order effect*) or when early questions invoke a social norm that affects the way later questions are answered (i.e., a *normative-based order effect*). The following examples illustrate how each of the effects in Figure 7.2 can occur in a survey.

Priming

One example of priming was found in an administration of the National Health Interview Survey on Disability. In an attempt to measure the prevalence of chronic conditions in the population, the researchers randomly assigned respondents to one of six condition checklists. After the checklists were administered, all respondents were asked questions about disabilities, including whether they had a disability and, if so, what caused it. In response to the question about what caused their disability, nearly 49% of respondents who had previously been asked about sensory impairments on their checklist reported such conditions as the cause of their disability compared to only 41% of those who had not been asked about sensory impairments. The same pattern held for a number of other types of chronic conditions. Overall, respondents who reported having disabilities were more likely to attribute their disability to conditions they had been asked about previously in the interview than to alternative conditions (Todorov, 2000). The early questions made certain conditions more accessible for consideration in the later questions, a priming effect that resulted in assimilation.

FIGURE 7.2   Common cognitive and normative-based sources of question order effects.

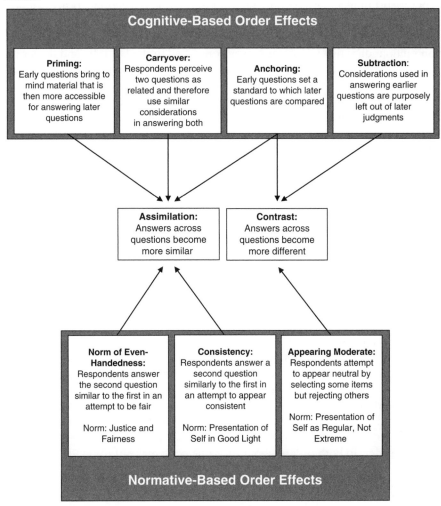

Carryover

An instance that created a carryover effect occurred in a survey in which respondents were presented with two questions: "How would you describe your marriage?" and "How would you say things are these days?" Answers to these two questions varied greatly depending on which was asked first. When the marriage question was asked first, 70% said their marriage was very happy (compared to pretty or not too happy), and 52% went on to say they were very happy in response to the general question. But when the general question was asked first, only 38% answered that they were generally very happy. Thus it appears that when the marriage question was asked first, respondents' thoughts about the happiness of their marriage were carried over into their general judgments about how things were going (Schuman & Presser, 1981).

Anchoring

Whereas priming and carryover result in assimilation effects, anchoring can produce either assimilation or a contrast effect, as shown in Figure 7.2. An example of anchoring that produced an assimilation effect comes from a general population random digit dial telephone survey conducted in the fall 1996 and the spring of 1997 (Herek & Capitanio, 1999). Respondents were administered feeling thermometers in which they rated their feelings toward "men who are homosexual" and "women who are lesbian, or homosexual" (p. 350) on a 101-point scale with higher ratings indicating more favorability. Half of the sample was administered the feeling thermometers for gay men first, followed by lesbian women, and the other half were administered the thermometers in the opposite order. Results are shown in Figure 7.3. When asked about gay men first, the average score for gay men provided by White male respondents was about 32 and the average score for lesbian women was about 34. By comparison, when asked about lesbians first, the average score for gay men was about 37 and the average score for lesbians was about 41. In other words, White male respondents were less favorable about both gay men and lesbians when they were asked first about gay men and were more favorable about both gay men and lesbians when they were asked first about lesbian women. The first category they experienced acted as an anchor to which the second category was then calibrated, resulting in the two estimates moving in the same direction, an assimilation effect.

Results from a Pew Research poll conducted in October 2003 show how anchoring can also lead to a contrast effect (see Figure 7.4) (Pew Research Center for the People & the Press, n.d.). In this case, respondents were asked whether they favored or opposed allowing gays and lesbians to enter into legal agreements that gave them the same rights as married couples, and whether they favored or opposed allowing gays and lesbians to marry. A random half of the respondents were assigned to be asked the gay marriage question first and the legal arrangements second and the other half received the questions in the opposite order. In both orders, about the same percentage of respondents favored

FIGURE 7.3 Example of anchoring leading to an assimilation effect where changing the order of the questions causes both estimates to shift in the same direction.

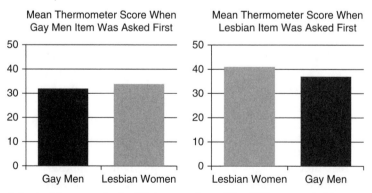

Source: Adapted from results for White men from "Sex Differences in How Heterosexuals Think About Lesbians and Gay Men: Evidence From Survey Context Effects," by G. M. Herek and J. P. Capitanio, 1999, *Journal of Sex Research, 36*(4), 348–360.

FIGURE 7.4 Example of anchoring leading to a contrast effect where changing the order of the questions causes the estimates to spread further apart.

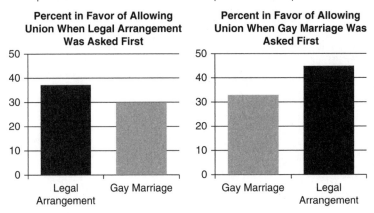

Source: Adapted from *Question Order*, by Pew Research Center for the People & the Press, n.d. Retrieved December 9, 2013, from http://www.people-press.org/methodology/questionnaire-design/question-order

allowing gays and lesbians to marry (30% to 33%), but the percentage favoring allowing them to enter into legal arrangements differed considerably depending on the order of the questions. A higher percentage (45%) favored allowing legal arrangements when they were asked this item after the gay marriage item than when it came before the gay marriage item (37%). Fewer people supported legal arrangements when asked about them first, but more supported them after having been asked about gay marriage, a contrast effect in which gay marriage served as an anchor to which legal arrangements were compared.

In both of these examples, the standard formed by the subject in the first question was applied to the second question, which changed how people answered the second question. So why did one result in an assimilation effect and the other a contrast effect? The answer is likely that when people were asked the thermometer items about gay men and lesbian women, they focused on the similarities between these two groups, but when asked the policy question about gay marriage and legal arrangements, they focused on the differences between the two options. When asked about legal arrangements outside of the gay marriage context, many people opposed them, but when asked about them within the gay marriage context, legal arrangements came to be seen as a much less problematic alternative and thus received more support and less opposition.

Subtraction

Mason, Carlson, and Tourangeau (1994) asked respondents how they would describe the economic situation in their community over the next 5 years and how they felt about the economic situation in their state over the next 5 years. They found that 7% to 10% more people said the state economy would get better when the state economy was presented before the community economy question. The reason for this difference is that once people answer the first question, they tend to subtract out reasons used to justify their answer from their reasoning on the second question. In this particular case, when the question about the community economy came first, new industry was a factor that strongly influenced respondents to say that their community's economy would get better. New industry also strongly influenced responses about the state economy when that question came first, but when the state economy question came after the community question, new industry did not play as large of a role for the state question (i.e., it was subtracted out of the considerations). The result was a subtraction effect, whereby important considerations used to answer an earlier question are taken out of considerations for a later question.

Norm of Evenhandedness

Students at Washington State University were asked two questions about the consequences of plagiarism. One asked whether a student who had plagiarized should be expelled. The other asked whether a professor who had plagiarized should be fired. When the professor question was asked first, 34% indicated on the following question that a plagiarizing student should be expelled. However, when the professor question was asked second, only 21% indicated that the student should be expelled (Sangster, 1993). The likely cause of this difference is that once the students had judged someone from outside their group harshly for plagiarizing (i.e., by recommending firing), they then felt they must apply the same standard to someone within their group.

This phenomenon of adjusting answers to be evenhanded or fair was first noticed in a classic study in 1948 in which respondents were asked whether communist reporters should be allowed to report on visits to the United States and whether U.S. reporters should be allowed to report on visits to the Soviet Union. When the question about communist reporters reporting on visits to the United States was asked first, only 37% of respondents said yes. However, when this question followed the question about U.S. reporters reporting on trips to the Soviet Union, 73% said yes (Hyman & Sheatsley, 1950).

Another instance is shown in a 2008 Pew Research poll (Pew Research Center for the People & the Press, n.d.) in which respondents were asked whether Republican leaders should work with or stand up to President Obama on important issues and whether Democratic leaders should work with or stand up to Republican leaders on important issues. Only 66% thought Republicans should work with the president when asked this question first and subsequently 71% said Democratic leaders should work with Republican leaders. However, the percentage saying Republicans should work with the president increased to 81% when this question was asked after the question about Democratic leaders working with or standing up to Republican leaders. This was because 82% had answered that Democratic leaders should work with Republican leaders. After having taken this stance, it would have been difficult to not also say that Republicans should work with the president.

Consistency

Dillehay and Jernigan (1970) administered three questionnaires pertaining to *policies* toward criminals to three sets of students. One was strongly biased toward leniency for criminals, another was strongly biased toward harshness for criminals, and the third was constructed to be neutral. All of the students were then asked to complete scales measuring their *opinions* about criminals. The results indicated that those who initially completed the questionnaire biased toward leniency later displayed more lenient opinions toward criminals than did those who initially received the harsh or neutral questionnaire. Thus, it appears that these students, after being swayed by a biased questionnaire into supporting a very lenient stance toward criminals, adjusted their answers to opinion questions about criminals to be more consistent with their original responses.

Appearing Moderate

As part of an experiment, a group of students were told the study they were taking part in was concerned with language and the structure of speech. The students were then introduced to the topics of euthanasia and reduced training for doctors through a questionnaire that asked them whether they stood for or against these controversial practices. Half of the students were then informed that they would be participating in a face-to-face interaction with another participant about either euthanasia or reduced training for doctors. They were told the topic they would be discussing as well as the position the other participant would take. The other half were informed that they would be listening to a recording of another participant's views on one of the two topics, and they were then informed of their particular topic and the other participant's views. All of the students were then told that more information was needed before beginning and were asked to complete a set of four questions on each topic. The results from these questions showed that students who expected to have to talk in person with another participant about their topic rated that topic more moderately than those who expected to only have to listen to a recording (Cialdini, Levy, Herman, & Evenbeck, 1973). When confronted with a more social situation, respondents avoided presenting themselves as extreme by moderating their answers.

In addition to these question order effects, a body of research has emerged that summarizes the effects of asking general or summary items—such as "How would you rate the overall quality of life in your community?"—prior to and after asking about a number of specific domains such as streets and roads, education, and police protection. Studies have found that the summary question tends to be scored lower by respondents when asked before a list of specific domain questions and higher when asked after the specific domain questions (Willits & Saltiel, 1995).

Although much of the research that has been conducted on question order effects predates the development of web surveys, we expect these effects to occur in all modes. However, we expect more cognitive-based order effects when it is easy to remember the questions that have come previously (i.e., in visual modes) and normative-based order effects when interviewers are present to evoke social norms (i.e., telephone and face-to-face surveys).

Regardless of mode, the extent to which these effects occur often depends on whether respondents think they are supposed to consider the questions together or separately, which is something we can influence through questionnaire design. For example, in all modes, question order and verbal cues can be used to communicate to respondents whether they should consider items in isolation or together, as shown in Figure 7.5.

Visual design can also be used in web and mail surveys to influence whether items are perceived as belonging together or separately. Grouping questions on one screen or page and/or enclosing them in a common region can encourage respondents to perceive the questions as related and make it easier to identify relationships between them. Tourangeau, Couper, and Conrad (2004), for example,

FIGURE 7.5 Examples of how question order and verbal cues can be used to signal whether items should be considered in isolation or together as a group.

Question order encourages respondents to consider their life as a whole separately from other domains	Question order encourages respondents to consider other domains when assessing their life as a whole
1. On a scale from 1 to 10, how satisfied are with your life as a whole? ☐ **(1–10)**	1. On a scale from 1 to 10, how satisfied are you with your work? ☐ (1–10)
2. On a scale from 1 to 10, how satisfied are you with your work? ☐ (1–10)	2. On a scale from 1 to 10, how satisfied are you with your leisure activities? ☐ (1–10)
3. On a scale from 1 to 10, how satisfied are you with your leisure activities? ☐ (1–10)	3. On a scale from 1 to 10, how satisfied are you with your marriage? ☐ (1–10)
4. On a scale from 1 to 10, how satisfied are you with your marriage? ☐ (1–10)	**4. On a scale from 1 to 10, how satisfied are you with your life as a whole?** ☐ **(1–10)**
Verbal cues encourage respondents to consider their life as a whole separately from other domains	Verbal cues encourage respondents to consider other domains when assessing their life as a whole
1. On a scale from 1 to 10, how satisfied are you with your work? ☐ (1–10)	1. On a scale from 1 to 10, how satisfied are you with your work? ☐ (1–10)
2. On a scale from 1 to 10, how satisfied are you with your leisure activities? ☐ (1–10)	2. On a scale from 1 to 10, how satisfied are you with your leisure activities? ☐ (1–10)
3. On a scale from 1 to 10, how satisfied are you with your marriage? ☐ (1–10)	3. On a scale from 1 to 10, how satisfied are you with your marriage? ☐ (1–10)
4. **Aside from** your work, leisure activities, and marriage, how satisfied are you with your life as a whole? ☐ (1–10)	4. **Including** your work, leisure activities, and marriage, how satisfied are you with your life as a whole? ☐ (1–10)

showed that items are more highly correlated when they appear together on one screen as opposed to being spread across several screens. In contrast, isolating the questions by enclosing them in separate regions or locating them across pages or screens can encourage respondents to perceive them as unrelated and make it more difficult for them to carry the context and memory of previous questions along as they process these questions.

While these tactics will help minimize question order effects, there is limited evidence that question order effects can occur even when questions are widely separated. When one suspects question order effects may occur, it may be judicious to consider constructing half the questionnaires with one order and half with another.

The computerization that underlies many web and telephone surveys makes this quite easy to do. In fact, in computerized modes, one can randomly order all of the questions, although we generally would not recommend doing so without very good reason. When respondents have been randomly assigned to different question orders and one knows which respondents were assigned to which question order, one can assess whether the order made a difference in responses. In addition, varying the order across respondents can reduce, and in some cases cancel out, error attributable to question order. It is also possible to vary the order of questions for mail surveys through the use of intelligent printing; however, doing so requires somewhat more preparation and management of packaging and mailing on the part of the surveyor since less of the mail survey process can be automated. At a minimum, one ought to recognize in reports of findings the possibility that question order may have influenced responses.

Once a question order that minimizes order effects has been determined, it is always a good idea to go back through the questions to make sure that any changes meant to minimize order effects have not undermined the parallel goal of getting respondents engaged with and committed to the questionnaire. Deciding which questions follow others can be an iterative process whereby one attempts to balance the sometimes competing goals of motivating respondents and minimizing question order effects.

No matter how hard one has worked in order to build a good questionnaire, the final essential test is what happens when respondents come face-to-face with the survey itself. Thus, once one has established questions and ordered them in a way thought to reduce unintentional order effects, it is a good idea to stop and test whether the questions are really working as intended. There are several testing methods that can be used to do this.

TESTING QUESTIONS AND QUESTIONNAIRES

The benefit of testing questions and questionnaires is that it helps one diagnose and solve problems before the survey goes into the field. In every questionnaire that we have subjected to testing, the testing has revealed problems that we did not expect. Oftentimes the solution is a simple change, but had the problem gone undiagnosed and the change not made, the potential for increased error is great.

One such instance occurred in a cognitive interview in which a respondent who had recently earned her PhD was entering answers into a newly developed web version of the National Science Foundation's Survey of Earned Doctorates. When she arrived at the following question, the respondent became visibly upset:

C14. What is your racial background?
- ❐ American Indian or Alaska Native (Please describe on next page)
- ❐ Native Hawaiian or other Pacific Islander
- ❐ Asian
- ❐ Black or African American
- ❐ White
- ❐ Decline to answer

Turning to the interviewer, she said, "I am of mixed racial heritage, and it really makes me angry when you force me into one category. Why do you write questions like this?"

Several minutes of discussion followed as she elaborated on her concerns, including that her mother and father were of different races. Finally, the interviewer asked her to take another look at the question and see if there was any way she might be able to register an answer that was acceptable to her. It was then that her original concern turned to embarrassment as she realized the HTML check boxes in front of the answer categories allowed her to choose as many answers as she liked for that question. The respondent was quite aware of this web page construction convention, but because she was so focused on the question wording, she completely missed what the answer spaces allowed her to do (Altheimer & Dillman, 2002).

The solution to this problem was to add the words "You may choose more than one response." This simple and cheap fix very likely avoided a lot of respondent frustration that could have led to increased measurement error on this item, or worse yet, item nonresponse or survey terminations. This example illustrates the importance of evaluating questions and questionnaires prior to the start of data collection.

Traditionally, the term *pretesting* referred to delivering a questionnaire to individuals with special knowledge of the topic or members of the survey population and asking them to complete it and report any problems they experienced (i.e., an expert review). In recent years, a variety of specific procedures have evolved for evaluating different kinds of questions and questionnaires. Many of these procedures are described in Presser et al. (2004), and each contributes to the evaluative process in ways that the other procedures cannot. All are important for comprehensively testing questions and questionnaires, and as such we offer guidelines here that emphasize the strengths and weaknesses of each.

The testing methods that we discuss here are all useful for better understanding how a survey will work and where it can be improved. They are important in evaluating the design of the questions and the questionnaire, as is the focus of this chapter, but also for assessing the impact of various aspects of the implementation procedures and survey design, which we discuss in Chapters 8, 9, and 10 for telephone, web, and mail surveys and in Chapter 11 for mixed-mode surveys.

It is important to recognize that the various testing methods are not interchangeable. Each one provides different information. The pretesting method that should be used depends heavily on what one wants to learn. If the goal is to learn how people understand questions as they are written or how they navigate the questionnaire, a cognitive interview will work great. Learning how a planned implementation will work will require a small field test, while learning which of several strategies will be most effective is best done with an experiment. As such, the first step in testing should be determining exactly what the goal of the testing is and what method will allow one to best reach that goal.

Guideline 7.7: Obtain Feedback on the Draft Questionnaire From Content, Questionnaire, and Analysis Experts (i.e., expert reviews)

Some people are able to look at questions and provide feedback on the content, such as whether the appropriate language is used and the survey actually measures the concepts that the surveyor intends to measure. Others will recognize when important constructs are missing from the questionnaire or when there are technical problems that those who are not experts in a field might miss. As an example, we once had a reviewer comment simply that the preamble to a question was not true: the phrase "Police in this community are responsible for arresting and fining people who violate traffic laws" was inaccurate. Although police arrest people, it is the judicial system that actually levies fines. In another instance a reviewer with knowledge of the population to be surveyed informed us that it was very unlikely that all members of a survey population could answer a few specific questions among a series of items, and recommended that "don't know" and "does not apply" categories be added. Obtaining feedback from these content experts is necessary to ensure that the questionnaire will be perceived positively and will make sense to respondents.

However, many content experts are not well trained in survey questionnaire design. While they are invaluable for identifying the types of problems mentioned here, they may not be able to identify important problems such as the potential for unintended question order effects or when the scale that is provided might bias responses. For this reason, it is equally important to seek feedback from experts in questionnaire design.

It is also important to get feedback from people who approach their review from more of an analytic perspective. For example, in one instance an expert reviewer recognized that the categories a student researcher was providing with a household income question were not very distinctive, because the highest category was only $20,000 per year and higher. Because the reviewer approached the review from more of an analytic perspective, he recognized that most responses would be clustered in the highest category, which would limit the analytic usefulness of the data, even though the question stem was written in a way people could understand and answer.

Others might have considerable knowledge about how questions are asked in large national surveys such as the American Community Survey, and will be able to provide feedback about whether data that are collected could be compared to those surveys. This is often a concern with demographic items that will be used for benchmarking or weighting, but can also be important when trying to examine how attitudes in a local population compare to those reported from national surveys or polls.

It would be quite unusual for a single person to have the ability to identify all of the potential problems with questions and a questionnaire. Testing questionnaires for these items requires getting evaluations from people with technical knowledge about the survey topic, how demographic data are collected in comparison surveys, statistical analysis techniques, survey mode effects, questionnaire design, and characteristics of the population to be surveyed.

Many studies fail to achieve their objectives because surveyors limit this phase of pretesting only to colleagues down the hallway who are experts in some aspect of survey construction or, at the other extreme, to people who are members of the study population. But questionnaires fail for many reasons, and having a systematic approach to obtaining feedback from a variety of knowledgeable people on a complete draft of the questionnaire is essential for evaluating, in a preliminary way, potential survey design problems.

Guideline 7.8: Conduct Cognitive Interviews of the Complete Questionnaire in Order to Identify Wording, Question Order, Visual Design, and Navigation Problems

Cognitive interviewing emerged in the early 1990s as a means of determining whether respondents comprehend questions as intended by the survey sponsor and whether questions can be answered accurately (Forsyth & Lessler, 1991; Willis, 1999; Willis, 2004). Cognitive interviews have now become the dominant mode of testing questions and questionnaires. Some organizations, such as the U.S. Census Bureau, which does many continuing surveys, have even mandated that before question wording changes can be made they must be tested. Cognitive interviews are considered an appropriate procedure for evaluating such changes, often providing insights that a pilot field test cannot (Dillman & Redline, 2004).

In think-aloud cognitive interviews, participants are asked to respond to a questionnaire in the presence of an interviewer. While they are going through the questionnaire, they are instructed to think aloud; that is, to tell the interviewer everything they read and what they are thinking about at all times. By listening to what respondents say and probing where necessary, the interviewer can get an understanding of how questions are being processed and understood, how answers are being formed, and whether the surveyor's intent for each question is being realized.

When a think-aloud cognitive interview begins, the interviewer explains to the respondent that she will be asked to complete a questionnaire in a special way, which is outlined in Figure 7.6. The respondent is told that this includes telling the interviewer everything she is thinking as she develops and reports her answers. The respondent is then asked to complete some practice questions in order to learn the technique. This part of the interview is critical, and we commonly ask one and sometimes both of these questions:

How many residences have you lived in since you were born?

_____ Number of residences

How many windows are in your home?

_____Number of windows

The first question is often difficult for people to answer, especially if they have lived in many different locations. Typically some people start counting from birth, whereas other people make an estimate. It has been our experience in more than 400 interviews in which this question has been used that some people will think of cities in which they have lived, whereas others will think about individual residences. Regardless of which way people answer, we explain to respondents that when we have asked this question in such interviews some people have answered each way. We also explain that when we learn that people interpret the question differently it tells us that the question needs to be improved, and that is why we do interviews of this nature.

People's answers to the question on windows usually allow us to begin to probe, for example, asking whether they counted a sliding glass door, what they may have done with any multiple-pane windows, and so on. By the time this practice questionnaire is complete, respondents have usually learned what the interview is designed to do and have become comfortable with thinking aloud. In addition, the entire interview experience has become far less threatening to them than it may have appeared at the beginning of the interview session. Practice questions shift the emphasis from providing answers that are correct, and that may reflect on the respondent's competence, to helping the interviewer identify problems with the questions written by the surveyor. In sum, the practice questions define expectations for the interview, provide respondents with the reasons for an outloud answering process that probably seems unnatural to them, and help them

FIGURE 7.6   Example of protocol used for testing U.S. Census questionnaires.

A. Introduction

Thank you for coming here today to help us out. The reason we asked for your help is that every 10 years the U.S. Census Bureau conducts a complete count of everyone who is living in the United States. All residences are mailed the Census form with the request that people who live there complete and return it. Today I am going to ask you to look at Census forms that are being evaluated for possible use in the 2010 Census. Your reactions to these forms will provide us with information that will help make the form as easy to complete as possible. Okay?

B. Hand Respondent Confidentiality Form

The first thing I need to do is to ask you to read and sign this consent form. But first let me explain what it is about. This interview is voluntary. It is being conducted by us for the U.S. Census Bureau, which is located in Washington DC. Everything you write on the Census form is confidential. The only people who can see the information you provide are employees of the Census Bureau and those of us at Washington State University who will be conducting the interviews. We have been sworn by the Census Bureau to keep individual answers confidential, and we can be fined if we reveal peoples' specific answers in any way that makes the person identifiable. The statement we are asking you to sign indicates that you have volunteered for this interview. I will also sign it as well since I am the person conducting the interview and I want to assure you in writing of my promise to keep all of your information confidential.

C. Explain Procedure

In a couple of minutes, I am going to hand you a Census form in an envelope. When I do, I would like you to talk out loud about your reactions to the form as you read questions and fill it out. I would like to know everything you think about it. Talking out loud about these sorts of things may seem a little unusual, so before I give you the Census mailing, I have a really short *practice* mailing. When I give it to you, please tell me everything you are thinking as you look at the envelope, and start deciding what to do with it and the form inside. I would like to know any thoughts you have about whether it strikes you in a favorable or unfavorable way, whether it is clear about what to do or not do, and so forth.

D. Hand Respondent Practice Mailout

Okay, please read the questions out loud and tell me everything you are thinking about while you fill it out.

(Provide positive reinforcement, e.g., "*Good, that's what we need to know.*")

(Encourage the respondent to provide other information, e.g., "*When you do the real Census form just be sure that you tell us about your reactions to everything, the envelope, the way the whole thing looks, whether it's clear what to do or not do, anything you don't understand, or anything that seems strange.*")

FIGURE 7.6 *(continued).*

E. Hand First Mailout to Respondent

Now here is the envelope that might arrive in the mailbox at the address for which you are completing the Census form in 2010. Please take your time and tell me any reactions you have to everything that you see in front of you. (Note: If person is responding for someone else, e.g., an elderly friend, mark here ☐ and make sure respondent understands our expectations.)

1. Any reactions to the mailing package:
2. Did respondent read the cover letter?
    - ❏ Fully
    - ❏ Partially
    - ❏ Not at all
3. Did respondent react at all to the opportunity to fill out the form electronically (from the cover letter)? If so, how?

F. Ask Respondent to Fill Out the Form Contained Inside

Now, please fill out the census form and talk out loud about your impressions of it. We would like for you to read whatever you would read at home while filling it out; however, if there is anything you wouldn't read, don't read it here. We'd like for you to fill it out just like you would at home, except that you should talk out loud about it, and anything you read to yourself should be read out loud. Please go ahead.

Probes that might be used:
- *What are you thinking right now?*
- *Remember to read aloud for me—it's up to you what you read, but whatever you decideto read please do aloud so I know what you are looking at.*
- *Can you tell me more about that?*
- *Could you describe that for me?*
- *Don't forget to tell me what you are thinking as you do that.*

G. Record Relevant Comments, Errors, Hesitations, and Other Indicators of Potential Problems During Completion (to be used to frame follow-up questions).

1. Did respondent read the note about filling out the form electronically?
    - ❏ Yes
    - ❏ No
2. What reactions did respondent volunteer, if any?
3. Did respondent read the roster instructions?
    - ❏ Fully
    - ❏ Partially
    - ❏ Skimmed
    - ❏ Not at all
4. Any reactions/hesitations/questions to the roster instructions?

FIGURE 7.6   (*continued*).

H. Debriefing Questions (first form)

1. Overall how easy or difficult was the form to complete?
   - ❏ Very easy
   - ❏ Somewhat easy
   - ❏ Somewhat difficult
   - ❏ Very difficult

2. Was there anything unclear or confusing about how to fill out this Census form?
   - ❏ Yes → (If yes) please explain:
   - ❏ No

3. If this form arrived at your residence in the mail, how soon do you think you would respond?
   - ❏ The same day
   - ❏ In 1–2 days
   - ❏ In a week or so
   - ❏ Two weeks or more
   - ❏ Not at all

understand why the surveyors are conducting the interviews. These crucial beginnings are designed to train respondents to think aloud as well as motivate them to be active participants in the process.

When the questionnaire to be evaluated is handed to respondents (or appears on the screen for web surveys), they are encouraged to continue to do what they have been doing with the practice questions. Detailed examples of protocols and questionnaire evaluations we have done that have utilized think-aloud techniques, along with technical reports providing the interpreted results, are available from this website: www.sesrc.wsu.edu/dillman/.

Sometimes cognitive interviews are aimed primarily at evaluating whether people are interpreting the wording of questions in the same way and understanding the questions (Parsons, Mahon-Haft, & Dillman, 2007). In other cases, they may be aimed at determining whether people are able to navigate through a questionnaire appropriately (Dillman & Allen, 1995). When the latter is our primary concern, we have sometimes used a retrospective interviewing technique in which we ask people to complete a questionnaire silently, just as they might if they were home by themselves and we simply observe the answering process and, in particular, whether mistakes get made. At the end of the questionnaire we are likely to ask them probing questions about how they experienced certain aspects of the questionnaire.

The reason for using this process in these situations is that asking them to think aloud seems likely to encourage respondents to read questions slower and with greater attention to the wording and visual layout than they would at home. The retrospective technique enables us to get a better sense of how the graphical layout of a questionnaire is guiding respondents. With web surveys, this technique has allowed us to pick up mannerisms (e.g., forward and backward clicking as a means of trying better comprehend question context) to understand different ways that respondents navigate through questionnaires when not having to divide their attention between the interviewer, reading questions aloud (which is slower than doing it silently), and providing substantive answers (Sawyer & Dillman, 2002).

We cannot recall having completed a set of cognitive interviews without identifying at least a few potential problems with question wordings or questionnaire layouts, regardless of how much effort went into the initial design. However, it is also important to recognize that cognitive interviewing, as typically practiced, exhibits a number of shortcomings. Respondents tend to be volunteers obtained through advertisements or personal recruitment, because of being asked to come to a central location for the process to take place, and cannot be thought of as a random sample of a larger study population. Also, doing interviews is labor intensive, and as a general rule the number of such interviews conducted is often quite small (e.g., less than 20). Further, inasmuch as problems are often associated with particular characteristics of the respondent, conclusions are often based upon only one person having that particular characteristic. In our experience it has been disconcerting to listen to strong recommendations for change from someone who has conducted interviews and then learn that the recommendation is based upon an occurrence in only one or perhaps two interviews or an interview with one respondent with a particular characteristic of interest. Under these circumstances it is difficult to know whether any problem that has been identified is a small isolated problem or something that will affect a significant number of respondents, and whether changing the question might then create problems for other respondents.

Another problem is that the labor-intensive nature of cognitive interviews often leads to their being conducted by entry-level personnel who are able to ask and record responses from individuals but who lack the skills or training needed for comprehending underlying causes of the problems and asking appropriate follow-up questions. A friend described it as the difference between a medical patient being examined by a physician and the physician's office assistant. Although the assistant may have medical training and as a result be able to ask appropriate questions, he probably lacks the in-depth knowledge needed for formulating additional questions necessary to rule out certain possibilities and better isolate the critical problems. We have observed some interviewers who are tremendously skilled at teasing out when interpretations of wording are problems and interacting with the respondent to identify words and phrases that are easier to understand. However, these same individuals are unable to pick up on the consequences of visual layout problems and how they might be corrected. The opposite situation also occurs. It is essential that individuals assigned to the cognitive interviewing task of evaluating surveys be knowledgeable in both of these areas.

Well-done cognitive interviews also require detailed reporting of procedures and evidence, just as is required for writing quantitative data reports. Doing so allows others to read the evidence and draw their own conclusions about its strength. Few things are as disconcerting as having the conductor of 20 cognitive interviews select a problem from one interview and simply declare that a question must be changed. Evidence is needed on what did or did not happen in the other 19 interviews to avoid making a correction to fix a problem experienced by one person, only to find that the revision creates problems for other respondents. This concern has led us to develop the practices of making sure probes on the same topics are administered in as many interviews as possible, summarizing individual interviews in reports, and ensuring that considerable detail is given in all reports so that others can fairly assess the evidence (Dillman, Parsons, & Mahon-Haft, 2004; Parsons & Dillman, 2008).

The term *usability study* emerged in the past decade to describe tests of web surveys. These tend to be one-on-one interviews in which an individual attempts to complete a web survey. Initially, such usability studies tended to focus on the challenges individuals faced in using a computer to register responses. This practice has, over time, become somewhat blurred with cognitive interviews as evaluators have attempted to combine evaluation of the wording and sequence of questions with the manner in which they are presented and responded to while on a computer. In recent years the term *usability* has also been applied to evaluating paper questionnaires.

Occasionally, when we have proposed conducting cognitive interviews to evaluate a questionnaire, the survey designer has thought we were planning to do focus groups, in which a number of people are brought together in order to talk about questions in a questionnaire (Morgan, 1997). There is a considerable difference between cognitive interviews and focus groups. The latter tend to be a social experience in which people not only express their own opinions but listen to the opinions of others, which then may be taken into account as they express additional opinions. The group orientation of such interviews may lead to inappropriate conclusions when cultural considerations are related to the issue being studied.

Such an effect appeared to happen in a set of focus groups conducted in anticipation of a response rate experiment conducted in 1995. In preparation for the 2000 Decennial Census, an extensive set of experiments was conducted with the aim of identifying factors that would improve response rates (Dillman, 2000). Prior to the field experiment, four focus groups in two different cities were conducted to determine whether messages included in a box on the outgoing envelope would increase response rates. They were unanimous in concluding that the message "U.S. Census Form Enclosed; Your Response Is Required by Law" would not affect response rates and that the message "It Pays to Be Counted" would be more effective. When the field test experiments were done, the factor that increased response rates most compared to 15 others—such as respondent-friendly design, a prenotice letter, a postcard reminder, and a replacement questionnaire—was the message "U.S. Census Form Enclosed; Your Response Is Required by Law." Response rates increased by about 10 percentage points when this message was included. The alternative message that was so popular with the focus groups had absolutely no effect on the response rate (Dillman, Singer, Clark, & Treat, 1996).

Guideline 7.9: Conduct Experimental Evaluations of Questionnaire Components

Once, when another critical decision was about to be made at the U.S. Census Bureau on the Decennial Census questionnaire, one of us was approached by a senior statistician who wanted to know the following: "Can't you just do a few cognitive interviews to find out whether it's okay to change to the newly proposed questionnaire format?" Doing that instead of an experiment would have been less costly and could have been completed much more quickly.

This incident illustrates a common dilemma faced in federal agencies as the practice of testing questions before changing them becomes a common expectation but costs and time are of the essence. Well-designed experiments can provide quantitative estimates of the effects of proposed changes in questionnaires and survey implementation procedures that are representative of the entire survey population, whereas cognitive interviews cannot. When a survey design decision needs to estimate the magnitude of a change in design, experimentation is needed. An example might be when one is considering changing the way a question is asked in a longitudinal survey where trends are being tracked. In this case, it is absolutely necessary to know how much any change in reports is due to the new way of asking the question and how much is actual change in the construct over time. Only an experimental evaluation can tell us this.

Experiments on question wording and questionnaire layout are not something that should be considered only when conducting national surveys for policy purposes. We have frequently interacted with survey designers in universities and private sector firms who have produced a questionnaire and have wanted to know whether people will give better answers to questions worded or laid out in a new way. Because of the unique combination of content, length, and implementation procedures, it is usually impossible to provide anything other than a vague estimate of effects based on previous literature or experiences. Thus, experimentation can play an essential and influential role in evaluating questions and questionnaires.

Although many surveyors may be reluctant to commit resources to doing experiments, the up-front costs of doing an experiment can often save considerable costs during the final data collection. For example, if methods can be found to increase early response, by improving the design of the questionnaire or making changes to early contacts, the number of expensive follow-up mailings or telephone callbacks can be reduced. These types of cost savings are most likely to be realized in surveys with large sample sizes or in longitudinal surveys. Thus, an experiment involving a few hundred respondents can often provide insightful information that will prevent much larger amounts of money from being spent in pursuit of an unachievable objective. When surveyors are unsure whether the design of a particular question (or implementation procedure) will help or hurt response and absolutely cannot afford to conduct an experiment ahead of time, we often encourage them to conduct an experiment during the main data collection, provided they have a large enough sample size to make doing so worthwhile. While the results of the experiment will not help them with the current study, they might help with future studies, and to the extent that they are shared, help others determine how best to implement their surveys.

Because they each yield very different types of information, the parallel use of experimental and cognitive interview methods is a particularly powerful way to evaluate survey questions and questionnaires. Dillman and Redline (2004) reported three cases in which parallel experimental and cognitive interview studies were completed. Although the results of each of these companion efforts tended to point toward similar conclusions about the questions and procedures being tested, the experimental and cognitive interviews provided quite different kinds of information. The experiments allowed conclusions to be drawn about what would actually happen if a procedure were to be adopted, but provided only minimal insight into why those differences occurred. In contrast, the cognitive interviews proved to be a rich source of hypotheses about the reasons those differences occurred. Neither method of testing can substitute for the other.

Guideline 7.10: Conduct a Small Pilot Study With a Subsample of the Population to Evaluate the Questionnaire

A pilot study refers to a mini-study in which the proposed questionnaire is tested on the survey population in an attempt to identify problems. The goal is to determine whether the proposed questionnaire and procedures are adequate for the larger study. Although it is possible that experiments can be embedded in a pilot study, we distinguish between these methods of testing here because a pilot study provides critical information regardless of whether experiments are embedded in the design. It constitutes a final test of the exact questionnaire and implementation procedures to be used in a study.

Pilot studies can provide valuable information about how individual items in a questionnaire are performing and how the overall construction of the questionnaire is working. For example, from a pilot study, one can calculate the item nonresponse rate for each item on the survey, which will reveal if any items are particularly prone to being overlooked or skipped. One can also examine response distributions to ensure that the items discriminate well and the final data will have enough variation to be useful (i.e., that all or most respondents are not registering the same response, making the item useless in analyses). In addition, the pilot data can be used to figure out if respondents are able to navigate skip instructions correctly for surveys that include them. One can also look over any notes respondents write in the margins or in comment boxes. These notes will often reveal questions that do not make sense to respondents or sets of response options that are not exhaustive. Finally, in telephone administered surveys, it is often useful to debrief with the interviewers after a pilot study to learn if any items were particularly problematic for them to administer and what the source of any problems might be. Similarly, pilot studies allow for the assessment of interviewer performance to see if additional changes or training is needed before the full study.

In addition to testing aspects of the questionnaire, pilot studies can yield valuable information about how the study procedures will work in practice, and in particular, how well all of the parts will work together. First, they can give one a sense of how sample members will react to the contacts and any materials provided, what proportion will answer the questionnaire, and what problems or areas of confusion will arise. They are particularly useful for making quantitative estimates of response rates and thus may help in setting sample sizes for the full study. They may also give one a sense of whether only certain types of people are responding leading to increased potential for nonresponse error.

Second, they can give the surveyor a better understanding of how well coordination of the implementation process works on the surveyor's side. For example, a pilot study will give a surveyor a good sense of how long each step in the process will take, what staffing level is needed, whether the system for tracking and monitoring progress is sufficient, how communication and coordination between staff members in charge of the various parts of the survey works, and a variety of other processes that are part of the survey design. It will also give staff a chance to practice all of the procedures and on the same timeline that they will need to be executed in the final design. Further, since pilot studies are also a full test of the questionnaire and implementation procedures, they can be especially valuable for obtaining cost estimates for the actual survey.

Pilot studies are often deemed essential when a new survey questionnaire or new implementation procedures are to be used for a survey or when implementation requires many different individuals and divisions to coordinate activities within an organization (as is the case with most mixed-mode studies), although they can also be very useful for smaller surveys as well. Pilot studies can be quite expensive, but even a study with a small sample size will allow for the full survey procedures to be tested from start to end (from sampling to completing the interviews and reviewing the data). And like experiments, pilot studies may save substantial money that would have been spent during the main data collection when the results uncover procedures that are inefficient or ineffective and thus can be modified before being deployed in the main study. If an organization is unable to conduct a pilot study, we at minimum recommend that a pilot is simulated by testing all of the materials used, the programming and data being transferred, and the coordination of staff needed at each step in the process.

Guideline 7.11: Use Eye Tracking to Learn How Respondents Are Visually Processing Questionnaires

Surveyors often struggle to figure out the best ways to organize information to ensure that it all gets seen and processed, and that the parts are processed in the correct order. Eye tracking can provide one way to find out what parts of a question or questionnaire respondents actually look at, and in which order they look at them, to help decide which of several formats might be most effective.

Figure 7.7 shows images from a recent eye-tracking study one of us conducted with a team of researchers in Nebraska (Ricci, Olson, & Smyth, 2013; Zhou, Smyth, & Olson, 2013). The black circles show the locations in which respondents fixated (i.e., their eyes paused on an area, in this case for a minimum of 100 milliseconds), while the numbers inside them indicate the order and duration of the fixations. Respondents are thought to be actively taking in information during fixations, but not when their eyes are moving between fixations (represented by the lines connecting the black circles) (Rayner, 1998). The grey circles represent mouse clicks, with the number inside them indicating the order in which they occurred. The top example in Figure 7.7 is from a respondent who skipped the first few words in the question stem, but thoroughly read the response options before registering an answer and advancing through the survey. The second example is from a respondent who only appears to have read one or two words in the question stem but then thoroughly processed the scale labels and each item within a grid and registered a response for each item.

The earliest use of eye tracking to understand questionnaire design of which we are aware was reported by Redline and Lankford (2001). They used this technology to see how respondents utilized different types of skip instructions in a paper survey. They found that respondents were most successful at following the skip instructions if they read them immediately prior to or after registering a response. Those who read them too early were more likely to fail to remember them accurately after registering their response or to follow them immediately, failing to register a response altogether. Moreover, some respondents did not look at the skip instructions at all.

In later work, Graesser, Cai, Louwerse, and Daniel (2006) found that rather than reading from left to right and top to bottom in a uniform and orderly way, respondents strategically look back and forth between the parts of a question to

FIGURE 7.7 Select images of fixations and gaze trails from an eye-tracked web survey.

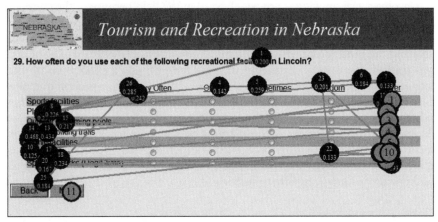

Note. These images were selected to illustrate how eye tracking can help surveyors understand what questionnaire features are being processed by respondents and the possibilities of eye tracking for testing questionnaires. They are not representative of how people process these particular types of questions.

make sense of and answer it. This finding reinforces the importance of holistic design (see Chapters 5 and 6). Graesser et al. (2006) also found that respondents were more likely to give up on difficult than on easy to understand questions. Rather than dig in and do the work to process the questions, respondents, especially those with low verbal ability, utilized an early exit strategy in which they answered the question before reading all of it.

In later work, Galesic, Tourangeau, Couper, and Conrad (2008) examined how respondents process response options when they appeared in drop-down menus with no items initially visible, drop-down menus with the first five items initially visible, and as a set of radio buttons where all items are visible. In the drop-down version where the first five items were initially visible, respondents spent significantly more time fixating on these items, making them more likely to be selected than on the items that were not immediately visible. This effect was smaller in the radio button version where all response options were visible from the outset, and disappeared entirely in the drop-down version where no items were initially visible. The use of drop-down menus is discussed more in Guideline 5.8.

In additional work, Galesic et al. (2008) found that respondents were much more likely to look at definitions that were always visible in a web survey compared to definitions that only appeared when respondents rolled their mouse pointer over the term to which the definition applied. On average, 10% of respondents looked at each definition in the "rollover" condition compared to 78% in the "always on" condition. However, respondents in the rollover condition who accessed a definition spent more time fixating on the definitions than those in the always on condition who looked at it, and the more time a respondent fixated on a definition, the more it affected her response.

Each of these are examples of how surveyors have been able to use eye tracking to better understand how respondents are processing questionnaires in web and mail surveys. Others have examined how adding smiling and frowning faces to a satisfaction scale impacts respondents (Libman & Smyth, 2012) and how low and high literacy respondents process survey questions (Nuttirudee, 2012; Smyth, Powell, Olson, & Libman, 2012).

As of yet, eye tracking is not widely used in the field because of the considerable challenges involved in implementing it. One of those challenges is that it is costly, both in terms of the expense of obtaining the needed equipment and software and the time and expense of bringing people into a laboratory to have their eyes tracked. However, because eye tracking can give one a good sense of what people are and are not processing and the order in which they process questionnaire elements, it seems especially well suited for use by survey researchers who are trying to figure out how to design questionnaires, and we expect its use to increase. Further, like other testing methods, eye tracking can be especially useful when used in combination with other methods, such as experiments or cognitive interviews, as it provides additional information that may help explain what researchers are finding from testing using other methods.

Guideline 7.12: Conduct Testing in the Mode or Modes That Will Be Used to Complete the Questionnaire

Because the type of communication used in a mode has such a large effect on the way survey questions are cognitively processed, it is important to test in the same mode that the survey will be conducted in. We have observed people pretesting telephone surveys by sitting down opposite of a colleague and administering the survey to them. They generally reason that this is not too different from what respondents will experience over the telephone. But in reality, it is quite different because when we communicate face-to-face we use much more than just spoken words. Eye contact, facial expressions, and body language communicate considerable information in addition to the words we speak, none of which will be available to interviewers and respondents when the survey goes live on the telephone.

Similarly, testing what will be a web survey using paper is ill advised because it will not be possible to tell how the technological features of the questionnaire, such as input fields and navigation, will work. And testing what will be a mail survey over the phone will not allow one to learn how the questionnaire will work when respondents can actually see the questions and response options, or how respondents will navigate the questionnaire without assistance. For these reasons, tests should be conducted in the mode or modes in which the questionnaire will ultimately be completed by respondents.

In addition to testing questionnaires, expert review, cognitive interviews, experimentation, pilot studies, and eye tracking can all be used to better understand what implementation materials and procedures are and are not working well. Because implementation materials and procedures vary so drastically across telephone, web, mail, and mixed-mode surveys, we return in Chapters 8, 9, 10, and 11 to discuss the use of these testing methods for implementation in each mode separately.

Guideline 7.13: Document and Archive All Aspects of the Survey Design

One of the most important aspects of all scientific research is the ability to understand the procedures used to generate the results so that the study can be replicated. We cannot emphasize enough the importance of documenting and archiving all aspects of the survey design, including the final questionnaires, contact materials, sampling frame, sample design, and any post-survey adjustments or weighting that were used, so that people can understand how the survey was conducted. We recommend documenting and archiving procedures as the study is being conducted and decisions are made to ensure that everything is recorded accurately and details are not forgotten, as commonly happens when researchers wait weeks or months to document the methods used.

The methodology report or statement should include a very detailed description. What may seem like small details at the time, such as the exact background color used for the web survey or how the components of the mailing were folded and packaged, are important aspects of the implementation that may influence whether and how people respond. Describing the specific procedures used and how they connect to one another is especially important when using a holistic design, where communication across different contacts and the questionnaire are made to work together. We are often asked to review methodology statements and nearly always we find ourselves wanting more detail than was included and asking additional questions about how the survey was conducted and the specific materials used. Thus, we encourage surveyors to very carefully and thoroughly document the survey methodology and design.

We want to emphasize that the preceding recommendations apply mostly to internal documentation and archiving. When presenting methodology to different audiences (e.g., clients, journalists, scientists, etc.), it likely will be necessary to provide a more general summary of the methodology that is understandable to those less familiar with survey methodology. However, even here, methodology statements often provide too little rather than too much information. For more on data dissemination, see Granda and Blasczyk (2013).

One critical aspect of a survey's methodology that we often find has not been archived is copies of the actual questionnaires (as seen or experienced by respondents) and contact materials that were used. Production quality hard copies of any paper questionnaires should be saved and archived. For web and telephone surveys, screenshots of the questions, exactly as they appeared to respondents and interviewers, should be taken to document the appearance of the final questionnaire (if telephone interviewers used paper questionnaires, then those should be documented). Screenshots should be taken at the time the survey is being conducted because once a survey has been removed from the web or CATI program, it is often very difficult, if not impossible because of hardware and software upgrades, to repost it for viewing, especially if any amount of time has passed. The reality is that if screenshots were not taken to document the questionnaire, there may be no available record of the survey's appearance. For web surveys, screenshots of the final questionnaire should be taken using the most common computer settings and ideally using the various devices, platforms, browsers, and user-controlled settings that respondents are likely to use. Taking these screenshots can be done as part of the process of testing the questionnaire across different hardware and software configurations as discussed in Guideline 9.27. For telephone surveys, screenshots should be taken on the actual workstations interviewers use to administer the survey. And for both web and telephone surveys, the screenshots should capture all of the screens, not just those that display questions. This means capturing the welcome, closing, and error screens used in web surveys and the screens showing any introductory scripts and within-household selection procedures in telephone surveys.

Further, all materials provided during the implementation of the survey should also be archived, including copies of the actual envelopes, letters, brochures, and any other materials that are used. Ideally, these materials would be archived as they were packaged and prepared to illustrate how people would have experienced the mailing. Similarly, e-mail communications should also be archived as sampled members would have experienced them, including not only the content of the e-mail but also the subject line, sender name and e-mail address, and other details of the e-mail heading. Likewise, any supplemental materials used for telephone surveys such as scripts or FAQs, common persuaders, study-specific training materials, and any other documents provided to interviewers should be archived.

In general, we encourage everyone who conducts surveys to document and archive the procedures used so that others may fully understand how the survey was designed and when possible to make the documentation and actual data from the studies available to other researchers. Documentation and archiving is especially important in mixed-mode surveys, where there is a need to fully document the procedures for each mode and how they are built to work together, as we discuss in Guideline 11.23.

CONCLUSION

In our experience, there are many ways that a single survey question can be written, and the number of possibilities seems to grow exponentially as the number of people working on the questionnaire increases. In addition, order effects can be substantial and can be rooted in many different cognition issues. Questions can also be ordered in ways that make people unwilling to complete the questionnaire.

So how do we know which version is best? How do we know when a question is ready to be used? These are hard questions to answer definitively, but one thing we can say is that a question is not ready until it has been examined within the context in which it will appear on the questionnaire. We can also say with confidence that a collection of the best written questions will likely do poorly if respondents are not motivated to answer them, a problem that can be addressed, in part, by question ordering.

Finally, we do not consider a question to be ready for use until it has undergone at least some testing, whether by experts, through cognitive interviews, in an experimental comparison, or through eye tracking. Each of these methods can yield important insight into how well a question is working, what effect any problems may have on the final data, and in some cases, what might be done to improve the question.

LIST OF GUIDELINES

Question Order

Guideline 7.1: Group related questions that cover similar topics together
Guideline 7.2: Begin with questions likely to be salient to nearly all respondents and choose the first question carefully
Guideline 7.3: Place sensitive or potentially objectionable questions near the end of the questionnaire
Guideline 7.4: When a series of filter and follow-up questions are to be used, ask all of the filter questions before asking the follow-up questions
Guideline 7.5: Ask questions about events in the order the events occurred
Guideline 7.6: Avoid unintended question order effects

Testing Questions and Questionnaires

Guideline 7.7: Obtain feedback on the draft questionnaire from content, questionnaire, and analysis experts
Guideline 7.8: Conduct cognitive interviews of the complete questionnaire in order to identify wording, question order, visual design, and navigation problems
Guideline 7.9: Conduct experimental evaluations of questionnaire components
Guideline 7.10: Conduct a small pilot study with a subsample of the population to evaluate the questionnaire
Guideline 7.11: Use eye tracking to learn how respondents are visually processing questionnaires
Guideline 7.12: Conduct testing in the mode or modes that will be used to complete the questionnaire
Guideline 7.13: Document and archive all aspects of the survey design

Telephone Questionnaires and Implementation

Stand-alone single-mode surveys such as telephone, Internet, or mail surveys remain important. Such surveys will be done in the future just as they have been done in the past. This is the first of three chapters in which we discuss how each of these data collection modes can be used to implement single-mode surveys. These chapters also provide essential background information that is necessary for understanding how these modes can be coordinated and used in conjunction with each other in mixed-mode designs to improve response rates and data quality.

We begin in this chapter with the telephone. Once the dominant mode of surveying in the United States, it has become increasingly challenged as a means of collecting survey responses over the past 10 years. These challenges stem from an underlying shift in how people communicate that has been driven by the development of alternative online communication channels (e.g., e-mail, instant messaging, texting, and other online communication tools), the spread of mobile phones in the United States and many other countries, and the decline of landline phones (see Figure 8.1 for trends in telephone ownership in the United States).

As other means of communication have proliferated, fewer people have landline telephones and those who do may rarely, if ever, actually use or answer them. For example, the phone may only be connected to a security system or fax, or the phone service may have been included as part of a telecommunications package or bundle but is never used. Those who use their landline phones also now have a variety of technologies to help screen or block unknown callers and numbers (e.g., caller ID, call blocking, voice mail messages, etc.). For many households, landline telephone service has been replaced or supplemented by Internet-based phone services (ranging from to VOIP to Skype and FaceTime) or by cellular phones, and in many households each member (or at least each member older than a certain age) has his own cell phone so that as a whole, the household has several. Some people also carry business cell phones alongside their personal cell phones. These changes in how people communicate have had a substantial impact on how telephone surveys are conducted and, in particular, on the amount of effort needed to contact people and gain their cooperation. As discussed in Chapter 3, telephone samples in the United States and in many other countries now need to include cell phones to adequately cover the population. If cell phones are excluded, the survey's estimates may be significantly biased due to coverage error, especially for certain types of questions that are correlated with not having a landline or with other characteristics of people who do not have landlines. For example, questions about residential mobility patterns may be biased if cell-only households are not included because they are more likely to rent than own their homes and to move more often.

FIGURE 8.1 Changing patterns in telephone ownership, 2003–2013.

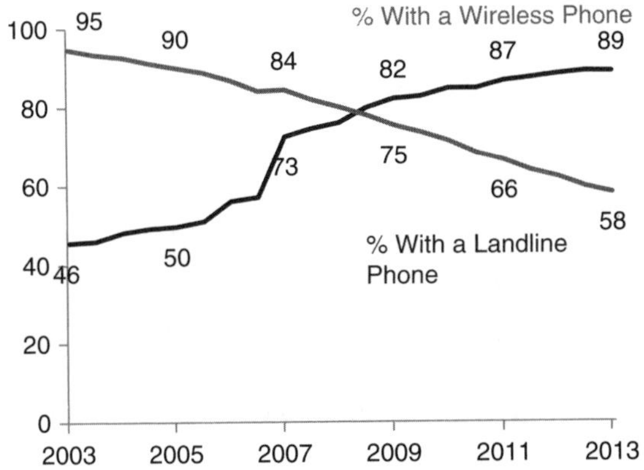

Source: Wireless Substitution: Early Release of Estimates From the National Health Interview Survey, January–June 2013, by S. J. Blumberg and J. V. Luke, 2013, National Center for Health Statistics. Retrieved from http://www.cdc.gov/nchs/data/nhis/earlyrelease/wireless201312.pdf. Based on households in the United States.

Telephone surveys have also faced significant challenges due to the decline in contact and cooperation rates. For example, the contact rate in a typical Pew Research Center survey declined from 90% in 1997 to 62% in 2012 and the cooperation rate declined from 43% to 14% (Keeter, Christian, Dimock, & Gewurz, 2012). As a result, the response rate is about a fourth of what it was in 1997, down from 36% to 9% in 2012 (see Figure 8.2). Although these numbers reflect the particular survey procedures used for the Pew Research political surveys, and some modifications to the calling procedures, including calling cell phones in 2008, they mirror broader trends seen in other surveys (Curtin, Presser, & Singer, 2005; Galea & Tracy, 2007). Because of the cost of including cell phones and the additional effort needed to contact sampled members and encourage them to participate, it costs more to complete an interview by telephone now than in the past.

Research has shown that low response rates to telephone surveys are not necessarily an indicator of nonresponse bias (Groves, 2006; Groves & Peytcheva, 2008; Keeter et al., 2012; Keeter, Kennedy, Dimock, Best, & Craighill, 2006; Keeter, Miller, Kohut, Groves, & Presser, 2000) if the nonrespondents do not differ from respondents on key variables of interest. However, any time response rates are quite low, there is concern about the threat of nonresponse bias, especially in studies that cover a variety of topics. In these situations, it is likely that at least a few of the estimates may be significantly impacted by the high rate of nonresponse.

Calling cell phones has introduced new challenges and operational considerations that must be considered when conducting telephone surveys. Cell phones are usually personal devices and are less likely to be shared than landline phones. Similarly, a cell phone is mobile and can be carried around throughout the day, wherever a person goes, whereas a landline phone is physically tied to a location. These differences, as well as legal limitations around calling cell phones, often result in calling procedures for cell phone numbers that are quite different than those for landline numbers. Also, introducing cell phones in telephone surveys can have substantial impact on the sampling, the design of the questionnaire (to add

FIGURE 8.2 Example of declining telephone contact, cooperation, and response rates in Pew Research Center surveys.

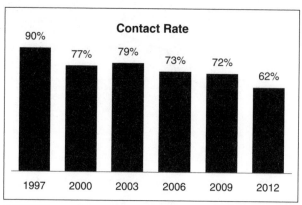

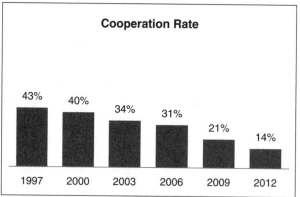

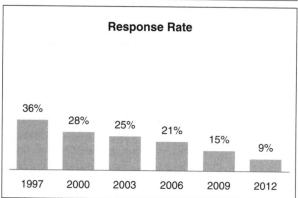

Notes. Rates shown are typical for surveys conducted in each year (but are not averages across all surveys that year) and were computed according to AAPOR's standard definitions. Contact rate is the percent of households sampled in which an adult was reached (AAPOR CON2). Cooperation rate is the percent of households contacted that yielded an interview (AAPOR COOP3). Response rate is the percent of households sampled that yielded a completed interview (AAPOR RR3).

Source: Adapted from "Nonresponse and the Validity of Estimates From National Telephone Surveys," by S. Keeter L. M. Christian, M. Dimock, and D. Gewurz, 2012. Paper presented at the annual conference of the American Association for Public Opinion Research.

any additional language or questions needed when calling cell phones), interviewer training, the calling protocols, as well as testing.

Considerable work has been done on conducting telephone surveys (Dillman, 1978; Groves & Kahn, 1979; Groves et al., 1988; Gwartney, 2007; Lepkowski, Tucker, Brick, & de Leeuw, 2007). However, much of this research was performed when most telephone surveys were conducted only by landline telephone and before many of the more recent challenges in contacting people and gaining their cooperation developed. The 2010 AAPOR Cell Phone Task Force Report addresses specific issues for incorporating cell phones into telephone surveys (AAPOR, 2010) but as of yet, there is not an integrated guide to conducting telephone surveys that include both landline and cell phone numbers.

This chapter provides an overview of issues that are important in telephone surveys. In particular, it presents guidelines for designing telephone survey questionnaires, interviewer procedures and training, developing calling rules and protocols, and testing and monitoring for telephone surveys. But due to space limitations, the chapter does not cover every technical detail needed for each step in the process when conducting telephone surveys. For example, general guidelines about calling are provided, but specific calling schedules are not. Similarly, key aspects of interviewer training are covered but not specific procedures for individual studies. We aim to provide a general overview while providing specific references to sources from which the reader can obtain additional information about these topics.

Developing and maintaining the infrastructure and interviewing staff needed to effectively conduct telephone surveys is quite expensive, making it difficult for most researchers to undertake on their own. As a result, generally we recommend that researchers seek the assistance of an organization that specializes in conducting telephone surveys and maintains the infrastructure and trained staff to do so. There are a variety of survey data collection organizations in the private sector and within many colleges and universities that conduct telephone surveys. Listings for many of these organizations can be found in the American Association for Public Opinion Research's *Blue Book* (AAPOR, n.d.) or the membership list of the Association of Academic Survey Research Organizations (AASRO, n.d.). The guidelines presented in this chapter include key questions researchers should ask when working with an external call center to develop the specific procedures for a study to ensure that it is administered effectively.

In this chapter we focus on surveys in which the telephone is the only mode used to contact and interview respondents. However, telephone surveys are often used in conjunction with other modes, in which case, additional considerations are needed. For example, designing a questionnaire that is to be administered only by telephone requires different considerations than one that will be administered by phone and web. Similarly, coordinating an implementation strategy that includes postal mail, e-mail, and telephone requires different procedures than one where only telephone will be used to contact sample members. Guidelines for designing mixed-mode questionnaires and implementation strategies that include telephone are discussed in Chapter 11. But even when telephone is used in combination with other modes, many of the guidelines presented here for designing questionnaires and contact strategies for telephone surveys are useful in effectively deploying this mode in mixed-mode surveys.

TYPES OF TELEPHONE-ONLY SURVEYS TODAY

Perhaps the most visible telephone surveys conducted today are public opinion surveys and election polls. We hear the results of these surveys when we turn on the TV or radio, open our laptop, get the latest political notification on our phone, or read the newspaper. Sometimes the findings from these surveys are even discussed in our conversations with friends and family. These surveys provide information about how people feel about the government, the economy, and other issues. They usually aim to describe the views of the general public or of voters in a specific area, whether that is the whole country or those living in a particular state or local area (often defined by electoral boundaries).

The majority of public opinion surveys in the United States, such as those sponsored by Gallup, the Pew Research Center, and national, state, and local news organizations, are still conducted exclusively by telephone, using RDD samples or voter registration lists. Although opt-in Internet surveyors, such as YouGov, Survey Monkey, and Google Consumer Surveys, are also increasingly conducting these types of surveys and releasing them publically.

Telephone has traditionally been the preferred mode for these types of surveys because it is often necessary to field the survey over a very short period (usually only 5 to 10 days) so that results can be reported quickly, when they are still considered fresh or current. The short field period is used to ensure that the interviews are conducted as close as possible to the release of the data and are less likely to be affected by external events occurring during interviewing, such as economic, political, or even weather events, that may influence the results. These constraints have made it very difficult to conduct these types of surveys by mail or in-person interviewing. Web surveys can provide an alternative that meets the quick turnaround needs; however, most available Internet options rely on opt-in or nonprobability sampling methodologies (with the exception of the few probability-based web panels), which some organizations are still hesitant to use, especially when they have long standing trends from surveys conducted by telephone.

But other types of surveys also employ a telephone-only design. Telephone surveys are frequently used for conducting surveys of listed samples, such as members of an organization, university alumni, or employees, where the list contains telephone numbers for everyone, or nearly everyone, on it. The Michigan/Reuters Survey of Consumer Sentiment, that asks a series of questions to estimate confidence among consumers, is conducted by telephone (and has employed a dual-frame design that includes landlines and cell phones since 2012). The Behavioral Risk Factor Surveillance System (BRFSS) is a collaboration between the Centers for Disease Control and state health programs and is conducted in all 50 states. The BRFSS includes questions about preventive health practices and risk behaviors that are linked to chronic and infectious diseases. The survey has been conducted by telephone since 1984, and since 2011 has employed a dual-frame RDD design sampling landlines and cell phones.

GUIDELINES FOR DESIGNING TELEPHONE QUESTIONNAIRES

One key difference between telephone surveys and paper and web surveys is the presence of an interviewer. Many of the tasks that the respondent must complete in a paper or web survey are carried out by the interviewer in telephone surveys. A telephone interviewer

- Calls the household and introduces the survey
- Encourages the household to participate
- Asks to speak with the selected household member (and administers any within-household selection procedures)
- Administers the questions (reads the introduction and transition statements, the question stem, the response options, and any additional instructions)
- Provides feedback and answers questions respondents may have
- Records the respondents' answers
- Probes inadequate answers
- Navigates the questionnaire (often with the help of a computer program)
- Submits the completed questionnaire

In this way, the interviewer is who presents the survey to the respondent and ensures the quality and accuracy of the answers respondents provide. Having an interviewer administer the questionnaire presents certain benefits and raises important challenges. Interviewers can help motivate respondents to participate, provide encouragement throughout the interview, answer respondent questions and help ensure that respondents comprehend the questions, and ensure that their answers are recorded accurately. However, interviewers can also negatively affect how respondents answer questions (as discussed in Chapter 4, Presence vs. Absence of an Interviewer).

Some telephone surveys are not administered by live interviewers. In interactive voice response (IVR) surveys, a prerecorded voice is used to administer the questions, and respondents either verbally say their response or input their response using the telephone keypad. These types of surveys remove the interviewer from the conversation—including any benefits the interviewer may provide as well as any errors that result from having an interviewer present.

Thus, designing effective telephone questionnaires requires viewing each question from the perspective of the respondent *and* the interviewer. By comparison, in self-administered surveys the focus is just on ensuring that the respondent can understand and answer the survey questions.

Interviewer confusion or misunderstanding about what they are supposed to do can have enormous impacts on respondents. Similarly, research has shown that when respondents are confused, interviewers are more likely to deviate from the script, have rough delivery, and make errors. In fact, signs of respondent confusion early in a survey are associated with poorer interviewer behaviors throughout the rest of the survey (B. Edwards, Schneider, & Brick, 2008).

As Japec (2008) pointed out, interviewers have to proceed through mental processes in order to administer questionnaires, much like respondents do in order to respond to them. Interviewers also experience burden, which increases substantially when they have to deal with respondent confusion. When that burden is too great, they look for ways to reduce it such as by skipping over questions; rewording items; or failing to clarify, probe, or otherwise work to obtain the optimal answer from respondents (i.e., interviewer satisficing). All of these behaviors have great potential to result in increased measurement error (i.e., interviewer bias and/or variance, as discussed in Chapter 4), and as such, should be avoided as much as possible.

Much like the visual design of self-administered questionnaires can help respondents navigate survey questionnaires and respond to individual questions, the visual design of telephone questionnaires can help interviewers administer the questionnaire. Many of the visual design guidelines that apply to paper and web surveys (discussed in Chapter 6) can be applied to designing telephone questionnaires. But in telephone surveys, the focus shifts to organizing information for the interviewer rather than the respondent. The respondent never sees the questionnaire.

The interviewer has to manage both visual (with the computer or paper) and verbal (with the respondent) communications. Interviewers must quickly look at the screen and determine what should be read and in what order, what additional clarification can be given, how to record the answers respondents provide, and whether and how they should probe responses (Japec, 2008). Further, they have to effectively navigate the questionnaire—moving from question to question on the page or across screens. Because interviewers have to do multiple things at once, it can make design more challenging, but we can also take advantage of the fact that we can teach and train interviewers to follow established protocols.

In most telephone surveys, a computer displays the survey question for an interviewer to read to the respondent. This process is called computer-assisted telephone interviewing or CATI for short. Most established telephone survey organizations operate specialized CATI software that is designed to present the questions one after another in the order specified during programming. The CATI software, or additional add-on programs, can also be used to keep track of sample telephone numbers, schedule and implement the calling procedures according to specified rules, prioritize calls and call them back at specified times, assign calls to interviewers, and close out each sample record.

Researchers who do not have access to specialized CATI software and systems have used web surveys or even paper questionnaires instead. These methods lack the sample and call management functionality found in dedicated CATI software, but can be made to work well for administering the questionnaire and recording responses, especially for studies with smaller sample sizes or with relatively simple survey procedures. In particular, web surveys still allow for more complicated programming and help ensure that a computer administers the skip routing and logic so interviewers do not have to determine the appropriate follow-up questions in addition to their other tasks.

Telephone surveys need to be designed to minimize burden on both the respondent and the interviewer and to make their interaction as easy and smooth as possible. One challenge is making sure that the questions are written so that they make sense to respondents and are easy enough for them to answer, especially when all of the communication between the interviewer and respondent is aural. This is particularly challenging for telephone surveys where respondents' memory and cognitive processing ability are already taxed. Further, we often find that telephone respondents are distracted, doing other things while on the phone, such as watching TV, cooking dinner, or responding to e-mails. We have found that listening to just a few telephone interviews provides key insights into the cognitive burdens and distractions that occur during a typical telephone survey.

The guidelines presented in Chapter 4 will help simplify questions for all modes, including telephone surveys (e.g., ask one question at a time, use simple and familiar words, use specific and concrete words, use as few words as possible, use complete sentences, etc.). In this chapter, we focus on additional ways to design telephone surveys that apply whether the questionnaire will be administered through a CATI, web, or paper instrument. These guidelines will help ensure that questions are delivered well and similarly across different interviewers and that respondents are given all of the information they need to respond, especially since they must rely exclusively on aural communication during the survey. Following these guidelines will help to minimize respondent confusion and improve the overall interaction between the interviewer and respondent.

Guideline 8.1: Break Complex Questions Into a Series of Simpler Questions

One of the most important ways to ease the cognitive burden in telephone surveys is by breaking complex questions into parts or a series of simpler questions. We discussed one example of breaking complex questions into simpler parts in Guideline 5.20 by branching bipolar ordinal scales to ease respondent burden. Another example is when questions ask respondents to include certain classes of events in their responses and exclude others. For example, many surveys ask how many people live in the household but only want certain types of people included in the count. In the 2010 Decennial Census, for example, this question was accompanied by the following complex instructions:

- "Count all people, including babies, who live and sleep here most of the time."
- "Do not count anyone living away either at college or in the armed forces."
- "Do not count anyone in a nursing home, jail, prison, detention facility, etc., on April 1, 2010."
- "Leave these people off your form, even if they will return to live here after they leave college, the nursing home, the military, jail, etc. Otherwise they may be counted twice."
- "If someone who has no permanent place to stay is staying here on April 1, 2010, count that person. Otherwise he or she may be missed in the census" (U.S. Census Bureau, 2010b).

Redline (2011) has shown that complex instructions like these are most likely to be followed when they are incorporated into a series of simple questions rather than presented as a complex instruction alongside one question. An example from Redline's work is shown in Figure 8.3. On this item respondents who received the single item shown in the top of the figure in an IVR survey reported an average of 2.6 residents living or staying at their home, but the mean number of residents calculated for respondents who received the questions in the bottom of the figure was 2.2. The smaller mean for those who received multiple questions suggests that respondents followed the instructions, which focused primarily on who to exclude from the count.

While Redline's examples focused on questions in which respondents were instructed to exclude certain cases from their counts, Fowler (1995) provided examples of situations in which respondents might need to be reminded to include certain events in their counts. One such example is when asking for reports of income. A complex instruction reminding respondents to include commonly forgotten sources of income other than wages and salary (e.g., rent, interest, tips, etc.) would be difficult for telephone respondents to remember and apply; in lieu of providing such an instruction, one might simplify the process

FIGURE 8.3 Example of breaking a complex question into multiple simple questions.

Question with complex exclusion instructions

1. How many people are currently living or staying at your home address? Do not forget to count yourself. For the purposes of this question, a person is defined as someone 18 years or older. Do not include children 17 years or younger. Do not include anyone who is living somewhere else for more than 2 months, such as a college student living away or someone in the Armed Forces on deployment.

Simpler questions that incorporate exclusion instructions

1. The first question is about people at your home address. How many people are currently living or staying at your home address?
2. When you reported the number of people living or staying at your home address, counting yourself, how many of them were 18 years or older?
3. When you reported the number of people living or staying at your home address, how many of them were children 17 years or younger?
4. When you reported the number of people living or staying at your home address, how many of them, if any, are currently living someplace else for more than 2 months, like a college student or someone in the Armed Forces on deployment?

Source: Adapted from *Clarifying Survey Questions*, by C. Redline, 2011. Unpublished dissertation, the Joint Program in Survey Methodology, University of Maryland, College Park, MD.

by asking a separate question for each source of income and then summing the results to generate a measure of total income. However, it is also important to remember that many people consider income to be sensitive information (and people are more likely to refuse to answer income than other questions) so asking a series of questions about income sources should only be done if precise income information is needed to achieve the survey's goals.

Guideline 8.2: Avoid Question Formats That Tax Respondents' Memory

One ought to avoid complex question formats in telephone surveys for the same reasons as avoiding complex question wording; respondent memory is more taxed because of their having to remember the question while answering. One example of a question format that should be avoided because it strains the memory too much over the telephone is the check-all-that-apply format (also see Guideline 5.12 for reasons we suggest avoiding the check-all-that-apply format in most instances). Instead, a forced-choice format should be used for multiple-answer questions because it allows the respondent to focus on and consider each item individually.

Ranking questions, especially those with more than three or four options, should also be avoided since it would require telephone respondents to remember all of the items to be ranked as well as to compare and rank them. Instead, one of the simpler alternatives, such as a paired comparison, discussed in Guideline 5.9, should be considered.

Nominal questions with many response options or with particularly complex response options should also be avoided since respondents are unlikely to be able to remember all of the necessary information to provide an optimal answer to these questions. Likewise, any question requiring summation should be avoided since it would require respondents to perform mental math.

All respondents will be unnecessarily burdened by these types of questions. Some will still be able to answer them adequately, but others will struggle. When several respondents struggle with the same question, interviewers may try to help them or to prevent problems for future respondents by rewording the question; decomposing the question into smaller, more manageable pieces; inferring responses from respondents' mumbling rather than working to get the correct answer; or even skipping the difficult question. While the interviewers are trying to be helpful and relieve burden for respondents, all of these behaviors result in lower data quality.

For this reason, it is important during the design stage to anticipate which question formats will be problematic for respondents and find ways to ask for the same information in less taxing ways. Doing this work up front will ease respondent burden and will eliminate the need for interviewers to take corrective action, thus helping to ensure that every respondent receives the same stimulus.

Guideline 8.3: Make Sure the Words the Interviewer Reads Clearly Convey What Is Being Asked

Remember, in telephone surveys, respondents will be unable to see lists of response options or what answer spaces look like. As such, it is even more important in this mode to ensure that the material the interviewer reads aloud communicates all of the information respondents need in order to answer the question.

Respondents need to know whether the question is open- or closed-ended, whether one or multiple responses should be given, what options are being offered as choices, and for open-ended questions the format or units in which a response should be given. Typically this information can be provided by carefully wording the question stem; it usually does not require a separate instruction. However, if there are extra instructions or definitions, they will need to be read out loud. Additionally, for closed-ended questions, the response options will often need to be read to the respondent, but as we discussed in Guideline 4.10, they should often be moved to the end of the question to improve processing.

Guideline 8.4: Provide Clear and Simple to Recognize Cues to the Interviewer About What Material Must Be Read, What Is Optional, and What Should Not Be Read to the Respondent

Figure 8.4 shows examples of telephone survey questions as they might appear on a CATI screen. Interviewers would read the questions and, in some cases the response options, and then enter the code that corresponds with the respondent's answer into the box below the item. In the left-hand column of this figure, there are no visual cues to help interviewers figure out what to read. For example, in the

FIGURE 8.4 Example telephone survey questions with and without visual cues to help interviewers.

Without visual cues to help interviewers	With visual cues to help interviewers
1. What do you think is the most important problem facing the country today? Record verbatim response. Probe for clarity but do not probe for additional mentions. Record in order mentioned. 　1　Open text box 　D　Don't know 　R　Refused 　☐	1. What do you think is the most important problem facing the country today? 　1　Open text box 　　**[INTERVIEWER: RECORD VERBATIM RESPONSE. PROBE FOR CLARITY BUT DO NOT PROBE FOR ADDITIONAL MENTIONS. RECORD IN ORDER MENTIONED.]** 　D　DON'T KNOW 　R　REFUSED 　☐
2. Now, thinking about the nation's economy ... How would you rate economic conditions in this country today? As ... 　1　Excellent 　2　Good 　3　Fair, or 　4　Poor 　D　Don't know 　R　Refused 　☐	2. Now, thinking about the nation's economy ... How would you rate economic conditions in this country today? As ... 　1　Excellent 　2　Good 　3　Fair, or 　4　Poor 　D　DON'T KNOW 　R　REFUSED 　☐
3. A year from now do you expect economic conditions in the country as a whole will be better than they are at present, worse, or just about the same as now? 　1　Better 　2　Worse 　3　About the same 　D　Don't know 　R　Refused 　☐	3. A year from now do you expect economic conditions in the country as a whole will be better than they are at present, worse, or just about the same as now? 　1　BETTER 　2　WORSE 　3　ABOUT THE SAME 　D　DON'T KNOW 　R　REFUSED 　☐

first question, interviewers have to recognize for themselves that the instruction to "record verbatim response" is for them and should not be read to respondents. The same is true for the last question. Likewise, there are no cues telling interviewers that they should read the response options aloud for the second question, but not for the third. And in the last question, they have to read an instruction telling them not to read the response options. It is also not clear whether they should explicitly offer the "don't know" and "refused" categories or not mention that these are options. Designing telephone questionnaires in this way makes the interviewer work much harder than is necessary, will likely result in slow and rough delivery of the questions, will lead to errors, and will considerably heighten the chance that respondents receive different stimuli from different interviewers.

FIGURE 8.4 (continued).

Without visual cues to help interviewers	With visual cues to help interviewers
4. We'd like to get your overall opinion of some people in the news. As I read each name, please say if you have a favorable or unfavorable opinion of these people—or if you have never heard of them.	4. We'd like to get your overall opinion of some people in the news. As I read each name, please say if you have a favorable or unfavorable opinion of these people—or if you have never heard of them.

Without visual cues to help interviewers

4. We'd like to get your overall opinion of some people in the news. As I read each name, please say if you have a favorable or unfavorable opinion of these people—or if you have never heard of them.

☐ The first name is Barack Obama. Do you have a favorable or unfavorable opinion of Barack Obama or have you never heard of him?

☐ The second name is Michelle Obama. Do you have a favorable or unfavorable opinion of Michelle Obama or have you never heard of her?

How about (NAME)?
Do you have a favorable or unfavorable opinion of (NAME) or have you never heard of (HIM/HER)?

☐ Joe Biden
☐ Mitt Romney
☐ Ann Romney
☐ Paul Ryan

Choices are 1=Favorable 2=Unfavorable 3=Never heard of D=Don't know R=Refused

5. What kind of activities do you do online?

Do not read answer categories. Code and probe for at least three activities.

1 Use e-mail
2 Facebook
3 Twitter
4 Stream music
5 Stream movies or TV shows
6 Read the news
7 Make purchases
8 Research products
9 Research restaurants
10 Look up health information
11 Other
12 None

☐☐☐☐☐☐☐☐☐☐☐

With visual cues to help interviewers

4. We'd like to get your overall opinion of some people in the news. As I read each name, please say if you have a favorable or unfavorable opinion of these people—or if you have never heard of them.

[INTERVIEWER: CHOICES ARE 1=FAVORABLE 2=UNFAVORABLE 3=NEVER HEARD OF D=DON'T KNOW R=REFUSED]

☐ The first name is Barack Obama. Do you have a favorable or unfavorable opinion of Barack Obama or have you never heard of him?

☐ The second name is Michelle Obama. Do you have a favorable or unfavorable opinion of Michelle Obama or have you never heard of her?

<How about (NAME)?>
<Do you have a favorable or unfavorable opinion of (NAME) or have you never heard of (HIM/HER)?>

☐ Joe Biden
☐ Mitt Romney
☐ Ann Romney
☐ Paul Ryan

5. What kind of activities do you do online?

[INTERVIEWER: CODE AND PROBE FOR AT LEAST THREE ACTIVITIES]

1 USE E-MAIL
2 FACEBOOK
3 TWITTER
4 STREAM MUSIC
5 STREAM MOVIES OR TV SHOWS
6 READ THE NEWS
7 MAKE PURCHASES
8 RESEARCH PRODUCTS
9 RESEARCH RESTAURANTS
10 LOOK UP HEALTH INFORMATION
11 OTHER
12 NONE

☐☐☐☐☐☐☐☐☐☐☐

In the second column, these problems are solved through the use of visual cues that indicate what should and should not be read. In this case the interviewers would be trained to follow the following rules:

- Information bolded, enclosed in brackets (i.e., [ ]), and preceded by "INTERVIEWER:" is interviewer instructions. Follow these instructions, but do not read them to respondents.
- Read all unbracketed information presented in sentence or lower case to the respondent in the order in which it appears.

- Do not read information presented in all caps.
- Read information enclosed in less than (i.e., <) or greater than (i.e., >) signs if you think doing so will help the respondent; it is optional.

Following these rules would ensure that each interviewer reads the same parts of each question. It also makes it much easier for interviewers to determine quickly what they are supposed to read aloud and what they should read silently to themselves, which will help them deliver the questions fluently. Moreover, lengthy written out directions about what should and should not be read can be eliminated. In other words, the use of visual cues in this way helps routinize the interviewer's interactions with the questionnaire so that they do not have to read instructions or make decisions about how to administer each and every question and its response options.

Every telephone survey does not have to use these exact rules and design strategies. Some may prefer using color and others may use different fonts (for more on how to use visual design effectively, see Chapter 6). What is important is that some method of quickly and efficiently communicating to interviewers what should and should not be read aloud is established and then used consistently to routinize their interaction with the questionnaire and minimize the amount of burdensome processing they have to do. Thus, it is often beneficial to standardize the rules within a call center so interviewers do not have to learn different rules for each study. That undermines their usefulness to help improve how interviewers interact with the questionnaire.

Guideline 8.5: Locate Interviewer Instructions Where They Are Needed by Interviewers

Much like for respondents, it is important to provide instructions to interviewers where they are needed. Interviewers who are trying to manage a respondent and the CATI system do not need the extra burden of having to go back and make changes because they did not see an instruction. Placing interviewer instructions where they are needed by interviewers will help ensure that they see them at the right time, follow them, and thus are able to provide the necessary feedback to respondents when it is needed to ensure accuracy. It can also help reduce the amount of searching needed to find necessary information. For example, in the first question in Figure 8.4, the instruction to enter a verbatim response is moved from the question stem to the answer item to which it applies. In the fourth question, the answer choices are moved from the bottom of the question, where they are hidden from view to just prior to the first item, making them more easily accessible the first time the interviewer needs them. Generally speaking, instructions about who should answer a question or how it should be read should be located prior to the question and instructions about how to enter a response or how to probe should be placed near the answer space.

Guideline 8.6: Include Conversational Cues and Short and Simple Transition Statements to Help Interviewers Administer the Questions

One key to ensuring that a telephone survey proceeds smoothly is to use a design that facilitates conversational turn-taking and discourages respondent interruptions that can take interviewers off script. In normal, everyday conversation, we use transitions to cue others about when we intend to keep talking and when we are almost done talking. For example, when trying to determine what to make for dinner, a parent might ask a child, "Do you want a hamburger, macaroni and cheese, pizza, or a sandwich?" In this question, the word "or" serves a very important purpose; it tells the child that the list is almost complete and it will be his turn to speak very soon. We insert transitions like this in everyday conversation effortlessly and often without even thinking about them, but when we write survey questions we often get very direct and forget to use these helpful transitions.

Figure 8.5 shows examples of how questions designed for self-administered modes can be revised to work better in a telephone survey by adding in a few simple transitions. In the first and second example, the transition "would you say"

FIGURE 8.5 Examples of the use of transitions to improve the delivery of survey questions over the telephone.

Typical Mail or Web Wording	Revised Wording for Telephone
Overall, how satisfied are you with living in this area? ○ Very satisfied ○ Somewhat satisfied ○ Neither satisfied nor dissatisfied ○ Somewhat dissatisfied ○ Very dissatisfied	Overall, how satisfied are you with living in this area? **Would you say . . .** ○ Very satisfied, ○ Somewhat satisfied, ○ Neither satisfied nor dissatisfied, ○ Somewhat dissatisfied, **or** ○ Very dissatisfied
How has the availability of jobs that provide a livable wage changed in the past five years? ○ Increased ○ Stayed the same ○ Decreased ○ Not sure	How has the availability of jobs that provide a livable wage changed in the past five years? **Would you say it has. . .** ○ Increased, ○ Stayed the same, ○ Decreased, **or** ○ **Are you unsure**
How do you currently obtain your prescription medications? ○ They are delivered to your home ○ You pick them up ○ Someone else picks them up for you ○ Other (specify) ○ Don't know/Don't remember	How do you currently obtain your prescription medications? ○ **Are they** delivered to your home, ○ **Do you** pick them up, ○ **Does** someone else pick them up for you, ○ **Do you get them some other way, or** ○ **Do you not know?**
Do you feel that each of the following descriptions does or does not describe Washington State University? Yes No Farm/Agriculture School ○ ○ Party School ○ ○ Electronic or "wired" university ○ ○ Competitive in Pac 12 sports ○ ○ Conservative university ○ ○ Politically charged/socially conscious ○ ○ Religious ○ ○ Outdoors oriented ○ ○ World class university ○ ○ Diverse ○ ○	I am going to read a list of descriptions. Please indicate whether you feel that each description does or does not describe Washington State University. The first description is farm or agriculture school. Do you feel this description does or does not describe Washington State University? The second description is party school. Do you feel this description does or does not describe Washington State University? [The next description is…] [Do you feel this description does or does not describe Washington State University?] Electronic or wired university? Competitive in Pac 12 sports? Conservative university? Politically charged or socially conscious? Religious? Outdoors oriented? World class university? Diverse?

is added to let the respondent know that the interviewer is going to read a set of options. In addition, the transition "or" is added to tell the respondent that the next option read will be the last one and it will be her turn to speak. Using transitions such as these consistently throughout a questionnaire will help respondents figure out when a question is closed-ended, requiring them to wait patiently to hear the response options, and when it is open-ended, requiring them to volunteer their answer as soon as they have one.

We have listened to a number of surveys where the lack of transitions resulted in respondents interrupting interviewers with a response after they read the question stem, but before they could read the response options. The interviewers then had to go off script to explain that they needed to read the response options. Because of these interactions early in the questionnaire, these same respondents later mistakenly waited silently for response options to be read when the question was actually open-ended, causing the interviewers to once again have to go off script to tell them that an open-ended response was needed. Using transitions to minimize these types of confusion and interruptions will ease the burden on both the respondent and the interviewer, reduce incidences of going off-script, and help the survey progress smoothly.

Another aspect of paper and web questions that does not work well over the telephone without some conversational improvements is providing nonsubstantive (e.g., don't know, not sure, etc.) and catch-all (e.g., other) categories. In paper and web surveys, we can just add these on to the end of the list of response options, but doing so makes for very awkward delivery in telephone surveys and often results in interviewers improvising to reduce the awkwardness. When asking a child about dinner, one would never say, "Do you want a hamburger, macaroni and cheese, pizza, a sandwich, other specify?" Instead, one would end the list of dinner options with something a little less stunted and more conversational like, " ... or something else?" The same should be done with survey questions that are to be asked over the telephone. Examples are shown in the second and third questions in Figure 8.5.

The final question in Figure 8.5 gives an example of how conversational content can be added to a forced-choice question to help communicate to respondents what is expected of them, but also be efficient. If an interviewer were to read just the items as they are presented in the paper or web version, many respondents would lose the context of the question and be unsure about how to answer. Conversely, reading the entire question stem for each of the 10 items would be unnecessarily repetitive and awkward.

In the telephone revision of this question, we find a middle ground between these two options by telling respondents what is about to happen and then reading the full question stem for the first two items to get them oriented before shortening the stimulus to only the items themselves. For these types of questions, we often give our interviewers the discretion to read all or part of the question stem as needed to reorient respondents should they become confused about what they are being asked. In this example, the optional material is presented in brackets and italics. Providing this scripted way for interviewers to get back on track if something goes wrong helps ensure that they do not each correct problems in their own ways but instead deliver the questionnaire similarly.

Each of the revisions provided in this figure adds extra wording in an effort to make delivery less awkward and encourage staying on script. But what is important to note is that the additional words do not add difficulty to the questions. Nor do they change the nature or meaning of the questions or bias responses. They are simply tools to help the survey conversation unfold in a more conversational way that facilitates the question and answer process. As such, these types of revisions can easily be made in web and paper modes as well as when these modes are used alongside telephone surveys in mixed-mode designs.

Similar to conversational cues within the question, transition statements to indicate a change in topic will help prepare respondents for questions on a different subject. Just like when we change the subject in everyday conversation, we want to add transitions such as "On a different subject" or "Now, thinking about (new topic)," or even a simple "Next" to help notify the respondent of a topic change. Scripted transition statements that help lead respondents from one topic to another will help interviewers stay on script, rather than adding their own transitions statements, and will improve the overall conversational flow between the interviewer and respondent.

Guideline 8.7: Avoid the Use of Abbreviations and Special Characters and Include Pronunciations for Difficult Words, Names, or Places

Abbreviations (for example, etc., e.g., i.e., and others) and special characters (e.g., -, (), %, #, &, /, etc.) are likely to be read in different ways by different interviewers. As a simple example, some interviewers will read words that appear in parentheses, but others will consider them optional and skip over them. Some may read the (character as "open parenthesis" and others might add interpretive words like "for example" in its place. In short, unless interviewers have been trained to handle abbreviations and special characters in prescribed ways, using them introduces uncertainty about whether and how items should be read, something we want to avoid in standardized surveys. If you look closely at the two versions of the fourth question in Figure 8.5, you will see that the special characters that appear in the paper and web version are all removed in the telephone version, resulting in a set of items that can easily be read word for word with very little decision making on the interviewer's part.

In addition, it is also important to include pronunciations for difficult words, names, or places to ensure that interviewers read and respondents hear exactly what the researcher intended. For example, in a survey about the country's political leadership, interviewers would need to know that the last name of the 61st Speaker of the U.S. House of Representatives, John Boehner, is pronounced BAY-ner. Names and places are two of the most common types of words that need pronunciations. In general, it is better to err on the side of providing a pronunciation if there is concern that the interviewer may not say the word or name correctly.

Guideline 8.8: Include a "Don't Know" or "Refused" Option for Every Question

Often CATI systems will require a response to a question in order to move to the next question. This can be problematic if for some reason a respondent is unable or unwilling to answer the question. In this case, the interviewer either has to continue to push for a response, which could anger the respondent or result in them giving a suboptimal answer, make up a response themselves, or end the survey. None of these are good options as they are likely to lead to nonresponse or measurement error on the item at hand and also possibly on later items.

To avoid this problem and to help the interviewer maintain proper rapport with respondents, it is important to give them a way to move forward in the questionnaire in these situations. This is commonly done by including options like "don't know" or "refused" on each question in the survey (see Figure 8.4). We typically call these *interviewer protected* or *volunteered* categories because they are generally not explicitly offered to respondents, but can be recorded by the interviewer when volunteered by respondents. Interviewers should be trained to probe for a substantive response, but to also recognize when they have reached an impasse and it is more productive to use one of these types of nonsubstantive response options than to jeopardize data quality or the rest of the survey.

Guideline 8.9: Provide Ways for Interviewers to Respond to and Record the Outcome of Every Possible Scenario That Can Be Anticipated

Although some people may think telephone surveys follow a specific script, at least once, and often many times during every interview, the respondent will say or do something to take the conversation away from the script. For example, the person on the phone may hang up, ask if they can finish the interview at another time, indicate that they are at a business and not a household, request more information about the study, or want to change a previous answer. Interviewers need to be able to respond appropriately and follow the correct path in the questionnaire. Thus, the questionnaire needs to be designed to anticipate these possible scenarios and provide interviewers specific options to respond to them.

In the preceding examples, interviewers would need a way to record that the person hung up the phone or requested to be called back at another time. If the interviewer talks with someone and realizes that they have reached a business, which is ineligible for the current study, they would need a way to record that a business was reached and if needed to ask any further follow-up questions to collect the name or type of business reached. Similarly, for the respondent who requested further information, the interviewer would need to know where to go in the CATI to find information about the study and/or responses to frequently asked questions (for more on this, see Guideline 8.10) to give to the respondent. Lastly, to respond to those who wanted to change their answers, the interviewer would need the ability to move backward in the interview to change a response to a previous question and then come back to where they had left off. Thinking ahead about these possible scenarios is important, especially when interviewers are using CATI or a web survey to administer the questionnaire, because these types of scenarios need to be programmed into the survey itself.

As some of the preceding examples demonstrate, it is important that the interviewer be able to accurately record the outcome of the call. Not only do interviewers work to complete the interview with potential respondents but when that process is interrupted for any reason, interviewers need a systematic way for recording these types of outcomes so all interviewers record them in the same way. It is important that interviewers can record these outcomes accurately, as discussed further in Guideline 8.24.

Guideline 8.10: Provide Standardized Scripts for Responses to Questions Respondents May Ask and to Address Any Special Procedures for the Study

For nearly all telephone surveys, it is important to provide information about the study to interviewers so they know how to respond to questions they receive. Generally, most researchers also provide a list of questions that they think people may ask about the study and the language or talking points they would like the interviewers to use in answering them. These are sometimes called FAQs (Frequently Asked Questions). The types of questions that it may be helpful to provide standardized scripts for are

- Who is conducting the study?
- How is the study funded?
- What is the study about?
- Why should I participate?
- How will the study benefit me?
- How did you select me for this study?

It is important that the responses provided to these questions do not bias the results of the study, which is why it is essential that the researchers instruct interviewers on what to say. The information that interviewers can disclose may vary depending on what point it is in the interview and other considerations. For example, a survey sponsor may not want to inform respondents that the study on environmental impact is being conducted by the major oil company in the region, at least until after the respondent has completed the interview. Thus, instructions or scripts for how interviewers should respond may vary depending on where the respondent is in the interview process.

Further, it is important that this information be accessible to interviewers so they do not have to recall it from memory, along with the other tasks they are executing to administer the interview. The information should be easily accessible, either within the CATI system by pressing a button or hot key that routes them to the screen with this information or for less automated telephone surveys, a printed sheet should be easily accessible at the interviewer's workstation.

Guideline 8.11: Display Each Individual Question on Its Own Screen to Reduce Clutter and Support Efficient Processing

As is apparent from the examples in Figure 8.4, the presentation of questions for telephone surveys can get quite complex. In addition to the question and response options, interviewers working with CATI software will also have other information on their screens such as details about the record being called and the call outcome; the question number and code; and hot keys or buttons that lead to things such as frequently asked questions, definitions, and space to leave notes about what happened in the interview. Interviewers have to sort through all of this information and decide what needs to be used and when. Placing multiple questions on one screen compounds this problem and thus should be avoided. Displaying each question on its own screen will reduce the number of elements vying for interviewers' attention and help them stay focused on administering the question at hand.

Guideline 8.12: Include Additional Questions Needed for Screening and Weighting Surveys That Include Cell Phones

There may be a need to ask additional questions when calling cell phones. First, one of the most important additional questions asked is whether the person is an adult so that calls with minors can be terminated (unless the survey is targeting minors, in which case, parental consent is nearly always required). Also, a very important step when talking to people on their cell phones is to ensure that they are in a safe place and are able to talk. This can be done with a question such as, "Are you driving a car right now or doing any other activity requiring your full attention? If so, I need to call you back later." Similarly, for surveys covering sensitive topics, additional questions may be needed to determine where the respondent is when taking the call and whether the interviewer should set up another time to call the person back to ensure that he can answer privately (AAPOR, 2010).

Surveys of particular geographies, such as cities, counties, or states, may also need to include an additional screening question to ensure that respondents currently live in the areas targeted by the survey. Figure 8.6 shows the results of a study in which respondents' self-reported zip codes were compared to geographic information on the sample frame (i.e., the geographic information associated with the telephone number) in six general population surveys (Christian, Dimock, & Keeter, 2009). The study found that the geographic information associated with landline phone numbers was quite accurate at the broader geographic levels of census regions and states as well as at the more precise geographic level of counties, but the geographic information associated with the cell phone numbers was much less accurate at the county level. Given the inability to precisely know where cell phone respondents live based on the phone number or information provided

FIGURE 8.6 Accuracy of geographic information from landline and cell phone sample frames.

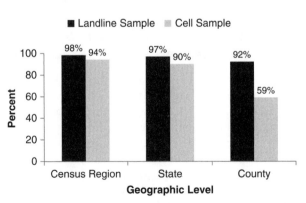

Percent of Cases Where Self-Reported Zip Code Matched Sample Frame Information by Geographic Level

Source: Adapted from *Accurately Locating Where Wireless Respondents Live Requires More Than a Phone Number*, by L. M. Christian, M. Dimock, and S. Keeter, 2009. Retrieved from http://pewresearch.org/pubs/1278/cell-phones-geographic-sampling-problems

with the sample, it is important to include any necessary questions to collect their zip code or full address to ensure they live in the target area of the survey.

Lastly, dual-frame RDD surveys, in which the final sample combines landline and cell phone numbers, will also need to ask questions about what types of phones people use and how they use them, as well as information about the people in the home who use those phones. In some surveys, these questions might be used to screen out respondents (e.g., to only interview respondents reached on their cell phone who do not have a landline). But for all dual-frame surveys, these types of questions are needed to ensure that the data can be weighted properly. Surveys generally ask for at least the first three pieces of information listed here:

- Presence/number of landline phones in the home (that receive calls)
- Presence/number of cell phones used by members of the home
- Number of adults/people in the household
- How people use their phones (many researchers use the National Health Interview Survey Question for people with a landline and cell phone to identify which phone they use more, or now use some variation of that question)
- Whether cell phones are shared with other members of the household

Guideline 8.13: Consider Offering Cell Phone Respondents Reimbursement for Their Minutes Used

Because some people pay for their cell phone use in minutes and they may incur a financial burden for the interview, many surveyors offer some small amount, such as $5 or $10, to reimburse respondents for their cell phone minutes. For longer surveys, larger amounts may be needed. It was recommended in AAPOR's 2010 Cell Phone Task Force to reimburse cell phone respondents to help ensure that respondents do not incur any additional burden for taking part in the survey. An example of how to offer this type of reimbursement in the survey introduction is: "I know I am calling you on a cell phone. If you would like to be reimbursed for your cell phone minutes, we will pay all eligible respondents (INSERT AMOUNT) for participating in this survey."

GUIDELINES FOR ADMINISTERING TELEPHONE QUESTIONNAIRES

The previous section focused on designing telephone questionnaires to help respondents and interviewers. In this section, we turn to guidelines for how interviewers should administer the questionnaire. We focus on the interviewers' role, including what is expected of them, how they should try to encourage participation, and how they should administer the questionnaire to the sampled households. These guidelines focus on strategies for ensuring interviewers accurately administer the questionnaire as the surveyor intended but also to focus on the respondents and what they are saying throughout the interview.

Guideline 8.14: Provide a Short, Clear, and Persuasive Introduction to the Survey

One of the most challenging aspects for interviewers is the first few minutes of the telephone interview. Once someone answers the phone, her decision about whether to participate in the survey may be made in just a few seconds. Thus, the survey introduction and how interviewers deliver it, even the first few words they say, can have a substantial impact on whether someone decides to stay on the line and continue with the survey or simply hang up the phone. The introduction to a telephone survey needs to introduce the survey (and generally the interviewer) and motivate people to participate. But because of the time pressures in telephone surveys mentioned earlier, the interviewer needs to be able to deliver the introduction in a few short sentences while also working to create a personal connection with the person on the phone.

While an introductory script is often provided for interviewers, it is important that they be given the latitude to deviate from that script as needed to immediately respond to any concerns raised by the respondent. If, for example, the respondent interrupts the reading of the introductory script with "I'm not buying anything," the interviewer needs to be able to quickly reassure the respondent that this is not a sales call. To ignore this objection and continue reading the script would almost surely result in a hang-up.

It is also important that interviewers express all of the key points included in the introduction, but not necessarily that they read it verbatim or even in the order in which it is organized in the script. Rather, at this very delicate point in the call, they need to be able to adjust to the interaction as it unfolds with the respondent. Likewise, interviewers need to be able to deliver the introduction in a smooth and natural sounding way rather than sounding mechanical or automated in order to make the interaction feel more natural and comfortable. Introductions that are less scripted and more tailored have been found to be more effective at gaining cooperation (Groves & Couper, 1998; Groves & McGonagle, 2001; Morton-Williams, 1991).

The survey introduction may include the name of the person being surveyed, if known, and should include the name of the interviewer and the name of the organization conducting the study (the actual sponsor may be revealed later if there is concern about how it may impact responses). It should also include information about the purpose of the study, benefits of participation, and information about the survey process. It is often helpful to include statements that address possible concerns people may have. For example, it can be particularly helpful in telephone surveys to include a statement that emphasizes the call is a request to complete a survey and not a sales or marketing call. Lastly, some organizations may need to include statements mandated by legal departments, institutional review boards, or the Office of Management and Budget; usually interviewers must read these statements verbatim so this should be clearly specified (although they often negatively impact cooperation). See Figure 8.7 for some examples of telephone survey introductions.

Guideline 8.15: Read Questions Fully and Exactly, in Order, as They Appear in the Questionnaire

One of the most important tasks the interviewer carries out is to read the questions to respondents. While the introduction can be less scripted and more conversational, in a standardized interview, it is essential that interviewers read the questions fully and exactly as they appear in the questionnaire (and pronounce each word correctly and clearly). That is, they should not deviate from the script at this point in the survey. This standardization ensures that a common stimulus

FIGURE 8.7 Examples of telephone survey introductions.

General introduction:
Hello, I'm (interviewer's name) calling on behalf of (organization name).
We are doing a survey and are asking questions about (topic of survey questions).
The information provided will be used to (describe purpose of study).
We are not trying to sell you anything. Your phone number has been chosen
(describe random or purposive sampling) to be included in the study.

You don't have to answer any question you don't want to, and you can end the
interview at any time. The interview takes only about (estimate number of
minutes) and any information you give me will be confidential. If you have
questions about this survey, I will provide you with a telephone number for you
to call to get more information.

Introduction to Behavioral Risk Surveillance Factor Survey (2011):
Hello, I am calling for the (health department). My name is (interviewer's name).
We are gathering information about the health of (state) residents. This project is
conducted by the health department with assistance from the Centers for Disease
Control and Prevention. Your telephone number has been chosen randomly, and
I would like to ask some questions about health and health practices.

Introduction to Pew Research Center surveys:
Hello, I am (interviewer's name) calling for (name of survey organization
conducting the study). We are conducting a study about some important issues
today and would like to include your household.

is provided and that results are comparable across different interviewers. Interviewers should not modify the questions by changing words or adding or deleting
information (unless instructed that this type of practice is allowed for a particular
survey) because small changes in the wording of questions and response options
can lead to differences in how respondents answer (as discussed in Chapters 4 and
5). To effectively administer the questions, the interviewer needs to understand
exactly what should and should not be read, as well as any additional information
that can be provided to respondents (e.g., optional instructions, clarifications, etc.).
This is why it is so important for the design of the questionnaire to provide visual
cues to help distinguish the different types of information (see Guideline 8.4).

Because the order of the questions should be carefully designed to improve the
conversational flow and minimize order effects (see Chapter 7), it is also important
for interviewers to ask the questions in the order the researcher intended (i.e., in
the order in which they are displayed in the questionnaire or by the CATI system).
Interviewers should not skip questions or move through the questionnaire in a different order. Even if interviewers believe they know how a respondent will answer
a question (usually based on a previous response/interaction in the survey), they
must ask the question as intended and get an answer from the respondent, rather
than providing what they think the answer should be. Interviewers can reduce
the awkwardness of asking questions that respondents have previously answered
by explaining that asking every question as it is written and in the right order is a
requirement of their job. For example, they might say "I'm sorry, but I am required
to read every question as written even if it is about something we have already discussed" or "As part of our commitment to quality research, it is important that we

ask every question of every household in the same way." These sorts of explanations help explain what would otherwise be awkward conversational behavior (i.e., asking a question that has already been answered) and help train the respondents about the rules of the survey conversation (Fowler & Mangione, 1990).

Asking questions in order is especially critical since many telephone questionnaires include extensive filtering or branching, where follow-up questions are dependent on responses to previous questions (e.g., "Did you vote in person, by mail, or some other way?" If voted in person, "Did you vote on election day or before election day?"), or fills, in which the wording of a subsequent question is based on information provided in a previous question (e.g., "How would you describe your stay at the Westin Hotel near the Atlanta airport?" where the respondent had previously reported staying at that particular hotel).

Guideline 8.16: Record Answers Exactly as Respondents Provide Them

Not only is it important for interviewers to read the questions fully and exactly as written, but they also need to accurately record respondents' answers. The survey researchers are usually not able to fully review each interview (by listening to a recording or reviewing a transcript) so the main source of information they have about how respondents answered the questions is through the answers that interviewers record and that ultimately end up in the final data set. Recording responses accurately may be relatively easy for closed-ended questions, where the interviewer simply needs to select the category corresponding to the respondent's answer. Although, even for these types of questions there can still be errors when interviewers code a response incorrectly, think they can infer a response based on how respondents answered an earlier question, or simply miss-key the response (e.g., accidentally pressing "2" instead of "1" because they are side by side on the keyboard).

For open-ended questions, it is important that interviewers type the responses exactly as respondents said them and record the full response without paraphrasing, interpreting, or inferring what respondents may have meant. That includes trying to minimize typographical and other errors that may impact how the respondents' answers are eventually coded and analyzed by the survey researcher. Open-ended questions can create longer pauses on the telephone, so one interviewer technique we have often observed is to simply say, "Thank you. Please give me a few moments to type in your response accurately" or a similar statement to give respondents feedback and inform them that the interviewer heard their response so that they do not feel compelled to fill the silence by repeating or elaborating on their response. Interviewers can also read the response back as they type it to achieve the same end.

Guideline 8.17: Focus on the Respondent and Practice Active Listening

One of the most important tasks for the interviewer is to be engaged with and listen to the respondent at all times throughout the interview. Active listening involves not only focusing on what respondents say and the specific words they use but also attending to how they say it, such as the pitch and tone of their voice and other paralinguistic cues (Gwartney, 2007). It also entails observing details in the background to understand aspects of the respondents' environment that might affect their ability to respond accurately. Overall, the conversational flow between the telephone interviewer and the respondent is improved when interviewers are listening actively because they can quickly decide what to do next and how to respond to any questions or comments raised by the respondent. Lastly, not only does listening involve hearing what respondents say, but also then incorporating that information into how the interviewers respond. It is this final step that helps keep respondents engaged in the survey since the interviewer is actively attending to what they are saying and showing that their responses are valued.

Guideline 8.18: Use a Controlled Speaking Pace and Manage the Pitch and Tone of Your Voice

An interviewer's ability to speak in a controlled pitch and tone is one of the key aspects of a successful interview. It is also important for interviewers to convey professionalism and confidence in their voice throughout the interview. Respondents will notice nervous utterances (e.g., um, okay, etc.), long pauses, and other inflections in the interviewer's voice and may interpret those as indicators that the interviewer is inexperienced or is not taking the interview seriously. For example, Oksenberg and Cannell (1988) found that interviewers who spoke quickly, loudly, and with perceived confidence had lower refusal rates than interviewers who spoke more slowly, in a softer tone, and with less confidence. This is likely because respondents found them more credible and competent and thus more persuasive.

Interviewers who are prepared and well-trained are often better at managing their voice (interviewer training is discussed more in Guideline 8.20). Specifically, interviewers who know and have practiced the script, especially the introduction and key general persuaders, are usually more effective at gaining people's cooperation. In addition, familiarity with the flow of the survey, the topics covered, and the specific terminology and language used will help interviewers manage the pace of the interview and anticipate what comes next so they can modify the pitch and tone of their voice as needed.

This same preparation is essential for helping interviewers control the pace of the survey conversation. Generally a normal or slightly fast pace that attempts to minimize pauses or lapses in the conversation is best for phone interviews (Gwartney, 2007). However, interviewers should also listen to cues from the respondent and adjust their pace as needed. If a respondent asks the interviewer to repeat information, especially multiple times, the interviewer will likely want to slow her speaking pace. By contrast, for respondents who are in a hurry, and are showing they easily understand the questions, the interviewer might want to speed up her speaking pace.

Throughout the years we have heard many telephone interviewers complain that a small cold or the symptoms of seasonal allergies will impact their cooperation rates. When they have a scratchy throat or need to pause more often to clear their throat, cough, or catch their breath it disrupts the pitch and tone of their voice and the pace they can maintain, which impacts their ability to persuade people to participate and effectively administer the survey.

Guideline 8.19: Provide Encouragement and Targeted Feedback to Respondents

To be successful at gaining and maintaining respondent cooperation, interviewers need to provide encouragement and feedback to respondents as they complete the interview. This is especially critical at the beginning of the survey, when the focus is explicitly on encouraging people to participate and establishing a connection with them. However, it is also important to continue providing encouragement as respondents move through the interview to inform them they are performing well or help guide their behavior so they perform better. Respondents notice when interviewers take the time to show that they have heard their response. This type of feedback is especially important if interviewers notice any hesitation or confusion by respondents or when they encounter more difficult questions in the survey.

Although feedback is important in helping to facilitate the interview process, it is critical that interviewers provide feedback that is neutral and not leading (Fowler & Mangione, 1990). Feedback should not influence how respondents answer the question in any way. Interviewers should not sound like they are approving or disapproving of what the respondent is saying or that they are favoring one response over another, by providing feedback like "yes," "good," or "I disagree."

Providing neutral feedback can be as simple as repeating what the respondent said or saying "thank you." Similarly, task-related feedback such as "I want to make sure I recorded your response accurately" or "I am typing exactly what you are saying" can also help let respondents know that their responses are important and the interviewer is taking the time to ensure the data are accurate.

Probing is a particularly important type of feedback that interviewers provide to help respondents answer more fully and accurately. In fact, the ability of interviewers to probe to gain additional clarity or detail from respondents about their answers is one benefit of interviewer-administered surveys compared to self-administered surveys.

Probing is especially important to help ensure that respondents provide high-quality answers to open-ended questions, as discussed in Guideline 5.4. But probing can also be important in closed-ended questions, especially when there is confusion about which category a respondent chooses. This usually happens when respondents give a response that does not clearly fit within the response options (e.g., answers "not very satisfied" on the scale very satisfied, somewhat satisfied, somewhat dissatisfied, very dissatisfied) or gives a range when an exact number is needed (e.g., "between 4 and 5"). In these cases, interviewers usually need to probe to get a more clear answer, and the probes interviewers use need to be nondirective.

One strategy that can be effective for encouraging respondents to elaborate or clarify their responses without influencing them is simply pausing and allowing a short silence after respondents provide their answer. Alternatively, repeating the question stem and/or response options for respondents can help them think more about how they want to respond or clarify which option they wanted to select. Generally, interviewers should be instructed to repeat the full question stem and/or read all of the response options; this helps ensure that respondents fully perceive the information and can then complete the rest of the steps in the question–answer process (Fowler & Mangione, 1990). Other more direct probes, such as "Is there anything else?" or "Please be more specific" can also help encourage respondents to clarify their response or provide more detail without influencing their response.

Guideline 8.20: Train Interviewers Before They Start Calling Sample Members and Provide Regular Follow-Up Trainings

Training is critical to ensuring that telephone interviewers can perform their jobs effectively. Generally, telephone interviewers receive extensive training when they first start as an interviewer, usually extended over several days or weeks. These trainings often start in the classroom but also can include online or other training methodologies. Once the classroom training is complete, telephone interviewers usually spend several days or weeks shadowing more experienced interviewers and interviewing on their own using a practice sample (i.e., calling members of the target population who are not in the actual sample and using the collected data only for practice or testing). Engaging in supervised practice is especially important; it has been shown to reduce poor interviewer behaviors like reading questions incorrectly, failing to probe, and using directive probes (Fowler & Mangione, 1990). In general, we have found that interviewers look forward to training and practice. They learn more about how to be successful, which gives them confidence and can directly impact their cooperation rates (and may impact their compensation in some call centers). Also, it is often an opportunity for interviewers to better understand why questions are worded a certain way or why they need to be asked in a particular order.

The initial training usually covers general information about how to administer the questionnaire, including how to use the CATI software and interact with any other systems needed for the interviewing process; the general layout of the questionnaire and rules about how to distinguish what information should and should not be read (as discussed in Guideline 8.4); strategies for encouraging people to participate, including commonly used persuaders that can be used to help interviewers overcome common objections; and information about how questions should be read and general probing techniques. The classroom training usually includes extensive time spent listening to and evaluating previous interviews, as well as role-playing, where people trade off being the interviewer and the respondent. This helps interviewers gain familiarity with the pace and flow of the interviews before interviewing real respondents. Also, many training courses have assessments or examinations that interviewers must pass before they are allowed to begin interviewing.

In addition to the initial training, it is important for interviewers to receive continuous feedback and training as they conduct live interviews. Ongoing monitoring and feedback helps interviewers hone their skills, but it also communicates to them that quality data collection is a high priority (Fowler & Mangione, 1990). This training is important for both newer interviewers who are still learning and more experienced interviewers who are further removed from their initial training and as a result may become more careless in reading questions as written or probing appropriately.

As part of the ongoing quality review, surveyors should monitor interviewer performance and provide them with timely feedback (for more on this, see Guideline 8.33). In addition, many call centers provide ongoing training updates or discussions with interviewers each day before they begin calling or more extensive refresher courses to help interviewers remember what they learned during the initial training and to provide any new information needed for the surveys they are currently interviewing on. Generally, any time interviewers start on a new study, they should receive training specific to that study so they understand the goals, their role, and what is expected of them. This is also where interviewers receive training on the specific script for that study and on any study-specific procedures, especially if they deviate from standard procedures. For more on interviewer training, see Alcser and Clemons (2013).

GUIDELINES FOR ESTABLISHING CALLING RULES AND PROCEDURES

One of the key aspects of implementing telephone surveys is deciding how to call the sampled telephone numbers. This includes rules about how many times and when numbers will be called, as well as the timing between calls, and whether numbers will be dialed by an autodialer or manually by interviewers. Not only are rules needed, but so are mechanisms for capturing the outcome of each call and tracking progress across multiple attempts.

When developing the calling procedures for a specific survey, it is important to remember that procedures will vary considerably depending on the population and topic of the survey, the survey's budget, and various aspects of the survey design, especially the length of the study period. Household surveys may have different calling procedures than surveys of businesses. Surveys that provide precise estimates for the government and inform decisions about how to allocate funding often have a longer field period and more rigorous calling procedures than surveys of voters and consumers, which often need to be conducted in just a few days. Likewise, surveys that recruit people to participate in a panel, in which participation is ongoing, may have more rigorous calling procedures than surveys that recruit people to complete a single survey because any errors or bias in the initial recruitment of the panel will carry through to subsequent waves and thus need to be minimized. These different goals and survey characteristics influence decisions about how many times and how often to call a number.

In addition, because people use landline and mobile phones differently, calling procedures are often different for landline and cell phone numbers. For example, a cell phone is mobile and can be carried around throughout the day, wherever a person goes, whereas a landline phone is physically tied to a person's home. This may affect the times of day an organization calls the number or what types of questions may need to be asked to ensure that the person is in a safe location (as discussed in Guideline 8.12). Similarly, cell phones are often considered personal devices and are less likely to be shared than landline phones. Thus, some procedures that are effective on landline phones may be less effective for cell phones. For example, refusal conversion attempts to landline telephone numbers often are successful because a new person in the sampled unit can be reached, but these procedures may not be as effective for cell phones since calling back often results in reaching the same person who refused initially.

The following guidelines focus on how to develop effective calling rules and procedures. In them, we highlight differences that should be considered when calling landlines versus cell phones.

Guideline 8.21: Make Multiple Attempts to Reach Someone at Each Sampled Telephone Number

One of the most successful ways to increase response, across different modes, is to make more than one attempt to reach and persuade each sampled member to participate. For all telephone surveys, but especially those that contact and survey respondents *only* by telephone, that means making multiple attempts to the sample member's phone number(s).

The length of the interviewing period has one of the largest impacts on the decision about the number of attempts to make and how long to wait between attempts. For example, a study with a 5-day interviewing period may make 7 to 10 attempts per number and most numbers will be attempted more than once a day. However, a study where interviewing is spread over several months may attempt each number 15 to 30 times, with several days or even weeks between attempts.

Another factor that affects the number of and duration between attempts is the outcome of the previous attempt (i.e., a nonworking number, nonresidential, no answer, busy, voice mail, refusal, language callback, etc.). For example, once a number is determined to be nonworking or nonresidential, only one or two additional attempts will be made to the number, usually just to confirm that the number is not working (some surveys may skip this practice and just move on to the next number). Far more attempts are usually made to numbers that were busy, where no one answered, or where a voice mail message was encountered. The additional call attempts are made to more accurately determine whether the number is working and if an eligible person can be reached at that number, and, if so, to give the sample member every opportunity to make an informed decision about whether to participate or not. For numbers that were busy or where no one answered, another attempt is often made the same day. But when a voice mail message is encountered, particularly if the interviewer leaves a message, or if the interviewer talked with someone in the household, it is better to wait at least a day or two, if not longer, before calling the number again.

For households that refused, one more attempt, sometimes called a refusal conversion attempt, may be made to try to encourage the home to participate. These types of refusal conversion attempts are generally not made to numbers where the person reached was irate or asked specifically not to be called again—so-called hard refusals—but are generally only made to soft refusals where there is more of a chance to persuade the reluctant person to participate. This attempt is often conducted by a more experienced interviewer and usually is not made until after a cooling off period of at least 7 to 10 days after the initial call (Groves, 1989). These types of refusal conversion attempts have been shown to help increase the representativeness of the final sample (Curtin, Presser, & Singer, 2000).

The number of and timing between attempts can also be different for cell phones than for landlines. For example, at many organizations, the maximum number of attempts is higher for landline numbers than for cell phone numbers. This is related to the fact that landline phones tend to be household devices where cell phones are more likely to be personal devices. Thus, when calling a cell phone, it is more likely that each attempt will be to the same person, whereas for landlines, it is more likely that different people in the household may be reached on subsequent attempts.

For all studies, it is important to respect the respondents when thinking about the appropriate number of attempts and the timing between them. Making too many attempts, especially in a short period of time, risks frustrating and alienating people rather than increasing the likelihood they cooperate. Also, with caller ID and cell phone records, it is now easier for people to track how many times an organization is calling them. It is important for telephone surveyors to understand the legal limitations and rules around calling telephone numbers, and how they vary across different states within the United States and across different countries, as discussed further in Guideline 8.23.

Guideline 8.22: Vary the Days of the Week and Times of the Day That Call Attempts Are Made to Each Sample Member

In addition to making multiple call attempts, one of the most successful ways to maximize the potential of reaching someone by phone is to vary the days and times that calls are made. Because people have different schedules, calling at different times of day and on different days of the week helps to maximize the potential to reach people when they are at home or available to talk by phone. For example, calling a number every weeknight at 7:00 will likely continue to produce non-contact for someone who works an evening shift, but calling the same number at 10:00 in the morning or on a weekend will improve the chances of the call being answered.

Generally, the calling window—or the times of day a number is called—is based on the local time zone associated with the phone number, but determining an accurate location for telephone numbers has become increasingly difficult with number portability and the increasing use of the Internet for telephone service (e.g., VOIP). This is especially difficult for cell phones that are inherently mobile in nature. Whether because they are traveling or keeping the same cell phone number after they move, a substantial share of cell phone users are in different areas than where their numbers would suggest. Surveyors may wish to adjust calling windows to address this type of error and train interviewers how to react to these situations.

When deciding what days and times to call, it is also important to think about the population of interest. For surveys of households, weekday evenings and weekends are often the best times to reach someone at home, so more attempts are often made during these periods than during daytime hours during the week, especially when calling landlines phones. Researchers may be less restricted when calling cell phones. Weekends have traditionally been effective times to reach people on their cell phones, but since many people continuously have their cell phones with them, surveyors can also reach people on weekdays during the day and in the evening.

However, for surveys of businesses or establishments the best time to reach someone is often during weekday business hours, although the call scheduling may need to be further adjusted based on the type of business. For example, a survey of elementary schools may necessitate calling at very different times than a survey of after-school programs. Likewise, a survey of family-style restaurants may be more successful if calls are placed during normal business hours while a survey of fine-dining dinner establishments may be most successful if calls are placed later in the day.

In addition, sometimes researchers may decide not to make calls for their survey on various holidays, during particular religious periods, during big events, at times when many people are on vacation, or other times when contact or cooperation rates are expected to be very low or when calling may affect responses. One funny example is that many surveyors in Nebraska avoid placing calls to Nebraska residents on Huskers football Saturdays in the fall; contact and cooperation rates on these days are exceptionally low across the state, and those who are contacted tend to be distracted or annoyed about the intrusion during their tailgating or game-watching activities.

Weather can also be a concern. One of us was surveying just before the 2012 U.S. presidential election when Hurricane Sandy hit the Northeast coast. We had to quickly respond to issues that arose. Thankfully, the actual call centers being used for the survey were outside the affected area, but many of the people working on the data collection effort were displaced by the storm or experienced loss of power and connectivity (Internet and/or cellular). We had to quickly develop alternative procedures to ensure that the survey was still carried out effectively, even under these circumstances. In addition, we monitored the completed interviews in the affected areas to ensure that we were able to reach and represent people in those regions; had we not been able to, we would have considered whether the results were reliable and should be used. This was a national survey, where people living in the affected areas made up a relatively small portion of the sample, but if we had been conducting a local survey in one of the affected cities or states, we likely would have stopped data collection altogether because of both feasibility and concerns about representativeness. We have also talked with other surveyors who have experienced similar issues in the aftermath of storms, whether hurricanes, tsunamis, or tornadoes.

Designing and implementing an effective telephone survey involves carefully detailing out the calling procedures, including how they should vary depending on the outcome of the previous call and how different types of calls should be prioritized. It also often involves programming the dialer/scheduler and/or CATI software to schedule and implement the calling procedures, according to the specified rules. The programming and logic for the calling procedures can often be quite complex. It is important that the programming is examined carefully since these guidelines will be used when the scheduler is reviewing the outcome for each call, determining the current status, scheduling the next attempt (if there is one), and then actually assigning and delivering the call to the interviewer.

Guideline 8.23: Decide How Telephone Numbers Will Be Dialed and Review Legal Rules About Calling

To increase efficiency, many survey organizations use automatic dialers to dial the sampled phone numbers and then transfer calls to interviewers only when a live person is on the phone. The autodialer is programmed to call numbers and route them according to the study's specifications. Automatic dialers can call numbers much more quickly and efficiently than interviewers dialing numbers by hand. Some autodialers also allow for the outcome of some calls to be determined by the dialer without involving the interviewer, including when a phone line is busy, when no one answers, or when an answering machine, rather than a live person, is encountered. Since interviewers are not dialing the numbers and determining the outcome of many of the calls, they can focus on interacting with the person who answers the phone, to gain the household's participation, and then administer the survey to the appropriate household member. However, it is important to ensure that the call is transferred from the dialer to the interviewer as quickly as possible so that the interviewer can begin delivering the interview quickly, reducing the likelihood that the person hangs up the phone.

For many types of calls, the interviewer is the one coding the outcome of the attempt in the CATI system, and it is important that she understands how this should be done and is able to do it correctly. This is one of the hardest aspects of training interviewers. It requires constant feedback and ongoing training (see Guideline 8.20 for more on training interviewers). What makes this difficult is that interviewers have to be able to respond to a variety of situations they may encounter, and some of these may vary considerably depending on the survey they are working on that day, the areas they are calling, and other aspects of the survey design that differ from survey to survey. One particularly challenging area for interviewers is how to respond to automated messages from telephone companies, which are changing all the time and vary considerably by company and region. For example, recently one interviewer heard the message "You've reached a Whistle Phone" and was unsure how to code this outcome. Later research revealed that this is an app used for making telephone calls over Wi-Fi. One of the reasons we emphasize in Guideline 8.9 the design of the CATI screen, and ensuring that the various situations that can be expected to occur are programmed for, is to help make this often difficult process for interviewers easier.

When calling cell phones in the United States, it is illegal to use an autodialer. The Telephone Consumer Protection Act (TCPA), established in 1991 and updated since then, includes several limitations on calling cell phones. TCPA not only prohibits the use of automatic dialers but also prevents surveyors from legally leaving prerecorded voice messages and sending text messages to cell phones. The limitation on autodialing also means that interactive voice response, where a recorded voice reads the questions and response options and respondents state their response, are not allowed on cell phones since they usually rely on an autodialer to dial the numbers and connect the person to the recorded interview. Because of these limitations, it is important the surveyors identify which numbers are for landlines and which are for cell phones. Neustar is a service that can be used to help identify numbers in the landline frame that have been ported to wireless service so they can be removed from the landline frame.

The TCPA law does allow an autodialer and prerecorded messages to be used once a person has given permission for an organization to call her cell phone, implicitly by providing her number to the organization or by giving explicit consent to be contacted on that phone. But that means that until that consent has been granted, organizations must have interviewers manually or physically dial all cell phone numbers by hand or face significant penalties. New additions to the TCPA in 2013 require "signed" written consent for sending text messages to people.

There is a great deal of variation in rules regarding calling landlines and cell phones across countries and across states within the United States. While the TCPA sets the minimum national restrictions in the United States, state laws may be more restrictive about how and how often numbers can be called, what times of day researchers can call people, and what types of messages can be sent to cell phones. Thus, it is important to carefully review the laws in all areas that the study will be calling, and, because these types of laws are changing, to update these reviews continuously so as to always be in compliance.

Guideline 8.24: Implement a System for Tracking Every Call Attempt and Assign Each Sample Member a Unique ID Number

In telephone surveys it is important to record details about each call or attempt to every phone number in the sample. At minimum, the date and time of the attempt and the outcome or disposition should be recorded. CATI surveys today generally can be programmed to collect this information automatically as part of the interviewing process; however, for surveys where interviewers are administered using paper questionnaires or when interviewers are hand-dialing numbers, call tracking forms, such as the one shown in Figure 8.8, should be used to track the history of attempts and outcome of each call. Accurately capturing this information allows

FIGURE 8.8 Example of a call outcome tracking form.

Study Name

Telephone Number: (___) ___ - ____

Attempt#	Date	Time	Disposition Code	Interviewer ID
1	__/__	__:__	_____	_____
2	__/__	__:__	_____	_____
3	__/__	__:__	_____	_____
4	__/__	__:__	_____	_____
5	__/__	__:__	_____	_____
6	__/__	__:__	_____	_____
7	__/__	__:__	_____	_____
8	__/__	__:__	_____	_____
9	__/__	__:__	_____	_____
10	__/__	__:__	_____	_____

Comments

1 _____
2 _____
3 _____
4 _____
5 _____
6 _____
7 _____
8 _____
9 _____
10 _____

surveyors to use it to know whether to call the number again and when it should be called again (e.g., no follow-up, dial number again in 2 hours, dial number again in 1 day, etc.). In addition, data containing the full history of attempts for every sampled member can be used to help analyze the effectiveness of the survey design and the survey responses themselves.

It is also important that a final outcome for each sampled member is recorded, because it is used when calculating contact, cooperation, refusal, and response rates. For some sampled members, a number may only be dialed once for a final outcome to be determined (e.g., if on the first call, a number is determined to be a business or if the sampled member completes the survey). But more often, multiple attempts are made to a number and the final outcome summarizes information from across all of the attempts. In these cases, knowing the outcome of every call attempt to a number is essential to being able to provide a final outcome or disposition for that sampled number. In most cases, the most recent attempt is given more weight in determining the final outcome than earlier attempts. For example, a number for which all attempts yielded busy or no answer outcomes would be considered a noncontact. But if the first few attempts yielded no answers and then someone answered and refused to complete the survey, the final outcome would be a refusal.

That said, it is not enough to only know what happened on the final call attempt. This is because it is possible that two numbers that both have the same outcome from the final call attempt can receive very different final outcome codes depending on what happened in previous call attempts. For example, one can have two numbers in which the final call attempt resulted in a ring-no-answer, but the final outcome codes would differ if a previous call attempt to one of them had resulted in a scheduled call-back (i.e., contact but noncooperation) but none of the previous call attempts to the other had ever been answered (i.e., noncontact).

AAPOR's standard definitions provide a list of commonly used outcome or disposition codes for the major survey modes, including telephone surveys (AAPOR, 2011). As noted in the disposition codes for telephone surveys, there may be some outcomes that are specific to landline or cell phones and some that are shared across both types of phones. The standard definitions also explain how each of the various disposition codes should be treated when calculating contact, cooperation, refusal, and response rates. Figure 8.9 shows examples of final dispositions codes for RDD telephone surveys.

As for all types of surveys, it is important that each sample member is assigned a unique ID number. We have often seen telephone numbers being used as the ID number in telephone surveys, but we recommend creating a different unique ID number because doing so can help track attempts. For example, an ID number that differs from the telephone number can help keep track of complex situations such as when a new number is obtained during the fielding period (e.g., when a cell respondent requests to be called back using a landline number). In addition, using a unique ID allows the phone number and all other identifying information to be removed from the final data set to protect the privacy and confidentiality of sample members.

Guideline 8.25: Decide Whether to Provide a Phone Number or Description That Displays on Caller ID

Many people now have caller ID and can use it to screen their calls, including nearly all cell phone users since this feature is built into most mobile phones. Survey researchers should consider whether to provide a number that will display for people with this technology, rather than make the number private or otherwise hide the number. Displaying a number for those who have caller ID has been shown sometimes to increase response rates when calling landlines (Trussell & Lavrakas, 2005) and cell phones (Callegaro, McCutcheon, & Ludwig, 2005). If a number is provided, it is also helpful, if the number displayed is one that people can actually call back to ask questions or complete the survey, especially when calling cell phones.

Further, for caller ID technology that allows a text description, the name of the organization or survey (e.g., "GALLUP" or "UNIV OF GA") can be provided in addition to a phone number. M. Barron and Khare (2007) found that a shortened version of the survey organization name (in this case "NORC U CHICAGO" for the National Opinion Research Center at the University of Chicago) was more effective than more generic text that telephone companies assign to toll-free numbers. Providing a phone number and a short description or name can help inform

FIGURE 8.9   Examples of final disposition codes for RDD telephone surveys.

Interview
- Complete
- Partial

Eligible, Noninterview
- Refusal
  - Break-off
  - Household level refusal
  - Known respondent refusal
- Noncontact
  - Respondent never available
  - Telephone answering device (if confirms residential household)
- Other
  - Deceased
  - Physically or mentally unable
  - Language problem (household or respondent level)
  - Audio quality issues
  - Unable to complete interview (b/c driving/location/activity)

Unknown Eligibility, Noninterview
- Unknown if housing unit
  - Always busy
  - No answer
  - Telecommunication technological barriers
  - Technical phone problems
- Housing unit but unknown if eligible respondent
  - No screener completed
- Other

Not Eligible
- Nonworking number
  - Nonworking
  - Disconnected
  - Temporarily out of service
- Out of sample
- Fax/data line
- Cell phone/Landline phone (depending on frame)
- Number changed/Call forwarding
- Nonresidential
  - Business, government office, other organization
  - Institution
  - Group quarters
- No eligible respondent
- Other

Source: Adapted from *Standard Definitions: Final Dispositions of Case Codes and Outcome Rates for Surveys*, by American Association for Public Opinion Research, 2011. Retrieved from http://www.aapor.org/AM/Template.cfm?Section=Standard_Definitions2&Template=/CM/ContentDisplay.cfm&ContentID=3156

the person about who is calling. However, there is substantial variation in how these types of descriptions actually display to people because of differences in people's phones and how telephone companies convey this information.

Guideline 8.26: Consider Leaving a Voice Mail Message, Especially When Calling Cell Phones

Surveyors should carefully consider whether to leave a voice mail message, because research regarding the effectiveness of voice mail messages is quite mixed. Some researchers have found that leaving an answering machine message can substantially increase response rates to landline surveys (Koepsell, McGuire, Longstreth, Nelson, & van Belle, 1996; Xu, Bates, & Schweitzer, 1993). However, other studies, especially those using RDD samples, have found that leaving answering machine messages has little impact on response rates (Benford, Lavrakas, Tompson, & Fleury, 2010; Link & Mokdad, 2005; Tuckel & Schulman, 2000). When it comes to the content of the message, most researchers have found little difference when testing different messages (Tuckel & Schulman, 2000; Xu et al., 1993).

When calling cell phones, voice mail messages may be more helpful (AAPOR, 2010). Since addresses cannot generally be linked to cell phone numbers, it is often difficult to mail an advance letter or notify people of the survey by another mode, a practice that can improve response, as discussed in more detail in Chapter 11. Thus, a short voice mail message can be used to inform people about the survey or the sponsor and to distinguish the request from sales calls. If possible, leaving a call-back number can also be helpful (especially if the number that appears on caller ID does not allow inbound calls). An example of a voice mail message used when calling cell phones is "I am calling for [name of research organization]. We are conducting a research study about some important issues today and would like to include you. This is *not* a sales call. We will try to reach you again. Thank you."

Voice mail messages should only be used once or at most a few times during the calling period and should not be left on every attempt to a phone number to avoid being overly intrusive. Usually, a message is left the first or second time voice mail is encountered. Some surveyors may also decide to leave a message near the end of the study, on one of the last attempts. Since we do not recommend leaving a message on every attempt a voice mail is reached, it is important to have the prior call attempt history and outcomes for properly scheduling when interviewers should and should not leave a voice mail message.

Guideline 8.27: Establish Procedures for Dealing With Inbound Calls

If one offers a call-in number, either displayed on caller ID, included in a voice mail message, or as part of the survey interview, it is important to establish procedures for handling inbound calls. This is also important for mixed-mode surveys that involve telephone since often the mail and e-mail communications may include a call-in number. One of the most difficult aspects of inbound calls is that you do not know when they are going to occur, unlike outbound calling that is heavily planned and scheduled. However, if a call-in number is offered, it is important for people to be able to reach someone when they call, at times that are convenient to them based on the area/time zone they live in. Thus, we recommend having someone available during the day and at least part of the evening, as well as on at least one weekend day (typically Saturday).

The interviewers handling inbound calls need to be familiar with the study and trained to answer questions about the survey, similar to outbound interviewers. Ideally, interviewers would also have the ability to administer the full interview when someone calls in. The best option is for the person who answers the phone to also be able to administer the interview so there is no hand off of the call, but at minimum other interviewers (who handle the outbound calling) should be available to complete the interview. This is important in helping to ensure that the contact is maintained with the household so they can be encouraged to participate at the time when they are most likely to be available and willing. If an interviewer is not available and there is a need to call the person back to complete the interview, then there is some chance that the person will not be available or will not be willing to complete the survey at that time.

Guideline 8.28: Maintain an Internal Do Not Call List

Although survey research is exempt from the U.S. Federal Trade Commission's National Do Not Call Registry, most survey organizations maintain their own internal Do Not Call (DNC) list. These lists include numbers accumulated across multiple studies where someone at that number has explicitly asked not to be called again by that organization. These internal DNC lists are then used to scrub samples for telephone surveys prior to calling so that the numbers are removed and not dialed. In most cases, people on the DNC list should be treated as refusals since they refused to be called for the study at all.

There is a great deal of variation in how these DNC lists are maintained. But if an organization maintains a DNC list, it should train interviewers on what to do when someone asks not to be called again. It is also important to establish processes for how numbers get added to the list, whether it can be automated or if interviewers need to make special notes for it. Further, decisions should be made about how long DNC numbers should stay on the list. For example, some organizations never remove numbers from their DNC list whereas others may decide to remove numbers after 3, 5, or 10 years.

QUALITY CONTROL AND TESTING GUIDELINES FOR TELEPHONE SURVEYS

One of the final steps in developing effective telephone surveys is testing the dialer, questionnaire, database, and any other systems needed for interviewing and monitoring. While the guidelines for testing questionnaires from a cognitive and usability perspective presented in Chapter 7 should also be applied to telephone-only surveys, here we focus on testing implementation procedures for telephone surveys and how well those procedures interact with the questionnaire. It is through testing the survey design from end to end that the researcher understands how well different aspects of the design work together, in addition to how each individual feature works. We also present guidelines for ensuring that the telephone questionnaire and calling systems are fully operational and that there is a system in place for monitoring the study's performance, as well as how individual interviewers are doing.

Guideline 8.29: Obtain Expert Review and Conduct Cognitive Interviews, Experimental Evaluations, and Pilot Studies of Implementation Materials and Procedures

Survey designers make a variety of decisions when designing an implementation strategy for telephone surveys. Oftentimes these decisions can be guided by what was done for the same survey in the past, experience designing other implementation protocols, best practices in the field, and previous scientific research. But other times it is difficult to know what will work best in the particular survey situation. What is the difference if I make 10 versus 15 attempts? What times should I call to maximize reaching this population? I cannot send cash up front, so will contingent or promised incentives be effective? Does leaving a voice mail message on the first attempt work better than leaving one on the second attempt? What should my interviewers say first when the phone is answered?

These and many of the other questions that arise when designing implementation procedures are often best answered through testing. In Chapter 7, we introduced a variety of testing methodologies. Nearly all of these can be used when testing components of the implementation process. For example, an expert review with people who know the population may help identify times that are best targeted to reach the population of interest. Cognitive interviews can be used to help researchers find the most persuasive introductory statements to use for the survey. Experimental evaluations are especially helpful for assessing implementation procedures because they allow researchers to identify the effects of specific implementation strategies on the data in a quantitative way. For example, a 2 × 2 experimental design testing the effect of 10 versus 15 call attempts and a 7 versus 14 day calling period would include four experimental groups where sample members would be randomly assigned to each group:

- 10 call attempts in 7 days
- 10 call attempts in 14 days
- 15 call attempts in 7 days
- 15 call attempts in 14 days

We discuss many of the benefits of pretests, experiments, and pilot studies in Chapter 7. They are especially helpful when making substantial changes to implementation procedures, such as the length of the calling period, the maximum number of call attempts, or not conducting a refusal conversion. Because all of these can have a substantial impact on nonresponse error, it is important to test their effects so one can understand the impact of these changes. As we discuss in Guidelines 7.9 and 7.10, although there are costs to conducting pretests, experiments, and pilot studies, they also can provide substantial savings, especially for larger surveys, since they can help identify issues with the questionnaire or implementation procedures that would have severely impacted the main study if not identified beforehand.

Guideline 8.30: Test the Programming of the Autodialer, CATI Software, and the Database as Well as Interviewer Workstations

The programming of a telephone survey needs to be thoroughly checked and tested (just like for other computer-administered questionnaires, such as web surveys). Testing the questionnaire involves ensuring that the wording of the questions, response options, and instructions are all correct (and for all languages the survey is being administered in). It also entails testing all possible routes through the questionnaire by going through the survey screen by screen and selecting every option to see that the appropriate follow-up questions are asked. Since it is interviewers who interact with the CATI software, it can be helpful to engage them in the testing process. In addition, if an autodialer is used, the programming of the dialer needs to be tested as well, including the interaction between the autodialer and the CATI program (if different systems are used).

Testing the response database is also important because it ensures that the responses to every question are coded correctly. This step is often done in combination with testing the survey itself, where questionnaire testers enter responses and record what they entered as they review the survey pages, so the responses can then be verified in the database. Testing the database involves ensuring that a response is collected for every question, that the correct code (text or numeric) is coded in the database for the response(s) selected, that open-ended responses are not being truncated, and that any other response coding unique to the survey is working correctly. Reviewing the database and running analysis on the test data can also help to identify routing and logic issues in the survey. If any paradata is collected, as recommended in Guideline 8.32, it is also important to test that it is being recorded accurately in the database.

Each interviewer workstation should be thoroughly checked to ensure that any hardware interviewers need is working correctly, such as headsets, dial pads, and the computers, if being used to administer the survey. As part of the CATI testing, interviewers should also ensure that they can properly log in to their workstations and access any study-specific information they will need during the interview.

Guideline 8.31: Implement a System for Monitoring Progress and Evaluating Early Calling

It is helpful in all surveys to monitor the progress and review the data being collected each day. In addition to monitoring systems, we also recommend having a way for interviewers to directly provide feedback about any issues they have encountered. Reviewing the data and running some basic analyses can help uncover issues in the design or administration of the survey. For example, looking at break-offs or dropouts and reviewing interviewer feedback can help inform the researcher whether a particular statement or question is causing problems, such as encouraging people to break off. Further, analyzing the call outcomes and dispositions can help ensure that the calling procedures are programmed and working correctly.

It is important to monitor progress at all stages throughout the survey, but especially at the beginning with a focus on identifying and prioritizing any potential issues and solutions that can be implemented for the remainder of the calling to improve the final data quality. We have found it helpful to have daily meetings in the beginning of a study to review progress and discuss any issues; these can often be weekly or even less frequent after the first few weeks of a study. As this discussion illustrates, monitoring systems need to be in place before calling begins so that early calls can be reviewed.

Many CATI systems have built-in monitoring features that can help researchers track progress and easily review a summary of the call outcomes. These monitoring systems also often allow researchers to analyze outcomes by week, day, day part, or some other increment. We also recommend that any monitoring systems be tested, similar to the testing of the questionnaire and database, as discussed in Guideline 8.30, a task that can be done in parallel with the questionnaire and database testing process.

Guideline 8.32: Collect Paradata That Provides Feedback About the Questionnaire and Implementation Process Whenever Possible

Surveyors are increasingly collecting paradata or additional process information that can be gathered as part of the survey implementation and response process (Kreuter, 2013). In computer-administered interviewer surveys, information can be collected about how interviewers interact with the CATI system, including the time it takes interviewers to read a question and record a response, whether interviewers have to move forward and backward a lot or change the responses entered. This information can then be used to identify problematic areas in the questionnaire. This is similar to how paradata is used in web surveys to understand how the respondent interacts with the questionnaire, as discussed in Guideline 9.16.

In telephone and in person interviews, the interviewer is also a key source of information about the survey process. Interviewers can be asked to answer questions about the process, including confirming whether they spoke with a live person, reporting on the respondent's behavior while completing the questionnaire (such as what language was used to administer the survey, how comfortable the respondent was in that language, how engaged respondents were, and whether they felt respondents encountered any difficulty answering the questions or whether they were distracted). In interviewer-administered surveys, interviewers can also observe characteristics about the location (e.g., house or business) or about the people encountered. A key strength of this type of paradata is that some information can be collected for both respondents and nonrespondents and thus can be helpful in understanding differences between those who decide to respond and those who are never reached or choose not to respond.

Guideline 8.33: Monitor Interviewer Performance to Ensure Quality, Identify Areas for Retraining, and Develop Metrics for Tracking Interviewer Performance

One essential step in conducting telephone surveys is monitoring interviewer performance to ensure the quality and accuracy of the data they are collecting. Many call centers have team or shift leaders who monitor interviewers on every shift, live, as the interviews are being conducted. This type of interviewer monitoring is critical for being able to provide immediate feedback to interviewers, should it be needed, and to make the feedback very specific to the issues encountered during a call.

In addition, many researchers (or sometimes a separate quality department in larger call centers) monitor interviewer performance by listening to recorded interviews. Recordings can be especially useful because they allow the researcher to move forward and backward, and repeat parts of the interview, to help in accurately identifying any quality issues. However, when recording interviews, it is important to follow the appropriate legal procedures in the areas one is calling, which may involve asking the person on the phone for their explicit consent to record the interview. Also, it is important for interviewers not to know which calls are being recorded so they do not try to perform better on that call than they otherwise would normally.

Most organizations also track interviewer performance across a variety of metrics, such as cooperation and refusal rates, refusal conversion rate, average length of completed interview, number/frequency of quality issues identified, completeness of respondents' answers, and other metrics. These are often used directly in evaluating interviewer performance but also to reward interviewers who are performing well and identify those who need additional training or other intervention to help them perform better.

Guideline 8.34: Validate That Interviews Were Conducted Accurately

When possible, it is important to validate that the interviews that were not monitored in real time were actually completed with a real respondent and that the respondent's answers were recorded accurately. This process can be completed with recorded interviews. For some studies, we also recommend validating a portion of interviews that were not completed or calls where contact was not made to ensure that the final dispositions were recorded accurately. For most survey researchers, we recommend, at minimum, recording a subsample of interviews so that they can be reviewed and validated for completeness and quality. As mentioned earlier, when recording interviews, it is important for interviewers not to know which calls are being recorded for validation.

Another way to validate surveys is to actually reinterview a subsample of respondents to confirm they were interviewed and re-ask a subset of questions from the original survey. Researchers usually include the key indicators from the survey and a few demographics so that these responses in the reinterview can be compared to those in the original survey. One issue with this type of validation survey is that depending on the types of questions being re-asked, differences between the original and validation responses may occur because respondents' answers actually changed since the original interview rather than because their original answer was recorded incorrectly by the interviewer. Sometimes this happens because the context of the reinterview is different, which can affect how people respond. Usually to not overburden respondents and to save costs, only a subset of questions are asked from the original survey, which can change the context in which the questions were asked on the original survey. Attitudinal questions are more likely to be affected by these changes in context than behavioral or demographic questions. Further, it is never the case that everyone selected for the validation study will respond, which may introduce bias into the validation study. In general, these types of reinterview surveys are useful for checking that a valid interview occurred and that a few key characteristics of the respondents match, with a focus on those that are unlikely to have changed.

CONCLUSION

The telephone is no longer the dominant survey mode. The societal shift of the telephone from a household to an individual device, the ability of people to port a telephone number to new residences in different states, caller ID, answering machines, and other issues continue to whittle away at its adequacy for conducting surveys. Yet, our use of the telephone for survey purposes is far from over. The telephone will continue to be used for opinion, and in particular voter preference, surveys where timing is critical with weighting and other adjustments being made to compensate for noncontact and nonresponse issues. In addition, compared to other modes, the telephone has great strengths when it comes to selecting respondents, allowing interactive exchanges to occur between interviewers and respondents, seeking elaboration from respondents, and answering their questions that are limited in other modes.

However, we expect that another important role of the telephone, and perhaps its predominant role, will be as a mode that is used alongside other modes in mixed-mode surveys. In some respects, this role will not be new. Telephone and postal mail have been used together for quite some time such as when advance contact is made by mail to legitimize an upcoming telephone request to be interviewed or when responses are collected by telephone from those who did not respond to a mail request. We elaborate on these uses and provide guidelines for adapting the telephone for use in mixed-mode surveys in Chapter 11.

LIST OF GUIDELINES

Guidelines for Designing Telephone Questionnaires

Guideline 8.1: Break complex questions into a series of simpler questions

Guideline 8.2: Avoid question formats that tax respondents' memory

Guideline 8.3: Make sure the words the interviewer reads clearly convey what is being asked

Guideline 8.4: Provide clear and simple to recognize cues to the interviewer about what material must be read, what is optional, and what should not be read to the respondent

Guideline 8.5: Locate interviewer instructions where they are needed by interviewers

Guideline 8.6: Include conversational cues and short and simple transition statements to help interviewers administer the questions

Guideline 8.7: Avoid the use of abbreviations and special characters and include pronunciations for difficult words, names, or places

Guideline 8.8: Include a "don't know" or "refused" option for every question

Guideline 8.9: Provide ways for interviewers to respond to and record the outcome of every possible scenario that can be anticipated

Guideline 8.10: Provide standardized scripts for responses to questions respondents may ask and to address any special procedures for the study

Guideline 8.11: Display each individual question on its own screen to reduce clutter and support efficient processing

Guideline 8.12: Include additional questions needed for screening and weighting surveys that include cell phones

Guideline 8.13: Consider offering cell phone respondents reimbursement for their minutes used

Guidelines for Administering Telephone Questionnaires

Guideline 8.14: Provide a short, clear, and persuasive introduction to the survey

Guideline 8.15: Read questions fully and exactly, in order, as they appear in the questionnaire

Guideline 8.16: Record answers exactly as respondents provide them

Guideline 8.17: Focus on the respondent and practice active listening

Guideline 8.18: Use a controlled speaking pace and manage the pitch and tone of your voice

Guideline 8.19: Provide encouragement and targeted feedback to respondents

Guideline 8.20: Train interviewers before they start calling sample members and provide regular follow-up trainings

Guidelines for Establishing Calling Rules and Procedures

Guideline 8.21: Make multiple attempts to reach someone at each sampled telephone number

Guideline 8.22: Vary the days of the week and times of the day that call attempts are made to each sample member

Guideline 8.23: Decide how telephone numbers will be dialed and review legal rules about calling

Guideline 8.24: Implement a system for tracking every call attempt and assign each sample member a unique ID number

Guideline 8.25: Decide whether to provide a phone number or description that displays on caller ID

Guideline 8.26: Consider leaving a voice mail message, especially when calling cell phones

Guideline 8.27: Establish procedures for dealing with inbound calls

Guideline 8.28: Maintain an internal do not call list

Quality Control and Testing Guidelines for Telephone Surveys

Guideline 8.29: Obtain expert review and conduct cognitive interviews, experimental evaluations, and pilot studies of implementation materials and procedures

Guideline 8.30: Test the programming of the autodialer, CATI software, and the database as well as interviewer workstations

Web Questionnaires and Implementation

Surveys that are completely electronic, relying only on e-mail contacts to obtain Internet responses, are the fastest growing form of surveying occurring in the United States, as well as throughout most of the world. As a stand-alone mode of data collection, web is especially attractive because of speed, low cost, and economies of scale. However, despite these benefits, many barriers to realizing them also exist and are discussed in this chapter. Through this discussion of how to design and implement web surveys, we focus on both the benefits and the current limitations of using only the Internet and e-mail invitations to request and obtain responses.

A large majority of the population in the United States and a growing number internationally now use the Internet. As of 2013, 85% of adults in the United States use the Internet and 70% have broadband Internet access in their homes (see Figure 9.1, data from Pew Internet & American Life Project, 2013b, 2013c). People have also become more familiar with computers and engaging in various activities online. For example, in 2001 just 18% of Internet users did any banking online; that increased to 61% in 2011 (Pew Internet & American Life Project, 2013a). Similarly, the percent of people who buy products online, make travel reservations online, and look for job information online have also increased dramatically (see Figure 9.1). Many now prefer to conduct their business electronically rather than pick up a phone, write a letter, or go in person, and many companies make it difficult to contact them any other way than electronically.

The increasing use of mobile devices—especially smartphones and tablets—has further fueled the growth in online behavior, especially as these devices have become the primary way that some people connect to the Internet. Nearly all adults (91%) have cell phones, up from 75% in 2007 (Duggan, 2013). And people are now far more likely to send text messages and access the Internet on their cell phones than they were just 5 years ago (see Figure 9.2). Smartphone ownership has increased from 35% to 56% among U.S. adults in just 2 years (from 2011 to 2013), and tablet ownership increased from 10% to 35% during the same period (see Figure 9.2, data from Pew Internet & American Life Project [Rainie & Smith, 2013; A. Smith, 2013a]). Further, 21% of cell phone owners say they *mostly* access the Internet using their phone, rather than other devices (Duggan & Smith, 2013).

The fact that people have become more accustomed to completing various daily activities online could be good for survey researchers interested in

FIGURE 9.1 Internet usage over time.

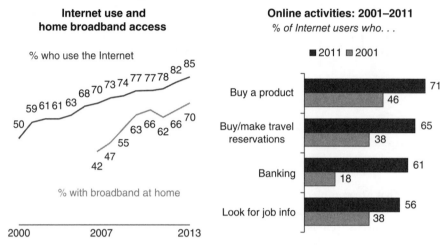

Source: Adapted from Pew Research Center's Pew Internet & American Life Project, 2013a, 2013b, 2013c. Figures based on adults in the United States.

FIGURE 9.2 Growth in use of mobile devices.

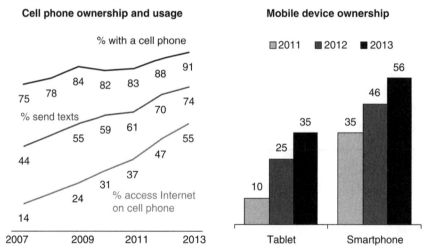

Source: Adapted from Pew Research Center's Pew Internet & American Life Project (Duggan, 2013; Rainie & Smith, 2013; Smith, 2013a). Figures based on adults in the United States.

conducting web surveys, since people may also have become more receptive to completing surveys online. However, it also means that web surveys are constantly changing as the ways in which people interact with computers and mobile devices also continues to evolve. The rise in mobile devices requires survey designers to reconsider aspects of questionnaire design to accommodate the smaller screen. Many people may also receive and quickly scan e-mail and texts on their phone but then wait to follow-up on requests that need more attention until they get to their desktop or laptop. The range of devices (from desktop to netbook to tablet to phablet to smartphone), operating systems and browsers (and different versions), and customized settings available to users also continues to expand, making designing and implementing web surveys more challenging than it was even a few short years ago.

Web surveys continue to pose many challenges and benefits for surveyors, much like they did in their early days (Couper, 2000). Typically, responses can be gathered from large numbers of people in a very short amount of time. Web surveys can also often be conducted at a fairly low cost, especially when e-mail is the only form of communication with sample members. Thousands or even tens of thousands of questionnaires can be completed in a single day with the results available for review and analysis immediately.

For this reason and others, the use of web and mobile surveys continues to grow. The proliferation of opt-in panels and other nonprobability online survey methodologies has further fueled the increase in web surveys. But surveys of special populations with high levels of computer ability, such as college students, policy experts, and business executives, also are increasingly being conducted online, using web alone or in combination with another mode. Lastly, surveyors have increasingly been using web surveys in mixed-mode designs of the general public where sample members are contacted by another mode (e.g., mail) and asked to complete the web survey (Smyth, Dillman, Christian, & O'Neill, 2010). Designing questionnaires and implementation strategies for mixed-mode surveys that include web is discussed in Chapter 11.

In this chapter, we present guidelines for designing web and mobile questionnaires and for implementing web surveys in which e-mail is the only method used to contact people, but these guidelines will also be helpful to those who are conducting mixed-mode surveys that include e-mail contacts or web data collection. These guidelines are aimed at helping surveyors work their way through the development and design of a web survey in ways that will encourage responses from many types of respondents. These guidelines address many of the technological issues of constructing web and mobile surveys as well as decisions about formatting and displaying the questionnaire to respondents. The implementation guidelines focus on designing e-mail strategies and contacts to maximize response, as well as monitoring responses (and nonresponse) and evaluating the survey process. Additionally, we discuss guidelines for testing and ensuring the quality of web surveys.

GUIDELINES FOR DESIGNING WEB AND MOBILE QUESTIONNAIRES

Most web surveys are browser based, where respondents interact with the survey through their Internet browser (such as Chrome, Firefox, Internet Explorer, and Safari). The web survey is made up of a web page or series of web pages containing survey questions programmed most commonly in hypertext markup language (HTML) that are stored on a server. Users with the proper URL can access them through their computers or mobile devices and an Internet or cellular connection. Surveyors send requests, often by e-mail, but also by mail or telephone, to the person (or unit) from whom a response is desired and provide the link or URL for the web survey (and often an individual identification code). Respondents click on the URL or enter it into their browser's address bar. Alternatively, QR codes (or quick response codes) provide mobile device users with a matrix barcode that can be read or scanned by such devices to take them directly to the web survey. Survey website URLs and a QR code are illustrated in Figure 9.3.

FIGURE 9.3   Example URLs and QR code.

URL

www.wiley.com/WileyCDA/WileyTitle/productCd-1118456149.html

Shortened URL

http://tinyurl.com/tailored-design

QR code

Once sample members click on the URL, they are usually routed to a welcome or introductory screen that briefly describes the survey and asks them to proceed with the questionnaire. Once they begin the survey, pressing the "submit" or "next" button on a page sends their answers back to the web server. Their responses may be reviewed by the survey software and are stored in a database on the server. What this means, in essence, is that surveyors have to translate their questionnaire designs into computer code to be stored on a server. They also have to design databases that will store survey responses in an accurate, organized, meaningful, and accessible way on the server.

This can be done by programming the survey and creating the databases from scratch (using unique code) or by using preexisting software, most of which provide fairly simple point-and-click interfaces. Programming the survey and databases from scratch provides the most design flexibility and ability to innovate, but it requires bringing together two very specialized skill sets—computer programming and survey methodology—and is often the most complex and expensive option.

Those who cannot program from scratch or who prefer other options have an almost dizzying array of software options to choose from. The available software programs vary along four dimensions that are important to consider.

1. *Design flexibility and difficulty.* Almost all survey software programs provide question templates that can be used. In some programs the template must be used as is, but other programs allow the surveyor to alter the underlying programming to customize the design. For some, customization can be done in standard programming languages like HTML and cascading style sheets (CSS), but others require one to use specialized programming languages developed for the particular software. In addition, some software packages include either mobile optimization or mobile app support and others do not, so it is important to review all of the features that a program has to offer before selecting one.

2. *Control over the data.* Some programs only allow the data to be collected and stored on the software company's servers while others allow collection and storage to take place on the surveyor's servers. Others provide both options. This raises the ethical considerations of how secure the data are and exactly who has access, issues that need to be considered carefully in light of any restrictions within one's organization and before promising anonymity or confidentiality to respondents.

3. *Data access and reporting.* Some programs limit the analysis to simple frequencies and cross tabulations while others provide raw data sets that can be analyzed however the surveyor desires (these come in a variety of formats). Similarly, some packages also offer various automated monitoring and reporting features that may make it easier to track progress and quickly look at results.

4. *Cost.* Cost underlies all these dimensions. Available software packages range from free to costing tens of thousands of dollars per year. Many software providers have tiered pricing structures in which the higher cost tiers grant more design flexibility for the survey itself and more control over the resulting data. Generally speaking the design flexibility required to conduct a good web survey comes with a higher price tag.

Reviewing the various software programs along these dimensions, as well as the questionnaire design and implementation guidelines presented throughout this chapter, can help in carefully evaluating the best software option for a specific survey or organization's needs.

There are several ways, other than a browser-based survey, for researchers to collect survey data over the web. For example, survey apps can be used for those who are on mobile devices (as discussed more in Guideline 9.4). Alternatively, other electronic options, such as fillable PDFs or embedded e-mail or text/SMS surveys, can sometimes be effective. With fillable PDFs, respondents can enter answers directly into a PDF file that is then e-mailed back to the surveyor (or returned some other way). In some cases, such as in surveys of establishments, this is desirable because PDF files can easily be printed to keep copies for one's records or to pass around to all the people who need to answer the questions.

Another option is to embed the survey directly into an e-mail or text message (Schaefer & Dillman, 1998). The major advantage of this strategy is its low cost, as it eliminates considerable programming costs. However it is difficult to control the visual appearance of such surveys because of the variety of ways people read their e-mail and SMS messages (i.e., web-based e-mail providers, local software programs, on mobile devices and phones, etc.) and because entering responses shifts their content around. Lastly, these types of surveys are quite difficult for those completing them on mobile devices, unless they are kept very short (only one to three questions).

Despite these drawbacks, it is important to evaluate whether one of these alternatives may be more appropriate for one's survey needs, as they are often less costly than fully interactive web surveys. The guidelines for designing web questionnaires presented here are primarily focused on browser-based web surveys, but we also highlight ways in which the design may need to be modified and optimized for a mobile experience. Designing survey questionnaires for mobile devices is still in its infancy and more research is needed to understand how people complete web questionnaires on their mobile devices.

If one chooses a browser-based web survey, it is important to remember that designing a web survey is very different from designing a website. Although some aspects of visual design, as discussed in Chapter 6, apply either way, others differ because people's motivation and purpose for going to a typical website are quite different from their motivation and purpose for visiting a web survey site (or using a web survey app). Most of the time, people visit websites to get information, and are self-motivated to find what they are looking for. In contrast, most respondents go to a web survey because someone else asked them to; their own motivation may be low. In addition, in a web survey, respondents' primary task is to provide, rather than seek, information. Thus, it is critical that web surveys be designed to make the response task as easy as possible while obtaining accurate measurement. Doing so may require different design strategies than might be suggested by the more general website usability literature. Moreover, design errors that may be tolerated when someone is looking for information or trying to pay their bills online may more easily trigger break-offs in a web survey.

Guideline 9.1: Decide How the Survey Will Be Programmed and Hosted

It is important to assess whether an organization has the capability of conducting and implementing a web survey that meets the desired goals. Some people have the training that allows them to design and program all aspects of their own web surveys and are located in an organization that provides the needed server capabilities and protection (including backups) to host the survey, receive the data, and send contacts to sample members. In addition, they or others in the organization can troubleshoot and manage survey and technical issues that may arise in the process.

If one's organization does not have the capabilities to design, host, and implement a wide range of web surveys, there are several other alternatives, as we discussed earlier, for programming and hosting a web survey. Designing and hosting surveys has also become an activity in which some people and organizations have become specialists. There are a variety of survey data collection organizations in the private sector and within many colleges and universities. Listings for many of these organizations can be found in the American Association for Public Opinion Research's *Blue Book* (AAPOR, n.d.) or the membership directory of the Association of Academic Survey Research Organizations (AASRO, n.d.). It may be necessary to contract out the programming and hosting of the survey to such people or organizations. Others may instead decide to purchase a software package that can help with designing and managing the implementation of the survey, particularly if they plan to conduct a large number of web surveys (see earlier discussion for issues to consider when purchasing such software). Lastly, some may choose to use one of the many online survey sites that allow them to design the questionnaire, send contacts to sample members, and collect responses using the website's servers. It is important for surveyors to think about the expectations they have for collecting data and choose from these alternatives for designing and hosting web surveys commensurate with those needs.

Guideline 9.2: Evaluate the Technological Capabilities of the Survey Population

Every web survey should be designed with the survey population in mind. Survey populations vary in their access to the necessary technology to complete a web survey and their understanding of how the technology and the process works (see Chapter 3 for more on coverage and access issues with web surveys). People differ in their adoption of new technology. Older people, those in rural areas, and those with lower education all tend to lag behind their counterparts in the adoption of the Internet, the use of mobile devices, and the speed of their connections. Even among those who have Internet access, some may not be familiar with completing web surveys (Stern, Adams, & Elsasser, 2009) and will need more instruction or even another mode of response. In contrast, for surveys of some populations, such as college students, business executives, and computer engineers, one should expect a very high level of technical proficiency with the Internet and possibly a greater use of mobile devices to complete the survey. Thus, it is important to assess the technological capabilities of the population for each survey that is conducted, recognizing variation in the speed at which technological changes are being adopted across many populations.

Guideline 9.3: Take Steps to Ensure That Questions Display Similarly Across Different Devices, Platforms, Browsers, and User Settings

One challenge with web surveys is that there is wide variation in how respondents might experience any given web survey. The types of devices available for accessing the Internet (including desktop computers, laptops, tablets, smartphones, and other types of devices—all with varying screen sizes and with a range of processors, memory, and hard drive sizes) and the browser software available for viewing websites—have grown considerably in recent years. The situation is further complicated by the constant release of updates and new plug-ins that affect whether and how web pages are displayed, and by the fact that some people install these updates and others do not. Moreover, as people become more computer savvy, they are more likely to customize their settings in ways that can affect how a website looks to a respondent. As such, the manner in which web surveys are displayed can vary widely across respondents. This makes it necessary to take additional steps to try to control the effects of devices, software, and settings on the visual display of questions in an effort to try to ensure that every respondent receives the same stimulus.

Screen sizes and resolution are one element that varies considerably across respondents and can have significant impacts on the visual appearance of web surveys. To try to minimize the impact of screen size, program web surveys for the lowest likely screen resolution. HTML programming relies on underlying tables made up of rows and columns to locate content on the screen. Setting the main HTML table to the lowest likely screen resolution will ensure that the content will appear in the intended way on the screens of most users, and will minimize the need for them to scroll (although surveyors may want to consider using web and mobile versions that are optimized differently). Currently, most general population Internet users have screen resolutions that are at least 800×600 pixels (StatCounter Global Stats, 2013b). Thus, a design in which the question fits in this size area will work for the vast majority of respondents. Among more technologically savvy populations with more current hardware, this can be increased to 1024×768. Similarly, most mobile Internet users have a screen resolution that is at least 320×240 pixels (StatCounter Global Stats, 2013a). See Figure 9.4 for a summary of common screen resolutions. Importantly, as time passes the recommended width and height will change because the hardware in use by most people will change. But the underlying recommendation to try to determine the minimum screen resolution used by the sample members, and to program for this resolution, should still apply.

Center-aligning the main survey questionnaire region horizontally on the page will also help ensure that the questions look similar across different screen resolutions. Within the HTML tables that make up a web page, the column widths can be manipulated to minimize the effects of changes in screen or window size on the visual appearance of the web page. Column widths can be set as either fixed widths or proportions. When they are fixed, the width of the columns does

FIGURE 9.4   Screen resolution of common devices.

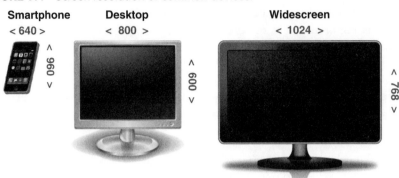

not change across different screens or when the window size is adjusted by a user. When they are set as proportions, the column widths adjust to the screen and browser window sizes. Setting the column widths as proportions can help ensure that the page is visible across many screen and window sizes, but as the columns shrink to accommodate smaller resolutions or window sizes, the information in them will wrap, sometimes in undesirable ways. If one has programmed for the lowest likely screen resolution as suggested earlier, the way columns are set will have minimal effect, but if this has not been done it will have a significant effect and should be considered carefully.

In addition to screen size and resolution, there are a number of user settings that may differ across respondents. CSS can help standardize web survey appearance across variations in user browsers and settings. CSS controls the stylistic elements (e.g., fonts, font sizes, color, widths, alignment, and other aspects of visual presentation) of a web page without affecting the content. The programmer can use CSS to specify the order and precedence in which various styles should be applied depending on user configurations and settings such as screen resolution. In other words, they allow the programmer to tailor how information is presented to different types of devices, browsers, and other equipment used to display web surveys in an effort to minimize variations in how web pages appear visually. In this way, they allow the design to respond to help optimize the user's experience.

As a simple example, which is illustrated in Figure 9.5, if one respondent has a high screen resolution, which makes items on the screen appear small, the CSS programming can be used to provide a larger font (e.g., 20 point). If another respondent has a very low screen resolution, which tends to make items on the screen look big, the CSS programming can be used to provide a smaller font (e.g., 12 point). Despite the respondents' different screen resolutions, the size of the text will appear very similarly for both of these respondents because the CSS programming adjusts the display to make up for differences due to resolution. CSS and other options in web programming give web surveyors greater control over how web questionnaires appear to survey respondents.

While we advocate standardizing the visual appearance of the questionnaire as much as possible across respondents, we also caution that website accessibility limitations should also be considered (i.e., respondents with decreased vision may need the larger font in order to be able to read the questions). In fact, federal agencies are required by Section 508 of the Rehabilitation Act to make websites accessible to those with disabilities or to provide comparable access to information

FIGURE 9.5 Example of how CSS can help minimize differences in web survey appearance.

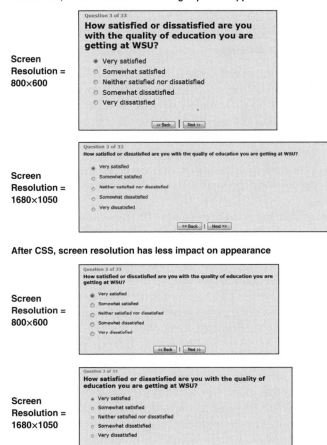

contained in the websites. The World Wide Web Consortium (W3C) Web Accessibility Initiative (n.d.) is one source for information on how web pages can be made more accessible for people with disabilities. For more on Section 508 compliance, also see www.section508.gov

Additional programming through client- and server-side scripting allows for even greater flexibility and customization. Client-side scripting is program code that is run by the respondents' browser (e.g., JavaScript). One of its key benefits is that whatever is programmed to happen can do so immediately within the browser and without the browser interacting with the web server. By contrast, server-side scripting is run by the web server (e.g., ASP, ColdFusion, PHP), so the respondent must submit the page to the server (i.e., click the "submit" or "next" button) for the feedback to occur. As a result, server-side scripting tends to be a little slower and less dynamic. Because client-side scripting is so dynamic, it can be used in a number of ways in web surveys (some of these will be discussed below) that can be helpful to web survey respondents; however, since about 1 to 5% of

Internet users have JavaScript disabled, we recommend having a no-script option or server-side backup in place so that the questionnaire pages will still be functional for those who have disabled JavaScript or other client-side scripting.

Guideline 9.4: Offer a Questionnaire Optimized for Mobile (Browser or App Based)

Smartphone penetration in the United States continues to grow—56% of adults now have smartphones (A. Smith, 2013a)—making it more likely that people will complete web surveys on their mobile devices. In most web surveys today, 10% or fewer are completing the survey on a smartphone, but the proportion completing the survey on a mobile device can range from 1% to 40%, depending on the survey population and topic. We expect the proportion answering web surveys on mobile devices to continue to increase given the rapid rise in tablet and smartphone adoption and the increasing use of mobile phones for many everyday activities.

This means that for many web surveys, it is important to include a separate option for mobile users—whether that is a browser-based version that is optimized for mobile or an app that people can download and then use to complete the survey. As discussed further in Guideline 9.16, it is important to collect the user agent string (browser and version information) so that people accessing the survey on a mobile device can be routed correctly to the mobile alternative.

For most one-time surveys, we generally recommend providing a version of the questionnaire that is optimized for mobile but that can still be viewed in a respondents' Internet browser (see Figure 9.6). Because app-based mobile surveys require asking people to download and install the app, it can be a substantial burden for a one-time survey. However, apps offer a very flexible design environment and several features that might be useful for particular survey goals, especially for those that establish longer term relationships with respondents (e.g., panel surveys). Survey apps, like other apps, can push surveys to respondents, send other types of notifications, work with the phone's GPS to collect geo-location tracking, allow the respondent to easily upload pictures or video, and offer other functionality that is not available in a browser survey (Link, 2011).

New hybrid or app-like browser surveys are emerging that contain app-like functionality and design capability but where respondents are still using their browser (Buskirk & Andrus, 2012). Although this design might not include the full functionality of a survey app, it allows for the design of the questionnaire to be far improved over a traditional browser-based mobile experience. However, the app versions of web surveys, and even the new hybrid versions, tend to look far different from a browser-based web survey. Thus, if it is expected that most respondents will still be completing the survey on a larger screen, perhaps the browser-based version, optimized for mobile, should be chosen to minimize the effects of any visual design differences when combining responses from those completing on various screen sizes. Further, HTML5 offers even more flexibility in the browser-based design.

When designing for mobile devices, the landscape is constantly changing but as of 2013, Android and Apple's iOS were the two most dominant mobile operating systems, although some users also have Windows, BlackBerry, and other devices (A. Smith, 2013b). Thus, when designing mobile options, we recommend designing at least for these dominant operating systems (Apple and Android).

FIGURE 9.6   Example of web survey displayed in a standard browser versus a browser optimized for mobile devices.

Standard web browser

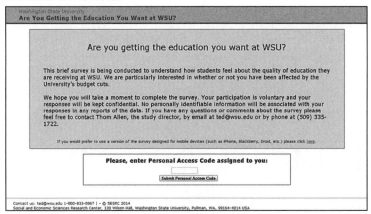

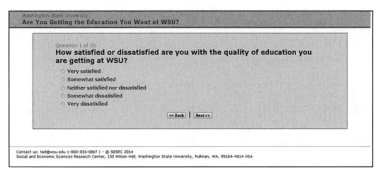

Browser optimized for mobile devices

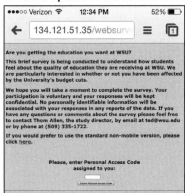

Guideline 9.5: Decide How Many Questions Will Be Presented on Each Web Page and How Questions Will Be Arranged

One of the most important decisions in designing a web questionnaire is how many questions will be presented on each screen or page. Web surveys can present one question per page, multiple questions per page, or all of the survey questions on one page. However, several important implications need to be considered when deciding how many questions will be presented on each page.

Most web surveys present each question on its own page and require respondents to click a button to move from page to page as shown in the example in Figure 9.7. In this format responses can be saved to the server database each time the "next" or "submit" button is pressed. One strength of a single-question-per-page design is that it gives web surveyors more control over how each question

FIGURE 9.7 Screens from a page-by-page web survey.

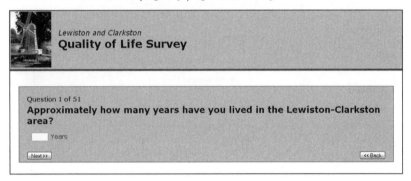

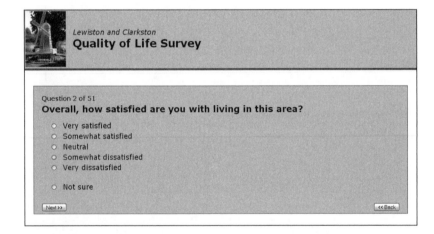

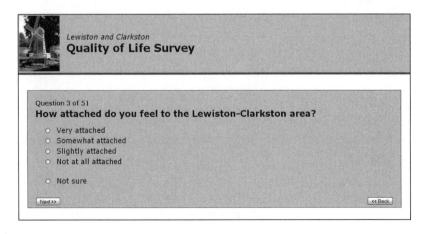

will appear to respondents. Another benefit of the page-by-page design is that responses are submitted to the server and stored in the database after every question (since the respondent has to hit a button to navigate to the next page). Thus, surveyors receive responses to each question answered as respondents progress through the survey, even if they choose not to complete the entire survey (which can be helpful in understanding where, and sometimes why, people are terminating the survey). Because of this continuous interaction with the server, more interactive capabilities can be utilized, such as automatically branching respondents to subsequent follow-up questions, modifying questions based on responses to previous questions, or collecting certain paradata for each question (see later discussion under Guideline 9.16).

The page-by-page design format is also best for questionnaires with complex skip patterns because it gives the surveyor control over which questions come next rather than having to rely on the respondent to correctly interpret and execute branching instructions. An additional benefit is that with page-by-page construction it is often easier for respondents to know where to focus their attention because every question can appear in the same location (horizontal and vertical alignment) on the pages, an element of consistency that can reduce item nonresponse (see Guideline 9.8).

On the negative side, questionnaires that are constructed with each question on its own page often take longer to complete (Couper, Traugott, & Lamias, 2001; Manfreda, Batagelj, & Vehovar, 2002). In addition, because the questions are viewed in isolation, respondents may have difficulty remembering the context established by previous questions and may need to review their previous responses to remind themselves of that context. This may happen as respondents proceed through the questions, but is especially likely to happen when they temporarily quit the survey and then come back later to complete it. Likewise, respondents who need to remember their answers to a previous question in order to answer a subsequent question or ensure they are not being redundant will face extra difficulty because reviewing previous questions in the page-by-page format is much more difficult than in a scrolling design. Thus, it is important for respondents to be able to move both forward and backward in the survey and to be able to see their previous answers when questions are presented on their own pages. However, even when respondents can move backward in the survey, effort needs to be made to make sure each question can stand alone and be understood without needing to refer to previous questions.

By contrast, when all of the questions are presented on one page, as shown in Figure 9.8, the web questionnaire more closely approximates a paper survey because the respondent can preview the entire questionnaire before answering questions and then scroll forward and backward within it while answering (Dillman, 2000). It has been argued that respondents can make a more informed decision about whether to complete the survey when they can see the entire questionnaire (Crawford, Couper, & Lamias, 2001). However, this format also has several limitations. Depending on the length of the survey, respondents may have to scroll through many questions in the questionnaire, thus increasing the chances that they will miss questions or even entire sets of questions. Branching formats or skip patterns may also be difficult for respondents to execute, similar to paper surveys. A scrolling design is also very difficult for respondents viewing the survey on a mobile device.

FIGURE 9.8 Screens from a scrolling web survey with dotted line to indicate where scrolling was required.

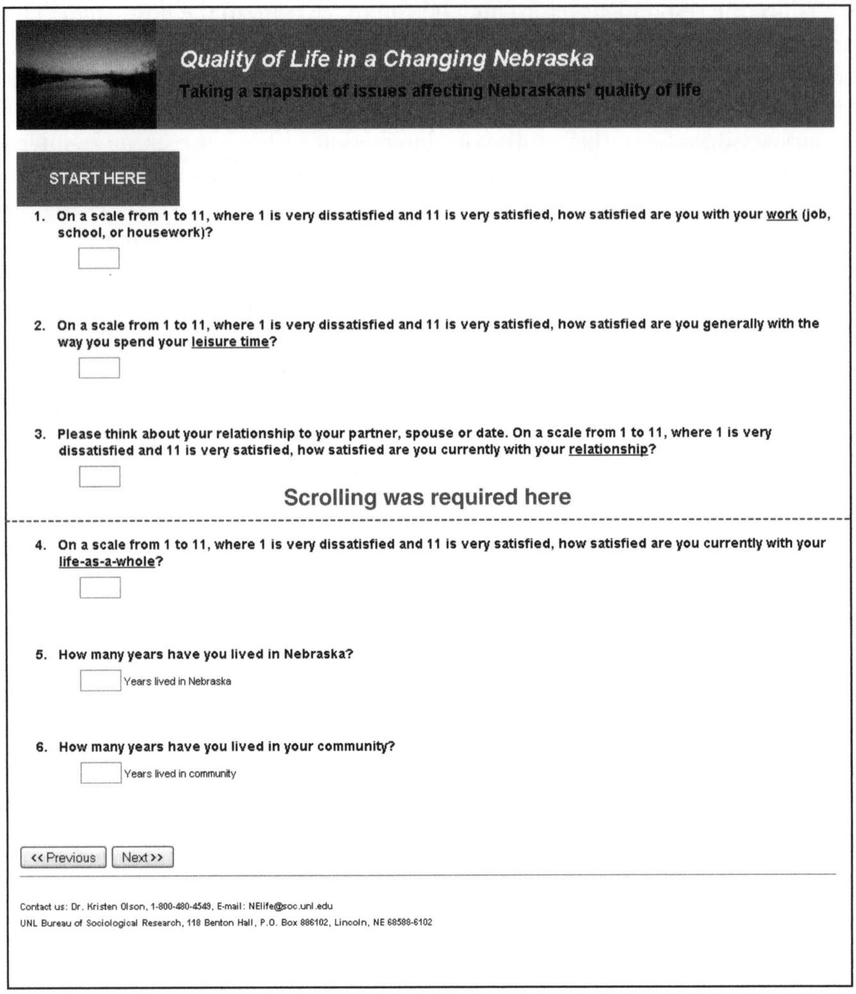

In addition, responses are usually not submitted to the server and stored in the database until the respondent completes all of the questions and clicks a button to submit the responses. Thus, any data respondents provide will be lost if they break off before submitting their responses at the end of the survey. Client-side scripting or other programming technologies can be used to capture responses more often in scroll designs, but some people disable this scripting on their computers and these types of programming may not always work effectively on mobile devices.

Lastly, this format limits the ability to use many of the interactive features of web surveys (e.g., asking follow-up questions based on previous answers, performing automatic calculations, etc.) for the same reason. That is, many interactive features rely on client-side scripting or related programming that can be disabled by respondents, so no-script backup options must be provided for these people.

Some web surveyors are using a hybrid of this scrollable web survey format in which more interactive features can be programmed into the survey, and responses can sometimes be saved before the entire questionnaire is completed. For example, once respondents start answering, inapplicable questions can be grayed out, in effect deemphasizing them and signaling the respondent to skip them (Potaka, 2008; Statistics New Zealand, 2006), or after a response to a question is given, follow-up or subsequent questions can appear. But once again, such interactive features depend on client-side scripting that can be disabled by respondents.

A final format for constructing web questionnaires is that in which multiple questions are presented on one page and respondents navigate between multiple web pages. This format is often used when surveyors want to group related questions (e.g., several questions about a current job position) or questions that use a common scale format (e.g., a grid) or when they want to ask one or two follow-up questions based on the response to a previous question. Grouping questions can help respondents as they answer the questions and can reduce the number of pages that respondents need to navigate (particularly with longer questionnaires). However, similar to findings on paper surveys (Schwarz, 1996), research on web surveys has shown that when questions appear on the same page, there is a higher correlation among answers across the questions (Couper et al., 2001; Tourangeau et al., 2004). Thus, when choosing to group multiple questions on the page, it is important to select questions that are related, otherwise respondents may infer connections across questions that the researcher does not intend. Further, for mobile devices, it is best to limit to no more than three questions per page.

In today's world of web surveying, which of these formats is used depends on the particular needs of each survey. Presenting each question on its own page is the most common questionnaire format for web surveys. It is typically used because it is easy to integrate complex skip patterns or other interactive features and works effectively for mobile devices. Constructing web surveys with multiple questions per page is often used for longer surveys and for surveys in which grouping questions on a page can help respondents process them.

Guideline 9.6: Create Interesting and Informative Welcome and Closing Screens That Will Have Wide Appeal to Respondents

The welcome or opening screen is important in a web survey because it gives sample members immediate and clear confirmation that they have found the correct screen for the study they were invited to participate in when they enter the survey URL or click on the link provided in an e-mail. The welcome screen is the first experience the respondent has with the actual questionnaire, and for many ambivalent respondents it is where they either make a commitment to start the survey or decide against doing so. As such, it should welcome and encourage sample members in ways that have wide appeal. In doing so, it should help orient respondents by providing a description of the survey and instructions for how to proceed.

One of us recently received a survey in which the first text on the opening screen stated the following: "No parts of this survey may be copied or used without written permission of [company name]. Requests should be mailed to [company name and address]. Use of this survey without written permission is punishable by law." Starting off with this somewhat cold tone is not what one wants to do if trying to convince undecided respondents who have reached the opening screen to go ahead and launch into the questionnaire. It immediately subordinates the respondent to the interests of the surveyor in a quite threatening manner and implies that the respondent and the surveyor have conflicting interests. If this type of information must be included to protect proprietary survey measures (as was probably the case in this instance) or for any other reason, it should be placed after a more welcoming message and perhaps even downplayed through the use of properties such as font size or color.

Figure 9.9 shows an example of an opening page from a survey of Washington State University undergraduates that was designed in a much more welcoming manner. The text on this opening screen describes the survey in a nonthreatening way. As in this example, the opening screen should include the title of the survey, a brief description of its purpose, and instructions for how to proceed. Most opening screens also include a space for respondents to enter individual access codes, a topic covered in more depth in Guideline.9.24. This particular screen also includes additional information about confidentiality and contact information that can be used if they have questions. The photo that is displayed was selected very carefully because of its appeal to those in the target population; the clock tower shown

FIGURE 9.9   Examples of interesting and informative welcome and closing pages for a web questionnaire.

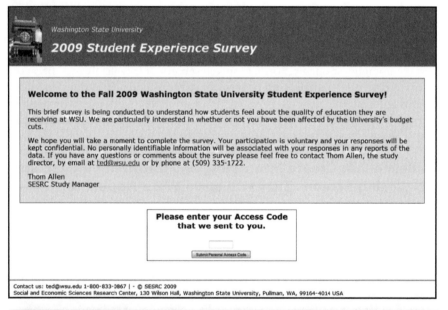

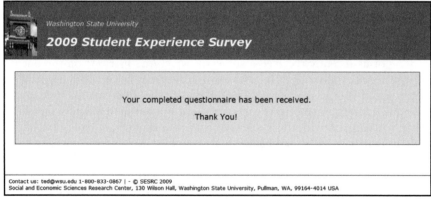

is centrally located and widely known on campus. Such photos, however, should only be used after careful consideration of how they may affect both the decision to respond and the responses people give to individual questions. Moreover, any such information should be easily connected with other implementation features described later in this chapter.

Surveyors also frequently place sponsorship and other information on the welcome screen to encourage respondents to begin the survey. However, information of this sort should be arranged so that it does not interfere with the major function of the page, which is getting respondents into the survey. For example, respondents should not have to scroll past a logo that is included only for branding purposes in order to enter their access codes and move to the next screen. Logos and images can take up most if not all of the screen on mobile devices, requiring respondents to need to scroll to see *any* other information (Orr, 2012). If used, logos and images should be resized and the resolution adjusted for the mobile screen (Nielsen & Budiu, 2013).

The opening screen should clearly connect to the e-mails that sample members receive. For example, it may have a similar visual or graphic to one included in the e-mail contact or simply repeat the title of the survey that was also included in the e-mail message. Another way the welcoming page can connect to the e-mail message is by asking people to please enter their access code included in the e-mail. Finally, the substantive content of the welcome page should very closely parallel the messages sent in the invitation e-mail and follow-ups. These connections to all of the previous information respondents have received about this survey will help them quickly realize that they have accessed the correct web page.

The message in the closing screen should also be written in a friendly, professional manner and should both tell the respondents that they have completed the survey and convey gratitude. In the example shown in Figure 9.9, respondents are informed that their questionnaire has been received. In addition, consistent with social exchange, the final message respondents receive from the surveyor is a reward—gratitude for the effort they have put forth with a simple thank you.

Guideline 9.7: Develop a Screen Format That Emphasizes the Respondent Rather Than the Sponsor

When designing web questionnaires, it is important to approach design from the respondents' perspective. Pages should be designed so they are appealing and interesting to respondents, similar to the welcome screen discussed previously. For example, repeating the title from the opening page and choosing a simple graphic that respondents identify with to repeat across each page can help encourage participation by focusing attention on respondents (see Figure 9.10).

In contrast, a survey that includes a title such as "Annual Federal Assessment of Juvenile Delinquency" and images of multiple delinquent behaviors focuses more on the sponsor's needs and why the survey is being conducted than on the respondent. In addition, the use of selected images may even bias how respondents answer individual questions. For example, it has been found that people rate their own health better in web surveys when presented with an image of a person who looks sick, and worse when presented with an image of a person who looks healthy (Couper, Conrad, & Tourangeau, 2007). Similarly, in the previous example, people may rate their own behavior differently depending on what delinquent behaviors are pictured.

FIGURE 9.10 Example of questionnaire screens that emphasize the respondent.

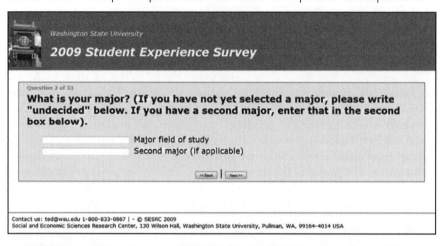

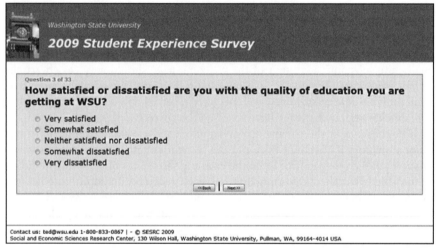

Overall, it is important to focus on the respondent when designing web questionnaire screens, both in the choice of title and any imagery, as well as in how information is presented on the page. Focusing on the respondent not only includes connecting and engaging with him, but also organizing the information in a way that allows the respondent to concentrate on the task at hand, as discussed more in Guideline 9.8.

Guideline 9.8: Use a Consistent Page Layout Across Screens and Visually Emphasize Information That Is Essential to Completing the Survey While Deemphasizing Inessential Information

A consistent page layout across screens helps respondents easily process the basic organization of information on the screen and focus on the task of answering the questions. This can be especially important as the type of information requested and the question format changes across screens. In the example in Figure 9.10, background colors, lines, and contours help respondents segment the page into three regions: the header or banner region, the main question area, and the footer.

The header and footer regions are often consistent across all screens. For the survey in Figure 9.10, the header region includes the name of the university and the title of the survey in white font against a dark green background. This area may also include a small, very carefully selected graphic to help respondents identify with the survey. The footer region contains contact information for use by respondents who have questions for the surveyor or who would like additional information about the survey. This information is the least used by respondents so it is located at the bottom of the page, similar to contact or designer information for many websites. It is set on a white background, and the text is in smaller black font to make it less visible (because not all respondents will need this information), but it can still be easily located by those who are looking for it and is available on every page of the survey. Given the small screen size of many mobile devices, the header and footer region may need to be reduced or eliminated from the design of the questionnaire to maximize the space reserved for the question area.

The main question area or *respondent region* contains all of the elements respondents need to answer the survey question and move to the next question: the question stem, any additional instructions, the response options or answer spaces, and the navigation buttons. If these elements are consistently located in the respondent region page after page, respondents will quickly learn to focus their attention in this area and not be distracted by other parts of the page, which will help them stay focused on the task. This area takes up most of the page, is located in the center of the page, and is defined by a colored background (in this particular survey it was light green) that helps draw attention to it. Locating all of the components of each question in the same region (defined by the contours and the green background color) creates a clear separation between this area and the other elements on the page. Defining a clear question region also encourages respondents to see the question stem, any additional instructions or definitions, and the answer categories or spaces as a group that belong together.

Every question in the survey is designed following the guidelines for the visual design of questions discussed in Chapter 6 (i.e., darker and larger print for the question stem, spacing to create subgrouping, visually standardized answer spaces, etc.). Looking across the question screens in Figure 9.10 also reveals, however, that great care was taken to ensure consistency in the visual appearance of the questions across screens. For example, the start of the respondent area and the question counter (i.e., Question 2 of 33) are located in the same location on every screen (both vertically and horizontally).

The question stem is presented in the largest font and is bolded; it is the most visually dominant element on the page to help draw respondents' attention to it. The response options and spaces are in a smaller font and indented underneath the question stem. The visual design and layout of the question stem and response options/answer spaces are consistent across each question page. Such consistency eases the response task as it allows the respondent to learn what to expect in the first screen or two and then apply that knowledge to the rest of the survey rather than having to reorient at every screen.

In many web surveys, designers provide custom navigation buttons for respondents to use when moving through the survey (i.e., different buttons from the "back" and "forward" buttons in their Internet browser). The benefit of these navigation buttons is that they allow greater control over how answers are saved as respondents proceed through the survey. As Figure 9.10 illustrates, the navigation buttons, if used, should be located in the main question area to make them more accessible to respondents as they move through the survey.

In this survey we placed the navigation buttons in the middle of the screen. In some of our previous surveys we have placed the "next" button on the left side of the screen directly under the answer spaces and the "back" button on the same horizontal line on the right side (see Figure 9.7). We have done this to make the "next" button easier and quicker to access to encourage forward movement through the survey. Locating the "back" button on the right side of the screen places it outside of the foveal view so that only those who truly need it go look for it. Limited research has indicated that locating the buttons in this way decreases backward movement through the questionnaire (Baker & Couper, 2007, as cited in Couper, Baker, & Mechling, 2011), and respondents seem to quickly learn where the buttons are and use them appropriately. Other alternatives that seem effective at keeping respondents moving forward in the questionnaire are to place the "next" button directly below the answer spaces with the "back" button underneath it or to differentiate and downplay the "back" button by making it a hyperlink instead of a button and locating it to the right of the "next" button (Couper, Baker, et al., 2011). What is most important, however, is that the location of the navigation buttons be consistent across screens as in the example in Figure 9.10.

Although screen layouts may differ somewhat from the one described here, the design of the web pages should help the respondent to organize the information on the page. Thus, it is important that surveyors use a consistent visual layout across web pages to aid respondents as the type of question or task changes and respondents move through individual pages or screens in the questionnaire.

Guideline 9.9: Allow Respondents to Back Up in the Survey

An important goal in web survey design is to keep respondents moving forward in the survey; however, there are instances when they may need to back up. This can happen, for example, if they realize they made a mistake or forgot to report something and want to correct it or if they have lost track of the flow of the survey conversation and need to revisit prior items to get reoriented. In these cases, allowing respondents to back up can improve data quality. While most respondents will not use the "back" button or will use it very little (Couper, 2008), research has shown that eliminating this option significantly increases break-offs (Couper, Baker, et al., 2011).

Guideline 9.10: Do Not Require Responses to Questions Unless Absolutely Necessary for the Survey

The design and programming of web surveys allow surveyors to require responses to every question. Sometimes requiring responses to one or a few key questions can be essential to the goal of the survey and can save time and expense, such as when screening respondents for a particular characteristic or when they would have to be called back by telephone to collect missing responses to key questions. However, for most surveys, requiring responses before respondents can move to the next screen, particularly for every question, can have detrimental effects on respondent motivation, on measurement, and on the likelihood that respondents will complete the entire survey. When respondents do not have an answer to a question but are required to provide one anyway, they have two options: get frustrated and terminate the survey or lie and provide an answer that is not true for them. The first option will increase the likelihood of nonresponse error in the data, and the second will introduce measurement error.

Putting respondents into a situation where they feel they have to lie to get past a question may also have the undesirable side effect of making them more likely to provide inaccurate answers for questions later in the survey. An example of this was witnessed during a cognitive interview on a question that required people to indicate the degree they received from the community college they attended. One respondent explained that she only took one course, so could not answer the question. When the error message appeared telling her that she had to provide a response, she laughed and said that it was a nice little college, and she always wanted a degree from there, so she guessed that she now had one. She then wondered out loud about what year she should say she got it. (Altheimer & Dillman, 2002).

In addition to increasing nonresponse and measurement error, requiring answers may be problematic for other reasons. For one, many institutional review boards require surveys to be designed so that respondents can skip questions they prefer not to answer (i.e., that each question is voluntary). Also, when web surveys are used as part of a mixed-mode survey with a mail component, requiring answers may lead to different stimuli, and ultimately responses, across the two modes because answers cannot be required in mail surveys.

When we advise against requiring responses, we are often asked about situations in which respondents need to provide a response to an initial question so they can be routed to the appropriate follow-up question. Requiring answers may be the only solution when the questions are used to screen the sample and determine eligibility for the survey (although in these cases, there should be an explanation for why a response is needed). But for most questions, the respondent can be branched appropriately even when a response to the initial question is not provided. In fact, it is important to consider where people who leave an item blank should go next for every question. It may require more thought on the part of the surveyor to think about which questions the respondent should be asked next, but it will often improve the quality of responses received.

Regardless of the topic, most surveys have a few—and some have many—questions that cannot be honestly answered by respondents. As we have discussed, requiring responses often leads to nonresponse and measurement biases that can far outweigh the benefits of collecting responses for every question. If a response is going to be required to a question, it is important to ascertain whether this is necessary for the survey and what effects it will have on respondent behavior. In addition, it may be useful to include options such as "This question does not apply to me," "Prefer not to answer," or "Don't know" so that rather than choose a response that does not fit for them, respondents will be able to move on without having to provide an inaccurate answer or quit the survey out of frustration. Another option is to give respondents who leave an item blank a prompt to go back and answer it (often with a motivational message or explanation as well), but then allow them to move on if they choose to leave it blank a second time.

Guideline 9.11: Design Survey-Specific and Item-Specific Error Messages to Help Respondents Troubleshoot Any Issues They May Encounter

Sometimes technical issues may occur that require communicating with respondents what has happened and what they should do next. For example, respondents may not have entered their identification or access code correctly or they may not be able to view a page in the survey because it does not load, particularly if there are a lot of complex features and the respondents are on a slow connection. In another scenario, a respondent may be trying to return to the survey after answering a phone call or experiencing another interruption, but the survey may have timed out, making the person unable to continue.

In these cases, standard messages are often sent to respondents by the browser or server. However, these generic error messages are usually not specific enough to help respondents troubleshoot the issue. For example, a generic message may say "This page cannot be found" and give some standard ways to try to fix the error. These messages are usually in a white background with black or red text and look very different from the survey pages. To the extent that these generic messages are unhelpful for the specific survey situation, they may frustrate respondents and cause some to stop trying to access the survey.

To help respondents troubleshoot these types of issues, we recommend designing and programming survey-specific messages that load in a new window and inform respondents of exactly what happened and how to get back on track. In our own web surveys we design survey-related error pages with the same look and feel of the regular survey pages. We do this so that instead of feeling as if they have left the survey, respondents mentally connect the error message to the rest of the survey.

The first example in Figure 9.11 shows a survey-specific error message that respondents might receive if they enter an incorrect access code. In this case, the respondent is told what he has done wrong (i.e., the user ID is invalid) and is given two options that are very specific and tailored to the survey—contact the sponsors for assistance, or return to the login page to try again. If the survey times out, one might explain in the message that the survey has timed out in order to conserve server resources but that respondents can resume where they left off by reentering the access code on the login page. Likewise, if a page cannot load or there is another type of programming issue, an error page may say "We are sorry, but a programming error has occurred while answering the survey. By clicking here and reentering your ID number you will be returned to the correct page. If you have any questions, please contact us at _____." Regardless of the cause of the error message, it is important to always provide a link on the error page that will take respondents to where they need to go next. In social exchange terms, doing so will reduce the costs to respondents by making the process of getting back into the survey as easy as possible (thus increasing the likelihood they will continue with the survey).

The second example in Figure 9.11 shows a screenshot of a custom-designed error page that respondents may encounter as they try to find the correct survey from the outset. Rather than a generic error message appearing, this page appears if respondents make a mistake in entering a survey's URL but get the domain correct. It provides immediate notification to the respondent that she is on the right track

FIGURE 9.11 Examples of customized error messages.

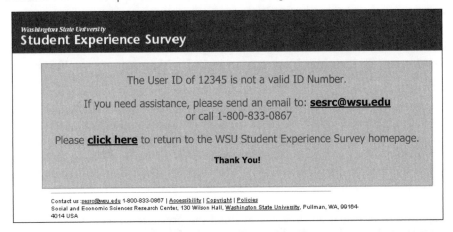

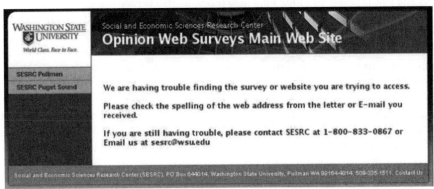

but may have made a slight error. It also provides contact information in case the respondent cannot resolve the problem.

In addition to these general survey-specific error messages, individual questions may require specific messages if the respondent's answer does not match the criteria programmed in a validation step. For example, if a response is needed for a particular question but a respondent leaves it blank, rather than using a generic message that says "Response required" or "You must provide a response to this question," a survey-specific message using the same page layout as the survey pages might explain why the response is required. For example, the surveyor may explain that "A response is needed so that we can determine … the appropriate questions to ask you" or "whether you are eligible for the survey." If additional options are provided, such as "Prefer not to answer" or "This question does not apply to me," it may be helpful to remind respondents that they can provide these types of responses so they are able to move on to the next page.

Overall, these survey-specific and item-specific error messages can help improve respondent motivation when issues are encountered that would otherwise negatively impact respondent behavior. This is especially important to prevent respondents from terminating the survey, particularly if they are likely to be unfamiliar with web surveys or when responses are required for some of the questions in the survey.

Guideline 9.12: Evaluate Carefully the Use of Interactive Features, Balancing Improvements in Measurement With the Impact on Respondent Burden

Common interactive web features include saving responses, branching respondents to appropriate questions based on their responses to previous questions (or previously collected data), and providing error message pages that communicate information about how to troubleshoot issues that may arise. Most of these types of features are considered essential for web surveys and should be included in all surveys.

Additional interactive features are available as well. One example is that early responses or information already available from previous surveys or from sample records can be used to tailor later questions in the survey (i.e., fills). This practice is especially common in establishment surveys and longitudinal surveys for which extensive information is available about the respondents ahead of time. An example is that question wording can be customized, similar to computer-assisted telephone interviewing and computer-assisted personal interviewing (e.g., "When you began your vacation in *July 2013* to *Tennessee*, did you drive your *Toyota Highlander* or your *Ford Focus* or travel there some other way?"). In some surveys, an enormous amount of information can be brought forward to frame questions in a more direct manner for respondents. Although this ability can be incredibly useful, each of these fills requires programming that should be extensively checked to make sure it is working properly.

In addition, web surveys can be designed so that if answers are not within a specified range, error messages are sent to respondents asking for corrections (i.e., validation steps). Although validation steps can improve the quality of the final dataset for the surveyor and save data cleaning and editing time, they are usually designed from the viewpoint of the surveyor rather than the respondent. As such, they can be quite problematic for respondents. First, frequent error messages can be frustrating and burdensome, possibly leading to poor response behavior or even break-offs. Second, it often happens that scenarios the surveyor did not anticipate apply to some respondents. In these cases, the data validation step often creates a roadblock that requires certain respondents to either give inaccurate data or quit the survey. Including data validation steps can also have negative effects for the surveyor. First and foremost, these steps are difficult to program, are very prone to mistakes that can have larger negative impacts on data quality, and are very expensive. In addition, the process of cleaning and editing data can be very informative with respect to how respondents interpret the questions being asked of them. Interactive validation steps, in essence, erase this potentially useful information.

Other types of interactive features have been (and continue to be) developed for the web, and the amount of research on these features varies greatly. Features such as drop-down menus, links to definitions or examples, automatic calculation tools, and visual analog scales have all been tested in web surveys and were discussed in Chapter 5. When deciding which interactive features to use, it is important to consider which are necessary and which are more of a novelty and not terribly helpful to respondents. This issue was summed up by a designer of many establishment surveys who commented that some respondents who completed the same survey each year expected such features to be included, especially for the purpose of avoiding subsequent requests for the information but that the same respondents often became frustrated when too many of such features and feedback messages appeared in the survey.

Oftentimes these interactive features cost more and take more time because they require more advanced programming and because the likelihood of programming errors increases. In addition, many of them require respondents to have JavaScript or other client-side scripting technologies enabled in order to work correctly, so no-script options (i.e., a different measurement stimulus) must also be programmed for those who have scripting disabled. Further, some of these features may not work properly on mobile devices and need to be thoroughly tested before using them in mobile surveys (Orr, 2012). Many of these features are not available in other modes so their use in web surveys that will also be used in mixed-mode designs should be carefully considered (see Chapter 11 for more on designing mixed-mode questionnaires). Most important, these features should be tested with respondents to see how they interact with them and whether the features help with or hinder survey completion.

Guideline 9.13: Do Not Include a Graphical Progress Indicator

Another interactive feature that is included in many web surveys is a graphical progress indicator. These graphics provide a visual indication of how much of the survey has been completed. The simple example in Figure 9.12 shows that about half of the survey has been completed and half remains to be completed. The same information can be communicated in a number of other formats such as pie charts or even text (e.g., "You have completed 50% of the survey") and is typically displayed prominently at the top or bottom of web survey screens.

The idea behind progress indicators is that if respondents can track their progress in the survey, they will be less likely to quit in the middle (i.e., break off), but a number of studies examining the effectiveness of progress indicators show that they rarely have the desired effect of decreasing break-offs (Couper et al., 2001; Crawford et al., 2001; Heerwegh & Loosveldt, 2006). They only tend to be

FIGURE 9.12 Example of a progress indicator and counter.

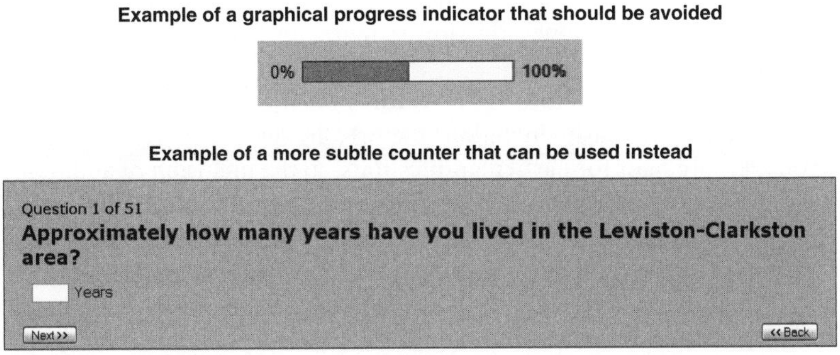

Example of a graphical progress indicator that should be avoided

0% 100%

Example of a more subtle counter that can be used instead

Question 1 of 51
Approximately how many years have you lived in the Lewiston-Clarkston area?

Years

Next >>   << Back effective in very short surveys, presumably because it is encouraging for respondents to see how quickly they are progressing through the survey. In long surveys they may be more discouraging than encouraging. In addition, most progress indicators reflect the number of questions answered out of the total number possible, making them quite inaccurate for surveys in which respondents are skipped past questions or where some items (e.g., grids) require far more responses (and time) than others.

Many web survey software programs are set to include graphical progress indicators by default. For all but the shortest of surveys, we recommend changing this setting and eliminating them. One alternative to a progress indicator that we sometimes use to help respondents know where they are in the survey in a more subtle way is a counter included with the question number (see Guideline 6.18 for discussion of the importance of numbering questions in web surveys). An example is shown in the bottom half of Figure 9.12. In addition to being more subtle, an advantage of this type of counter over a progress indicator is that the programming for it is much simpler, which reduces the amount of testing that is needed and the chances of programming errors happening.

Guideline 9.14: Use Audiovisual Capabilities of the Web Sparingly, and Evaluate the Differential Effect They May Have on Respondents

The web allows for enhanced audiovisual capabilities that are not possible in any other survey mode, other than perhaps face-to-face interviews. This has made the web an ideal mode for evaluating videos and pictures on a large scale. Many web surveyors are also interested in using audio and video to make the web more similar to interviewer-administered modes. For example, a survey may have a video of an interviewer who reads the questions or may include an audio recording of the question alongside the text version on the screen. Some have even explored using animated interviewing agents or avatars to conduct surveys (Malakhoff & Jans, 2011).

Although these features are generally included in an effort to assist respondents, they can be quite problematic for several reasons. First, outside of web panels where many panelists are used to encountering audio and video, some respondents may not be expecting audio or video content (and may have their volume turned down or off) and others may not even have the necessary computer hardware capabilities, software, or additional plug-ins to run the video or audio components. In addition, these files often require longer download times, which can be problematic for those completing the survey using a slow connection or on their mobile device via the cellular network, where download times can vary extensively and are generally slower than most download times for PCs (Orr, 2012).

Moreover, research on these new features on the web is still rather limited. And as discussed previously, including pictures in surveys can have detrimental effects on measurement for particular questions, so the inclusion of audio or video may also have unknown effects on measurement or nonresponse. Thus, it is important to evaluate the effects of including audio or video components on respondent motivation and on the concepts being measured. In addition, previous research on interviewer features may be important in evaluating audio-video web components that include an interviewer reading the questions to respondents.

Guideline 9.15: Allow Respondents to Stop the Survey and Finish Completing It at a Later Time

Most web survey respondents will complete the survey at one time rather than coming back and finishing it later, particularly if the survey is short and only one person is needed to answer the questions. However, sometimes people are interrupted (e.g., because of power outages or loss of Internet connectivity, to answer the phone, to respond to an urgent e-mail, to have a conversation with another person in the household, etc.) and need to finish the survey at another time. In addition, for more complex and longer surveys or for establishment surveys for which multiple people often need to be consulted to answer all of the questions, it is absolutely essential for respondents to be able to easily discontinue the survey and resume it later.

Most software packages make it possible to allow respondents to quit and return to the survey later. When respondents return to the survey welcome page and enter their identification code, it is usually helpful to then route them to the page where they left off so they do not have to click through multiple screens to find where they stopped answering. However, it is also a good idea to allow respondents to go backward from the point they left off so they can remind themselves of the topic of the previous few questions if needed before proceeding with the remaining questions.

For establishment surveys and other complex surveys that are likely to be completed in multiple sessions, section headings or other types of tabs that describe the type of information requested may also help orient respondents when they resume the survey or when they are asked to complete a section they are particularly qualified for by someone else who has already completed another section. Section headings or tabs can allow these respondents to move directly to the relevant questions. For example, in an establishment, survey headings may be organized by position (e.g., human resources, communications, research, accounting etc.), or in an individual survey they may be organized based on the type of information requested (e.g., biographical information, employment history, political attitudes, etc.).

Overall, providing the ability to resume the survey at a later time shows that the surveyor is responsive to respondents' needs and is thinking about how they will complete the survey. As we mentioned, this feature is absolutely essential for surveys on particular topics, of longer lengths, and for particular types of populations. However, we recommend it for most surveys, even if only a few respondents may need to take advantage of this feature.

Guideline 9.16: Whenever Possible, Collect Paradata That Provide Feedback on How the Respondent Interacts With the Questionnaire

One especially useful tool in web surveys is the ability to collect server-side and client-side paradata that records the server's and client's interactions with the questionnaire (Couper, 1998; Heerwegh, 2003; Heerwegh & Loosveldt, 2002a). The type of information that can be collected includes how long it takes respondents to answer each question (and the entire survey), whether and how answers to each question are changed, and the sequence of clicks that respondents make on each page. This information can provide important feedback about how the respondents access, process, and answer specific questions. Also, one key strength of paradata is that it can be collected for all respondents, rather than only for a select few as is the case with laboratory studies or cognitive interviews, thus allowing for analysis in the population as a whole and in important subgroups.

Another key aspect of paradata is that it includes the user agent string. This information is collected as part of the respondents' interaction with the server and provides the name and version of the browser that they are using to access the survey. This is critical for surveyors who wish to route people who are completing the survey on a mobile device to a separate mobile optimized questionnaire.

Beyond the browser information, extensive paradata can be collected about how respondents interact with each screen, the clicks they make, and how long they spend on each page. The following are ways in which paradata have been used to better understand questions and questionnaires.

- Christian, Parsons, and Dillman (2009) observed that respondents take longer to answer scalar questions when they are provided with a number box into which they must type the number corresponding with their response versus when they are provided with a labeled scale with radio buttons that correspond to each scale point.
- Smyth, Dillman, Christian, and Stern (2006) found that, on average, respondents to check-all-that-apply questions answer more quickly than respondents to forced-choice questions. In further analyses they were able to determine that those answering check-all questions the most quickly were also more likely to select options appearing in the top of the lists, indicating that they may have been satisficing (see Chapter 5, Guideline 5.12).
- Stern (2008) found that students were having considerable trouble discerning between two responses in a check-all-that-apply question: "libraries" and "library instruction." When "library instruction" was presented before "libraries," many students selected that response but later changed it when they saw the "libraries" option. However, this was not a problem when "libraries" was presented first.

Overall, we have found that paradata can be a very valuable resource for evaluating responses to web surveys. One cautionary note, however, is that when paradata are collected, a large amount of information can be recorded, so it is particularly important to identify where paradata can be most useful in understanding response behavior in order to be able to focus the analyses. However, simple information such as response time is easy to compute, and many web surveyors now regularly include total response time when describing their web survey as well as question response times when reporting analyses from individual questions. Some web survey software packages also can routinely collect certain paradata. For more on paradata and its uses in interviewer-administered surveys see Guideline 8.32, and for more on paradata in all survey modes see a recent edited volume on the topic (Kreuter, 2013).

GUIDELINES FOR WEB AND MOBILE SURVEY IMPLEMENTATION

Web survey implementation includes procedures for contacting sample members by e-mail, tracking who has responded, and monitoring the survey's progress. In this chapter, we focus specifically on web surveys in which e-mail is the only method used to contact sample members. This approach can be effective when surveying certain populations, when responses are needed quickly, and for online panels where a preexisting relationship has already been established.

In other situations, such as for general population surveys using an address-based frame where e-mail addresses for sample members are not available, sample members can only be approached by another mode (e.g., mail or phone) and then be asked to access the survey on the web. For some populations, multiple ways can be used to contact sample members (e.g., mail and e-mail, etc.). Implementation strategies for these types of mixed-mode strategies are discussed in Chapter 11, but we have found that including a postal mail contact, especially to deliver an incentive, can be quite effective for many web surveys and should be strongly considered when postal addresses are available.

In general, one needs to think very carefully about these multiple situations when starting to work on a web implementation system, because the mode of contact has serious consequences for other implementation features, such as the extent to which and how personalizing elements are used, whether and what type of incentives can be delivered, and how the delivery of contacts will be timed.

Guideline 9.17: To the Extent Possible, Personalize All Contacts to Respondents

Personalizing all contacts in web surveys is important for the same reasons as in other survey modes—it establishes a connection between the surveyor and the respondent that is necessary to invoke social exchange, and it draws the respondent out of the group. However, the type of personalization one uses depends very much on the type of contact one is sending, and e-mail contacts can be particularly difficult to personalize, in part because e-mail is considered by many to be a less personal form of communication. In addition, many Internet users are keenly aware of the ease with which personalized e-mails can be mass produced. In fact, for experienced e-mail users, the appearance of one's name in certain locations within an e-mail—the subject line, for example—is an immediate indication that the message may be spam. Thus, the importance of striking a balance between adequately personalizing and overpersonalizing contacts may be even greater with e-mail contacts. However, similar strategies can be used for e-mail and postal mail contacts. That is, write the e-mail contacts as if writing an e-mail to a business acquaintance who is not well known. Doing so will help to strike the right tone and achieve the proper amount of personalization so that it is obvious that the message is from a real person (i.e., not computer generated) and that the request is legitimate and appropriate.

The effectiveness of e-mail invitation personalization was tested in a sample of first-year university students in Belgium. Students were randomly assigned to receive either a personalized ("Dear [First name] [Last name],") or an impersonalized ("Dear Student,") e-mail invitation to participate in a web survey. The personalized invitations resulted in nearly an 8 percentage point increase in response rates over the impersonalized invitations (Heerwegh, 2005). In another study, university students were asked to join an online survey panel for their university. Personalizing the invitation with "Dear [First name]" resulted in a 4.5 percentage point increase in the number of students joining the panel than did the less personal salutation "Dear Student" (Joinson & Reips, 2007). Further experimentation with the same panel also indicated that personalization has a stronger effect when survey invitations are sent from powerful individuals (e.g., professor and vice chancellor) than from less powerful individuals (Joinson & Reips, 2007).

Another strong indication that one is getting personal attention with e-mails is receiving individual, not bulk, messages. Stated another way, receiving a bulk e-mail (i.e., one sent to multiple recipients at once) is an immediate sign to individual recipients that they are unimportant. In this situation, it is easy for respondents to conclude that someone else will comply with the request and that their own response is not all that important, thus diffusing responsibility to others in the group. The same conclusion, however, is much more difficult to reach when the request is targeted to one individual in a more personal way.

Barron and Yechiam (2002) conducted an experiment to test this phenomenon. They e-mailed a simple question (i.e., "Is there a biology faculty in the institution?") to faculty, administrative staff members, and graduate students at a university, all of whom were likely to know the answer to such a question. Some of the requests were sent to groups of five individuals at a time, whereas others were sent to single individuals. Among those individuals who were sole recipients of the request for this information, about 65% replied, but among those who received the request as part of a group, only about 50% replied. Moreover, those who received individual requests provided longer and more helpful responses to the question than did those who received the request along with others. This effect is much like the bystander effect that has long been studied in psychology, whereby the presence of bystanders decreases the likelihood of any one person stepping forward to help someone in need. Barron and Yechiam argued that virtual bystanders, represented by the presence of their e-mail addresses in the "To" field, invoke much the same effect.

In addition, the appearance of the e-mail addresses of multiple sample members in the "To" field raises serious ethical considerations, as confidentiality can no longer be ensured and increases the likelihood that a message will be flagged as spam. As a result, in order to be ethical, to minimize the chance that contacts will be treated as spam, and to personalize contacts, avoid sending bulk e-mail contacts.

Guideline 9.18: Consider Sending an Incentive Electronically With the Survey Request

Inasmuch as one of the largest contributors to improved response rates is the appropriate use of prepaid token financial incentives, it stands to reason that the same would be true for web surveys. However, Internet surveys that only use e-mail contacts raise special problems for delivering prepaid financial incentives in that cash cannot be sent via e-mail. As a result, researchers have begun to explore different ways of delivering incentives, such as through electronic gift certificates, gift cards, or money through such services as PayPal (Birnholtz, Horn, Finholt, & Bae, 2004).

Incentives such as these have been shown to increase response rates only modestly compared to sending no incentive. In a meta-analysis of 26 studies comparing incentive use to no incentive use in web surveys, Göritz (2006) found that providing material incentives increased the response rate by an average of 4.2 percentage points. This is likely a low estimate of the effect of material incentives, because most of the studies included in this meta-analysis utilized promised incentives, which tend not to be as effective as advance or prepaid incentives.

The limited success of money and gift certificates sent electronically may very well stem from the added difficulty (i.e., costs) of redeeming them. For example,

PayPal charges the recipients of money a fee to issue them a check (Birnholtz et al., 2004). In addition, it takes a fair amount of time, effort, and knowledge to set up an account with such services or to redeem gift certificates with particular online merchants. Moreover, there may be additional costs to respondents if the amount of the incentive only covers part of the cost of the item they are buying (Birnholtz et al., 2004). The costs (monetary and social exchange) of redeeming electronic incentives may be particularly high, and perhaps even prohibitive, for sample members who are relatively inexperienced with the Internet.

Another common response to the difficulty of providing incentives via e-mail is to utilize a lottery or prize drawing instead of a prepaid incentive. However, the research on the effectiveness of lotteries in web-based surveys has generally shown that lotteries and prize drawings do not increase response rates significantly (Brennan, Rae, & Parackal, 1999; Cobanoglu & Cobanoglu, 2003; Porter & Whitcomb, 2003), with few exceptions (Bosnjak & Tuten, 2003). Overall, then, the evidence strongly suggests that prize drawings and lotteries are not as effective as traditional cash incentives or material incentives (Singer & Ye, 2013), but there is some evidence to suggest that their effectiveness can be improved somewhat by informing respondents that they will receive the results of the prize drawing or lottery immediately upon completing the survey (Tuten, Galesic, & Bosnjak, 2004).

In all survey modes, a prepaid cash incentive appears to be most effective at increasing response rates (Singer & Ye, 2013). Such an incentive, however, requires the surveyor to use a mode other than the web to contact respondents and provide them with the incentive (see Chapter 11). When a mixed-mode strategy is not possible, and e-mail is the only contact option, an electronic incentive sent to all sample members with the survey request is likely the best option.

Guideline 9.19: Use Multiple Contacts and Vary the Message Across Them

Sending multiple contacts to potential web survey respondents is one of the most effective ways to increase response rates (Cook, Heath, & Thompson, 2000). As an illustration, in one study of college undergraduates, using four follow-up contacts resulted in a 37 percentage point increase in response rate over sending only a survey invitation and no follow-ups (Olsen, Call, & Wygant, 2005). However, little research has been done on the optimal combination of contacts to use for web surveys.

The web survey implementation sequence generally starts with a survey invitation; a prenotice is rarely used. This initial e-mail invitation is then often followed up with a number of reminder e-mails. Because sending additional e-mail contacts is relatively inexpensive, one can often leave the final decision on the number of follow-ups to send until well into the fielding process. If both the first and second follow-ups yield significant gains, a third follow-up may be useful as well. However, if previous follow-ups have only yielded a handful of responses, additional follow-ups may not be warranted as they may only irritate sample members (unless these follow-ups take a significantly different approach than previous contacts). The fact that one can send several e-mail reminders very cheaply does not mean it is appropriate to send them every day; they should be spaced out during the field period.

It is important to vary the stimulus across e-mail contacts. Sending the same e-mail over and over is unlikely to be effective at convincing sample members to reply. Moreover, if the first message gets flagged as spam, a repeat message is likely to meet the same fate. Varying the content of the e-mails both appeals in different ways to respondents and reduces the likelihood that all of the messages will be sorted out by spam filters.

In many ways the content of the e-mails can parallel the content that would be used in other modes. For example, the original e-mail invitation should clearly state what is being asked of respondents, why they were selected, what the survey is about, who is conducting it, and how sample members can contact someone to get any questions they have answered. It should also state that the data will be kept confidential. One key difference between web surveys and other modes is that information should also be provided about how to access the survey (including a URL). The first e-mail reminder message should explain that a survey invitation was sent, thank those who have responded, and ask those to respond who have yet to do so. Additional follow-up e-mails should provide personalized feedback (e.g., "We've not heard from you") and emphasize the importance of the recipient's response. It is important to remove those who have already responded to the request from the mailing list for every contact after the initial invitation, so that they do not receive additional requests to complete the survey.

An example of a five-contact e-mail strategy that demonstrates some of these features and was used in a recent survey of university students is shown in Figure 9.13.

FIGURE 9.13 *Examples of e-mail contacts.*

Invitation

From: Don Dillman [don.dillman@wsu.edu]
Sent: Tuesday, November 10, 2009 9:00 AM
To: tchambers5@wsu.edu
Subject: WSU Student Experience Survey Invitation

Dear Tyson,

I am writing to ask for your help with the 2009 WSU Student Experience Survey. You are part of a random sample of undergraduates that has been chosen to complete a brief questionnaire about your experiences as a WSU student. A goal of this survey is to understand how students rate the quality of education they are receiving at WSU. We are especially interested in learning how recent events, ranging from the University's budget cuts to the swine flu, have affected students.

The questionnaire is short, only 33 questions, and should take about ten minutes to complete. To begin the survey, simply click on this link:

> http://www.opinion.wsu.edu/studentexperience

And then type in the following access code:

> Access Code: **11568**

This survey is confidential. Your participation is voluntary, and if you come to any question you prefer not to answer please skip it and go on to the next. Should you have any questions or comments please contact Thom Allen, the study director, at the Social and Economic Sciences Research Center, (509) 335-1722 or ted@wsu.edu.

We have been conducting this survey since 2002 in order to better understand how student life at WSU is changing, and really appreciate your help with this year's survey.

Many Thanks.

Don Dillman

Don A. Dillman
Regents' Professor and Deputy Director
Social and Economic Sciences Research Center
Washington State University

FIGURE 9.13   (*continued*).

First reminder

From: Don Dillman [don.dillman@wsu.edu]
Sent: Friday, November 13, 2009 9:00 AM
To: tchambers5@wsu.edu
Subject: Voice Your Opinions about WSU

Dear Tyson,

Earlier this week we sent an e-mail to you asking for your participation in the 2009 WSU Student Experience Survey.

We hope that providing you with a link to the survey website makes it easy for you to respond. To complete the survey, simply click on this link:

> http://www.opinion.wsu.edu/studentexperience

And then enter your access code to begin the questionnaire: **11568**

We have been conducting the WSU Student Experience Survey periodically since 2002. It seemed particularly important to do the survey this semester because of the current economic conditions facing the state and the university, and the lack of information about how students are being affected by them.

Your response is voluntary and we appreciate your considering our request.

Sincerely,

Don Dillman
Don A. Dillman
Regents' Professor and Deputy Director
Social and Economic Sciences Research Center
Washington State University

Second reminder

From: Don Dillman [don.dillman@wsu.edu]
Sent: Thursday, November 19, 2009 9:00 AM
To: tchambers5@wsu.edu
Subject: How Do You Rate WSU?

Dear Tyson,

Recently we sent you an e-mail asking you to complete a survey about how students may have been affected by recent changes at WSU. If you have already completed this survey, we would like to thank you very much. We truly appreciate your help.

If you have not answered the questionnaire yet, we'd like to urge you to do so. It should only take about ten minutes to complete. Simply click on the link below and use your access code to begin answering questions.

> http://opinion.wsu.edu/studentexperience
> Access Code: **11568**

The 2009 WSU Student Experience Survey is important; current students are the only source we have for getting truly representative opinions of the undergraduate experience at WSU. If you have questions or comments, please contact Thom Allen, the study director, at (509) 335-1722 or ted@wsu.edu. Thank you for your help, and best wishes for an enjoyable Thanksgiving break.

Sincerely,

Don Dillman
Don A. Dillman
Regents' Professor and Deputy Director
Social and Economic Sciences Research Center
Washington State University

FIGURE 9.13 *(continued).*

Third reminder

From: Don Dillman [don.dillman@wsu.edu]
Sent: Tuesday, December 8, 2009 9:00 AM
To: tchambers5@wsu.edu
Subject: Help WSU Understand the Student Experience

Dear Tyson,

In November we contacted you asking for your help with the Fall 2009 Student Experience Survey. We are writing to you again because our ability to accurately describe how WSU students may have been affected by recent University changes depends on hearing from those who have not yet responded. We need your help to ensure the results are as precise as possible.

To fill out the questionnaire, click on the web address link below and then enter your access code.

> http://opinion.wsu.edu/studentexperience
> Access Code: 11568

Responses to the survey are confidential and will not be connected to your name in any reports of the data. If you have any questions about the survey, please contact the study director, Thom Allen. He can be reached via e-mail at ted@wsu.edu or by telephone at (509) 335-1722. You may wonder why we are asking you to complete this survey so near to the end of the semester. We do this for the same reason that course evaluations are usually done at this time; we hope this will allow you to take into account as much of the semester as possible when reflecting on the quality of your WSU education.

Thanks for considering our request during this very busy time of year.

Sincerely,

Don A. Dillman (signature)

Don A. Dillman
Regents' Professor and Deputy Director
Social and Economic Sciences Research Center
Washington State University

Fourth and final reminder

From: Don Dillman [don.dillman@wsu.edu]
Sent: Monday, December 14, 2009 9:00 AM
To: tchambers5@wsu.edu
Subject: Last Chance to Help WSU Understand the Student Experience

Dear Tyson,

We are writing to follow up on the message we sent last week asking you to participate in the Fall 2009 WSU Student Experience Survey. This assessment of the impacts of University changes on students is drawing to a close, and this is the last reminder we are sending about the study.

The URL and your personal access code are included below to provide an easy link to the survey website.

> http://opinion.wsu.edu/studentexperience
> Access Code: 11568

We also wanted to let you know that if you are interested in seeing a summary of results, we hope to have them posted on the SESRC website in mid-January. In the meantime, we want to wish you an enjoyable winter break.

Sincerely,

Don A. Dillman (signature)

Don A. Dillman
Regents' Professor and Deputy Director
Social and Economic Sciences Research Center
www.sesrc.wsu.edu

---

1. November 10: The invitation e-mail introduces the recipients to the survey, explaining how they have been chosen and emphasizing why their response is important. It also provides the essential information needed for them to find and enter the survey (including the URL and their access code).
2. November 13: The second e-mail message serves as a reminder to those who have not yet completed the survey and repeats the URL and access code. It gives the same general reason for the study, but expresses it in slightly different terms, including mentioning how this survey fits in a longer tradition of student surveys and why the timing of this particular survey is important.
3. November 19: The second reminder serves as a thank you to those who have completed the survey and a reminder that emphasizes why their response is important for those who have not. The purpose of the survey is only briefly mentioned; most of the focus is on why hearing from the sample member is important (i.e., students are the only source of the sought after information).
4. December 8: The third reminder also focuses on why hearing from those who have not responded is important, but emphasizes more clearly the need to hear from those who have not responded and frames the request to complete the survey as a request for help. This contact also takes a slightly different approach to describing why the study is important in that it focuses on the importance of conducting the survey late in the semester for learning about the student experience.
5. December 14: The final reminder contact takes a different tone altogether, focusing in a friendly way on the fact that the study is drawing to a close and the short amount of time that is left to complete the survey before the winter break.

As is illustrated in these contacts, some features typical in postal letters can be omitted from e-mail contacts. For example, the use of a date and inside address is less important in e-mail than in a postal letter because these features are not conventional in e-mail correspondence. In addition, this information is usually automatically included by e-mail software. Likewise a blue ballpoint pen signature is not possible in e-mails (although it can be replaced with a very high-quality scanned copy of one's signature but this often requires sending e-mails in HTML so images can be used).

Although e-mail contacts may seem more relaxed, it is still important to maintain the professionalism of the contacts. To that end, one should avoid four e-mail practices commonly employed in other settings:

1. The first is ignoring common grammatical rules such as when to use capitalization or writing without punctuation. Another example is using punctuation in unconventional ways, such.as.uisng.periods.instead.of.spaces.between .words.
2. THE SECOND PRACTICE TO AVOID IS WRITING IN ALL CAPITAL LETTERS. NOT ONLY DOES THIS MAKE THE TEXT MORE DIFFICULT TO READ, BUT IT ALSO MAY GIVE THE IMPRESSION THAT ONE IS YELLING AT RESPONDENTS.
3. A third practice to avoid is using acronyms that have increased in popularity with the use of e-mail, text messaging, and instant messaging (e.g., BTW =

by the way; FYI = for your information; LOL = laughing out loud; u r gr8 = you are great; etc.) but that instantly portray a lack of professionalism.

4. A fourth practice is to avoid special characters or other symbols. These types of characters do not always appear the same across different computers, devices, and operating systems so it best to avoid these in e-mail communications.

Guideline 9.20: Carefully and Strategically Time All Contacts With the Population in Mind

Each contact for a web survey is designed to meet a specific goal but also has to work well within the entire set of contacts, and timing is important to the overall effect. For example, respondents need to be given adequate time to respond before reminders begin arriving, and waiting to send reminders gives the surveyor an opportunity to identify and address problems if they are occurring. However, one should not allow so much time to pass that the initial requests are forgotten.

The optimal timing sequence for web surveys varies considerably depending on the goals and needs of the study, as well as the population being surveyed. As a result, we provide general guidelines for planning the timing of web survey contacts. First, the tempo of web surveys is fairly quick—responses can come in quite quickly after an e-mail request is sent (see Figure 9.14). That, and the somewhat faster pace people interact with web and mobile devices, when compared with postal mail, means that follow-up contacts can be sent more quickly. But various studies have different needs. In one study, three e-mail contacts might be sent in just 2 weeks, whereas for other studies four to six e-mail contacts might be sent over a month. The faster timing of e-mail communication is also important; e-mails are often more quickly dismissed and forgotten than a piece of mail that physically lingers around the house until it is thrown away.

FIGURE 9.14 Contribution of each contact to the response rate for the 2009 WSU Student Experience Survey.

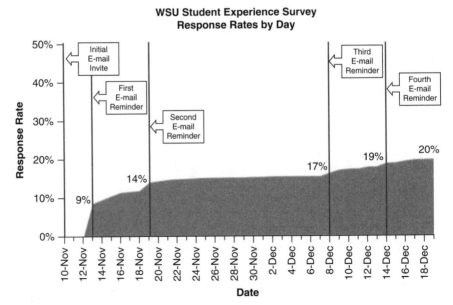

However, we have heard of several instances when two, three, and even four reminders were sent in only a couple of days or even in the same day. Unless there is a very strong survey- or population-related reason for doing this, we generally advise against such rapid-fire reminder sequences. The danger of sending multiple reminders too quickly is that they will seem pushy and irritate respondents. When thinking about contact timing, it might be useful to return to the comparison with how one would communicate with business acquaintances whom one does not know very well. One would not likely send the same request to such acquaintances multiple times in 1 day or even in 2 days for fear of alienating them. The same should be true for survey sample members.

Second, using e-mail contacts means surveyors can carefully control the time of day that the message is delivered. One has no control over what time mail is delivered to sample members, but e-mail messages will likely arrive in respondents' inboxes within minutes or even seconds of their being sent. There is some indication that e-mail invitations are most successful if they are delivered to recipients' inboxes early in the morning. In one study, e-mail contacts were intended to be sent before work hours on a Monday morning, but a technical difficulty resulted in only half of them being sent then and the rest being sent during lunchtime. Those who received the invitation midday were significantly less likely to respond than those who received it before working hours (Trouteaud, 2004). The likely explanation for this finding is that an e-mail request received first thing in the morning can be handled before one gets into the major demands of the day, whereas an e-mail received midday is in direct competition with the ongoing demands of the day. However, this may be further complicated by mobile devices where people may quickly check e-mails on their smartphone, deleting some, filing some, and marking others to return to later when they have more time or are at a computer. Thus, one should consider when sample members are most likely to check their e-mail and be free from other demands and then attempt to have e-mail invitations delivered to their inboxes just prior to this time. However, these concerns are secondary to concerns about sending e-mails in batches to avoid overloading servers (see Guideline 9.25).

Guideline 9.21: Keep E-Mail Contacts Short and to the Point

The key to getting respondents to read all of the important information in the e-mail invitation and follow-ups is to keep these contacts short and engaging. Whereas one page is the standard length for a printed letter, e-mail communications tend to be shorter on average. As a result, the survey contacts should provide the information that is required for respondents to understand what is being asked of them, why they are being asked, and what they should do, but the contacts should do this in as short of a format as possible in order to increase the likelihood that they will be read in their entirety. Also, varying the message in each contact can help reduce length by not repeating the same information in each contact.

Keeping e-mails short is increasingly important as more and more people read their e-mail on mobile devices. The amount of information sample members will see on their screen is very small so it is important that the first few lines of the e-mail highlight the key information, such as the sponsor, topic, any incentive, and the link to the survey. Some of this key information can be part of the sender address (e.g., organization name) or subject line and then does not need to be repeated in the body of the e-mail (see Guideline 9.22 for more about selecting the sender name and subject line). It is important to include the survey link as early in the e-mail as possible, so that sample members can see clearly what the next step or action is. This is particularly important for those reading the e-mail on a mobile device. One suggestion we have heard is to think of an e-mail on a mobile device more like a text message and try to reduce the length accordingly. Also, consider a shortened URL to reduce the amount of space it takes up on the screen.

Guideline 9.22: Carefully Select the Sender Name and Address and the Subject Line Text for E-Mail Communications

Once an e-mail gets past spam filters and delivered into an inbox, the recipient generally has only two sources of information to use in determining whether to open the message: the text that appears in the "From" field and the subject line. As a result, these two pieces of information need to convince the respondent that this is an important message from a reputable sender. Thus, it is important to send the e-mail requests from a professional-appearing e-mail sender and address. For example, leah.christian@xyzuniversity.edu or @abcresearch.org seems much more reputable than lotusgal@yoga_enthusiast.com. Likewise, it is advisable to have a full, formal name appear in the "From" field rather than a nickname (i.e., Leah Christian vs. lotusgal).

In addition to communicating the professionalism of the e-mail, the material in the "From" line should also help respondents make connections between the various e-mails they will receive about a survey. For this reason, all contacts should be sent from the same e-mail address so that they are recognizable to respondents and so that respondents can quickly sort their messages by sender to find related e-mails. Also, when possible, it is desirable to have the "From" line match the person's name and organization conducting the survey mentioned in the body or signature of the e-mail communication.

The subject line should also be professional and informative. It should immediately tell the respondent that the e-mail is about a survey, who the sponsor is, and what the topic is (e.g., "Survey of College Presidents"). Consistent with the social exchange perspective, some research has found that stating the subject as a request for help rather than an offer to let respondents share their opinions results in increased response. For example, Trouteaud (2004) found that the subject line "Please help [name of company] with your advice and opinions" resulted in a 5% increase in response rates compared to the subject line "Share your advice and opinions now with [name of company]."

It is best to keep subject lines short. In the viewing window on most e-mail applications, especially on smartphones, subject lines are truncated to fit within the allotted space so sample members may only see the first few words of the subject line until they click on the e-mail.

Guideline 9.23: Take Steps to Ensure That E-Mails Are Not Flagged as Spam

Almost all of us who regularly use e-mail have had an important message get routed by our e-mail software to a "junk" or "bulk" mail folder because it was mistaken for *spam* (i.e., unsolicited bulk messages for which there is no preexisting relationship between the sender and recipient). Oftentimes we do not even know we missed the important message until the sender contacts us in another way and brings it to our attention. Although all of us appreciate them for what they do, spam filters pose special problems for web surveyors. The problem of e-mail contacts being labeled as junk mail is particularly severe, because the decision is often not in sample members' hands, but rather the e-mail system's spam filtering rules. Rather, spam filters can prevent large segments of the sample from receiving contacts altogether.

A quick search will turn up long lists of advice for how to minimize the likelihood of survey e-mails being flagged as spam. Some common examples include the following:

- Talk to your Internet service provider or survey vendor—make sure the Internet protocol (IP) address you will be sending from is not already flagged by major e-mail providers your sample members use. This may involve opening e-mail accounts with those providers and sending yourself simple test messages. If the IP address is flagged, resulting in your not receiving the test messages or their being routed to junk mail folders, insist on a different IP address for your survey mailings.
- Use plain text communications rather than HTML messages because many people and spam filters closely associate the formatting and graphics available in HTML messages with spam.
- Send individual e-mails rather than using bulk mailing options, and do not use the "CC" or "BCC" fields.
- Avoid words such as *offer, free, cash, win, promo, prize,* and so on.

The list could go on and on. In fact, many spam filters use hundreds and even thousands of criteria to create scores to classify messages as legitimate or as spam. To complicate matters further, the advice provided here may quickly be out of date, because spam filters are constantly being updated to catch increasingly creative spammers. Therefore, perhaps the most useful advice we can give is to research spam filters close to the time one will be doing the survey and to test the messages using a spam analyzer, a number of which are now available on the web. These programs will examine the message for common content that is known to trigger spam filters. They then provide feedback on how likely the message is to be flagged as spam and what components of the message are particularly problematic so that one can make appropriate changes.

Guideline 9.24: Assign Each Sample Member a Unique ID Number

Assigning respondents a unique identification number is important for all modes, including web surveys. It allows the surveyor to keep track of who has responded and to remove respondents' contact information from follow-up databases so that they do not continue to receive reminders. In web surveys, the unique identification number can also serve an additional function in that it can be used as a unique access code that can, and should, be required in order to enter the web survey. Requiring respondents to enter a code in order to access the survey helps protect the integrity of the sample and survey data by ensuring that unsampled people who stumble upon the survey are not able to access it. It also provides a way to ensure that each respondent answers the survey only once, as the access code can be deactivated after the respondent submits the completed survey.

Some respondents, however, legitimately need to stop the survey and return to it at a later time to finish. As a result, deactivating access codes after they have been entered once is not a desirable practice. For this reason, we typically program our surveys so that if respondents stop before completing the survey and then come back to it later, they are returned to the question where they previously quit (as discussed in Guideline 9.15). They can leave and reenter the survey in this way as many times as they desire. However, once respondents submit the completed survey, their access code is deactivated. We have found this to be a quite useful strategy because most respondents who start the survey will finish it all at once if there are no offensive questions or technical difficulties that lead to artificially high break-off rates. Although this seems to work well for most of our surveys, other strategies may be more appropriate in other situations.

That one should assign an access code raises the issue of how one should require that access code to be used. Currently two main strategies are used: manual and automatic login. In manual login, respondents are sent a URL and access code. Once they get to the introductory web page using the URL, they are asked to key their access code into a designated space to gain access to the survey. In automatic login, the unique access code is contained within the URL so that entering the URL in their web browser (or clicking on it if it is sent by e-mail) will automatically gain respondents entrance into the survey.

Several studies have compared these two strategies. Crawford et al. (2001) found that providing an automatic login significantly increased response rates by nearly 5 percentage points over a manual login condition in which respondents had to enter both a password and access code. Heerwegh and Loosveldt (2003) reported a similar but nonsignificant finding (a 3-percentage-point advantage for automatic login). However, they also found that a semiautomatic login procedure in which the password was included in a URL but the respondent still had to key in an access code resulted in an 8-percentage-point increase in response rate over the manual login procedure. Both of these studies as well as an additional study by Heerwegh and Loosveldt (2002c) also reported some evidence that respondents who log in manually (or semiautomatically) provide more complete data. In particular, Heerwegh and Loosveldt (2002c) reported that respondents who log in manually are more likely to complete more of the survey and are more likely to provide substantive answers to sensitive questions, an effect they attributed to respondents believing their data are more secure when they have to key in an access code.

Based on these findings, it seems advisable to require respondents to key in an access code rather than to provide automatic login. But it is also important to use access codes large enough that one is unlikely to wrongfully enter the survey, whether by accident (i.e., a typo in entering one's own code) or by guessing a code. If, for example, one wants to use a four-digit numerical access code (where each digit can range from 0 to 9), the total number of possible codes that can be generated is 10,000. If one is surveying 1,000 respondents, 1 in every 10 possible access codes will be assigned to a respondent. With a five-digit access code, however, there are 100,000 possibilities, meaning that only 1 in every 100 possible codes will be assigned to a respondent. The likelihood of somebody wrongfully accessing the survey by guessing an access code or making a typo in entering his own code is considerably less with a five-digit access code.

However, the use of longer access codes should be balanced with considerations of the difficulty of transferring the access code from the e-mail to the website.

Although long access codes can be copied and pasted, many people will still type in the code, and the more digits they have to enter, the greater the likelihood for error.

In addition to considering the length of the access code, one should also be sure to avoid using adjacent numbers for different respondents. For example, using the access codes 10001, 10002, 10003, and so on would make it quite simple for a respondent to answer the survey multiple times by simply altering his own access code by one digit. Thus, it is important to build in an interval greater than 1 between access codes. However, one should also avoid regular intervals, as in the following sequence: 10101, 10201, 10301, and so on. Instead, a random interval of between 50 and 300 digits should be used; this can be easily accomplished using the random functions included in common software.

It is also important to make sure that the access codes one provides are not easily mistaken with other codes respondents deal with on a daily basis. For example, we once sent e-mail invitations for a student experience survey to a sample of undergraduate students. The invitation included a clickable link to the survey and respondents' ID number for accessing the survey. Shortly after sending the first batch of e-mails, we began getting messages back from students claiming that their ID did not work. It was only when one student included her ID number in her message that we realized that the students were entering their school ID numbers rather than the randomly generated ID numbers we had sent them in the e-mail. When surveying this type of group, we now make it a point to refer to the survey ID numbers as access codes to help differentiate them from what students more commonly think of as their ID. We also now specify "Please enter your access code listed in the e-mail we sent you" on the login page rather than the less specific "Please enter your ID." The types of specialized groups who can be surveyed via the web oftentimes have preexisting ID numbers, membership numbers, or access codes that they use regularly. It is good practice to look into this ahead of time and take steps to differentiate survey access codes from these more common, group-specific identifiers.

Guideline 9.25: Work Within the Capabilities and Limits of the Web Server(s)

Although conducting a survey using computer and Internet technology gives one a wealth of new possibilities, it also means that one is constrained by the limits of those technologies. One of those limits that can be very damaging to a survey project if exceeded is the capacity of the web server(s). Web servers can only handle so much outgoing or incoming traffic before they begin to bog down or even crash. As a result, it is important to know ahead of time what effect sending or receiving mass amounts of survey-related information might have on one's server(s) and to plan accordingly.

Based on the advice of our information technology professionals, we very rarely send e-mail survey invitations or reminders to the entire sample at one time (the exception is for small samples) because, although our e-mail program will allow us to do so, our server cannot handle that many outgoing e-mails at once. The risk is that some of the messages will be lost or will be bounced back to the sender, leading to the incredibly complex task of trying to sort through who got the e-mail and who did not. Instead, we send our e-mail communications in batches of a few hundred at a time over the course of a day or, better yet, in the late evening when the servers are less busy and the messages can arrive before recipients check their e-mail the next morning. This is slightly more labor intensive, but it is not nearly the amount of work that sorting out bounced e-mails would be.

In addition to considering the effects of outgoing communications, it is also important to consider the effects of incoming survey activity on the server(s). The nature of the Internet is such that many sample members can receive their invitations at virtually the same time, and all of them can immediately try to access and complete the survey. However, if too many people try to access the same survey on the same server all at once (or if responses are coming into the same server for different surveys all at once), the likely results could range from significant slowdowns that might lead some to quit the survey to a server crash that would cut every respondent off. Neither of these outcomes, nor any point in between, is desirable. When we have large survey projects that pose such challenges, we send invitations in batches over longer time periods so that the responses come in smaller waves rather than in one large spike. Another strategy we often employ is to have our server disconnect from respondents' computers if the computers are idle for a specified amount of time. We do this so that server resources can be devoted to respondents who are actively completing the questionnaire. When the idle respondents return to their computers and try to continue, they are provided with a friendly message that explains what happened and tells them how to return to their previous place in the survey.

The main point, though, is that it is important to know the limits of the hosting server(s) and plan accordingly. The best advice we can give here is to consult one's information technology professional or Internet service provider well in advance to work out an implementation and survey management strategy that works well within the limits of the server(s) one will be using.

QUALITY CONTROL AND TESTING GUIDELINES FOR WEB AND MOBILE SURVEYS

A great deal of technology is involved in producing and fielding a web survey, meaning there are many things that can go wrong. Careful testing can catch and allow surveyors to correct most problems ahead of time so that they do not compromise the final data. In Chapter 7 we discussed general methods for testing questionnaires. Here we discuss how those same methods should be applied to web surveys specifically, including how to make sure web and mobile questionnaires are fully functional and how to test implementation procedures.

Guideline 9.26: Obtain Expert Review and Conduct Cognitive Interviews, Experimental Evaluations, and Pilot Studies of Web Implementation Materials and Procedures

Surveyors make many decisions when designing the communications that will be used to contact and recruit sample members to complete a web survey. As the previous discussion indicated, everything in the e-mails from the sender name to the signature line should be carefully thought out and strategically designed to try to entice as many sample members as possible to respond. In addition, issues such as the number of contacts to send and when they should be sent have to be decided. The goals that drive all of these decisions are to maximize response and minimize nonresponse and measurement error. But in most cases it is not possible to know how the decisions being made will contribute to reaching these goals without testing the implementation features.

How well the various features of the implementation protocol will work can be assessed using many of the same methods that are used to test questionnaires including expert reviews, cognitive interviews, experiments, and pilot studies (see Chapter 7). For example expert reviews with topic experts or people who are familiar with the target population can help identify compelling ways of presenting the argument to convince sample members to respond or features of the implementation system that may negatively affect cooperation. Cognitive interviews with members of the target population can achieve similar ends, but can also be used to understand what features of the contacts inhibit response and how they might be altered (e.g., moving the URL and access code earlier in the e-mail). Cognitive interviews might also be used to better understand how easy or difficult it is for people to use the information in the contacts to access the questionnaire on a mobile device versus a computer.

In many cases, the surveyor will have to choose between multiple options with each having its own pros and cons. For example, one might wonder whether an electronic gift certificate to Amazon will work as well as transferring money to respondents through a service like PayPal. This is the type of question that is best answered through a small experiment in which sample members are randomly assigned to one of two treatments that then receive these different types of incentives. The benefit of such experiments is that they allow the surveyor to learn exactly what, if any, effect the different designs will have on important outcomes like response rates and the composition of the final sample.

Pilot studies can also be very useful for web surveys as they give the surveyor the opportunity to test the entire survey process from start to finish and to assess its success in a number of useful ways. For most pilot studies of implementation procedures, the outcome of primary interest is the response rate, as this can be used to decide if additional improvements need to be made in the final data collection in order to achieve the survey's goals (e.g., adding another contact, using an incentive, etc.) and if the planned sample size is adequate. But any number of other things can be learned about a web survey from a pilot study as well. For example, a pilot study gives the surveyor an opportunity to test procedures for conducting the mail merge that will be used to send e-mail contacts. One can also test the capability of the servers to handle outgoing e-mail traffic when the contacts are sent and incoming traffic when responses come in (Guideline 9.25). A pilot study can also give one a sense of how quickly responses might come in after requests are sent so that the surveyor can determine whether requests need to be sent in batches to avoid overloading servers or whether all requests can be sent at one time. Systems for tracking incentives (see Guideline 9.29) and managing respondent inquiries (see Guideline 9.30) can also be assessed and improved through a pilot study, and any paradata collected during the pilot can be examined for indications of problems in the questionnaire (e.g., questions that take a long time to answer or that have a lot of answer changes—see Guideline 9.16).

In addition to learning how well the systems used to carry out the web survey work, a pilot study can give the researcher a good sense of how respondents experience the survey. Inquiries respondents send, comments they make in the survey, and data about who does and who does not respond after each contact is sent can all be examined to get a better sense of how the entire package of survey materials from contacts to questionnaires is working and what might need to be improved.

Guideline 9.27: Test the Survey Using a Variety of Devices, Platforms, Connection Speeds, Browsers, and User-Controlled Settings, and Test the Database to Ensure That Items Are Collected and Coded Correctly

Testing the web survey is one of the most important steps in the design process. Although paper surveys look the same for all respondents, web surveys cannot be standardized in the same way and are dependent on the respondents' individual setups. All of the hard work in designing and programming the survey does not matter if the survey does not work effectively on a variety of devices, hardware and software configurations, and across various connection speeds. Thus, it is important to test the survey using various technological configurations as determined earlier when assessing the capabilities of the survey population.

It should be standard web survey procedure to test the survey using all (or at least most) of the possible combinations of settings that potential respondents may use to complete the survey (i.e., the most popular and current platforms for the population of interest). Moreover, testing needs to be a systematic process whereby every page in the survey is viewed using these different combinations by multiple people and from different locations. One of the most important things to test is page download times to ensure that most pages download very quickly (ideally less than 5 to 10 seconds), even with slower connection speeds and processors. This is especially important when interactive features, images, or video are used.

Another very important thing to test is what happens if scripting is disabled. It is critical to both make sure that the web survey does not crash when accessed by a browser with scripting disabled and to ensure that a no-script option is available for each JavaScript (or other script) function in the survey. Although it is not ideal to have some respondents experiencing the JavaScript version and others experiencing the no-script version because the stimulus may differ between the two, JavaScript enables many important web survey functions and therefore is likely to be included to some degree in almost all web surveys. When JavaScript is used, the survey should be able to detect if a respondent has scripting disabled. One option is to provide those who have it disabled a polite explanation as to why scripting needs to be enabled for the survey and how to enable it.

Often web survey designers and programmers are on the cutting edge of new computer technology. They have the newest devices, the most recent versions of web browsers, and are adept at customizing their own user settings. However, it is important to design and test the web survey from the respondent perspective; the respondent may not be as computer savvy or familiar with being online. In one of our recent student surveys, we decided to send a tester out to a number of different computer labs at our university because many respondents would be completing the survey on campus. In the process of testing, it was discovered that two labs on campus had not updated their browsers in 5 years. Although many students were aware of that and avoided using those labs, others did not know and may have completed the survey on those computers with the outdated browsers.

We believe this situation is not unique and that even more variation exists in types and versions of browsers and in other hardware and connection speeds, as individual users have control over their own machines and how they run them. Under these conditions, seemingly small problems in the testing phase will often become much larger problems once the survey goes live. Generally, differences across browsers or versions of a browser result in subtle differences that can be tolerated, but sometimes testing can reveal far larger issues with the way a question design displays across different browsers and versions. For example, in one study we worked on, the ability to toggle back and forth between English and Spanish was only functional in some versions of specific browsers.

In addition to testing the survey itself, it is also important to test the database. This step can be done in combination with testing the survey. As testers view the survey pages, they should enter responses and record what they entered so the responses can then be checked in the database. Every response option for every question should be tested at least once. Testing the database involves ensuring that a response is collected for every question, that the correct number is coded in the database for the response(s) selected, that open-ended text boxes are not truncating responses (unless desired by the researcher), and that any other response coding that may be unique to the survey is working correctly.

Guideline 9.28: Establish a Procedure for Dealing With Bounced E-Mails

Whenever we field a web survey using e-mail contacts, we expect that many of the e-mails, even sometimes hundreds, will bounce back to us as undeliverable. Some come back because the e-mail address is unknown, others because the recipients' mailboxes are full, and still others for a variety of other reasons. A similar thing happens with undeliverable postal mail, but with e-mails it occurs with much higher frequency and much more rapidly. The benefit is that some problems can be addressed quickly and the e-mails re-sent, even the same day as the original message. The downside, though, is that tracking the delivery status of e-mails and following up with potentially hundreds of bounced e-mails can be a very daunting process. For this reason, the fielding period is not the time to be trying to figure out how to deal with bounced e-mails. The procedures that will be followed should be planned before the first set of contacts is sent out.

We have found that in many cases, the problems that cause the e-mail to be returned to us are only temporary, and the message can be re-sent at a later date. But depending on how much later the message is sent, this may mean that future contacts have to be delayed as well. In other cases, it may be necessary to examine the e-mail addresses for errors or to attempt to contact respondents by an alternative mode.

Guideline 9.29: Establish Procedures for Tracking Incentives

When using electronic incentives, it is important to carefully track the incentives that have been sent and whether they have been used or not. This may mean remembering, months after the survey has been completed, to work with the cash card company or other provider of electronic incentives to retrieve the value of the incentives that were not used before they expired, assuming such an arrangement was made in the beginning. Forgetting these follow-through steps may entirely nullify any cost savings of using these types of incentives in the first place and is simply not good business.

Guideline 9.30: Establish Procedures for Dealing With Respondent Inquiries

The need to respond to inquiries is important in all modes, and it is important to monitor feedback through any method provided (e.g., call-in number, e-mail, etc.). One of the best ways for the surveyor to know about any difficulties people are having is by paying close attention to what respondents are saying in their inquiries. For example, the mix-up of university student ID numbers and survey access codes discussed previously was recognized as the cause of many login errors only because a student e-mailed an inquiry in which she listed her student ID as her access code. The project director recognized the difference in the number of digits and followed up, only then identifying the problem that so many respondents were having. Had this e-mail been skipped over or even just ignored for a day or two, many more respondents may have had the same problem and may have written off the survey. In another instance, we received the following e-mail:

> Dear Professor Dillman,
>
> When I enter my access code into the window that says, "Welcome to the WSU Student Experience Survey" I enter my number and it opens up the same window??? I'm not real sure if this is a system error or an operator error?
>
> Thanks,
> Kayla

After some investigation, it was discovered that this error was occurring for respondents with common free, web-based e-mail accounts because this e-mail program was putting a frame around the survey web page that was interfering with the survey programming. Once this was recognized, the respondents who e-mailed were advised to copy and paste the link into their browser instead of clicking on it in order to avoid the frame. Similar advice was then included in the next e-mail contact to the entire group of nonrespondents. A short time later a programming solution was discovered to automatically break out of such frames. Given the large portion of students who had their university e-mail forwarded to this and other e-mail providers that also use frames, this was an issue that could have caused major problems had it gone undetected or unacknowledged. Respondents are often are best source for information about issues they are having or about how to improve the study. Reviewing feedback from them is critical throughout the study period, but especially in the beginning, so appropriate action can be taken while there is still time.

Guideline 9.31: Implement a System for Monitoring Progress and Evaluating Early Completes

One of the most powerful aspects of web surveys is the fast pace with which things begin to happen when a web survey goes live. People can start completing the survey immediately after the e-mail is sent and often returns come in within minutes or the first hour of sending the initial e-mail invitation. By contrast, in a mail survey there are usually a few days of lag while the letters make their way through the mail to their destination and the completed surveys make their way back to the surveyor. If the surveys are being sent a great distance, this lag can be a week or longer.

The fact that web survey responses come in very fast and that they are already in electronic form means that surveyors can more quickly and easily monitor the progress of the study. However, it also means that the surveyor has to be ready and have systems for monitoring progress in place immediately when survey notices go out. Many established research organizations have web pages on which the survey sponsor and project managers can monitor results as they come in, and many survey software packages include similar tools. In one organization, these progress-monitoring web pages are jokingly referred to as the sanity pages because they allow the surveyors to watch closely to ensure that their costly projects are going well.

Such a page might include a summary of response dispositions (i.e., partial completes, completes, refusals, return to sender, and nonresponse rates) that updates as additional information comes in. Another good feature for progress monitoring is a list of case IDs that have accessed the survey, the date each accessed it, and the outcome (i.e., the last question completed). Having this information available and updated regularly makes it possible to quickly find problem areas if they exist. For example, if a large proportion of those who access the survey drop out at a specific question, one can reexamine that question and the survey programming underlying it to determine what the problem may be. In web surveys, changes to the questionnaire can be made very quickly even after the survey is fielded to correct any problems due to question wording, design, or programming, provided these problems are identified and fixed very early in the fielding process.

Unfortunately, not every surveyor has the resources to also have a progress monitoring website that automatically updates as surveys come in. But even if one is not available, it is still important to set up some sort of system for this type of monitoring. At the very least, a manual accounting of case dispositions and break-off points for those returning partially completed surveys should be taken once daily starting when the survey goes live. Regardless of how and how often the progress monitoring is going to occur, one should have the system or protocol in place before the survey goes live. If one has to take the time to establish a system while the survey is in the field, by the time she gets around to actually looking closely at the returns, there is little time left to resolve any issues and likely any damage would have already occurred, affecting the quality of the data.

In addition to monitoring completion rates and break-off points, one should also closely monitor the data. In one of our surveys that included open-ended questions we inadvertently set a character limit on the answer box so that only the first 255 characters that were entered got recorded into the database, a mistake that was caught by examining early returns. It is also important to monitor server logs to see what types of errors are being registered, as these logs will let the researcher know if respondents are experiencing things like browser incompatibilities, data transfer errors, or other obscure errors that may have been missed in the testing phase. In one instance we mistakenly had a maximum byte limit set for each record (i.e., respondent) so that an error occurred if people tried to submit too much information. Checking too many items on a check-all question or entering too much text into text boxes triggered these errors. One cannot catch these types of problems by looking at completion rates or even the data, but server logs of errors can reveal that such problems are occurring. It is imperative to examine the data set and the server logs throughout the fielding process. Again, such monitoring should commence immediately when returns start coming in so that corrective action can be taken quickly to minimize the damage caused by easy-to-make mistakes like these examples.

Guideline 9.32: Develop Procedures to Ensure Data Security

Surveyors need to ensure that procedures are in place when collecting and transmitting data online to ensure that the data is kept safe. Organizations may want to consider consulting with data security experts, especially when developing initial procedures that are used across studies, or working with any other internal groups at their organization who also work on securing data. We generally recommend establishing procedures that can be used for all studies and modifying them as needed to meet the goals of a particular study that may require stricter data handling procedures.

Some common steps that researchers should take to ensure data security are to store any identifying information separately from the survey responses. This is another key benefit of using unique access codes since they can be used to link the responses to any identifying information when needed. Another key step is to secure all information being collected and transferred using encryption (e.g., SSL, Secure Socket Layering), rigorous firewalls, and other technologies at each stage in the process. Organizations should also maintain control of who has access to the data and ensure those with access sign a pledge of confidentiality (including people inside and outside the research team who are granted access). As mentioned earlier, one of the concerns of using some of the online web survey vendors is that the data are stored on their servers, making it difficult to directly ensure the security of the data.

Data security is important because breaches can have substantial consequences. People may publicly identify those who responded and the answers they provided. People's contact information may be compromised and used for other purposes. Fabricated responses can impact the quality of the data provided. And finally, researchers can be held culpable for damages and for not protecting and securing people's data. Thus, it is important for surveyors, especially those conducting web surveys, to take steps to ensure the security of the data collected.

CONCLUSION

Much success coexists with considerable frustration as one considers today's reality of conducting standalone e-mail/Internet surveys. The proportion of households with Internet access continues to rise and individuals are more likely to carry Internet-connected devices with them everywhere. However, the usability of such devices for responding to surveys is in many cases limited, and the Internet has become a very competitive space in which to attempt communication with people. Response rates have remained low for most web-only surveys, as discussed throughout this chapter.

There is reason for considerable optimism that growth of web survey acceptance among potential respondents will continue to improve, but whether we will see acceptable response rates with low nonresponse error is less certain. The much anticipated hope for a smooth transition from telephone, now an expensive mode, to the web has not occurred except for specialized use in certain highly educated survey populations.

Substantial research, which we discuss in the next chapters, suggests that web surveys are more effective when used in combination with other modes, especially mail surveys since both modes are self-administered and visual. We describe methods for using the web in mixed-mode survey designs in Chapter 11.

LIST OF GUIDELINES

Guidelines for Designing Web and Mobile Questionnaires

Guideline 9.1:   Decide how the survey will be programmed and hosted

Guideline 9.2:   Evaluate the technological capabilities of the survey population

Guideline 9.3:   Take steps to ensure that questions display similarly across different devices, platforms, browsers, and user settings

Guideline 9.4:   Offer a questionnaire optimized for mobile (browser or app based)

Guideline 9.5:   Decide how many questions will be presented on each web page and how questions will be arranged

Guideline 9.6:   Create interesting and informative welcome and closing screens that will have wide appeal to respondents

Guideline 9.7:   Develop a screen format that emphasizes the respondent rather than the sponsor

Guideline 9.8:   Use a consistent page layout across screens and visually emphasize information that is essential to completing the survey while deemphasizing inessential information

Guideline 9.9:   Allow respondents to back up in the survey

Guideline 9.10:   Do not require responses to questions unless absolutely necessary for the survey

Guideline 9.11:   Design survey-specific and item-specific error messages to help respondents troubleshoot any issues they may encounter

Guideline 9.12:   Evaluate carefully the use of interactive features, balancing improvements in measurement with the impact on respondent burden

Guideline 9.13:   Do not include a graphical progress indicator

Guideline 9.14:   Use audiovisual capabilities of the web sparingly, and evaluate the differential effect they may have on respondents

Guideline 9.15:   Allow respondents to stop the survey and finish completing it at a later time

Guideline 9.16:   Whenever possible, collect paradata that provide feedback on how the respondent interacts with the questionnaire

Guidelines for Web and Mobile Survey Implementation

Guideline 9.17:   To the extent possible, personalize all contacts to respondents

Guideline 9.18:   Consider sending an incentive electronically with the survey request

Guideline 9.19: Use multiple contacts and vary the message across them
Guideline 9.20: Carefully and strategically time all contacts with the population in mind
Guideline 9.21: Keep e-mail contacts short and to the point
Guideline 9.22: Carefully select the sender name and address and the subject line text for e-mail communications
Guideline 9.23: Take steps to ensure that e-mails are not flagged as spam
Guideline 9.24: Assign each sample member a unique ID number
Guideline 9.25: Work within the capabilities and limits of the web server(s)

Quality Control and Testing Guidelines for Web and Mobile Surveys

Guideline 9.26: Obtain expert review and conduct cognitive interviews, experimental evaluations, and pilot studies of web implementation materials and procedures
Guideline 9.27: Test the survey using a variety of devices, platforms, connection speeds, browsers, and user-controlled settings, and test the database to ensure that items are collected and coded correctly
Guideline 9.28: Establish a procedure for dealing with bounced e-mails
Guideline 9.29: Establish procedures for tracking incentives
Guideline 9.30: Establish procedures for dealing with respondent inquiries
Guideline 9.31: Implement a system for monitoring progress and evaluating early completes
Guideline 9.32: Develop procedures to ensure data security

Mail Questionnaires and Implementation

Without a doubt, the Internet and cellular telephone technology have revolutionized the way people in the U.S. communicate, especially the young. Private communications via postal mail have been almost entirely replaced by electronic communications in the form of e-mails, text messages, or updates and messages sent through social networking sites. Postal letters that were once used to keep in touch with distant friends and family members are now rare. Even birthday and holiday cards sent through the mail have been replaced with electronic versions that can be e-mailed or posted to one's wall.

With this change has come a tendency among many surveyors to abandon mail as a survey mode. Many adamantly argue that people with a clear preference for electronic communication in other parts of their life will be unwilling to complete a paper survey and return it by mail. They argue that people, especially the young, will be more likely to complete a web survey or will prefer to answer surveys via an app on their smartphone. They are wrong.

A number of recent studies have shown that mail surveys can achieve reasonable response rates. For example, in 2007 we surveyed residents of two adjacent cities in Washington and Idaho about the quality of life in their community using a mail survey. With a $5 prepaid incentive and four mailings, we achieved a 70% response rate (Smyth, Dillman, Christian, & O'Neill, 2010). In 2009, one of us surveyed Nebraska residents about the quality of life in that state. This survey used five mailings but no incentive and yielded a 54% response rate (Olson, Smyth, & Wood, 2012). In a 2008 survey of Washington State residents about community satisfaction and quality of life issues and a 2009 survey in the same state about economic conditions, 57% and 59%, respectively, responded to the mail survey. Both of these surveys utilized a $5 incentive and four mailings (Messer & Dillman, 2011). Finally, a 2012 survey of Washington residents about water issues in their state yielded a 53% response rate. A parallel survey of Nebraska residents about water issues in Nebraska yielded a 58% response rate. Both of these surveys used four mailings with a $4 prepaid incentive and an additional $2 incentive included with the third mailing (Edwards, Dillman, & Smyth, 2013a, 2013b).

Each of these studies demonstrates that when carefully planned and implemented, mail surveys can do reasonably well and achieve response rates of 50% or higher. Other research has also shown that when respondents are given a choice of answering by mail or another mode, they most commonly choose mail, at least when the paper questionnaire is included with the mailing. For example, in an experimental treatment in our survey of residents from the two adjacent cities in Washington and Idaho, we gave sample members the choice of answering by mail or web. Half answered by mail and only 13% answered by web (Smyth et al., 2010). In an earlier study, sample members to a 1993 national test Census conducted by the U.S. Census Bureau were given the option of responding by mail or calling in to respond by telephone. In this case, about 64% responded by mail and only 6% by telephone (Dillman, West, & Clark, 1994).

These studies indicate that people are willing to complete well-designed mail surveys, and many prefer responding to a paper questionnaire than to other modes. But even those who claim to prefer other modes seem willing to complete mail surveys (Olson et al., 2012), as discussed more in Guideline 11.14. Also, the delivery sequence file (DSF) discussed in Chapter 3 provides good coverage of households in the United States, making mail surveys of the general public quite effective. But in addition to asking people to respond by mail, each of these studies had a number of other characteristics that contributed to their success. Most of them used prepaid incentives but some did not. They used different numbers of mailings and the sponsoring organization differed across them. They each also differed in appearance and how they were packaged and delivered to sample members.

In this chapter, we focus on how to design effective mail-only surveys like those just described. This includes considerations for designing mail question- naires that have not been covered in the previous chapters and discussion of how to field that questionnaire in ways that will maximize response rates and reduce nonresponse error. While we focus heavily on mail surveys (i.e., paper surveys that will be delivered via postal mail), the questionnaire design guidelines we provide apply equally well for paper surveys that will be delivered through means other than postal mail (e.g., paper and pencil intercept surveys or those administered in a classroom setting).

GUIDELINES FOR DESIGNING PAPER QUESTIONNAIRES

When the first edition of this book was published in 1978, it was quite difficult to use graphical design features effectively to guide respondents because paper questionnaires were typically produced in black and white using typewriters. Ver- tical spacing, leader dots, and hand-drawn lines were among the few features that could be used in a design. Rapid computer and printer technological advancement means we now have a whole host of graphical possibilities at our fingertips, includ- ing, among other things, the ability to use color, bolding, font variation, graphics, and shading in the design of our questionnaires. We can even customize paper questionnaires by inserting variable information into them while they are being printed, resulting in each respondent getting a unique questionnaire. Thus, we now have choices that were considered impossible not long ago.

However, paper surveys also have certain limitations that distinguish this mode from others. They lack the computerization and interviewers of other modes, meaning we have to communicate to respondents how to follow skip instructions on their own and it is not possible to incorporate answers to earlier questions into later questions in helpful ways. Nor is it possible to provide automatic totals or feedback when answers to questions are inconsistent with answers to previous items (e.g., when the total number of people in the household is inconsistent with the number of people enumerated). In addition, it is easy for paper respondents to peruse the entire questionnaire to get a sense of its length and the topics covered and to answer questions out of the intended order. These limitations mean we have to be very strategic on our design of paper surveys in order to help respondents get through them as we intend.

Guideline 10.1: Determine Whether Keypunching or Optical Imaging and Scanning Will Be Used, and Assess the Limitations That May Impose on Designing and Processing Questionnaires

Keypunching (i.e., entering the data from a questionnaire into an electronic database) has become an increasingly significant cost for those using paper questionnaires. It is now possible to avoid much of that cost by using software to design, scan, and process questionnaires optically. Current optical scanning options scan an image of the entire questionnaire into a computer and then read the marks on the page into a data spreadsheet. A threshold can be set for entering or flagging items. For example, if the software is not 99% (or 95% or 90%) sure of the intention of a mark (i.e., that it is intended for a specific answer space or what letter or number it is), it will flag the case to be looked at and interpreted by a human. In this way, most of the data entry can be handled by software, with people only having to intervene on the most difficult cases, saving time and money at the data-entry stage. Whereas in the past the optical scanning software and hardware severely restricted questionnaire design, new systems allow much more design flexibility.

Although different software packages require different kinds of marks, it is important to recognize that the shape and size of spaces one provides send a message about what kind of mark is desired. For example, as shown in Figure 10.1, a small circle (or oval) encourages respondents to fill in the space entirely with a pencil or pen, whereas large ovals encourage ticks or check marks. Check marks are a preferred mark in some cultures because of Xs being associated with receiving a bad mark in school. When one wants respondents to use an X, as is desired in other cultures, a square box should be provided. However, if this box is too small, it will encourage the use of check marks as respondents attempt to "hit" the small box with the bottom of the check mark. Such marks are often problematic for processing because of their less controlled nature, which results in the long line after the point reversal, interfering with the reading of nearby answer spaces. In addition, intensive observation of completed questionnaires has revealed that rectangles encourage the use of check marks that produce similar interference with nearby response areas.

A significant barrier to the early development of scannable questionnaires was the entrenched belief that respondent handwriting would be too divergent to ever allow software to read it effectively. In retrospect this turned out to be a case of defining a problem incorrectly. Rather than avoiding scanning, respondents just needed to be encouraged to write more clearly, for example, by printing instead of using cursive. The use of narrow lines or tick marks to segment answer boxes into a series of connected one-character spaces encourages people to print letters rather than use cursive (Dillman, 1995). It has also been observed that the use of colored backgrounds to surround white answer spaces encourages further improvements in writing by helping people stay inside the answer spaces. Likewise, it is important

FIGURE 10.1 Graphical designs of answer spaces that affect respondent writing and make optical scanning more effective.

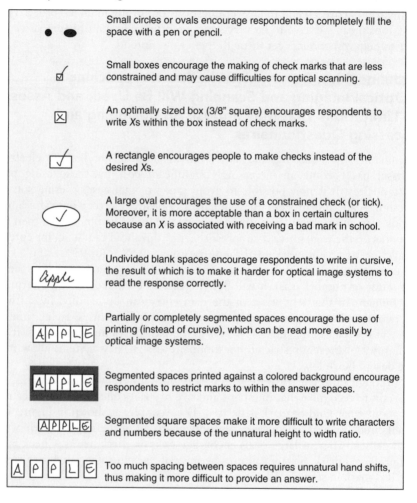

that spaces for printed characters and numbers have greater height than width to accommodate people's natural way of writing. Thus, good questionnaire design can encourage people to write in a way that facilitates software accurately reading characters, words, and numbers (these practices can also help human data enterers in the event that scanning is not used). The recording and processing of longer responses to open-ended questions is facilitated by providing larger blank spaces in which people can write their responses. Once the entire field is imaged into a computer, a trained data entry person can simply process all of the answers to a particular question as a group, typing or coding one answer after another (Dillman, 2000).

If one does not have the equipment for optical scanning or decides to use hand data entry for other reasons, it is important to implement quality control procedures. The most common of these is conducting double entry (i.e., the data are keyed in twice). The two sets of data are compared to catch possible keying errors. Several software packages are available to facilitate this process and offer the advantage of working in pre-created forms rather than spreadsheets where one has to make sure to enter information into the correct row and column and mistakes are easily made.

Guideline 10.2: Construct Paper Questionnaires in Booklet Formats, and Choose Physical Dimensions Based Upon Printing and Mailing Considerations

To put it simply, questionnaires should be presented in conventional formats that people are used to handling when reading several pages of information. In the United States, the most common format is a book or booklet with pages. People are used to opening booklets and reading from left to right and top to bottom as well as to turning pages from right to left, and more importantly, to reading both sides of every page. This is not always the case with other formats. Stapling in the upper left corner of pages or using multiple folds (Z folds or accordion folds) should be avoided as doing so often leads to entire pages of questions being overlooked.

When working on the U.S. Decennial Census in the 1990s, one of us was asked to design alternative single-page forms that could be unfolded so that answers to all of the questions could be scanned in a single operation. Although many formats were extensively tested (including accordion folds, soft-folds [first in half and then in quarters], and a booklet with a single fold-out page), none worked as well as a simple booklet (Dillman, Jackson, Pavlov, & Schaefer, 1998). After observing pages left blank and refolded questionnaires that would not fit into envelopes, one colleague made the amusing but accurate observation that when questionnaires look like maps, people treat them like maps; that is, they are unable to refold them in their original form.

When using booklets, it is important to factor in several issues related to designing, printing, and mailing differently sized booklets. First, it is important to print questions in a portrait rather than landscape format. When the paper is longer than it is wide, it helps to reinforce the vertical format and conventional reading patterns. Second, when one uses booklet construction, pages have to be added or deleted in units of four. Thus, the decision to add or delete a sheet of paper (i.e., four pages) often has consequences for the costs of mailing and printing the questionnaires. Many office printers can now print and staple booklets, although paper size requirements may need to be met. For example, some common printers will print questionnaires on legal-size paper (8.5″ × 14″) with two pages on each side, fold, and then staple the resulting booklet so that individual questionnaire pages are 8.5″ × 7″ (see Figure 10.2). These questionnaires can then be folded lengthwise to fit into regular #10 business mail envelopes (4.125″ × 9.5″), which is an envelope size commonly used for correspondence.

A more common format prints the questionnaire pages using 11″ × 17″ paper, which can then be folded into a conventional 8.5″ × 11″ booklet and fit into 9″ × 12″ clasp envelopes for mailing. This size booklet is more commonly encountered by respondents, and its larger size often makes it easier for respondents to use. If one chooses to go to a professional printer, one's options are expanded, and even more paper and color options may be available. However, it is important to assess the effect of the size of the questionnaire on printing and mailing costs, as discussed in more detail in Guideline 10.14.

FIGURE 10.2 Example of booklet questionnaire made from 8.5″ × 14″ (legal-size) and 11″ × 17″ paper.

Example of booklet made from 8.5″ × 14″ (legal-size) paper

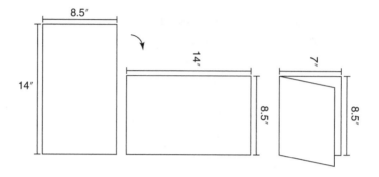

Example of booklet made from 11″ × 17″ paper

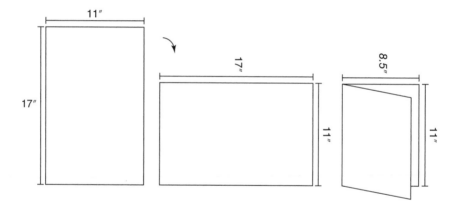

Guideline 10.3: Decide Question Layout and How Questions Will Be Arranged on Each Page

Once the size of the booklet has been decided, the next step is determining the graphical layout of individual pages. In the legal-size folded format shown in Figure 10.2, the questions should be aligned in a single column on each page. If the larger size booklet is used with questionnaire pages that are 8.5″ × 11″, the page can be divided into two columns so that the span of type being read does not extend entirely across the page. The example in Figure 10.3 shows relatively short questions for which the two-column format works well because it allows more questions per page and contributes to more accurate reading and comprehension of each question (see Guideline 6.5).

A one-column format can also be used with the larger size booklet, particularly when longer or more complex questions are included; however, this format can be difficult for some respondents as lines of text extend all the way across the page and a larger eye motion is needed to move from the end of one line to the beginning of the next. One benefit of this format is that it can more closely emulate web survey screens, which are usually constructed with questions that read all the way across the width of the screen. In addition to using a one-column format, the

FIGURE 10.3 Example of double-column pages from an 8.5″ × 11″ booklet questionnaire.

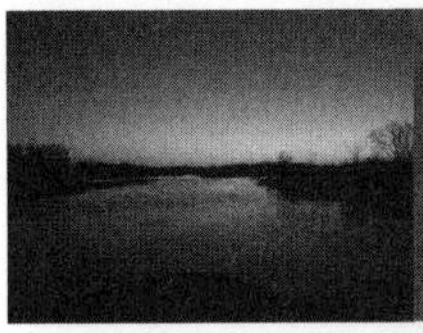

Quality of Life in a Changing Nebraska

Taking a snapshot of issues affecting Nebraskans' quality of life.

START HERE

1. **On a scale from 1 to 11, where 1 is very dissatisfied and 11 is very satisfied, how satisfied are you with your work (job, school, or housework)?**

   ☐

2. **On a scale from 1 to 11, where 1 is very dissatisfied and 11 is very satisfied, how satisfied are you generally with the way you spend your leisure time?**

   ☐

3. **Please think about your relationship to your partner, spouse or date. On a scale from 1 to 11, where 1 is very dissatisfied and 11 is very satisfied, how satisfied are you currently with your relationship?**

   ☐

4. **On a scale from 1 to 11, where 1 is very dissatisfied and 11 is very satisfied, how satisfied are you currently with your life-as-a-whole?**

   ☐

5. **How many years have you lived in Nebraska?**

   ☐ Years lived in Nebraska

6. **How many years have you lived in your community?**

   ☐ Years lived in community

Family

7. **How many adults ages 19 and older are living in your household?**

   ☐ Number of adults living in household

8. **What is your marital status?**

   ☐ Married → **Go to # 10**
   ☐ Never married
   ☐ Widowed
   ☐ Divorced
   ☐ Separated

9. **Are you currently living with someone in a marriage-like relationship?**

   ☐ No
   ☐ Yes

10. **Do you have any children aged 18 or younger at home?**

    ☐ No → **Go to # 13**
    ☐ Yes

11. **If yes, do you think your children will stay in Nebraska when they grow up?**

    ☐ No
    ☐ Yes → **Go to #12**

12. **Do you want your children to stay in Nebraska when they grow up?**

    ☐ No
    ☐ Yes

13. **Do you think that children today will be better off or worse off if they stay in Nebraska?**

    ☐ Better
    ☐ Same
    ☐ Worse

1

example shown in Figure 10.4 encloses each question in a separate region, more similar to how questions would appear in a page-by-page web survey. This format was developed for a mixed-mode survey that is discussed in more depth in Guideline 11.2.

All three of these different formats can be developed using common word processing programs that are available to most surveyors. The examples shown incorporate the guidelines for visually designing questionnaire pages discussed in Chapter 6, although in somewhat different ways.

Grouping questions on one page in paper questionnaires presents both challenges and opportunities. As mentioned previously, there is a considerable risk that when people turn pages, they do not carry over information well from the previous page. As such, related questions, such as a series of queries about one's job

FIGURE 10.3 (continued).

36. If you received a request to do another survey like this one, would you <u>find it most enjoyable answering questions</u> in...

☐ An in-person interview at your home
☐ An interview on your home phone
☐ An interview on your cell phone
☐ A paper survey sent by mail
☐ A survey on the internet

37. In an average year, approximately how many surveys do you think you answer in each of the following ways? If none, enter zero.

In-person interviews at your home ☐

Interviews on your home phone ☐

Interviews on your cell phone ☐

Paper surveys sent by mail ☐

Surveys on the internet ☐

38. Did you receive help from anyone when completing <u>this</u> questionnaire?

☐ No
☐ Yes

About You

39. What is your sex?

☐ Male
☐ Female

40. In what year were you born?

☐ Year born (YYYY)

41. Which income category describes your total family income in the last 12 months?

☐ Under $20,000
☐ $20,000 – $39,999
☐ $40,000 – $59,999
☐ $60,000 – $79,999
☐ $80,000 – $99,999
☐ $100,000 or more

42. What is the highest degree or level of school you have completed?

☐ No diploma
☐ High school diploma / G.E.D.
☐ Some college, but no degree
☐ Technical / Associate / Junior college
☐ Bachelor's degree
☐ Graduate degree

43. What is your ethnicity?

☐ Hispanic or Latino
☐ Not Hispanic or Latino

44. What is your race? Check all that apply.

☐ White
☐ Black or African American
☐ Asian
☐ American Indian or Alaska Native
☐ Native Hawaiian or Other Pacific Islander

45. If you have any additional comments, please enter them here. Feel free to attach more pages.

Thank you!!
Please return your survey in the enclosed envelope or use the following address.

Dr. Kristen Olson
Bureau of Sociological Research
118 Benton Hall
P.O. Box 886102
Lincoln, NE 68588-6102

Unique ID

4

experiences after college graduation, need to be grouped on one page or on two facing pages. In contrast, placing information on different pages allows items to be separated when there is concern about respondents referring back to earlier questions when answering later ones or when surveyors prefer that one question does not immediately impact the context for another related question. Placing questions in individual enclosed regions as done in Figure 10.4 can also discourage respondents from looking back and forth between them. In sum, it is important to contemplate individual page content as both a challenge and an opportunity for which a balanced solution needs to be found. Unfortunately, responding to this challenge is sometimes made more difficult when using booklet designs where two pages are often viewable at a time; however, these facing pages are more conducive for complex series of questions where multiple pages are needed to present all of the questions in the sequence.

FIGURE 10.4 Example of a paper questionnaire designed to emulate a page-by-page web questionnaire for a mixed-mode study (8.5″ × 11″ booklet).

Q1. Approximately how many years have you lived in the Lewiston-Clarkston area?

☐ Years

Q2. Overall, how satisfied are you with living in this area?

○₁ Very satisfied
○₂ Somewhat satisfied
○₃ Neutral
○₄ Somewhat dissatisfied
○₅ Very dissatisfied

○₆ Not sure

Q3. How attached do you feel to the Lewiston-Clarkston area?

○₁ Very attached
○₂ Somewhat attached
○₃ Slightly attached
○₄ Not at all attached

○₅ Not sure

Q4. During the past five years, how much better or worse do you think Lewiston-Clarkston has become as a place to live?

○₁ A lot better
○₂ Somewhat better
○₃ No change
○₄ Somewhat worse
○₅ A lot worse

○₆ Not sure

Q5. How much better or worse do you think the local economy has become in the past five years?

○₁ A lot better
○₂ Somewhat better
○₃ No change
○₄ Somewhat worse
○₅ A lot worse

○₆ Not sure

Q6. How much better or worse do you think the area's natural environment has become in the past five years?

○₁ A lot better
○₂ Somewhat better
○₃ No change
○₄ Somewhat worse
○₅ A lot worse

○₆ Not sure

1

Overall, the most important decisions to make when constructing paper questionnaires are how the questionnaire will be presented to respondents (in a booklet format or not), what size the questionnaire will be, and how the questions will be arranged on the page.

Guideline 10.4: Use Symbols, Contrast, Size, Proximity, and Pagination Effectively When Designing Branching Instructions to Help Respondents Correctly Execute Them

Getting some people to skip questions they should not answer while convincing other respondents not to skip ahead remains one of the most perplexing problems facing mail survey designers. With no computerization or interviewer, respondents must execute skip instructions on their own. Several experiments have been conducted on how best to design such instructions (Gohring & Smyth, 2013; Redline, Dillman, Carley-Baxter, & Creecy, 2005; Redline, Dillman, Dajani, & Scaggs, 2003). Treatments from one of these studies are shown in Figure 10.5.

This experiment was included in a field test of about 12,500 households using the 2000 U.S. Decennial Census Long Form, which contained 53 questions, 19 of which included branching instructions (Redline et al., 2003). In each treatment a combination of factors designed to get people to correctly follow branching instructions were tested. In the control treatment, the response option is followed by an arrow leading to the skip instruction, which is displayed in the same font as the response option. In the prevention method the answer boxes are moved from the left of the answer categories to the right so that the skip instructions could be located within the respondents' foveal view when focusing on the answer box. The arrow and the skip instruction are also displayed in larger, darker print and the question stem is preceded by an instruction reminding respondents to look for a skip instruction. In the detection treatment, the arrow and the skip instruction are also presented in a large, dark font, but here arrows are used next to both response options to direct people from their answer either to the next question or to the skip instruction. In addition, words were used at the beginning of the next question to remind respondents who should and who should not answer it (e.g., "If Yes").

FIGURE 10.5 Examples of different branching instruction designs used in classroom experiment and national census test in the 2000 Decennial Census.

Treatments	Images	Classroom Error Rate	Census Error Rate
Control form: Standard format used in Decennial Census with written instructions	30 a. LAST YEAR, 1999, did this person work at a job or business at any time? ☐ Yes ☐ No → Go to 31 b. How many weeks did this person work in 1999?	22.3%	25.8%
Prevention method: Advanced verbal warning, shift answer box to right, and larger, bolder font	30 Attention: Remember to check for a "Go to" instruction after you answer the question below. a. LAST YEAR, 1999, did this person work at a job or business at any time? Yes ☐ No ☐ → **Go to 31** b. How many weeks did this person work in 1999?	11.3%	17.5%
Detection method: Arrows, larger and bolder fonts, and verbal feedback	30 a. LAST YEAR, 1999, did this person work at a job or business at any time? ☐ Yes ☐ No → **Go to 31** b. (If Yes) How many weeks did this person work in 1999? Count paid vacation, paid sick leave, and military	12.3%	21.7%

* Statistically significant difference in error rates between the control form and each of the two methods ($p < .01$).
Note. Error rates shown here include commission errors (not skipping ahead when directed) and omission errors (skipping ahead when not directed). Advanced verbal warning used only in the Classroom Experiment.
Source: Adapted from "Improving Navigational Performance in U.S. Census 2000 by Altering the Visual Administered Languages of Branching Instructions," by C. D. Redline, D. A. Dillman, A. N. Dajan and M. A. Scaggs, 2003, *Journal of Official Statistics, 19*, 403–419.

The detection method reduced the proportion of branching errors by one third, lowering commission errors (i.e., not skipping ahead when directed to do so) from 21% to 13% and omission errors (i.e., skipping ahead when not directed to do so) from 5% to 4%. The total error rates (commission and omission error rates combined) were lower for both the detection and prevention groups compared to the control group, where errors were made nearly 26% of the time (see Figure 10.5). The conclusions drawn from these experiments were that both of these methods were effective in helping respondents follow the desired navigational path. This research also revealed that branching instructions would most likely be ignored when they extended from one page to the next (Redline et al., 2005). Thus, we work hard to avoid having the last question on a page branch any respondent somewhere other than to the first question on the next page. We will even slightly reorder questions if needed to avoid that situation. In addition to helping better understand ways to design skip instructions, this research provides evidence of the substantial effects that the combined use of symbols, wording, size, contrast, and proximity can have on task-oriented processing.

Figure 10.6 shows an example of another way to format skip instructions. The top panel shows a typical skip instruction format. In the bottom panel, the response options are reversed so that "no" is listed first and "yes" is listed second. This reversal allows for the placement of arrows to the right of both response options (i.e., in the natural reading direction) that lead to the appropriate next question. This format also incorporates indentation that visually sets the follow-up question (i.e., the question that only a subset of respondents will answer) apart from the main pathway through the questionnaire thereby establishing a hierarchy in the questions. In an experimental test, this format significantly reduced skip errors in three of six comparisons (Gohring & Smyth, 2013). Note that if response options are reversed to accommodate an item with a skip instruction in this way, they should also be reversed on all other items of this nature (i.e., yes/no questions in this case) throughout the survey to avoid unnecessary inconsistencies in the design.

Guideline 10.5: Create Interesting and Informative Front and Back Cover Pages That Will Have Wide Appeal to Respondents

Imagine you come home one day and find a questionnaire enclosed with your utility bill. A cover letter very nicely explains that the survey is part of a study aimed at finding out people's perceptions and feelings about "green" or energy efficient homes. You unfold the survey and are greeted with the title, "Determining the Largest Energy Offenders in Existing Residential Structures." Would you fill it out? Would you fear that you might be arrested or otherwise punished if you gave the wrong answers? What if there was another survey in the mail that day titled, "The Continuous Measurement Survey." Would this survey interest you? Would you know what it was about? Would you complete it?

Both of these examples illustrate a tendency that is common among surveyors both big and small: giving their surveys titles that describe the purpose from the perspective of the surveyors but that have no meaning whatsoever (or worse yet, negative meaning) to respondents. The first comes from a survey a PhD student was proposing for his dissertation. In this case, we advised the student to find a title that would have more appeal and would be less threatening; he wisely changed it to,

FIGURE 10.6 Example of using indentation to support a skip instruction.

__Skip instruction without indentation__

4. Have you had interaction with an employee of the Nebraska Department of Roads within the past year?
   - ☐ Yes
   - ☐ No → **Go to question #6**

5. How courteous was the employee?
   - ☐ Very courteous
   - ☐ Somewhat courteous
   - ☐ A little courteous
   - ☐ Not at all courteous

6. How satisfied or dissatisfied are you with the Nebraska state highway system?
   - ☐ Very satisfied
   - ☐ Somewhat satisfied
   - ☐ Neutral
   - ☐ Somewhat dissatisfied
   - ☐ Very dissatisfied

__Skip instruction with indentation__

4. Have you had interaction with an employee of the Nebraska Department of Roads within the past year?
   - ☐ No → **Go to question #6**
   - ☐ Yes ⌐

        5. How courteous was the employee?
           - ☐ Very courteous
           - ☐ Somewhat courteous
           - ☐ A little courteous
           - ☐ Not at all courteous

6. How satisfied or dissatisfied are you with the Nebraska state highway system?
   - ☐ Very satisfied
   - ☐ Somewhat satisfied
   - ☐ Neutral
   - ☐ Somewhat dissatisfied
   - ☐ Very dissatisfied

"Energy Use in Rural America." The second example comes from the U.S. Census Bureau's efforts in the 1990s to replace the Decennial Census Long Form, which collected detailed information from one in six U.S. households every 10 years, with a survey that would collect this information from a few hundred thousand households on a yearly basis. The results of this survey are incredibly important for the United States because it produces reliable demographic estimates and information related to education, occupations, commuting behavior, and income for most cities and counties in the United States, except for small ones. Getting good response is absolutely essential. When it was pointed out to the director of the Census Bureau that the title "The Continuous Measurement Survey" would be unappealing to most people, it was retitled "The American Community Survey," which it remains today.

The survey title needs to describe what a survey is about but also have broad appeal to the sample members who receive it. At the same time, care must be taken not to use a title that makes the questionnaire appeal to some types of people while being a turn-off to others. Thus, one would not title a survey on political views "The Problems With the Current Presidential Administration." That would seem likely to attract people who do not like the president and turn off those who do.

In addition to a good title, it is important to design questionnaire covers that look interesting and appeal to as wide of a spectrum of the survey population as possible. The front cover should have a clear title that respondents can understand, identify the sponsor, and encourage respondents to want to complete the survey. The back cover should express gratitude toward respondents for the effort they have expended, give them a place to add any additional comments, and provide a return address. The comment space is offered as a courtesy so that respondents have a chance to voice thoughts that are important to them after having answered all the questions that were important to the surveyor. In addition, we have found information provided in this space to be of great value for understanding respondents' perspectives on substantive issues as well as on the survey itself and therefore include it on nearly all of our surveys. We have also found that providing the return address is important for paper questionnaires that will be returned by mail because some people will misplace the return envelope we enclose. Finally, it is important for the questionnaire covers to connect to the other implementation materials such as the cover letters.

Figure 10.7 shows an example of a cover page we designed to appeal to those sampled for a survey of residents of the state of Nebraska about water and water management (Edwards et al., 2013a). The title of this survey was simply "Water in Nebraska." The front cover included six photos related to water, one of which is a sandhill crane. The sandhill crane is widely recognized in Nebraska because every year about 500,000 of these cranes descend on the Platte River in the center of the state to feed for about five weeks during their annual migration (Nebraska Game and Parks, 2013), creating a natural spectacle that draws tourists from around the world. The cover also included a map of the state, a brief statement describing the study in general terms, and contact information for the sponsor. The back cover of the questionnaire thanked respondents for completing the questionnaire, provided an opportunity for them to add any additional comments about the study, and listed contact information in case of questions. These cover pages enclosed 10 pages of questions.

Figure 10.8 shows a very similar cover page. The difference is that this survey was designed to understand people's opinions on water and water management in the state of Washington (Edwards et al., 2013b). As a result, the Nebraska map is replaced with a map of Washington State, and the image of the sandhill crane is replaced with an image of migrating salmon. The title is also altered to refer to Washington. These changes help tailor the questionnaire to make it much more appealing and salient to Washington residents.

When a full page can be devoted to creating front and back cover pages such as these, doing so is advisable; however, in many instances there is not enough space to do so. Figure 10.3 showed the first and last pages of a questionnaire that was only four pages long. In this case, it was not possible to devote two full pages to opening and closing covers. Instead, the front cover was reduced to an attractive banner at the top of the first page and all of the elements of a closing page were included at the end of the questionnaire.

FIGURE 10.7 Examples of interesting and appealing front and back cover pages for a survey about water and water management in Nebraska.

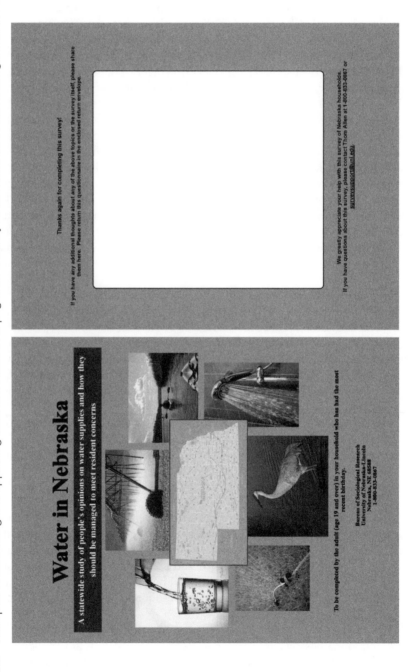

FIGURE 10.8 Examples of interesting and appealing front and back cover pages for a survey about water and water management in Washington.

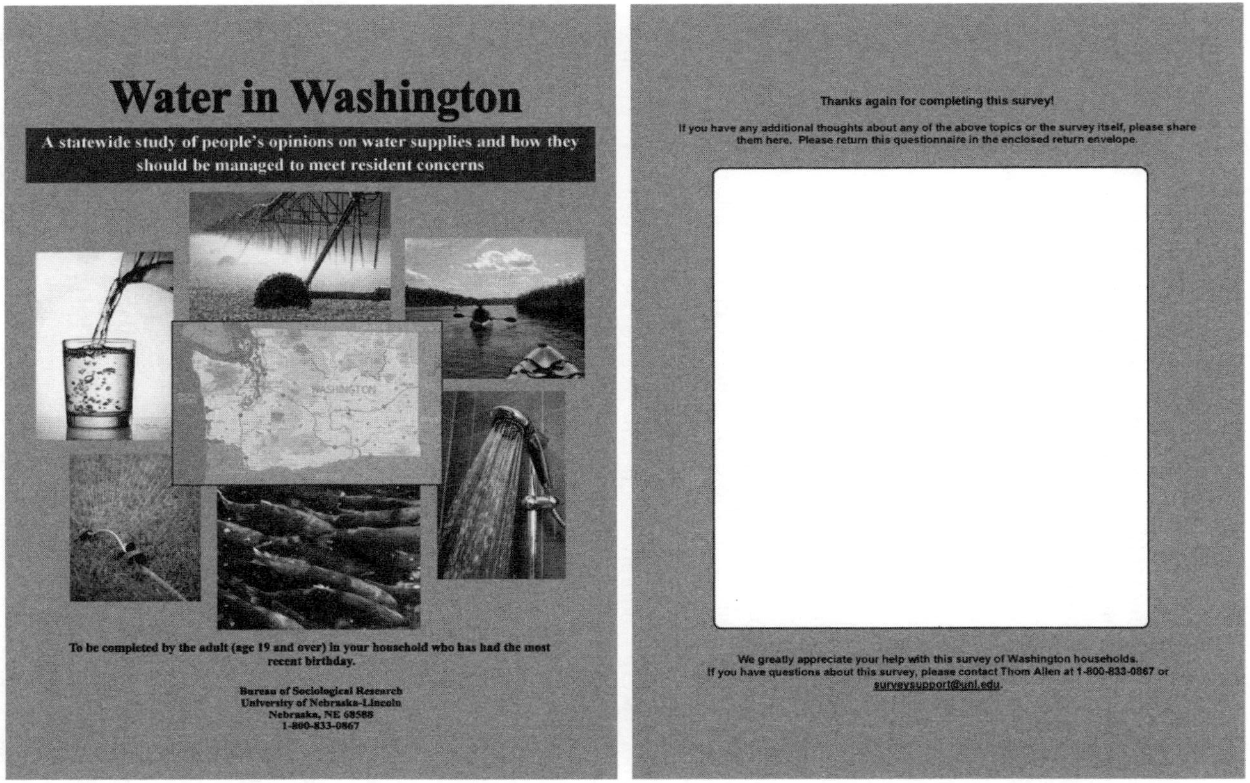

Water in Washington

A statewide study of people's opinions on water supplies and how they should be managed to meet resident concerns

To be completed by the adult (age 19 and over) in your household who has had the most recent birthday.

Bureau of Sociological Research
University of Nebraska–Lincoln
Nebraska, NE 68588
1-800-833-0867

Thanks again for completing this survey!

If you have any additional thoughts about any of the above topics or the survey itself, please share them here. Please return this questionnaire in the enclosed return envelope.

We greatly appreciate your help with this survey of Washington households.
If you have questions about this survey, please contact Thom Allen at 1-800-833-0867 or surveysupport@unl.edu.

GUIDELINES FOR IMPLEMENTING MAIL QUESTIONNAIRES

The surveys we mentioned in the introduction to this chapter all had response rates ranging from 50% to 70%. Their success was due in large part to the fact that they had questionnaires designed in the ways discussed in this and previous chapters. But it was also because the implementation procedures for these studies were carefully designed and planned. For each of them, an enormous amount of effort was devoted to developing multiple aspects of the survey implementation as a means to create appeal for many different types of sample members. The success of these studies was not due to any one characteristic or element of the survey or implementation; rather, it reflects a whole package of design and implementation decisions, the goals of which were to remove barriers to response and motivate as many sample members to complete the questionnaire as possible (i.e., to minimize costs, maximize rewards, and promote trust). The details of implementation are essential elements in the success of a mail survey and therefore must receive considerable thought and planning. The survey will not be successful if the implementation plan and materials are hastily thrown together at the last minute.

We turn now to guidelines for mail survey implementation designed to help surveys appeal to as many sample members as possible. We utilize the survey discussed briefly in Guideline 10.5 and shown in Figure 10.7 as an example that will illustrate how many of these guidelines can be implemented. In an effort to examine different possibilities for conducting general population surveys, the researchers designed several experimental treatments for this survey and sampled households were randomly assigned to receive one of them. We will focus here on one of those designs in which sample members were asked to complete a mail survey. Other mixed-mode designs for this study are discussed in Chapter 11.

The sample for the mail survey was comprised of a list of 600 Nebraska residential addresses drawn at random from the U.S. Postal Service DSF described in Chapter 3. On April 13, 2012, sampled addresses were sent by postal mail a request to respond to the 12-page (8.5″ × 11″) booklet questionnaire shown in Figure 10.7. This questionnaire contained 47 questions that requested up to 132 responses on issues related to water use and governance in the state of Nebraska. Over the course of the next month sampled addresses were sent three additional contacts, all by postal mail, to try to encourage them to respond. In the end, 58% of sample members responded to this survey. Results from this study were sufficiently promising that, in many cases the guidelines we present in this chapter use examples from it. Nevertheless, the guidelines remain broad enough to be applied in a wide variety of survey situations.

Guideline 10.6: To the Extent Possible, Personalize All Contacts to Respondents (Even When Names Are Unavailable)

Social and behavioral scientists have long known that in emergency situations, the more bystanders there are, the less likely anyone is to step forward and help out. It is for this reason that many first aid courses emphasize the importance of personally singling out individuals to make requests for help: "You, go call 911!" Although less dramatic, the goal of personalizing survey contacts is quite similar: to draw the respondent out of the group. Personalization with a person's name can make a survey request feel less like a form letter and reduce the social distance between the surveyor and the sample member. If the request is not personalized, it is very easy for respondents to ignore it, using the rationale that others in the group will surely respond. Moreover, personalization can be used to establish the authenticity of the survey sponsor and the survey itself and to gain the trust of respondents, both of which should improve the likelihood of response.

Correspondence can be personalized in many ways—the use of real letterhead printed on high-quality paper, names instead of a preprinted salutation of "Dear Resident," blue ink signatures, or simply replacement mailings with the message "To the best of our knowledge you have not yet responded." Thus, in addition to using names when they are available, it is also important to look for other ways to personalize.

In the Water in Nebraska study, the use of the address-based sampling frame meant that only addresses and not individual names were available, yet personalization played heavily in the design. The survey was strongly personalized to the state through the use of recognizable graphics. This was further enhanced through the use of questions that made meaningful reference to specific issues and events that occurred in Nebraska, in particular the Ogallala Aquifer and the proposed TransCanada Keystone XL oil pipeline. In addition, the request to complete the survey was framed as a request for help that only residents of this state could provide. Finally, rather than using the generic "Dear Resident" salutation, a more personalized salutation that made mention of the sample members' location was used (e.g., "Dear Lincoln Resident"—see Figure 10.10, which is further discussed later, under "The Tailored Design of Contacts for the Water in Nebraska Study").

However, because it is easy to use computer technology to insert information into form letters and e-mails, it is possible and very easy to over-personalize, as in the following example: "Dear Jolene Smyth, I am writing to inform you that the XYZ Company has created a new Kayak rack that will hold both of the Sundance Kayaks you won in the Nebraska Great Parks Pursuit in 2009 and will fit your 1997 Chevy Silverado perfectly. This rack will allow you to pack your two Trek mountain bikes and other camping gear in the truck bed so you can take everything you need along with you your annual June camping trip from Lincoln, Nebraska, to Lake McConaughy." Such letters are impersonal precisely because of the extreme effort made to insert personal references. Therefore, it is important to strike a balance between producing generic contacts that could be sent to anyone and overpersonalizing contacts in a way that makes them seem intrusive. Personalization might best be thought of as what one would do in a letter sent to a business acquaintance who is not well known. It provides the look and feel of being from a real person rather than a carefully programmed computer, but it maintains professional distance.

A significant body of research has found such personalization to be an effective means for modestly increasing response to mail surveys. As just one example, Dillman et al. (2007) reported the results of nine experiments testing the effects in mail surveys of contacts that are personalized (insertion of name and address, use of sponsor's stationery, and blue ink signatures in each letter) versus nonpersonalized (mass-copied letters with group salutations). The surveys included one nationwide survey, a statewide survey, three county or city surveys, and four surveys of special interest groups (e.g., Oregon ATV owners, New Hampshire mountain bikers, etc.). In the general population surveys, the personalization had a consistent and modest impact on response rates, increasing them from 3 to 12 percentage points. The effects of personalization in the surveys of special interest groups were less clear, however. In some cases appealing to the person's special interest (e.g., Dear ATV Owner), which may be considered a different kind of personalization, resulted in higher response than using the person's name, but this was not always the case and there was no predictable pattern in the data for when this effect may occur.

We mentioned earlier that we were unable to use sample members' names in the salutation of the contacts for the Water in Nebraska study, but even if we did have names, we would not have used them in this particular survey because we were using a within-household selection method to choose a respondent from within each household. The use of specific names when this is being done is inadvisable because it encourages the named person to take ownership of and answer the questionnaire rather than following the within-household selection instructions.

When there is no preexisting relationship between the sender and receiver but the gender is known, salutations such as "Dear Ms. Adamson" or "Dear Mr. Adamson" are appropriate. However, it is increasingly difficult to determine gender from a name (e.g., Pat, Chris, Kelly, Terry, etc.), and many names appear simply as initials. In such cases, the surveyor should omit the salutation rather than risk offending the recipient. If a personalized salutation cannot be used because names are not available or because a within-household selection method is being employed, every attempt should be made to personalize in the other ways discussed previously.

As more and more daily interactions occur with computers (i.e., automatic teller machines, self-check-out at stores, global positioning system units that give driving directions, etc.) or products of computers (e.g., mass-produced letters and questionnaires), we believe that true authentic personalization will become more rare, thus making it even more important and effective when it is achieved. Inasmuch as authenticity and trust are integral parts of the social exchange method, so too is personalization a central component of tailored design.

Guideline 10.7: Send a Token of Appreciation With the Survey Request

One of the largest contributors to improved response rates, second only to multiple contacts (to be discussed later), is the appropriate use of prepaid token financial incentives. The token incentive serves two functions. It brings social exchange into play and encourages respondents to reciprocate by completing the survey. Equally important, though, it is a novel and unexpected gesture that can get sample members to read and contemplate the survey materials rather than just tossing them away, giving surveyors another chance to make their case. Some examples of the effectiveness of various advance incentives on student and general public populations can be seen in Figure 10.9.

Perhaps more important than its influence on response rates is the effect that a token financial incentive has on nonresponse bias. Research is beginning to demonstrate that such incentives reduce nonresponse bias by pulling in respondents who otherwise might not answer the questionnaire.

For example, Groves et al. (2006) found that respondents who reported high interest in birding were more likely than those who were uninterested in birding to respond to a mail questionnaire about birding, thus artificially inflating estimates of the prevalence of this activity among the population. When the surveyors included a prepaid token financial incentive with their survey request, however, more respondents who were relatively uninterested in birding completed the questionnaire, thus adjusting estimates of its prevalence down toward what one might expect the true value to be.

FIGURE 10.9 Examples of the effects of advance token incentives in mail surveys.

Population (year, survey director)	Sample Size	Experimental Groups	Response Rate
Oregon State University students who left the College of Agricultural Sciences without graduating (1997, Lesser)	133 130 125	$0 $2 Check $2 Bill	28% 44% 53%
Recent graduates of the College of Agricultural Sciences at Oregon State University (1998, Lesser)	129 135 141	$0 $2 Bill $5 Bill	59% 67% 81%
Oregon State University distance education students (1997, Lesser)	249 91 92 87 97	$0 $2 Check $2 Bill $5 Check $5 Bill	20% 25% 32% 31% 32%
Oregon State University June 1997 graduates (1998, Lesser)	231 234	$0 $2 Bill	52% 65%
New residents of Washington who obtained a state driver's license (1994, Dillman)	368 357	$0 $2 Bill	44% 63%
New residents in Iowa who obtained an Iowa state driver's license (1997, Lorenz)	317 313 313	$0 $2 Singles $2 Bill	42% 70% 73%
New residents of Idaho aged 50 to 70 (1996, Carlson)	526 526 524	$0 $2 Bill $300 Lottery	53% 72% 58%
Centre County Pennsylvania Residents (1998, Willits)	470 288	$0 $2 Bill	39% 62%

Source: *Quantifying the Influence of Incentives on Mail Survey Response Rates and Nonresponse Bias*, by V. M. Lesser, D. A. Dillman, J. Carlson, F. Lorenz, R. Mason, and F. Willits, 2001, Atlanta, GA: American Statistical Association. Retrieved from http://www.sesrc.wsu.edu/dillman

In an effort to save valuable resources, many surveyors opt to utilize promised or contingent incentives (i.e., payments sent after the questionnaire is completed and returned, also known as post incentives) instead of advance incentives. However, the question of advance versus promised incentives is one for which the evidence is quite clear. Token financial incentives included with the original survey request have been shown to be significantly more effective than much larger payments promised to respondents after they complete their questionnaires. As just one example, James and Bolstein (1992) achieved a 71% response rate with a four-contact response strategy including a $1 prepaid incentive but only a 57% response rate with the same contact strategy and a promised payment of $50 for those returning questionnaires. Likewise, in a meta-analysis of 38 experimental studies, Church (1993) found no statistically significant effect of promised incentives.

The problem with promised incentives is that many people view them as financial remuneration for answering a survey: "If you complete this questionnaire,

I will pay you for it." In an economic exchange of this kind, if the price is too low or the person simply is not interested in doing the survey at any price, it is culturally acceptable not to respond. In contrast, token incentives provided in advance change the terms of exchange from economic to social, as discussed in Chapter 2. Sending a small amount of money with the questionnaire is a goodwill gesture that puts the sponsor and questionnaire in a positive light, helps get letters read so that respondents have more information on which to base their response decision, and sets the stage for the respondent to reciprocate by completing the questionnaire.

Because the incentive is meant to invoke a social exchange rather than a financial exchange, the value of the incentive can be kept quite small. From a practical standpoint, $1 is the smallest amount one can easily send because coinage is heavy and difficult to process. Some studies have found that larger amounts are more effective (Trussell & Lavrakas, 2004), but there are clearly diminished returns with far more of an increase coming from the first dollar than from 5 or 10 times that amount. Based on both evidence and experience, we recommend an incentive amount between $1 and $5 for surveys of most populations. One exception is with physicians—for whom incentives of $25 to $100 have been found to be effective—but this is a very specialized population (VanGeest, Johnson, & Welch, 2007).

Most studies offer cash incentives only once during the data collection sequence. However, a recent test of sending a second $5 incentive to nonresponding households in a statewide survey (after already sending $5 with the initial request) resulted in increasing the response rate 9 percentage points from 59% to 68% (Messer & Dillman, 2011). The additional $5 incentive was included in the third contact that also contained a second copy of the questionnaire. A test conducted 1 year earlier in a similar statewide survey on a different topic sent a $5 incentive only in the first contact, and produced a 13 percentage point improvement in response over sending no incentive, from 39% to 52% (Messer & Dillman, 2011). Our interest in considering the use of a second cash incentive stems from the possibility that the second incentive will stimulate the careful reading and evaluation by the recipient of the follow-up survey request. Increasingly, we expect to use different kinds of appeals in later letters, in order to increase the likelihood that people underrepresented in the early returns will respond. Using incentives of this nature more than once represents an important issue for which additional research is needed. We return to this issue in a mixed-mode context in Guideline 11.13, where we believe it takes on additional significance.

Many surveyors include nonmonetary, material incentives rather than cash incentives with their questionnaires. In some cases they use cash cards or gift cards to approximate a cash incentive. Other incentives that have been used to encourage response are packets of coffee, chocolate, ballpoint pens, regional park passes, phone cards, postage stamps, key rings, tea bags, and trading stamps, among other things. The reasons for opting to send such token gifts in lieu of a cash incentive vary widely. In some cases, material incentives are used because surveyors are bound by rules prohibiting them from sending cash. For example, cash cannot be sent through the mail in New Zealand or the Netherlands. In other cases, surveyors have opted to send material incentives because they can be bought in bulk, which saves money (e.g., buying a large number of $5 phone cards for $2.50 each; Teisl, Roe, & Vayda, 2005) or because the surveyor can be refunded for unused cash cards, whereas cash itself is gone for good once it is mailed (Bailey, Lavrakas, & Bennett, 2007).

The research, however, is consistent on the effects of such cash card and material incentives: They generally do increase response rates, but not as much as a small prepaid cash incentive. The aforementioned meta-analysis by Church (1993) found that material incentives improved response rates by 8 percentage points compared with 19 percentage points for token financial incentives. Likewise, Bailey et al. (2007) found that even a cash card worth twice the value resulted in significantly lower response rates than a $5 cash incentive. In addition, in a heterogeneous sample, it may be difficult to find a material incentive that will appeal similarly to everyone in the sample in the way that cash might. For example, one study in New Zealand found that chocolate increased response among young respondents, whereas postage stamps increased response among older respondents (Gendall & Healey, 2007). Thus, when it is allowable, providing a small token cash incentive has the largest effect on response rates, but when cash cannot be used, providing carefully selected material incentives can be beneficial.

Another incentive that has increased in popularity among surveyors is lotteries or prize drawings where respondents have a chance to win large-ticket items such as iPads or airline tickets. However, it appears that these offers have relatively small, if any, effects on response. A comparison by Carlson (see Figure 10.9) of a $2 bill, a chance to win $300 in a lottery, and no incentive in a survey of new residents of Idaho resulted in a response rate of 53% for the control group compared to 58% for the lottery and 73% for the cash incentive. Another study that compared lotteries, cash, and contributions to charities showed that only prepaid cash incentives made a difference in response rates (Warriner, Goyder, Gjertsen, Hohner, & McSpurren, 1996). In another study, high school students were randomly assigned to experimental treatments offering them no incentive or one of four lottery conditions in which the prizes were a $50, $100, $150, or $200 Amazon.com gift certificate. On average across the incentive groups, 16% responded, which is only a slight and nonsignificant increase compared to the 14% who responded in the no-incentive control group (Porter & Whitcomb, 2003). Taken together, this research strongly suggests that even if prizes or lotteries can boost response a small amount, the effect when compared to sending a token cash incentive is quite small.

In summary, the primary function of incentives, whether sent with the initial request or in a follow-up request, is to invoke a sense of reciprocal obligation. In addition, their presence with the cover letter (see Guideline 10.9) increases the likelihood that one's carefully constructed cover letter will be carefully read and considered.

Guideline 10.8: Send a Postage Paid Return Envelope With the Questionnaire

A postage paid return envelope is a very important element to be included whenever a paper questionnaire to be returned by mail is sent to sample members. Within the social exchange framework, such an envelope serves three functions. First, it reduces costs to the respondent by making the return of the questionnaire as easy as possible. She does not have to expend her own time and resources to find an envelope and stamp. Second, it encourages trust that the questionnaire is important, perhaps encouraging the respondent to think "Why else would this person have sent a stamped envelope that I can use for something else?" Third, sending a real stamp represents a goodwill gesture; the sender has sent something of value that the recipient can use for some other purpose if she likes. In addition, it is culturally difficult for many people to throw away something that has any monetary value. As a result, the enclosure of a stamped reply envelope seems likely to encourage the sample member to go ahead and complete the survey or at least to keep it around until the thank you postcard arrives.

One may be tempted to save money by using business reply envelopes rather than blank envelopes with real stamps. Such envelopes are processed by the U.S. Postal Service for a small annual charge for the permit necessary to use this service, and postage is paid only for envelopes that are returned. The use of business reply envelopes is becoming so common that receiving one will not seem unordinary. Further, there is evidence that using a stamped envelope can improve response rates by a few percentage points over sending a business reply envelope (Armstrong & Lusk, 1987; Dillman, Clark, & Sinclair, 1995; Tarnai, Schultz, Solet, & Pfingst, 2012). Responses also tend to come in more quickly with stamped envelopes, sometimes providing an advantage of 5 to 7 percentage points early in the fielding process so fewer incoming questionnaires cross in the mail with outgoing replacement questionnaires. Business reply envelopes are processed differently by the post office than are first-class stamped envelopes. Because the post office has to keep an account of how many business reply envelopes are mailed back so that they can bill the organization correctly, it tends to hold them longer so that it can process them in groups. As a result, the returns to the surveyor are delayed and clustered much more than the small amount of delay and clustering that happens with first-class mail on the weekends and holidays.

Occasionally, in surveys that go to business employees, users of the tailored design method have objected to the use of stamped return envelopes and even business reply envelopes on the basis that outgoing postage is essentially free to the respondent. Such an interpretation places the stamp in an economic rather than social exchange framework, much like the argument that incentives should be paid after the return of a questionnaire. It is the immediate effect on the recipient's mind-set and behavior that is important when enclosing these items of small but real monetary value. Even when surveying organization executives, we normally use return envelopes with real stamps.

Guideline 10.9: Use Multiple Contacts, Each With a Different Look and Appeal

Multiple contacts are essential for maximizing response to mail surveys. They increase the likelihood that sample members are informed of the survey, especially in cases where early notices were not delivered or did not make it to the correct person in the household or organization. In addition, they provide opportunities to tell respondents about different features of the survey and make the case for why they should respond.

A key to ensuring that the use of multiple contacts achieves the intended goal of increasing response is to ensure that the content of the contacts is varied; they should not simply repeat the same information over and over. Information that did not convince sample members to respond the first time it was presented is unlikely to convince them if it is presented again. Rather, as discussed in Chapter 2 under social exchange, stimuli that are different from previous ones are generally more powerful. As such, each communication should differ from the previous one and convey a sense of appropriate renewal of an effort to communicate.

Another key to the success of multiple contacts is that all of the relevant information does not need to be presented in every contact. Rather, information should be presented so that respondents have what they need when they need it. For example, it makes little sense to alert respondents to the sensitive nature of questions, the length of the questionnaire, or the estimated time it will take to answer the questions if they do not have the questionnaire in hand. This information can be conveyed when the questionnaire is delivered and should not come before in a prenotice.

In previous editions of this book we have encouraged the use of a five-contact mailing strategy that included a prenotice letter, questionnaire mailing, thank-you postcard, replacement questionnaire mailing, and a final reminder. Increasingly we have come to believe that the strategy of using multiple carefully designed contacts that are strategically timed (see Guideline 10.10) is more important than using this exact system of contacts.

The contact strategy used should reflect the characteristics of the survey and the culture in which the survey is being conducted. As an example, because people are increasingly inundated with messages and requests, sending a prenotice letter may not be as effective now as it once was. Because of this, we have opted in several recent surveys to forgo the prenotice in favor of an additional reminder mailing that respondents receive when they have the questionnaire in hand and can answer it.

While replacing the prenotice with an additional reminder has been effective for some of our surveys, there are other situations when we think sending a prenotice is still a good idea. In surveys that are contracted to another organization for data collection, it may be useful to have a prenotice come from the study sponsor on its stationery if that sponsor is expected to be well regarded. An example is when a government agency contracts with a private firm to conduct the survey. A prenotice provides an opportunity to explain briefly that the survey is being conducted for that government agency by the private company, thereby invoking the exchange elements of authority and legitimacy discussed in Chapter 2. In this case, the prenotice should be sent as a letter instead of a postcard because a letter can contain more trust-inducing elements (e.g., stationery, personalized address, blue ink signature, etc.) and because it takes longer for sample members to open and attend to a letter, which will help ensure that it is committed to long-term memory. A postcard can be looked at, flipped over, and laid aside in only a few seconds.

The Tailored Design of Contacts for the Water in Nebraska Study

Consistent with our strategy of tailoring the contacts to the specific study, the Water in Nebraska study discussed earlier used only four contacts: an invitation packet, letter reminder, follow-up replacement questionnaire packet, and a final letter. In constructing all of these contacts, we followed the guidelines discussed earlier in this section and in Chapter 2. Each contact was personalized as much as possible. We included an incentive in the initial invitation and a second incentive in the third mailing, postage paid return envelopes were enclosed with the questionnaire, and all of the contacts were printed on university letterhead to help assure sample members that the request was legitimate and could be trusted. The contacts were also all made to look professional through the use of an inside address, date, and salutation. Each contact also expressed the request to do the survey as a request for help to try to take advantage of the tendency for people to like to be helpful, as discussed in Chapter 2. The contacts also included a set of within-household selection instructions to select a respondent from among all household members as described in Chapter 3 and confidentiality assurances that communicated the necessary information with a low level of urgency that was appropriate for a survey about water management and that would not unnecessarily alarm sample members. Finally, all of the letters contained multiple types of contact information and appropriate expressions of gratitude.

The Initial Invitation. The invitation letter can be seen in Figure 10.10. It was sent with a copy of the questionnaire, a postage paid return envelope, and a $4 token incentive (consisting of two $2 bills) to encourage careful attention to the cover letter and other enclosures. As the initial contact, this letter was designed to deliver the questionnaire for the first time and the critical pieces of information to convince sample members to respond and tell them how to do so. In other words, it needed to communicate in a brief and engaging way what people were being asked to do, why they were being asked to do it, how they should do it, and

FIGURE 10.10 Survey invitation cover letter used for the Water in Nebraska survey.

Lincoln

BUREAU OF SOCIOLOGICAL RESEARCH

April 13, 2012

Lincoln Area Resident
55 Nebraska Street
Lincoln, NE 68510

Dear Lincoln Resident,

Every person in Nebraska needs water. In many parts of the state, the same sources of water are used by households, businesses, farms, and wildlife areas. Sometimes it may be possible to meet all of these water requests, but at other times, doing so may be quite tough. One of the challenges Nebraska faces is how to balance many different water uses.

I am writing to ask for your help in improving our understanding of residents' views on water issues in Nebraska. The best way we know how to do this is by asking people throughout the state to share their thoughts and opinions with us. Your address is one of only a small number that have been randomly selected to help in this study.

To make sure we hear from all different types of people who live in the state, please have the adult (**age 19 or over**) in your household who has had the **most recent birthday** be the one to complete the enclosed questionnaire. Please return the completed questionnaire in the enclosed stamped envelope. Your responses are voluntary and will be kept confidential. Your names are not on our mailing list, and your answers will never be associated with your mailing address. If you have any questions about this survey please contact Thom Allen by telephone at 1-800-833-0867 or by email at surveysupport@unl.edu.

By taking a few minutes, you will be adding greatly to our understanding of residents' opinions on water decision-making. I hope you enjoy completing the questionnaire and I look forward to receiving your responses.

Many Thanks,

Jolene D. Smyth

Jolene D. Smyth
Project Director
University of Nebraska-Lincoln

P.S.   We have enclosed a small token of appreciation as a way of saying thanks for completing the survey!

Research and Administrative Offices, 301 Benton Hall, P.O. Box 886102, Lincoln, NE 68588-6102
402-472-3672 • Fax: 402-472-4568 • bosr@unl.edu • http://bosr.unl.edu

what benefit would come from it, within only one page of text. The text starts by explaining the purpose of the survey, emphasizing that it is asking about a topic that affects everyone in the state. The description given in the first paragraph is meant to be consistent with the topic as conveyed through the questionnaire cover and in the first few questions so that sample members can easily recognize the common theme across the materials. This is followed by the request for a response, within-household selection instructions, information about confidentiality, and instructions for how to return the questionnaire.

The Thank-You Reminder.   This first letter was followed about a week later by the thank-you reminder letter shown in Figure 10.11. This follow-up was sent

FIGURE 10.11   Thank-you reminder used for the Water in Nebraska survey.

UNIVERSITY OF
Nebraska
Lincoln

BUREAU OF SOCIOLOGICAL RESEARCH

April 20, 2012

Lincoln Area Resident
55 Nebraska Street
Lincoln, NE 68510

Dear Lincoln Resident,

Last week, we mailed you a letter asking for your help with a study about how water decisions should be made in Nebraska.

If you or someone in your household has already completed the questionnaire, please accept our sincere thanks. If not, please have the adult (**age 19 and over**) with the **most recent birthday** complete and return the questionnaire as soon as possible. We are especially grateful for your help with this important study.

If you do not have a questionnaire, or if you have any questions, please contact Thom Allen by phone at 1-800-833-0867 or by email at surveysupport@unl.edu.

Many Thanks,

Jolene D. Smyth

Jolene D. Smyth
Project Director
University of Nebraska-Lincoln

Research and Administrative Offices, 301 Benton Hall, P.O. Box 886102, Lincoln, NE 68588-6102
402-472-3672 • Fax: 402-472-4568 • bosr@unl.edu • http://bosr.unl.edu

to help remind people about the survey, especially for those who intended to answer the survey but had not yet done so. Many people will lay a survey aside with the vague intention of looking at it later, but as each day passes, the survey becomes a lower priority until it is completely forgotten, lost, or thrown away. A carefully timed contact can remind them to complete the survey before it is thrown out. This reminder should be timed to arrive just after the original mailing has produced its major effect but before each person's questionnaire has had time to be buried too deeply under more recent mail or to be thrown away. One week is an appropriate interval of time for making an appeal that, if carefully worded, conveys a sense of importance without sounding impatient or unreasonable.

For the Water in Nebraska survey we opted to send this reminder as a letter enclosed in an envelope rather than in the postcard format that we often use for this mailing. The reason for this was because this mail survey was part of an experiment that contained several treatments asking for a web response. The letter format was needed for those treatments so that individual login information could be kept out of public view. More information about the mixed-mode treatments for this study can be found in Chapter 11.

Most of the time, we choose the postcard format over a letter so that it contrasts with the previous letter(s) because new stimuli have a greater effect than repeated stimuli. The letter format is used for any prenotice that is sent because it takes longer for the respondent to process cognitively and thus has a greater likelihood of being stored in long-term memory and recalled when the questionnaire arrives. In contrast, the function of this reminder is simply to jog one's memory, so the fact that it can be quickly turned over and read is a benefit.

The wording of the letter shown in Figure 10.11 is quite similar to what we would put on a postcard. It is kept very short and positive. The first lines simply state that a questionnaire was sent to the household the previous week and why. This may appear to be a waste of precious space; however, for some people this is the first time they learn that a questionnaire was sent to them. The reasons for the original questionnaire not reaching the intended recipient extend well beyond it getting lost in the mail. The previous mail-out is sometimes addressed incorrectly or is not forwarded, whereas for some unexplained reason the postcard is. In still other cases, another member of the household opens the envelope containing the questionnaire and fails to give it to the desired sample member. Alternatively, it may have been skipped over when the sample member was looking through the mail and not opened at all. Whatever the reason, we sometimes get telephone calls or letters after the thank-you reminder is mailed stating that the sample member would be willing to fill out a questionnaire if one were sent to him.

Most people who do not recall receiving a questionnaire will not bother to ask for one when they get the thank-you reminder. However, the knowledge that one was sent may stimulate them to query other members of their household (or organization) and may lead to its discovery. For others, the reminder may increase receptivity when a questionnaire finally does arrive in the mail, if it has been delayed. For those sample members who are fully aware of having received the questionnaire and still have it in their possession, the lead paragraph serves to remind them of it by coming quickly to the point.

The second paragraph of the reminder contains the crucial message that the letter is designed to convey. People who have already returned their questionnaires are thanked, and those who have not are asked to do so right away. The urgency conveyed by asking for a response "as soon as possible" (or alternatively providing a time referent like "today") is consistent with the importance one wants to convey.

Because we used the letter format for this particular study, we printed the letter on the same university stationery as the invitation letter and included a date, inside address, and salutation. Had we used the postcard format, we would have printed any identifying logos and the respondent's name and address on the reverse side and would not have repeated it on the message side because of the space limits of the postcard format. In addition, when it is appropriate and not expected to influence answers to the survey questions, we sometimes include a relevant photograph or graphic on the reverse side of the postcard to help it stand out in the mail.

We sent this thank-you reminder to all sample members, whether they had responded or not, because it was more practical to do that than to try to send it only to nonrespondents. About one week after the initial mailing is when the maximum number of returns usually arrive. Even in small surveys with a sample of a few hundred, there is usually no time to wait until a significant number of returns are in before addressing the follow-up reminder and still get it mailed on schedule. Moreover, the monetary savings of doing so would be very small compared to the risk of sending the reminder too late. Another significant advantage of the blanket mailing is that the reminder letter or postcards can be (and should be) printed and addressed even before the first mail-out and stored so that this work does not interfere with the task of processing early returns.

The effect of the thank-you reminder varies. A large factorial experiment of the preletter–postcard reminder sequence and a stamped return envelope on a national test of Census questionnaires (where people were informed in a letter that their response was required by law) showed that the postcard reminder added 8 percentage points to the final response rate, compared with 6 percentage points for a preletter when tested alone (Dillman, Clark, et al., 1995). The combination of preletter and postcard added 13 percentage points, suggesting clearly that the effects are additive. The use of all three elements added 14 percentage points.

In a more recent examination of the effects of follow-up procedures, Roose, Lievens, and Waege (2007) reported a 12 percentage point increase in cooperation rates as a result of sending a postcard reminder to respondents who had responded to a brief questionnaire at a cultural performance and then been given a longer mail questionnaire to take home and complete. The cooperation rate for those who received no follow-up was 70% compared to 82% for those receiving only a postcard follow-up, 83% for those receiving both a postcard follow-up and a replacement questionnaire, and 89% for those receiving a postcard and two replacement questionnaire follow-ups.

Another experiment confirmed the importance of the format of the reminder contrasting with that of the prenotice. In this experiment, very similar postcards were used for the prenotice and reminder. Independently, the prenotice postcard improved response rates by 4 percentage points, and the reminder postcard improved them by 7 percentage points. In a treatment in which the prenotice and reminder postcards were both used, the response rate increased by 7 percentage points, the same as when the reminder was used alone (S. Ohm, personal communication, August 8, 1998). These results contrast sharply with the additive effect achieved in the Census test mentioned previously, which relied on a prenotice letter and reminder postcard, and they provide additional evidence that contrasting stimuli are better for response than are repeated stimuli.

The Follow-Up Reminder. Fourteen days after the thank-you reminder was sent for the Water in Nebraska study, the follow-up reminder letter shown in Figure 10.12 was sent to all nonrespondents. A replacement questionnaire and return envelope were enclosed with this letter because we expected that most of the original questionnaires had likely been lost or thrown away by this point. This expectation is based on the experience of having mistakenly omitted a replacement questionnaire a number of years ago and receiving many cards and letters requesting a copy of it (Dillman, Christenson, Carpenter, & Brooks, 1974). In this instance, even after all of the effort of responding to these requests, the total response was only half that usually obtained for the second follow-up when a questionnaire was included.

FIGURE 10.12 Follow-up reminder letter used for the Water in Nebraska survey.

UNIVERSITY OF
Nebraska
Lincoln

BUREAU OF SOCIOLOGICAL RESEARCH

May 4, 2012

Lincoln Area Resident
55 Nebraska Street
Lincoln, NE 68510

Dear Lincoln Resident,

About three weeks ago, we sent you a survey request asking for your opinions on how Nebraska's water supplies should be managed. To the best of our knowledge, we have not yet received your responses. From irrigation to drinking water, Nebraska faces the challenge of balancing many competing uses of water. Our hope is that this study will provide Nebraska leaders with a better understanding of how residents think these decisions should be made.

We are writing again because of the importance that your household's responses have for helping to get accurate results. It is only by hearing from nearly everyone in the sample that we can be sure that the results truly represent Nebraska residents. Thus, we hope the adult (**age 19 or over**) in your household who has had the **most recent birthday** will fill out the survey soon.

Simply complete the enclosed questionnaire and return it in the stamped envelope provided. Your responses are voluntary and will be kept confidential. Your names are not on our mailing list, and your answers will never be associated with your address in any way. If you have any questions about this survey please contact Thom Allen by telephone at 1-800-833-0867 or by email at surveysupport@unl.edu.

The enclosed token of appreciation is yours to keep whether you choose to complete the survey or not. Thank you so much for your help with this very important issue.

Many Thanks,

Jolene D. Smyth
Project Director
University of Nebraska-Lincoln

Research and Administrative Offices, 301 Benton Hall, P.O. Box 886102, Lincoln, NE 68588-6102
402-472-3672 • Fax: 402-472-4568 • bosr@unl.edu • http://bosr.unl.edu

While the packet of materials sent in this follow-up mailing closely resembled those sent in the initial mailing, the letter had a tone of insistence that the previous contacts lacked. Its strongest aspect was the first paragraph, in which recipients were told that their completed questionnaire had not yet been received. This message is one of the strongest forms of personalization, communicating to sample members that they are indeed receiving individual attention. It reinforces messages contained in three previous contacts that the respondent is important to the success of the survey.

Most of this letter was devoted to a restatement of each respondent's importance to the study in terms quite different from those used in previous mailings. The social usefulness of the study was also reemphasized, implying that the usefulness of the study is dependent on the return of the questionnaire. This letter also included brief mention of a second incentive that was enclosed with the letter. This second incentive, this time consisting of a single $2 bill, was used to encourage respondents to actually read the letter before disposing of it. Mentioning the incentive in the letter is intended to draw attention back to the incentive in order to build trust, provide a benefit, and invoke reciprocity as discussed in Guideline 10.7.

In developing the obviously stronger tone of this letter, it is important to neither over- nor undersell. It needs to show a greater intensity than preceding letters, but not be so strong that sample members become disgruntled or angered. The letter appears sterner and a little more demanding when considered in isolation than when read in the context of having already been asked to make a significant contribution to an important study. If the study lacked social importance or had a frivolous quality about it, the letter would probably seem inappropriate to the respondent and could produce a negative reaction.

Ordinarily this letter is not produced until questionnaires are returned from previous mailings in considerable quantity. The lapse of time provides an excellent opportunity to gather feedback on problems encountered by sample members. For every person who writes to ask a question, it is likely that many more have a similar question but do not take time to write. Thus, information is sometimes included in the follow-up letter in hopes of answering questions that may have been suggested to the researcher by such feedback. When used in this way, it will help reinforce that the study is important by indicating that the researcher is examining early returns and trying to deal with people's concerns.

A replacement questionnaire creates certain processing challenges. It is possible that someone may fill out two questionnaires instead of only the one intended or may perhaps give the questionnaire to a spouse or friend to complete. Although this occasionally happens (as evidenced by returns with duplicate identification numbers and different handwriting), the frequency is so low as to be of little concern. Perhaps the greatest difficulty rests with those respondents who did fill out and return the earlier questionnaire, only to be informed that the researcher did not receive it. This underscores the great importance of an accurate identification system (discussed further under Guideline 10.17) and the need to hold the follow-up mailing to the last minute so that respondents whose questionnaires have just been received can be removed from this mailing.

The Final Reminder.   The final contact used for the Water in Nebraska study is shown in Figure 10.13. This letter contains several elements intended to induce response that were discussed in Chapter 2, such as the suggestion that time is running out and an appeal for help. The benefits of the study are also highlighted

FIGURE 10.13 Final reminder letter used for the Water in Nebraska survey.

Nebraska
UNIVERSITY OF
Lincoln

BUREAU OF SOCIOLOGICAL RESEARCH

May 14, 2012

Lincoln Area Resident
55 Nebraska Street
Lincoln, NE 68510

Dear Lincoln Resident,

In recent weeks, our research team has asked you, as part of a random selection of Nebraska residents, to let us know how you think water decisions should be made in your state. We plan to start summarizing results later this month, so we hope that all questionnaires will be completed by then.

You can help us by filling out the questionnaire we mailed to your household last week and returning it in the provided stamped envelope.

For many years, we have heard people in Nebraska and all across the U.S. talk about water – how it should be protected, managed, owned, and used. In the future, we believe that water issues will receive even more attention. We hope that this study will contribute to these conversations and provide insight into Nebraska residents' views on water.

This is the last contact we will be sending you about this survey, as we are bringing this phase of the project to a close. A summary of preliminary results from this study will be available on our website www.opinion.unl.edu/nebraskawater/results this summer. If you have any questions about this survey please contact Thom Allen by telephone at 1-800-833-0867 or by email at surveysupport@unl.edu.

Many thanks for considering our request.

Respectfully and with appreciation,

Jolene D. Smyth
Project Director
University of Nebraska-Lincoln

Research and Administrative Offices, 301 Benton Hall, P.O. Box 886102, Lincoln, NE 68588-6102
402-472-3672 • Fax: 402-472-4568 • bosr@unl.edu • http://bosr.unl.edu

in this letter in a slightly different way than in the previous letters; it focuses on the contributions the study can make to future debates about water use, suggesting that the study will continue to be beneficial into the future. Finally, a URL is provided where respondents can learn about the outcome of the study. In addition to being a benefit for those sample members interested in this particular topic, the URL shows a commitment on the part of the surveyors to sharing and making use of the results, a trust inducing factor.

Because of budget constraints, this final contact was sent by first-class mail and a reminder questionnaire was not included. When budget allows, we prefer to include another questionnaire with this mailing in case the previous ones have been misplaced or discarded. We also prefer to utilize an alternative form of delivery with special packaging and faster delivery speed. The packaging and delivery speed will both be noticed before the package is even opened and will differentiate this final contact from the previous contacts in ways that increase the perception of importance and legitimacy.

There are several alternative forms of mail delivery one might use. The original total design method (TDM) book (Dillman, 1978) suggested using certified mail, which was subsequently shown to increase response rates between 10 and 20 percentage points (de Leeuw & Hox, 1988), but we no longer use certified mail except in special circumstances because it requires that someone be available to sign for the delivery. If nobody can sign for the letter, as is the case with many of today's households where no one is home during the day, an attempted delivery notice is left and the individual may either sign that note and leave it for delivery the next day or go to the post office and pick up the letter. We consider it undesirable both from an exchange perspective and out of concern for the welfare of respondents to require people to go to the post office, which some recipients may be inclined to do. In addition, many alternatives to certified mail are now available that do not require signatures for delivery. They include courier delivery by one of several private companies such as Federal Express or United Parcel Service (UPS) and priority mail delivery or special delivery by the U.S. Postal Service. The sole situation in which certified mail is recommended for use is when one is confident that someone is always present when postal deliveries are made, as might be the case in a business office.

An early study by D. E. Moore and Dillman (1980), which tested the use of special delivery and telephone follow-up calls (see Chapter 11) as individual alternatives to certified mail, found that both alternatives worked about the same as certified mail (no significant difference), and both worked much better than another first-class mailing. We have observed many other tests of priority mail by courier in which an increment of additional response is attributable to use of courier or two-day priority U.S. Postal Service mail. For example, Brick et al. (2012) found that sending a final reminder via priority mail resulted in about a 5 percentage point advantage over sending it via first-class mail.

In recent years, there have been many reports of response rates to surveys being improved significantly by the use of Federal Express instead of a U.S. Postal Service contact (Hager, Wilson, Pollak, & Rooney, 2003; Kasprzyk, Montaño, St. Lawrence, & Phillips, 2001; Mamedova & McPhee, 2012). One of the strengths of using a Federal Express delivery system is that the request for a response enters the household or business in a different way than regular postal contacts, even when they are sent by priority mail. The survey request is delivered individually by a personal visit, and thus seems more likely to get attention than a letter that is interspersed with other mail. We believe that the individual attention increases the likelihood that a written request to respond to a survey will be opened and examined. Even if the package is left at the door, it is generally separate from other mail.

This kind of contact, which also might be sent by UPS, seems to have considerable potential in today's world in which it is increasingly difficult to get people's attention by a straightforward phone, Internet, or mail contact. However, such contacts tend to be expensive; they may range from about $5 per questionnaire up to as much as $25, or even more when faster delivery times are requested and a signature is required. Charges also vary by distance, time of day that delivery is requested, whether a special promotional offer is being made, whether the sponsor has a special contract or volume discount with the provider, and how many questionnaires are being sent.

In addition, sending the final contact by special mail requires using out-of-the-ordinary mailing procedures, which sometimes include different mailing forms and labels. Therefore, if one is contemplating using a particular service, it is imperative to talk with the provider. These delivery services are normally not set up to receive large numbers of such mailings at one time, and computerized procedures may be available for streamlining the process.

When considering these special contact methods, it is important to remember the total effect one is attempting to accomplish with this mailing. A new look is achieved by using a different outside container than in any previous mailings. An example is the light cardboard 9″ × 12″ envelope used by some couriers. One also depends upon the special handling to convey that an attempt for rapid, assured delivery is being made. These attributes convey to the respondent that the survey is important and are depended upon to get the recipient to read the letter, which differs significantly from the previous letters in that it is typically written in a softer tone, addresses any aspects of the survey that have been problematic for respondents, and includes an explanation of why the special contact procedure was used. In addition, enough time is allowed to elapse since the previous contact so that little, if any, overlap occurs between this mail-out and late returns from the previous contact.

In summary, the promise of Federal Express and United Parcel Service for stimulating mail survey responses is substantial but requires careful planning and cost analysis. There likely will be significant changes that occur in how these special contact procedures are used in the coming years as all providers of in-person deliveries seek to lower costs, which may impact the effectiveness of this alternative method of delivery.

Guideline 10.10: Carefully and Strategically Time All Contacts

As the previous discussion illustrated, each contact is intended to meet a specific goal. But each contact also has to work well within a set of other contacts. Sometimes it is the combined effects of multiple contacts that can be most powerful, and timing is central to those combined effects. For example, if a prenotice is to be used, it should be given enough time to arrive and be processed before the questionnaire arrives, but it is important to ensure the questionnaire is received before the prenotice is forgotten. Therefore, the first questionnaire mailing should be sent only a few days to a week after the prenotice and by first-class mail. In this way, when the respondent gets the questionnaire, he should immediately be able to make the connection between it and the prenotice letter he recently received: "Oh, this is the questionnaire they said they would be sending."

Likewise, the effectiveness of the thank-you reminder depends strongly on its arriving after the original request but before the questionnaire has been discarded or irretrievably lost. Therefore, it should be sent a few days to a week after the questionnaire. Scheduling the first replacement questionnaire follow-up a full 2 to 4 weeks after the thank-you reminder mailing is useful because it allows initial responses to dwindle to a small trickle, considerably lowering the chance that respondents who have just recently sent back their questionnaires will receive another one. Furthermore, the additional time, and subsequently smaller number of required follow-ups, reduces postage and clerical costs considerably. The strategy of waiting 2 to 4 weeks before sending the final contact serves the same purpose.

Guideline 10.11: Select All Mail-Out Dates With the Characteristics of the Population in Mind

Generally speaking, very few survey mail-out date rules apply to all populations. One exception might be that one should avoid certain holiday periods such as between Thanksgiving and Christmas, because people are often busier in these times. In addition, during this time as well as the day after any federal holiday, the U.S. Postal Service experiences higher than usual volume, which can create delivery problems. Other than these major holidays, the time of year or day of the week that a questionnaire is mailed does not seem to affect response rates.

Rather than attempting to find and follow general rules for mail-out timing, one should select a mail-out date based on the known characteristics of the population and the study's objectives. For example, in a survey of farm families, periods of planting and harvest, which are typically quite hectic, should be avoided. In northern climates this almost always means not doing such surveys in the spring or fall. Likewise, one should probably attempt to do surveys of grade school parents during the school year rather than in the summer because such a survey is more likely to be salient to the parents at that time. For targeting homogeneous groups such as these, thinking about salience and availability are prime considerations, and both are factors that make it difficult to develop general rules that work when surveying the general population.

Guideline 10.12: Place Information in the Mailing Exactly Where It Needs to Be Used

Initially, it is important to contemplate where the information to be included in the questionnaire mail-out best fits. For example, we have seen some questionnaires that provided information inside the questionnaire cover about who should respond and how. This information was then repeated almost word for word in the cover letter, a decision that contributed to the letter becoming three pages long! Sometimes separate sheets of instructions on how to answer certain questions are included. We have also seen mailing packages that included a second cover letter that was intended as support for the study but probably did no more than contribute to the bulk of the mail-out package. The complexity of mailing caused by multiple enclosures, often with redundant information, tends to cause a delay in reading that information and, ultimately, nonresponse.

For these reasons, construction of the mail-out package begins by deciding what information should and should not be included and in which element it should be expressed. As noted in Guideline 6.6, there are compelling reasons for placing information exactly where it is to be used. If this is done, it tends to reduce the total number of words as well as the number of separate pieces that must be included in the mail-out, thereby reducing both stuffing and shipping costs. It is also useful to determine which, if any, information needs to be repeated in multiple locations. One example is that the address to which the survey should be returned should be placed on the return envelope to ease the task of replying and also on the questionnaire itself in case the return envelope is misplaced. However, if it is in both of these locations, it does not need to be included in the invitation letter. Likewise, it is sometimes useful to repeat within-household selection instructions both in the letter and on the questionnaire to help ensure that they get noticed and followed appropriately.

Guideline 10.13: Take Steps to Ensure That Mailings Will Not Be Mistaken for Junk Mail or Marketing Materials

When a legitimate survey arrives in mailboxes, it is among a whole host of other pieces of mail such as merchandise catalogs, credit card offers, charity requests, campaign materials, messages from advocacy groups, personal correspondence, and bills, all vying for the recipients' attention. Because there are direct consequences attached to ignoring personal correspondence and bills, both of these are likely to get top priority from recipients, with the rest of the mail left to compete for attention and much of it thrown away unopened. Thus, it is important to differentiate the survey request and reminders from everyday junk mail. Doing so is absolutely critical when using address-only (i.e., no names) mailings, because the lack of a name in the address is an immediate indicator to recipients that a piece of mail is probably junk. In order to contribute to the impression that the survey is legitimate, authentic, and important, we recommend differentiating survey mail by professionalizing it while also making it stand out as different from all other mailings, in these ways:

- Avoid envelopes with flashy colors, those made of glossy paper, or those that are *artificially* made to look like express mail, air mail, or courier delivered.
- Provide a complete return address that clearly identifies the sender, in a way that is recognizable to respondents.
- If possible, use a recognized and respected logo with the return address.
- Except for the logo, limit print to standard colors such as black or charcoal gray.
- Avoid marketing buzzwords and phrases on envelopes such as *free gift, easy, hurry, urgent, immediate attention required,* or *open at once.*

Most of the tactics used by senders of junk mail are easily recognized as such by recipients. Thus, for the surveyor, it is useful to think of the envelope in a traditional sense, as a means to deliver an *enclosed* message to sampled members. See Figure 10.14 for examples of personalized envelopes that convey professionalism. Except for those features meant to portray professionalism and perhaps sponsorship, the message one is delivering should be kept inside the envelope.

It is common to use a standard #10 business envelope (4.125″ × 9.5″) for many mail surveys, but sometimes the decision is made to use a larger envelope to draw attention to the mailings. In the Water in Nebraska survey we used a 6.5″ × 9.5″ natural color (i.e., light tan) envelope for questionnaire mailings and #10 official stationery envelopes for other contacts. The contrast between these two envelopes seems desirable from the standpoint of getting them opened. In other studies we have conducted in recent years, we have used a standard 9″ × 12″ envelope to avoid the need to fold the questionnaire. In a recent experiment, Tarnai et al. (2012) found that using a 6.5″ × 9.5″ envelope increased response rates 1 to 6 percentage points over a standard #10 envelope, depending on whether an incentive and real stamp were also used. The larger sized envelopes help draw attention to the mailings, but it is also important to realize that they will increase the costs of mailing the survey.

FIGURE 10.14 Examples of personalized envelopes.

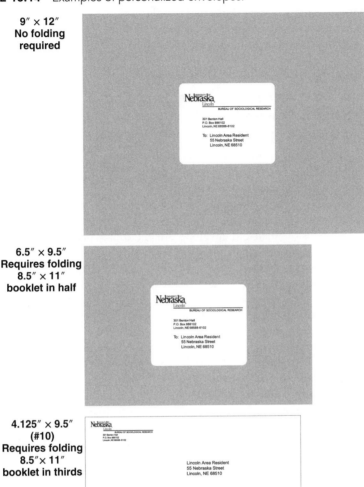

9″ × 12″
No folding
required

6.5″ × 9.5″
Requires folding
8.5″ × 11″
booklet in half

4.125″ × 9.5″
(#10)
Requires folding
8.5″× 11″
booklet in thirds

Guideline 10.14: Evaluate the Impact of Size and Weight of Mailing Materials on Mailing Costs

An unpleasant reality for mail surveyors in the United States is that postal expenses continue to increase. Whereas in the past postage was determined based on the weight (in ounces) of a mailing, in the round of postal price changes implemented in May 2007 package size and shape also became elements used to determine postal costs for fairly standard types of mail (i.e., there have long been extra fees for irregular mail requiring special handling). For example, in the United States in 2014 the rate for a standard letter or card (length, 5″ to 11.5″; height, 3.5″ to 6.125″; thickness, ≤.25″; weight, up to 3.5 oz.) sent first class was 49 cents for 1 ounce and an additional 21 cents for each additional ounce. If mailed in a large envelope (length, ≥11.5″; height, ≥6.125″; thickness, ≤.75″) the first ounce cost 98 cents, with each additional ounce adding 21 cents. Given the reality of tight survey budgets, it is now important to consider both weight and size when calculating survey costs. Mailings that cannot fit into a standard #10 business envelope will be significantly more costly than those that can. However, those costs may be worth it since a larger envelope may mean it is more likely to be noticed and, since the materials do not have to be folded, they are easier for people to open and process.

Guideline 10.15: Assemble the Mailings in a Way That Maximizes the Appealing Aspects of Each Element When the Package Is Opened

When it comes time to prepare each mail-out (except for the postcard), the first step is to assemble and insert the components—questionnaire, cover letter, return envelope, and (if appropriate) the token incentive. Often the planning of this step is ignored, leaving it up to the personnel who do it to find the most efficient way. However, this step is important and should be considered just as carefully as the content of the cover letter and the survey itself. Two things need to happen when the recipient opens the mail-out envelope: All enclosures need to come out of the envelope at once, and the appealing aspects of each element need to be immediately visible. Neither of these details should be left to chance; efforts should be made to overcome limitations around how the mailings are prepared and packaged.

In cognitive interviews designed to test mail-out packages, it has been observed repeatedly that one or more components often gets left in the envelope when the other contents are removed (Dillman et al., 1998). As a result of the desire to be as efficient as possible when assembling the mail-out, personnel typically fold the components individually and place them on top of one another before inserting them into the envelope. When the envelope is opened, the questionnaire typically gets removed because of its bulk, but the cover letter may be left in the envelope, which is often discarded before anyone realizes the mistake. When this happens, people have no explanation for why the questionnaire has been sent or what they are supposed to do with it. This can be particularly troublesome if the cover letter specifies who in the household is supposed to complete the questionnaire.

Fear of something getting lost has led to solutions that may compound the problem. One surveyor decided to insert a $2 bill into the reply envelope, reasoning that respondents would see it when inserting their completed questionnaires. This unfortunate decision did not take into account the importance of the sample member being able to see the token incentive immediately when opening the envelope in order to invoke social exchange. Moreover, those who decided not to complete the survey likely discarded the materials, including the return envelope with the incentive. Another surveyor decided to hide the incentive inside the pages of the booklet questionnaire, reasoning that the respondent would find it while answering the questions. Here again, the incentive was not immediately visible so that it could serve its social exchange function and, therefore, was probably unknowingly discarded by many.

Depending upon the size and shape of enclosures, somewhat different solutions are needed to avoid these problems. First, if one is using an 8.5″ × 7″ booklet questionnaire (i.e., legal-size paper folded in half the short way) with a standard 8.5″ × 11″ cover letter and a #10 business envelope, the following procedure is recommended. Fold the questionnaire vertically with the front cover on the outside of the fold. Insert the $2 bill on top of the folded questionnaire, and place the stamped reply envelope underneath. Then lay all three components on the middle

FIGURE 10.15   Examples of ways to assemble mailings so that all pieces come out of the envelope at once and are immediately visible.

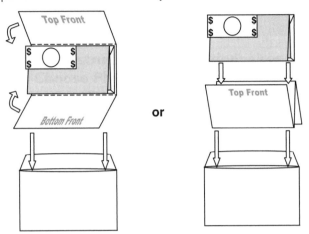

third of the face-up cover letter. Fold the bottom third of the cover letter up and over these three components and complete the process by folding the top third of the cover letter down. The entire set of materials can then be picked up easily and inserted into the mail-out envelope (see the left panel of Figure 10.15). The advantage of this type of fold is that all materials must be removed together from the envelope. When the packet is unfolded, the respondent will simultaneously see every component.

Another possibility is to use a Z fold, whereby the bottom third of the cover letter is folded upward over the middle third, and the top third is folded backward, so the paper forms a Z shape. The folded cover letter is then flipped over so that the top third of the letter is visible (and the portion of the letter on it is right side up), and the questionnaire and other materials are placed between the top and middle thirds so that they rest in the V formed by the fold. Placing the package into the envelope with the top portion of the letter right side up and facing forward ensures that when the letter is removed from the envelope, all of the other materials will come with it (see the right panel of Figure 10.15).

A thin 8.5″ × 11″ questionnaire printed in the two-column format can be similarly folded. However, when initially folded for insertion, it should be done in accordion (or Z-fold) fashion so that the top of the front page displaying any masthead appears on the top of the fold, and underneath the token incentive, before being tucked inside the cover letter for insertion into the envelope.

When the questionnaire has too many pages to allow for folding, flat mailouts or U.S. Postal Service priority mail envelopes are often used. The chance of something getting left in this type of mail-out envelope is even greater. In these instances we are likely to use stickers to attach the token incentives to the cover letter or first page of the questionnaire. Attaching the mail-out components together with a metal binder clip is usually not done because of potential envelope tears from postal processing machines. However, the use of simple paper clips to place cash incentives on top of the mail is generally okay, if we are convinced that they will go through postal service processing machines without causing paper tears. That usually means showing what we propose to do to Postal Service staff, and making sure that our paper envelopes are of high enough quality to use the paper clips.

An important quality control issue surfaces during the folding and insertion process. The use of an identification number on the questionnaire for sample tracking purposes means that the right questionnaire has to be packaged with the right personally addressed cover letter and envelope (lest the wrong person be removed from the mailing list once the questionnaire is returned). In addition, the handling of cash (or checks written to individuals) requires that all of the right elements get into every mail-out in order for the implementation system to work (including occasionally different amounts of cash if $2 is provided for some households and $5 to others). This is not a process that can be delegated to an organization's newest hires and forgotten. Like the rest of tailored design, it requires attention to detail.

We often print and organize our materials (questionnaires, cover letters, envelopes, labels, incentives, etc.) in batches of 50. We then stuff 50 questionnaires at a time. If everything is done correctly, we should run out of cover letters, incentives, questionnaires, and return envelopes at the same time. Only then do we seal the envelopes. If we are left with too few or to many of a specific insert (this sometimes happens, for example, when crisp new dollar bills stick together), we know we have made an error. Stuffing everything in batches of 50 ensures that we do not have to search back through hundreds or thousands of envelopes to find and correct that error. It gives us an extra quality-control step every 50 items.

When one is faced with the prospect of assembling thousands of mail-outs, rather than hundreds, or when one has access to machine assembly, it is tempting to forgo these methods in favor of separately folding and inserting each item as the machines encourage. We have observed many different mechanical processes and urge that anyone considering using them study prototype results carefully to control as much as possible whether and how people will be exposed to the results. The quality control for getting the right components in every mail-out package also needs to be carefully examined before committing to their use.

Guideline 10.16: Ensure That All Addresses in the Sample Comply With Current Postal Regulations

One relatively easy way to streamline a mail implementation system is to ensure that all addresses comply with current postal regulations prior to mailing. Doing so will considerably reduce the number of undeliverable pieces of mail returned by the post office. Some common rules to follow for mailing within the United States include the following (regulations may differ for other countries):

- Left-justify the delivery address
- Capitalize everything in the delivery address
- Use two-letter abbreviations for states
- When possible, use zip+4 for more efficient delivery
- Do not use punctuation (periods or commas) in the delivery address, except for the hyphen in the zip+4

For example, "S.W. 705 Marcel St." should be changed to "705 SW MARCEL ST". In addition, the address should be printed large enough that it can be read when held at arm's length. Commercial software that will detect and correct errors is available. With this software, it is much easier and more efficient to correct addresses ahead of time than to deal with individual pieces of returned mail once the survey is in the field, a topic to which we return later.

Additional detail on where the delivery address should be placed on envelopes is available online from the U.S. Postal Service. The increasing emphasis on auto-mated processing of mail makes attention to the details provided there essential.

Guideline 10.17: Assign an Individual ID Number to Each Sample Member

Each questionnaire should have an individual identification number printed on it or printed on a label and affixed to it. An ID number is included so that follow-up mailings, an essential aspect of tailored design, can be sent only to nonrespon-dents (with the exception of returns that cross with the follow-up letter in the mail). Removing those who have already responded from the follow-up mailing list ensures that they are not inconvenienced, confused, or irritated by additional mailings that do not apply to them.

The ID number should be placed on the front or back cover of the question-naire in plain view. Because some respondents are likely to tear off identification numbers, it is wise to place them in the corner of the questionnaire where their removal does not eliminate answers to questions (be sure to look at what is on the back side of the page, too). Attempting to hide the numbers by placing them in small type on an inside page; embedding them into something that might be referred to as a *form*, *approval*, or *processing number* (e.g., "Approved Form 91854"); or printing them using invisible ink that will show up only under ultraviolet or other special light is unethical and inconsistent with the premise of making an honest effort to communicate openly with recipients. These are not trust-inducing strategies, and if respondents notice such attempts to hide ID numbers, their dis-trust will be heightened and their likelihood of participating reduced. That said, simply printing the number in a font size that matches that used elsewhere in the questionnaire is the best practice.

If one is concerned that respondents will strongly object to the ID number, it might be best to disclose to them up front the reason for including such a number: "An identification number is printed on the back cover of the questionnaire so that we can check your name off of the mailing list when your questionnaire is returned. The list of names is then destroyed so that individual names can never be connected to the results in any way." Informing respondents of the presence of an identification number in this way does not seem to have a serious negative effect on response rates, especially when compared to not being able to use the tailored follow-up that it facilitates.

QUALITY CONTROL AND TESTING GUIDELINES FOR MAIL SURVEYS

Once a reasonable and affordable implementation protocol has been established, it is important to test it to ensure that it will work as intended. This is the topic to which we turn next. The testing procedures for questionnaires presented in Chapter 7 work very well and should be applied to mail-only surveys. Rather than repeat these, we focus here on testing procedures aimed at assessing implemen-tation procedures for mail surveys and how well these procedures work alongside the questionnaire. After all, as we have said previously, how well all of the design features work together is just as important, if not more so, than how well any one individual feature works.

Guideline 10.18: Obtain Expert Review and Conduct Cognitive Interviews, Experimental Evaluations, and Pilot Studies of Implementation Materials and Procedures

In the abstract, designing implementation procedures for a mail survey sounds pretty simple. One needs to decide how many contacts to send, how to send them, how to time them, and what incentive, if any, will be used. It is often not until one sits down to actually write the letters and address the envelopes that she realizes just how many decisions need to be made to produce the final products. Even though we have designed many implementation protocols for mail surveys and have much of the scientific literature about how to do so at our fingertips, we still regularly find ourselves unsure about which of our ideas will produce the best effect: "If I explain the study this way, will it be more convincing than explaining it that way? I cannot send cash, so what kind of material incentive will be most motivating? Which delivery method will work best for my final contact? Will this cover image have broad appeal or will it only appeal to certain types of people?" We can obtain considerable information to make good decisions about these and many of the other questions that arise when designing implementation procedures using expert review, cognitive interviews, experiments, and pilot studies.

Topic area experts, for example, can provide valuable feedback about whether letters will make sense to and resonate with sample members. They may also have a practical perspective that the surveyor lacks. For example, when one of us once suggested including a token cash incentive to increase response rates to a survey of defense contractors, it was quickly pointed out that the resources that would have to be expended by the contractors to appropriately account for the incoming money would far outweigh the benefit of receiving it. Including an incentive would have likely produced considerable frustration, the opposite of what we wanted to do. Only someone with a close understanding of the rules and regulations defense contractors must abide by could give us this valuable perspective.

Cognitive interviews can also be helpful for understanding how details of the implementation procedures might impact response. For example, watching cognitive interview participants open and remove materials from envelopes can be very instructive for figuring out how best to arrange the materials in the envelopes so that they all come out together and the most important pieces will be quickly noticed. Cognitive interviews can also be used to learn how people read and react to the messages included in contacts. For example, in the 1990s the U.S. Census Bureau commissioned an outside firm to design two new mail-out envelopes and questionnaires, one of which was rolled out publicly as a new Census design to be used in the Decennial Census. Cognitive interviews revealed that people were not noticing the message "Your response is required by law" because it was graphically hidden in the new print formats. Inasmuch as the words in this message had previously been shown to increase response rates by as much as 10 percentage points, the cognitive interviews suggested that neither of the graphical designs were likely to work well (Dillman, Jenkins, Martin, & DeMaio, 1996).

This same example can also illustrate how useful experimental tests can be for testing mail implementation systems. An experimental test on the effectiveness of the new mail-out envelopes that was run at the same time as the cognitive interviews were conducted showed that indeed the two new designs lowered response rates by 9% and 5%, respectively, both of which were considered dramatic declines (Leslie, 1996). Inasmuch as a considerable commitment had been made by agency leadership to the new designs, it seemed quite unlikely that their use would have been rejected had only the cognitive interview report been available. However, the experimental results from a random sample of U.S. households provided an unquestioned quantitative basis for rejecting the designs. Together, the experiment and the cognitive interviews revealed that fewer people would respond if the new designs were used and why this was the case (Dillman & Redline, 2004).

Pilot studies can also be incredibly informative about how well a mail survey will work, and in particular, how well all of the parts will work together. Pilot studies can yield two types of valuable information. First, they can give one a sense of how sample members will react to the materials, what proportion will answer the questionnaire, and what problems or areas of confusion will arise. They are particularly useful for making quantitative estimates of response rates and thus may help in setting sample sizes for the full study. They may also give one a sense of whether only certain types of people are responding leading to increased potential for nonresponse error. Second, they can give the surveyor a better understanding of how well coordination of the implementation process works on the surveyor's side. For example, a pilot study will give a surveyor a good sense of how long it will take to stuff the mailings, what staffing level is needed, whether the accounting system for tracking outgoing and returned incentives is sufficient, how well the system for tracking returned questionnaires works, how communication between staff members in charge of the various parts of the survey works, how much time data entry (whether hand entry or scanning) will take, and so on. It will also give staff a chance to practice procedures. Pilot studies are also especially valuable for obtaining cost estimates for the actual survey.

Pilot studies are often deemed essential when a new survey questionnaire or new implementation procedures are to be used for a survey or when implementation requires many different individuals and divisions to coordinate activities within an organization, although they can also be very useful for smaller surveys as well.

Guideline 10.19: Test All Systems for Producing and Mailing Contacts and Questionnaires and Closely Examine Production Quality Proofs of All Materials

Experience tells us that a lot of hard work can be quickly undone by glitches in the production process. For example, we once spent considerable time and effort perfecting a full-color questionnaire that we then had printed outside our shop. We understood that colors often look very different on computers screens than in print, so we made a special trip to review the actual hard printed copies of the questionnaire rather than PDF proofs. The printed proofs looked excellent, and we approved them for final printing. Later when we went to pick up the full order of printed questionnaires, they looked terrible! The background color was quite different from what we had approved; it was unattractive and did not have the proper contrast with the text and answer spaces to make reading easy. We learned in this case that the proofs we had approved were printed on a good color desktop printer, but the full order was printed on a larger production printer. The two printers rendered the same background color very differently. In another instance, we received a large number of returns in which pages of the questionnaire were left blank because wet ink had caused the facing pages to stick together. Many respondents had not even noticed they missed pages. These experiences and others like them have led us to be very careful to print and examine proofs of all of our materials (questionnaires, letters, envelopes, postcards, etc.) before we print the large final orders. We also make sure that any proofs are printed at production quality so that we can see exactly what our sample members will be seeing.

In addition to checking these materials for appearance, we also check the variable aspects of the printing. The most common of these is the mail merge that adds names, addresses, and ID numbers to materials, but we sometimes also print variable information within the questionnaire that needs to be closely checked as well. In addition to making sure that the right information is being pulled into the right places on materials, we also double-check that all of the files we are using to merge information onto questionnaires, letters, envelopes, and any other materials are sorted in the same order so that we can group materials in batches for quality control during stuffing (see Guideline 10.15). We also test procedures for folding and stuffing materials. If we are doing this by hand, the test involves processing a couple of packages to see how well each step of the system will work. If we are using automated machines to do any folding or stuffing, we do some practice runs to ensure that everything is working properly. Either way, we want to make sure that materials are getting into envelopes in ways that ensure that they will come out of the envelopes well for sample members. This is also a good time to double-check the weight of the fully stuffed packages to ensure that enough postage is applied so they will be delivered without problems.

Once the fielding period begins, tasks have to be completed on schedule in order to ensure that the contacts are mailed on time to have the largest impact. The goal in this testing is to ensure that all systems are in place and working so things stay on schedule. In addition to testing the mechanics of the mail processing system, it is important to ensure that all materials (i.e., properly sized paper and envelopes, stamps, incentives, printer toner, etc.) are on hand at this stage so that scheduled mailings are not disrupted by the need to order and have materials delivered in the middle of the fielding period. A plan should also be in place for obtaining and securing incentives prior to mailing them. Finally, during this testing, any hardware and software that will be used to track and process returns and to enter data should be prepared and tested so that it is fully operational when completed surveys start coming back.

Guideline 10.20: Establish Procedures for Dealing With Undeliverable Mail

Usually one of the initial problems to present itself once mail-outs have been sent is the return of undelivered mail. Use of the U.S. Postal Service CDSF (see Chapter 3) has greatly decreased the number of undelivered letters, because residences are not included unless mail is currently being delivered to that address. However, people often move on short notice, and a certain number of postal returns are inevitable. The first solution to this problem is to do everything possible to prevent it from happening, but despite the best of efforts some mail is still likely to be returned as undeliverable. Giving immediate attention to this mail often makes re-mailing possible and prevents wasting scheduled follow-ups.

The reasons provided by the U.S. Postal Service for nondelivery generally fit into three categories. The first relates to a change of residence by the household.

Occasionally people move without leaving a forwarding address. Others leave forwarding addresses, but the U.S. Postal Service only keeps them on record for 18 months. If the move was within the same city or county, it is sometimes possible to locate the person by consulting the local telephone directory or other listings (although this is now far more difficult because so many people no longer have a landline phone and thus are not included in these types of directories). If only a telephone number is available, it may be necessary to call the household to get a mailing address. Through these efforts, it is often possible to re-mail a sizable portion of the contacts that were not forwarded.

The second reason for undelivered mailings is categorized here as "possible errors." This categorization seems appropriate because the main causes for return postal codes of "addressee unknown," "no such street," "no apartment number," "no residential delivery," and so on are clerical errors. When a mailing is returned for any of these reasons, processing procedures and sample sources need to be checked to see if an incorrect address was used. If this procedure does not identify the problem, then an attempt should be made to locate the respondent's telephone number and to call the household or business, thus reverting to the procedures used to locate those known to have moved. Some problems are unique to certain surveys. In one of our statewide surveys, nearly all of the letters for one rural community were returned. The reason for this problem was that the addresses reported in the sample list were different from those used by the U.S. Postal Service. A call to the local post office helped solve the problem.

The third category of problems reported in the notation system used by the U.S. Postal Service is that of letters that are refused or unclaimed. Generally, refusals are not a problem until later mailings when people recognize the envelope and presumably choose not to accept delivery. The questionnaires that are unclaimed from earlier mailings may have simply lain in the mailbox for a period of time without being picked up. This result suggests that the person may be temporarily gone, and re-mailing at a later time is often effective. However, some are clearly refusals, or the person chooses to leave the envelope in the mailbox. Out of respect for their rights, these people should not be contacted again. Finally, the U.S. Postal Service marks letters of persons who are deceased with that notation and returns them to the sender unless other arrangements for handling the deceased person's mail have been made.

The remailing of questionnaires requires establishing new mail-out dates for follow-up correspondence, creating additional work and complexity for the implementation of the study. However, the end result can be a significant increase of several percentage points in the final response rate and often in the representativeness of the final sample.

We recommend using the American Association for Public Opinion Research's system for assigning disposition codes to cases while they are in the field and at the end of the field period (AAPOR, 2011). These codes help researchers keep track of the outcome for each sample member and ultimately calculate their final response rates following industry best practices. Documentation and instruction for how to use these codes can be found at www.aapor.org.

Guideline 10.21: Establish Procedures for Dealing With Returned Incentives

In addition to creating a method for tracking and responding to returned mail, it is also important to establish a procedure for dealing with returned incentives.

We sometimes have people who send their incentive back to us because they do not want it, because they do not feel like they need an incentive to respond, or for other reasons. Likewise, incentives will come back in undeliverable mail. On one occasion a box of returned envelopes that could not be re-mailed sat unopened in the mail center for weeks as other more pressing business was conducted. While on the way to discard these mailings, one of us decided to open one of the envelopes and found that it contained a $2 cash incentive. It turned out that all of the envelopes in the box contained cash. As with this case, many surveyors are quite careful to account for every dollar when incentives are mailed out, but they often forget to plan ways to account for the money that is returned in undeliverable mail or by sample members. A system needs to be in place to deal with such returns and make sure all money is properly accounted for on a timely basis.

Guideline 10.22: Establish Procedures for Dealing With Respondent Inquiries

Another activity for which the researcher must be prepared is to answer respondent inquiries and comments. Each mailing is likely to bring reactions other than a completed questionnaire. Among the more frequent are the following:

- "The person you want is out of town for a month and cannot do it until she returns."
- "I would do the questionnaire except for the identification number on it."
- "I would answer except for the personal questions, which I don't think are any of your business."
- "I have only lived here for a few months, so I don't know enough about this community to answer your questions."
- "I'm too old, but my son will fill it out if you really need it."
- "I filled out a questionnaire like this one 6 months ago and don't want to do it again."
- "Tell me how you got my name, and I'll do your questionnaire."

It would hardly be fair, or ethical, to send a questionnaire asking 50+ questions to someone and then ignore or refuse to answer one or two resulting inquiries. People's questions, even strange ones, deserve a response. Thus, we make a point to answer each of them, but our response is determined by both philosophical concerns and response considerations. We explain why an identification number is used, why it is important to have old people as well as young people in the study, why the son would not be an acceptable substitute, and how the recipient's name was obtained. In general, one should respond to these types of queries as a well-trained interviewer would, attempting to convince people of their importance to the study. The most appropriate approach is to be straightforward and honest and to always thank the person for writing or calling.

In addition to these types of comments, letters are sometimes written by second parties on behalf of the questionnaire recipients. The most common of these indicate that the desired respondent is physically incapable of completing the survey, usually because of the infirmities of old age. Another fairly typical request comes from the spouse of the requested respondent, who reports that the person is temporarily out of town. These letters are responded to in much the same way that other inquiries are answered, except that the acknowledgment letters are sent to the second parties who reported that the desired respondent cannot complete the questionnaire. The aim of these letters is to thank them and also to assure them that the person will be removed from the sample list and will not be contacted again, if that action is appropriate.

Still another kind of inquiry we have grown accustomed to seeing occasionally is from individuals who have simply heard about the study, perhaps because a friend showed them a questionnaire. These sometimes come from media people or from those who would find the results useful in their work. These inquiries are handled in as helpful a way as possible, consistent with the study's objectives. It is particularly important for large-scale surveys to be prepared with a policy for handling requests for interviews or news stories. An appropriate approach is to respond to such requests in much the same way one would answer sample members' questions, emphasizing the social usefulness of the study, the importance of every individual responding, and so on.

Guideline 10.23: Evaluate Early Returns for Problems That Can Be Addressed Midstride

When returns begin to come in, one of the first priorities is to open the return envelopes and scrutinize the questionnaires. Besides providing for the quick location of items of concern that must be given attention in follow-up letters, this allows certain problems to be identified. For example, in one study mentioned earlier, it was learned that the ink used in printing the questionnaires caused some pages to stick together, resulting in sets of facing pages being skipped in many of the returned questionnaires (i.e., high item nonresponse). The immediate identification of this problem led to instituting a procedure whereby the missing two pages were photocopied, marked with the appropriate identification number, and returned to the respondent with a personalized note: "In our routine check for completeness we noticed two pages were missed. It appears they may have stuck together and thereby been inadvertently missed. … " Nearly two thirds of those contacted returned the missing pages, significantly improving the quality of the data. Usually, problems of this nature are not anticipated, making the close monitoring of early returns essential.

Each survey is different, with the survey topic, population, and sampling procedures all contributing to the existence of a unique set of circumstances. As a result, the implementation procedures that will be needed for each survey will also differ. Applying the same procedures to every survey will not work well. Implementation procedures need to be tailored to each specific survey situation in order to minimize barriers and costs of responding and maximize rewards and trust.

While the implementation procedures needed for each survey differ based on the characteristics of the survey, the procedures that can be afforded also differ based on the available budget. Because of this, most surveyors have to pick and choose from among the many implementation options available to them. For some, for example, it may be necessary to choose between providing an incentive or sending an additional contact. For those on even tighter budgets, neither the incentive nor the additional contact may be an option. What are they to do? While incentives and multiple contacts do improve response considerably, it is also important to remember that the less expensive strategies we have discussed here can also pay off by increasing response rates. For example, in a mail survey experiment using a 12-page questionnaire about a local metropolitan area, three mailings, and no incentive, Tarnai et al. (2012) got a 19% response rate using a standard #10 outgoing envelope and providing a business reply return envelope. A second treatment with the same standard outgoing envelope but with a stamped return envelope produced a 23% response rate, an increase of 4 percentage points. An additional 3 percentage points were gained, bringing the response rate to 26%, in a third treatment in which the standard outgoing envelope was replaced with a larger 6.5″ × 9.5″ envelope. This study clearly shows how a series of smaller and less expensive implementation strategies can add up to rather substantial increases in response.

CONCLUSION

Mail surveys have experienced a considerable reversal of fortune in recent years. Although response rates are now somewhat lower than in the past, when used alone as a data collection method, a surveyor can expect that they will be much higher than can usually be achieved by telephone or the Internet, when each of these modes is used alone. Response rates often range from 50% to 65%, as indicated by multiple recent studies discussed in this chapter. In addition, whereas address lists that cover all households in the United States did not used to be available, address-based samples now have as good of coverage as telephone surveys (and far higher than telephone surveys that only include landlines) but often the contact possibilities are far greater. And, since no available sampling frame exists for Internet surveys, using an address-based frame to contact people by postal mail provides a way of contacting people and asking them to respond by web, as discussed in more detail in the next chapter.

At the same time, certain limitations remain. In particular, controlling respondent navigation through paper questionnaires is difficult, and many people incorrectly execute complicated branching and skip patterns thus making it difficult to administer complicated questionnaires using this mode. Responding to paper surveys may also be particularly difficult for those who cannot read and understand the language(s) that the questionnaire is provided in. In addition, obtaining high response rates and quality depends upon multiple contacts that are carefully designed and coordinated, which may be far more expensive than administering a web-only survey.

The coverage and contact capabilities of mail make it especially useful in mixed-mode data collection designs. Postal mail is particularly effective at encouraging response to other modes, such as phone and Internet, especially since token cash or other incentives can often be delivered in the mailing. Thus, understanding procedures for postal mail contacts is essential for many mixed-mode surveys. The next chapter focuses on designing questionnaires and implementation procedures for mixed-mode surveys that include mail, web, and/or telephone modes.

LIST OF GUIDELINES

Guidelines for Designing Paper Questionnaires

Guideline 10.1: Determine whether keypunching or optical imaging and scanning will be used, and assess the limitations that may impose on designing and processing questionnaires

Guideline 10.2:   Construct paper questionnaires in booklet formats, and choose physical dimensions based upon printing and mailing considerations

Guideline 10.3:   Decide question layout and how questions will be arranged on each page

Guideline 10.4:   Use symbols, contrast, size, proximity, and pagination effectively when designing branching instructions to help respondents correctly execute them

Guideline 10.5:   Create interesting and informative front and back cover pages that will have wide appeal to respondents

Guidelines for Implementing Mail Questionnaires

Guideline 10.6:   To the extent possible, personalize all contacts to respondents (even when names are unavailable)

Guideline 10.7:   Send a token of appreciation with the survey request

Guideline 10.8:   Send a postage paid return envelope with the questionnaire

Guideline 10.9:   Use multiple contacts, each with a different look and appeal

Guideline 10.10:   Carefully and strategically time all contacts

Guideline 10.11:   Select all mail-out dates with the characteristics of the population in mind

Guideline 10.12:   Place information in the mailing exactly where it needs to be used

Guideline 10.13:   Take steps to ensure that mailings will not be mistaken for junk mail or marketing materials

Guideline 10.14:   Evaluate the effect of size and weight of mailing materials on mailing costs

Guideline 10.15:   Assemble the mailings in a way that maximizes the appealing aspects of each element when the package is opened

Guideline 10.16:   Ensure that all addresses in the sample comply with current postal regulations

Guideline 10.17:   Assign an individual ID number to each sample member

Quality Control and Testing Guidelines for Mail Surveys

Guideline 10.18:   Obtain expert review and conduct cognitive interviews, experimental evaluations, and pilot studies of implementation materials and procedures

Guideline 10.19:   Test all systems for producing and mailing contacts and questionnaires and closely examine production quality proofs of all materials

Guideline 10.20:   Establish procedures for dealing with undeliverable mail

Guideline 10.21:   Establish procedures for dealing with returned incentives

Guideline 10.22:   Establish procedures for dealing with respondent inquiries

Guideline 10.23:   Evaluate early returns for problems that can be addressed midstride

Mixed-Mode Questionnaires and Survey Implementation

WHEN SINGLE-MODE SURVEYS ARE NOT ACCEPTABLE

Single-mode surveys remain important in many situations, as discussed in Chapters 8, 9, and 10. However, in other circumstances such surveys, regardless of whether telephone, web, or mail, are likely to produce inadequate results. Three discussions with survey sponsors illustrate the compelling need to consider mixed-mode approaches, and how these mixed-mode designs require changes to be made in the procedures for single-mode designs that we have covered in the preceding three chapters.

A university faculty member approached one of us to discuss his plan to conduct a mail-only random sample survey of university students. He believed that significant differences were likely to have occurred in alcohol and marijuana use among undergraduates since he had conducted a similar survey in 1995. He wanted to compare results from a new survey with his previously collected data to assess change among students. For the original survey, he had obtained a complete mailing list of local addresses for students from the university registrar; at that time, addresses were updated at the beginning of each semester during registration. Nearly two thirds of the students sampled completed the 12-page paper survey.

For the new survey, postal addresses were no longer automatically updated by the university; that task is now left to the students, and many do not update their address information. As a result, some mailing addresses are the same as those reported when students first applied for university admission, thus increasing the likelihood that a nonrandom subset of students was unlikely to receive a questionnaire mailed to that address. In addition, some students may have an updated address but are unlikely to check postal mail regularly. It seemed probable that repeating the same procedures used a decade earlier would not obtain acceptable results. Instead, a plan was made to obtain e-mail and postal addresses for students, as well as their telephone numbers. By using all three modes of contact, the expectation was that he would increase his chances of making contact with sample members and get them to do the survey, overcoming the weaknesses that each mode has when used alone. The faculty member was also encouraged to obtain responses mostly over the Internet using e-mail communication, supported by postal letters and token cash incentives, a mixed-mode methodology described later in this chapter.

Another discussion involved staff of a state agency that regularly conducted random digit dial telephone surveys to measure the general public's concerns with state roads and highways. The agency was committed to continuing those surveys using a landline sampling frame as they had done in previous years. We discussed whether the systematic decline in response rates that had been occurring in recent years was acceptable to the agency. An agency representative pointed to research showing that response rates are not necessarily correlated with nonresponse error, and suggested that the declining response rates were not a problem. It was also noted that one of the successful aspects of their past surveys was that the results showed respondents' concerns were changing over time. The agency did not want to make changes in survey mode, question wording, or other features of the survey that might disrupt the trend lines. The response to this situation began with a description of the rapid decline in use of landline phones (according to the latest estimates from the National Health Interview Survey in 2013, only 58% of households in the United States have landline phones [Blumberg & Luke, 2013]), and how this could result in a substantial number of households not being covered by their frame. The trend lines were perhaps more a reflection of the fact that the sample frame was becoming less and less representative of the desired statewide population of households than a result of true change.

In considering alternative methods, we discussed the possibility of including cell phones, and the related concern that a significant number of cell phones (and some landlines) would belong to people who no longer lived in the state, and that the frame would miss many new residents who kept their area codes from the state they previously lived in. It was also noted that other ways in which calling cell phones can be more expensive (as discussed in Chapter 8), thus increasing the overall costs of conducting the survey. Ultimately, the suggestion to the agency was to consider sampling postal addresses and sending a survey request with a token cash incentive by mail. With the postal request, they could either ask sample members to respond to a paper questionnaire, or ask them initially to respond by web and then in a later reminder provide nonrespondents with a paper questionnaire as an alternative response mode. The expectation was that the change to address-based sampling would significantly improve household coverage as well as the response rate, compared to that obtained by using landline RDD procedures alone.

The third discussion was with a business that periodically conducted client surveys over the Internet on a variety of topics. This group reported having e-mail addresses for nearly 90% of their clients. Their standard practice was to send the initial e-mail contact followed by one reminder a few days later. To compensate for the low number of returns (less than 10%), they increased their sample size so that many clients were being approached with a request once a month. However, response rates had declined over time, a possible result of being surveyed so frequently. In addition, it was noted that those who responded tended to report either a negative experience or positive one, so that the response distributions were becoming somewhat bimodal, causing them to wonder if the results were representative of all clients, or only those at the two extremes. After some discussion, we learned that this organization had mail and telephone contact information for most of their clients in addition to the e-mail addresses they were using.

The discussion with this group focused on how they might survey individuals less frequently. This required increasing response rates so that smaller samples could be drawn for each survey. The suggested approach involved encouraging people to respond over the Internet by using a postal letter to bring attention to the e-mail request that they were about to receive, which included an electronic link for the survey, and by using a telephone reminder call. The possibility of using a design that would include an invitation to provide answers over the telephone in the follow-up phone calls was also introduced. However, inasmuch as many of the questions asked in some of the surveys focused on client opinions (e.g., very satisfied, somewhat satisfied, etc.), collecting some responses by telephone raised the likelihood that answers would be different than those collected over the Internet simply because of the change in modes, a topic to which we return to in Guideline 11.8 (Christian, Dillman, & Smyth, 2008).

Conversations like these have become increasingly common over the last few years, as many surveyors try to repeat or emulate single-mode methods they have successfully used in the past, and others try to use new technologies to reduce costs or overcome some of the response and coverage challenges associated with only using the Internet to contact and survey respondents. In each of these cases, it appeared as if a multiple-mode survey might be a better, and sometimes perhaps the only, way to accomplish the goals of each study.

Prior to the beginning of the 21st century, mixed-mode survey designs were used, but generally were uncommon as most surveys were conducting by a single mode (Dillman, 2000; Dillman & Tarnai, 1988). The generally good quality of single-mode survey designs, and the huge time-consuming challenge of coordinating data collection across multiple modes in a noncomputerized and less connected environment, made their use infrequent. But as technology was developed that made coordination across modes easier, and response rates to single-mode surveys declined, researchers began exploring in detail the ways in which survey modes could be mixed and the consequences of mixing them (de Leeuw, 2005; Dillman & Christian, 2005).

In Chapter 2, we advised readers to use multiple modes of communication (Guideline 2.4) and multiple modes of response (Guideline 2.5) to affect the benefits, costs, and trust balance in ways that would encourage response. But, as these conversations illustrate, undertaking a mixed-mode survey in these ways is likely to be significantly more challenging than designing a single-mode survey. It requires understanding not only the intricacies of questionnaire construction, contacts, and implementation procedures appropriate for each of the survey modes (as discussed in Chapters 8, 9, and 10), but also coordinating when and how those modes are to be used. Thus, the methodological knowledge requirements are greater, as are the organizational efforts needed for success. Yet despite all these complications and challenges, the reasons for considering mixed-mode designs have become more and more compelling in recent years.

WHY CONSIDER A MIXED-MODE SURVEY DESIGN

Surveyors often turn to mixed-mode survey designs when it is difficult to achieve the desired results using a single mode alone. As mentioned in the earlier chapters, individual modes may have limitations that prevent surveyors from using a single mode to achieve the high-quality data results they need. When this happens, mixed-mode surveys may be the answer. The following are common reasons surveyors might be motivated to use a mixed-mode design (for more detail, see de Leeuw, 2005).

Lower Costs

One of the most compelling reasons for considering the use of multiple survey modes is to lower costs. Many mixed-mode survey designs begin with less expensive modes and then move to more costly modes for those who do not respond initially. An example of using multiple modes to reduce survey costs is the U.S. 2010 Decennial Census, for which questionnaires are mailed to all U.S. households to get initial responses (nearly 70%), and then more costly personal enumeration is used to collect the remaining responses. Additional examples of using mixed-mode designs to lower costs are discussed in Guideline 11.18.

Improve Timeliness

Mixed-mode surveys may also allow surveyors to collect responses more quickly. For example, a longitudinal survey of doctoral degree recipients conducted by the National Science Foundation (NSF) asked which mode (web, paper, or telephone) respondents preferred in a 2003 data collection and then offered the preferred method in 2006. This significantly shortened the length of time needed to complete the follow-up (Hoffer, Grigorian, & Fecso, 2007).

As another example, the Current Employment Statistics (CES) survey, conducted each month by the Bureau of Labor Statistics, uses six different modes (mail, computer-assisted telephone interviewing, fax, touchtone data entry, electronic data exchange, and web) to collect employment data from businesses. Businesses are matched with the mode that is most convenient for them to respond by in an effort to improve the speed of response because a 14-day turnaround is critical for reporting the national employment data collected by this survey (Rosen, 2007).

Reduce Coverage Error

In addition to reducing survey costs and improving timeliness, mixed-mode surveys are also used to improve coverage when a single mode cannot adequately cover the population of interest, or when contact information is not available for the desired mode of data collection. For example, a number of studies we will discuss in this chapter use postal mail to contact sample members and ask them to respond to a web survey because e-mail addresses are not available. To improve coverage, paper questionnaires are also mailed to respondents who are unable to respond via the web. As another example, a number of web panels have been built by using an alternative mode, such as in-person or telephone interviews, to enroll members so that all households, including those who do not have Internet access, can be covered. Those without the Internet are typically either provided with web access or surveyed via another mode, such as paper.

Another example is a series of WSU Student Experience Surveys conducted via the web almost annually from 2002 to 2011. In the earlier years of these studies, e-mail addresses were only available for about two thirds of the students.

Therefore, building the sample frame from this list would have resulted in serious undercoverage. Instead, the sample frame was built using postal addresses, which were available for almost all students. E-mail addresses were then appended to it. This allowed us to contact all respondents by postal mail and follow up by e-mail with those for whom an e-mail address was available.

Improve Response Rates and Reduce Nonresponse Error

One of the core reasons for using mixed-mode surveys is to improve response rates and reduce nonresponse error. One of the most effective ways of improving response rates in surveys, as discussed in Chapters 2 and 10, is to provide token cash incentives of a few dollars at the time of the survey request. Postal mail can be an effective way to provide small cash incentives for modes where cash incentives cannot otherwise be easily delivered (e.g., for telephone or web data collection), as discussed in Guideline 11.12. But there are other ways in which multiple modes can be used to improve response. For example, assigning respondents to one mode ahead of time based on their preference, if it is known, can be useful for improving responses.

Offering people the mode they prefer increases the speed by which they respond and has been shown to increase response rates in some modes. We discuss the issue of mode preference in greater detail in Guideline 11.14. Likewise, offering a second or even third mode to nonrespondents can improve response rates and reduce error by encouraging responses from people who are difficult to reach or unable or unwilling to respond via the initial mode. Often the second or third mode also adds a new and different contact to the survey request, increasing the likelihood that even those who may have missed a previous contact will notice this one.

However, achieving high response rates does not always mean that nonresponse error is reduced (Dillman et al., 2009; Groves, 2006). Thus, it is important that the use of multiple modes actually help to improve the representativeness of the responses received such that nonrespondents are not different in significant ways from those who do respond. For example, if people included in a particular survey population are unskilled computer users or are uncomfortable with responding to web surveys, offering a second mode such as mail or telephone may serve as an important way of reducing nonresponse error, as we discuss further in Guideline 11.16.

Reduce Measurement Error

Using mixed-mode surveys to reduce measurement error may be one of the oldest and most generally recognized reasons for conducting mixed-mode surveys. When in-person interviews were the primary means of collecting data, respondents often had to provide answers aloud, in the presence of other household members, in addition to the interviewer, which often led to more socially desirable responses for sensitive questions (e.g., sexual behaviors or the use of drugs and alcohol). The need to ask sensitive questions in ways that were not embarrassing led to the practice of handing people a brief paper questionnaire for them to record their responses without saying their answers aloud. A modern version of this practice is to simply offer respondents the same computer or tablet used by the interviewer to record their answers so they have the opportunity to read and answer the questions themselves (i.e., mixing computer-assisted personal inter-viewing with computer-assisted self-administration). In a more advanced version, respondents can be provided with earphones to listen to questions, and can answer them by marking answers on a screen where no one, including the respondent, can see the questions (Tourangeau & Smith, 1996). This practice is particularly common in health interview surveys.

Combined Effects

In general, it would be a mistake to attribute the trend toward using multiple modes to only one of these reasons. More often, a combination of concerns leads to the decision to use a mixed-mode survey design. The substantial increase in the use of mixed-mode surveys throughout the world has been fueled by survey-ors balancing the often competing demands of budget and time while striving to improve data quality by reducing coverage, sampling, nonresponse, and measure-ment errors.

What error source(s) are minimized and whether costs and field time are reduced depends heavily on how the modes are mixed. For example, using one mode to contact sample members and encourage a response by a different mode can improve coverage and response rates with no negative effect on measurement, but will likely increase costs. In comparison, using alternative modes for different respondents in the same survey may minimize coverage and nonresponse error and can also decrease survey costs, but, depending on how it is done, may also increase measurement error because respondents answering in the different modes may experience the survey differently. Having interview respondents answer sen-sitive questions in a self-administered mode will not impact coverage error, but has real potential to decrease measurement error. Thus, the way modes are mixed should be determined based on consideration of the ultimate survey goal and why using multiple modes was seen as the best solution. Creating the best survey design involves choosing the optimal mode or combination of modes, and utilizing them in ways that minimize overall total survey error.

The wide variety of ways that modes can be mixed for surveys can be catego-rized into three overarching strategies:

1. Use of multiple *contact* modes to encourage response for data to be collected by a single response mode.
2. Use of multiple *response* modes to collect respondent answers, while using only one mode of contact.
3. Use of multiple *contact and response* modes for the same study.

Within these three strategies, there are many options for how to mix modes, as initially discussed in Chapter 2. For example, all three of the main survey modes—telephone, mail, and Internet (or e-mail) may be used either as a contact mode or a response mode, which opens up an enormous number of potential combinations that can include mixing some or all of these modes at the contact, response, or both contact and response stages. This chapter builds upon the foundation provided in Chapters 8, 9, and 10 for telephone, web, and mail surveys and provides specific guidelines for designing questionnaires and implementation procedures for mixed-mode surveys that involve more than one mode of contact and/or response.

GUIDELINES FOR DESIGNING QUESTIONNAIRES THAT WILL MINIMIZE MEASUREMENT DIFFERENCES ACROSS SURVEY MODES

It is necessary to understand questionnaire design for each mode, as discussed in Chapters 8, 9, and 10, in order to design a questionnaire for a mixed-mode survey. But while some of the best practices for design in those chapters will work well in mixed-mode surveys, others will not. In mixed-mode surveys, the biggest questionnaire design challenge is figuring out how to bring design together across modes without introducing measurement error.

The most significant barrier to doing this is the tradition of working in single modes. Typically, surveyors using a particular mode worked separately from those using other modes, with the goal of maximizing the fit of each question with their survey mode. For telephone questionnaires that meant, for example, including answer choices in the questions that were read to respondents and providing extra response options (e.g., "no opinion," "refused") that the interviewer could offer only when needed. Mail questionnaire designers, on the other hand, tended to offer all response categories up front, including options like "no opinion," so that people needing those responses could select an appropriate answer without having to leave the question blank. Internet questionnaire designers also designed in mode-specific ways. For example, they quickly started introducing new response mechanisms such as slider scales that required respondents to complete several motions (i.e., click, hold, and move) to register an answer. Writing questionnaires for mixed-mode surveys requires rethinking many of these practices. If we do not, it is likely that the differences in how questions are asked across modes will inadvertently result in different answers (i.e., increased measurement error when responses are combined).

Guideline 11.1: Use the Same Question Format and Wording Across Modes

Using different question wordings and formats across modes is one of the most significant barriers to conducting successful mixed-mode surveys. Figure 11.1 provides examples of questions suited for one mode, but not others, and how these questions can be revised to work across modes. The top example shows a question using a telephone format we mentioned earlier, where the "don't know" option is available for interviewers to use but is not explicitly offered to respondents up front. It is not possible to use this same format in self-administered modes; since there is no interviewer present, the category needs to either be offered to respondents or not. For a mixed-mode survey involving telephone and a self-administered mode, the sponsor has two options. One is to withhold the "don't know" response from all respondents. This will likely result in higher item nonresponse rates in the self-administered mode. Another option is to provide the "don't know" option to everyone, a change that is likely to increase the percentage of respondents choosing that category across all modes. The solution we suggest is to explicitly provide "don't know" (or similar categories such as "no opinion") in both versions, thus unifying the items offered to respondents across modes.

The second example in Figure 11.1 starts with a question about marital status that had been asked for many years in multiple telephone surveys by a national

FIGURE 11.1 Examples of unified mode construction to create similar stimuli across all survey modes.

A telephone format that does not work well for mail or web

How satisfied are you with the community in which you live? Would you say . . .

1 Very satisfied
2 Somewhat satisfied
3 Slightly satisfied
4 Not at all satisfied
5 (DON'T KNOW—read only if respondent cannot decide)

A revised unified format for use in all three modes

How satisfied are you with the community in which you live? Would you say . . .

O_1 Very satisfied
O_2 Somewhat satisfied
O_3 Slightly satisfied
O_4 Not at all satisfied, or
O_5 Are you not sure?

A telephone format that does not work well for mail or web

What is your marital status?
(INTERVIEWER: RECORD APPROPRIATE CATEGORY BUT DO NOT READ)

1 Single
2 Married
3 Separated
4 Divorced
5 Widowed

A revised unified format for use in all three modes

Which of the following best describes your marital status?

O_1 Single
O_2 Married
O_3 Separated
O_4 Divorced
O_5 Widowed

A web or mail format that does not work well for telephone

Why did you join the retirement community Recreation Association? (check all that apply)

☐ To meet new people

☐ To be more active

☐ To spend more time with friends

☐ To participate in a specific activity it offered

A revised unified format for use in all three modes

Please indicate whether or not each of the following is a reason you joined the retirement community Recreation Association.

	Yes	No
To meet new people	O_1	O_2
To be more active	O_1	O_2
To spend more time with friends	O_1	O_2
To participate in a specific activity it offered	O_1	O_2

---

polling organization. When a survey was switched from telephone to web and the closed-ended version was asked, it was immediately noticed that the proportion reporting being divorced, widowed, or separated increased while the proportion reporting being single or married decreased. What is so different about these two questions to cause people to report their marital status, which is a very concrete construct, differently? The major difference between them is that the telephone version is asked as an open-ended question, where respondents were not read the response options, while the web version is asked in a closed-ended format where respondents could see the response options. When asked for their marital status in an open-ended format, many respondents likely decided that it was sufficient to report that they were married or single. For those who were single, the more detailed categories of separated, divorced, or widowed likely never came to mind. In this case, offering all of the categories in both the telephone and web modes was a simple solution to the problem, but when this solution was posed to the survey sponsor, it was met with hesitation. There was a real concern that changing the telephone version of the question would disrupt trend lines that had been measured for many years. The use of questionnaires delivered in two or more modes requires us to think differently about what question formats are best and, oftentimes, to confront the reality that what was done in the past may not work well now.

The third example in Figure 11.1 shows another question construction that was commonly used in some modes, but does not work in others. Check-all-that-apply questions were frequently used in mail surveys in order to make the response task easier (e.g., no need to select an answer to every item), but their use significantly increased when surveyors began asking questions on the web because the html design feature of square check boxes was easy to use and allowed for choosing multiple answers. However, check-all-that-apply formats are seldom used in telephone because they are difficult to administer. Reading all of the options and having respondents report which ones apply requires more working memory capacity than most people have, and the alternative of reading one item at a time is awkward, since respondents might or might not respond to each item, which makes it difficult for the interviewer to know when to move to the next item. Research we discussed in Guideline 5.12 makes it clear that answers tend to differ between the check-all and forced-choice (i.e., yes/no) formats, but that the forced-choice format seems to transfer well across interviewer and self-administered modes, and allows for the items to be subject to deeper processing.

There are many other examples of question formats that tend to work in one mode but not others. In mixed-mode designs, these mode-specific differences in question construction should be identified and eliminated. Unified mode design of question and answer formats is critical.

Guideline 11.2: Use Similar Visual Formats Across Modes

Until the late 1990s there was virtually no research that showed how dramatically different visual layouts for questions affected responses to mail and web surveys. Substantial research since that time has made it clear that responses are significantly affected by the size of open-ended response spaces; spacing between response categories; verbal labels accompanying answer boxes; and the use of color, spacing, delineation of response fields; how branching instructions are provided; and a variety of other issues (as discussed in Chapter 6). It has also become clear that the effects of visual information (i.e., graphics, symbols, words, and numbers) are generally similar for web and mail surveys. These findings suggest the desirability of building questions similarly for both web screens and the pages of paper questionnaires to minimize mode differences.

The need for similarity goes beyond the design of individual questions; overall page format is important as well and can be standardized to a great degree across the web and mail modes. Figure 11.2 shows examples of screens and pages from a mixed-mode survey that used web and mail modes (the Lewiston and Clarkston Quality of Life Survey). The web version of this questionnaire used page-by-page construction to keep respondents focused on one question at a time. The paper version was designed to emulate the page-by-page construction of the web survey by placing each question in an enclosed region with a colored background and boundaries. This design decision was made because of the tendency for respondents to see information within each region as separate from information in other

FIGURE 11.2 Example of web and paper questionnaires for a mixed-mode study in which the paper questionnaire was designed to emulate the web questionnaire.

Screens from original web version*

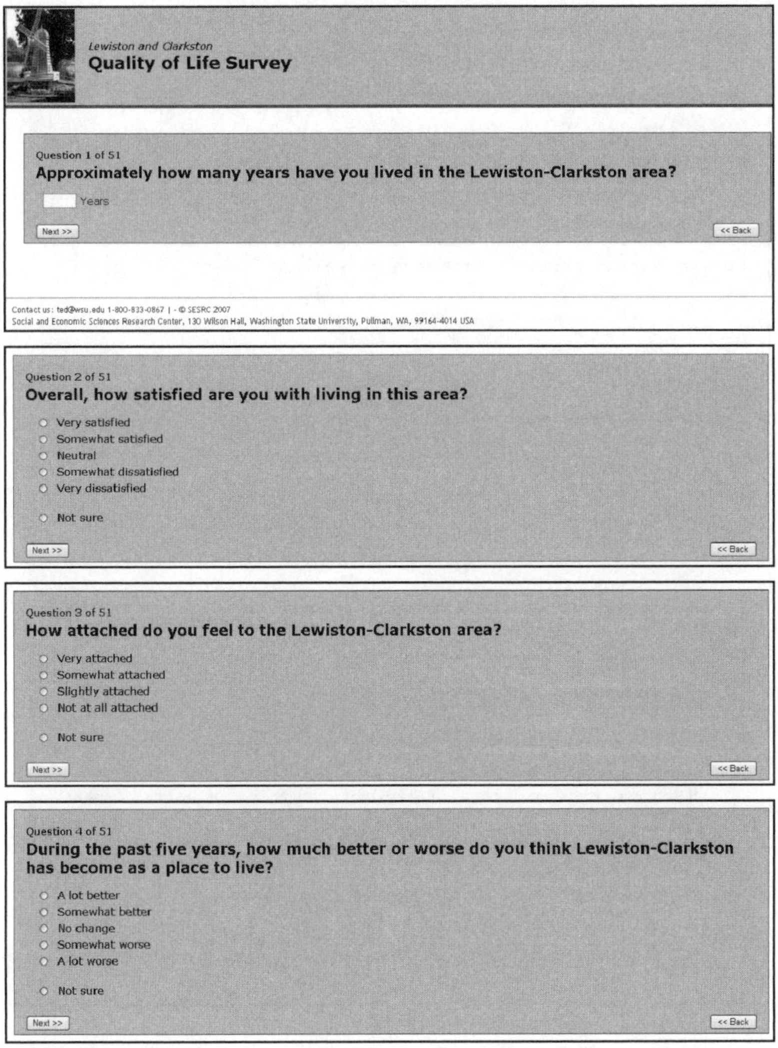

Lewiston and Clarkston
Quality of Life Survey

Question 1 of 51
Approximately how many years have you lived in the Lewiston-Clarkston area?

☐ Years

Next >>　　　　<< Back

Contact us: ted@wsu.edu 1-800-833-0867 | - © SESRC 2007
Social and Economic Sciences Research Center, 130 Wilson Hall, Washington State University, Pullman, WA, 99164-4014 USA

Question 2 of 51
Overall, how satisfied are you with living in this area?

○ Very satisfied
○ Somewhat satisfied
○ Neutral
○ Somewhat dissatisfied
○ Very dissatisfied

○ Not sure

Next >>　　　　<< Back

Question 3 of 51
How attached do you feel to the Lewiston-Clarkston area?

○ Very attached
○ Somewhat attached
○ Slightly attached
○ Not at all attached

○ Not sure

Next >>　　　　<< Back

Question 4 of 51
During the past five years, how much better or worse do you think Lewiston-Clarkston has become as a place to live?

○ A lot better
○ Somewhat better
○ No change
○ Somewhat worse
○ A lot worse

○ Not sure

Next >>　　　　<< Back

* The second through fourth images have been cropped to save space.

regions, as described in Dillman, Gertseva, and Mahon-Haft (2005). The goal of this design was to have respondents to both the paper and web questionnaires process the questions one at a time. Answer categories were also aligned vertically, rather than horizontally, which could have been easily accomplished for the paper questionnaire pages because of the unused space in each field. This was done to match the vertical format used on the individual web pages (Smyth, Dillman, Christian, & O'Neill, 2010).

In the survey shown in Figure 11.3 (Quality of Life in a Changing Nebraska survey), the design goal was different. Here, the web questionnaire was built to mirror the paper version, where multiple questions appeared on the page. In this case, the researchers only had enough money to print and mail a four-page

FIGURE 11.2 (*continued*).

Paper version designed to emulate web version

Q1. **Approximately how many years have you lived in the Lewiston-Clarkston area?**

☐ Years

Q2. **Overall, how satisfied are you with living in this area?**

○₁ Very satisfied
○₂ Somewhat satisfied
○₃ Neutral
○₄ Somewhat dissatisfied
○₅ Very dissatisfied

○₆ Not sure

Q3. **How attached do you feel to the Lewiston-Clarkston area?**

○₁ Very attached
○₂ Somewhat attached
○₃ Slightly attached
○₄ Not at all attached

○₅ Not sure

Q4. **During the past five years, how much better or worse do you think Lewiston-Clarkston has become as a place to live?**

○₁ A lot better
○₂ Somewhat better
○₃ No change
○₄ Somewhat worse
○₅ A lot worse

○₆ Not sure

Q5. **How much better or worse do you think the local economy has become in the past five years?**

○₁ A lot better
○₂ Somewhat better
○₃ No change
○₄ Somewhat worse
○₅ A lot worse

○₆ Not sure

Q6. **How much better or worse do you think the area's natural environment has become in the past five years?**

○₁ A lot better
○₂ Somewhat better
○₃ No change
○₄ Somewhat worse
○₅ A lot worse

○₆ Not sure

1

questionnaire for their mail version. As a result, it was necessary to use a two-column page format to fit all of the questions. Once this paper version of the questionnaire was designed, the web version shown in Figure 11.3 was designed to emulate it. In this case, a scrolling design was needed on the web to match the paper version, but the questionnaire was long enough that putting it all on one screen seemed ill advised. Instead, page breaks were put into the web survey at every section heading that was used in the paper questionnaire. This helped ensure that the same questions were visually grouped together in the paper and web versions, although by slightly different means. In addition, the same banner style, image (the sun setting on the Platte river), colors, title, and so on were used in both modes to further unify the design.

Once, when involved in discussions at the U.S. Census Bureau on building an Internet version of the Decennial Census form, a strong case was made by a committee that the web page would look better if it were done with blue background

FIGURE 11.3 Example of paper and web questionnaires for a mixed-mode study in which the web questionnaire was designed to emulate the paper questionnaire.

Original paper version

Quality of Life in a Changing Nebraska
Taking a snapshot of issues affecting Nebraskans' quality of life.

START HERE

1. On a scale from 1 to 11, where 1 is very dissatisfied and 11 is very satisfied, how satisfied are you with your <u>work</u> (job, school, or housework)?

2. On a scale from 1 to 11, where 1 is very dissatisfied and 11 is very satisfied, how satisfied are you generally with the way you spend your <u>leisure time</u>?

3. Please think about your relationship to your partner, spouse or date. On a scale from 1 to 11, where 1 is very dissatisfied and 11 is very satisfied, how satisfied are you currently with your <u>relationship</u>?

4. On a scale from 1 to 11, where 1 is very dissatisfied and 11 is very satisfied, how satisfied are you currently with your <u>life-as-a-whole</u>?

5. How many years have you lived in Nebraska?
   ☐ Years lived in Nebraska

6. How many years have you lived in your community?
   ☐ Years lived in community

Family

7. How many adults ages 19 and older are living in your household?
   ☐ Number of adults living in household

8. What is your marital status?
   ☐ Married → **Go to # 10**
   ☐ Never married
   ☐ Widowed
   ☐ Divorced
   ☐ Separated

9. Are you currently living with someone in a marriage-like relationship?
   ☐ No
   ☐ Yes

10. Do you have any children aged 18 or younger at home?
    ☐ No → **Go to # 13**
    ☐ Yes

11. If yes, do you think your children will stay in Nebraska when they grow up?
    ☐ No
    ☐ Yes ▸ **Go to #12**

12. Do you want your children to stay in Nebraska when they grow up?
    ☐ No
    ☐ Yes

13. Do you think that children today will be better off or worse off if they stay in Nebraska?
    ☐ Better
    ☐ Same
    ☐ Worse

1

fields, rather than the yellow fields that were used in the 2000 Decennial Census paper form. Doing that would have resulted in the yellow paper form being mailed to households looking dramatically different than the form that they were going to be encouraged to complete on the Census web page. This mismatch likely would have increased the possibility for error, because putting the forms into quite different colors (and graphic families) would have been confusing to some recipients, especially those using more than one mode (e.g., those who use the paper form to draft answers and then transfer them to the web survey). Others may have filled out the questionnaire twice, thinking that the yellow paper form and blue

FIGURE 11.3 *(continued).*

Scrolling web version designed to emulate paper version

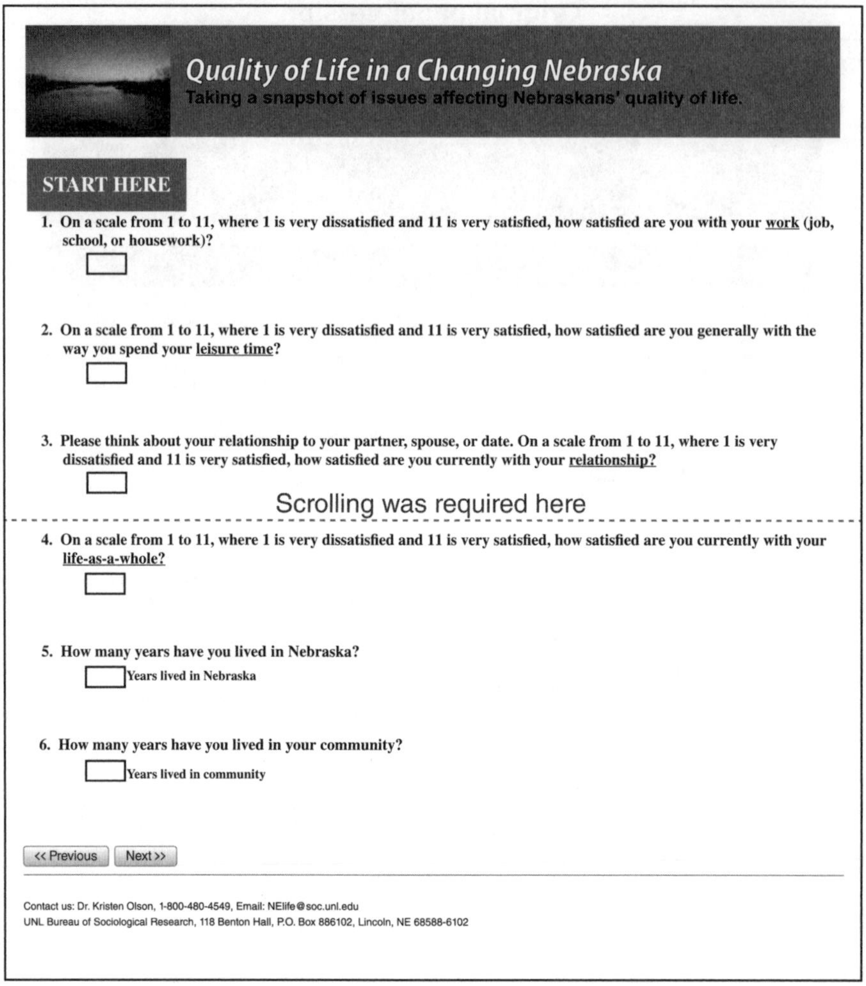

web form were for different surveys. This visual consistency problem was resolved by changing the paper form so that it utilized a blue background similar to the one desired for the web survey.

Guideline 11.3: Use Similar Wording and Visual Formats Across Web and Telephone Surveys

Building a web survey with a screen-by-screen design will result in questions being perceived individually rather than as a group, similar to how they are experienced by respondents in a telephone survey. In addition, for some telephone interviews conducted in mixed-mode surveys, where web is also a mode of response, interviewers may use the web instrument, rather than a separate CATI system, to administer the questionnaire. A page-by-page construction is closer to a traditional CATI screen, so it should help ensure that the interviewers ask the questions in the right order and do not get distracted or confused by extra information on the screen. To a somewhat lesser degree, a similar effect can be accomplished in paper surveys by putting each question into its own region as was done in the questionnaire shown in Figure 11.2.

If one is using only telephone and web as response modes, and therefore is not limited by the lack of computerization in mail surveys, there is much more that one can do to unify these two modes. In these modes respondents may easily be routed to different follow-up questions based on how they answer each question, a task that requires complex visual design instructions in paper surveys. In addition, the answer one gives to an early question, for example, the city that one visited, may be used in a later question, for example, "When did you visit <u>Atlanta, Georgia</u>?" Further, it is occasionally important for responses to a question (or series of questions) to equal a total. Providing an automated calculation tool for interviewers or respondents to use is generally beneficial and should be used in both telephone and web surveys. These types of changes can improve response accuracy, but are only a few of the features that can be used when mixed-mode surveys are conducted by telephone and web.

A survey conducted several years ago by the Research Triangle Institute (Wine, Cominole, Heuer, & Riccobono, 2006) illustrates how a unified mode questionnaire construction approach can be used to bring results from telephone and web surveys together. Their implementation involved encouraging people to respond initially by web, with a telephone interview follow-up to everyone who did not do so. To achieve mode equivalency, the researchers used the same screens for telephone interviews as those used for web respondents. This required building the screens in ways quite different from typical telephone questionnaire screens. The new screens did not include common features such as interviewer prompts and instructions that are not to be read to respondents. This meant that the interviewers had to adjust to the new design. Follow-up analyses by the authors indicated that this unified design produced virtually no differences between modes.

Even if additional information is still needed by interviewers to effectively administer the questionnaire, the web questionnaire can be leveraged for the telephone interviewing. For a recent survey of college presidents that one of us worked on, we created a copy of the web questionnaire, and then added additional information that interviewers needed to each screen so that they would still have the information that was important to them while administering the questionnaire. This approach saved substantial time from programming a separate CATI questionnaire and helped ensure that the design of the questions and how the responses were entered was similar across modes.

Guideline 11.4: When Mixing Mail and Web, Leverage Web Technologies When They Will Help Respondents Navigate the Questionnaire or Reduce Errors, But Not When They Will Likely Result in Measurement Differences

The web offers a number of design options that are not available in mail surveys. Some of these options should be used in web and mail mixed-mode surveys. Others should not. For example, one should allow the web survey programming to automatically navigate respondents through skip instructions even though those responding by mail will not receive this assistance. Likewise, one should use automatic calculation tools on the web to show totals even though the same cannot be done on the mail.

Alternatively, drop-down menus and embedded links to definitions or additional information should not be used on the web because the same cannot be done on the mail. So what is the difference? Why would we suggest using automatic calculation tools, but not drop-down menus? The answer is that the first two examples—navigation assistance and automatic calculation tool—will help respondents avoid making errors or correct those they have already made, but will not fundamentally affect the way a question is asked or what information is presented to respondents.

In contrast, a drop-down menu changes the way respondents see the response options in a question, possibly making certain options more visible than others, which will in turn make them more likely to be selected (as discussed in Guideline 5.8). Similarly, since links may contain information that other respondents also may need, they can change the fundamental context of the question. If the definitions or other information is important, it should be presented to respondents in all modes as part of the question. It is these types of unnecessary changes in the measurement stimulus across modes that we want to avoid in mixed-mode surveys.

Guideline 11.5: When Mixing Web or Paper With Telephone, Give Priority in Both Modes to the Short and Simple Stimuli Needed for Telephone

A number of design elements that are necessary for telephone administration can and should be incorporated into web or mail modes if these modes are to be used alongside the telephone in a mixed-mode design. For example, respondents in all modes can benefit from short and simple question stems and from breaking complex response tasks down into simpler tasks (although one should be careful if this results in a lot of branching in paper surveys). Other design elements may not be ideal for the web or paper, but may still be necessary to create a stimulus that parallels what is used in the telephone mode, such as using fewer scale points and separating grids into a series of items that can stand on their own (because the grid format cannot be administered over the telephone). Each of these is an example of using a unified mode design to ensure that the stimulus is kept as similar as possible across the modes.

Guideline 11.6: When Mixing Web or Mail With Telephone, Build in Conversational Cues and Transition Statements to Unify the Design Across Modes

However, in some instances where mail or web is mixed with telephone, including additional information is helpful. Adding conversational cues to telephone questionnaires can help make it easier for interviewers to read and administer questions and avoid untimely respondent interruptions that can take the conversation off script in ways that might affect measurement. In addition, when each question appears on its own screen, whether by telephone or web, occasional transitions help focus the respondent's (and interviewer's) attention. As mentioned in Guideline 8.6, these include transitions that inform respondents of topic changes as well as transitions within questions that tell respondents when it is their turn to speak. In the interest of unified mode design, these same transitions can be added to mail or web surveys. If done correctly, the addition should take very little space and should not add to respondent burden. Including these transitions in web or mail questionnaires is particularly important when one intends to have interviewers use them to administer the questions by telephone.

Guideline 11.7: If There Is Even a Small Chance of Mixing Modes in the Project, Design the Questionnaire for the Possibility of Mixed-Mode Data Collection

We have come across many surveyors who plan to conduct their survey using a single mode such as web, but when response rates are not as high as desired, may decide to start calling sample members late in the field period and administer the questionnaire over the telephone. Because they did not plan for aural adminis-tration when designing the questionnaire, they end up asking questions that are awkward over the telephone. Oftentimes these surveyors have to quickly change the wording, add information, or modify the questions in some other way to make the questions work over the telephone. This undermines the important goal of standardizing the stimulus across respondents. If there is even the slightest chance that the telephone will be used to follow up with nonrespondents, one should consider this possibility from the outset of the design. Several of the guidelines presented for telephone surveys can be implemented during the design of the ini-tial web or mail questionnaire that will make administering it by telephone much easier and more standardized.

A similar challenge is commonly faced by those conducting web surveys that ask for a great deal of complex information, especially information that needs to be gathered from records or collected from several different people. In many cases, the way information is stored in records does not match the order in which that information is asked for in the web questionnaire (for more on this, see Snijkers, Haraldsen, Jones, & Willimack, 2013). In this case, many respondents will want a paper version of the questionnaire that they can use to organize and collect all of the responses on, prior to entering them into the web questionnaire. If one consid-ers the potential for this need from the outset and designs accordingly, response burden can be decreased considerably. For example, a print-friendly version of the web survey that incorporates the guidelines for designing paper surveys can be made available, or a parallel paper version of the questionnaire can be offered. However, if one does not anticipate this need, respondents may be stuck trying to make do with a web instrument that is just not built to be printed. Imagine, for example, how much work would be involved in having to individually print every page of a page-by-page web survey, especially for longer surveys. Alternatively, one may decide to design a printable version of the questionnaire quickly to respond to these types of requests.

We also know of instances in which in an effort to obtain responses only over the Internet, individuals have been sent a sample paper questionnaire to illustrate the kinds of questions asked in the survey. This can be a successful means for reduc-ing mid-questionnaire cut-offs for Internet response. Similar efforts have been made to improve response to follow-up telephone calls. In each of these instances it is important that unified mode construction be applied to the questionnaires produced for each mode.

Guideline 11.8: Recognize That Even With Unified Mode Design, Some Measurement Differences May Still Occur Across Modes

Even when one has taken all steps to create a unified design across questionnaires, there are still situations in which a true mode effect will occur. That is, there will be a difference in measurement across the modes that cannot be explained by unnecessary variations in design across the modes. For example, many of the interviewer effects discussed in Chapter 4, such as social desirability, acquiescence, and interviewer characteristics (e.g., gender, age, or race), may still contribute to measurement error when mixing interviewer and self-administered modes. Further, utilizing some of the programming available in telephone and web surveys may improve measurement enough in those modes to balance any additional measurement error that may occur because these features are not available in the paper survey.

Another example concerns responses to scalar questions. For more than two decades, studies have shown substantial differences in responses to scalar questions when asked by telephone versus visual modes, an effect that was confirmed in a recent meta-analysis by Ye, Fulton, and Tourangeau (2011). This research has demonstrated that respondents provide more positive responses when surveyed by telephone than when presented with a visual scale (in mail and web surveys, or in face-to-face surveys when show cards are used).

An example from one of these studies is shown in Figure 11.4, where responses to 10 questions about long distance telephone service were compared across four modes: mail, web, telephone, and IVR. Five of the questions were scalar questions presented in a polar-point scalar format where only the end points of the scale were verbally labeled (e.g., "Overall how satisfied are you with your long distance company? Please use a 1 to 5 scale where 1 means not at all satisfied and 5 means extremely satisfied."). The results indicated that telephone and IVR respondents provided more positive responses than mail and web respondents for all 5 polar-point questions (Dillman et al., 2009). It should also be noted that the direction of

FIGURE 11.4 Example of more frequent selection of the extreme positive category in scalar questions in interviewer than self-administered modes.

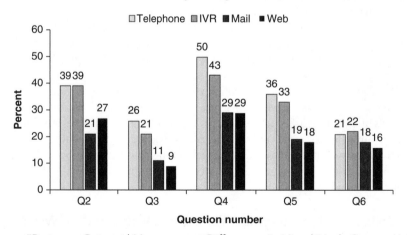

Percent choosing the positive labeled end point for five satisfaction questions about long distance telephone service, by survey mode

Source: "Response Rate and Measurement Differences in Mixed-Mode Surveys Using Mail, Telephone, Interactive Voice Response, and the Internet," by D. A. Dillman, G. Phelps, R. Tortora, K. Swift, J. Kohrell, J. Berck, and B. L. Messer, 2009, *Social Science Research, 38*(1), 1–18.

the scalar categories was reversed for half of the telephone sample, and no evidence of a recency effect was found.

Similar findings were reported by Dillman and Mason (1984), who found that face-to-face and telephone respondents from the general population were more likely than mail respondents to choose the extreme positive option on nine items (differences ranged from 4 to 9 percentage points). Also, Tarnai and Dillman (1992) reported the same type of differences among college students (ranging from 13 to 38 percentage points), and Krysan, Schuman, Scott, and Beatty (1994) found the same effect when comparing face-to-face to mail general population respondents (7 to 17 percentage points).

Consistent with these previous findings, in two mixed-mode telephone and web surveys of college undergraduates conducted in 2004 and 2006, telephone respondents provided significantly more positive ratings than web respondents for 36 of the 46 scalar questions across various types of response scales and a variety of different question topics and scale labels (Christian, 2007). This happened (a) regardless of whether all of the categories or only the endpoints were verbally labeled, (b) regardless of whether all of the categories were presented in one step or in two steps (the first step asked respondents to report the direction, positive or negative; the second step asked respondents to evaluate the strength of their position), (c) across a variety of scale lengths, and (d) across a variety of topics and types of scales (e.g., satisfaction, agreement, likelihood, and a variety of construct-specific scales). In other words, the effect was not eliminated by manipulating the presentation of the scales.

Social desirability, acquiescence, and primacy and recency effects have all been offered as explanations for these findings, but are not able to adequately account for them. The extremeness in aural modes has been found consistently on questions that would not seem particularly sensitive or otherwise subject to social desirability, as well as across many types of scales that would not seem prone to acquiescence. In addition, three studies comparing responses to scalar questions across interviewer-administered surveys found that respondents were more likely to select the extreme positive category when surveyed by telephone than when surveyed face-to-face by an interviewer with show cards used to visually display the scale (de Leeuw, 1992; Groves & Kahn, 1979; Jordan, Marcus, & Reeder, 1980). Because interviewers were present in all of these comparisons of telephone and face-to-face responses, social desirability and acquiescence would not seem likely to have caused these differences. In fact, if these social norms were the culprit, we would generally expect higher use of the extreme category in the face-to-face survey, where the interviewer is physically present, rather than in the telephone survey. Similarly, primacy or recency cannot explain these findings, because in several studies the extremeness occurred regardless of whether the positive or negative end of the scale was presented first. Thus, it seems that the differences are due to the different stimulus (i.e., aural versus visual) across modes.

The results of all of these studies indicate that the same scalar questions may produce more positive responses when no visual display of the scale is present, and these differences can sometimes be quite large in magnitude. The likelihood that these differences will occur cannot be ignored. The consistency of the evidence across various types of attitude and opinion items is such that we caution against mixing aural and visual modes for surveys containing a lot of scalar questions, or where the scalar questions are used for answering the central research question.

EXPANDING THE RESEARCH BASE FOR DESIGNING MIXED-MODE SURVEYS

Mixing modes raises a number of other complicated challenges, in addition to necessitating unified questionnaire designs. One has to decide what mode or modes to use to contact respondents. If multiple modes are used for contact, it then becomes important to decide how many will be sent/made by each mode, as well as the order, timing, and content of each contact. Likewise, one has to decide what mode or modes to use to collect responses, and, if using multiple modes, whether they should both be offered simultaneously (concurrently where multiple modes are offered up front) or sequentially (where only one mode is offered initially and another is offered later). For sequential mixed-mode designs, questions arise such as which mode should be offered first and how long to wait before offering alternative modes of response.

In Chapter 2 we introduced the WSU Doctoral Student Experience Survey (Millar, 2013). This study attempted to maximize benefits, minimize costs, and build trust to the extent possible in a situation where e-mail and postal addresses were both available (for most respondents) and where the target population was very familiar with using computers and the Internet. To do this, a mixed-mode approach was used at both the contact stage (to increase the likelihood that students would receive, attend to, and ultimately cooperate with the survey request) and the response stage (to increase response while getting as many people to respond by web as possible to save costs). A great strength of the design for this particular survey was sending an e-mail with the survey link to support the initial postal contact and remove a significant barrier to responding by web (i.e., the need to transfer the URL from a postal letter to a web browser). In this study, in addition to good response and data quality, it was also essential to maximize web responses and minimize the time and expense spent processing the mail responses. The study was successful in this regard; a final report was sent to the study sponsor within 45 days of when data collection began. This study was successful because it brought together the right mix of design elements for the target population of doctoral students within the time and budget constraints for the study.

Surveying the general public, a population for which high response rates are increasingly difficult to obtain, raises different kinds of challenges with regard to how elements might be combined into an effective design, especially given the coverage and sampling challenges for most modes of contact, with the exception of postal mail. In 2007 we began a series of experiments aimed at testing the effectiveness of combining various elements together to encourage general public responses over the Internet. These experiments included using multiple postal mail contacts, token cash incentives, and a focus on the visual and verbal design of the contacts and questionnaires. We tested these elements in multiple surveys sent to households in local communities and states that were selected using address-based sampling, which provided 95% to 97% coverage of households in the geographic areas being studied. Results from the early experiments were used to refine the procedures used in the later ones. In addition, certain tests were repeated across experiments and new tests were added. The results from these studies have been described in detail elsewhere (M. L. Edwards, 2013; Messer, 2012; Messer & Dillman, 2011; Messer, Edwards, & Dillman, 2012; Olson, Smyth, & Wood, 2012; Smyth et al., 2010), but the guidelines that follow draw heavily on what we have learned from these studies.

Most of these tests were made using 12-page mail questionnaires (containing 10 pages of questions) and web questionnaires consisting of between 50 and 60 individual pages. The items within these questionnaires requested a total number of individual responses that ranged from 70 to 150, which we estimated would take 20 to 25 minutes to complete. This questionnaire length was chosen because of research on paper questionnaires that suggested a significant decline in response when longer booklet questionnaires were used (Leslie, 1996). Each study was also conducted on a different topic, ranging from community satisfaction and economic issues to preferences for electricity production and concerns about water management. This variation was deemed important so that we could gain insight into the robustness of the general approach for studying multiple issues, but all of the topics were public policy issues that seemed relevant to community, state, and societal concerns. For most of the studies, the sponsor was Washington State University. One exception was a study conducted by researchers at the University of Nebraska–Lincoln using a four-page questionnaire containing 45 questions (75 individual items) about the quality of life in Nebraska.

GUIDELINES FOR USING MULTIPLE CONTACT MODES TO ACHIEVE MORE EFFECTIVE COMMUNICATION WITH POTENTIAL RESPONDENTS

For too long, many survey designers have viewed mode of response as synonymous with mode of contact—a phone call to get a response by telephone, a postal letter to obtain a response by mail, and now an e-mail to obtain a web response. At first look, it seems logical that great efficiency would be obtained by only having to deal with a single mode of contact and response, inasmuch as the transition from contact to responding to the questionnaire in the same mode is generally more seamless and natural. However, limiting a survey to contacts by the desired response mode has become one of the major stumbling blocks preventing surveyors from obtaining higher response rates to all survey modes. Increasingly, telephone calls from strangers do not get answered, e-mails from unknown sources are ignored or deleted, and people may check for postal mail only occasionally.

When it comes to increasing response rates, mixed-mode survey designs have the advantage of allowing for the use of additional modes to send contacts, making them less likely to be ignored. Contact by a different mode may reach a sample member when contacts sent via the original mode did not, or may allow for the delivery of an advanced token incentive that will help shift the perceived balance of rewards and costs in favor of response. In addition, a second mode of contact may be instrumental for building trust that the survey is legitimate and not a scam. Also, synergy between contacts by multiple modes can be achieved to further increase the likelihood of receiving responses. This was the case with the e-mail used to deliver an electronic link that followed a postal letter (that also contained a token cash incentive) in the WSU Doctoral Student Experience Survey example discussed in Chapter 2.

In many cases, the utilization of multiple contact modes will improve response rates more than offering alternative modes of response, as is often done, for example, when surveyors are trying to increase response rates by offering different modes so people can respond how they prefer, a topic to which we return to later in this chapter. Outlined here are several guidelines for harnessing the power of mixing contact modes, either to support response by one mode or to offer alternative ways of responding. All of these guidelines will require knowledge of the implementation procedures discussed in Chapters 8, 9, and 10 for telephone, web, and mail surveys. Successful mixed-mode implementation will also require some creative thinking about how to use these procedures in new ways, especially to build synergy with other aspects of the mixed-mode design.

Guideline 11.9: Obtain Contact Information for More Than One Survey Mode Whenever Possible

There was a time when providing contact information for mail and telephone was viewed as important, even mandatory. It was generally assumed that others had a right to contact individuals, so such information was readily provided. Many organizations spent large sums of money periodically updating contact information for employees, customers, students, and others. When e-mail and cell phones came into the picture, people became more inclined to reserve one or more means of contact for certain individuals or groups (e.g., I only share this e-mail account with my close friends and family and have another account for online shopping, coupons, etc.). In addition, rather than actively initiating and carrying out updates of contact information, organizations began leaving it up to their employees, customers, students, clients, and so on to update their own contact information when they see fit. Complicating matters further, people were increasingly able to change their e-mail addresses and telephone numbers and did so more often. Perhaps even more important for how people communicate, the distinction between e-mail and telephone began to blur as a growing segment of the population now primarily uses one device—a smartphone—for making calls, checking e-mail, texting, browsing the Internet, and consuming media.

In the past, surveyors maintained a list of contact information associated with the survey mode in which people were being asked to respond, and did not ask for or compile contact information for additional modes. Increasingly, it is not possible to obtain lists with the same type of contact information available for every person on the list. Rather, many lists have e-mail addresses for some people, telephone numbers for others, and postal addresses for other people, making it difficult to contact, and even more importantly reach, everyone in the sample by a single mode. We recommend routinely obtaining contact information for as many ways of reaching people in the sample as possible. This allows for the use of a second or third contact mode when others do not work, and even more importantly, facilitates building synergy between one mode of contact and alternative ways of responding.

Guideline 11.10: Use Multiple Contact Modes to Increase the Likelihood of Contacts Being Received and Attended to by the Sample Members

When contacting people by mail, e-mail, or telephone, at least some people may not be reachable by or have access to that mode. Survey requests that do not reach people cannot obtain responses, no matter how convincing or well designed they are. If only one contact mode is used to deliver the survey request and encourage people to respond, there is little that can be done when the request never reaches anyone (e.g., when postal mail is returned undeliverable and some letters may never be opened, e-mails bounce back or are deleted or routed to spam filters before they are read, or phone calls go unanswered and voice mail messages ignored).

Introducing an additional contact mode provides a second opportunity to communicate with sample members, increasing the number of contacts overall, which has long been shown to increase response rates (Heberlein & Baumgartner, 1978). However, changing the mode of delivery when making the additional contact makes it more likely to be noticed than an additional contact in the same mode because by altering the physical medium in which the contact is delivered, it adds freshness to one's request that cannot be achieved by sending another contact in the original mode. This is supported by research that suggests repeating the same message over again in multiple contacts is less effective than varying the messages across contacts (Dillman, 2000; S. Ohm, personal communication, August 8, 1998). Thus, not only should the wording of requests and the nature of the appeals be changed between contacts, but introducing an additional mode can also help to increase the likelihood that at least one of the contacts will be attended to by the sample member. Once the recipient of the survey request has received a contact and decided to attend to it, each contact mode can facilitate different strategies for convincing the sample member to cooperate. For example, both telephone and e-mail contacts make it possible to contact people and answer questions quickly and efficiently. Postal contacts are slower, but they allow for the delivery of a prepaid token incentive, in particular cash incentives, and also make it easy to include other information or materials.

Previous research has found that contacting sample members by different modes can help improve response. For example, a special contact by telephone or certified mail was shown to be effective for improving response rates in mail surveys (Brick et al., 2012; de Leeuw & Hox, 1988; D. E. Moore & Dillman, 1980). In particular, the switch to telephone to contact respondents provides considerable contrast to the repetitive mail contacts. In this case, interviewers inform sampled members that a questionnaire was sent to them previously, encourage them to respond, and answer any questions they may have about the study and the questionnaire. In some cases, people may be given the opportunity to complete the survey on the telephone or told that another paper questionnaire can be sent again if the previous one has been thrown away. When such a contact is used, it is important to time the call such that people will still remember and hopefully have the paper questionnaire that was sent. Also, these types of calls are often more effective when they can be conducted by more experienced interviewers, rather than those who are instructed only to read a simple reminder notice to the questionnaire recipient. As this example shows, it can often be helpful to link together the contacts by different modes so that the telephone call can be used to support the completion of the paper questionnaire, even if responses are not collected by telephone.

Guideline 11.11: Use Contact by a Mode Different Than the Response Mode to Increase Trust That the Survey Is Legitimate and Useful

People frequently receive e-mails from sources that are not what they pretend to be, and thus are often skeptical of requests from unknown or suspicious sources. For example, in recent months we have received e-mails asking us to click on a link and fill out forms to update bank account information, click on a link and enter personal information so that we can obtain a parcel at the Post Office that could not be delivered to our home, enter our computer password to get access to e-mail that was not delivered because of an allegedly full inbox, enter personal information to get a $100 gift card for a well-known box store, and others. None of these requests was legitimate and many times the apparent sponsor was known but the request actually originated from a different source. These attempts to access one's personal information are incredibly creative. Oftentimes they even provide a link one can use to verify the legitimacy of the request that sends one to a fake web page created for that purpose.

In this environment it should not be surprising that people become quite suspicious of requests from unknown or unverified sources, especially those that contain attachments or links, which many e-mails asking for people to complete web surveys include. Since many of these types of requests appear to come from known sponsors, even e-mails from organizations a person knows may be viewed with suspicion. In addition, many Internet users are cautious about providing any personal information over the Internet because of hacking concerns and even simply to avoid getting on e-mail marketing lists.

Trust is not an issue that only applies to Internet surveys. Answering a phone call from an unknown survey sponsor, or even one whose name is known, carries some risk that the call is not legitimate or that the request is actually a sales call rather than one for a research study. In addition, the common practice of not telling people the topic(s) of the survey questions (or sometimes the sponsor) may raise concerns as to whether the call is legitimate. It is also possible that senders of postal mail may misrepresent themselves and send out marketing materials under the guise of a survey.

Using multiple contact modes provides opportunities to provide information that can be used by the sample member to confirm that the survey is legitimate. For example, postal letters can provide the name and phone number of sponsors (something that is seldom provided in deceptive e-mails). It is also possible to provide website addresses that contain considerable detail about who the sponsor is, the nature of the survey, why it is being conducted, and how the results will be used. An example would be the website for the American Community Survey (U.S. Census Bureau, n.d.). Websites with restricted domain names like .gov or .edu are likely to engender more trust than others.

Phone calls that come without any warning are easily ignored and when answered, the time pressure means that people often have little opportunity to learn more about the study and assess whether to participate. Advance letters sent by postal mail have been shown to be effective across multiple studies in giving notice ahead of time that a phone call is coming, thereby reducing the surprise and uncertainty associated with getting an unexpected telephone survey request. Further, often more information can be provided in a letter than in a short introduction to a telephone survey, and as mentioned earlier, prepaid token cash incentives can be included with the postal contact.

In a meta-analysis of 29 individual studies, de Leeuw et al. (2007) showed that sending an advance letter increased telephone survey cooperation rates by 11 percentage points on average (from 64% to 75%) and response rates by 8 percentage points (from 58% to 66%). Such letters have long been used for telephone surveys when addresses are available, but one of the challenges of traditional RDD surveys today is the lack of availability of addresses for most sampled phone numbers.

In sum, when postal addresses are available for telephone surveys, advance letters can help build trust that the survey is legitimate, and help communicate that the results may be beneficial to individuals or groups with whom they identify in a positive way.

Just as postal letters can help improve response rates to mail surveys, telephone calls, when numbers are available, can help improve response rates to web and mail surveys. In particular, phone calls can be made after contacts by other modes to learn whether previous contacts sent by e-mail or postal mail have been received, to answer any questions or address any concerns recipients may have, and to encourage response. Such follow-up phone calls can help convey the legitimacy of the study as well its potential benefits. Telephone calls can also be effective up front in surveys of establishments to help inform them about the study and identify the appropriate people within the organization who should respond to the survey request (e.g., which people at the organization know or handle the information requested as part of the survey).

Guideline 11.12: Send a Token Cash Incentive With an Initial Postal Mail Contact to Increase Trust in the Survey

As discussed in Chapter 10, research on mail surveys has consistently shown over many years that small cash incentives sent with the survey request have a strong positive effect on response rates (Church, 1993; P. Edwards et al., 2002; Heberlein & Baumgarter, 1978). In lieu of cash, small gifts sent with a survey request also have a positive, albeit somewhat smaller, effect. By contrast, post-paid or contingent incentives sent only to those who complete the questionnaire are much less successful at increasing response. Research has also suggested that the use of token cash incentives increases response more among reluctant or uninterested sample members (Groves et al., 2006) and among younger recipients than older ones (Miller, 1996). These effects are not limited to mail surveys. A recent report on nonresponse in social science surveys by the National Research Council (2013) concludes, based upon work by Singer (2011), that incentives, especially prepaid incentives, increase response rates to surveys in all modes.

One of the difficulties faced with initial contacts by either telephone or e-mail is that prepaid cash incentives cannot be delivered by those modes in order to encourage consideration of the request, which is usually presented in a hurried fashion over telephone or in an abbreviated fashion by e-mail. However, a token cash incentive can easily be included in a postal letter that asks the recipient to go to the Internet or informs her to expect a phone call in the near future. Two experimental tests of sending letters asking for responses over the Internet have shown that such an approach is quite effective. In one survey of undergraduates at Washington State University, a $2 bill included with the postal request to respond over the Internet nearly doubled the response rate, from 21% to 38%, compared to sending either an e-mail or a postal letter without an incentive (Millar & Dillman, 2011).

In another survey conducted on households in Washington State, including a $5 incentive in a postal letter improved both mail and web responses (Messer & Dillman, 2011). In one group, where sampled members were first asked to respond over the Internet and mail was introduced in the fourth and final contact (web+mail, i.e., web first), including a $5 incentive in the postal letter increased responses by web from 13% to 31%. The overall response rate (combining the

FIGURE 11.5 Effect of a $5 token cash incentive with the initial survey request in web+mail and mail+web sequential mixed-mode designs.

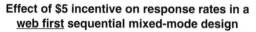

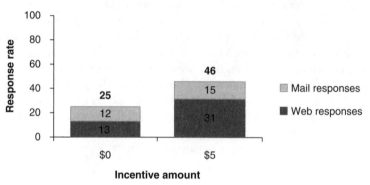

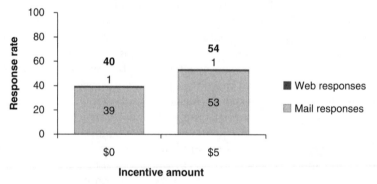

Note. Results from an address-based sample survey of Washington State households. In the web+mail treatment, web was offered as the first response mode with the mail alternative withheld until the fourth and final contact. In the mail+web treatment, mail was offered as the first response mode with the web alternative withheld until the fourth and final contact.

Source: "Surveying the General Public Over the Internet Using Address-Based Sampling and Mail Contact Procedures," by B. L. Messer and D. A. Dillman, 2011, *Public Opinion Quarterly, 75*(3), 429–457.

responses by mail) increased 21 percentage points, from 25% to 46%. In a control group where response was initially requested by mail, and a web alternative was not provided until the fourth contact (mail+web, i.e., mail first), a $5 incentive produced a smaller but significant improvement in the overall response rate, from 40% to 54%, an increase of 14 percentage points as shown in Figure 11.5.

The fact that the incentive had a larger effect when web was the initial mode offered and the primary mode of response is understandable. Significant effort (a cost to respondents) and trust are required to go from a mail request to a computer or other device and to manually enter a URL in order to respond over the Internet (i.e., to switch from one mode of contact to a different mode of response). The incentive with the request fosters trust and encourages recipients to make this effort. Responding to a mail request by filling out an enclosed paper questionnaire requires less effort and can likely be done with less apprehension, meaning more people may complete the request even when no incentive is provided. The lower burden for those responding by mail is supported in the same study; more people responded by mail than web when it was offered first or second and regardless of whether an incentive was offered. For example, when given a $5 incentive, 53% of those responded by mail when that mode was offered first compared with 31% who responded by web when it was offered first (as shown in Figure 11.5).

Reflecting the importance of looking at the implementation procedures holistically, in this study the group that had the highest overall response rate, 54%, was that which received the $5 incentive but also were offered the paper rather than web questionnaire first (overall response rate was 46% when web was offered first). In this case, the incentive was not the only aspect of the design that impacted response; the overall response rate reflects multiple aspects of the implementation process, not just the inclusion of the incentive. The convenience (or lower costs) of not having to switch modes for those asked to complete the paper questionnaire (mail+web) combined with the effect of the $5 incentive to produce the highest response rate. It is also important to note that while providing a mail response option after web produced improved response rates and overall representation, offering web after a mail request produced virtually no improvement in response rates, a topic we discuss further in Guideline 11.16.

Some might wonder if an electronic incentive sent by e-mail would have the same effect as a cash incentive sent by postal mail. Research shows that electronic incentives do not have as strong of an effect as a prepaid cash incentive delivered by mail. For example, Birnholtz et al. (2004) randomly assigned members of their web survey sample (all of whom were very experienced Internet users) to receive either (a) a $5 cash incentive with a survey invitation via postal mail, (b) a $5 Amazon.com gift certificate with a survey invitation via postal mail, or (c) a $5 Amazon.com gift certificate with a survey invitation via e-mail. The results showed that 57% of those receiving the cash incentive via postal mail completed the survey compared to 40% of those receiving the gift certificate via postal mail and only 32% of those receiving the gift certificate via e-mail.

In summary, the most powerful stimulus for getting people approached by one mode to respond by another is a token cash incentive sent with the survey request. The incentive does not need to be large, but its presence engenders trust and encourages recipients to attend to the other information provided, including the surveyors' appeal to respond. Yet, as the Messer and Dillman (2011) study demonstrated, it is not the only factor entering into the cost, benefit, and trust considerations used by sample members to decide whether and how to respond.

Guideline 11.13: Consider Including a Second Cash Incentive in a Later Contact to Improve Response Rates

Sending a second cash incentive, in a later contact, is not something that surveyors have typically done. Some argue that they do not want to reward people for not responding when the first incentive was offered. However, in today's environment for household surveys, where address-based samples do not include names, respondent selection instructions are included in the survey instructions, and mode changes are being made between early and late contacts, including a second cash incentive will strengthen the likelihood that later communications will be read, and hopefully acted upon, thereby increasing overall response. Additional experimental treatments by Messer and Dillman (2011) tested the effects of a second incentive on response rates. One treatment included an additional $5 incentive when those who had not responded by web were sent the paper questionnaire and given the option of responding by mail (in the third of five contacts). The final response rate was higher, 52% compared to 48%, in the treatment that received the second incentive. More responses were returned by mail for the group that received the additional incentive (18% vs. 15%), but that difference was also not statistically significant. However, as noted in Chapter 10, the second incentive was quite effective in the treatment group that was only asked to respond by mail and never offered a web option. The overall mail response rate for this group was 68%, compared with 59% for the group that did not receive the second incentive.

Additional research needs to be done to examine whether offering a second incentive is effective for different types of studies, and particularly to determine whether the quality of data is improved by reducing differences in a meaningful way between respondents and nonrespondents, an issue not evaluated by Messer and Dillman (2011). The use of additional incentives, provided later in the field period, may be especially useful in adaptive designs, to target the incentives toward certain groups or types of nonrespondents.

GUIDELINES FOR PROVIDING ALTERNATIVE RESPONSE MODES

Offering alternative response modes is another way that mixed-mode designs can improve response compared to single-mode surveys. However, the decisions on which modes to use, whether to offer those modes simultaneously as a choice or sequentially by offering one mode initially and withholding the alternative mode until later, and how to support the offering of multiple modes with appropriate contacts are complicated. In this section we provide guidelines for offering alternative response modes aimed at improving data collection strategies.

Guideline 11.14: Utilize Information on Respondent Mode Preferences When Practical, but Recognize That Improvements in Response Rates and Data Quality May Be Quite Modest

Research has shown that individuals can and do express preferences to respond by particular survey modes (Groves & Kahn, 1979) and that catering to this mode preference can be of limited benefit. For example, respondents to the 2008 Nebraska Annual Social Indicators Survey were asked in a telephone survey which mode they would prefer for future surveys; about 49% reported preferring telephone, 25% mail, and 20% Internet (Olson et al., 2012; Smyth, Olson, & Millar, forthcoming). In 2009, these same respondents were surveyed again with some being asked to complete a survey in the mode they previously reported

FIGURE 11.6   Results from a study examining the effects of catering to mode preferences on response rates.

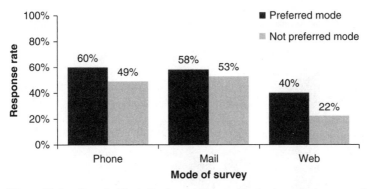

Response rates in phone, mail, and web surveys, by whether respondents received their preferred mode

Source: "Does Giving People Their Preferred Survey Mode Actually Increase Survey Participation? An Experimental Examination," by K. Olson, J. D. Smyth, and H. Wood, 2012, *Public Opinion Quarterly, 74*(4), 611–635.

preferring and others being asked to complete a survey in a different mode (Olson et al., 2012). Those who received their preferred mode responded more quickly, and, as Figure 11.6 shows, response rates were higher among those who received their preferred mode than those who did not receive their preferred mode, significantly so in the telephone and web modes. However, it is also important to notice that web achieved a lower response rate than mail or phone. Even among those who preferred this mode the response rate was only 40%, which is lower than both the phone and mail response rates among those who did not prefer these modes (49% and 53%, respectively). Put a different way, the study received higher response rates among those surveyed by nonpreferred phone and mail modes than among those surveyed by their preferred mode of web.

Time and time again, we have heard surveyors insist that they need to offer a web mode of response because young people will prefer this mode and will be unwilling to respond by other modes (and we are now starting to hear the same argument made about surveys on mobile devices). While our research suggests that young people do, in fact, prefer the web mode (Millar, O'Neill, & Dillman, 2009; Smyth et al., forthcoming; Smyth, Olson, & Richards, 2009), the findings shown in Figure 11.6 suggest that catering to this preference for the web may not be advisable because of the overall lower response rates this mode produces compared to phone and mail. It is for this reason that we say that catering to mode preference can be of limited benefit.

We are also cautiously optimistic about the promise of catering to mode preferences for another reason. Figure 11.7 shows the reported mode preferences of those who responded to the 2008 Nebraska Annual Social Indicators Survey (NASIS), which was conducted by telephone, and the reported mode preferences for the same people when they answered the 2009 Quality of Life in a Changing Nebraska (QLCN) survey, which was conducted by mail and Internet. In 2008, when they were being surveyed over the telephone, the majority of these respondents chose home phone as their preferred survey mode, but in 2009 when

FIGURE 11.7 Example of how reported mode preferences are influenced by the survey mode in which the mode preference question is asked.

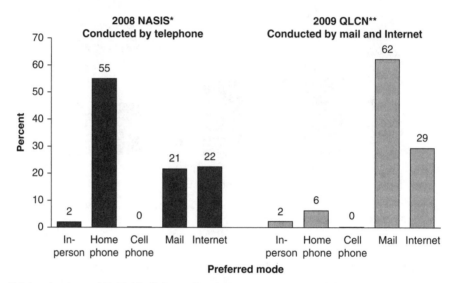

Percent reporting a preference for each mode in the 2008 NASIS and 2009 QLCN

*Nebraska Annual Social Indicators Survey.
**Quality of Life in a Changing Nebraska Survey.
Source: "Measuring Mode Preference: Question Wording and Question Order Experiments," by J. D. Smyth and K. Olson, 2010. Paper presented at AAPOR May 13–16, 2010, Chicago, IL.

they were being surveyed either over the mail or Internet, the majority chose mail as their preferred survey mode with Internet coming in second. These data also reveal that in the 2009 QLCN, 80% of those who answered by mail reported that mail was their preferred mode and 80% of those who answered by web reported that web was their preferred mode (Smyth & Olson, 2010). Similar results were obtained when respondents were asked to report their mode preferences in a mail and web mixed-mode survey in adjacent towns in Washington and Idaho in 2007. In this case, 65% reported preferring mail, 35% web, and 1% telephone, but 87% of those surveyed by mail chose mail as their preferred mode and 90% of those surveyed by web chose web as their preferred mode (Millar et al., 2009). These results suggest that reports of mode preference are highly influenced by the mode in which people are asked the question and their thoughts about their current experience of being surveyed in that mode.

Additional insight into the effect of mode preferences is available from a treatment group in the Lewiston and Clarkston Quality of Life study, in which recipients of the survey request were told that the mode of response (web or mail) was entirely up to them and complete information was provided with each contact to allow either mode of response. In this mode-choice treatment, 63% of the households returned questionnaires. Of these, 80% responded by mail while only 20% chose to respond by Internet (Smyth et al., 2010). This 4-to-1 ratio of mail to web responses is consistent with findings from other research. It suggests a clear preference for mail when the mail contact offers both a web or mail response.

It has also been found that preferences for mode vary with respondent characteristics. For example, Smyth et al. (forthcoming) show that younger people clearly prefer the web. In addition, being highly educated, a heavy Internet user, and having Internet access at home all predict having a web preference. While this research shows that the young tend to prefer the web over other modes, it is also important to remember that not all young people have access to the Internet. Two percent of 18- to 29-year-olds and 8% of 30- to 49-year-olds are not Internet users (Pew Internet & American Life Project, 2013d). In addition, some who are Internet users may not have the skills to use it well and others may simply be unwilling to respond in that way (e.g., those with low literacy or vision impairments). For these young people, mode preference may be based less on liking and more on ability to respond in a mode. Thus targeting modes to young people based on an age variable on the sample frame or to people who live in areas with high concentrations of young people based on census data may introduce some risks if other modes of responding are not provided.

In conclusion, clearly people have mode preferences and they can make a difference in whether they are willing and/or able to respond by that mode, but at the same time mode preferences for some people are not strongly held and there is variation in mode preferences within demographic groups. As a result, offering multiple modes of responding (web plus mail) may produce higher response rates than using a web-only single mode, as found by Olson et al. (2012). As this discussion implies, providing alternative response modes is one way to attempt to cater to mode preference, but how those alternatives are provided is likely to have a significant impact on the quality of results, as we discuss in the following sections.

Guideline 11.15: Avoid Offering a Simultaneous Choice of Response Modes Unless Barriers to Responding in Both Modes Are Removed

We are often asked why we should not just offer multiple modes and let people choose how they prefer to respond, especially if people have modes that they prefer over others. Many surveyors have offered multiple modes of response at the same time and allow people to choose a mode of response (known as a *simultaneous* or *concurrent* mixed-mode design). A meta-analysis of 19 such surveys that offered web and mail alternatives found that response rates are lower when the two modes are offered simultaneously than when mail is the only mode offered (Medway & Fulton, 2012). Only one of those surveys exhibited an increase in response rates, and it was conducted under a very different set of conditions. One explanation for this finding of lower response rates is that offering respondents a choice may complicate the response decision, causing some to defer the decision (Tversky & Shafir, 1992). Additionally, some may not respond to the mail option because they intend to respond later over the Internet, but never find it convenient to do so. Offering options may also encourage some to consider additional options, such as not responding at all (Schwartz, 2004).

An experiment conducted among college undergraduates by Millar and Dillman (2011) evaluated the effects of providing a choice of response modes. The student population was chosen for this experiment because Internet literacy was likely to be high for all members of the population, thus removing low Internet skills as a factor influencing the decision of whether to respond by that mode. In this study, three of four groups were contacted exclusively through postal mail contacts.

The treatment group that was asked to respond by mail achieved a 51% response rate, the treatment that requested web response resulted in a 42% response rate, and 48% responded in the group where respondents were given the choice of responding by web or mail. Thus, in this Internet-savvy population, providing the choice produced a statistically significant higher response rate than asking for responses solely by web, but a lower response rate than asking for responses solely by mail.

A fourth treatment in this experiment requested responses by web, but added an e-mail contact after each of the first and fourth postal mail contacts. The e-mail explained that the surveyor was following up "to provide an electronic link, which we hope will make it easier to respond." This treatment produced a response rate of 60%, which was significantly higher statistically than the response rates for each of the other groups. Thus, a design with a single mode of response (web) and multiple modes of contact (postal and e-mail) produced by far the highest response rate, 18 percentage points higher than the design requesting response by the web.

A follow-up experiment a few months later (also detailed in Millar & Dillman, 2011) further explored the effects of choice of response mode, using a similar questionnaire on the same student survey population. Among the treatments in this experiment were two groups given the choice to respond by mail or web, one group asked only to respond by mail, and one group asked only to respond by web. One of the choice groups received up to five postal contacts, each of which offered a choice of web or mail response modes, and produced a 41% response rate. The other choice group also received up to five contacts, but the second and fifth contacts were sent by e-mail rather than postal mail, in order to provide an electronic link to the web survey, and thereby reduce the effort students would need to expend to access the survey (i.e., reduce costs). This design resulted in a 47% response rate, significantly higher than the 41% response achieved when no e-mail contacts were used. The mail-only group, which received five postal contacts, produced a 44% response rate, and the web-only group, which also received five postal contacts, produced a 38% response rate.

These experiments show that it is sometimes possible to turn choice, which was shown by the Medway and Fulton (2012) meta-analysis to be a negative, into a positive, by using multiple contact modes to remove barriers to respond by each of the modes. From a social exchange standpoint, the first contact used in these experiments reduced the effort required to respond by mail by providing the paper questionnaire and return envelope, and the second contact (by e-mail) reduced the effort to respond over the Internet by including a clickable link to the website, thus removing the need to switch modes and manually enter a URL in order to respond by web. This same process was also repeated later in the implementation sequence. This method, which we label e-mail augmentation, allows choice to become a catalyst for response rather than a barrier to response. However, to effectively use this approach, both postal and e-mail addresses of sample members are needed.

As we have discussed previously, the pairing of postal and e-mail contacts may also lend credibility and legitimacy to the request to complete a web survey, and, in these studies, it also allowed a prepaid token cash incentive to be sent. In sum, multiple aspects of the implementation process were leveraged in an attempt to create trust and lower the costs of responding to the survey. Adoption of this procedure for augmenting postal contacts with e-mail follow-ups provided the basis for the implementation method used in the doctoral student survey discussed in detail in Chapter 2.

Guideline 11.16: Offer a Mail Response Option After a Web Response Option in Sequential Mixed-Mode Designs to Increase Response Rates and Improve Data Quality

We have tested offering modes sequentially as a means of improving response in five different experiments, one on residents of two adjacent cities in Washington and Idaho (Smyth et al., 2010), two on Washington State residents (Messer & Dillman, 2011), one on Nebraska residents (Smyth & Olson, n.d.), and one on Washington State University students—a very web-literate population (Millar & Dillman, 2011). Results from each of these experiments are shown in Figure 11.8. In all five experiments, offering a mail questionnaire in follow-up to an initial web questionnaire increases response rates substantially. The increases range from 8 to 41 percentage points. Throughout the rest of this chapter, we refer to this as a *web-first* design, although it has also been referred to in the literature as *web+mail* or *web-push* (to emphasize that a goal of this design is to push as many respondents as possible to respond via web). All five studies in Figure 11.8 also show that offering a web questionnaire in follow-up to an initial mail questionnaire (i.e., *mail-first*,

FIGURE 11.8 Effect of order in which modes are offered in web and mail sequential mixed-mode designs.

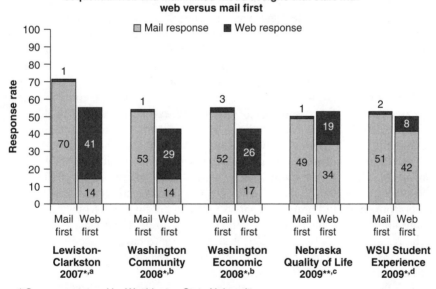

Response rates by treatment from five studies comparing sequential web and mail mixed-mode designs that start with web versus mail first

* Survey sponsored by Washington State University
** Survey sponsored by the University of Nebraska–Lincoln

Sources: (a) "Using the Internet to Survey Small Towns and Communities: Limitations and Possibilities in the Early 21st Century," by J. D. Smyth, D. A. Dillman, L. M. Christian, and A. C. O'Neill, 2010, *American Behavioral Scientist, 53*, 1423–1448. (b) "Surveying the General Public Over the Internet Using Address-Based Sampling and Mail Contact Procedures," by B. L. Messer and D. A. Dillman, 2011, *Public Opinion Quarterly, 75*(3), 429–457. (c) Unpublished data by J. D. Smyth and K. Olson, n.d. (d) "Improving Response to Web and Mixed-Mode Surveys," by M. M. Millar and D. A. Dillman, 2011, *Public Opinion Quarterly, 75*(2), 249–269.

mail-push, or *mail+web*) has little to no effect on responses rates (differences of 1 to 3 percentage points). These findings suggest that it makes little sense to expend the resources to program a web version of the questionnaire if it will be used to supplement an initially offered mail mode, because the increase in response does not justify the extra costs. It is far more effective when one is leading with the web mode and supplementing it with the mail mode.

Additional analysis of the responses to the Lewiston-Clarkston, Washington Community, and Nebraska Quality of Life surveys in Figure 11.8 showed that offering mail as a follow-up to web in the web-first design encouraged different kinds of people to respond (older, less educated, more likely to live alone, and having lower incomes) than those who had responded by the web (Messer & Dillman, 2011; Smyth et al., 2010). Additional analysis by Messer and Dillman (2011) also showed that respondents to the web-first design were demographically quite similar to respondents from the mail-only designs who were included in these studies and to benchmarks for Washington resident characteristics obtained from the American Community Survey. Smyth and Olson (n.d.) have also found in web-first sequential designs that the two modes bring in different types of respondents and that, when combined, respondents to this treatment are demographically very similar to those in a mail-only treatment. Thus, the lower response achieved by the sequential web and mail mixed-mode design does not appear to be producing results of a lesser quality (i.e., substantially different completed samples).

However, it should also be noted that even when using the guidelines discussed in this chapter, the web-first mixed-mode designs in these studies produced response rates that were somewhat lower than those obtained by the mail-first mixed-mode treatments (Figure 11.8) and mail-only treatments (Figure 11.9). Across these experiments, we obtained average mail-first or mail-only response rates of 52%, with individual studies ranging from 38% to 71%. By comparison, the web-first approach produced a mean response rate of 44%, with individual studies ranging from 31% to 55%.

One of our interests in this line of research was to see if we could encourage a greater portion of respondents to respond by web rather than mail. One way we tried to do this was by withholding the mail response mode for even longer in the implementation period. Whereas our early studies withheld this mode until the third of four contacts, our later studies withheld it until the fourth of four contacts (in the QLCN study, mail was withheld until the fourth of five contacts). Comparing the Washington and Pennsylvania Electricity studies in the top and bottom charts in Figure 11.9 shows that withholding mail from the web-first groups until later in the implementation process appears to push a greater portion of the respondents to the web. But, it also appears to have reduced the response rate in Washington and increase it slightly in Pennsylvania. This, too, is a topic in need of additional research.

In light of the higher response rates obtained for the mail-only surveys and the fact that the demographic characteristics of the completed samples are so similar in the web-first and mail-only treatments, we are often asked why not stick to a mail-only approach. Mail currently has a clear response advantage and is obtaining a much higher response rate than can now be obtained by either telephone or web alone. However, mail responses come in quite slowly and sometimes the speed of web response is needed. Also, the cost of printing and mailing questionnaires continues to increase, while the technology to host and design web surveys

FIGURE 11.9 Response rates for mail-only versus web-first designs in a series of experiments.

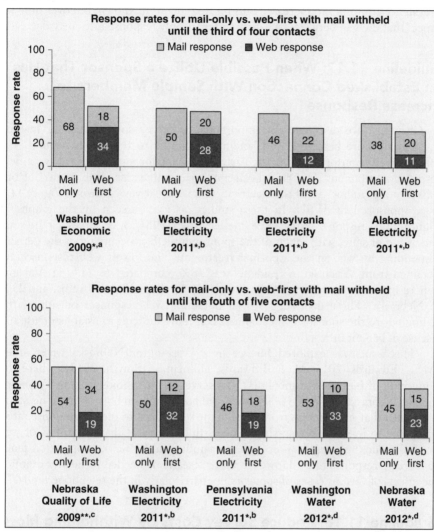

* Survey sponsored by Washington State University.
** Survey sponsored by the University of Nebraska-Lincoln.
Sources: (a) "Surveying the General Public Over the Internet Using Address-Based Sampling and Mail Contact Procedures," by B. L. Messer and D. A. Dillman, 2011, *Public Opinion Quarterly, 75*(3), 429–457. (b) "Pushing Households to the Web: Experiments of a 'Web+Mail' Methodology for Conducting General Public Surveys," by B. L. Messer, 2012. Unpublished doctoral dissertation, Washington State University, Pullman, WA. (c) Unpublished data, by J. D. Smyth and K. Olson, n.d. (d) "Effects of Survey Sponsorship on Internet and Mail Response: Using Address-Based Sampling," by M. L. Edwards, D. A. Dillman, and J. D. Smyth, 2013c, May. Paper presented at the American Association for Public Opinion Research (AAPOR) annual meeting, Boston, MA.

is becoming more available and at a lower cost. Over time, we expect more and more surveying to continue to shift toward the web mode as Internet literacy and prevalence continues to increase. This future remains unknown, but over time we expect that the gap between web-first and mail-only response rates may decrease.

Guideline 11.17: When Possible Utilize a Sponsor That Has an Established Connection With Sample Members to Increase Response

In Chapter 2 we discussed the importance of survey sponsorship for making responding more beneficial and lending legitimacy to the survey request. We think survey sponsorship is particularly important for surveys that have a web response component. We have been able to examine this issue in two of our mixed-mode studies. All of the electricity and water surveys shown in Figure 11.9 were sponsored by WSU. In these studies, as can be seen by the graphs in Figure 11.9, response rates were higher when WSU was surveying in state versus out of state, with much of the sponsorship effect occurring in the percent responding by web in the web-first treatment. The lowest web response rate obtained from Washington residents was 28%, compared to 11% in Alabama (where Internet penetration was lowest), 12% to 19% in Pennsylvania, and 23% in Nebraska. These data suggest that obtaining web responses outside of the region where the sponsor is located makes it more difficult to establish trust and a sense of benefit in responding.

This issue was explored further in a Washington/Nebraska water study (M. L. Edwards, 2013; M. L. Edwards, Dillman, & Smyth, 2013c) where the University of Nebraska–Lincoln (UNL) surveyed households in both Washington and Nebraska while WSU also surveyed households in both states. This study confirmed that sponsorship from outside the state tends to reduce response rates, compared to in-state sponsorship. These studies suggest that regardless of web or mail mode, utilizing a sponsor that is familiar to the survey population tends to increase response rates. However, more research is needed to further examine the effects of various types of sponsorship, particularly in the telephone mode.

Guideline 11.18: Reduce Survey Costs by Withholding More Expensive Response Modes Until Later in the Implementation Process

A primary driver of nearly all survey designs is cost. Introducing a second or third mode into data collection seems likely to increase costs, simply because of having to coordinate the construction of unified questionnaires, develop contacts for different modes, manage data collection across modes, and integrate the results. But, if higher response can be achieved by first using lower cost modes and reserving the most costly and presumably effective modes of contact or data collection for final follow-up, then cost savings may result. This is the compelling reason that the Decennial Census, which counts all U.S. households (currently over 155 million), has traditionally first surveyed by mail to get most responses and then uses enumerators to personally contact nonresponding households and administer the survey. Another survey that uses this strategy is the Agricultural Resource Management Survey, conducted by the U.S. Department of Agriculture National

Agricultural Statistics Service. This survey obtained responses from about 40% of the approximately 30,000 farm operations it surveys by mail prior to sending interviewers to follow up with nonrespondents (Beckler & Ott, 2006).

A survey of foreign policy experts (members of the Council on Foreign Relations) conducted by the Pew Research Center in 2009 utilized a different mixed-mode design, where web was offered first since it was the less expensive mode and then telephone as a follow-up to those who did not respond by web. Sampled members were first contacted by postal mail and asked to complete the survey online (and also provided a call-in number if they had questions or wanted to complete the survey by telephone). Follow-up contacts were sent by e-mail (to encourage web response) and by telephone (to encourage response by web or phone). The survey yielded a response rate of 64%; 79% of the completed interviews were from the web and 21% from telephone (Pew Research Center, 2009).

A survey of the same population was conducted four years later but achieved a far lower response rate, just 39% (Pew Research Center, 2013). For this survey, sampled members were still initially contacted by postal mail and asked to complete the web survey, with additional follow-up contacts by e-mail. But the additional contacts by telephone and the option of completing the survey by telephone were eliminated; this likely contributed to the sharp decline in the response rate.

Until 2013, the American Community Survey, which replaced the Decennial Census long form in 2000, used a slightly different approach than the Decennial Census in order to achieve cost savings. Households were first contacted by mail and asked to complete a paper questionnaire and return it by mail, which produced about a 55% response rate. Nonresponding households for which a telephone number could be matched to the address were then called to complete the survey by telephone, adding an additional 7 percentage points to the response rate. Finally, the remaining households that had not yet responded were sampled for follow-up by an in-person interviewer. Beginning in 2013 this procedure was changed in an effort to reduce costs even more. Under the new design, households are first contacted by mail but with the request to complete the questionnaire over the Internet, and then followed up by mail, telephone, and the in-person request. This new design is still being evaluated to see how it compares to the previous design.

Research is mixed on whether first requesting responses using a postal mail contact that includes the paper questionnaire and only later providing other modes of data collection actually reduces survey costs. A careful accounting of all costs in the Messer and Dillman (2011) surveys of Washington State residents in the summer and fall of 2008 showed that the total cost of the web-first treatment was somewhat higher on a per respondent basis than the costs of the mail-first and mail-only treatments. This happened for two reasons. First, the costs of printing and mailing the postal mail contacts were similar across all treatments (i.e., no money was saved in the web-first treatment because postal mail contacts were still used). Second, the web-first treatment produced a lower response rate, meaning that in the end, more money was spent per completed questionnaire in this treatment.

A different perspective on costs is provided by an NSF National Survey of College Graduates reported by Finamore and Dillman (2013). This survey used three modes of data collection—telephone, mail, and web—varying the order in which modes were sequentially used. The sample was drawn from respondents to the American Community Survey. A total of 16 postal and telephone contacts were attempted over the course of 42 weeks of data collection. Response rates were quite similar, ranging from 75% for the mail-first methodology to 77% for the web-first methodology. A web/mail choice group was also included and achieved a slightly lower response rate of 73%, as expected based upon past research.

In this study the cost per response was much lower for the web-first methodology ($48/complete) compared to the mail-first methodology ($66/complete) and the telephone-first methodology ($75/complete). The web-first design was more cost-effective in this study because its target population was college graduates, a population with high rates of Internet access and use. Seventy percent of those who responded to this treatment did so over the Internet, thus eliminating considerable interview and data entry costs for most of that group. Over time, as Internet access increases and people get better at using it, we expect the web-first methodology to become more cost effective.

Guideline 11.19: When Using Multiple Contact and Response Modes, Choose Software and Management Tools That Facilitate an Integrated Design and Implementation Process

A major barrier to conducting mixed-mode surveys, and in particular those involving both contact and response by different modes, can be the management of the data collection process. Survey management systems developed when single-mode survey designs dominated are generally not easily integrated across different modes, making it difficult to keep track of what is done and who has responded across multiple modes on a daily basis. This has been especially problematic in large data collection organizations where mail, telephone, and web surveys were administered through different divisions, often in different physical locations and with different systems used for data collection.

However, many software systems have now been developed for designing and implementing surveys across different modes, and some also include features for compiling results quickly and effectively. These types of integrated software programs are available especially for designs that combine telephone, web, and/or computer-assisted in-person surveys. Often systems for mail surveys are different since the questionnaires need to be processed before they can be added to the database (rather than be added directly as the interview is being completed, as it can be for these other modes). Using such systems for mixed-mode surveys is desirable if not essential. These types of integrated systems are absolutely critical for those using adaptive design procedures that rely on information from the various modes to inform the next step in the implementation process.

FROM INDIVIDUAL GUIDELINES TO PRACTICAL STUDY DESIGNS

Throughout this book, and especially in this chapter, we have introduced specific guidelines relevant to the design of mixed-mode surveys. However, there is more to designing mixed-mode data collection efforts than simply checking off whether guidelines have been met. Some guidelines are more important than others or will get enacted differently depending on the particular survey. Further, bringing the relevant guidelines together to evoke trust, increase the benefits of being a survey respondent, and reduce the perceived costs of carrying out that task involves considering how the guidelines can be brought together in supportive ways.

Applying the Mixed-Mode Guidelines

In the Washington–Nebraska water surveys, we brought together what we had learned from the series of prior of studies about mixed-mode designs to increase overall response rates and to get as many people to respond via the web as possible. We describe here how the guidelines discussed throughout this book, and particularly those in this chapter, were applied to the mixed-mode design of this study using illustrations from the Washington State University–sponsored survey of Washington households, details of which are reported elsewhere (M. L. Edwards, 2013).

The Contacts

In this study we used a four-contact postal mail implementation strategy. Consistent with Guideline 11.12, we included a $4 incentive with the initial request. This amount was slightly lower than used in previous tests, because of budget constraints, but it was deemed acceptable inasmuch as previous research shows a large effect of going from no incentive to any incentive with only small increases in response rates as the amount of the incentive increases. A second cash incentive of $2 was included in the third contact (consistent with Guideline 11.13). In previous tests, the second incentive had been delivered with the alternative mail questionnaire, producing an increase in mail response (Messer & Dillman, 2011), but in this study, it was used with the repeated web request in the third contact, consistent with our goal of increasing the response by web.

The initial contact for this survey is shown in Figure 11.10. In developing this and the other contacts, we followed the guidelines described in Chapters 9 and 10.

- The letter was printed in color on professional-appearing letterhead that emphasizes the sponsor, with a blue signature for personalization and red font for the access code for easy visibility.
- To make it easier to remember and enter into the web browser, the URL was designed using meaningful words rather than strings of unrelated characters.
- Names were not available on the sample frame and a within-household selection method was used, so the letters were personalized to the address and community where the sampled household was located.
- The message in the letter framed the task as a request for help.
- It also stated the survey topic clearly and simply, explaining that the questionnaire was about water management issues involving rainfall and a core river system that provides hydroelectric power, irrigation, migratory fish runs, and recreational opportunities (the Columbia–Snake system) to the state.
- Contact information was provided for the sponsor, including a telephone number that was answered during normal working hours and an e-mail address that was monitored daily. Although the Social and Economic Sciences Research Center (SESRC) website could have been provided for additional legitimation of the study, we chose not to do that in order to avoid having the SESRC URL compete with the survey URL, which may have confused recipients.

FIGURE 11.10 First contact letter asking Washington residents to respond to the Water in Washington survey over the Internet.

WASHINGTON STATE
UNIVERSITY

Social and Economic Sciences Research Center

April 13, 2012

Seattle Area Resident
55 Rainier St.
Seattle, WA 98119

Dear Seattle Resident,

Every person in Washington needs water. In many parts of the state, the same sources of water are used by households, businesses, farms, and wildlife areas. Sometimes it may be possible to meet all of these water requests, but at other times, doing so may be quite tough. One of the challenges Washington faces is how to balance many different water uses.

I am writing to ask for your help in improving our understanding of residents' views on water issues in Washington. The best way we know how to do this is by asking people throughout the state to share their thoughts and opinions with us. Your address is one of only a small number that have been randomly selected to help in this study.

To make sure we hear from all different types of people who live in the state, please have the adult (**age 19 or over**) in your household who has had the **most recent birthday** be the one to complete the survey. We hope that you will be able to complete the survey on the Internet so that we can summarize results more quickly.

First, enter this address into your Internet browser's address bar:
http://www.opinion.wsu.edu/washingtonwater

Next, enter your access code: **Your Access Code: 11856**

Your responses are voluntary and will be kept confidential. Your names are not on our mailing list, and your answers will never be associated with your mailing address. If you have any questions about this survey please contact Thom Allen by telephone at 1-800-833-0867 or by email at survey.support@wsu.edu.

By taking a few minutes, you will be adding greatly to our understanding of residents' opinions on water decision-making. I hope you enjoy completing the questionnaire and I look forward to receiving your responses.

Many Thanks,

Don A. Dillman
Project Director
Washington State University

P.S.   We have enclosed a small token of appreciation as a way of saying thanks for completing the survey!

Research and Administrative Offices, 133 Wilson-Short Hall
PO Box 644014, Pullman, WA 99164-4014 • 509-335-1511 • Fax: 509-335-0116

- The incentive included with this letter was intended to encourage recipients to read the letter and attend to who should respond and how to do it. Its presence was mentioned in the footnote, with no mention of the amount, consistent with it being a gift rather than a payment.

Figure 11.11 shows the second contact used for this survey. This letter was designed to connect with the first contact and to arrive while there was still a reasonable chance that the first letter was still in the household, whether it had been opened or not, and had not been entirely forgotten. If the timing was successful, this second letter may have encouraged recipients to open and review

FIGURE 11.11 Second contact letter asking Washington residents to respond to the Water in Washington survey over the Internet.

Social and Economic Sciences Research Center

April 20, 2012

Seattle Area Resident
55 Rainier St.
Seattle, WA 98119

Dear Seattle Resident,

Last week, we mailed you a letter asking for your help with a study about how water decisions should be made in Washington.

If you or someone in your household has already completed the questionnaire, please accept our sincere thanks. If not, please have the adult (**age 19 and over**) with the **most recent birthday** complete the survey online as soon as possible. We are especially grateful for your help with this important study.

To complete the survey, just enter this web page address in your Internet browser and then type in your access code to begin answering questions.

http://www.opinion.wsu.edu/washingtonwater   Your Access Code: 11856

If you have any questions, please contact Thom Allen by phone at 1-800-833-0867 or by email at survey.support@wsu.edu.

Many Thanks,

Don A. Dillman
Project Director
Washington State University

Research and Administrative Offices, 133 Wilson-Short Hall
PO Box 644014, Pullman, WA 99164-4014 • 509-335-1511 • Fax: 509-335-0116

the initial request in the first mailing, where they would see the presence of the incentive.

This second letter was modeled after the postcard reminder discussed in Chapter 10, but it was sent as a postal letter because it included the survey URL and the sample household's individualized access code. Putting this information inside an envelope rather than on a postcard was done to ensure that anyone else who saw the mailing was not able to enter the questionnaire designated for a specific household, and thus prevent the selected respondent from answering it. The within-household selection instructions were also emphasized in this brief follow-up.

FIGURE 11.12 Third contact letter asking Washington residents to respond to the Water in Washington survey over the Internet.

WASHINGTON STATE
UNIVERSITY   Social and Economic Sciences Research Center

May 4, 2012

Seattle Area Resident
55 Rainier St.
Seattle, WA 98119

Dear Seattle Resident,

About three weeks ago, we sent you a survey request asking for your opinions on how Washington's water supplies should be managed. To the best of our knowledge, we have not yet received your responses. Given the many competing uses of water in Washington, our hope is that this study will provide state leaders with a better understanding of how residents think water decisions should be made.

We are writing again because of the importance that your household's responses have for helping to get accurate results. It is only by hearing from nearly everyone in the sample that we can be sure that the results truly represent Washington residents. We would greatly appreciate your help by having the adult (**age 19 or over**) in your household who has had the **most recent birthday** fill out the survey.

You can complete the survey online at http://www.opinion.wsu.edu/washingtonwater. This address should take you to our survey login page, where you can then enter your personal access code in the space provided. Your Personal Access Code is: 11856.

A few people have emailed or called to say they are unable to find the web survey. We learned most had accidentally put our address, http://www.opinion.wsu.edu/washingtonwater, into the Google, Yahoo, or Bing space by mistake. Here's an example of where the address should and should not go:

Hopefully this will work for you, but if it doesn't please call or email Thom Allen at 1-800-833-0867 or survey.support@wsu.edu. Your responses are voluntary and will be kept confidential. Your names are not on our mailing list, and your answers will never be associated with your address in any way.

The enclosed token of appreciation is yours to keep whether you choose to complete the survey or not. Thank you so much for your help with this very important issue.

Many Thanks,

Don A. Dillman
Project Director
Washington State University

Research and Administrative Offices, 133 Wilson-Short Hall
PO Box 644014, Pullman, WA 99164-4014 • 509-335-1511 • Fax: 509-335-0116

The third contact, shown in Figure 11.12, built upon the previous contacts, but was somewhat longer. It was also more strongly worded; the recipient was informed that a response had not been received from his household. This letter was not written until shortly before it was sent. This gave us time to review all of the inquiries we had received to identify common difficulties respondents were having. In this particular study, getting access to the web questionnaire was the most important issue sample members were facing. We decided to address this problem, which a number of people had called or written to ask about, in this third contact in case it would be helpful to others who may have had the same problem, but not contacted us about it. To do so, we added the illustration of where to enter (and where not to enter) the URL. This gave this letter a quite noticeable visual aspect that differentiated it from the previous letters. In other surveys when no problems like this needed to be addressed, we have included additional information about how results from the survey will be used or expressed appreciation for the high level of response already received, building upon the Cialdini (1984) principle of conveying that others have responded (see Chapter 2).

A second token of appreciation was included in this mailing in an effort to convey the importance of the study and encourage recipients to read this letter. The letter contained new information (but was consistent with what was previously sent) on what the study is about and the importance of hearing from those who have not responded. It also included information from previous contacts, expressed in somewhat different prose, such as who should respond, how to do it, and how to contact the study sponsors. The helpful feedback, second incentive, and new information were all efforts to adapt the design in order to reach individuals who were different from those who had already responded.

The fourth contact, which is shown in Figure 11.13, was sent 10 days after the third contact and was designed to make a fresh appeal by including an alternative paper questionnaire. The questionnaire dominated the mailing, requiring a large envelope that was quite different in appearance from previous mailings. The inclusion of the paper questionnaire also gave reluctant recipients an opportunity to glance through the questionnaire and see what it was all about. The wording of this letter acknowledged that a number of sample members had contacted us previously to ask that a mail questionnaire be sent, thus showing responsiveness to respondent needs and building additional rapport and trust. The wording was also aimed at those who had not yet responded. We also added to this letter a URL where sample members would be able to find out some of the results of the study. If people found the questions of particular interest, knowing they would be able to see the results may have had reward value, as discussed in Chapter 2.

It is important that the nature and content of these contacts be considered in relation to one another. Each of the four contacts is designed by itself to be a strong communication, having salient aspects not included in any of the previous contacts—the token of appreciation with requests, reference to previous contacts, and a request for response by a different mode. Yet, none is written independently of the other contacts; they all share certain elements—the common letterhead and sponsorship information, similar descriptions of the purpose of the study, similar personalization, and so on—and the message in each contact builds off of what was communicated in previous contacts.

The writing of contacts for many surveys, including mixed-mode surveys, often seems to get left to the last minute, and sometimes contacts for the same study are written by different people. For example, the contacts referring to a web response often get composed by those who implement the web portion of the survey, while those referring to a mail response are prepared by those coordinating the paper questionnaire and mailings. But with the complexity of mixed-mode surveys, especially those in which contact by one mode is being used to ask for response by another or when requests for different modes of responding are being sent at different times, coordinating the writing of these requests is absolutely critical so that the design and messaging work together.

FIGURE 11.13   Fourth and final contact letter asking Washington residents to respond to the paper version of the Water in Washington survey.

WASHINGTON STATE
UNIVERSITY   Social and Economic Sciences Research Center

May 14, 2012

Seattle Area Resident
55 Rainier St.
Seattle, WA 98119

Dear Seattle Resident,

In recent weeks, our research team has asked you, as part of a random selection of Washington residents, to let us know how you think water decisions should be made in your state. We plan to start summarizing results later this month, so we hope that all surveys will be completed by then.

Some people have asked us if they could complete a paper survey instead of using the Internet. The answer is yes, and we are enclosing a paper questionnaire in hopes that it makes it easier for you to respond. You can help us by filling out this questionnaire and returning it in the provided stamped envelope.

For many years, we have heard people in Washington and all across the U.S. talk about water – how it should be protected, managed, owned, and used. In the future, we believe that water issues will receive even more attention. We hope that this study will contribute to these conversations and provide insight into Washington residents' views on water.

This is the last contact we will be sending you about this survey, as we are bringing this phase of the project to a close. A summary of preliminary results from this study will be available on our website www.opinion.wsu.edu/washingtonwater/results this summer. If you have any questions about this survey please contact Thom Allen by telephone at 1-800-833-0867 or by email at survey.support@wsu.edu.

Many thanks for considering our request.

Respectfully and with appreciation,

Don A. Dillman
Project Director
Washington State University

Research and Administrative Offices, 133 Wilson-Short Hall
PO Box 644014, Pullman, WA 99164-4014 • 509-335-1511 • Fax: 509-335-0116

The Questionnaires

It was critical in this study to coordinate the development of the web and paper questionnaires. We carefully followed Guidelines 11.1 and 11.2, creating unified mode construction in the question wording and in the visual design and layouts across the two questionnaires.

The mail questionnaire, which was only seen by those who had not responded by the time the fourth contact was sent, began with a carefully designed questionnaire cover (see Figure 11.14). When it was received, we expected people's attention to oscillate between the cover letter and the questionnaire itself. As a

FIGURE 11.14 Paper questionnaire cover and web survey entry page from the mixed-mode Water in Washington survey.

result, it was important to create an interest-getting title that connected thematically to pictures conveying the theme of the study, in this case different uses of water (irrigation, household use, and the migration of salmon) in Washington State. We also restated instructions for who should complete the survey on the questionnaire cover, and we included the sponsor's name and address so that even if the return envelope was lost, the respondent would still know where to return the questionnaire.

FIGURE 11.14 *(continued).*

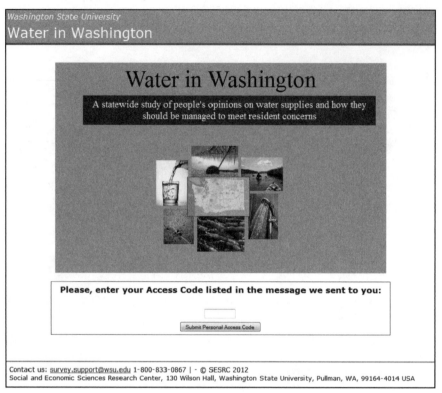

As Figure 11.14 also shows, the welcome page of the web questionnaire uses the same colors, titles, and images as the paper questionnaire to ensure that the web respondents received a very similar stimulus as the paper respondents. However, the images and title are smaller and less bold and the within-household selection instructions have been omitted. In addition, the sponsorship information and address is minimized to the bottom of the screen. These differences were driven by both practical constraints and strategic considerations. Sample members will have attended to some of these details in the cover letter before ever getting to this welcome page. As a result, these details did not need to be repeated here. Given this, the primary purposes of the welcome page were to keep sample members interested (hence the use of the title and imagery) and to get them to enter their access code and move forward to the questions. The images were reduced in size so that more focus would be put on where to enter the access code.

The first questions in this survey are shown in Figure 11.15. They concern the community where people live, how respondents feel about the safety of their water, and whether it has a bad taste and/or odor. A great deal of discussion and pretesting went into selecting these first questions. We wanted them to be simple, interesting, and relevant to most respondents, as discussed in Guideline 7.2. In essence, we attempted to bring people into the water management issues that were our main interest with questions that respondents could quickly and easily answer and that focused on the final use of water (water from the tap) that comes closest to how most people experience water in their daily lives.

FIGURE 11.15 Examples of questionnaire design used in the paper and web versions of the mixed-mode Water in Washington survey.

Cropped screenshots from web questionnaire

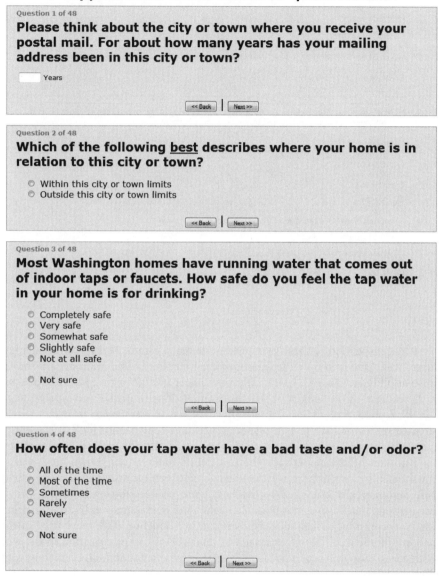

The paper and web questions both appear in similar colored (light blue) background fields, as was discussed in Guideline 11.2 and shown with a different survey in Figure 11.2. Our purpose for this use of enclosures in the mail questionnaire is to focus people's attention on only one question at a time and discourage them from looking forward or behind in the questionnaire, in order to create a stimulus that is as similar as possible to that provided by the page-by-page design of the web questionnaire. The background fields and question layout are nearly the same across the paper and web modes to reduce the likelihood of unintentional measurement differences.

FIGURE 11.15 (*continued*).

Cropped first page from paper questionnaire

Q1.	**Please think about the city or town where you receive your postal mail. For about how many years has your mailing address been in this city or town?**

☐ Years

Q2. **Which of the following __best__ describes where your home is in relation to this city or town?**

   O₁ Within this city or town limits
   O₂ Outside this city or town limits

Q3. **Most Washington homes have running water that comes out of indoor taps or faucets. How safe do you feel the tap water in your home is for drinking?**

   O₁ Completely safe
   O₂ Very safe
   O₃ Somewhat safe
   O₄ Slightly safe
   O₅ Not at all safe

   O₆ Not sure

Q4. **How often does your tap water have a bad taste and/or odor?**

   O₁ All of the time
   O₂ Most of the time
   O₃ Sometimes
   O₄ Rarely
   O₅ Never

   O₆ Not sure

Close inspection of these two questionnaires in Figure 11.15 will reveal a few differences. One is in how the questions are numbered. The numbers are shown in isolation (e.g., Q1, Q2, Q3, etc.) on the paper questionnaire, but they are put in the context of the length of the entire questionnaire in the web version (e.g., 1 of 48, 2 of 48, 3 of 48, etc.). This difference was introduced to provide a subtle progress indicator for the web respondents, since they cannot look at the entire questionnaire and see how many questions remain, like the mail respondents can.

Another difference between the two questionnaires (not shown here) was in how branching or skipping was handled. In the web questionnaire, respondents were automatically branched to the next appropriate question based on previous answers, but this was not possible in the mail questionnaire. Instead, instructions incorporating visual cues, as discussed in Guideline 10.4, were used in the mail questionnaire. Taking advantage of this perk of computerization in the web mode, even though it could not be duplicated in the mail mode, is consistent with Guideline 11.4.

The Outcome

This web-first survey achieved a final response rate of 43% with slightly more than three quarters of the responses (77%) obtained over the web. It is our sense from this and the studies proceeding it, as well as our expectation that the Internet will increasingly be used in other areas of people's lives, that the web-first methodology will continue to be effective and possibly become even more effective.

More remains to be learned about the potential of this mixed-mode methodology. One of the potential additions that might be used for important studies is to follow up by telephone in hopes of achieving even higher response rates, especially encouraging response from households whose members have lower levels of education or for whom literacy is a problem and may be less likely to respond to a paper or web survey. Additional research on optimal levels of incentives and other ways of motivating sampled households to open and act upon the communications they receive is also needed.

GUIDELINES FOR TESTING MIXED-MODE SURVEYS

Many of the guidelines for questionnaire testing discussed in Chapter 7, and for testing implementation procedures for telephone, web, and mail single-mode surveys covered in Chapters 8, 9, and 10 also apply to mixed-mode surveys. However, additional considerations are needed, especially to ensure that procedures used for each mode are tested and documented, as well as to ensure that efforts are coordinated effectively across modes.

Guideline 11.20: Review and Test the Questionnaires for Each Survey Mode Being Used

Testing the questionnaires is absolutely essential in mixed-mode surveys. As we discussed in Guidelines 11.1 to 11.7, it is important to achieve a common measurement stimulus across modes. Thus, the questionnaire testing for mixed-mode surveys should focus specifically on what formats work effectively across modes and ensuring that the unified mode design is carried through to what the respondent will actually experience in each mode. A common issue that continues to occur in mixed-mode surveys is that, even when survey designers have the best intentions, inadvertent differences in questionnaire design happen across modes. Within a single month while writing this book, we observed two studies in which the surveyors were strongly committed to unified mode construction but had unintentionally relied on their usual mode-specific design practices, and as a result, caused the designs across modes to diverge significantly.

- In one instance, a series of yes/no questions from a telephone questionnaire were converted to a check-all-that-apply format in the web survey. As we showed in Guideline 5.12, if this was not identified during testing, this variation would have produced different results across the modes.
- In the other instance, the question numbering on a paper questionnaire was removed from the web version of the questionnaire because using question numbers was not standard practice for the web designers. This change, if implemented, would have made it more difficult for anyone who saw both versions of the questionnaires to know they were actually the same questionnaire, or for anyone to use the paper questionnaire to collect information that would later be entered into the web questionnaire.

Thus, in addition to testing the questionnaire in each mode using cognitive interviewing, eye tracking, and other techniques discussed in Chapter 7, it is essential to have someone familiar with all the survey modes being used for that study review the questionnaires for these types of inadvertent modifications. Further, an expert review by individuals who are sensitive to measurement differences likely to occur across modes and are familiar with the research literature pertaining to such differences can also be especially helpful in identifying questions that may not perform similarly across modes or when these types of inadvertent changes have been made.

Guideline 11.21: Test All Implementation Procedures, Especially the Coordination Across Modes

Using multiple modes means that the systems and procedures supporting each mode being used need to be thoroughly tested (as described in Chapters 8, 9, and 10). But for mixed-mode surveys, this also includes the coordination that is necessary across modes to effectively administer and monitor the progress of mixed-mode surveys. When multiple people are working on a survey and especially in organizations where each group has separate procedures and where people are often separated structurally and/or physically, activities need to be carefully coordinated across these different groups to ensure that each is completing the necessary procedures to successfully execute the mixed-mode design. This coordination is especially important when the action of one unit affects that of another, as it does for most mixed-mode surveys.

A mixed-mode study that one of us worked on involved substantial coordination across groups and systems—including in-person interviewing staff, telephone surveying staff, those who do the printing and mailing, as well as the information technology staff who support the systems for each of these groups—many of whom who had not worked together before. Working across these different groups to standardize questionnaires and procedures, including developing several new procedures, was a substantial undertaking. Just one example of the coordination needed happened when the letters requesting response by web (or paper) were sent out with identification codes for accessing the web survey, but the codes were not loaded to the website so people received errors when trying to log in to the web survey. This was only discovered when people handling the inbound calls for the study were unable to log in using the codes as well. The codes were quickly loaded to the website once the issue was identified, but it is unknown how many people were affected before the issue was fixed.

Another example of the coordination needed in mixed-mode designs is when pairing a mail contact that sends an incentive with a near immediate e-mail to provide an electronic link in order to encourage quick web responses. The process of sending these communications needs to be carefully coordinated by the different units who may be responsible for them to ensure that the desired timing between contacts is achieved. Recently, in a very large survey, it was learned too late that the postal mailing with an incentive that was being sent (from another city) had been delayed. As a result, web staff had sent the follow-up e-mail ahead of the postal mailing (assuming the postal mailing went out on time). For all of the elements of a mixed-mode design to work properly, it requires substantial coordination and the types of issues discussed here need to be anticipated and avoided. If one has not previously implemented a carefully coordinated mixed-mode study in which contacts and requests have to be precisely timed and take into account the content, as well as when other contacts were sent and who has already responded, it is critical to develop these procedures and test them extensively so that mistakes are prevented when implemented on a larger scale.

Guideline 11.22: Plan an Initial Pilot Test, Especially If Testing a New Mixed-Mode Design

Testing is so critical in mixed-mode surveys that we generally recommend a pilot test, especially if the mixed-mode design is new or a substantial change from a previous design. When undergoing major changes in survey design, it is important to ensure that all systems are working correctly, as discussed in Guideline 11.21, but then to fully test the questionnaires and procedures with actual members of the survey population. For example, the National Household Education Survey conducted several pilot tests when considering a move from a landline RDD telephone survey to a two-phase mail survey using address-based sampling methodology (Brick, Williams, & Montaquila, 2011).

These types of pilot tests are important when evaluating whether to make a change in design and what impact the change in design may have on the survey's estimates. They can also be helpful in estimating sample sizes needed and expected response to the new design. Further, we cannot emphasize enough the kinks or issues that arise when conducting mixed-mode surveys, and that the more the procedures are tested, the greater the likelihood that these issues will be identified and accounted for in the design.

Guideline 11.23: Document and Disclose the Methodology Used and the Results Achieved

The flexibility of mixed-mode designs results in a great deal of variation in how different modes are deployed and the procedures used. Indeed, this is also one of the key strengths of mixed-mode surveys—that they can be tailored to effectively meet the survey's needs. However, it also means that it is especially important to document the specific methodological procedures used and the results achieved with the design. Although this is important in single-mode surveys as well, it becomes critical in mixed-mode designs so people can understand how each of the modes was used, how many responses were received by each mode, and so on.

For each study, we recommend archiving the final questionnaires and contact materials used in all modes, as well as a summary of the overall design and specific procedures used in each mode. Disclosing the specific materials and procedures used in each mode and how they were designed to work together is critical for people to understand how the survey was conducted. This is not only important if the design is to be repeated, but also is especially helpful in evaluating the survey design and identifying areas for improvement. And internal documentation should be very detailed, especially when describing any new procedures developed for the mixed-mode design that are not documented elsewhere.

CONCLUSION

One of the most substantial changes in survey methodology over the past decade is the growth in the use of mixed-mode designs. Surveyors are increasingly turning to mixed-mode designs to balance considerations of cost and timeliness while aiming to reduce coverage, nonresponse, and measurement error. In some ways, mixed-mode studies used to be a luxury but are now a necessity for most surveys to achieve the high-quality data needed. This increased use of mixed-mode surveys has resulted in a growing research area where studies demonstrate specific ways in which multiple modes can effectively be used for contacting and surveying respondents.

Designing effective mixed-mode surveys requires getting past the individualistic mode orientation that has dominated survey data collection for many decades. Many of the single-mode construction and administration methods described in Chapters 8, 9, and 10 have to be modified, as described throughout this chapter, in order for modes to fit with one another in mixed-mode designs. In addition, the coordination of contact and response modes is an essential requirement for achieving the potential of mixed-mode designs for improving response rates and response quality.

It remains to be seen whether mixed-mode surveys will continue to expand in their prominence, or whether we will move into a new era in which the modes we know today morph into something quite different, just as how cell phone and Internet communication have now begun to blend together. We see this discussion of mixed-mode designs not as a culmination, but rather as more of a beginning of what future survey designs might be, the topic to which we turn to in Chapter 12.

LIST OF GUIDELINES

Guidelines for Designing Questionnaires That Will Minimize Measurement Differences Across Survey Modes

Guideline 11.1:   Use the same question format and wording across modes

Guideline 11.2:   Use similar visual formats across modes

Guideline 11.3:   Use similar wording and visual formats across web and telephone surveys

Guideline 11.4:   When mixing mail and web, leverage web technologies when they will help respondents navigate the questionnaire or reduce errors, but not when they will likely result in measurement differences

Guideline 11.5:   When mixing web or paper with telephone, give priority in both modes to the short and simple stimuli needed for telephone

Guideline 11.6:   When mixing web or mail with telephone, build in conversational cues and transition statements to unify the design across modes

Guideline 11.7:   If there is even a small chance of mixing modes in the project, design the questionnaire for the possibility of mixed-mode data collection

Guideline 11.8:   Recognize that even with unified mode design, some measurement differences may still occur across modes

Guidelines for Using Multiple Contact Modes to Achieve More Effective Communication With Potential Respondents

Guideline 11.9:   Obtain contact information for more than one survey mode whenever possible

Guideline 11.10:   Use multiple contact modes to increase the likelihood of contacts being received and attended to by the sample members

Guideline 11.11:   Use contact by a mode different than the response mode to increase trust that the survey is legitimate and useful

Guideline 11.12:   Send a token cash incentive with an initial postal mail contact to increase trust in the survey

Guideline 11.13:   Consider including a second cash incentive in a later contact to improve response rates

Guidelines for Providing Alternative Response Modes

Guideline 11.14:   Utilize information on respondent mode preferences when practical, but recognize that improvements in response rates and data quality may be quite modest

Guideline 11.15:   Avoid offering a simultaneous choice of response modes unless barriers to responding in both modes are removed

Guideline 11.16:   Offer a mail response option after a web response option in sequential mixed-mode designs to increase response rates and improve data quality

Guideline 11.17:   When possible utilize a sponsor that has an established connection with sample members to increase response

Guideline 11.18:   Reduce survey costs by withholding more expensive response modes until later in the implementation process

Guideline 11.19:   When using multiple contact and response modes, choose software and management tools that facilitate an integrated design and implementation process

Guidelines for Testing Mixed-Mode Surveys

Guideline 11.20:   Review and test the questionnaires for each survey mode being used

Guideline 11.21:   Test all implementation procedures, especially the coordination across modes

Guideline 11.22:   Plan an initial pilot test, especially if testing a new mixed-mode design

Guideline 11.23:   Document and disclose the methodology used and the results achieved

Responding to Societal Change and Preparing for What Lies Ahead

Throughout this book, we have proposed an approach for conducting sample surveys that responds to the current cultural and communication environment and addresses many of the challenges faced by those conducting surveys today. The central features of this approach are summarized in these eight conclusions:

1. *The quality of sample survey results* depends upon the joint contributions of the surveyor and respondents to reducing coverage, sampling, measurement, and nonresponse error.
2. *Using tailored designs* that are customized to the survey population, topic, burden, and contact possibilities, as well as the budget and length of time available for conducting the study, will be more effective than attempting to use the same data collection procedures for all situations.
3. *Social exchange*, with its emphasis on improving trust in the legitimacy and purpose of the survey and improving the ratio of benefits to costs for respondents, provides an effective framework for improving response rates and quality.
4. *A holistic approach to design* that coordinates the multiple ways in which information is communicated to people throughout the implementation process, from the contact materials to the survey questionnaire itself (including visual design), is necessary to improve response rates and quality.
5. *Using different modes of contact* increases the likelihood that the selected sample members will receive survey communications and attend to them.
6. *Successful mixed-mode surveys* depend greatly upon how the mode of contact and mode of response are coordinated and applied.
7. *Unified mode construction* of survey questions improves data quality in mixed-mode surveys by structuring questions similarly across survey modes and attempting to overcome differences in how people process visual and aural modes of communication.
8. *Single-mode surveys are adequate* for certain studies, but many others require multiple modes. Methods for designing and implementing single-mode surveys are essential in understanding how these modes can be used in mixed-mode designs.

We believe these eight conclusions, and the practical guidance we have provided throughout this book for achieving them, will help surveyors deal with the immense challenges they currently face, such as encountering increasing demand for more sophisticated survey data in the face of a reluctant public and constraining budgets. These challenges are closely tied to our current culture and recent technological developments. But meeting these challenges will not be simple. We also recognize that culture and the technology that is relevant to surveys are constantly changing. Cultural and technological shifts occurring in the 1970s were reflected in the first edition of this book published in 1978, and these shifts have continued to occur into the present. As a result, much of the content of this book has changed with each new edition as we have attempted to help surveyors deal with and, in some cases, take advantage of these changes. The same is true in this edition.

The constant churning of ideas and constraints impacting the conduct of surveys that has characterized the past 40 years shows little or no sign of stabilizing (Stern, Bilgen, & Dillman, in press). Despite this cultural and technological churn a couple of things have remained consistent across all editions of this book, including this one. One of these is the application of social exchange theory to the conduct of surveys. While the exact costs, benefits, and trust-inducing factors have changed somewhat with the times, the key premises and the framework this theory gives us for thinking through how to conduct surveys and for making informed strategic decisions has remained across all editions because it continues to be useful. The future may make some things more important than others in the costs, benefits, and trust balance, but we anticipate that careful consideration of these key elements in a culturally informed way will help surveyors make their data collections successful. In particular, with continued electronic data exchange and communication, we expect trust to continue to be of primary importance to convincing sample members to cooperate with survey requests and to provide accurate information.

Another element that has been consistent in this book since the 2000 edition is the importance of tailoring. It is tailored design that allows one to leverage costs, benefits, and trust-inducing factors within their cultural context to modify approaches for different survey populations, topics, and goals to make surveys more successful. This, we expect, will continue to be true well into the future.

We have talked mostly in this book about a very standard type of survey—one-time-only cross-sectional surveys primarily of individuals and households—and we have given many practical guidelines for how to make this type of survey successful. One of the key changes in the survey field that we have emphasized in this current edition is the increasing need for mixed-mode designs that give surveyors new ways of building trust, increasing benefits, and reducing the barriers to response. In order to deal with this well, we brought the telephone mode back into this edition. Aside from a few mentions here and there, it had not been discussed in this book since the 1978 edition, but we felt it was necessary to bring it back in now because it is commonly used for certain types of surveys and is important in mixed-mode survey designs.

The full integration of mixed modes, including bringing the telephone back in, meant that other topics we have devoted significant space to in previous editions had to be left out of this edition. This includes panels and longitudinal surveys, business surveys, diaries, and customer satisfaction surveys. We briefly discuss each of these and a few newer topics here in this final chapter because they represent creative ways researchers are trying to deal with some of the current challenges of collecting data, including through the increasing use of mixed-mode survey designs. Substantial resources are being invested in evaluating the potential for these methods to meet many of society's survey needs. In addition, we firmly believe that the principles discussed in this book can and should be used to improve these types of efforts.

Because we cannot give each of these the full attention they deserve in the allotted space, we will point the reader to more thorough treatments of them where possible. We are fortunate that some very good references about several of these topics have become available since the last edition of this book was published, and we hope our readers will be able to benefit from these resources as well.

During the writing process, it was apparent that many of the strategies traditionally used to conduct sample survey data collection are viewed quite differently by surveyors and sample members. One of the underlying ideas that motivated much of the guidance we have provided in this book is that surveyors need to take a more respondent-centered approach to designing their survey data collection efforts than they have in the past. We end this chapter and the book with more discussion of this key point.

PANELS AND LONGITUDINAL SURVEYS

Panel surveys continue to play an important role in surveying today. As the costs of recruiting people to participate in surveys continue to rise, surveyors are increasingly turning to survey designs where people are asked to participate in multiple surveys, typically on different topics, over time, rather than just to complete a single survey.

One of the key areas of growth is panel surveys in which the Internet is the primary mode of survey response. Internet panels have become especially attractive in countries where there is high penetration of reliable Internet connections, although it appears there are differences across countries in how such panels can be used. Many Internet panels recruit members through nonprobability sampling methodologies (discussed in more detail in the next section) but a substantial number also recruit members through probability sampling methods. Many also utilize multiple modes for recruitment. Although recruitment of sample members and the building and maintenance of panels represents a considerable expense, the ultimate goal is to take advantage of the low costs of contacting people by e-mail to respond to web surveys on a regular basis.

The LISS (Longitudinal Internet Studies for the Social Sciences) panel created in the Netherlands in 2007 is one of the best-known examples. The LISS panel is made up of a probability sample of Dutch households drawn from the population register by Statistics Netherlands, the nation's primary statistical agency. About 90% of Dutch households have Internet access, currently the highest of any European country (Mohorko, de Leeuw, & Hox, 2013). For those LISS panel members without Internet access, a computer and Internet connection are provided (Das, Ester, & Kaczmirek, 2010). The 5,000 panel members are asked to complete online questionnaires about once a month, and are paid a modest amount for each completed questionnaire. Attempts to develop similar panels in other countries with high Internet penetration are being considered or are now underway.

In the United States, probability-selected Internet-only household panels have also existed for some time. An example is the GfK KnowledgePanel. When the 2009 addition of this book was published, recruitment for this panel was conducted predominately by telephone using RDD sampling methodologies. Since then, the recruitment has shifted to mail and telephone using a sample from an address-based sampling frame. This mixed-mode design was chosen to overcome some of the coverage and response rate limitations associated with telephone-only RDD surveys (GfK-Knowledge Networks, n.d.).

Similar to the LISS Panel, the KnowledgePanel also provides a computer and Internet access to recruited panelists who do not already have them. An alternative favored by some organizations is to offer those who are unable or unwilling to respond over the Internet another mode of response, such as paper or telephone, so that they can still participate in the panel. This is a model that is followed by the Gallup Organization in the United States (Rookey et al., 2008) and is being introduced by the Leibniz Institute for the Social Sciences in Germany (Gesis Panel, n.d.).

In addition to the time and costs savings of having a sample recruited and ready to answer multiple surveys, the substantial effort undertaken to recruit panelists and maintain a relationship with them opens up opportunities for other types of measurement. For example, Nielsen asks panel members to allow them to install meters on their TVs that collect what programs they watch. This viewing information is supplemented with survey information about the household, such as the demographics and interests of the people in the home. Other panels ask people to install programs on their mobile devices that track the use of different apps, their viewing behavior, online purchases, or their location and movements. It is possible to get panel members to cooperate with these types of requests, which might seem invasive in other circumstances, because a trusting relationship has been developed and sustained over time.

Panels seem to work best on a large scale (i.e., a nationally representative panel rather than one that is representative at the state or local level or of a specific population like students or members of an organization) because the costs of establishing and operating them are substantial. In addition, many surveys of both national and more localized areas have very specific population and eligibility requirements that are difficult to justify building an entire panel around. Some surveyors use panels because they can sample specific types of people (e.g., college graduates or middle-aged men), but the ability to target other low-incidence and hard-to-reach populations (e.g., low-income households, households with children of certain ages, people with specific health conditions, same-sex couples, etc.) is limited because in order to do so the panel has to be quite large. In addition, requiring sample selection methods to be somewhat general makes it difficult for many surveyors to accomplish their purpose within the constraints of the panel's normal operations and procedures. It also seems unlikely that many established surveys would be willing to abandon their independent samples in favor of one sample shared by others and controlled by an outside organization that becomes an intermediary surveyor.

Longitudinal surveys, which have been used since the early years of surveying, are another type of panel survey. In longitudinal surveys individuals are surveyed with the same or similar questions periodically over months or years, allowing researchers to track trends and understand the causes and consequences of societal and individual change. Such surveys have become of even greater interest in recent years as the technology for locating previous respondents and conducting follow-up surveys has improved and it has become increasingly evident that many conditions of human existence, from education and health to family formation and wealth accumulation, cannot be well understood without understanding change over time.

Sponsors of longitudinal surveys often find it difficult to maintain the same modes of data collection over time, particularly if their surveys continue over many years or even decades. But switching modes across different measurements presents particular challenges for longitudinal and other panel surveys. This was a major reason we introduced a discussion of mixed-mode designs in the third edition of this book. Introducing a new mode in longitudinal and other panel surveys can affect the ability to accurately measure change because response differences may be a result of the differences in modes used to survey respondents rather than actual change in people's responses (Dillman & Christian, 2005). It is for this reason that for longitudinal and panel surveys that are just beginning, it is important to try to anticipate likely mode changes up front so the questionnaire can be designed to minimize differences when it is administered in a different mode in the future (for more on unified mode design, see Chapter 11).

The complexities involved in designing and conducting longitudinal surveys are substantial. A book edited by Peter Lynn (2009) provides a much-needed overview and discussion of the multiple and complex issues involved. Topics range from designing the original sample and questionnaire construction to locating people for follow-up and the use of incentives and other procedures for gaining and maintaining cooperation. Also discussed are weighting, analysis, and the handling of attrition over time. Conducting longitudinal surveys requires additional design considerations that go beyond those needed for cross-sectional surveys in nearly all stages of development and implementation. It is a rapidly growing specialty area of surveying.

Due to the high costs of recruiting people to participate in surveys, an increasing number of researchers are drawing their study samples from households that have responded to other surveys. For example, the National Survey of College Graduates (NSCG) now uses the list of households that answered the American Community Survey as its sampling frame. The NSCG is itself longitudinal, but the fact that its sample comes from respondents to a previous survey suggests that some carryover from the original survey may occur. Several Pew Research Center studies have also used lists of respondents from previous surveys as a sample source along with other sources, such as new landline and cell phone RDD numbers. In this case, the advantage of using a sample from a previous survey is that it allowed the researchers to rely on responses from the previous surveys to identify people belonging to certain hard-to-reach populations, such as Muslims and Asian Americans, for in-depth surveys of these subpopulations. While these surveys are able to leverage previous surveys to reduce the costs of sampling and ensure certain groups are included in their studies, one weakness of these designs is that any undercoverage or nonresponse that existed in the initial surveys is highly likely to carry over into the new survey. Whether or not these problems manifest in error depends on whether the differences between those who were covered and not covered and between those who responded and did not respond in the first survey are related to the items and characteristics being measured in the new survey.

All of these types of surveys (panels, longitudinal surveys, and drawing sample from respondents to previous surveys) involve repeated questioning of the same individuals over time, often relying on payments to maintain cooperation. A special concern in these types of surveys is conditioning, or how being a previous survey participant affects answers later on (Sturgis, Allum, & Brunton-Smith, 2009). This is an area that is not yet fully researched or understood, especially with respect to attitudes and opinions, which are especially sensitive to such effects. Further, conditioning effects may be exacerbated as the time between surveys decreases. As such, panel conditioning may be particularly problematic in Internet-only panels where people are surveyed frequently (i.e., monthly, weekly, or even more often). With this high frequency of surveying, there is an increased likelihood that later answers and styles of responding to questions will be affected by earlier experiences. Do people get into a mind-set that encourages them to read questions more superficially and thus miss important details? When responding is viewed simply as an obligation for earning routine payments, does lack of interest in particular questions cause them to straight-line answers or satisfice in other ways? Do early responses on particular topics cause individuals to pay more attention to those topics in their daily lives, resulting in changes in behaviors, changes in answers to future questions on similar topics, or both? In sum, the effects of being surveyed repeatedly, sometimes in short intervals, and other times years or even decades apart, raises questions for which answers are needed if surveyors are to use these methods with confidence.

While they each have their limits and challenges, we expect these types of surveys to continue in the long run because they represent methods of responding to the difficulties being faced by individual survey modes or can answer questions that regular cross-sectional surveys cannot. The use of Internet panels seems particularly likely to increase because of the cost savings opportunities they present, especially as Internet use continues to expand. In the future, we expect to see more surveys drawing their samples from previous surveys for the same reason. Each of these methods introduces complications and challenges that go above and beyond those faced by surveyors conducting cross-sectional surveys with their own sample, and as such, drawing on social exchange theory and using tailored designs may be particularly valuable for these types of surveys.

NONPROBABILITY SAMPLING

The framework for surveying that has guided the writing of this book is probability sampling. That means that everyone in the sampling frame has a known and possible chance of being selected to participate, and a probability method is used to select the actual sample members from the frame. It is this probability sampling basis that allows surveyors to use inferential statistics to estimate the distribution of characteristics of interest in the target population. There is a long history of attempting to use alternatives to probability sampling that seek responses from volunteers or others who are recruited and selected unsystematically. Terms applied to such selection have included convenience sampling, mall or person-on-the-street intercept surveys, or simply volunteer samples.

The distinction between probability and nonprobability sampling has been diminished by the reduced coverage and high nonresponse associated with the use of some survey data collection approaches. The lack of complete coverage for telephone and Internet household samples, combined with low response rates for telephone-only and e-mail/Internet-only surveys raises serious questions with regard to whether these surveys achieve a probability sample of households, or are more akin to volunteer samples.

The problem with samples selected using nonprobability methods is that there is a high likelihood that those who do not volunteer to participate differ in important ways from those who do because no probability mechanism is used to help ensure that the sample is representative of the target population. Also, response rates are often quite low. Most importantly, surveys that use nonprobability sampling have no scientific or theoretical basis for making meaningful statistical inference from those who were surveyed to the population they are supposed to represent, as described by Baker et al. (2013) in the recent AAPOR Task Force on Non-Probability Sampling report.

However, nonprobability methods are becoming much more sophisticated with regard to who is asked to participate. There is a substantial difference between how nonprobability methods were designed and implemented in decades past and the efforts now being made to construct samples that match the characteristics of participants to known characteristics of populations of interest. Modeling is generally used to identify the characteristics most correlated with response, and statistical adjustments are made to account for different propensities of various types of individuals to be selected and respond to the survey requests. As noted by the AAPOR task force, there is evidence that nonprobability samples have performed well in predicting elections, but their performance is less clear in other domains (Baker et al., 2013). However, it is important to note that nonprobability samples are more accepted in some areas, such as market research, and in some countries, than others.

Much of the interest in developing and using nonprobability samples has been fueled by the low costs of sending e-mails and surveying people via the Internet compared to other methods. Much of the cost is absorbed by setting up procedures for the first few respondents, so that significant economies of scale can be achieved when the decision is made to survey thousands instead of a few hundred. We expect the search for topics and situations where nonprobability surveys work and research applying sophisticated principles of selection and response encouragement that are outside of a strictly probability selection framework will continue.

NEW MOBILE DEVICES AND TECHNOLOGY

Technological changes and their adoption are occurring at an unprecedented rate. The Apple iPad was released in April 2010, more than a year after the third edition of this book was published. Within 3 years more than 170,000,000 iPads had been sold (Panzarino, 2013) and 35% of U.S. adults owned a tablet computer of some kind (Rainie & Smith, 2013). Also, as of May 2013, 56% of American adults had a smartphone, with roughly equal proportions having iPhones and Android phones, which were first released in October 2008, and far fewer using other types of smartphones (Smith, 2013a). Fully 91% of adults have a cell phone of some kind, 81% of whom send or receive text messages on their cell phone, 60% of whom access the Internet, and 52% of whom send or receive e-mail on their phones (Brenner, 2013). These mobile devices have advanced and been adopted quite quickly, and we expect changes in them to continue, as well as for new devices to be developed, although it is uncertain which new devices will catch on and which will not.

Mobile devices with small screens present special challenges to surveyors because they have changed the ways in which people communicate and how survey questionnaires need to be designed. Many of the traditional question formats relied on by web surveyors are difficult to display on these small screens. An example is the grid format, which is usually too large to display on smartphone screens. For such questions to work on smartphones, it is generally necessary to instead ask them as a series of individual questions. In addition, open-ended questions that ask for lengthy detailed answers, which can easily be provided on computers, are likely to obtain greatly abbreviated answers, more akin to a texting response, by people responding on mobile devices. Adapting questions from full-size computer screens or paper questionnaire pages is challenging because of the space constraints, the touch input methodology that most mobile devices use, and the wide variety of devices that must be accommodated. But, it also raises issues with regard to finding a unified mode construction that works the same across different devices and modes.

New electronic devices not only change how people respond to individual survey questions but also when and where they can respond. Someone may receive a survey request while checking e-mail on her mobile device. If she tries to access the survey and is unable to because of connectivity issues, or cannot understand or navigate the questionnaire because it is not optimized for mobile, then she must remember to go back and access the survey from a desktop or laptop computer to respond. The need to switch devices is an additional barrier and cost associated with responding, which will reduce the chances she will respond.

Mobile devices are not always compatible with completing complex tasks that require sustained concentration. While smartphones have been constrained to a size people can comfortably carry nearly everywhere, work and home offices are equipped with large screens or multiple screens that allow people to simultaneously see and process multiple pieces of information. Thus, a division of labor often develops between what people feel they can do effectively on their mobile device and what they feel they can do effectively on a computer with a larger screen. Paper is also used in many situations because it helps people better understand the geography of the argument contained within (Sellen & Harper, 2002, as cited in Korkki, 2012). In the near term, how people divide their tasks across different means—whether smartphone, landline, tablet, desktop, or paper—is part of the environment that must be considered when selecting and using modes to contact and survey people. It also illustrates how the development of technology, and how people learn to depend on it, introduces new possibilities and constraints for surveying.

So far, attempts to convince people on a widespread basis to use their smartphone for responding to surveys have only been modestly successful (Callegaro & Macer, 2011). Our own attempt to obtain smartphone survey responses in 2011 took place in an undergraduate student population in which about half of the students were known to have smartphones. Each of four contacts encouraged students with a smartphone to respond on it. Although about half of the students sampled responded to the survey, only 7% of those who responded did so over a smartphone (Millar & Dillman, 2012).

However, the expectation that mobile devices will eventually be used by many to answer surveys and the optimism about their potential is reflected in the fact that those conducting several large national surveys have begun to seriously consider and test whether mobile devices can be used to improve data collection. For example, a recent report from the National Research Council (2013) that detailed the difficulties of obtaining consumer expenditure reports using interviews and paper diaries in the U.S. Bureau of Labor Statistics–sponsored Consumer Expenditure Survey recommended testing tablets to produce more accurate and timely reporting. Additional research is being conducted under the BLS Gemini project to examine how smartphones may be used in such reporting (Edgar,

Nelson, Paszkiewicz, & Safir, 2013). It will take several years to work through and appropriately test a new methodology to replace the current design that was developed and has been used since the early 1980s. Nielsen has also tested using a mobile app and website where people can self-report their TV viewing behavior as an alternative to the paper diary that is currently used today (Link, Lai, & Bristol, 2013). As these examples of trying to develop electronic reporting suggest, there is a compelling need to think constantly about how new devices and technologies can improve surveys and about the prevalence of their use in coming years.

One of the obstacles survey research faces is how to successfully connect the request to complete a survey with the unprecedented availability of devices that can be used for responding. The challenges associated with achieving that suggest to us that future surveying is likely to remain mixed-mode and involve not only contacting people by one survey mode to encourage them to respond to another, as emphasized in this book, but also contacting them by one device and encouraging them to go to another device to respond.

SUPPLEMENTING QUESTIONNAIRES WITH MEASUREMENT USING ELECTRONIC DEVICES

The willingness of respondents to use and carry electronic devices has not gone unnoticed by surveyors. Nielsen Audio (formerly Arbitron), which for decades has used paper diaries to identify which radio stations people were listening to, developed a new device to measure listening passively so people do not have to self-report what radio stations they listen to and when. The Portable People Meter (PPM) is a device that people carry with them throughout the day that detects audio codes inserted in radio and television broadcasts. The PPM has replaced the self-reported paper diary methodology in many cities. Nielsen utilizes a similar approach for measuring TV viewing in which devices are installed on TV sets and computers in the home. Using devices such as these means that the listening and viewing estimates are less subject to recall error and individual differences in reporting.

This is a highly specialized use of a technology, and it can work because the television and radio stations have a vested interest in obtaining accurate measurement of what programs and stations people are watching and listening to (and thus are willing to embed codes in their broadcasts that can be picked up by these devices). Self-reporting viewing and listening information at the level of detail requested in the TV and radio paper diaries over the time period requested (usually about a week) can be quite difficult and prone to error because people may not always know, with accuracy, what programs and stations are watched or listened to at all times of the day.

Similar use of devices to supplement survey measurement seems likely for surveys on various other topics. Pocket or clip-on devices—sometimes called wearable devices—are now used to measure physical activity such as walking and running, routes walked, and sleeping duration and soundness. Information from those devices can be uploaded and analyzed daily if people are willing to allow researchers to access the data. People can also apply self-administered medical tests to themselves, the results of which can be shared with those participating in research studies. Cell phones can now track individuals' movement from one location to another via GPS, which has great potential for transportation and consumer behavior surveys. In fact, survey methodologists are currently using this capability to study how face-to-face interviewers travel between sampled households to complete their workload (Olson & Wagner, 2013). In addition, cell phones can be used to pay for purchases, making it possible to collect and transmit transaction information using this technology instead of consumer diaries to measure consumer purchases.

Efforts to use such devices to record behaviors are likely to continue to involve mixed-mode survey designs because most participants in this research are recruited using a variety of modes. Further, survey questions are usually asked of these participants with the survey data being used to better understand the data recorded by the devices. Participants are asked to report demographic characteristics, interests or attitudes, and additional information about the behaviors recorded by the devices. For example, a phone's GPS might be used to collect data about where the person goes, but it cannot tell why he goes there or how satisfied he is with what he encounters there, which is information that can be collected in a survey. In fact, the ability to combine survey data with data from the electronic devices is a powerful strength of these approaches. As such, it seems quite likely that the survey design and implementation methods described in this book, and especially those for mixed-mode surveys, will continue to be used to both enable the use of electronic devices for data collection (i.e., recruitment, building trust to gain cooperation, etc.) and to supplement and make the data collected by these devices more useful.

BIG DATA AND ADMINISTRATIVE RECORDS

In addition to devices that measure different behaviors passively, there is a variety of existing organic or big-data sources available to be used to better understand behavior. Organic data are collected as part of people's interactions in daily life such as registering for a driver's license, purchasing items, engaging in online searches, and posting content on social media sites. As more of our transactions become computerized and communication moves online, more and more data are collected in large databases that record these interactions and transactions, as well as supplementary information (such as the date, time, or location of the transaction or posting) also available at the time of the interaction. These databases can now easily be preserved for decades.

After learning about the availability of these data, a student in a survey design class posed what seemed like a straightforward question, "With big data, why would we ever need or want to do a survey?" The response to that question was equally straightforward. Surveys are undertaken because we have a question for which we do not have an answer. Surveys can be used to collect information that does not exist for the population the survey sponsor is interested in or information that is needed to understand relationships among variables but that is not available in a single existing data source. In addition, surveys might be used when the desired information exists, but is not available from those who have previously collected it, or when it is enormously difficult and costly to extract. Also, surveys are particularly useful for collecting information about what people are thinking or doing now. This type of information is generally not available in most databases. The exception is data from social media posts which are very good for capturing what people are thinking or doing at a particular time, but in many instances are limited to only those who use these sites (i.e., to the extent that users and nonusers of social media sites differ, the conclusions drawn from such data may only generalize to social media users).

Despite the explosion of information that is recorded each second of every day in highly automated systems, the resultant data have not proved to be an effective substitute for survey data to answer a large number of questions that researchers attempt to answer. Rather, as with data collected by electronic devices, the most exciting possibilities for big data might be using them in conjunction with survey data to learn things that neither data source on its own can reveal or to reduce the number of questions that need to be asked on questionnaires in order to ease the burden of responding to them. Big data that are available at the individual level where they can be more easily linked or matched to survey data may be particularly effective for these types of uses. However, additional research about how to integrate big data with survey data is needed.

In sum, there can be little doubt that businesses, government, and other organizations will increasingly attempt to answer questions on a variety of topics through the analysis of big data. However, it's not likely that this will eliminate the need for sample surveys. The more likely scenario for the immediate future is that administrative records collected on individuals and other types of big data will be connected with survey data, which will require collaboration across agencies and organizations and surveyors to work with those who manage big data, which can be a substantial undertaking.

Because using existing administrative data can reduce the amount of information that must be collected in surveys, linking administrative records and survey data across different government agencies is of particular interest for government survey efforts. Doing so requires individual agency approval and also may require informed consent on the part of individuals whose records are being matched to their survey responses (Sakshaug, Couper, Ofstedal, & Weir, 2012). Research has suggested that many respondents are willing to approve the linkage of their answers to government-sponsored surveys with data obtained from administrative records in other agencies (Bates, 2005). Yet, the potential for linking data from different sources goes far beyond government. Such linkages can be done with membership and customer lists, credit history files, customer transaction and loyalty program data, and many other sources of information. However, trust in the legitimacy of the research being conducted with such linkages and a belief that the benefits of allowing the linkage outweigh the costs of doing so will be key to obtaining the public's cooperation with such efforts.

One of the challenges associated with both big data and administrative records as replacements for surveys is that the populations for which they are covered are inherently limited (e.g., to a specific store's customers, people who post to a particular social media site, etc.), and it is often difficult to estimate the coverage of the target population by the data source. Because of this limitation of using data from a single source, it is often helpful to combine data from multiple sources (e.g., purchasing behavior across several stores to track the food a family buys or license data across several states). However, working with these large data sets to standardize formats and combine data can be quite difficult and the barriers to convincing people and organizations to permit large-scale transfers of information are substantial. Further, data are often collected with a certain regularity or may cover only a certain time period. Taken together, these errors that may arise from a variety of sources and the sheer size and complexity of the data, as well as data security issues raise huge challenges. These challenges mean that substantial research is still needed about how big data can be used alone and in combination with other data sources, including surveys.

DATA SECURITY

Data security is a fundamental concern for nearly all survey undertakings. The attention being given to data security of all types is probably greater now than at any time in history. This is likely because increased electronic connectivity has led to the rapid transfer of large amounts of electronic information, including a lot of highly sensitive information (e.g., telephone records, credit card transactions, medical records, Internet use, etc.). Information, including sensitive information, can be compromised on an enormous scale.

There are several types of security concerns relevant to conducting surveys. First, entering and answering web surveys sometimes requires remembering and typing complicated security codes and other information that itself becomes a barrier to responding. Examples include lengthy codes that entail random combinations of capital and lowercase letters, numbers, and symbols, such as this 12-digit code one of us was asked to use to enter a survey: NuC4$&@K?Z0c. We have also observed surveys in which a URL that was 50 or more characters had to be transferred from a paper letter to a computer browser to access the survey.

A different type of security concern is raised when Internet surveys are hosted and data are collected using servers that are not controlled by the surveyor, as is the case with many free online survey hosting sites. Institutional review boards and sponsoring organizations often require that surveyors promise data protection and confidentiality, but because of its storage location some of that protection is outside the surveyor's control. It is important to understand data ownership when promising confidentiality to survey respondents. Additionally, no matter how many layers of security are in place to protect survey data from outsiders, organizations may always be open to the occasional "inside job" whereby someone who works for an organization steals survey data.

These types of data security threats worry surveyors and respondents alike that confidentiality cannot be kept as promised, which likely dampens people's willingness to respond to surveys in general and to answer certain questions, especially sensitive ones. The magnitude of the threat to survey data security in the coming years seems especially difficult to predict as it depends on what happens with worldwide electronic connectedness, the efforts of governments, security developments in the private sector, the ability and willingness of individuals to take steps to protect their transactions with others, and the creativity and determination of those with nefarious intent to overcome these efforts as technology also changes. How these issues will change and affect surveyors in coming years remains to be seen.

SPECIALIZED PURPOSE SURVEYS

Some uses of surveys are so specialized that they have become a subfield of survey methodology. An example is business or establishment surveys, in which the unit of analysis is a business or establishment and people provide answers as a representative of that organization rather than as individuals representing themselves (Cox et al., 1995). The application of social exchange concepts and the use of tailored design strategies may be more important in business and establishment surveys than in many other types of surveys. For a business the costs of doing a survey are real financial costs (i.e., someone has to complete the survey while on the company clock) that can reduce productivity and cut into the bottom line. Additionally, the information requested is often quite complex, difficult to obtain and report, and oftentimes sensitive (Snijkers, Haraldsen, Jones, & Willimack, 2013).

Despite their incredible difficulty, business surveys are among the most critical surveys done in societies throughout the world. They are used to assess many important phenomena such as the amount of new housing constructed, employment practices, money borrowing, research and development expenditures, the societal production of scientists and engineers, energy use, manufacturing output, and imports and exports, among many other things. In the United States, they are relied upon to provide information that is critical to providing statistical guidance to the Federal Reserve Board and other entities responsible for maintaining the smooth operation of national and international economies. They also provide information relied on for developing new laws and government regulations. Thousands of such surveys are conducted each year in the United States and elsewhere.

Traditionally, business surveys were conducted by paper with forms sent to organizations to be completed and returned. Because the adoption rate for the Internet has been much faster in businesses, some business surveys have been moved directly from paper to web. However, the process of contacting businesses and obtaining responses has and continues to be inherently mixed-mode, leveraging mail, web, and telephone as needed to ensure a high quality result.

The tradition of conducting business surveys by self-administered modes inspired considerable research and development of the visual design and layout principles reported in Chapter 6 of this book and elsewhere (Dillman, Gertseva, & Haft, 2005; Morrison, Dillman, & Christian, 2010). A recent book, *Designing and Conducting Business Surveys* by Snijkers et al. (2013), has expanded on those principles. In addition, it summarizes the key issues that one needs to attend to when designing business surveys, including how surveying businesses differs from surveying individuals (with explicit consideration of the different cost, benefit, and trust issues encountered in business surveys) and considerations involved in listing and sampling businesses, questionnaire design, and implementation. This work provides much-needed detailed methods for conducting business surveys, including emphasis on electronic reporting and mixed-mode methods where appropriate.

Another specialized form of surveying, and one that is rapidly changing, is the customer behavior and satisfaction survey. The Internet has helped fuel a substantial increase in the number of customer satisfaction surveys conducted, and the variations in the type of customer satisfaction surveys has also expanded greatly. Some surveys are aimed at providing regular feedback about satisfaction with a product, such as one's cable or telephone service or a store's loyalty program. Others are aimed less at assessing customer satisfaction and more at shaping the customer experience. It is increasingly likely that one's travel will be followed by a request to comment on that experience, especially if travelers have shared their e-mail addresses when making travel arrangements.

We have also observed that many customer satisfaction surveys have changed from a random sample survey used to assess experiences with a company to feedback devices employed after every transaction (e.g., trip, visit, purchase, etc.) or only when there has been a problem. Instead of a periodic general survey to assess satisfaction, some organizations now conduct special surveys of all customers who have experienced a problem. For example, we commonly receive e-mails asking us for feedback about flights that experienced problems like late departures or mechanical issues, but rarely receive such requests when all goes well. In other cases, we have had a hotel company survey us after every visit to one of their hotels. Data collected via these mostly electronic surveys are also connected immediately to administrative records maintained by the organization, sometimes leading to personalized responses. Companies have also shifted to greater use of electronic modes of contact and response with mail and telephone interspersed in support of such methods to measure customer satisfaction.

Business and consumer satisfaction surveys are only two examples of the many areas of specialized surveying that now exist and are likely to expand in future years. Both involve mixed-mode designs but also illustrate how e-mail and web are shouldering greater portions of the data collection responsibility. And the success of both can be greatly improved through the application of social exchange concepts to tailor the survey designs for these very particular types of surveys.

INTERNATIONAL AND CROSS-CULTURAL SURVEYS

Archimedes, an ancient mathematician and physicist, is reputed to have said, "Give me a place to stand I will move the earth" (Pappus of Alexandria, AD 340, quoted in *The Lever*, n.d.). His description referred to the power of the lever and fulcrum for moving heavy objects. The imagery of a lever so long that when manipulated with an appropriately-placed fulcrum it could move an impossibly large object is powerful. It might also serve as a good metaphor for using a small sample of the Earth's 7 billion people to describe their characteristics. Collecting sample survey information that would make it possible to estimate on a worldwide basis the interests, opinions, and problems people face, including differences within countries, and to compare these estimates across different countries and regions is an intriguing challenge. Yet, from a sampling theory standpoint is quite feasible.

Our interconnected world now makes it possible for news media to report events from and to nearly every place on the globe on a daily, and sometimes on an hourly or minute-by-minute basis. Decisions of national and international leaders increasingly reflect events happening in other countries. In our global economy, countries compete with one another for the development and retention of jobs. Terrorist threats are as likely to originate from far places as they are locally. The effective monitoring of behaviors, economic conditions, environmental concerns, and well-being is no longer just a local or even a country-specific concern.

Like moving the earth, the challenges of undertaking worldwide surveys are by no means small. The large number of languages and the cultural differences in how people respond to surveys need to be understood for cross-national surveys to be effective (Harkness et al., 2010; Harkness, van de Vijver, & Mohler, 2003; de Leeuw et al., 2007). As people continue to move between countries, understanding language and cultural differences that affect response is critical even for surveys of a single country. Other challenges include understanding and working with the governments that have to provide permission to conduct the survey and ensuring the safety of survey staff in some countries among many other things. Nonetheless, steady progress is being made. In the European Social Survey, the same survey questions are now being asked regularly in over 30 countries (European Social Survey, n.d.). The Pew Research Center also conducts surveys in many different countries throughout the world, from which they regularly release results (Pew Research Center's Global Attitudes Project, n.d.)

One of the most ambitious global surveying efforts is the Gallup World Poll, which routinely conducts sample surveys in up to 160 countries (Gallup, n.d.). Most countries on all continents are now being surveyed regularly. This effort, like all cross-national surveys, requires the use of different sampling strategies and survey response modes appropriate to the country, ranging from in-person to telephone and the Internet. Gallup reports have provided country-by-country estimates of the participation of people in paid work, their interest in migrating to a different country, satisfaction with their local and national governments, the number of children parents would like to have, and other characteristics of widespread interest. Reports from the Gallup World Poll sometimes make worldwide estimates. In other cases, they focus on comparisons between countries and regions of the world (Ray, 2013).

The countries in which Gallup surveys for the World Poll include both the richest and poorest in the world and have populations that vary from the most to the least literate and who speak a wide variety of languages. A great deal of effort has been made to try to make the survey questions meaningful and answerable across all of these languages and cultures and in the different modes used across countries. Work focused on meeting that challenge continues, but great progress is being made in producing survey results that can provide a meaningful knowledge base for better understanding the human condition across the globe and affecting public policy decisions across country boundaries. The power of survey sampling, as a lever for understanding the people and conditions around the globe, and perhaps acting on that knowledge, no longer seems an impossible dream.

Thinking about costs, benefits, and trust and tailoring design is essential to being able to conduct effective international surveys. As an extreme but all too common example, in some countries the personal costs of criticizing one's government are such that questions about the government should not even be asked, and if they are, the data collected will certainly be biased. What is considered sensitive information or taboo in one country may be a perfectly acceptable topic to discuss in another. Likewise, things that motivate people in one country to respond may discourage people in another from responding. Balancing these cultural and national differences with the need for a minimal level of standardization is the primary challenge of these surveys. It is a challenge on which a lot of progress has been made and on which considerably more work and research is needed.

THE CHALLENGE OF CONNECTING WITH EMPOWERED BUT DIVERSE RESPONDENTS

Too often the methods used by surveyors have treated sampled households and individuals as being willing to serve the study and interviewer needs in an unquestioning way. In addition the surveyor has sometimes forgotten to view the process from the perspective of the respondent, deciding to use long and difficult-to-answer questionnaires that greatly exceed people's willingness and even ability to answer. Surveyors have also tried to minimize the burden and costs to themselves of implementing their surveys. That has sometimes meant restricting survey designs to a single mode of contact and response and treating all respondents exactly the same irrespective of what is best for them.

For many years the surveyor had the upper hand and was able to work in this way. People were inclined to give those who approached them with a request to answer questionnaires the benefit of the doubt. They were also more likely to think of answering survey questions as an extension of how they interacted cooperatively with others who approached them with requests for help. It made it easier that people were also typically accessible by different means, so that surveyors seldom needed to use multiple means of contact in order to locate and gain the attention of individuals. In addition, the cadence for conducting and reporting survey results was somewhat slower by comparison to today's rapid-fire communication environment.

Surveyors can no longer think of a sampled household or individual as becoming a participant only on the surveyor's terms, while giving no recognition to the sample member's desires or interests. Responding to nearly all surveys is voluntary, and the respondents' power to say "no" and the likelihood of their acting on that ability have never been greater. When recipients of survey requests sense that this norm of voluntary cooperation is being violated, reactions are sometimes public, in addition to being privately expressed. Today's surveyors must work within this voluntary culture in order to conduct successful surveys.

This does not mean, as we have shown in this book, that we must abandon our efforts to design and carry out successful probability-based sample surveys. However, it does mean that we must design and implement our surveys in ways that take into account people's needs and preferences. Surveyors must be responsive to sample members' needs just as businesses and other enterprises that depend on customers must be responsive to their customers' needs. The survey requests and the questions themselves need to be seen by the empowered sample members as understandable, reasonable, and, when possible, interesting. The approach we have offered is a respondent-centric one—to utilize our social exchange framework to design surveys that offer benefits while reducing the costs associated with responding and improve trust in the legitimacy of the survey and that the eventual rewards will outweigh the costs.

One of the biggest current challenges to achieving this is reducing respondent burden. The surveyor's appetite for additional questions has at times seemed insatiable. We have observed a blank page in paper questionnaires suddenly be filled with new questions during a final review. Similarly we have observed survey investigators come to periodic review meetings with new questions to be asked, but seldom arrive with proposals for eliminating as many questions as they hoped to add. More recently, we have witnessed investigators expressing their pleasure that the Internet makes the number of questions mostly invisible to respondents, thinking that they could pretty much ignore length considerations. When in-person interviews were dominant in society, surveyors felt impunity with regard to number of questions. Extending the interview a few minutes was unlikely to reduce response rates, and the costs of going back to collect additional data later was substantial. That world has disappeared twice—first with the telephone, and second with the Internet. People today expect communication to be shorter and to occur in more frequent bits.

More than 40 years ago the director of the nation's most prominent survey research center made the observation, "We always seem to end up collecting far more data than ever gets analyzed" (P. Rossi, personal communication, 1971). This is still true today. Recently, a doctoral student went through a year-long process of developing a dissertation mail questionnaire. Each meeting with her advisers and pretest volunteers resulted in adding additional questions. These additions were defended with comments about only some of the respondents needing to answer them; it was reasoned that they were not really making the questionnaire longer for most respondents. Ultimately the additions led to the need to reduce the font size and fill all blank spots until the maximum content for a 12-page booklet questionnaire had been reached. After her dissertation defense, she was asked what she would have done differently if she were starting the project over. Her answer was simply, "I would have asked fewer questions. I only analyzed some of the data, and the sample sizes were so small for some of the branched questions that I did not think the analyses would be meaningful."

A somewhat different survey situation existed when one of us was part of a group reviewing a national survey about energy use in residences. Many new questions were proposed in order to update the survey, but strong defenses were offered for keeping nearly all of the current questions. However, it was also noted during these meetings that many of the more detailed questions of less current relevance were deemed lower priority by the agency. Results for these questions were not released until several years after the data were collected. For this survey and many others, there are constant pressures to keep old questions and add new ones, which come from investigators who want increasingly comprehensive but precise analytic models, interest groups who want specific data for their purposes, and survey professionals who care about maintaining trend lines over many years. These pressures have often meant sacrificing explanations and other trust- and benefit-inducing features in favor of asking an additional question or two without having to increase the stated length of the survey. The respondents are those who ultimately pay the price of accommodating everyone's wishes, unless they choose not to respond at all. Like many things in life, questionnaire design needs to strike a balance between competing interests with the goal of keeping questionnaire length to a minimum in order to minimize respondents' burden and avoid wasting their time collecting data that will never be used.

There is a broad cultural appeal for making questionnaires shorter than many surveyors would like for them to be. There is also broad cultural appeal in the United States for token cash incentives that can be included with the request to complete surveys; both response rate improvements and the general lack of objections suggest that sending them fits with the general culture. Also a general part of the culture is to communicate politely, identify oneself honestly, provide contact information, and inform people how they can get answers to questions. Efforts to be helpful and make responding easier also have general appeal. These and other considerations can positively affect some recipients of survey requests without negatively affecting most others.

At the same time, there are many differences among those asked to respond to a particular survey. Some may be attracted to colorful questionnaires with pictures, while others see no difference from black-and-white renditions. Some people are skeptical of anything government. Others are equally skeptical of all things business. The mode of contact, whether by telephone, mail, or web, may make some people apprehensive, but not others. Also, some people are very community oriented, and others are much more oriented to their own self-interest. It is important to appeal to these different types of people in our survey requests to reduce the risk of nonresponse error. Doing so means incorporating a number of respondent-centric features into our designs.

Early research has suggested that adaptive designs, which develop later implementation procedures and contact materials to try to obtain responses from different kinds of people than those who have already responded, can help reduce nonresponse error (Wagner, 2008). Strategies offered here under the social exchange framework for carrying out adaptive design include obtaining contact information for as many modes as possible and communicating the survey request using multiple modes, offering different modes of response, and packaging requests so that each introduces new elements of potential value into the communications to affect the balance of benefits, costs, and trust. A half century ago it was observed for mail surveys that multiple contacts are the most effective means of improving survey response rates (e.g., Scott, 1961). Mixed-mode designs with emphasis on changes in mode of contact and response and the coordination among them represent a means of achieving even greater effectiveness and quality because they allow adaptations to be made that have great potential to appeal to different types of sample members. In other words, they allow the surveyor to respond to needs and desires.

As surveyors react to the continued technological changes that affect how people communicate, it will remain ever important to be appreciative of the contribution that respondents make to the success of surveys. We must also be respectful of their needs and desires as well as how those needs and desires might differ among various groups in our survey populations.

References

Ajzen, I., & Fishbein, M. (1980). *Understanding attitudes and predicting social behavior*. Englewood Cliffs, NJ: Prentice Hall.

Alcser, K., & Clemons, J. (2013). Interviewer recruitment, selection, and training. In *Cross-cultural survey guidelines*. Retrieved from http://ccsg.isr.umich.edu/iwerselection.cfm

Altheimer, I., & Dillman, D. A. (2002). Results from cognitive interviews of NSF earned doctorate web survey (Technical Report No. 02-30). Pullman: Washington State University, Social and Economic Sciences Research Center.

Amaya, A., Skalland, B., & Wooten, K. (2010). What's in a match? *Survey Practice 3*(6). Available at http://www.surveypractice.org/index.php/SurveyPractice/article/view/148/pdf

American Association for Public Opinion Research. (n.d.). *Blue book*. Retrieved January 4, 2014, from http://www.aapor.org/source/bluebooksearch/pdf.cfm

American Association for Public Opinion Research. (2010). *Cell phone task force report*. Retrieved from http://www.aapor.org/AM/Template.cfm?Section=Cell_Phone_Task_Force_Report&Template=/CM/ContentDisplay.cfm&ContentID=3189

American Association for Public Opinion Research. (2011). *Standard definitions: Final dispositions of case codes and outcome rates for surveys*. Retrieved from http://www.aapor.org/Standards_and_Ethics/5102.htm#.Uma3HBCUZc4

American Community Survey. (2008). *2008 American Community Survey 1 year estimates: Washington*. American FactFinder, U.S. Census Bureau. Retrieved from http://factfinder.census.gov/servlet/DatasetMainPageServlet?_program=ACS&_submenuId=&_lang=en&_ts=

Andrews, F. M. (1984). Construct validity and error components of survey measures: A structural modeling approach. *Public Opinion Quarterly, 48*, 409–442.

Aquilino, W. S. (1994). Interview mode effects in surveys of drug and alcohol use: A field experiment. *Public Opinion Quarterly, 58*, 210–240.

Armstrong, F. M., & Lusk, E. J. (1987). Return postage in mail surveys: A meta-analysis. *Public Opinion Quarterly, 51*(2), 233–248.

Association of Academic Survey Research Organizations. (n.d.). *Member organizations*. Retrieved January 4, 2014, from www.aasro.org/current-members

Avdeyeva, O. A., & Matland, R. E. (2013). An experimental test of mail surveys as a tool for social inquiry in Russia. *International Journal of Public Opinion Research, 25*(2), 173–194.

Baer, J., Kutner, M., & Sabatini, J. (2009). *Basic reading skills and the literacy of America's least literate adults: Results from the 2003 National Assessment of Adult Literacy (NAAL) supplemental studies* (NCES 2009-481). National Center for Education Statistics, Institute of Education Sciences, U.S. Department of Education. Washington DC. Retrieved from http://nces.ed.gov/pubs2009/2009481.pdf

Bailey, J. T., Lavrakas, P. J., & Bennett, M. A. (2007, May). *Cash, credit, or check: A test of monetary alternatives to cash incentives*. Paper presented at the annual conference of the American Association for Public Opinion Research, Anaheim, CA.

Baker, R., Brick, J. M., Bates, N. A., Battaglia M., Couper, M. P., Dever, J. A., … Tourangeau, R. (2013). *Report of the AAPOR Task Force on Non-Probability Sampling*. Retrieved from http://www.aapor.org/AM/Template.cfm?Section=Reports1&Template=/CM/ContentDisplay.cfm&ContentID=6055

Baker, R. P., & Couper, M. P. (2007, March). *The impact of screen size and background color on response in web surveys*. Paper presented at the General Online Research Conference (GOR'07), Leipzig, Germany.

Bates, N. (2005). Development and testing of informed consent questions to link survey data with administrative records. *Proceedings of the Survey Research Methods Section of the American Statistical Association*, pp. 3786–3793.

Battaglia, M. P., Link, M. W., Frankel, M. R., Osborn, L., & Mokdad, A. H. (2005, August). *An evaluation of respondent selection methods for household mail surveys*. Paper presented at the Joint Statistical Meetings, Minneapolis, MN.

Barron, G., & Yechiam, E. (2002). Private email requests and the diffusion of responsibility. *Computers in Human Behavior, 18*, 507–520.

Barron, M., & Khare, M. (2007). Manipulating caller ID for higher survey response in RDD surveys. *Proceedings of the Survey Research Methods Section of the American Statistical Association*, pp. 3957–3962.

Beckler, D., & Ott, K. (2006). Indirect monetary incentives with a complex agricultural establishment survey. *Proceedings of the Survey Research Methods Section of the American Statistical Association*, pp. 2741–2748.

Belli, R. F. (1998). The structure of autobiographical memory and the event history calendar: Potential improvements in the quality of retrospective reports in surveys. *Memory, 6*(4), 383–406.

Benford, R., Lavrakas, P. J. Tompson, T. N. & Fleury, C. (2010). *An experiment testing the impact of leaving voice messages in cell phone surveying*. Paper presented at the annual conference of the American Association for Public Opinion Research, Chicago, IL.

Biemer, P. P. (1997). [Health insurance finance agency evaluation]. Unpublished data. Research Triangle, NC: Research Triangle Institute.

Biemer, P. P., & Lyberg, L. E. (2003). *Introduction to survey quality*. Hoboken, NJ: Wiley.

Bilgen, I., & Belli, R. F. (2011). *The effect of interviewer experience on item non-response: A verbal behavior study*. Paper presented at the Annual Conference of the American Association for Public Opinion Research, Phoenix, AZ.

Birnholtz, J. P., Horn, D. B., Finholt, T. A., & Bae, S. J. (2004). Cash, electronic, and paper gift certificates as respondent incentives for a web-based survey of technologically sophisticated respondents. *Social Science Computer Review, 22*, 355–362.

Blasius, J. (2012). Comparing ranking techniques in web surveys. *Field Methods, 24*(4), 382–398.

Blau, P. M. (1964). *Exchange and power in social life*. New York, NY: Wiley.

Blumberg, S. J., & Luke, J. V. (2006). *Wireless substitution: preliminary data from the January–June 2006*. National Health Interview Survey, U.S. Department of Health and Human Services Centers for Disease Control and Prevention, National Center for Health Statistics. Retrieved from www.cdc.gov/nchs/products/pubs/pubd/hestats/wireless2006/wireless2006.htm

Blumberg, S. J., & Luke, J. V. (2013). *Wireless substitution: Early release of estimates from the National Health Interview Survey, January–June 2013*. National Center for Health Statistics. Retrieved from http://www.cdc.gov/nchs/data/nhis/earlyrelease/wireless 201312.pdf

Bosnjak, M., & Tuten, T. L. (2003). Prepaid and promised incentives in web surveys: An experiment. *Social Science Computer Review, 21*, 208–217.

Boyle, J., Bucuvalas., M., Piekarski, L. & Weiss, A. (2009). Zero banks: Coverage error and bias in RDD samples based on hundred banks with listed numbers. *Public Opinion Quarterly, 73*(4), 729–750.

Bradburn, N. M., & Miles, C. (1979). Vague quantifiers. *Public Opinion Quarterly, 43*(1), 92–101.

Bradburn, N. M., Sudman, S., & Blair, E. (1979). *Improving interview method and questionnaire design*. San Francisco, CA: Jossey-Bass.

Brennan, M., Rae, N., & Parackal, M. (1999). Survey-based experimental research via the web: Some observations. *Marketing Bulletin, 10*, 57–65.

Brenner, J. (2013). *Cell phone activities 2013*. Retrieved from http://pewinternet.org/Reports/2013/Cell-Activities.aspx

Brick, J. M., Andrews, W. R., Brick, P. D., King, H. Mathiowetz, N. A., & Stokes, L. (2012). Methods for improving response rates in two-phase mail surveys. *Survey Practice*, 5(3). Available at http://www.surveypractice.org/index.php/SurveyPractice/article/view/17/pdf

Brick, J. M., Brick, P. D., Dipko, S., Presser, S., Tucker, C., & Yuan, Y. (2007). Cell phone survey feasibility in the U.S.: Sampling and calling cell numbers versus landline numbers. *Public Opinion Quarterly*, 71(1), 23–39.

Brick, J. M., Williams, D., & Montaquila, J. M. (2011). Address-based sampling for sub-population surveys. *Public Opinion Quarterly*, 75(3), 409–428.

Buskirk, T. D., & Andrus, C. (2012). Smart surveys for smart phones: Exploring various approaches for conducting online surveys via smartphones. *Survey Practice*, 5(1). Retrieved from http://surveypractice.wordpress.com/2012/02/21/smart-surveys-for-smart-phones/

Buskirk T. D., Gaynor, M., Andrus, C., & Gorrell, C. (2011). *An app a day could keep the doctor away: Comparing mode effects for a iPhone survey related to health app use.* Paper presented at the annual conference of the American Association for Public Opinion Research, Phoenix, AZ.

Callegaro, M., & Macer, T. (2011). *Designing surveys for mobile devices: Pocket-sized surveys and yield powerful results.* Short course presented at the annual meeting of the American Association for Public Opinion Research, Phoenix, AZ.

Callegaro, M., McCutcheon, A., & Ludwig, J. (2005). *Who's calling? The impact of caller ID on survey response.* Paper presented at the Second International Conference on Telephone Survey Methodology.

Catania, J. A., Binson, D., Canchola, J., Pollack, L. M., & Hauck, W. (1996). Effects of interviewer gender, interviewer choice, and item wording on responses to questions concerning sexual behavior. *Public Opinion Quarterly*, 60(3), 345–375.

Centers for Disease Control and Prevention. (1991). Current trends pilot study of a household survey to determine HIV seroprevalence. *Morbidity and Mortality Weekly Report*, 40(1), 1–5. Retrieved from http://www.cdc.gov/mmwr/preview/mmwrhtml/00001871.htm

Chaiken, S., & Eagly, A. H. (1976). Communication modality as a determinant of message persuasiveness and message comprehensibility. *Journal of Personality and Social Psychology*, 34(4), 605–614.

Chestnut, J. (2008). *Effects of using a grid versus a sequential form on the ACS basic demographic data* (Memorandum Series Chapter No. ASC-MP-09). Washington DC: U.S. Census Bureau, DSSD American Community Survey Methods Panel.

Christian, L. M. (2003). *The influence of visual layout on scalar questions in web surveys.* Unpublished master's thesis. Retrieved from Washington State University, Social and Economic Sciences Research Center website: http://www.sesrc.wsu.edu/dillman/papers/2003/theinfluenceofvisuallayout.pdf.

Christian, L. M. (2007). *How mixed-move surveys are transforming social research: The influence of survey mode on measurement in web and telephone surveys.* Unpublished doctoral dissertation, Washington State University, Pullman.

Christian, L. M., & Dillman, D. A. (2004). The influence of graphical and symbolic language manipulations on responses to self-administered questions. *Public Opinion Quarterly*, 68(1), 58–81.

Christian, L. M., Dillman, D. A, & Smyth, J. D. (2007a, May). *After a decade of development: A visual design framework for how respondents process survey information.* Paper presented at the annual conference of the American Association for Public Opinion Research, Anaheim, CA.

Christian, L. M., Dillman, D. A., & Smyth, J. D. (2007b). Helping respondents get it right the first time: The influence of words, symbols, and graphics in web surveys. *Public Opinion Quarterly*, 71(1), 113–125.

Christian, L. M., Dillman, D. A., & Smyth, J. D. (2008). The effects of mode and format on answers to scalar questions in telephone and web surveys. In J. M. Lepkowski, C. Tucker, J. M. Brick, E. D. de Leeuw, L. Japec, P. J. Lavrakas, ... R. L. Sangster (Eds.), *Advances in telephone survey methodology* (pp. 250–275). Hoboken, NJ: Wiley.

Christian, L. M., Dimock, M., & Keeter, S. (2009). *Accurately locating where wireless respondents live requires more than a phone number*. Retrieved from http://pewresearch.org/pubs/1278/cell-phones-geographic-sampling-problems

Christian, L. M., Keeter, S. Purcell, K., & Smith, A. (2010). *Accessing the cell phone challenge*. Paper presented at the annual conference of the American Association for Public Opinion Research, Chicago, IL. Available at http://www.pewresearch.org/2010/05/20/assessing-the-cell-phone-challenge/.

Christian, L. M., Parsons, N. L., & Dillman, D. A. (2009). Designing scalar questions for web surveys. *Sociological Methods and Research, 37*(3), 393–425.

Church, A. H. (1993). Estimating the effect of incentives on mail survey response rates: A meta-analysis. *Public Opinion Quarterly, 57,* 62–79.

Cialdini, R. B. (1984). *Influence: The new psychology of modern persuasion.* New York, NY: Quill.

Cialdini, R. B. (2009). *Influence: Science and practice.* Boston, MA: Pearson.

Cialdini, R. B., Levy, A., Herman, P., & Evenbeck, S. (1973). Attitudinal politics: The strategy of moderation. *Journal of Personality and Social Psychology, 25*(1), 100–108.

Cobanoglu, C., & Cobanoglu, N. (2003). The effect of incentives in web surveys: Application and ethical considerations. *International Journal of Market Research, 45*(4), 475–488.

Cochran, W. G. (1977). *Sampling techniques* (3rd ed.). New York, NY: Wiley.

Comley, P. (2006, November). The games we play: A psychoanalysis of the relationship between panel owners and panel participants. *Proceedings from the ESOMAR World Research Conference, Panel Research 2006: Vol. 317* (pp. 123–132). Amsterdam, The Netherlands: ESOMAR.

Conrad, F. G., Couper, M. P., Tourangeau, R., & Galesic, M. (2005). Interactive feedback can improve quality of responses in web surveys. *Proceedings of the survey research methods section of the American Statistical Association,* pp. 3835–3840. Retrieved from http://www.amstat.org/sections/srms/Proceedings/

Conrad, F. G., Tourangeau, R., Couper, M. P., & Zhang, C. (2010). *Professional web respondents and data quality*. Paper presented at the American Association for Public Opinion Research 65th Annual Conference, Chicago, IL.

Converse, J. M., & Presser, S. (1986). *Survey questions: Handcrafting the standardized questionnaire.* Beverly Hills, CA: Sage.

Cook, C., Heath, F., & Thompson, R. L. (2000). A meta-analysis of response rates in web- or Internet-based surveys. *Educational and Psychology Measurement, 60*(6), 821–836.

Council of American Survey Research Organizations. (2011). *Code of standards and ethics for survey research*. Retrieved from http://c.ymcdn.com/sites/www.casro.org/resource/resmgr/casro_code_of_standards.pdf

Couper, M. P. (1998). Measuring survey quality in a CASIC environment. *Proceedings of the Survey Research Methods Section of the American Statistical Association,* pp. 41–49.

Couper, M. P. (2000). Web surveys: A review of issues and approaches. *Public Opinion Quarterly, 64,* 464–494.

Couper, M. P. (2008). *Designing effective web surveys.* Cambridge, MA: Cambridge University Press.

Couper, M. P., Baker, R., & Mechling, J. (2011). Placement and design of navigation buttons in web surveys. *Survey Practice, 4*(1). Available at http://www.surveypractice.org/index.php/SurveyPractice/article/view/93/pdf

Couper, M. P., Conrad, F. G., & Tourangeau, R. (2007). Visual context effects in web surveys. *Public Opinion Quarterly, 71,* 623–634.

Couper, M. P., Kennedy, C., Conrad, F. G., & Tourangeau, R. (2011). Designing input fields for non-narrative open-ended responses in web surveys. *Journal of Official Statistics, 27*(1), 65–85.

Couper, M. P., Tourangeau, R., Conrad, F. G., & Crawford, S. D. (2004). What they see is what we get: Response options for web surveys. *Social Science Computer Review*, *22*(1), 111–127.

Couper, M. P., Tourangeau, R., Conrad, F. G., & Singer, E. (2006). Evaluating the effectiveness of visual analog scales: A web experiment. *Social Science Computer Review*, *24*(2), 227–245.

Couper, M. P., Tourangeau, R., Conrad, F. G., & Zhang, C. (2013). The design of grids in web surveys. *Social Science Computer Review*, *31*, 322–345.

Couper, M. P., Traugott, M. W., & Lamias, M. J. (2001). Web survey design and administration. *Public Opinion Quarterly*, *65*(2), 230–253.

Cox, B. G., Binder, D. A., Chinnappa, B. N., Christianson, A., Colledge, M. J., & Kott, P. S. (1995). *Business survey methods*. New York, NY: Wiley.

Crawford, S. D., Couper, M. P., & Lamias, M. J. (2001). Web surveys: Perceptions of burden. *Social Science Computer Review*, *19*, 146–162.

Curtin, R., Presser, S., & Singer, E. (2000). The effects of response rate changes on the index of consumer sentiment. *Public Opinion Quarterly*, *64*, 413–28.

Curtin, R., Presser, S., & Singer, E. (2005). Changes in telephone survey nonresponse over the past quarter century. *Public Opinion Quarterly*, *69*, 87–98.

Das, M., Ester, P., & Kaczmirek, L. (2010). *Social and behavioral research and the Internet: Advances in applied methods and research strategies*. New York, NY: Routledge.

de Leeuw, E., Callegaro, M., Hox, J., Korendijk, E., & Lensvelt-Mulders, G. (2007). The influence of advance letters on response in telephone surveys: A meta-analysis. *Public Opinion Quarterly*, *71*(3), 413–443.

de Leeuw, E. D. (1992). *Data quality in mail, telephone, and face-to-face surveys*. Amsterdam, The Netherlands: TT Publications.

de Leeuw, E. D. (2005). To mix or not mix data collection modes in surveys. *Journal of Official Statistics*, *21*(5), 233–255.

de Leeuw, E. D., & Hox, J. J. (1988). The effects of response-stimulating factors on response rates and data quality in mail surveys: A test of Dillman's Total Design Method. *Journal of Official Statistics*, *4*, 241–249.

de Leeuw, E. D., & van der Zouwen, J. (1988). Data quality in telephone and face-to-face surveys: A comparative analysis. In R. M. Groves, P. P. Biemer, L. E. Lyberg, J. T. Massey, W. L. Nicholls II, & J. Waksberg (Eds.), *Telephone survey methodology* (pp. 283–299). New York, NY: Wiley.

DeMaio, T. J. (1984). Social desirability and survey measurement: A review. In C. F. Turner & E. Martin (Eds.), *Surveying subjective phenomena* (Vol. 2, pp. 257–282). New York, NY: Russell Sage Foundation.

DeMaio, T. J., & Bates, N. (1992). Redesigning the Census long form: Results from the 1990 alternative questionnaire experiment. *Proceedings of the Survey Research Methods Section of the American Statistical Association*, pp. 784–789.

Dillehay, R. C., & Jernigan, L. R. (1970). The biased questionnaire as an instrument of opinion change. *Journal of Personality and Social Psychology*, *15*(2), 144–150.

Dillman, D. A. (1978). *Mail and telephone surveys: The total design method*. New York, NY: Wiley-Interscience.

Dillman, D. A. (1995). *Image optimization test: Summary of 15 taped interviews in Moscow, Idaho, Pullman, Washington, and Spokane, Washington* (Technical Report No. 95-40). Pullman: Washington State University, Social and Economic Sciences Research Center.

Dillman, D. A. (2000). *Mail and Internet surveys: The tailored design method* (2nd ed.). New York, NY: Wiley.

Dillman, D. A. (2008). The logic and psychology of constructing questionnaires. In E. D. de Leeuw, J. J. Hox, & D. A. Dillman (Eds.), *International handbook of survey methodology* (pp. 161–175). New York, NY: Psychology Press.

Dillman, D. A., & Allen, T. B. (1995). Census booklet questionnaire evaluation test: Phase I—Summary of 20 taped interviews (Technical Report No. 95-41). Pullman: Washington State University, Social and Economic Sciences Research Center.

Dillman, D. A., Brown, T. L., Carlson, J. E., Carpenter, E. H., Lorenz, F. O., Mason, R., ... Sangster, R. L. (1995). Effects of category order on answers in mail and telephone surveys. *Rural Sociology, 60*, 674–687.

Dillman, D. A., Christenson, J. A., Carpenter, E. H., & Brooks, R. (1974). Increasing mail questionnaire response: A four-state comparison. *American Sociological Review, 39*, 744–756.

Dillman, D. A., & Christian, L. M. (2003). *The influence of words, symbols, numbers and graphics on answers to self-administered questionnaires: Results from 18 experimental comparisons*. Paper presented at the American Association for Public Opinion Research Annual Conference, Nashville, TN.

Dillman, D. A., & Christian, L. M. (2005). Survey mode as a source of instability across surveys. *Field Methods, 17*(1), 30–52.

Dillman, D. A., Clark, J. R., & Sinclair, M. D. (1995). How prenotice letters, stamped return envelopes, and reminder postcards affect mailback response rates for Census questionnaires. *Survey Methodology, 21*, 1–7.

Dillman, D. A., Dolsen, D. E., & Machlis, G. E. (1995). Increasing response to personally-delivered mail-back questionnaires by combining foot-in-the-door and social exchange methods. *Journal of Official Statistics, 11*(2), 129–139.

Dillman, D. A., Gertseva, A., & Mahon-Haft, T. (2005). Achieving usability in establishment surveys through the application of visual design principles. *Journal of Official Statistics, 21*(2), 183–214.

Dillman, D. A., Jackson, A., Pavlov, R., & Schaefer, D. (1998). *Results from cognitive tests of 6-person accordion versus bi-fold census forms* (Technical Report No. 98-15). Pullman: Washington State University, Social and Economic Sciences Research Center.

Dillman, D. A., Jenkins, C., Martin, B., & DeMaio, T. (1996). *Cognitive and motivational properties of three proposed decennial census forms* (Technical Report No. 96-29). Pullman: Washington State University, Social and Economic Sciences Research Center.

Dillman, D. A., Lesser, V., Mason, R., Carlson, J., Willits, F., Robertson, R., & Burke, B. (2007). Personalization of mail surveys for general public and populations with a group identity: Results from nine studies. *Rural Sociology, 72*(4), 632–646.

Dillman, D. A., & Mason, R. G. (1984, May). *The influence of survey method on question response*. Paper presented at the annual conference of the American Association for Public Opinion Research, Delevan, WI.

Dillman, D. A., Parsons, N. L., & Mahon-Haft, T. (2004). *Connections between optical features and respondent friendly design: Cognitive interview comparisons of the Census 2000 form and new possibilities* (Technical Report No. 04-030). Pullman: Washington State University, Social and Economic Sciences Research Center.

Dillman, D. A., Phelps, G., Tortora, R., Swift, K., Kohrell, J., Berck, J., & Messer, B. L. (2009). Response rate and measurement differences in mixed-mode surveys using mail, telephone, interactive voice response, and the Internet. *Social Science Research, 38*(1), 1–18.

Dillman, D. A., & Redline, C. D. (2004). Testing paper self-administered questionnaires: Cognitive interview and field test comparisons. In S. Presser, J. M. Rothgeb, M. P. Couper, J. T. Lessler, E. Martin, J. Martin, & E. Singer (Eds.), *Methods for testing and evaluating survey questionnaires* (pp. 299–317). Hoboken, NJ: Wiley-Interscience.

Dillman, D. A., Sangster, R. L., Tarnai, J., & Rockwood, T. H. (1996). Understanding differences in people's answers to telephone and mail surveys. In M. T. Braverman & J. K. Slater (Eds.), *New directions for evaluation series: Vol. 70. Advances in survey research* (pp. 45–62). San Francisco, CA: Jossey-Bass.

Dillman, D. A., Sinclair, M. D., & Clark, J. R. (1993). Effects of questionnaire length, respondent-friendly design, and a difficult question on response rates for occupant-addressed census mail surveys. *Public Opinion Quarterly, 57*, 289–304.

Dillman, D. A., Singer, E., Clark, J. R., & Treat, J. B. (1996). Effects of benefit appeals, mandatory appeals and variations in confidentiality on completion rates of Census questionnaires. *Public Opinion Quarterly, 60*(3), 376–389.

Dillman, D. A., & Tarnai, J. (1988). Administrative issues in mixed-mode surveys. In R. Groves, P. P. Biemer, L. E. Lyberg, J. T. Massey, W. L. Nicholls II, & J. Waksberg (Eds.), *Telephone survey methodology* (pp. 509–528). New York, NY: Wiley.

Dillman, D. A., & Tarnai, J. (1991). Mode effects of cognitively-designed recall questions: A comparison of answers to telephone and mail surveys. In P. P. Biemer, R. M. Groves, L. E. Lyberg, N. A. Mathiowetz, & S. Sudman (Eds.), *Measurement errors in surveys* (pp. 73–93). New York, NY: Wiley.

Dillman, D. A., West, K. K., & Clark, J. R. (1994). Influence of an invitation to answer by telephone on response to Census questionnaires. *Public Opinion Quarterly, 58*, 557–568.

DiSorga, C., Dennis, M., & Fahimi, M. (2010). On the quality of ancillary data available for address-based sampling. *Proceedings of the Survey Research Methods Section of the American Statistical Association*, pp. 4174–4183.

Duan, N., Alegria, M., Canino, G., McGuire, T. G., & Takeuchi, D. (2007). Survey conditioning in self-reported mental health service use: Randomized comparison of alternative instrument formats. *Health Services Research, 42*, 890–907.

Duggan, M. (2013). *Cell phone activities (selected surveys from each year chosen)*. Retrieved from http://pewinternet.org/Reports/2013/Cell-Activities.aspx

Duggan, M., & Smith, A. (2013). Cell Internet use 2013. Retrieved from http://pewinternet.org/~/media//Files/Reports/2013/PIP_CellInternetUse2013.pdf

Eckman, S. & Kreuter, F. (2011). Confirmation bias in housing unit listing. *Public Opinion Quarterly, 75*(1), 139–150.

Edgar, J., Nelson, D. V., Paszkiewicz, L, & Safir, A. (2013, June 26). *The Gemini project to redesign the consumer expenditure survey: Redesign proposal*. Bureau of Labor Statistics.

Edwards, B., Schneider, S., & Brick, P. D. (2008). Visual elements of questionnaire design: experiments with a CATI establishment survey. In J. M. Lepkowski, C. Tucker, J. M. Brick, E. D. de Leeuw, L. Japec, P. J. Lavrakas, … R. L. Sangster (Eds.), *Advances in Telephone Survey Methodology* (pp. 276–296). Hoboken, NJ: Wiley.

Edwards, M. L. (2013). *Measuring public perceptions of water governance in Nebraska and Washington*. Unpublished doctoral dissertation, Washington State University, Pullman.

Edwards, M. L., Dillman, D. A., & Smyth, J. D. (2013a). *Attitudes of Nebraska residents on Nebraska water management* (Technical Report No. 13-020). Pullman: Washington State University, Social and Economic Sciences Research Center.

Edwards, M. L., Dillman, D. A., & Smyth, J. D. (2013b). *Attitudes of Washington residents on Washington water management* (Technical Report No. 13-019). Pullman: Washington State University, Social and Economic Sciences Research Center.

Edwards, M. L., Dillman, D. A., & Smyth, J. D. (2013c, May). *Effects of survey sponsorship on Internet and mail response: Using address-based sampling*. Paper presented at the American Association for Public Opinion Research (AAPOR) annual meeting, Boston, MA.

Edwards, P., Roberts, I., Clark, M., DiGuiseppi, C., Pratap, S., Wentz, R., & Kwan, I. (2002). Increasing response rates to postal questionnaires: Systematic review. *British Medical Journal, 324*, 1183–1191.

European Social Survey. (n.d.). *About the European Social Survey*. Retrieved December 28, 2013, from http://www.europeansocialsurvey.org/

Fahimi, M., Kulp, D., & Brick, J. M. (2009). A reassessment of list-assisted RDD methodology. *Public Opinion Quarterly, 73*(4), 751–760.

Fazekas, Z., Wall, M. T., & Krouwel, A. (2013). Is it what you say, or how you say it? An experimental analysis of the effects of invitation wording for online. *International Journal of Public Opinion Research*, online advance access. Retrieved from http://ijpor.oxfordjournals.org/content/early/2013/07/13/ijpor.edt022.extract

Festinger, L. 1957. *A theory of cognitive dissonance*. Stanford, CA: Stanford University Press.

Finamore, J., & Dillman, D. A. (2013, July). *How mode sequence affects response by Internet, mail, and telephone in the National Survey of College Graduates*. Paper presented at the European Survey Research Association Biennial Conference, Ljubljana, Slovenia.

Forsyth, B. H., & Lessler, J. T. (1991). Cognitive laboratory methods: A taxonomy. In P. P. Biemer, R. M. Groves, L. E. Lysber, N. A. Mathiowetz, & S. Sudman (Eds.), *Measurement errors in surveys* (pp. 393–418). New York, NY: Wiley.

Fowler, F. J. (1995). *Improving survey questions: Design and evaluation*. Thousand Oaks, CA: Sage.

Fowler, F. J., & Mangione, T. W. (1990). *Standardized survey interviewing: Minimizing interviewer-related error*. Newbury Park, CA: Sage.

Fox, R. J., Crask, M. R., & Kim, J. (1988). Mail survey response rate: A meta-analysis of selected techniques for inducing response. *Public Opinion Quarterly, 52*, 467–491.

Friedman, M. (1953). *Essays in positive economics*. Chicago, IL: University of Chicago Press.

Funke, F., Reips, U.-D., & Thomas, R. K. (2011). Sliders for the smart: Type of rating scale on the web interacts with educational level. *Social Science Computer Review, 29*(2), 221–231.

Galea, S., & Tracy, M. (2007). Participation rates in epidemiologic studies. *Annals of Epidemiology, 17*, 643–653.

Galesic, M., Tourangeau, R., Couper, M. P., & Conrad, F. G. (2007, March). *Using change to improve navigation in grid questions*. Paper presented at the General Online Research Conference (GOR'07), Leipzig, Germany.

Galesic, M., Tourangeau, R., Couper, M. P., & Conrad, F. G. (2008), Eye-tracking data: New insights on response order effects and other cognitive shortcuts in survey responding. *Public Opinion Quarterly, 72*(5), 892–913.

Gaziano, C. (2005). Comparative analysis of within-household respondent selection techniques. *Public Opinion Quarterly, 69*(1), 124–157.

Gallup. (n.d.). *World poll*. Retrieved December 28, 2013, from http://www.gallup.com/strategicconsulting/en-us/worldpoll.aspx?ref=f

Gendall, P., & Healey, B. (2007, May). *Alternatives to prepaid monetary incentives in mail surveys*. Paper presented at the annual conference of the American Association for Public Opinion Research, Anaheim, CA.

Gendall, P., & Healey, B. (2008). Asking the age question in mail and online surveys. *International Journal of Market Research, 50*(3), 309–317.

Gentry, R., & Good, C. (2008). *Offering respondents a choice of survey mode: Use patterns of an Internet response option in a mail survey*. Paper presented at the Annual Conference of the American Association of Public Opinion Research, New Orleans, LA.

Gesis Panel. (n.d.). *Sample and recruitment*. Retrieved December 28, 2013, from http://www.gesis.org/en/services/data-collection/gesis-panel/sample-recruitment/

GfK-Knowledge Networks. (n.d.). *KnowledgePanel*. Retrieved December 28, 2013, from http://www.knowledgenetworks.com/knpanel/

Griffin, D. H., & Clark, S. L. (2009, May 14–17). *Respondent effects associated with questionnaire designed to accommodate survey processing*. Paper presented at the American Association for Public Opinion Research Annual Conference, Hollywood, FL.

Gohring, N., & Smyth, J. D. (2013, May 16–19). *Using visual design theory to improve skip instructions: An experimental test*. Paper presented at the American Association for Public Opinion Research Annual Conference, Boston, MA.

Göritz, A. S. (2006). Incentives in web studies: Methodological issues and a review. *International Journal of Internet Science, 1*(1), 58–70.

Government Accountability Office. (2012). *Decennial Census: Additional actions could improve the Census Bureau's ability to control costs for the 2020 Decennial Census*. Retrieved from http://www.gao.gov/products/GAO-12-80

Graesser, A. C., Cai, Z., Louwerse, M. M., & Daniel, F. (2006). Question understanding aid (QUAID): A web facility that tests question comprehensibility. *Public Opinion Quarterly, 70*(1), 3–22.

Granda, P., & Blasczyk, E. (2013). Data dissemination. In *Cross-Cultural Survey Guidelines*. Retrieved from http://ccsg.isr.umich.edu/datadissem.cfm

Groves, R. M. (1989). *Survey errors and survey costs*. New York, NY: Wiley.

Groves, R. M. (2006). Nonresponse rates and nonresponse bias in household surveys. *Public Opinion Quarterly*, *70*(5), 646–675.

Groves, R. M., Biemer, P. P., Lyberg, L. E., Massey, J. T., Nicholls, W. L. II, & Waksberg, J. (1988). *Telephone survey methodology*. New York, NY: Wiley.

Groves, R. M., Cialdini, R. B., & Couper, M. P. (1992). Understanding the decision to participate in a survey. *Public Opinion Quarterly*, *56*, 475–495.

Groves, R. M., & Couper, M. P. (1998). *Nonresponse in household interview surveys*. New York, NY: Wiley.

Groves, R. M., Couper, M. P., Presser, S., Singer, E., Tourangeau, R., Acosta, G. P., & Nelson, L. (2006). Experiments in producing nonresponse bias. *Public Opinion Quarterly*, *70*(5), 720–736.

Groves, R. M., & Fultz, N. H. (1985). Gender effects among telephone interviewers in a survey of economic attitudes. *Sociological Methods and Research*, *14*(1), 31–52.

Groves, R. M., & Heeringa, S. G. (2006). Responsive design for household surveys: Tools for actively controlling survey costs and errors. *Journal of the Royal Statistical Society*, *169*(3), 439–457.

Groves, R. M., & Kahn, R. L. (1979). *Surveys by telephone*. New York, NY: Wiley.

Groves, R. M., & Lyberg, L. E. (1988). An overview of nonresponse issues in telephone surveys. In R. M. Groves, P. P. Beimer, L. E. Lyberg, J. T. Massey, W. L. Nichols II, & J. Waksberg (Eds.), *Telephone survey methodology* (pp. 191–211). New York, NY: Wiley.

Groves, R. M., & McGonagle, K. A. (2001). A theory-guided interviewer training protocol regarding survey participation. *Journal of Official Statistics*, *17*(2), 249–265.

Groves, R. M., & Peytcheva, E. (2008). The impact of nonresponse rates on nonresponse bias: a meta-analysis. *Public Opinion Quarterly*, *72*(2), 167–189.

Groves, R. M., Presser, S., Tourangeau, R., West, B. T., Couper, M. P., Singer, E., & Toppe, C. (2012). Support for the survey sponsor and nonresponse bias. *Public Opinion Quarterly*, *76*(3), 512–524.

Groves, R. M., Singer, E., & Corning, A. (2000). Leverage-saliency theory of survey participation: Description and an illustration. *Public Opinion Quarterly*, *64*(3), 299–308.

Gwartney, P. A. (2007). *The telephone interviewer's handbook: How to conduct standardized conversations*. San Francisco, CA: Jossey-Bass.

Hager, M. A., Wilson, S., Pollak, T. H., & Rooney, P. M. (2003). Response rates for mail surveys of nonprofit organizations: A review and empirical test. *Nonprofit and Voluntary Sector Quarterly*, *32*(2), 252–267.

Harkness, J. A., Braun, M., Edwards, B., Johnson, T. P., Lyberg, L. E., Mohler, P. Ph., … Smith, T. W. (2010). *Survey methods in multicultural, multinational, and multiregional contexts*. Hoboken, NJ: Wiley.

Harkness, J. A., van de Vijver, F. J. R., & Mohler, P. Ph. (2003). *Cross-cultural survey methods*. Hoboken, NJ: Wiley.

Hatchett, S., & Schuman, H. (1975). White respondents and race-of-interviewer effects. *Public Opinion Quarterly*, *39*(4), 523–528.

Haug, O. M. (1952). The relative effectiveness of reading and listening to radio drama as ways of imparting information and shifting attitudes. *Journal of Educational Research*, *45*(7), 489–498.

Healey, B. (2007). Drop downs and scroll mice: The effect of response option format and input mechanism employed on data quality in web surveys. *Social Science Computer Review*, *25*(1), 111–128.

Heberlein, T. A., & Baumgartner, R. (1978). Factors affecting response rates to mailed questionnaires: A quantitative analysis of the published literature. *American Sociological Review*, *43*, 447–462.

Heeringa, S. G., West, B. T., & Berglund, P. A. (2010). *Applied survey data analysis*. Boca Raton, FL: Chapman & Hall CRC.

Heerwegh, D. (2003). Explaining response latencies and changing answers using client-side paradata from a web survey. *Social Science Computer Review*, *21*, 360–373.

Heerwegh, D. (2005). Effects of personal salutations in email invitations to participate in a web survey. *Public Opinion Quarterly*, *69*(4), 588–598.

Heerwegh, D., & Loosveldt, G. (2002a, October). *Describing response behavior in web surveys using client side paradata*. Paper presented at the International Workshop on Web Surveys, Mannheim, Germany.

Heerwegh, D., & Loosveldt, G. (2002b). An evaluation of the effects of response formats on data quality in web surveys. *Social Science Computer Review*, *20*, 471–484.

Heerwegh, D., & Loosveldt, G. (2002c). Web surveys: The effect of controlling survey access using PIN numbers. *Social Science Computer Review*, *20*, 10–21.

Heerwegh, D., & Loosveldt, G. (2003). An evaluation of the semiautomatic login procedure to control web survey access. *Social Science Computer Review*, *21*, 223–234.

Heerwegh, D., & Loosveldt, G. (2006). An experimental study on the effects of personalization, survey length statements, progress indicators, and survey sponsor logos in web surveys. *Journal of Official Statistics*, *22*(2), 191–210.

Herek, G. M., & Capitanio, J. P. (1999). Sex differences in how heterosexuals think about lesbians and gay men: Evidence from survey context effects. *Journal of Sex Research*, *36*, 348–360.

Hochstim, J. R. (1967). A critical comparison of three strategies of collecting data from households. *Journal of the American Statistical Association*, *62*, 976–989.

Hoffer, T. B., Grigorian, K., & Fesco, R. (2007, July). *Assessing the effectiveness of using panel respondent preferences*. Paper presented at the Joint Statistical Meetings, Salt Lake City, UT.

Hoffman, D. D. (2004). *Visual intelligence*. New York, NY: Norton.

Holland, J., & Christian, L. M. (2007, October). *The influence of interactive probing on response to open-ended questions in a web survey*. Paper presented at the Southern Association for Public Opinion Research Annual Conference, Raleigh, NC.

Homans, G. (1961). *Social behavior: Its elementary forms*. New York, NY: Harcourt, Brace & World.

Hox, J. J. (1997). From theoretical concept to survey question. In L. E. Lyberg, P. Biemer, M. Collins, E. D. de Leeuw, C. Dippo, N. Schwarz, & D. Trewin (Eds.), *Survey measurement and process quality* (pp. 47–69). New York, NY: Wiley-Interscience.

Hyman, H. H., Cobb, W. J., Feldman, J. J., Hart, C. W., & Stember, C. H. (1954). *Interviewing in social research*. Chicago, IL: University of Chicago Press.

Hyman, H. H., & Sheatsley, P. B. (1950). The current status of American public opinion. In J. C. Payne (Ed.), *The teaching of contemporary affairs: Twenty-first yearbook of the National Council for the Social Studies* (pp. 11–34). New York, NY: National Education Association.

Iannacchione, V. G. (2011). The changing role of address-based sampling in survey research. *Public Opinion Quarterly*, *75*(3), 556–575.

Iannacchione, V. G., Staab, J. M., & Redden, D. T. (2003). Evaluating the use of residential mailing addresses in a metropolitan household survey. *Public Opinion Quarterly*, *67*, 202–210.

Israel, G. D. (2010). Effects of answer space size on responses to open-ended questions in mail surveys. *Journal of Official Statistics*, *26*(2), 271–285.

Israel, G. D. (2013). Combining mail and e-mail contacts to facilitate participation in mixed-mode surveys. *Social Science Computer Review*, *31*(3), 346–358.

Israel, G. D., & Taylor, C. L. (1990). Can response order bias evaluations? *Evaluation and Program Planning*, *13*, 1–7.

James, J. M., & Bolstein, R. (1990). The effect of monetary incentives and follow-up mailings on the response rate and response quality in mail surveys. *Public Opinion Quarterly*, *54*, 346–361.

James, J. M., & Bolstein, R. (1992). Large monetary incentives and their effect on mail survey response rates. *Public Opinion Quarterly*, *56*, 442–453.

Japec, L. (2008). Interviewer error and interviewer burden. In J. M. Lepkowski, C. Tucker, J. M. Brick, M. W. Link, & R. L. Sangster (Eds.), *Advances in telephone survey methodology* (pp. 187–211). Hoboken, NJ: Wiley.

Javeline, D. (1999). Response effects in polite cultures: A test of acquiescence in Kazakhstan. *Public Opinion Quarterly, 63*(1), 1–28.

Jenkins, C., & Dillman, D. A. (1997). Towards a theory of self-administered questionnaire design. In L. E. Lyberg, P. Biemer, M. Collins, E. D. de Leeuw, C. Dippo, N. Schwarz, & D. Trewin (Eds.), *Survey measurement and process quality* (pp. 165–196). New York: Wiley-Interscience.

Joinson, A. N., & Reips, U.-D. (2007). Personalized salutation, power of sender, and response rates to web-based surveys. *Computers in Human Behavior, 23*, 1372–1383.

Jones, W. H. (1979). Generalizing mail survey inducement methods: Population interactions with anonymity and sponsorship. *Public Opinion Quarterly, 43*, 102–111.

Jordan, L. A., Marcus, A. C., & Reeder, L. G. (1980). Response styles in telephone and household interviewing: A field experiment. *Public Opinion Quarterly, 44*, 210–222.

Kaczmirek, L. (2011). Attention and usability in internet surveys: Effects of visual feedback in grid questions. In M. Das, P. Ester, & L. Kaczmirek (Eds.), *Social and behavioral research and the Internet: Advances in applied methods and research strategies* (pp. 191–214). New York, NY: Routledge.

Kaplowitz, M. D., Lupi, F., Couper, M. P., & Thorp, L. (2012). The effect of invitation design on web survey response rates. *Social Science Computer Review, 30*(3), 339–349.

Kasabian, A., Olson, K., & Smyth, J. D. (2012, May 16–20). *Making a match: Exploring the impact of mode preference on measurement*. Presented at the annual meeting of the American Association for Public Opinion Research, Orlando, FL.

Kasprzyk, D., Montaño, D. E., St. Lawrence, J. S., & Phillips, W. R. (2001). The effects of variations in mode of delivery and monetary incentive on physicians' responses to a mailed survey assessing STD practice patterns. *Evaluation and the Health Professions, 21*(1), 3–17.

Keeter, S., Christian, L. M., Dimock, M., & Gewurz, D. (2012). *Assessing the representativeness of public opinion surveys*. Retrieved from http://www.people-press.org/2012/05/15/assessing-the-representativeness-of-public-opinion-surveys/

Keeter, S., Kennedy, C., Dimock, M., Best, J., & Craighill, P. (2006). Gauging the impact of growing nonresponse on estimates from a national RDD telephone survey. *Public Opinion Quarterly, 70*, 759–779.

Keeter, S., Miller, C., Kohut, A., Groves, R. M., & Presser, S. (2000). Consequences of reducing nonresponse in a national telephone survey. *Public Opinion Quarterly, 64*, 125–148.

Kessler, R. C., Wittchen, H-U., Abelson, J. A., McGonagle, K., Schwarz, N., Kendler, K. S., … Zhao, S. (1998). Methodological studies of the composite international diagnostic interview (CIDI) in the US National Comorbidity Survey (NCS). *International Journal of Methods in Psychiatric Research, 7*, 33–55.

Kish, L. (1949). A procedure for objective respondent selection within the household. *Journal of American Statistical Association, 44*, 380–387.

Kish, L. (1962). Studies of interviewer variance for attitudinal variables. *Journal of the American Statistical Association, 57*, 92–115.

Kish, L. (1965). *Survey sampling*. New York, NY: Wiley.

Koepsell, T. D., McGuire, V., Longstreth, Jr., W. T., Nelson, L. M., & van Belle, G. (1996). Randomized trial of leaving messages on telephone answering machines for control recruitment in an epidemiologic study. *American Journal of Epidemiology, 144*(7), 704–706.

Korkki, P. (2012, September 8). In defense of the power of paper. *New York Times*, p. BU8.

Kreuter, F. (Ed.). (2013). *Improving surveys with paradata: Analytic uses of process information*. Hoboken, NJ: Wiley.

Kreuter, F., McCulloch, S., Presser, S., & Tourangeau, R. (2011). The effects of asking filter questions in interleafed versus grouped format. *Sociological Methods & Research, 40*(1), 88–104.

Kreuter, F., Presser, S., & Tourangeau, R. (2008). Social desirability bias in CATI, IVR and web surveys. *Public Opinion Quarterly, 72,* 847–865.

Krosnick, J. A. (1991). Response strategies for coping with the cognitive demands of attitude measures in surveys. *Applied Cognitive Psychology, 5,* 213–236.

Krosnick, J. A. (2002). The causes of no-opinion responses to attitude measures in surveys: They are rarely what they appear to be. In R. M. Groves, D. A. Dillman, J. L. Eltinge, & R. J. A. Little (Eds.), *Survey nonresponse* (pp. 87–100). New York, NY: Wiley.

Krosnick, J. A., & Alwin, D. F. (1987). An evaluation of a cognitive theory of response-order effects in survey measurement. *Public Opinion Quarterly, 51,* 201–219.

Krosnick, J. A., & Berent, M. K. (1993). Comparisons of party identification and policy preferences: The impact of survey question format. *American Journal of Political Science, 37*(3), 941–964.

Krosnick, J. A., & Fabrigar, L. R. (1997). Designing rating scales for effective measurement in surveys. In L. Lyberg, P. Biemer, M. Collins, L. Decker, E. D. de Leeuw, C. Dippo, N. Schwarz, & D. Trewin (Eds.), *Survey measurement and process quality* (pp. 141–164). New York, NY: Wiley-Interscience.

Krysan, M., & Couper, M. P. (2003). Race in the live and the virtual interview: Racial deference, social desirability, and activation effects in attitude surveys. *Social Psychology Quarterly, 66,* 364–383.

Krysan, M., Schuman, H., Scott, L. J., & Beatty, P. (1994). Response rates and response content in mail versus face-to-face surveys. *Public Opinion Quarterly, 58,* 381–399.

Kutner, M., Greenberg, E., Jin, Y., Boyle, B., Hsu, Y., & Dunleavy, E. (2007). *Literacy in everyday life: Results from the 2003 National Assessment of Adult Literacy* (NCES 2007–480). Washington DC: National Center for Education Statistics, U.S. Department of Education.

Lai, J. W., Bristol, K., & Link, M. W. (2012). *Unlocking virtual badges as the key for respondent engagement in mobile app surveys.* Presentation at the annual meeting of the Midwest Association for Public Opinion Research, Chicago, IL.

Lavrakas, P. J. (2008). Listed number. In P. J. Lavrakas (Ed.), *Encyclopedia of survey research methods* (p. 433). Thousand Oaks, CA: Sage.

Lavrakas, P. J., Stasny, E. A., & Harpuder, B. (2000). A further investigation of the last-birthday respondent selection method and within-unit coverage error. *Proceedings of the Survey Research Methods Section of the American Statistical Association,* pp. 890–895. Retrieved from www.amstat.org/sections/srms/Proceedings/

Lenhart, A., Ling, R., Campbell, S. & Purcell, K. (2010). *Teens and mobile phones.* Pew Internet & American Life Project. Retrieved from http://pewinternet.org/~/media//Files/Reports/2010/PIP-Teens-and-Mobile-2010-with-topline.pdf

Lepkowski, J. M., Tucker, C., Brick, J. M., & de Leeuw, E. D. (2007). *Advances in telephone survey methodology.* Hoboken, NJ: Wiley.

Leslie, T. F. (1996). *1996 national content survey results* (Internal DSSD Memorandum No. 3). Washington DC: U.S. Census Bureau.

Leslie, T. F. (1997). Comparing two approaches to questionnaire design: Official government versus public information design. In *Proceedings of the American Statistical Association* (pp. 336–341). Anaheim, CA: American Statistical Association.

Lesser, V. M., Dillman, D. A., Carlson, J., Lorenz, F., Mason, R., & Willits, F. (2001). *Quantifying the influence of incentives on mail survey response rates and nonresponse bias.* Paper presented at the annual meeting of the American Statistical Association, Atlanta, GA. Retrieved from http://www.sesrc.wsu.edu/dillman

The Lever. (n.d.) A remark of Archimedes quoted by Pappus of Alexandria, Synagoge, Book VIII, AD 340. Retrieved from http://www.math.nyu.edu/~crorres/Archimedes/Lever/LeverIntro.html

Levy, P. S., & Lemeshow, S. (2008). *Sampling of populations: Methods and applications* (4th ed). Hoboken, NJ: Wiley.

Libman, A., & Smyth, J. D. (2012, May 17–20). *Turn that frown upside down: The use of smiley faces as symbolic language in self-administered surveys*. Paper presented at the annual meeting of the American Association for Public Opinion Research, Orlando, FL.

Lidwell, W., Holden, K., & Butler, J. (2003). *Universal principles of design*. Gloucester, MA: Rockport.

Link, M. W. (2011). *Evolving survey research: New technologies & the next steps forward*. Webinar conducted for American Association of Public Opinion Research.

Link, M. W., Battaglia, M. P., Frankel, M. R., Osborn, L., & Mokdad, A. H. (2008). Comparison of address-based sampling (ABS) versus random-digit dialing (RDD) for general population surveys. *Public Opinion Quarterly, 72*(1), 6–27.

Link, M. W., Battaglia, M. P., Giambo, P., Frankel, M. R, Mokdad, A. H., & Rao, R. S. (2005, May). *Assessment of address frame replacements for RDD sampling frames*. Paper presented at the annual conference of the American Association for Public Opinion Research, Miami Beach, FL.

Link, M. W., Lai, J. W., & Bristol, K. (2013). *From 1.0 to 2.0: Accessibility or simplicity? How respondents engage with a multiportal (mobile, tablet, online) methodology for data collection*. Paper presented at the annual conference of the American Association for Public Opinion Research, Boston, MA.

Link, M. W., & Mokdad, A. (2005). Leaving answering machine messages: Do they increase response rates for the Behavioral Risk Factor Surveillance System? *International Journal of Public Opinion Research, 17*, 239–250.

Lohr, S. L. (1999). *Sampling: Design and analysis*. Pacific Grove, CA: Duxbury Press.

Lohr, S. L. (2009). Multiple frame surveys. In D. Pfeffermann & C. R. Rao (Eds.), *Handbook of statistics, sample surveys: Design, methods and applications* (pp. 71–88). Amsterdam, The Netherlands: North-Holland.

Luiten, A. (2013, July 15–19). *Costs, timeliness, response and measurement errors: A review of mixed mode data collection in official population surveys*. Paper presented at the European Survey Research Association biennial conference, Ljubljana, Slovenia.

Lynn, P. (Ed.). (2009). *Methodology of longitudinal surveys*. Hoboken, NJ: Wiley.

Mahon-Haft, T., & Dillman, D. A. 2010. Does visual appeal matter? Effects of web survey screen design on survey quality. *Survey Research Methods, 4*(1), 43–59.

Malakhoff, L. A. & Jans, M. (2011). Towards usage of avatar interviewers in web surveys. *Survey Practice, 4*(3). Available at http://www.surveypractice.org/index.php/Survey Practice/article/view/104/pdf

Malhotra, N., Krosnick, J. A., & Thomas, R. K. (2009). Optimal design of branching questions to measure bipolar constructs. *Public Opinion Quarterly, 73*(2), 304–324.

Mamedova, S., & McPhee, C. (2012). *Return to sender: Improving response rates in two-stage mail surveys*. Paper presented at the Federal Committee on Statistical Methodology 2012 Research Conference, Washington, DC. Retrieved from http://www.fcsm .gov/12papers/Mamedova_2012FCSM_II-C.pdf

Manfreda, K. L., Batagelj, Z., & Vehovar, V. (2002). Design of web survey questionnaires: Three basic experiments. *Journal of Computer Mediated Communication, 7*(3). Retrieved from http://jcmc.indiana.edu/vol7/issue3/vehovar.html

Marketing Systems Group. (2013). *Pros and cons of address based sampling*. Retrieved from http://www.m-s-g.com/CMS/ServerGallery/MSGWebNew/Documents/GENESYS/ whitepapers/Pros-and-Cons-of-ABS.pdf

Martin, E. (2002). The effects of questionnaire design on reporting of detailed Hispanic origin in Census 2000 mail questionnaires. *Public Opinion Quarterly, 66*, 583–593.

Mason, R., Carlson, J. E., & Tourangeau, R. (1994). Contrast effects and subtraction in part-whole questions. *Public Opinion Quarterly, 58*(4), 569–578.

Maxim, P. S. (1999). *Quantitative research methods in the social sciences*. New York, NY: Oxford University Press.

Medway, R. L., & Fulton, J. (2012). When more gets you less: A meta-analysis of the effect of concurrent web options on mail survey response rates. *Public Opinion Quarterly*, *76*, 733–746.

Menold, N., Kaczmirek, L., Lenzner, T., & Neusar, A. (2013). How do respondents attend to verbal labels in rating scales? *Field Methods*. Advanced access doi: 10.1177/1525822X13508270

Messer, B. L. (2012). Pushing households to the web: Experiments of a "web+mail" methodology for conducting general public surveys. Unpublished doctoral dissertation, Washington State University, Pullman.

Messer, B. L., & Dillman, D. A. (2011). Surveying the general public over the Internet using address-based sampling and mail contact procedures. *Public Opinion Quarterly*, *75*(3), 429–457.

Messer, B. L., Edwards, M. L., & Dillman, D. A. (2012). Determinants of item nonresponse to web and mail respondents in three address-based mixed-mode surveys of the general public. *Survey Practice*, *5*(2). Available at http://www.surveypractice.org/index.php/SurveyPractice/article/view/45/pdf

Millar, M. M. (2013). *Determining whether research is interdisciplinary: An analysis of new indicators* (Technical Report No. 13-049). Pullman: Washington State University, Social and Economic Sciences Research Center.

Millar, M. M., & Dillman, D. A. (2011). Improving response to web and mixed-mode surveys. *Public Opinion Quarterly*, *75*(2), 249–269.

Millar, M. M., & Dillman, D. A. (2012). Encouraging survey response via smartphones: Effects on respondents' use of mobile devices and survey response rates. *Survey Practice*, *5*(3). Available at http://www.surveypractice.org/index.php/SurveyPractice/article/view/19/pdf

Millar, M. M., O'Neill, A. C., & Dillman, D. A. (2009). *Are mode preferences real?* (Technical Report No. 09-003). Pullman: Washington State University, Social and Economic Sciences Research Center.

Miller, K. J. (1996). *The influence of different techniques on response rates and nonresponse error in mail surveys*. Unpublished master's thesis, Western Washington University, Bellingham.

Mohorko, A., de Leeuw, E., & Hox, J. (2013). Internet coverage and coverage bias in Europe: Developments across countries and over time. *Journal of Official Statistics*, *29*(4), 609–622.

Molm, L. D., Takahashi, N., & Peterson, G. (2000). Risk and trust in social exchange: An experimental test of a classical proposition. *American Journal of Sociology*, *105*(5), 1396–1427.

Montaquila, J. M., Brick, J. M., Williams, D., Kim, K., & Han, D. (2013). A study of two-phase mail survey data collection methods. *Journal of Survey Statistics and Methodology*, *1*(1), 66–87.

Moore, D. E., & Dillman, D. A. (1980). *Response rate of certified mail and alternatives*. Unpublished paper, Pennsylvania State University, State College.

Moore, D. W. (1997). Perils of polling '96: Myth and fallacy. *Polling Report*, *12*, 1ff.

Morgan, D. L. (1997). *Focus groups as qualitative research* (2nd ed.). Thousand Oaks, CA: Sage.

Morrison, R. L., Dillman, D. A., & Christian, L. M. (2010). Questionnaire design guidelines for establishment surveys. *Journal of Official Statistics*, *26*(1), 43–85.

Morton-Williams, J. (1991). *Obtaining co-operation in surveys—The development of a social skills approach to interviewer training in introducing surveys* (Working Paper No. 3). London: Joint Centre for Survey Methods.

Mowen, J. C., & Cialdini, R. B. (1980). On implementing the door in the face compliance technique in a business context. *Journal of Marketing Research*, *17*, 253–258.

National Research Council. (2013). *Measuring what we spend: Toward a new Consumer Expenditure Survey* (D. A. Dillman & C. C. House, Eds.). Panel on redesigning the BLS

Consumer Expenditure Surveys. Committee on National Statistics, Division of Behavioral and Social Sciences and Education. Washington, DC: National Academies Press.

Nebraska Game and Parks. (2013). *Spring migration guide*. Retrieved from http://outdoor nebraska.ne.gov/wildlife/guides/migration/migration.asp

Nielsen, J., & Budiu, R. (2013). *Mobile usability*. Berkeley, CA: New Riders.

Noelle-Neumann, E. (1970). Wanted: Rules for wording structured questionnaires. *Public Opinion Quarterly, 34*(2), 191–201.

Norman, D. A. (1988). *The psychology of everyday things*. New York, NY: Basic Books.

Nuttirudee, C. (2012, November 16–17). *The effect of visual designs in web surveys on response process across literacy groups*. Paper presented at the annual conference of the Midwest Association for Public Opinion Research, Chicago, IL.

Oksenberg, L., & Cannell, C. (1988). Effects of interviewer vocal characteristics on nonresponse. In R. M. Groves, P. P. Biemer, L. E. Lyberg, J. T. Massey, W. L. Nicholls II, & J. Waksberg (Eds.), *Telephone survey methodology* (pp. 257–272). New York, NY: Wiley.

Olsen, D., Call, V., & Wygant, S. (2005, May). *Comparative analyses of parallel paper, phone, and web surveys with and without incentives: What differences do incentive and mode make?* Paper presented at the annual conference of the American Association for Public Opinion Research, Miami Beach, FL.

Olson, K., & Bilgen, I. (2011). The role of interviewer experience on acquiescence. *Public Opinion Quarterly, 75*(1), 99–114.

Olson, K., & Peytchev, A. (2007). Effect of interviewer experience on interview pace and interviewer attitudes. *Public Opinion Quarterly, 71*(2), 273–286.

Olson, K., Smyth, J. D., & Wood, H. (2012). Does giving people their preferred survey mode actually increase survey participation? An experimental examination. *Public Opinion Quarterly, 74*(4), 611–635.

Olson, K., Stange, M., & Smyth, J. D. (forthcoming). Assessing within—Household selection methods in household mail surveys. *Public Opinion Quarterly*.

Olson, K., & Wagner, J. (2013, May 16–19). *A field experiment using GPS devices to monitor interviewer travel behavior*. Paper presented at the American Association for Public Opinion Research annual conference, Boston, MA.

O'Muircheartaigh, C., English, E. M., & Eckman, S. (2007, May). *Predicting the relative quality of alternative sampling frames*. Paper presented at the annual conference of the American Association for Public Opinion Research, Anaheim, CA.

Orr, L. (2012). The rise of the smart phone: Are you leveraging mobile? 10 tips for mobile-friendly survey creation. *Alert, 52*(3) 32–34.

Otto, L., Call, V. R., & Spenner, K. (1976). *Design for a study of entry into careers*. Lexington, MA: Lexington Books.

Oudejans, M., & Christian, L. M. (2011). Using interactive features to motivate and probe responses to open-ended questions. In M. Das, P. Ester, & L. Kaczmirek (Eds.), *Social and behavioral research and the internet: Advances in applied methods and research strategies* (pp. 215–244). New York, NY: Routledge.

Palmer, S. E. (1999). *Vision science: Photons to phenomenology*. London: Bradford Books.

Panzarino, M. (2013, October 22). Apple announces 170M iPads sold, with 81% tablet usage share and 475K apps. *Tech Crunch*. Retrieved from http://techcrunch.com/2013/10/22/apple-announces-170m-ipads-sold-with-81-tablet-usage-share-and-475k-apps/

Parsons, N. L., & Dillman, D. A. (2008). *Alternative questions for reporting the time periods during which the NSRCG respondents took community college classes: A cognitive evaluation* (Technical Report No. 08-003). Pullman: Washington State University, Social and Economic Sciences Research Center.

Parsons, N., Mahon-Haft, T., & Dillman, D. A. (2007). *Cognitive evaluations of potential questions for SESTAT surveys to determine the influence of community college on educational and work choices: Round 2* (Technical Report No. 07-58). Pullman: Washington State University, Social and Economic Sciences Research Center.

Pew Internet & American Life Project. (2013a). *51% of U.S. adults bank online*. Retrieved from http://www.pewinternet.org/2013/08/07/51-of-u-s-adults-bank-online/

Pew Internet & American Life Project. (2013b). Broadband vs. dial up adoption over time. Retrieved from http://www.pewinternet.org/data-trend/internet-use/connection-type/

Pew Internet & American Life Project. (2013c). *Internet use over time* [Percent of adults who use the Internet]. Retrieved from http://www.pewinternet.org/data-trend/internet-use/internet-use-over-time/

Pew Internet & American Life Project. (2013d). *Internet user demographics*. Retrieved from http://www.pewinternet.org/data-trend/internet-use/latest-stats/

Pew Research Center. (2009). *America's place in the world 2009: An investigation of public and leadership opinion about international affairs*. Retrieved from http://www.people-press.org/files/legacy-pdf/569.pdf

Pew Research Center. (2013). *Public sees U.S. power declining as support for global engagement slips: America's place in the world 2013*. Retrieved from http://www.people-press.org/files/legacy-pdf/12-3-13%20APW%20VI%20release.pdf

Pew Research Center for the People & the Press. (n.d.). *Question order*. Retrieved December 9, 2013, from http://www.people-press.org/methodology/questionnaire-design/question-order/

Pew Research Center's Global Attitudes Project. (n.d.). *About the project*. Retrieved January 3, 2014, from http://www.pewglobal.org/about/

Peytchev, A., & Hill, C. A. (2010). Experiments in mobile web survey design: similarities to other modes and unique considerations. *Social Science Computer Review*, *28*, 319–335.

Porter, S., & Whitcomb, M. E. (2003). The impact of lottery incentives on student survey response rates. *Research in Higher Education*, *44*(4), 389–407.

Potaka, L. (2008). Comparability and usability: Key issues in the design of Internet forms for New Zealand's 2006 Census of populations and dwellings. *Survey Research Methods*, *2*, 1–10.

Presser, S., Rothgeb, J. M., Couper, M. P., Lessler, J. T., Martin, E., Martin, J., & Singer, E. (2004). *Methods for testing and evaluating survey questionnaires*. Hoboken, NJ: Wiley-Interscience.

Puleston, J. (2012a, January). Gamification 101—From theory to practice—Part I. *Quirk's Marketing Research Review* (article 20120126-1).

Puleston, J. (2012b, February). Gamification 101—From theory to practice—Part II. *Quirk's Marketing Research Review* (article 20120225-2).

Radloff, L. S. (1977). The CES-D scale: A self-report depression scale for research in the general population. *Applied Psychological Measurement*, *1*(3), 385–401.

Rainie, L., & Smith, A. (2013). *Tablet and e-reader ownership update*. Retrieved from http://pewinternet.org/Reports/2013/Tablets-and-ereaders.aspx

Ray, J. (2013). *Gallup's top 10 world news findings of 2013*. Retrieved from http://www.gallup.com/poll/166619/gallup-top-world-news-findings-2013.aspx

Rayner, K. (1998). Eye movements in reading and information processing: 20 years of research. *Psychological Bulletin*, *124*(3), 372–422.

Redline, C. (2011). *Clarifying survey questions*. Unpublished dissertation, the Joint Program in Survey Methodology, University of Maryland, College Park.

Redline, C. D., & Dillman, D. A. (2002). The influence of alternative visual design on respondents' performance with branching instructions in self-administered questionnaires. In R. Groves, D. Dillman, J. Eltinge, & R. Little (Eds.), *Survey nonresponse* (pp. 179–196). New York, NY: Wiley.

Redline, C. D., Dillman, D. A., Carley-Baxter, L., & Creecy, R. H. (2005). Factors that influence reading and comprehension of branching instructions in self-administered questionnaires. *Allgemeines Statistiches Archiv* (Journal of the German Statistical Society), *89*(1), 21–38.

Redline, C. D., Dillman, D. A., Dajani, A. N., & Scaggs, M. A. (2003). Improving navigational performance in U.S. Census 2000 by altering the visual administered languages of branching instructions. *Journal of Official Statistics, 19*, 403–419.

Redline, C. D., & Lankford, C. P. (2001, May). *Eye-movement analysis: A new tool for evaluating the design of visually administered instruments (paper and web)*. Paper presented at the American Association for Public Opinion Research Conference, Montreal, Quebec, Canada.

Ricci, K., Olson, K., & Smyth, J. D. (2013, November). *Evaluating the impact of visual design on speeders*. Paper presented at the annual meeting of the Midwest Association for Public Opinion Research, Chicago, IL.

Rizzo, L., Brick, J. M., & Park, I. (2004). A minimally intrusive method for sampling persons in random digit dial surveys. *Public Opinion Quarterly, 68*(2), 267–274.

Rockwood, T. H., Sangster, R. L., & Dillman, D. A. (1997). The effect of response categories in questionnaire answers: Context and mode effects. *Sociological Methods and Research, 26*(1), 118–140.

Rokeach, M. (1973). *The nature of human values*. New York, NY: Free Press.

Roloff, M. E. (1981). *Interpersonal communication: The social exchange approach*. Beverly Hills, CA: Sage.

Rookey, B. D., Hanway, S., & Dillman, D. A. (2008). Does a probability-based household panel benefit from assignment to postal response as an alternative to internet-only? *Public Opinion Quarterly, 72*(5), 962–984.

Rookey, B. D., Le, L., Littlejohn, M., & Dillman, D. A. (2012). Understanding the resilience of mail-back survey methods: An analysis of 20 years of change in response rates to national park surveys. *Social Science Research, 41*(6), 1404–1414.

Roose, H., Lievens, J., & Waege, H. (2007). The joint effect of topic interest and follow-up procedures on the response in a mail questionnaire: An empirical test of the leverage-saliency theory in audience research. *Sociological Methods and Research, 35*(3), 410–428.

Rosen, R. J. (2007, June). *Multi-mode data collection: Why, when, how*. Paper presented at the ICES III International Conference on Establishment Surveys, Montreal, Quebec, Canada.

Sakshaug, J. W., Couper, M. P., Ofstedal, M. B., & Weir, D. R. (2012). Linking survey and administrative records: Mechanisms of consent. *Sociological Methods and Research, 41*, 535–569.

Salant, P., & Dillman, D. A. (1994). *How to conduct your own survey*. New York, NY: Wiley.

Sangster, R. L. (1993). *Question order effects: Are they really less prevalent in mail surveys?* Unpublished doctoral dissertation, Washington State University, Pullman.

Saris, W. E., Revilla, M., Krosnick, J. A., & Shaeffer, E. M. (2010). Comparing questions with agree/disagree response options to questions with item-specific response options. *Survey Research Methods, 4*(1), 61–79.

Sawyer, S., & Dillman, D. A. (2002). *How graphical, numerical, and verbal languages affect the completion of the Gallup Q-12 on self-administered questionnaires: Results from 22 cognitive interviews and field experiment* (Technical Report No. 02-26). Pullman: Washington State University, Social and Economic Sciences Research Center.

Schaefer, D. R., & Dillman, D. A. (1998). Development of a standard e-mail methodology: Results of an experiment. *Public Opinion Quarterly, 62*, 378–397.

Schaeffer, N. C., & Presser, S. (2003). The science of asking questions. *Annual Review of Sociology, 29*, 65–88.

Schouten, B., Calinescu, M., & Luiten, A. (2013). Optimizing quality of response through adaptive survey designs. *Survey Methodology, 39*(1), 29–58.

Schuman, H., & Converse, J. M. (1971). The effects of black and white interviewers on black responses in 1968. *Public Opinion Quarterly, 35*, 44–68.

Schuman, H., & Presser, S. (1981). *Questions and answers in attitude surveys: Experiments on question form, wording, and context*. New York, NY: Academic Press.

Schwartz, B. (2004). *The paradox of choice: Why more is less*. New York, NY: Harper Perennial.

Schwarz, N. (1996). *Cognition and communication: Judgmental Biases, research methods, and the logic of conversation.* Mahwah, NJ: Erlbaum.

Schwarz, N., Grayson, C. E., & Knäuper, B. (1998). Formal features of rating scales and the interpretation of question meaning. *International Journal of Public Opinion Research, 10*(2), 177–183.

Schwarz, N., Hippler, H.-J., & Noelle-Neumann, E. (1992). A cognitive model of response-order effects in survey measurement. In N. Schwarz & S. Sudman (Eds.), *Context effects in social and psychological research* (pp. 187–199). New York, NY: Springer-Verlag.

Schwarz, N., Knäuper, B., Hippler, H.-J., Noelle-Neumann, E., & Clark, L. (1991). Rating scales: Numeric values may change the meaning of scale labels. *Public Opinion Quarterly, 55*(4), 570–582.

Scott, C. (1961). Research on mail surveys. *Journal of the Royal Statistical Society, 124,* 143–205.

Sellen, A. J., & Harper, R. H. R. (2002). *The myth of the paperless office.* Cambridge, MA: MIT Press.

Shin, H. B., & Kominski, R. A. (2010). *Language use in the United States: 2007* (American Community Survey Reports, ACS-12). Washington DC: U.S. Census Bureau.

Singer, E. (2011). Toward a cost-benefit theory of survey participation: Evidence, further tests, and implications. *Journal of Official Statistics, 27*(2), 379–392.

Singer, E., Hippler, H.-J., & Schwarz, N. (1992). Confidentiality assurances in surveys: Reassurance or threat? *International Journal of Public Opinion Research, 4*(3), 256–268.

Singer, E., von Thurn, D. R., & Miller, E. R. (1995). Confidentiality assurances and survey response: A review of the experimental literature. *Public Opinion Quarterly, 59,* 266–277.

Singer, E., & Ye, C. (2013). The use and effects of incentives in surveys. *Annals of the American Academy of Political and Social Science, 645*(1), 112–141.

Skalland, B., & M. Khare. (2013). Geographic inaccuracy of cell phone samples and the effect on telephone survey bias, variance, and cost. *Journal of Survey Statistics and Methodology, 1*(1), 45–65.

Smith, A. (2013a). *Smartphone ownership.* Retrieved from http://pewinternet.org/Reports/2013/Smartphone-Ownership-2013.aspx

Smith, A. (2013b). *Smartphone ownership* [2013 update]. Retrieved from http://pewinternet.org/Reports/2013/Smartphone-Ownership-2013/Findings.aspx

Smith, T. W. (1993). *Little things matter: A sampler of how differences in questionnaire format can affect survey response* (GSS Methodological Report No. 78). Chicago, IL: University of Chicago, National Opinion Research Center.

Smyth, J. D. (2008, May 15–18). *Unresolved issues in multiple-answer questions.* Paper presented at the American Association for Public Opinion Research, New Orleans, LA.

Smyth, J. D., Dillman, D. A., & Christian, L. M. (2007a). Context effects in web surveys: New issues and evidence. In A. Joinson, K. McKenna, T. Postmes, & U.-D. Reips (Eds.), *The Oxford handbook of Internet psychology* (pp. 427–443). New York, NY: Oxford University Press.

Smyth, J. D., Dillman, D. A., & Christian, L. M. (2007b, May 17–20). *Improving response quality in list-style open-ended questions in web and telephone surveys.* Paper presented at the American Association for Public Opinion Research, Anaheim, CA.

Smyth, J. D., Dillman, D. A., & Christian, L. M. (2008). Does "yes or no" on the telephone mean the same as "check-all-that-apply" on the web? *Public Opinion Quarterly, 72,* 103–113.

Smyth, J. D., Dillman, D. A., Christian, L. M., & McBride, M. (2006). *Open ended questions in telephone and web surveys.* Paper presented at the World Association for Public Opinion Research Conference, Montreal, Canada.

Smyth, J. D., Dillman, D. A., Christian, L. M., & McBride, M. (2009). Open-ended questions in web surveys: Can increasing the size of answer spaces and providing extra verbal instructions improve response quality? *Public Opinion Quarterly, 73,* 325–337.

Smyth, J. D., Dillman, D. A., Christian, L. M., & O'Neill, A. C. (2010). Using the Internet to survey small towns and communities: Limitations and possibilities in the early 21st century. *American Behavioral Scientist*, *53*, 1423–1448.

Smyth, J. D., Dillman, D. A., Christian, L. M., & Stern, M. J. (2006a). Comparing check-all and forced-choice formats in web surveys. *Public Opinion Quarterly*, *70*, 66–77.

Smyth, J. D., Dillman, D. A., Christian, L. M., & Stern, M. J. (2006b). Effects of using visual design principles to group response options in web surveys. *International Journal of Internet Science*, *1*(1), 6–16.

Smyth, J. D., & Olson, K. (n.d.). Unpublished data.

Smyth, J. D., & Olson, K. (2010). *Measuring mode preference: Question wording and question order experiments.* Paper presented at AAPOR May 13–16, 2010, Chicago, IL.

Smyth, J. D., Olson, K., & Millar, M. M. (forthcoming). Identifying predictors of survey mode preference. *Social Science Research*.

Smyth, J. D., Olson, K., & Richards, A. (2009, May 14–17). *Unraveling mode preference.* Paper presented at the annual meeting of the American Association for Public Opinion Research, Hollywood, FL.

Smyth, J. D., Powell, R., Olson, K., & Libman, A. (2012, May 17–20), *Understanding the relationship between literacy and data quality in self-administered surveys.* Paper presented at the annual conference of the American Association for Public Opinion Research, Orlando, FL.

Snijkers, G., Haraldsen, G., Jones, J., & Willimack, D. K. (2013). *Designing and conducting business surveys.* Hoboken, NJ: Wiley.

Stafford, L. (2008). Social exchange theories. In L. A. Baster & D. O. Braithwaite (Eds.), *Engaging theories in interpersonal communication: Multiple perspectives* (pp. 377–389). Thousand Oaks, CA: Sage.

Stange, M., Olson, K., & Smyth, J. D. (2013, May 16–19). *Using visual design to aid within-household selection in mail surveys: Does it lead to accurate selection and representative samples?* Paper presented at the annual conference of the American Association for Public Opinion Research, Boston, MA.

StatCounter Global Stats. (2013a). Top 10 mobile screen resolutions. Retrieved from http://gs.statcounter.com

StatCounter Global Stats. (2013b). Top 10 desktop screen resolutions. Retrieved from http://gs.statcounter.com

Statistics New Zealand. (2006). *2006 Census final questionnaire design.* Retrieved from http://www.stats.govt.nz/Census/about-2006-census/methodology-papers/2006-census-final-questionnaire-design.aspx

Stern, M. J. (2006). *How use of the Internet impacts community participation and the maintenance of core social ties: An empirical study.* Unpublished doctoral dissertation, Washington State University, Pullman.

Stern, M. J. (2008). The use of client-side paradata in analyzing the effects of visual layout on changing responses in web surveys. *Field Methods*, *20*(4), 377–398.

Stern, M. J., Adams, A. E., & Elsasser, S. (2009). Digital inequality and place: The effects of technological diffusion on Internet proficiency and usage across rural, suburban, and urban counties. *Sociological Inquiry*, *79*(4), 391–417.

Stern, M. J., Bilgen, I., & Dillman, D. A. (in press). The state of survey methodology. *Field Methods*.

Steve, K., Dally, G., Lavrakas, P. J., Yancey, T., & Kulp, D. (2007, May). *R&D studies to replace the RDD-frame with an ABS-frame.* Paper presented at the annual conference of the American Association for Public Opinion Research, Anaheim, CA.

Sturgis, P., Allum, N., Brunton-Smith, I. (2009). Attitudes over time: The psychology of panel conditioning. In P. Lynn (ed.), *Methodology of longitudinal surveys* (pp. 113–126). West Sussex, UK: Wiley.

Sudman, S., Bradburn, N. M., & Schwarz, N. (1996). *Thinking about answers.* San Francisco, CA: Jossey-Bass.

Tarnai, J., & Dillman, D. A. (1992). Questionnaire context as a source of response differences in mail versus telephone surveys. In N. Schwarz & S. Sudman (Eds.), *Context effects in social and psychological research* (pp. 115–129). New York, NY: Springer-Verlag.

Tarnai, J., Schultz, D., Solet, D., & Pfingst, L. (2012). *Response rate effects in an ABS survey for stamped vs. business reply envelopes, with and without incentives, and medium vs. standard size outgoing envelopes*. Paper presented at the annual meeting of the American Association of Public Opinion Research, Orlando, FL.

Teisl, M. F., Roe, B., & Vayda, M. (2005). Incentive effects on response rates, data quality, and survey administration costs. *International Journal of Public Opinion Research, 18*(3), 364–373.

Thibaut, J. W., & Kelley, H. H. (1959). *The social psychology of groups*. New York, NY: Wiley.

Thomas, R. K., & Couper, M. P. (2007, March). *A comparison of visual analog and graphic ratings scales*. Paper presented at the General Online Research Conference, Leipzig, Germany.

Todorov, A. (2000). The accessibility and applicability of knowledge: Predicting context effects in national surveys. *Public Opinion Quarterly, 64*(4), 429–451.

Toepoel, V., Das, M., & van Soest, A. (2006). Design of web questionnaires: The effect of layout in rating scales (CentER Discussion Series No. 2006-30). Tilburg, the Netherlands: CentER. Retrieved from http://papers.ssrn.com/sol3/papers.cfm?abstract_id=903740

Toepoel, V., Das, M., & van Soest, A. (2009). Design of web questionnaires: The effects of layout in rating scales. *Journal of Official Statistics, 25*(4), 509–528.

Tourangeau, R. (1992). Context effects on response to attitude surveys: Attitudes as memory structure. In N. Schwarz & S. Sudman (Eds.), *Context effects in social and psychological research* (pp. 35–48). New York, NY: Springer-Verlag.

Tourangeau, R., Couper, M. P., & Conrad, F. (2004). Spacing, position, and order: Interpretive heuristics for visual features of survey questions. *Public Opinion Quarterly, 68*, 368–393.

Tourangeau, R., Couper, M. P., & Conrad, F. (2007). Color, labels, and interpretive heuristics for response scales. *Public Opinion Quarterly, 71*(1), 91–112.

Tourangeau, R., Rips, L. J., & Rasinski, K. (2000). *The psychology of survey response*. New York, NY: Cambridge University Press.

Tourangeau, R., & Smith, T. W. (1996). Asking sensitive questions: The impact of data collection mode, question format, and question context. *Public Opinion Quarterly, 60*, 275–304.

Trouteaud, A. R. (2004). How you ask counts: A test of Internet-related components of response rates to a web-based survey. *Social Science Computer Review, 22*, 385–392.

Trussell, N., & Lavrakas, P. J. (2004). The influence of incremental increases in token cash incentives on mail survey response: Is there an optimal amount? *Public Opinion Quarterly, 68*(3), 349–367.

Trussell, N., & Lavrakas, P. J. (2005). *Testing the impact of caller ID technology on response rates in a mixed mode survey*. Paper presented at the annual conference of the American Association for Public Opinion Research, Miami Beach, FL.

Tuckel, P., & Schulman, M. (2000). *The effect of leaving different answering machine messages on response rates in a nationwide RDD survey*. Paper presented at the Joint Statistical Meetings, Indianapolis, IN.

Tulp, D. R., How, C. E., Kusch, G. L., & Cole, S. J. (1991). Nonresponse under mandatory versus voluntary reporting in the 1980 Survey of Pollution Abatement Costs and Expenditures (PACE). *Proceedings of the survey research methods section of the American Statistical Association* (pp. 272–277). Alexandria, VA: American Statistical Association.

Tuten, T. L., Galesic, M., & Bosnjak, M. (2004). Effects of immediate versus delayed notification of prize draw results on response behavior in web surveys. *Social Science Computer Review, 22*, 377–384.

Tversky, A., & Shafir, E. (1992). Choice under conflict: the dynamics of deferred decision. *Psychological Science, 6*, 358–361.

U. S. Census Bureau. (n.d.). *About the American Community Survey.* Retrieved January 1, 2014, from https://www.census.gov/acs/www/about_the_survey/american_community_survey/

U.S. Census Bureau. (n.d.). *What is the Census?* Retrieved January 6, 2013, from http://www.census.gov/2010census/about/

U. S. Census Bureau. (2010a). Decennial Census bilingual questionnaire. Retrieved from http://www.census.gov/2010census/pdf/2010_Bilingual_Questionnaire_Info.pdf

U. S. Census Bureau. (2010b). 2010 Decennial Census questionnaire. Retrieved from http://www.census.gov/2010census/pdf/2010_Questionnaire_Info.pdf

U. S. Census Bureau. (2011). *American Community Survey* [questionnaire]. Retrieved from http://www.census.gov/acs/www/Downloads/questionnaires/2011/Quest11.pdf

U.S. Postal Service. (2013). *2013 annual report to Congress.* Retrieved at http://about.usps.com/publications/annual-report-comprehensive-statement-2013/annual-report-comprehensive-statement-2013_v2.pdf

Valliant R., Dever, J. A., & Kreuter, F. (2013). *Practical tools for designing and weighting survey samples* (Statistics for social and behavioral sciences). New York, NY: Springer.

VanGeest, J. B., Johnson, T. P., & Welch, V. L. (2007). Methodologies for improving response rates in surveys of physicians: A systematic review. *Evaluation and the Health Professions, 30*(4), 303–321.

Wagner, J. (2008). *Adaptive survey design to reduce nonresponse bias.* Unpublished doctoral thesis, University of Michigan, Ann Arbor.

Waksberg, J. (1978). Sampling methods for random digit dialing. *Journal of the American Statistical Association, 73*(361), 40–46.

Ware, C. (2004). *Information visualization: Perception for design.* San Francisco, CA: Morgan Kaufmann.

Warriner, K., Goyder, J., Gjertsen, H., Hohner, P., & McSpurren, K. (1996). Charities, no; lotteries, no; cash, yes: Main effects and interactions in a Canadian incentives experiment. *Public Opinion Quarterly, 60*, 542–562.

West, B. T., & Olson, K. (2010). How much of interviewer variance is really nonresponse error variance? *Public Opinion Quarterly, 74*(5), 1004–1026.

Willis, G. B. (1999). Cognitive interviewing: A "how to" guide. Retrieved from http://www.hkr.se/PageFiles/35002/GordonWillis.pdf

Willis, G. B. (2004). *Cognitive interviewing: A tool for improving questionnaire design.* Thousand Oaks, CA: Sage.

Willits, F. K., & Janota, J. (1996, August). *A matter of order: Effects of response order on answers to surveys.* Paper presented at the meeting of the Rural Sociological Society, Des Moines, IA.

Willits, F. K., & Saltiel, J. (1995). Question order effects on subjective measures of quality of life. *Rural Sociology, 60*, 654–665.

Wilson, C. E. (1974). The effect of medium on loss of information. *Journalism Quarterly, 51*, 111–115.

Wine, J. S., Cominole, M. B., Heuer, R. E., & Riccobono, J. A. (2006). *Challenges of designing and implementing multimode instruments.* Paper presented at the Second International Conference on Telephone Survey Methodology, Miami, FL.

Witt-Swanson, L. (2013, May 19–22). *Design decisions: Can one reduce measurement error on paper/pencil surveys by using boxes or ovals?* Paper presented at the International Field Directors & Technologies Conference, Providence, RI.

World Wide Web Consortium. (n.d.). *Web accessibility initiative (WAI).* Retrieved January 4, 2014, from http://www.w3.org/WAI/

Xu, M., Bates, B. J., & Schweitzer, J. C. (1993). The impact of messages on survey partici-pation in answering machine households. *Public Opinion Quarterly*, 57(2), 232–237.

Ye, C., Fulton, J., & Tourangeau, R. (2011). More positive or more extreme? A meta-analysis of mode differences in response choice. *Public Opinion Quarterly*, 75(2), 349–365.

Zhou, Q., Smyth, J. D., & Olson, K. (2013, November). *The effect of the graphic layout of question stems and rating scales on respondents' behavior*. Paper presented at the annual meeting of the Midwest Association for Public Opinion Research, Chicago, IL.

Zickuhr K., & Smith A. (2013). *Home broadband 2013*. Retrieved from http://pewinternet.org/Reports/2013/Broadband.aspx

Author Index

Subject Index